ASCD publications present a variety of viewpoints. The views expressed or implied in this publication are not necessarily official positions of the Association.

Price: $19.95
ASCD Stock Number: 611-85362
ISBN: 0-87120-131-3
Library of Congress Card Catalog Number: 85-070037

Autumn 1985

Acknowledgements

"Exhilaration is that feeling you get just after a great idea hits you and just before you realize what's wrong with it."

WHEN I CASUALLY AGREED to edit *Developing Minds* I didn't realize the enormity of the task. I knew I was in trouble when my patient wife, Nancy, met me at the airport upon my return from an extended meeting with the ASCD editorial staff: "Your computer missed you," she greeted, with a detectable ingredient of caustic sarcasm. To her and for her I am eternally grateful.

I seem to have been preparing almost my entire professional career for the production of this book. I want to thank my many mentors on whose interaction, inspiration, guidance, and knowledge I've drawn: Arthur Wells Foshay, Howardine Hoffman, Paul Brandwein, J. Cecil Parker, Larry Lowery, Frances Link, Reuven Feuerstein, J. Richard Suchman, Jerome Bruner, Jean Piaget, Hilda Taba, and Bruce Joyce, to mention only a few.

Gratitude should be expressed to ASCD's Executive Director, Executive Council, and Publications Committee for their proactive leadership, foresight, and realization of thinking skills as a high priority in which this organization should invest maximum and immediate efforts. I believe that ASCD has created a national awareness of intellectual development as a valued goal of education. It has been an awesome display of how an organization can move almost an entire profession.

I wish to express appreciation to the many contributors to this publication. They are a veritable "Who's Who" of outstanding, contemporary cognitive educators. They have produced what I believe to be the most extensive, helpful, and scholarly publication on this topic to date. They've been patient with my prodding, determined with my deadlines, and agreeable to my editorial exclusions.

Finally, I wish to thank the ASCD editorial staff: Ron Brandt for his encouragement, thoughtfulness, and high standards; Nancy Modrak, Debbie Johnson, Jo Ann Irick, Fran Schweiger, and Pam Dronka for their attention to detail; and Al Way for his artistry.

Arthur L. Costa
Roseville, California

CONTENTS

Foreword ix
    Carolyn Sue Hughes

Introduction xi
    Arthur L. Costa

Part I.
The Need to Teach Students to Think 1

  1. Why Teach Thinking: A Statement of Rationale 3
     Jay McTighe and Jan Schollenberger

  2. Educational Outcomes for a K-12 Curriculum 7
     Sydelle Seiger-Ehrenberg

Part II.
Creating School Conditions for Thinking 11

  3. A Call for Staff Development 13
     James A. Bellanca

  4. Teaching For, Of, and About Thinking 20
     Arthur L Costa

  5. Are Teachers Motivated to Teach Thinking? 24
     Robert Garmston

  6. The Principal's Role in Enhancing Thinking Skills 29
     Arthur L. Costa

  7. Removing Impediments to Change 33
     John Barell

Part III.
What Is Thinking? Deciding on Definitions 41

  8. Thinking Skills: Meanings, Models, Materials 43
     Barbara Z. Presseisen

  9. The Good Thinker 49
     Allan A. Glatthorn and Jonathan Baron

  10. Goals for a Critical Thinking Curriculum 54
     Robert H. Ennis

  11. What Creative Thinking Is 58
     D. N. Perkins

  12. Toward a Model of Human Intellectual Functioning 62
     Arthur L. Costa

  13. The Behaviors of Intelligence 66
     Arthur L. Costa

Part IV.
A Curriculum for Thinking 69

   14. The Biological Basis of Thinking 71
        Lawrence F. Lowery

   15. Cognitive Levels Matching and Curriculum Analysis. 81
        Esther Fusco

   16. Developing Lesson Plans With Cognitive Objectives 87
        S. Lee Winocur

Part V.
Thinking Pervades the Curriculum 95

   17. Some Thoughts About Mathematics and Problem Solving 97
        Robert Wirtz

   18. The Thinking/Writing Connection 102
        Carol Booth Olson

   19. Reading and Thinking. 108
        Beau Fly Jones

   20. How Scientists Think When They Are Doing Science 114
        Arthur L. Costa

   21. Aesthetics: Where Thinking Originates 118
        Arthur L. Costa

   22. Thinking Across the Disciplines; Publications and Programs 120
        Arthur L. Costa

Part VI.
Teacher Behaviors That Enable Student Thinking 125
        Arthur L. Costa

Part VII.
Teaching Strategies Intended to Develop Student Thinking ...139

   23. Building a Repertoire of Strategies 141
        Arthur L. Costa, Robert Hanson, Harvey F. Silver, and Richard W. Strong

   24. Directive Strategies 144
        Arthur L. Costa, Robert Hanson, Harvey F. Silver, and Richard W. Strong

        Practical Strategies for the Direct Teaching of Thinking Skills 145
        Barry K. Beyer

   25. Mediative Strategies. 151
        Arthur L. Costa, Robert Hanson, Harvey F. Silver, and Richard W. Strong

           Dialectical Reasoning 152
           Richard W. Paul

           Concept Development 161
           Sydelle Seiger-Ehrenberg

           Other Mediative Strategies. 166
           Arthur L. Costa, Robert Hanson, Harvey F. Silver, and Richard W. Strong

   26. Generative Strategies 171
        Arthur L. Costa, Robert Hanson, Harvey F. Silver, and Richard W. Strong

           Creativity by Design 172
           D. N. Perkins

           Synectics: Making the Familiar Strange 175
           Arthur L. Costa, Robert Hanson, Harvey F. Silver, and Richard W. Strong

27. Collaborative Strategies 177
   Arthur L. Costa, Dee Dishon, and Pat Wilson O'Leary

      Cooperative Learning................................179
      Dee Dishon and Pat Wilson O'Leary

28. Summing Up 181
   Arthur L. Costa

Part VIII.
Programs for Teaching Thinking...........................183

29. Choosing the Right Program 185
   Robert J. Sternberg

30. SOI 187
   Mary N. Meeker

31. Instrumental Enrichment................................193
   Frances R. Link

32. Strategic Reasoning 196
   Howard Citron and John J. Glade

33. The CoRT Thinking Program 203
   Edward de Bono

34. Project IMPACT.......................................210
   S. Lee Winocur

35. Philosophy for Children 212
   Matthew Lipman

36. The California Writing Project 215
   Carol Booth Olson

37. Future Problem Solving 217
   Anne B. Crabbe

38. Teaching Decision Making with Guided Design............220
   Anne H. Nardi and Charles E. Wales

39. Odyssey: A Curriculum for Thinking 224
   Elena Wright

40. Learning to Learn 227
   Marcia Heiman

41. Creative Problem Solving...............................230
   Sidney J. Parnes

42. Great Books..233
   Howard Will

43. Building Thinking Skills 236
   John D. Baker

44. HOTS: A Computer-Based Approach 239
   Stanley Pogrow

45. BASICS 241
   Sydelle Seiger-Ehrenberg

46. Comparing Approaches to Teaching Thinking..............244
   Ronald S. Brandt

Part IX.
Computers and Thinking...............................247

47. The Potential of Computers for Teaching Thinking 249
   Carolee Matsumoto

48. Uses of the Computer for Teaching Thinking 255
   Chuck Wiederhold

49. CompuTHINK and Criteria for Selecting Software 256
   John Cradler

Part X.
Assessing Growth in Thinking Abilities 267

50. Test Results from Teaching Thinking 269
   Arthur Whimbey

51. Evaluating Efforts to Teach Thinking 272
   Stuart C. Rankin

52. California Assesses Critical Thinking 276
   Peter Kneedler

53. What Are We Looking For and How Can We Find It? 281
   Joan Boykoff Baron and Bena Kallick

54. How Can We Recognize Improved Student Thinking? 288
   Arthur L. Costa

Epilogue:
It's Our Move 291
   Rebecca van der Bogert

Resources for Teaching Thinking 293

A. Selected Bibliography 295
   Arthur L. Costa, Inabeth Miller, and Nelson "Pete" Quinby

B. Tests That Could Be Called Critical Thinking Tests 303
   Robert H. Ennis

C. Media, Newsletters, and Networks 305
   Arthur L. Costa

Appendices 307

A. A Glossary of Cognitive Terminology 309
   Arthur L. Costa and Barbara Presseisen

B. Classroom Observation Form 314
   John Barell

C. Self-Reflection on Your Teaching: A Checklist 315
   John Barell

D. How Thoughtful Are Your Classrooms? 317
   Arthur L. Costa

E. A Thinking Skills Checklist 319
   Barry K. Beyer

F. Classroom Observation Checklist 322
   S. Lee Winocur

G. Questionnaire: Are You Ready to Teach Thinking? 325
   Arthur L. Costa

H. Suggestions for Getting Started 327
   Sandra Black

I. Questions for System Planners 328
   Carolee Matsumoto

J. Overhead Transparency Masters 330
   Ronald S. Brandt

Contributing Authors 338

Index 341

Foreword

Our greatest national resource is the minds of our children.

—Walt Disney

Helping students become effective thinkers is increasingly recognized as a primary goal of education. Rapid expansion of knowledge points to the importance of curriculums that empower students to locate and process knowledge rather than simply memorize facts. The most recent Gallup Poll asked teachers and the public to rate goals of education as to their importance. At the top of teacher ratings and near the top of public ratings was developing the ability to think creatively, objectively, and analytically. When John Goodlad surveyed teachers, parents, and students, he found that intellectual development of students was consistently identified as the most important goal of schooling.

While the importance of cognitive development has been widely recognized, performance of students on existing measures of higher-order thinking ability has pointed to a critical need for students to develop the skills and attitudes of effective thinking. Interest of ASCD members in finding better ways to help students become more effective thinkers has been expressed in high registrations for National Curriculum Study Institutes and in the hundreds of inquiries to authors following publication of theme issues of *Educational Leadership* that focus on thinking.

Recognizing both the need and the opportunity to make a contribution to the profession in this area, the Executive Council of the Association for Supervision and Curriculum Development appointed a committee on teaching thinking, chaired by Stu Rankin. This committee planned and conducted an invitational conference for researchers and practicing educators at the Wingspread Conference Center in May 1984. The conference participants considered the state of professional knowledge and practice in teaching thinking in elementary and secondary schools and recommended ways in which ASCD could respond to the identified needs.

One of those recommendations was to publish a resource book that could be of immediate practical value to educators and school systems seeking to develop more effective student thinking. The book you now hold in your hands is the fulfillment of that recommendation. Included is consideration of school climate that fosters thinking, classroom teaching strategies, curriculum planning, assessment, and teacher education, as well as a guide to a variety of existing curriculums designed to teach thinking. We are fortunate to have had the talented leadership of Art Costa and writers with expertise in developing effective student thinking, who have contributed so generously of themselves to create this volume.

Other recommendations emerging from the Wingspread Conference are currently being implemented by ASCD. A series of videotapes on teaching thinking for use in staff development has been designed by a committee chaired by Jim Bellanca. A network of individuals interested in the teaching of thinking is operating under the leadership of John Barell. Collaborative efforts with other professional associations that share a common interest in developing more effective student thinking are finding a high degree of support from our colleagues in 15 other associations. I have the pleasure of chairing this stimulating exchange of ideas and expertise. We hope to be able to use our combined efforts to accomplish goals that individual associations are not likely to achieve in isolation.

The challenge of helping students become effective thinkers is one that holds promise for both students and teachers. A school climate that fosters and values thinking in students is also one where teachers' ideas are respected and where professional growth flourishes through collegial exchange. This book has been designed to help turn the challenge and the promise into reality.

Carolyn Sue Hughes
President, 1985-86
Association for Supervision and
Curriculum Development

Introduction

It takes much coaching for human movement to be performed with precision, style, and grace. It takes years of practice, concentration, and coaching to become a skilled gymnast or ice skater, for instance. Improvement is demonstrated by the increasing mastery of complex and intricate maneuvers performed repeatedly on command with sustained and seemingly effortless grace. The distinction between awkwardness and agility is obvious to even the most undisciplined observer.

Like strenuous movement, thinking is hard work. Similarly, we can assume that with proper instruction, human thought processes can become more broadly applied, more spontaneously generated, more precisely focused, more intricately complex, more metaphorically abstract, and more insightfully divergent. Such refinement also requires practice, concentration, and coaching. Unlike athletics, however, thinking is most often idiosyncratic and covert. Definitions of thought processes, strategies for their development, and assessment of the stamina required for their increased mastery are therefore illusive. Awkwardness and agility are not as easily distinguished in thinking as they are in athletics.

Today there is a growing realization worldwide, by educators as well as the general public, that the level of a country's development depends on the level of intellectual development of its people. Indeed, Luis Alberto Machado (1980), the former Venezuelan Minister of Intellectual Development, reminds us that all human beings have a basic right to the full development of their intellect. Furthermore, recent research in education, psychology, and neurobiology supports the belief of many educators that the increasing interest in teaching thinking is not just a backlash from the "back to basics" movement. Rather, it is an integral component of instruction in every school subject, and achievement depends largely on the inclusion of those mental processes prerequisite to mastery of that subject.

Just as the "Age of Aquarius" left its mark on education in the 1970s by vindicating *affect* as an essential consideration of learning, the greatest contribution of today's "Information Age" may well be the inclusion of *intellectual processes* as essential to all learning.

This resource book is dedicated to educators who believe that teaching is one of the most powerful mechanisms for developing intellectual prowess; that meaningful interaction with adults, peers, and the environment is essential in mediating the learner's intellectual development; that learning is a continual transformation of inner perceptions, knowledge, and experiences; and that all human beings have the potential to continually develop their intellectual powers throughout their lives. It is intended to help educational leaders—teachers, administrators, curriculum workers, staff developers, and teacher educators—infuse curriculum, instruction, and school organization with practices that more fully develop children's intellectual potentials.

Because the research in and development of cognitive education programs are progressing rapidly, this book is *not* intended to be complete. Rather, it is intended to serve as a practical resource to help initiate change, to validate the enhancement of intelligent behavior as a legitimate goal of education, to invite critical assessment of existing school practices for their contributions to children's intellectual growth, and to foster the expansion of thinking throughout the curriculum.

Practical Applications of this Book

Classification involves the separation of data and information into groups by commonalities and differences. The labels given to these groups should describe, as precisely as possible, their essential elements and attributes. Categorization, in contrast, involves a system of groupings; attributes of objects, events, and conditions are examined to determine which predetermined group they should be assigned to.

The categories chosen for this book were developed by classifying numerous concerns; expressions of interest; identified needs; and questions posed by teachers, curriculum workers; administrators, staff developers, psychologists, and teacher educators. Thus, we hope this resource book will give you practical assistance in initiating, improving, and evaluating your curriculum and instructional efforts to infuse thinking into your educational programs.

Developing Minds: A Resource Book for Teaching Thinking provides an organized space for information about curriculums intended to develop students' thinking abilities, instructional strategies, and behaviors that enhance their thinking. It offers the *beginning* of a categorization system into which additional helpful resources may be placed.

You may wish to create new classifications. You should also be alert to materials and resources that will help you develop instructional programs for thinking and, after examining their attributes, fit them into one of the categories provided.

We don't recommend reading this book from cover to cover. Regardless of your school or district situation, or the progress you may have already made in installing thinking skills instruction in your curriculum, this book will provide ideas, examples, definitions, and programs to give you a boost when you appropriately need one.

While we have also included resources on a national level, you may wish to conduct a similar search of your own local resources. Talented people, innovative programs, and provocative media are available in most schools and communities. The process begins wherever you are.

On the day of its publication, *Developing Minds* will be obsolete—prices will have increased, new programs developed, additional research generated, and new articles and books written and published. You should expect these changes.

Although this publication is copyrighted, most of its contents are contributions and descriptions of noncopyrighted ideas. You are therefore invited to duplicate those portions you find suitable for distribution to community groups, school staffs, boards of education, and so forth. We merely ask that you identify the book on all duplicated materials, and not use these materials for resale. For example, if you need a statement of philosophy or rationale to support your staff development or curriculum writing project, please duplicate or adapt the one contained in Part I. Give credit to the authors, Jay McTighe and Jan Schollenberger; then feel free to use it as a discussion starter for your own group. Our interest is to improve educational practices, using this book as a means of getting the word out.

Developing Minds is *not* a recipe book, nor does it provide easy answers. A curriculum for thinking, and therefore this book, is intentionally unfinished. Its design is symbolic of this field of educational inquiry today—controversial, tentative, incomplete, and fascinating. Several chapters present alternative approaches, multiple definitions, and differing points of view. This is purposeful. Instructional leaders, working with other educators and interested community members, will strive for improvement by continuing to stimulate dialogue, gathering additional resources and data, clarifying meaning, synthesizing definitions, and searching for better ways of learning to think through education. Out of this confusion comes enlightenment. Thus the *process* of developing curriculum, improving instructional strategies, and assessing students' growth in thinking abilities is, and should be, an intellectually stimulating experience.

Arthur L. Costa

REFERENCE

Machado, L. A. *The Right to be Intelligent*. New York: Pergamon Press, 1980.

PART I

The Need to Teach Students to Think

We must return to basics, but the "basics" of the 21st century are not only reading, writing and arithmetic. They include communication and higher problem-solving skills, and scientific and technological literacy—the think-ing tools that allow us to understand the technological world around us.

—Educating Americans for the 21st Century

● *Don't we already teach students to think?* Many ed-ucators believe that schools are already doing an adequate job of developing students' cognitive abilities.

● *Of course I teach thinking; why just yesterday I gave my students a lecture on the importance of thinking criti-cally.* Many teachers feel they are already doing an ade-quate job of educating the intellect.

● *Please . . . don't add anything more to the curricu-lum. We can't cover all that we're supposed to now!* Many administrators do not understand the place of thinking in the overall school day or the curriculum to be taught.

● *How does this new thinking skills curriculum in your schools meet the Economic Security Act—the Hatch Act? Is this one of the "sensitive subjects" I'm supposed to give my child permission to participate in?* Many parents don't understand the purposes of a cognitive curriculum.

● *I don't like those kinds of questions—they're too hard. Why don't teachers just tell us the answers they want us to have? Then we'll know if we're right so we can get a better grade in this class.* Many students don't realize that learning to think is the purpose of their education.

Even though *you* may be convinced, it is often neces-sary to persuade community groups, parents, other educa-tors, and boards of education that resources should be de-voted to educating the intellect. Part I of this resource book presents two statements of rationale. Their purpose is to explain why there is a need to include thinking in the cur-riculum and why the development of students' intellectual abilities is a valid goal of education.

1

Why Teach Thinking: A Statement of Rationale

Jay McTighe and Jan Schollenberger

The level of the development of a country is determined, in considerable part, by the level of development of its people's intelligence. . . .

       —Luis Alberto Machado

The goal of helping students become more effective thinkers is fundamental to American schooling and certainly not a new idea. John Dewey saw the development of an individual capable of reflective thinking as a prominent educational objective.[1] In 1937 the National Education Association's Educational Policies Commission included the following statement among its list of ten "imperatives": "all youth need to grow in their ability to think rationally, to express their thoughts clearly, and to read and listen with understanding."[2]

The rationale for teaching thinking that we present in this chapter allows readers to examine their existing needs in this area. This rationale serves at least four purposes. First, it provides a clear picture of the problem for both educators and the public. Second, it offers well-founded reasons for considering change. Why should an individual teacher, school, or entire district bother to alter its approach without due cause? Third, it helps to structure the philosophy, goals and objectives, and form of improvement efforts. Finally, it identifies expected outcomes, which is necessary for the selection or development of appropriate instruments for assessment.

Our rationale is based on three significant factors that point to the need for teaching thinking: the *characteristics of present and future societies,* which can help us identify the skills that will be needed to develop *students' thinking capabilities* by modifying or creating new *teaching methods.*

Characteristics of Present and Future Societies

Much has been written about America's movement from the industrial era into the "information age." This transition has been prompted in part by the extraordinary rate of emerging knowledge in today's world. It is estimated that the information half-life (the time period during which half of the information in a field becomes outdated) of certain fields is as short as six years. At present, 55 percent of the nation's workers are engaged in processing and communicating information, and the percentage is expected to increase in the future.[3]

The requirements of the information age clearly affect educational goals and practices. The National Science Board Commission on Pre-College Education in Mathematics, Science, and Technology declared in its report, *Educating Americans for the 21st Century:*

> We must return to basics, but the basics of the 21st century are not only reading, writing, and arithmetic. They include communication and higher problem-solving skills, and scientific and technological literacy—the *thinking* tools that allow us to understand the technological world around us. . . . Development of students' capacities for problem-solving and critical thinking in all areas of learning is presented as a fundamental goal.[4]

The Association for Supervision and Curriculum Development has also acknowledged the need for an expanded version of the basics in a 1984 resolution: "Further development and emphases are needed in teaching skills of problem solving, reasoning, conceptualization, and analysis, which are among the neglected basics needed in tomorrow's society."[5]

Additional support for this view resulted from the work of a committee of leaders from various organizations and industries. In 1982 the Education Commission of the

States directed this committee to identify those skills that would be considered basic for the future. They listed: "Evaluation and analysis skills, critical thinking, problem-solving strategies, organization and reference skills, synthesis, application, creativity, decision-making given incomplete information, and communication skills through a variety of modes."[6]

The rapid increase of available knowledge has particular significance for education. Content teachers frequently lament their ability to cover all the material in the content curriculums. The increased knowledge bases of many subjects quantitatively compound this task. It is clear that a different strategy is in order—one that emphasizes developing the life-long *learning* and *thinking* skills necessary to acquire and process information within an ever-expanding field of knowledge.

According to Robert Ornstein of the Institute for the Study of Human Knowledge,

Solutions to the significant problems facing modern society demand a widespread, qualitative improvement in thinking and understanding. We are slowly and painfully becoming aware that such diverse contemporary challenges as energy, population, the environment, employment, health, psychological well-being of individuals and meaningful education of our youth are not being met by the mere accumulation of more data or expenditure of more time, energy, or money. In view of the increasing pressures imposed on our society by these problems, many responsible thinkers have realized that we cannot sit back and hope for some technological invention to cure our social ills. We need a breakthrough in the *quality* of thinking employed both by decision-makers at all levels of society and by each of us in our daily affairs.[7]

Having identified the kinds of skills students need to develop now in order to function well in the future, it is imperative that we evaluate the capabilities that students presently possess.

Student Thinking Capabilities

Despite this need, results from numerous sources consistently indicate that "the percentage of students achieving higher-order [thinking] skills is declining."[8] For example:

● Reporting on the 1979-80 assessment of reading comprehension, the National Assessment of Education Progress concluded:

The most significant finding from this assessment is that while students learn to read a wide range of materials, they develop very few skills for examining the nature of the ideas that they take away from their reading. Students seemed satisfied with their initial interpretations of what they had read and seemed satisfied with their initial requests to explain or defend their points of view. Few students could provide more than superficial responses to such tasks, and even the better responses showed little

evidence of well-developed problem-solving strategies or critical-thinking skills.[9]

● Citing other National Assessment data, the National Commission on Excellence in Education warned:

Many 17-year-olds do not possess the higher order intellectual skills we should expect of them. Nearly 40 percent cannot draw inferences from written materials; only one-fifth can write a persuasive essay; and only one-third can solve a mathematics problem requiring several steps.[10]

● Much attention has been given to the recent decline in Scholastic Aptitude Test (SAT) scores. Contrary to public opinion, this decline does not indicate a drop in basic knowledge. According to Jencks, a breakdown of the SAT examination questions showed no significant decline in spelling, punctuation, reading recall, or basic mathematic skills. Students were less successful, however, with those questions requiring more complex thinking, such as making analogies and organizing concepts.[11]

Such results are no surprise to teachers of all levels who express concern that students are unable to argue effectively, examine complex problems carefully, or write convincingly. These feelings are shared by parents, employers, and others who recognize the importance of thinking in today's world.

Thus it is necessary to also examine *why* students are falling short in this area. If teachers are to be charged with developing students' thinking skills, the first step is to look at the methods teachers currently use to find what they actually accomplish and to identify new techniques.

Today's Teaching Methods

While many teachers value thinking and employ methods that encourage its development, a number of probing studies indicate that these teachers do not constitute the norm. For example, in 1978, the National Institute of Education commissioned the Center for the Study of Reading at the University of Illinois to investigate the development of reading comprehension at the elementary level. Visiting teams observed 39 classrooms in 14 school districts over a three-day period. Reading and social studies instruction was viewed for a total of 17,977 minutes. The general consensus was that the teaching of comprehension was practically nonexistent. There was no trace of comprehension being taught in any social studies session, and only 17 instances—involving 45 of 11,587 minutes—were devoted to teaching reading comprehension skills.[12]

In his book, *A Place Called School*, John Goodlad reports on an exhaustive study involving observations of more than 1,000 classrooms in a variety of communities throughout the country. A summary of results showed that an average of 75 percent of class time was spent on instruction. Approximately 70 percent of this time involved verbal interaction—with teachers "out talking" students by a ratio of three to one. Observers noted that *less than* 1 percent of this "teacher talk" invited students to engage in anything more than mere recall of information.[13]

Other studies have reached similar conclusions. Most teachers do not regularly employ methods that encourage and develop thinking in their students.

Recommendations for Schools

Recognition of these needs has led to an unusual consensus of opinion.

● In *An Agenda for Action,* the National Council of Teachers of Mathematics states:

The higher-order mental processes of logical reasoning, information processing, and decision making should be considered basic to the application of mathematics . . . problem solving [should] be the focus of school mathematics in the 1980's.[14]

● The National Council of Teachers of English highlights thinking skills in the publication *Essentials of English* by affirming that:

Because thinking and language are closely linked, teachers of English have always held that one of their main duties is to teach students *how* to think. Thinking skills, involved in the study of all disciplines, are inherent in the reading, writing, speaking, listening and observing involved in the study of English. The ability to analyze, classify, compare, formulate hypotheses, make inferences, and draw conclusions is essential to the reasoning processes of all adults. The capacity to solve problems, both rationally and intuitively, is a way to help students cope successfully with the experience of learning within the school setting and outside.[15]

● In the National Council for the Social Studies publication, *Developing Decision-Making Skills,* Kurfman and Cassidy observe:

Social studies classrooms have been dominated by attempts to transmit knowledge, often very specific knowledge, about people, places, dates, and institutional structure . . . There is no denying the importance of knowledge: the more capable we are of enjoying experiences; the more we know, the more likely we are to make sound decisions. But, as the overall purpose of social studies, knowledge attainment is not a sufficiently broad purpose to guide program development or to inspire modern students. . . .

They propose:

Learning only easily testable fact-finding skills will prove increasingly inadequate for life in the modern world. Much more than fact-finding skills—that is, *higher-level thought processes,* useful knowledge, and clear values—are needed for students to function effectively.[16]

● In her article, "Striving for Excellence in Arts Education," Leilani Duke describes the ways in which thinking skills can and should be promoted through the arts:

The goal of education in the arts should be to foster the learning of higher order intellectual skills through presenting arts instruction as a compound discipline. Such an integrated approach includes (a) aesthetic perception, (b) production or performing skills, (c) arts criticism, and (d) arts history. Attending to aesthetic perception, children can learn to analyze, criticize, and interpret sensory properties. Through production and performing skills, they can learn how to translate abstract concepts into tangible, visual, auditory, or kinesthetic expressions. In developing critical skills, children can learn to make and support discriminatory judgments. They can learn to draw facts and inferences about man and society by studying the cultural and historical contexts from which the arts spring.[17]

Conclusion

The goal of developing school graduates with the ability to think critically is significant, yet it should not constitute the sole justification for improvement efforts. Since thinking is essential to all school subjects, its development should be considered *a means* as well as *an end.*

Finally, the fundamental requirements of our democratic society provide a powerful rationale for focusing on thinking. Democracy, as envisioned by our nation's founders, rests on an informed and intellectually able citizenry. Edward Glaser observes:

For good citizenship in a representative democracy is not just a matter of keeping within the law and being a good and a kind neighbor. In addition good citizenship calls for the attainment of a working understanding of our social, political, and economic arrangements and for the ability to *think critically* about issues concerning which there may be an honest difference of opinion.[18]

Effective thinking is particularly important for contemporary democracy as local, national, and international issues become increasingly complex. Additional sources attesting to this need and making recommendations could be cited; however, the message is clear—educators need to take renewed action to bring about qualitative improvements in student thinking.

FOOTNOTES

[1]John Dewey, *How We Think* (Chicago: Henry Regenery Company, 1933).

[2]From a report of the Educational Policies Commission, Washington, D.C., National Education Association, 1937.

[3]"The Future World of Work," a report from the Long Range Planning Subcommittee on Environmental Scanning/Strategic Planning Development (Alexandria, Va.: United Way of America, 1981). For an excellent overview of demographic and social trends affecting society, see *A Profound Transformation,* a slide/tape presentation (Arlington, Va.: American Association of School Administrators, 1980). See also John Naisbitt, *Megatrends* (New York: Warner Books, 1984).

[4]*Educating Americans for the 21st Century* (Washington,

D.C.: The National Science Board Commission on Pre-College Education in Mathematics, Science, and Technology, 1983).

[5]"ASCD 1984 Resolutions," *ASCD Update* 26, 4 (May 1984).

[6]Education Commission of the States, Denver, Colo., 1982.

[7]Robert Ornstein, concept paper from The Institute for the Study of Human Knowledge, Los Altos, Calif., 1980.

[8]Education Commission of the States, Denver, Colo., 1982

[9]"Reading, Thinking and Writing," *The 1979-80 National Assessment of Reading and Literature* (Denver, Colo.: National Assessment of Education Progress, 1981).

[10]*A Nation at Risk: The Imperative for Educational Reform,* a report of The National Commission of Excellence in Education, Washington, D.C., 1983.

[11]C. Jencks, "The Wrong Answer for School Is," *The Washington Post,* February 1978, p. 42.

[12]From a study sponsored by the National Institute of Education, The Center for the Study of Reading, University of Illinois, 1978.

[13]John Goodlad, "A Study of Schooling: Some Findings and Hypotheses," *Phi Delta Kappan* (March 1983): 465-470.

[14]*An Agenda for Action* (Reston, Va.: National Council of Teachers of Mathematics, 1980).

[15]*Essentials of English* (Urbana, Ill.: The National Council of Teachers of English, 1982).

[16]D. Kurfman and E. Cassidy, *Developing Decision-Making Skills* (Arlington, Va.: The National Council for the Social Studies, 1977).

[17]Leilani Duke, "Striving for Excellence in Arts Education," *Design for Arts in Education* 85, 3 (January/February 1984).

[18]Edward Glaser, *An Experiment in the Development of Critical Thinking* (New York: Teachers College, Columbia University, 1941), p. 5.

2
Educational Outcomes For a K-12 Curriculum

Sydelle Seiger-Ehrenberg

The principal goal of education is to create men who are capable of doing new things, not simply of repeating what other generations have done—men who are creative, inventive, and discoverers. The second goal of education is to form minds which can be critical, can verify, and not accept everything they are offered.

—Jean Piaget

Traditionally, elementary and secondary school curriculum has been derived from arbitrary selections of content from the "scholarly disciplines": history, geography, mathematics, biology, and so forth. Yet every significant statement of the goals of education has been expressed in terms of *desired outcome characteristics of the student*—"effective problem solver," "responsible citizen," and the like. What we've been saying, in effect, is that if students learn all the subject matter content we've included in the curriculum, they will somehow become the kind of people we want them to become.

The Institute for Curriculum and Instruction's (ICI) Curriculum Model is based on a different premise. It says, "If you want students to develop certain behavioral characteristics, start with those and focus the entire curriculum on achieving them. View the scholarly disciplines as sources of needed information, ideas, and procedures. Select and use content only as needed to achieve the desired student characteristics." By taking this approach, not only is the same basic content "covered," but all of it is learned in a *relevant context*, as it applies to achieving the desired outcome characteristics.

The following is an introduction to the ICI Curriculum Model.[1] The Intended Outcome Statement is followed by a detailed analysis of its meaning.

Intended Outcome for Students

By the time students graduate from high school, they should be able to consistently and effectively take intelligent and ethical action to accomplish the tasks society legitimately expects of all its members and to establish and pursue worthwhile goals of their own choosing.

Consistently and Effectively Take Intelligent, Ethical Action

"Consistently" here means characteristically or without deviation, except under extraordinary circumstances. "Effectively" implies the ability to achieve desired results. "Intelligent, ethical action" refers to *planned behavior* undertaken as a result of having gone through a mental process such as:

● Clarifying what is to be achieved and why, the criteria and standards to be met and why.

● Obtaining sufficient valid, relevant, and reliable information to assess the current situation and deciding what, if anything, needs to be done.

● Analyzing alternative courses of action in terms of feasibility and possible short- and long-term consequences.

● Choosing the most appropriate, desirable courses of action considering what is to be achieved *and* the well-being of those involved.

● Making and carrying out the commitment to pursue one or more selected courses of action, evaluate the results and the way they were obtained, and accept and deal with

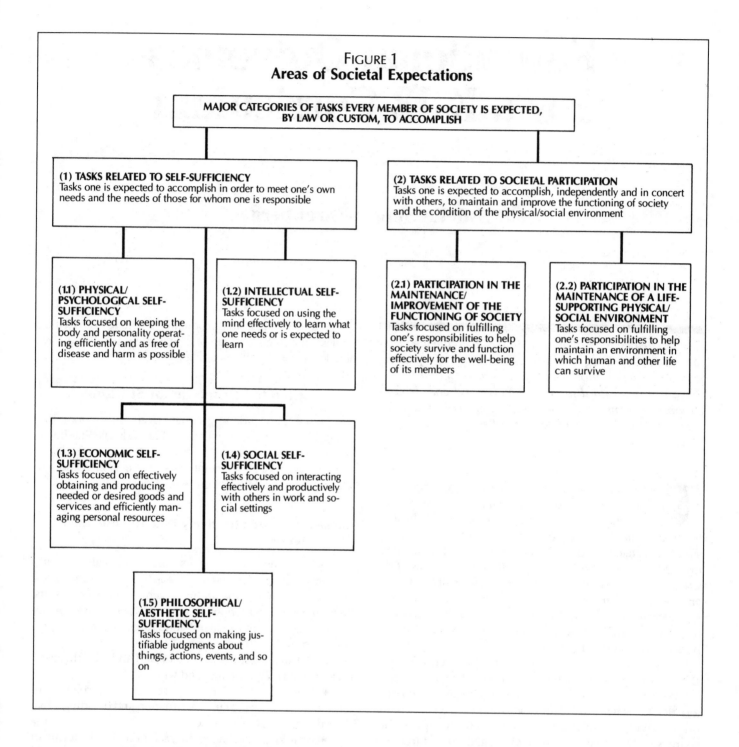

FIGURE 1
Areas of Societal Expectations

MAJOR CATEGORIES OF TASKS EVERY MEMBER OF SOCIETY IS EXPECTED, BY LAW OR CUSTOM, TO ACCOMPLISH

(1) TASKS RELATED TO SELF-SUFFICIENCY
Tasks one is expected to accomplish in order to meet one's own needs and the needs of those for whom one is responsible

(2) TASKS RELATED TO SOCIETAL PARTICIPATION
Tasks one is expected to accomplish, independently and in concert with others, to maintain and improve the functioning of society and the condition of the physical/social environment

(1.1) PHYSICAL/ PSYCHOLOGICAL SELF-SUFFICIENCY
Tasks focused on keeping the body and personality operating efficiently and as free of disease and harm as possible

(1.2) INTELLECTUAL SELF-SUFFICIENCY
Tasks focused on using the mind effectively to learn what one needs or is expected to learn

(2.1) PARTICIPATION IN THE MAINTENANCE/ IMPROVEMENT OF THE FUNCTIONING OF SOCIETY
Tasks focused on fulfilling one's responsibilities to help society survive and function effectively for the well-being of its members

(2.2) PARTICIPATION IN THE MAINTENANCE OF A LIFE-SUPPORTING PHYSICAL/ SOCIAL ENVIRONMENT
Tasks focused on fulfilling one's responsibilities to help maintain an environment in which human and other life can survive

(1.3) ECONOMIC SELF-SUFFICIENCY
Tasks focused on effectively obtaining and producing needed or desired goods and services and efficiently managing personal resources

(1.4) SOCIAL SELF-SUFFICIENCY
Tasks focused on interacting effectively and productively with others in work and social settings

(1.5) PHILOSOPHICAL/ AESTHETIC SELF-SUFFICIENCY
Tasks focused on making justifiable judgments about things, actions, events, and so on

the consequences using the same rational, ethical procedures used to decide on the selected course of action.

"Intelligent," in effect, means using rational thought processes to arrive at a decision to act (or not act). It does *not* imply "unfeeling" or "uncreative," nor does it exclude the use of intuition. This concept of intelligence or rationality views feelings, attitudes, values, and ideas—from whatever source—as key factors to be consciously recognized and reckoned with in the decision-making or action process.

"Ethical" means taking into account, when deciding or acting, the well-being of those involved and making a commitment to take courses of action that are likely to contribute to (or at least will not detract from) the well-being of

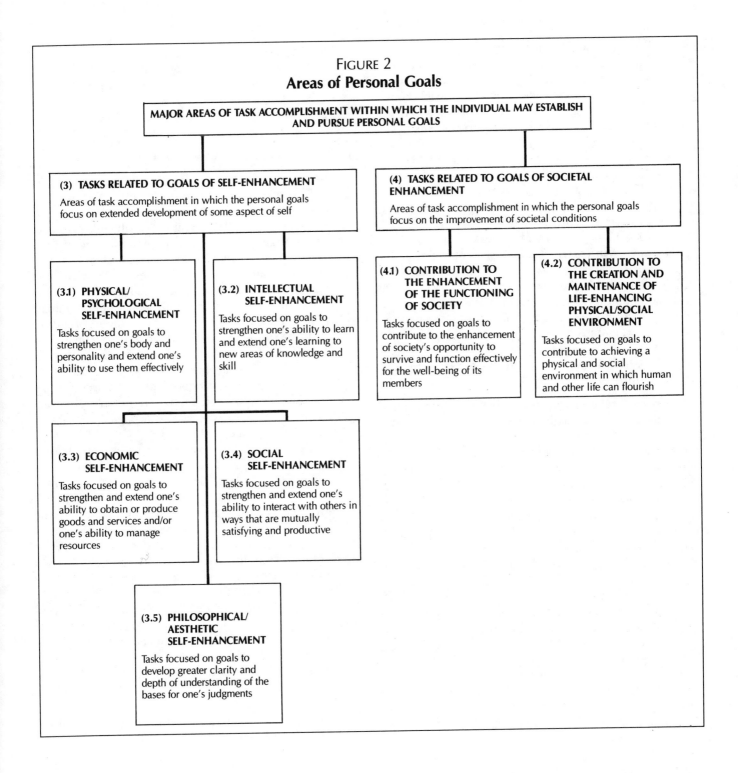

FIGURE 2
Areas of Personal Goals

MAJOR AREAS OF TASK ACCOMPLISHMENT WITHIN WHICH THE INDIVIDUAL MAY ESTABLISH AND PURSUE PERSONAL GOALS

(3) TASKS RELATED TO GOALS OF SELF-ENHANCEMENT

Areas of task accomplishment in which the personal goals focus on extended development of some aspect of self

(4) TASKS RELATED TO GOALS OF SOCIETAL ENHANCEMENT

Areas of task accomplishment in which the personal goals focus on the improvement of societal conditions

(3.1) PHYSICAL/ PSYCHOLOGICAL SELF-ENHANCEMENT

Tasks focused on goals to strengthen one's body and personality and extend one's ability to use them effectively

(3.2) INTELLECTUAL SELF-ENHANCEMENT

Tasks focused on goals to strengthen one's ability to learn and extend one's learning to new areas of knowledge and skill

(4.1) CONTRIBUTION TO THE ENHANCEMENT OF THE FUNCTIONING OF SOCIETY

Tasks focused on goals to contribute to the enhancement of society's opportunity to survive and function effectively for the well-being of its members

(4.2) CONTRIBUTION TO THE CREATION AND MAINTENANCE OF LIFE-ENHANCING PHYSICAL/SOCIAL ENVIRONMENT

Tasks focused on goals to contribute to achieving a physical and social environment in which human and other life can flourish

(3.3) ECONOMIC SELF-ENHANCEMENT

Tasks focused on goals to strengthen and extend one's ability to obtain or produce goods and services and/or one's ability to manage resources

(3.4) SOCIAL SELF-ENHANCEMENT

Tasks focused on goals to strengthen and extend one's ability to interact with others in ways that are mutually satisfying and productive

(3.5) PHILOSOPHICAL/ AESTHETIC SELF-ENHANCEMENT

Tasks focused on goals to develop greater clarity and depth of understanding of the bases for one's judgments

those affected and their opportunity to take intelligent, ethical action.

Intelligent, ethical action *excludes:*

• *Irrationality*—choosing a course of action knowing it is likely to produce an undesired outcome (a person who is dieting decides to eat a rich dessert knowing it will add unwanted calories).

• *Irresponsibility or recklessness*—choosing a course of action without concern for the predicted consequences (an overweight person chooses to eat a rich dessert knowing it will add calories, but not caring whether or not he or she gains additional weight).

• *Impulsiveness*—choosing a course of action without giving any consideration to alternatives or possible consequences (an overweight person chooses to eat a rich dessert without thinking of either the calories or his or her weight).

• *Immorality*—choosing a course of action knowing it is likely to have injurious consequences for those involved (telling an overweight person who is dieting that the dessert you prepared is safe to eat because it was made with low-calorie substitutes, knowing that the dessert is really made with high-calorie ingredients).

• *Lack of integrity*—choosing a course of action knowing that it violates avowed principles (an overweight person who publicly claims to be on a very strict diet eats rich snacks on the sly and says that there must be something wrong with his or her glands or the diet because there is no weight loss).

Accomplish Tasks Society Legitimately Expects of All Its Members

"Society" refers to any identifiable group of people of which an individual may be considered to be a member. This includes the broad human community and therefore embraces tasks that *any* human being is expected to accomplish, by law or custom, regardless of the time or place (maintaining good health, caring for dependents, maintaining a safe physical environment). It also includes one's national group, cultural or subcultural group, age group, family group, and so on, and implies any tasks legitimately required of any member of those groups.

While many possible tasks might legitimately be expected of every member of society, Figure 1 (p. 8) categorizes the tasks used in this curriculum design, which apply to membership in *any* societal group, broad or narrow.

A corresponding concern is *how* these tasks are performed. In our society, we hold two broad expectations:

1. Tasks will be performed within the framework of both the letter and spirit of the law (or rules).

2. Where there is no explicit law or rule relating to a given situation, tasks will be performed in a manner consistent with the traditional customs, ethics, values, and mores of the society:

a. With empathy and goodwill toward others, like and different from oneself.

b. With consideration of the rights of others (without becoming a burden on society or inhibiting others' rights).

c. With effort to do one's best.

d. With integrity and honesty.

e. With intent to live a productive, useful life.

f. With willingness to accept responsibility for personal behavior.

g. With intent to protect, defend, and improve society and its institutions.

Establish and Pursue Worthwhile Goals

Implied here is that intelligent, ethical action will be taken (1) to select areas of interest or desired accomplishment and (2) to develop one's knowledge and skills to achieve desired goals. The qualifier "worthwhile" is somewhat redundant, because if such goals are identified through intelligent, *ethical* action, they are likely to be selected with consideration of and interest in the well-being of self and others. The word is included for emphasis.

Generally, personal goals, rather than being in areas different from the tasks expected of all members of society, are really *extensions* of them. They are based primarily on particular individual interests and abilities, rather than on societal expectations. An analysis of this context (Figure 2, p. 9), therefore, is essentially the same as the previous one but with a slight change of focus from *required* task accomplishment to *self-selected* task accomplishment.

The most extreme implementation of the ICI Curriculum Model would require doing away with the traditional subjects of science, social studies, and so on, and replacing them with such subjects as Economic Self-Sufficiency, Intellectual Self-Enhancement, Participation in Functioning Society. A more moderate approach would be to retain the current subject areas but to use the student characteristics as the basis for selection of content and the way it is taught. For example, a high school biology course curriculum would be developed around the goal of students becoming prepared to contribute to the well-being of the living things in their environment. Students would be assessed accordingly—that is, they would be required to demonstrate that they have learned how to *use* certain knowledge and skills, rather than that they have simply acquired them. And isn't that, after all, what we *really* want curriculum to achieve?

REFERENCE

Ehrenberg, Sydelle D., and Lyle, M. *A Strategy for Curriculum Design—The ICI Model.* Coshocton, Ohio: Institute for Curriculum and Instruction, 1978, pp. 44-50.

FOOTNOTE

[1]The entire ICI Curriculum Model, too lengthy to include here, contains confirmation tasks, criteria, and standards for assessing student progress toward achievement of the intended outcome.

PART II

Creating School Conditions for Thinking

We should be teaching students how to think; instead we are primarily teaching them what to think.

—Jack Lochhead

To install thinking as a valid goal of education, the many components of the educational system must be tuned to work harmoniously. Years of experience with major efforts to improve educational practices demonstrate the ineffectiveness of change when these components are not "in sync." Materials of instruction, staff development, adopted curriculum, supervisory processes, evaluation measures, communication with parents, and so forth, must all be aligned and focused on a common goal. Recent school effectiveness studies demonstrate the benefits when they are.

Education of the intellect must, therefore, be installed as a value of the school and community. If teachers, parents, administrators, board members, and the community adopted thinking as a basic goal of education, the community-wide emphasis would be exhibited in several ways:

● Instructional materials would be developed and adopted based on their contributions to developing thinking.

● Supervisory personnel would be trained to recognize and evaluate the contributions of certain instructional practices to intellectual development.

● Staff development would be provided on how to describe, teach, and assess thinking.

● Problem solving would be discussed and debated in faculty, parent, and board meetings.

● Monies would be allocated to increase thinking skills programs.

● Community groups would complain that schools are not teaching enough thinking skills.

● Systems would be developed and installed to monitor and assess students' growth in thinking.

● Parent education would be provided to foster and support thinking at home.

● Incentives and rewards would be given to teachers, students, and administrators who excel in their use of intelligent behaviors.

In Part II of this resource book, we will examine some of these components in an effort to help curriculum leaders create a readiness in their classrooms, schools, and communities for the education of the intellect as a valued outcome of schooling.

3

A Call for Staff Development

James A. Bellanca

It must be remembered that the purpose of education is not to fill the minds of students with facts . . . it is to teach them to think, if that is possible, and always to think for themselves.

—Robert Hutchins

"I'd like you to give our faculty an inservice on thinking skills," the caller said. "This will be our inservice kickoff for the year."

Having received several similar phone requests in the past year, I interjected my questions. "When you say 'kickoff,' do you mean you're starting an extended inservice training program that will help your faculty develop new teaching methods?"

"Oh, no. We don't have time for that. We just want you to give one of those short, inspirational speeches for our first-day institute."

I needed more information. "Is there a reason you have selected the thinking skills topic?" I asked.

"Oh, yes. Our superintendent attended a conference and liked the thinking skills workshop best. Besides, a lot of the other curriculum directors in our area are talking about the importance of students' learning to think better."

A few more questions and my worst fears about faddish inservice were confirmed. "I'm sorry," I said. "I can't accept your invitation."

The caller's "Oh" was followed by a moment of silence. "Is there a special reason?" he asked.

"Yes," I responded. "There are several reasons. If you have the time, I'd be happy to outline them for you."

"Please do."

"First," I began, "in my nine years of working with the research on effective staff development, I've learned that most one-shot inservices are a waste of time and money—for me, for you, and for the teachers. I can sympathize with the teachers' need for energy builders and a district's need to introduce new ideas into a school, but the one-shot does not do that thoroughly or cost-effectively."

"But we have the superintendent's commitment. Surely that will motivate some faculty to adopt your ideas."

"Yes," I agreed. "The superintendent's support is essential. My concern is more basic."

"I don't know what you mean."

"Let me illustrate. I have a friend who is the superintendent of a 17-school district. She views her job as the district seer. She wants to predict the kind of education students in the district will need for success after graduation. She keeps her ear tuned closely to emerging issues, parental concerns, and educational developments. When a question of importance arises, such as 'Do our students know how to use computers?' or 'Are our reading scores up to snuff?' she avoids becoming what Naisbitt might call a 'fad maker,' an administrator who give a top-down, hastily conceived directive. Instead, she gathers principals and teachers together to study the issues and make a recommendation. She weighs that recommendation against other district priorities."

"But that could take months," objected the caller.

"I agree, and those months are necessary. If we are talking about meeting students' needs, we are talking about improving instruction. The one-shot inservice is planned quickly and as quickly forgotten. If we want to avoid reinforcing a 'This too shall pass' attitude about thinking skills, or any curriculum revision, the first requirement is the superintendent's commitment to a clear, well-conceived goal, not to a quick-fix fad."

"I don't see the distinction."

"Let me clarify. My friend is a good model. Recently she identified thinking skills as an important concern. She selected a task force and instructed this committee to assess what the district was already doing with thinking skills. Next, she outlined what she wanted within a set time, which was:

1. A recommendation on how the district could best improve students' thinking skills in the next three to five years.

2. A list of barriers that might impede progress.

3. Specific steps necessary to reach specific goals.

4. Timelines.

5. A proposed budget.

6. A description of responsibilities for everyone involved in implementing the process.

In addition, she provided funds for the committee so that members could visit schools that had operational thinking skills programs, attend pertinent workshops, review materials, and gather other helpful information."

"That sounds expensive for a committee report."

"That may be true," I said, "especially if the committee recommends killing the idea. If not, consider the benefits."

"I see the point. She built in expertise on thinking skills, informed a committed leadership group, and brought about a strategic plan with definite implementation tactics—and probably spent less money than I would have paid for your inspirational speech."

"Exactly," I responded. "And that is why I resist one-shot inservices however neatly packaged they might be. A district or school that studies the trend is ready to use its staff development money to cause *real and lasting improvement* in thinking skills; a district that rushes in on a whim gets hooked into the *fad.*"

"I see," said the caller, "but I'm not sure what happens if the committee says 'Go.'"

"Then," I said, "it's time for some sales work. My friend, aided by her task force, devised a plan for the school board, the PTA, and local union leadership. She concentrated on three elements: what she wanted to see students doing differently after three years; what administrators and teachers would be doing differently; and what it would cost in time, resources, and money."

"The old bugaboos!"

"I prefer to call them the marketing realities of school improvement. If we want a solid, well-conceived, and successful thinking skills program, bearing the expense is an essential part."

"And time," said the caller.

"Yes," I added. "It takes well-spent time to build a good foundation. A good idea without a solid, strategic plan will collapse."

"How much time are you proposing?"

"In the case I've been describing, about three hours work for the committee."

"Did their strategies work?"

"Yes, as they usually do. Even though the school board asked hard-money questions, as did union leaders."

"Can you be more specific? What was approved? Did the district get everything it requested?"

"I'll take the last question first," I said. "The committee didn't get *all* it requested. I've yet to see that happen. However, the substance of the recommendation remained intact."

"And what was that?"

"First, the plan focused on student outcomes. One example was 'Given the teachers' improved methods for developing thinking skills, the students would demonstrate significant gains on the New Jersey Test of Reasoning."

"Was there a reason for using that specific test?"

"Yes. While the committee described several assessment techniques, they knew the board would also want statistical measures. After reviewing several different instruments, the task force agreed that this test could be used to evaluate the measurable outcomes of their planned program."

"And those were. . . ."

The Operating Philosophy

"The committee endorsed the premise that *all* students, even those in special education, could move toward intelligent thought, could solve increasingly complex problems, and apply new skills to other content areas."

"What other bases did the committee establish?"

"Two others. First, the committee set the expectation that *all* staff—administrators, teachers, and support persons—could improve their own capabilities as thinkers and teachers of thinking. Second, they were convinced that a clear, schoolwide purpose, understood by all, was important to this project."

"I agree. One or two enthusiasts working alone don't make a winning team."

"That is why this basic operating philosophy is important. They didn't want thinking skills to be another 'add-on' to the curriculum. They wanted to see thinking skills integrated into what was already being done, and they wanted staff development to support this approach."

"What did they propose?"

"First, a K-12 curriculum that included a hierarchy of thinking skills."

"Can you give me an example?"

"Yes," I replied. "In the primary grades, the curriculum would introduce students to observing, sequencing, patterning, finding likenesses and differences, grouping, naming, attribute shifting, basic predicting, and goal setting. In middle school, the curriculum would reinforce the basic thinking skills by moving the youngsters from concrete examples to more abstract concept formation; teacher would introduce problem identification, cause-effect analysis, attribute shifting, solution design, and outcome prediction. In high school, the curriculum would call for students to practice their skills, master a variety of problem-solving processes, and tackle rudiments of inductive and deductive logic."

"But haven't schools always taught these skills and processes?"

"Indirectly, yes. But for the most part assessment data showed that only individual teachers here and there recognized what mental operations students were using—whether, for example, they were identifying patterns or identifying likenesses. The students used the skills, but they were often unaware of *how* they arrived at their conclusions."

"Is that so wrong?"

"It's not wrong, only limiting. When students are not aware of how they are thinking, they cannot formalize the skill; they can only react to a situation. They cannot elicit the principle governing the situation. As a result, they seldom transfer thinking skills learned in one context, such as math, to other subject areas. Worse yet, they fail to develop the concepts about thinking that could help them improve how well they think."

"Thinking about thinking? That is called metacognition, isn't it?"

"Yes. And labeling is an important first step in preparing students to think about their thinking."

"That seems sensible. What I don't understand is why you listed so few skills processes."

"You have a sharp eye. The list was restricted purposefully."

"Why?"

"The committee was looking for quality, not quantity. It saw no benefit in adding a host of skills to be covered. To prevent both the overload factor and the curriculum race syndrome, the committee argued for selected skills to be well taught at each grade level, carefully reinforced, and thoroughly transferred."

"How do you mean 'well taught'?"

Questioning Skills as Prerequisites

"We hear much talk about students acquiring *higher-level thinking* skills. We know this occurs most successfully when a teacher uses *higher-order teaching* skills. For instance, asking students questions that demand complex re-sponses—not just the simple recall of information—requires sophisticated teaching skills. Teachers must use very refined questioning skills to draw out and extend responses, especially from reluctant learners."

"Are you saying, then, that every teacher must be a skilled questioner?"

"If we expect every student to become a capable thinker, yes. The teacher's questioning skills are a prerequisite to better thinking."

"I am familiar with a variety of prepackaged thinking skills programs. Do they demand such skilled teaching?"

"Not all do. The poorest are no more than glossy mimeo worksheets. When a teacher floods the room with worksheets, the students may fill in the blanks and boxes without much thought, play games, or dawdle the time away. The best programs recognize that the development of thinking skills and the mastery of problem-solving processes depend on how teachers set up the activity and guide the discussion that follows. Whether the curriculum is prepackaged or devised by the district, the teacher's skill in asking questions and explicitly teaching thinking skills will determine the degree of the program's success."

"That seems so obvious."

"In theory, yes; in practice the purple plague of mindless, duplicated worksheets is more common."

"In other words, you are saying that just as it takes more skill to cook a soufflé than a hamburger, it takes more skill to lead an inquiry lesson than it takes to teach a direct instruction lesson."

"Yes. As long as you understand that the best teachers do both well, I would argue that good inquiry teaching is more difficult."

Measures of Success

"Suppose we structure the type of inquiry program you describe. Will we increase student achievement by the end of the year?"

"Probably not. One year is too short a time for such results. However, you could easily measure increased teacher knowledge, skill, and use of inquiry in the classroom—increased student participation, more thoughtful student behavior, and a greater value accorded thinking by all. By assessing those elements first, you could predict meaningful achievement increases in two or three years."

"That gives me a sense of relief."

"How so?"

"I was trying to think how we could do what you are suggesting. I'm now seeing the difference between the quick fix and mastery curriculum. You're asking us to integrate a formal thinking skills program. It would highlight a limited number of essential skills, emphasize transfer of those skills, and train teachers to spend more time helping students to apply their new skills and less time 'covering' material."

"Precisely. Most traditional curriculums give short shrift to teaching for transfer. Rather than introducing a multitude of thinking skills in each grade, it is more practical for each grade to introduce no more than six micro-thinking skills. More time should be spent helping students transfer the skills to their content areas and practicing previously learning skills by positive reinforcement and meta-cognitive discussion."

"I see. You value depth over breadth in teaching skills."

"Yes. Rather than an empty emphasis on coverage, I want each teacher to focus on an outcome—the students' use of the skill."

"You are saying, then, that teaching for transfer, along with inquiry skills, is a mark of the more skilled teacher?"

"Yes, and so is the teacher's ability to use metacognitive strategies."

"I understand the term metacognition, but what are metacognitive strategies?"

"They are teaching strategies, used regularly and consistently by the teacher, that promote metacognition. Art Costa outlined the most productive metacognitive strategies in *Educational Leadership* (November 1984)."

"Can you give me some examples?"

"Yes. When teachers explain to students that the lesson objective is a specific thinking skill, ask extending questions, or have students map their thinking patterns, they are promoting metacognition."

"Those procedures don't sound difficult."

"They aren't. The challenge comes in the teacher's discipline and finesse in causing students to examine how they think."

"Discipline?"

"Yes. Discipline is required to design a lesson that not only covers course content, such as science or literature, but integrates thinking skills, too. Planning this lesson will require that teachers take time to isolate the desired level of thinking, model the thinking skill, structure the thinking experience, question so that all students are involved, and encourage transfer of the skill to other academic areas."

"Can you give an example?"

"Yes. Suppose that Mrs. Fuller intends to introduce induction to her composition students. Her curriculum guide provides the 'Sherlock Holmes Mystery Student' activity. In this activity, she plans a series of 'what if' questions. Knowing that she has some students who need extra focus time, she structures her questions using small group whip-a-round. Every student in each group will answer at least twice. She'll follow this with a random report from each group. Each new idea will be listed on the board and she'll ask students to attempt generalizations about the specific ideas. This will lead to her explanation and definition of induction and the posting of her objectives. 'You will apply the inductive process to the writing of an essay about induction.' Because she knows that this is a complex objective, she encourages student questions."

"I see what you mean about time and discipline. I have teachers who would resist having to go to all that trouble."

"And that is why I would also argue they will have less success than Mrs. Fuller in teaching students how to think."

"Let me play the devil's advocate for my teachers by asking, 'Why not just give the definition and explain with some examples? The capable thinkers will get it; the others won't anyway.'"

"Ah, but remember our original expectation. Our intention is to improve the thinking capacity of all students. That cannot happen if we take the easy route of doling out information for the few. Furthermore, I'd question how well even the best students increase their capacity to think by memorizing definitions and examples. Mrs. Fuller took great care to motivate every student not just to memorize facts but actually to start thinking inductively. She structured the Sherlock Holmes activity to keep it going. Only when she was sure her students knew where they were going and why did she give precise instructions for the activity. In groups of three, students searched for planted clues around the classroom. After ten minutes, each group pooled its finds and formed hunches about the items. As students reported their hunches, Mrs. Fuller extended their thinking with clarifying and probing questions. Gradually, groups began to exchange clues, searching for patterns until finally they discovered the answers."

"That must have taken a lot more time than a lecture."

"You don't know the half of it—Mrs. Fuller continued with a metacognitive discussion. She asked each group to recall the thinking steps used to reach the final conclusion. She asked the groups to contrast the patterns; and as they listed their patterns on the blackboard, she helped them recognize the difference in the approaches each had used, places where thinking hit dead ends, and processes that led to the sound conclusions they ultimately drew. She concluded the lesson by asking each student to use the 'Thinking Journal' to compose a personal definition of induction along with an 'I learned' statement."

"And that was the end?"

"Of that two-period lesson, yes. Mrs. Fuller followed the basic lesson with shorter practices—another Sherlock Holmes activity to accompany a short story, another activity for a magazine article, and a third using the students' world history text. Each of the practice lessons was designed to promote transfer of the concept introduced in the first lesson. What could have more utility than transfer through related coursework? After the social studies lesson, Mrs. Fuller finally pulled all the pieces together with a biology text assignment and take-home newspaper assignment. The latter also served as the test, which revealed how well she had succeeded with *all* the students."

A Hierarchy of Teaching Skills

"Now I understand your emphasis on the more advanced skills needed to teach thinking skills. However, I wouldn't know where to begin to develop my staff."

"First, think about a hierarchy of teaching skills."

"Similar to the hierarchy of thinking skills?"

"Yes. First, there are the skills needed by a teacher to be effective with basic instruction: classroom management, lesson design, and learning theory."

"The methods of effective teaching."

"Yes. The concepts and methods that researchers have confirmed as the basics of quality instruction. However, they are only a starting point."

"What's next on your hierarchy?"

"Next is what I call the enabling behaviors. These are the teaching skills that enable all students to increase the quantity of active thinking in the classroom."

"What are some examples?"

"First, I'd go to the research. There I'd find wait time, equal distribution of student responses, selective reinforcement, equal cueing and encouragement, and the other strategies leading to equal opportunity to respond to questions."

"To promote the quantity of thinking, you are suggesting an approach similar to the Teacher Expectations and Student Achievement (TESA) behaviors."

"Yes, these enabling behaviors are simple but powerful tools that get amazing results. Without these enablers, the classroom is not a hospitable environment for good inquiry."

"Beyond basic teaching skills and enabling behaviors, what?"

"Quality. I'd move up a step in our teaching hierarchy to the metacognitive and transfer strategies. From there, I want to see the teacher helping students acquire more complex thinking skills, use the skills to develop more abstract concepts, and apply the skills for analytic and creative problem solving."

"If our district develops a thinking skills curriculum of this hierarchy of teaching skills, what should follow?"

"First, a needs assessment would identify the basic, enabling, and advanced skills each teacher uses successfully. A written test and classroom observations take care of this.

Next, you would use the needs data to teach any additional skills needed."

"That sounds easy enough."

"Don't be fooled. I can predict two difficulties. First, your teachers are used to the one-shot inservice. Second, you have always encouraged your teachers to identify and correct their own problems. They may balk at a focused program. If you want to model the 'thinking' approach, the design of your workshop will differ radically from past practices. The approach I recommend determines needs based on district priorities, observations, and in a sense, required inservice over an extended period of time."

"I see no problem there. Our district is committed to the idea of personal and school improvement. Also, I wouldn't gain support for any idea by asserting that there is something wrong with our teachers. I'd want an incentive program to concentrate on individual and school improvement rather than punitive measures, and as I see it, your hierarchy of teaching skills allows for an infinite scale of improvement. In contrast with the proscriptive repair of the 'medical model'—something's really wrong—the hierarchy of teaching skills presents improvement in a more positive light."

"I like your analysis."

Workable Workshop Design

"On the other hand, I'm not clear what you mean by a *radically* different workshop design. Our teachers are impatient with any workshop that doesn't produce immediate results."

"The way to do that is through the workshop design that 'walks its talk.' "

"Walks its talk?"

"Yes. Adults learning new ways to instruct students will grasp the content best from a model that demonstrates exactly what it teaches."

"Be more specific."

"Surely. Imagine that your desired outcome for the workshop is to have teachers identify situations in which they might use the enabling skills. Let me picture for you a design that will accomplish this objective." I then described the design shown on Figure 1 (p. 18).

"That is a very thorough and active design. I notice that the lesson not only teaches about the enablers, but demonstrates their use and promotes transfer."

"You are right on target. Moreover, this design allows for the trainers to introduce behavior coaching and peer support teams."

"What do you mean?"

FIGURE 1
Workshop Design Utilizing Enabling Skills

Focus: 1. "How many teachers remember the Lone Ranger?"

"Who can recall his horse's name? His companion's name?"

"How is the story line of that serial similar to TV soaps such as *Dallas*?"

2. "Explain how soap opera writers use the morphological grid to motivate their own divergent thinking."

Objective: To motivate divergent thinking so that we will explore new combinations of ideas.

Task: Develop a modern soap opera.

Instructions: 1. You are members of a TV production team assigned to develop a new soap opera for the networks. Observe your grid:

	Male Lead	Female Lead	Third Party	Action	Scene	Result
1)						
2)						
3)						
4)						
5)						
6)						
7)						
8)						
9)						
10)						

2. All brainstorm, column by column.

3. Take the last six digits of a randomly selected phone number and check the items.

4. In groups of three, use the elements to create a story line. Read select examples.

Objective: Apply the above process.

Task: Each group creates a grid similar to the one above for the following task areas:

1) Writing a short story.
2) Discovering a new _____.
3) Applying the scientific method.
4) Solving a math problem.
5) Promoting a new college loan program.
6) Building a house.

Instructions: Identify the variables (no more than six) for the top line of the grid. For instance, you might have the following variables for creating a lesson design: *Objective, Information, Activity, Discussion, Closure.*

Discussion: In your classroom, list some ways you might use the grid to promote divergent thinking among students. What are some other ways to promote divergent thinking? What are the advantages of using this approach with students? Disadvantages? How can divergent thinking help your students?

Closing Activity: Select one example from the discussion above and prepare a lesson for students. Use all the design elements previously learned in this workshop.

Sustaining Workshop Momentum

"If you are familiar with the best practices on effective staff development, you will recall that chances for the teachers to adopt newly learned skills increase dramatically if they observe each other using the skills and discuss their mutual experiences."

"Yes, but our teachers resist anyone coming into their classrooms to observe."

"I would, too, if the norms were the same as you have described in your system. Change the norms from the medical model you dislike. The positive improvement model you described earlier replaces 'We're going to fix up your bad teaching' with 'Let's help each other get even better.'"

"I guess I can't argue that point, but it won't be easy."

"Quality staff development is never easy."

"Did all this really work in your friend's district?"

"Yes, with a great deal of thought, planning, and hard work. The committee suggested that grade-level teams already working on curriculums receive the first training on thinking skills. In the first semester, they used the district's scheduled inservice time plus their monthly committee time for workshops in the enabling behaviors, microskills, and problem-solving models. The workshops included guided practice, peer feedback, and specific lesson planning to utilize new skills. With principals' help, team members scheduled peer observations and feedback sessions between each workshop."

"How did that work?"

"Very well. In addition to giving the teams a deeper understanding of the skills, a cadre was prepared to pilot the new curriculum and prepare assessment tools for colleagues. Also, each individual's development program was personalized. Thinking skill training, matched to individual needs, recognized what teachers already could do and thus did not teach skills to teachers who already had them. The old inoculation approach gave way to focused training, and both time and dollars were saved. Each teacher's program included input, cooperative practice, observation, feedback, and coaching so that teachers could achieve their own desired improvement targets."

"This all sounds great, but this exact model may not work in our district."

"I agree. Each district, even each building, is unique. Rather than slavishly copying any example of a thinking skills program, it's important that you follow a problem-solving process that adjusts your needs to your district's goals."

"To paraphrase *My Fair Lady*, I think I've got it."

"Let me check it out with you."

Looking Back, Looking Ahead

"First, we need to establish district goals for thinking skills instruction. That goal should clarify our definition, our assumptions, and our expectations.

Second, we must identify the specific microthinking skills for each grade and build a cohesive thinking skills curriculum. We could use a leadership committee to do this.

Next, we need to design lessons to teach each microskill. If we emphasize teaching the microskills with guided practice that helps students apply them, we will do better than if we overpack a curriculum stressing massive content coverage.

Fourth, we need to ascertain each teacher's ability to use the teaching behaviors that heighten student mastery of thinking skills.

Fifth, we must design multilevel staff development programs that ensure that all faculties blend the basic instructional skills, the enablers, and the metacognitive and transfer strategies into their content lessons.

Last, we must add coaching and clinical supervision to ensure high transfer of thinking skills instruction in the classroom practices. Our instructional lessons should model the inductive approach, allowing extensive time for focused questioning, metacognitive analysis, and activities to promote transfer."

"That is a thorough summary. You have identified the main points I wanted to make."

"Thank you. I'll happily trade my one-shot mentality for your better process, a sound thinking skills program based on systematic staff development."

4

Teaching For, Of, and About Thinking

Arthur L. Costa

Ron Brandt's editorial in the September 1984 issue of *Educational Leadership* is one of the most helpful organizers for the teaching of thinking I've found. He discusses a balanced, three-part program, which I interpret as follows.

Teaching FOR Thinking

Many authors and psychologists feel that children learn to think long before they come to school and that educators need to create the conditions for their natural, human inclination to think to emerge and develop. Indeed, Hart (1975) believes that schools are "brain incompatible." In their studies of creativity, Ghiselin and Gardner find that what young children do prior to entering school and what practicing scientists and artists do is more similar than anything that goes on in between.

Teaching for thinking simply means that teachers and administrators examine and strive to create school and classroom conditions that are conducive to children's thinking. This means that:

1. Teachers *pose problems, raise questions*, and intervene with paradoxes, dilemmas, and discrepancies that students can try to resolve.

2. Teachers and administrators *structure* the school environment for thinking—value it, make time for it, secure support materials, and evaluate growth in it.

3. Teachers and administrators *respond* to students' ideas in such a way as to maintain a school and classroom climate that creates trust, allows risktaking, and is experimental, creative, and positive. This requires listening to

students' and each other's ideas, remaining nonjudgmental, and having rich data sources.

4. Teachers, administrators, and other adults in the school environment *model* the behaviors of thinking that are desired in students.

Accomplishing all of the above alone would go far in encouraging students to use their native intelligence. However, there's more. Students haven't learned to think yet.

Teaching OF Thinking

Most authors and developers of major cognitive curriculum projects agree that direct instruction in thinking skills is imperative. Beyer, de Bono, Feuerstein, Lipman, and Whimbey would probably agree on at least one point: the teaching of thinking requires teachers to instruct students directly in the processes of thinking. Even Perkins believes that creativity can be taught—by design.

This does not mean that a curriculum program must be purchased, inserviced, and installed. While this is surely a viable option and should be considered, there are other ways of teaching students thinking skills: analyzing the subject areas or skills being taught in the normal curriculum for their prerequisite cognitive abilities and then teaching those skills directly, for example. The act of decoding in reading requires analysis, comparison, making analogies, inferring, synthesizing, and evaluating. Teaching of thinking, therefore, means that these cognitive skills are taught *directly* as part of the reading (decoding) program.

Critical thinking skills might be taught directly during a social studies unit on the election process. Steps in problem solving might be taught directly during math and science instruction. The qualities of fluency and metaphorical thinking might be taught directly during creative writing,

Figure 1
Staff Development Matrix for Thinking Skills

Levels of Skill Development	I. Teaching For Thinking: Creating school and classroom conditions conducive to full cognitive development	II. Teaching Of Thinking: Instructing students in the skills and strategies directly or implementing one or more programs	III. Teaching About Thinking: Helping students become aware of their own and others' cognitive processes and their use in real-life situations and problems
A. Awareness Developed by lectures, readings, witnessing demonstrations, and so on	I A	II A	III A
B. Knowledge and Comprehension Developed by modeling, practicing, comparing, discussing, interacting	I B	II B	III B
C. Mastery of Skills Developed by practicing with feedback and coaching	I C	II C	III C
D. Application Developed by extended use across subject areas, varieties of groups, demonstrations; critique and dialogue with others	I D	II D	III D
E. Trainer of Trainers Developed by creating, conducting, and critiquing inservice strategies; observing the training of other trainers	I E	II E	III E

and so forth. Creating conditions for thinking and teaching it directly are excellent procedures, but what about the application? Nothing yet has been taught about the transference of these thinking skills beyond the context in which they were learned. Students may be able to identify the steps in the problem-solving process and correctly distinguish between classification and categorization, but do they have any inclination to use these skills in real-life situations? There's more.

Teaching ABOUT Thinking

Teaching about thinking can be divided into at least three components: brain functioning, metacognition, and epistemic cognition.

1. *Brain functioning.* Recently neurobiological research has shed light on how our brains work. Teaching about thinking would include investigating such curiosities as: How do we think? How does memory work? What

causes emotions? Why do we dream? How do we learn? How and why do mental disorders occur? What happens when part of the brain is damaged? Restak's *The Brain*, Ornstein and Thompson's *The Amazing Brain,* and Russell's *The Brain Book* are sources of information. A recent public television series entitled "The Brain" has heightened this awareness and is available for use in schools.

2. *Metacognition.* Being conscious of our own thinking and problem solving while thinking is known as metacognition. It is a uniquely human ability occurring in the neocortex of the brain. Good problem solvers plan a course of action before they begin a task, monitor themselves while executing that plan, back up or adjust the plan consciously, and evaluate themselves upon completion.

Metacognition in the classroom might be characterized by having discussions with students about what is going on inside their heads while they're thinking; comparing different students' approaches to problem solving and decision making; identifying what is known, what needs to

FIGURE 2
I. Teaching FOR Thinking

Intersection	Competencies of Teachers
I A	Is aware of different levels of questions and various ways of organizing the classroom for instruction. Can describe alternative ways of responding so as to maintain and extend students' thinking.
I B	Plans lessons to incorporate levels of questions, response behaviors, and classroom organization for thinking. Seeks assistance, advice from others in methods and materials for teaching thinking.
I C	Invites others to observe a lesson, then to give feedback about questioning skills, classroom organization, and response behaviors. Volunteers to do the same for colleagues.
I D	Incorporates thinking skills across subject areas. Devotes maximum time to teaching for thinking. Shares ideas and materials with colleagues. Strives to model rational thinking processes in own behavior.
I E	Conducts inservice for colleagues. Videotapes own lessons and shares with colleagues. Plans, conducts, and evaluates staff development strategies. Analyzes school and classroom conditions for their conduciveness to and modeling of thinking. Works to improve them.

FIGURE 3
II. Teaching OF Thinking

Intersection	Competencies of Teachers
II A	Is aware of various programs intended to teach thinking directly. Is aware of definitions and distinctions among various thinking skills and strategies.
II B	Employs lessons intended to directly teach thinking skills. Incorporates thinking skills into content areas. Attends training in a curriculum program intended to teach thinking directly.
II C	Invites others to observe and give feedback about lessons in which thinking is taught directly. Applies knowledge learned in training programs to instruction. Devotes two to three hours per week to teaching thinking directly.
II D	Distinguishes among several major curriculums intended to teach thinking. Diagnoses students' cognitive deficiencies and provides experiences to remediate them. Analyzes the cognitive skills prerequisite for students to master school subjects, and incorporates instruction in those skills.
II E	Develops and implements inservice training in one or more of the major curriculum programs. Trains others in the development of lesson plans incorporating direct instruction of thinking skills and strategies. Surveys and recommends adoption of instructional materials that enhance thinking skills.

be known, and how to produce that knowledge; or having students think aloud while problem solving.

Metacognitive instruction would include learning how to learn; how to study for a test; how to use strategies of question asking before, during, and after reading. It might include knowing how to learn best—visually, auditorily, kinesthetically—and what strategies to use when you find yourself in a situation that does *not* match your best learning modality.

Metacognition is discussed more extensively later in this book. See also Costa (1984).

3. *Epistemic cognition.* Epistemology is the study of how knowledge is produced. In the curriculum it might include studying the lives, processes, and works of great composers, artists, scientists, and philosophers. Epistemological questions for discussion include:

● How does what scientists do differ from what artists do?

● What are the procedures of inquiry used by anthropologists as they live with and study a culture?

● What goes on inside a maestro's mind as he or she conducts an orchestra?

FIGURE 4
III. Teaching ABOUT Thinking

Intersection	Competencies of Teachers
III A	Is aware of differences in modality strengths, learning styles, and brain functioning. Can define such terms as metacognition and epistemology.
III B	Attempts metacognitive discussions with students. Discusses how the brain works. Selects materials on brain functioning and biographies of famous scientists and artists in an attempt to intrigue students.
III C	Invites colleagues to observe a lesson involving a philosophical/epistemological discussion and seeks feedback as to ways to improve. Reads and attends courses and lectures, watches video programs on philosophy, cognition, brain functioning, and so on. Discusses differences in learning strengths and modalities with students.
III D	Selects materials and conducts lessons in which comparisons are made of strategic reasoning, knowledge production, and creativity. Discusses with students such topics as artificial intelligence, the analysis of propaganda, and strategies of learning. Models metacognition overtly in the presence of students.
III E	Develops, conducts, and evaluates inservice strategies for colleagues for instruction on brain functioning, learning style differences, and metacognition. Develops curriculum incorporating materials and learning activities intended to have students learn to think and learn about thinking. Designs assessment tools and techniques to gather evidence of students' growth in intelligent behaviors.

● What was it about Mozart's genius that allowed him to "hear" a total musical composition before writing it down?

● What process do poets use to create?

● Why can't we use processes of scientific inquiry to solve social problems.?

Epistemic cognition is the study and comparison of great artists, scientists, and scholars and the differential processes of investigation, inquiry, and creativity that underlie their productivity. Lipman's Philosophy for Children program is especially well-suited for this. Other resources include Perkins' *The Mind's Best Work*, Madigan and Elwood's *Brainstorms and Thunderbolts: How Creative Genius Works*, and Gardner's *Art, Mind, and Brain*.

Installing a Program for Thinking

Installing a program of teaching for thinking does not happen overnight. It takes time, patience, and practice. Joyce and others have created a helpful paradigm for thinking about the steps and sequences in staff development efforts. They suggest a series of stages and levels of concern through which teachers proceed during the change process. Their procedure includes inservice techniques that help teachers raise their skill development levels in using new skills and behaviors.

The matrix for staff development presented in Figure 1 combines two components—*teaching for, of, and about thinking* and the *levels of skill development*. Figures 2, 3, and 4 provide examples of teacher competencies, skills, and knowledge as indicators of what might be included at each intersection in the matrix. Please consider these examples merely as helpful starting points to which you can add your own indicators of competence.

REFERENCES

Costa, Arthur L. "Mediating the Metacognitive." *Educational Leadership* 42 (November 1984): 57-62.

Gardner, Howard. *Art, Mind, and Brain*. New York: Basic Books, 1982.

Hart, Leslie. *Human Brain and Human Learning*. New York: Longman, 1975.

Madigan, Carol, and Elwood, Ann. *Brainstorms and Thunderbolts: How Creative Genius Works*. New York: Macmillan, 1983.

Perkins, David. *The Mind's Best Work*. Cambridge: Harvard University Press, 1981.

Restak, R. *The Brain: The Last Frontier*. New York: Warner Books, 1979.

Russell, Peter. *The Brain Book*. New York: E. P. Dutton, 1979.

5

Are Teachers Motivated to Teach Thinking?

Robert Garmston

What we call the beginning is often the end
And to make an end is to make a beginning
The end is where we start from.
— T. S. Eliot, "Little Gidding"

A principal and mentor teacher consider the staff at their school. Who are the risk takers? Who might be induced to attend inservice and join a team to teach higher-order thinking skills? Eleanor Gallagher is selected. As a high risk taker who wants to succeed, Eleanor works diligently with the principal and mentor teacher to make this critical thinking project work. Months later, an end-of-year post-test shows that higher-order thinking skills in 4th and 5th graders have increased significantly since midyear.

At another school, teachers bring mountains of raw data to an initial workshop. They sort, classify, analyze, and make propositions. The inside of a computer is displayed, and data base systems are introduced. A few months and four workshop days later, the teachers' journals demonstrate changes in *teacher thinking*. This thinking leads to teaching behaviors that facilitate higher-order student thinking skills.

As we review these and other examples of teachers approaching the teaching of thinking skills, we wonder if we really need to ask how we can motivate teachers. Clearly, such a question presumes that motivation is not present, and that teachers will only pursue a goal as a result of external action by administrators, mentor teachers, or other support staff. Lieberman and Miller (1984) observe that most of the literature on school change comes from this managerial perspective: "One gets the view that teachers can be infinitely manipulated like puppets on a string."

Instead, let us suppose that the motivation to teach thinking skills is *already* present in most teachers. After all, many will tell us they value teaching thinking skills and are already finding places in the curriculum to address it. These teachers may point out their use of higher-level questioning in reading comprehension and synthesis exercises in social sciences as examples. Other teachers might tell us that they value teaching for thinking, but can't find time to teach as much of it as they'd like.

However, teachers' examples of how they teach thinking skills may not always conform with what we have in mind. We may be sensitive to Goodlad's observation that schools are not very stimulating places (1984) or join Lipman (1984) in suspecting that the disappointing academic performances of many students are connected with their lack of cognitive skills. We may also agree with Feuerstein's assumption that intelligence is modifiable only through carefully constructed and *mediated* learning experiences that take place over long periods of time (Sternberg, 1984). In short, our impressions of teaching thinking may be more involved, complex, and intensive than what teachers have in mind when they assure us that they value the teaching of thinking.

Despite these possible differences in perception, the approach to teacher motivation I am proposing is to *act as if the motivation were already present*. The *as if* presumption is a strategy that can move us quickly toward an intended or desired state (McMaster and Grinder, 1980; Labarde, 1984). This proposal is appealing for several reasons.

• It shifts our attention from a subjective focus on motivation to an objective focus on implementation.

• It removes us from the dubious and uncomfortable role of motivator.

• It allows us to use knowledge we already have about the change process and to work on cognitive coaching with teachers as adult learners.

• It works.

Implementation—Not Motivation

Most teachers value the development of rational processes in their students and see schools as instruments to attain this goal. Some are avid on the subject and regard thinking as the primary purpose of formal schooling. Others regard different goals as predominant, such as facilitating self-actualization or focusing student energy on the restructuring of society. Still others hold a primary philosophical orientation toward academic rationalism or technology (Eisner and Vallance, 1974). Yet, regardless of their primary philosophies about what we should be teaching students, all but a few teachers agree that schools have a major responsibility to teach thinking.

By approaching our task by acting as if motivation were present, we acknowledge a value already existing in teachers and presume an alignment of our desires with theirs. This produces a natural setting for collaborative work, which has been repeatedly demonstrated to be superior to top-down or "grass-roots" approaches to change (Berman and McLaughlin, 1978; Peters and Waterman, 1982).

Removal from Motivator Role

Collegiality in program development presumes a commonality of vision about the direction or end product. This contrasts sharply with the vision of a mentor teacher or principal who motivates teachers to achieve or work toward a goal. Motivation in this latter context suggests acting on or extrinsically influencing others. Festinger (1957) shook our long-standing beliefs about the efficacy of reward with his experiments on cognitive dissonance. His subjects were more prone to incorporate into their own beliefs ideas that they were *not rewarded* to state. The subjects who were paid to adopt views they did not really hold kept their original beliefs intact. In their study on change, Berman and McLaughlin (1978) found evidence of this principle at work when they discovered that paying teachers to attend inservice functions had a negative impact on reaching inservice goals. They claim: "This strategy fails because it seriously misconstrues the motivations that lead most teachers to want to change their practices."

Freed from thinking that we need to *act on* teachers in order to motivate them to work toward our ends, we can turn our energy toward *working with* teachers, using a rapidly growing body of information and experiences about how to produce long-term change.

Using What We Know About Change

One conception of the change process is illustrated by a formula attributed to David Gleichey of Arthur D. Little Company: ch = $a \cdot b \cdot c > x$.

Change, in this formulation, equals the product of (a) a shared dissatisfaction, (b) a shared vision of an ideal state, and (c) knowledge of practical steps needed to attain the vision, provided this product is greater than (x) the cost of change. Using this approach, change agents analyze the situation and perform the functions that appear to be most needed next.

When applying this formula to teaching thinking skills, it is appropriate to first consider potential expenditures of time, energy, and financial resources. If our view of the desired state (b) is ambitious, the investment will be high. An example is Feuerstein's Instrumental Enrichment, for which we might want a commitment to inservice training over a three-year period and the acquisition of many new teaching strategies among most teachers. The (a) and (b) of our formula need to be quite strong and (c) quite practical and attainable for us to overcome the costs this vision suggests. Depending on local conditions, the change agent will either need to *create* a potent shared dissatisfaction or *facilitate* a forceful shared vision of the ideal.

Let us consider a possible ideal that includes better performance on academic achievement tests, more responsive student interaction in class, and more insightful essays. Teachers may still be disinterested at this point because we are describing change concerns that only reflect student needs. Teachers tend to give such concerns priority status only in the later stages of new program implementation (Hall, 1978). In the early stages, Hall notes that teachers, like all of us, are concerned for themselves—"How much time will this innovation cost me?" "What will I have to give up to do this?" "Am I *capable* of doing this?" Successful projects link teacher concerns like these with programmatic concerns (Lieberman and Miller, 1981). As change agents, can we build shared visions that incorporate teacher concerns? I propose that we can and often instinctively do.

An Example

An elementary school staff is examining its reading program. The principal observes that most of the 4th, 5th, and 6th grade teachers have little formal training in teaching reading and do not consider this their forte. Their methods are mainly sets of activities selected from the teacher editions of basal readers. Little staff communication or collaboration exists regarding reading, and student progress is limited. There is daily instruction, but it is unfocused, uninspired, and relatively ineffective.

To change this, the principal begins by building a sense of shared dissatisfaction by simply describing the existing circumstances. The principal reminds teachers that 4th grade classes have at least a four-year reading range and 6th grade classes at least six. To accommodate this range, teachers create three reading groups: high, medium, and low. They then make nine lesson plans for each reading hour (one directed instruction and two seatwork assignments for each reading group). Pragmatically, lesson planning is skimpy because there is so much to prepare. Seatwork assignments usually consist of completing workbook pages that have little or no relationship to the teacher's lesson. Instructional time for each reading group is dishearteningly limited. Out of an allocated 20 minutes per group, perhaps three minutes are spent coming to the group, three minutes collecting and correcting seatwork, one minute organizing and distributing materials for the lesson, and four minutes at the end making the next seatwork assignment and checking for understanding. This leaves nine minutes for instruction. Students must spend 40 minutes of the 60-minute reading period working independently. Time spent on relevant learning tasks is very limited, for lower-level students in particular.

In this manner, the principal highlights and elicits teacher elaboration on the classroom management horrors associated with a three-ring reading group program. Then the principal describes an ideal state, attainable by rearranging existing school resources, in which each teacher could hold an uninterrupted 50-minute class with a single homogeneous group. The number of daily lesson plans could be reduced from nine to one, guidance and assistance on lesson formats could be provided, and student learning could be accelerated.

Infused with both a powerful dissatisfaction and an ideal state, teachers planning collaboratively with this principal will work very hard to attain such results. As it does for most elementary school teachers, the three-group organization in this example prohibits extensive teacher preparation for reading lessons, seatwork that is a logical extension of teacher-directed activity, high student time-on-task, full student and teacher enjoyment of the reading period, and gains in student achievement.

Teamwork

What prevents teachers from focusing more intensely and skillfully on teaching thinking skills? Is it lack of teacher knowledge and skills? Poor classroom management systems? The pressure of other curricular demands? Im-

proper teaching materials? Unrealistic student groupings? Lack of planning time? Anxiety about immediate and practical support in the early stages of program implementation? These questions are illustrative of common teacher concerns in the early stages of a new program. Administrators who *creatively* address the incorporation of program concerns with teacher concerns can build program goals teachers will find worth fighting for.

Glickman (1985) describes this process as providing the glue with which we link individual teacher needs with organizational needs so that individuals within the school can work in harmony toward their vision of what the school should be. Laborde (1984), in her chapter on negotiating with others, defines this strategy as discovering other people's hierarchy of values and showing them how helping gain your outcome will satisfy their own highest value.

Using the change formula strategy, teacher concerns are matched with the administrator's designed program outcomes. In the reading program example, the principal increases student achievement and teacher sophistication and morale by momentarily heightening tensions teachers already possess. This is done within the context of a general plan.

The change agent is wise to think in detail about dissatisfaction, vision, and practical steps to take when designing a general tactical approach to teaching cognitive processes. However, the change literature is very clear that successful change takes place through the collaborative involvement of workers in the planning and implementation stages (Berman and McLaughlin, 1978; Peters and Waterman, 1982; Lieberman and Miller, 1981).

We *lead* by pointing the way. We *attain* by involving others in finding out how to get there. Judicious work at group efforts in departments, grade levels, and schools is the most efficient way to bring about change. The school, not the district, should be the organizational level for change (Goodlad, 1984).

Before we create and involve groups of teachers we need a tentative, overall plan that includes information about the major steps to be taken, who needs to be involved in what capacities (such as advisory, information, and decision making), and a timeline. Once embarked, we want to exercise "systematic ad-hocism," a process of monitoring and adjusting our approaches as new data appear (Lieberman and Miller, 1981).

Using What We Know About Adult Learners

If we want to involve teachers in helping design and implement thinking programs, we need to engage teachers themselves in thinking. Sprinthall and Theis-Sprinthall (1983), like Goodlad, suggest that schools are not very stimulating places for teachers and note that teachers, relative to other adult groups, mature less along intellectual lines. Presumably, this results from the isolation in which they work and our disposition to favor "make it/take it" workshops over those that engage teachers' minds.

Good program development evolves in ways that respect certain fundamental principles of adult learning. As part of implementing the $ch = a \cdot b \cdot c > x$ formula, the successful change agent follows acknowledged staff development procedures by engaging teachers in the identification of the content they need to learn, skills they need to acquire, and the best activities through which they can learn (Robbins and Garmston, 1984). We know that adults will try to learn the things they consider realistic and job-related and that they need to see the results of their learning. They fear external judgments and will resist learning situations that they believe attack their competence (Wood and Thompson, 1980). Good staff development is based on knowledge of such adult learner characteristics, and effective program development is synonymous with good staff development (McLaughlin and Berman, 1977).

Using What We Know About Cognitive Coaching

Trust is fundamental to any teacher-supervisor relationship in which the goals are increased teacher learning and autonomy (self-criticism, self-supervision, and self-learning, for example). All of the foregoing discussion concerning tactical approaches to implementing teaching cognition presumes the existence of trust in teachers' relationships with supervisors. Trust is the product of mutual respect, perceived confidentiality, and dependability and consistency in the behavior of the supervisor. It is the first goal in the attainment of learning and autonomy—one that must not only be initially attained by the supervisor, but monitored and maintained throughout the relationship (Costa and Garmston, 1984). Principals who add cognitive coaching tools to their clinical supervision practices are often surprised at the dramatic progress they make with teachers previously viewed as resistant. Trust and rapport are the initial critical factors in each case.

Supervisors must also have their desired outcomes clearly in mind as they work with individual teachers. Several exacting criteria must be met to reach these outcomes. While space prevents a full discussion of all of them, one subtle but profoundly influential criterion should be noted: the outcome the supervisor plans must incorporate the *positive* intentions of the teacher's present behaviors. When this condition is not met, the teacher will, either consciously or unconsciously, sabotage the project.

For example, teachers may resist implementing a thinking program if they view the expression of students' critical thinking as a threat to their own authority. We must help these teachers continue to achieve the goals they are currently realizing without teaching cognitive processes through the implementation of the new program. This requires individual counseling with the teacher, similar to the postconference in a clinical supervision sequence. The use of questioning strategies to clarify and probe inner meanings and intellectual functioning, stimulate thinking, and formulate new understandings will help us attain this goal.

Another cognitive coaching skill that facilitates teacher learning is the application of linguistic tools to help teachers see the limitations, deletions, and illogical assumptions present in their own thinking (Chomsky, 1957). Effective supervisors can do this by judiciously and gently challenging vague teacher statements. For example:

● *Teacher:* "They are to think critically...." *Supervisor:* "Critically? How, specifically?"

● *Teacher:* "The students are not demonstrating divergent thinking." *Supervisor:* "Which students?"

● *Teacher:* "These students don't think because they don't care." *Supervisor:* "Help me understand this interpretation. Has there ever been a time in which students don't think but still care?"

● *Teacher:* "I can't...." *Supervisor:* "What's stopping you...?"

● *Teacher:* "When students repeatedly demonstrate episodic learning, I don't know what to do." *Supervisor:* "What do you think of first when you're successful at figuring out a situation like this?"

Drever (1961) defines *motivate* as "to provide an incentive, to act as an incentive." Perhaps, in one sense, *we are the incentive*. Everything we do is important in our work with teachers (Block, 1981). We lead through our modeling. Our actions speak louder than our words.

Harvey (1970) analyzed teachers' levels of conceptual development and found that most were in stage one of a four-stage system. This stage, unilateral dependence, is one in which concepts are undifferentiated and do not account for ambiguity. Thought is concrete with dependence on authority.

In our interaction with teachers, do we model critical, creative, and higher-order thinking? Do we engage them and expect the same of them? Do we facilitate precision and clarity in their thinking through our own thinking and language skills? In other words, do we support the conceptual development of our own staffs for the complex array of decisions they make daily? (Costa and Garmston, 1985.) If we want teaching for thinking to infuse our curriculum, we must expect it of ourselves, strive for it, and model it. We must walk like we talk and think like we ought.

REFERENCES

Berman, P., and McLaughlin, M. *Federal Programs Supporting Educational Change, Vol. VIII: Implementing and Sustaining Innovations.* Santa Monica: The Rand Corp., 1978, p. 27.

Block, P. *Flawless Consulting: A Guide to Getting Your Expertise Used.* San Diego: University Associates, 1981.

Chomsky, N. *Syntactic Structures.* The Hague: Mouton, 1957.

Costa, A., and Garmston, R. "Supervision for Intelligent Teaching." *Educational Leadership* 42 (February 1985): 70-80.

Costa, A., and Garmston, R. "The Art of Cognitive Coaching: Supervision for Intelligent Teaching." Paper presented at the annual conference of the Association for Supervision and Curriculum Development, Chicago, March 1985.

Drever, J. *A Dictionary of Psychology.* Baltimore: Penguin Books, 1969, pp. 174-175.

Eisner, E., and Vallance, E. *Conflicting Conceptions of the Curriculum.* Berkeley: McCutchan Publishers, 1974.

Eliot, T. S. *Four Quartets.* New York: Harcourt Brace, 1984, p. 38.

Festinger, Leon. *A Theory of Cognitive Dissonance.* Stanford: Stanford University Press, 1957.

Glickman, C. *Supervision of Instruction: A Developmental Approach.* New York: Allyn and Bacon, 1985.

Goodlad, J. *A Place Called School: Prospects for the Future.* New York: McGraw Hill, 1984.

Hall, G. "The Study of Teachers' Concerns and Consequent Implications for Staff Development." *Staff Development Newsletter: A Forum for the Development of Human Resources.* Austin, Tex.: Professional Development Association, Spring 1978.

Harvey, O. J. "Beliefs and Behavior: Some Implications for Education." *The Science Teacher* 37 (December 1970): 10-14, 73.

Laborde, G. *Influencing With Integrity: Management Skills for Communication and Negotiation.* Palo Alto: Science and Behavior Books, Syntony, Inc., 1984.

Lieberman, A., and Miller, L. "Synthesis of Leadership on Improving Schools." *Educational Leadership* 38, 7 (April 1981): 583-586.

Lipman, M. "The Cultivation of Reasoning Through Philosophy." *Educational Leadership* 42, 1 (September 1984): 51.

McLaughlin, M., and Berman, P. "Retooling Staff Development in a Period of Retrenchment." *Educational Leadership* 35, 3 (December 1977): 191-195.

McMaster, M., and Grinder, J. *Precision: A New Approach to Communication.* Bonny Doon, Calif.: Precision Models, 1980, pp. 134-137.

Peters, T., and Waterman, R. *In Search of Excellence: Lessons from America's Best Run Companies.* New York: Harper and Row, 1982.

Robbins, P., and Garmston, R. "Toward Better Staff Development: A Cost Effective Training Program." *The Professional Educator* VII, 1 (Spring 1984): 1-4.

Sprinthall, N., and Theis-Sprinthall, L. "The Teacher as an Adult Learner: A Cognitive-Development View." In *Staff Development.* 82nd Yearbook of the National Society for the Study of Education. Edited by Gary Griffin. Chicago: University of Chicago Press, 1983.

Sternberg, R. "How Can We Teach Intelligence?" *Educational Leadership* 42, 1 (September 1984): 41.

Wood, F., and Thompson, S. "Guidelines for Better Staff Development." *Educational Leadership* 37, 5 (February 1980): 374-378.

6

The Principal's Role in Enhancing Thinking Skills

Arthur L. Costa

School effectiveness research supports what many educators intuitively know: the principal has a strong influence on the curriculum implemented, the instructional strategies employed, and, thus, on student achievement.

Nationwide efforts to infuse thinking skills into the curriculum, to include them in instructional strategies, and to assess schools' success in teaching thinking are capturing the attention and energies of boards of education, curriculum committees, and departments of education. Obviously, the role of principals in this endeavor is critical. Their behaviors are symbolic for staff members, students, and the community.

This chapter clarifies the principal's role and suggests how principals can exert their crucial influence in enhancing students' full intellectual functioning and development. Principals can approach this goal by (1) creating intellectually stimulating school conditions for staff and students, (2) using available resources to support a cognitive curriculum, and (3) modeling rational practices.

Creating Intellectually Stimulating School Conditions

If teachers are expected to teach for thinking, they need an environment in which their intellectual processes are stimulated. One role of the principal, therefore, is to create a school atmosphere that invites teachers' highest intellectual functioning (Sprinthall and Theis-Sprinthall, 1983). There are many ways principals can create intellectually stimulating environments. For instance, they can:

1. *Involve teachers, parents, and students in decision making.* Teachers in effective schools have opportunities to participate in making decisions that affect them. Mandates from above are among the greatest deterrents to thinking. Principals must encourage, facilitate, and protect teachers' rights to:
- Pursue self-studies.
- Develop goals.
- Plan personal staff development.
- Prioritize which thinking skills to emphasize.
- Select their own instructional materials.
- Invent methods to determine their own effectiveness.
- Determine indicators of student growth.
- Share and suggest solutions to problems.

As teachers participate in making decisions that affect them, the likelihood that those processes will infiltrate their classrooms greatly increases.

2. *Employ collegial supervision rather than evaluation.* Another way to inhibit thinking is to make value judgments about teachers' competencies, potentials, and ideas. Value judgments detract from motivation and produce stress (Lepper and Greene, 1978). Under stress, the brain's creative, analytical functions are extinguished and replaced with conformity (MacLean, 1978). Instead, withholding judgments and viewing teaching and learning as a continual problem-solving, creative method of inquiry build trust and challenge teachers to become experimental hypothesis makers. Supervision thereby becomes "brain compatible" (Hart, 1983; Costa and Garmston, 1985).

3. *Avoid recipes.* It is tempting to describe and evaluate the act of teaching in "five steps, four factors, and seven variables." Obviously, teaching and learning the complex strategies of higher-level thinking are more lengthy and

dignified than that. Teaching *by the number* is as creative as painting by the number. Participants must capitalize on this complexity, find richness in this confusion, and avoid simplistic answers.

4. *Explicate the dream.* Principals of effective schools have a vision of what their schools can become. They constantly assess all programs, each decision, and every new direction in order to help achieve that vision. In their pursuit of excellence, they strive to be thoughtful, rational, innovative, and cooperative. In addition, principals should seize every opportunity to articulate, refine, and magnify this vision by:

● Openly discussing it with the faculty, community, fellow administrators, and central office staff.

● Illuminating instruction that illustrates it.

● Finding materials that are consistent with it.

● Organizing classrooms to better achieve it.

Not only do these activities help clarify principals' intuitive perceptions, but they also make a strong public statement about their values.

5. *Constant reminders.* "Thought is Taught at Huntington Beach High" emblazons one school's memo pads. "The 'HOTS' (Higher-Order Thinking Skills) Committee will meet in the teachers' room at 3:30" resounds from another school's loudspeaker. A brightly painted banner exclaiming "Thursday is for Thinking" decorates one wall of the teachers' room as a not-so-subtle souvenir of their commitment to plan at least one thinking skills lesson each week. Lesson plan books list Bloom's taxonomical levels of thinking on the covers. "Just a Minute, Let Me Think" is the slogan on the bulletin board in yet another school's foyer. In a staff lounge, a butcher paper scope-and-sequence chart displays skill activities entered by each teacher at each grade level for each subject area. These are but a few of the many innovative ways principals strive to keep their staff members thinking about thinking.

Using Available Resources to Support Thinking

Resources are usually defined in terms of time, space, energy, and money. How principals allocate these limited resources is yet another significant expression to staff members, students, and the community of their value systems.

Most obvious is the principal's commitment of financial resources for thinking skills programs by purchasing materials and hiring consultants to assist the faculty in curriculum and staff development, sending staff members to conferences and workshops, and securing substitutes to facilitate peer observation.

Securing financial grants from local industries, philanthropic organizations, and national, state, and local education agencies is one way to increase this often limited resource.

Because time and energy are an administrator's most precious commodities, parceling them out wisely is crucial to their effectiveness. The following suggestions should attract administrators' highest priorities.

1. *Monitor instructional decision making.* Once the staff has defined how to effectively teach thinking, these indicators may be monitored in the instructional decisions teachers make, such as:

● Planning lessons that include cognitive objectives.

● Sequencing teaching strategies according to levels of thought.

● Selecting instructional materials that stimulate problem solving.

● Organizing the classroom for discussion of ideas.

● Developing learning activities that provoke thinking.

● Evaluating student growth in thinking abilities.

In these ways, administrators convey to teachers that *instruction* is the mechanism by which thought is taught; if instruction is improved, thinking will improve correspondingly.

2. *Coordinate the Curriculum.* Possessing a broad curriculum purview, principals are in a good position to effectively monitor the relationship between teachers' instructional decisions and the district's philosophical goals. They can search for ever-increasing complexity and abstraction of thinking required in learning activities at each grade level, coordinate resources with other schools in the district or community, and evaluate the long-range cumulative effects of cognitive instruction.

3. *Use precious faculty time to think and discuss thinking.* Too often, faculty meeting time is relegated to managerial tasks and information transmission. Discussing thinking as a total faculty, or in department- or grade-level meetings, is time well spent. Agenda items can include inviting teachers to:

● Report what they have learned from thinking skills courses, staff development activities, or research.

● Describe successes and problems in teaching for thinking.

● Discuss which thinking skills to focus on this year.

● Demonstrate instructional techniques that provoke thinking.

● Compare how they include thinking in each subject area.

● Describe how children increase the complexity of their intellectual skills throughout their development.

● Review and select materials to enhance thinking.

● Discuss ways to support each other's teaching with concurrent instruction (thinking across the curriculum).

● Invent alternative ways to assess students' growth in thinking abilities.

● Relate school goals to district priorities.

4. *Secure parental support.* Parents probably have the most effect on children's abilities and inclinations for mental development. Concerned parents model thinking; their language engages differential cognitive structures. Often what we do in schools to teach thinking is remedial for those students whose parents do not provide this mediation.

Principals are the primary link between schools and the community. They have the opportunity to involve parents in decision making, interpret school programs to the community, and educate parents in their dominant role as mediators of their children's cognitive development.

Some parents believe that schools should teach only the basics. They may judge modern education in terms of their experience as students—during a time when the value of thinking was not necessarily recognized. Principals can help parents enhance their aspirations for their children by stressing that reasoning is a basic for survival in the future, critical thinking is required for college entrance and success, cognitive processes are prerequisite to mastery in all school subjects, and career security and advancement are dependent on innovation, insightfulness, and cooperation.

Many parents appear to be realizing that reasoning is the fourth "R," and there is a definite trend toward increased parental concern for children's cognitive development (Gallup, 1984). Principals should engage parents to search for ways to encourage children to use thinking by stimulating their interest in school and learning, environmental issues, time and money planning, and so on.

Time and energy invested in parental education pay high dividends. Elementary school administrators may wish to involve their school psychologists and nurses in enhancing parental effectiveness. Secondary and college-level school administrators may consider including parenting classes in their curriculum. Possible offerings include instruction in such cognitively related understandings as: promoting language development, experiential stimulation, parent-child communication skills, good nutrition, child growth and development, rational approaches to discipline, supervising homework, providing home environments conducive to cognitive development, and modeling appropriate adult behaviors.

5. *Enhance personal thinking skills.* If any time and energy remain, principals themselves may wish to participate in staff development activities and learn more about cognitive education by: learning to distinguish among the many programs available, considering what to look for in teacher-student classroom interaction, studying how to apply criteria to the selection of instructional materials, understanding more about brain functioning, and increasing their own cognitive skills of problem solving, creativity, research, and cooperative planning.

Modeling in the Principal's Own Behavior

Imitation is the most basic form of learning. Emerson is often quoted as saying, "What you do speaks so loudly they can't hear what you say." Thus, when problems arise in the school, the community, and the classroom, the principal must be seen solving those problems in rational, thoughtful ways. If not, the principal may unknowingly undermine the very goals of curriculum to which commitment is sought. Evaluation of a teacher's or program's effectiveness may be performed by the very person who is rendering the program ineffective. Principals should emulate those rational competencies desired in students and taught by teachers through:

1. *Withholding impulsivity.* The environment of the school principal is analogous to living in a popcorn popper. It's easy to become tense, fatigued, and cognitively overloaded. Effective principals, however, develop self-awareness and biofeedback strategies to combat stress and to cope with irritating problems through patience, rationality, and poise.

2. *Demonstrating empathy for others.* One of the highest forms of mental ability is empathy. Behaving empathically requires overcoming one's own egocentricity, detecting another's subtle emotional and physical cues, and perceiving a situation from another's point of view—a complex set of cognitive processes. When dealing with parents, staff members, colleagues, and students, the administrator who demonstrates empathy will model the most potent intellectual process.

3. *Metacognition.* Metacognition is our ability to formulate a plan of action, monitor our own progress along that plan, realize what we know and don't know, detect and recover from error, and reflect upon and evaluate our own thinking processes. Administrators demonstrate metacognition when they publicly share their planning strategies, admit their lack of knowledge but describe means of generating that knowledge, and engage others in deliberating, monitoring, and evaluating problem-solving strategies.

Metacognition seems to be an attribute of effective problem solvers. Administrators can model effective problem solving by demonstrating their awareness of, discussing, and then inviting feedback and evaluation of their own problem-solving abilities (Costa, 1984).

4. *Cooperative decision making.* Democratic princi-

pals realize that their intellectual power multiplies when they draw on the power of others. They value group thinking in decisions facing staff members. This requires attitudes such as withholding judgment, coping with ambiguity, flexible thinking, tentativeness, evaluating alternatives, seeking consensus, taking another person's point of view, and employing hypothetical, experimental thinking. These are the same attributes of critical thinking and problem solving that we want teachers to instill in students.

5. *Believing that all children can think.* School effectiveness research indicates that teachers' and administrators' expectancies of student performance are correlated with achievement. Likewise, in programs of cognitive education, our expectancies become apparent. In many schools, however, children with low I.Q. scores are thought incapable of higher-level thought. Some schools employ thinking programs only for the gifted. Some children are "excused" from thinking because of the supposed inadequacies of home environment, culture, socioeconomic level, or genetic makeup. Indeed, those students who are reluctant to think—who recoil from mental activity because it's "too hard"—are the ones who need it most.

Modern cognitive theorists reject the notion of a static and unchanging I.Q. Rather, they adopt a dynamic theory of multiple intelligences that can be nurtured and developed throughout a person's life. Administrators must demonstrate the belief that, with proper mediation and instruc-

tion, *all* children can continue to increase their intellectual capacities (Gardner, 1983; Feuerstein, 1980; Whimbey and Whimbey, 1975).

REFERENCES

Costa, A. "Mediating the Metacognitive." *Educational Leadership* 42 (November 1984): 57-62.
Costa, A., and Garmston, R. "Supervision for Intelligent Teaching." *Educational Leadership* 42 (February 1985): 70-80.
Feuerstein, R. *Instrumental Enrichment.* Baltimore: University Park Press, 1980.
Gallup, G. "The 16th Annual Gallup Poll of the Public's Attitudes Toward the Public Schools." *Phi Delta Kappan* 66 (September 1984).
Gardner, H. *Frames of Mind.* New York: Basic Books, 1983.
Hart, L. *Human Brain, Human Learning.* New York: Longman, 1983.
Lepper, M., and Greene, D. *The Hidden Costs of Rewards.* Hillsdale, N.J.: Lawrence Erlbaum Associates, 1978.
MacLean, P. "A Mind of Three Minds: Educating the Triune Brain." In *Education and the Brain,* 77th Yearbook of the National Society for the Study of Education. Edited by J. Chall and A. Mirsky. Chicago: University of Chicago Press, 1978.
Sprinthall, N., and Theis-Sprinthall, L. "The Teacher as an Adult Learner: A Cognitive Developmental View." In *Staff Development,* 82nd Yearbook of the National Society for the Study of Education. Edited by G. Griffin. Chicago: University of Chicago Press, 1983.
Whimbey, A., and Whimbey, L. *Intelligence Can Be Taught.* New York: E. B. Dutton and Co., 1975.

7

Removing Impediments to Change

John Barell

Some people think that it is holding on that makes one strong. Sometimes it's letting go.

—Sylvia Robinson

Let us suppose that you have decided to challenge your students to think critically and creatively. You enter the classroom prepared to pose higher-level questions and probe for underlying meanings, principles, concepts, and relationships. Your students are going to work together cooperatively and not rely on you as the sole arbiter of truth.

If your success is to match your enthusiasm, there are several factors that you need to plan for: students' difficulties with complex thinking, your own difficulties with challenging students to think, supervisors' routines and organizational constraints, and community expectations and pressures.

Students' Difficulties with Complex Thinking

Student difficulties can be viewed from at least two different perspectives: the hidden or implicit curriculum and students' cognitive developmental levels.

The Hidden or Implicit Curriculum

Dewey called the hidden curriculum "collateral learnings": the knowledge acquired just by being a member of a classroom organization and a school system. Children quickly pick up a set of expectations, specific roles, rules, procedures, and outcomes toward which they are supposed to strive. For example, they learn, among other things, that:

● Teachers have the right answer and students are supposed to figure it out. Roby (1981) called this the Quiz Show Model.

● Teachers decide what to do, when, how, and what to think of it afterwards.

● Students' responses to questions should be short and as close to the right answer as possible.

● Students learn from the teacher and the textbook, not from each other.

Such behaviors militate against our challenging students to think in complex fashions. But there are ways to help students *unlearn* these behaviors and *learn* new ones. Let's examine a few specific teacher actions that can successfully introduce a new set of collateral learnings.

Possible Solutions

Teachers must create an environment for thinking and spend time focusing students' attention on those preconditions for thoughtfulness that must exist if students are to become independent thinkers. Teachers need to:

1. *Ensure that students know their classmates' names.* Students are more receptive to the opinions of people they know; too often classrooms at all educational levels are enclaves of anonymity.

2. *Spend sufficient time observing students as they listen and respond to their peers.* If students are unable or unwilling to respond to the reasoning of their classmates, they will not be challenged with perspectives and solutions to problems different from their own. They may thus miss out on what Sigel has called the "discrepant experience" that encourages inquiry. Johnson and Johnson (1979) said

that it is through repeated interpersonal controversies and arguments, where students must repeatedly take cognizance of the reasoning processes of others, that cognitive development occurs.

To stimulate listening and responding, teachers can create structured learning experiences (see, for example, Johnson and Johnson, 1982), for instance, by requiring each student who speaks to paraphrase or build on what the previous student said.

These communications experiences help to create an environment in which communications are multidirectional, not just between one student and the teacher. They focus on all students' responding not only to the so-called right answer but *to the reasoning involved in obtaining any answer, viewpoint, or question* (for example, "How did you arrive at your conclusion?"). If by critical thinking we mean "the cognitive activity associated with the evaluation of the products of thought" (Yinger, 1980), then we must devote time to creating the conditions wherein students can attend to and comment critically on what their peers are saying and why.

3. *Clearly delineate their objectives for thinking.* Students need to know that they will be challenged to use information as raw material for more productive thought: generating ideas and many solutions to problems, relating complex ideas to each other, and probing for *why* someone has made a statement through the use of clarifying questions.

4. *Provide time for students to think in response to complex questions.* This means providing sufficient wait time (more than three seconds). It might also mean giving students five minutes to write down an answer to a question such as "What alternative courses of action might have been undertaken with what consequences?" Once students have analyzed the problem and generated some responses, they can work in small groups to share their answers, achieve consensus, list priorities, or probe for reasons why they arrived at these conclusions.

5. *Model thinking.* Students enjoy speculating with a teacher about how the teacher approaches real problems. One of the best times to do this is when a student asks an unanticipated question. In addition to noting that such thinking is creative, unusual, or productive, teachers might seize this opportunity to engage in inquiry: "I wonder how we could find out . . . how might we solve that problem . . . how might we solve this another way. . . . Let's think this through together." Thinking aloud with students is one of the best ways to communicate the value of thoughtfulness.

6. *Encourage students to pose questions.* This is easily done by presenting complex problems and asking "What do we know?" and "What don't we know that we should or might want to know?" Asking for students' questions about,

for example, solving the energy crisis or about Macbeth's motivations might lead to individual or group projects. In this way students share some instructional control with the teacher and have more of a stake in their own learning.

7. *Identify excellent thinking when it occurs.* When students demonstrate higher-order thinking, the teacher should occasionally recognize the quality of thinking and probe to discover *how* students arrived at their conclusions. In other words, teachers should directly teach what assumptions are and what makes a good assumption.

8. *Evaluate for thinking.* Teachers send confusing messages to students if they pose challenging thought questions during classes, but then test primarily for lower level recall of information. Teachers must reward good thinking by communicating through their evaluations that they and the school value more complex thinking. Yes, identification or recall of information is important—but *using* such information critically and creatively is equally important.

Students' Cognitive Developmental Levels

We should know at what levels our students are thinking. Several kinds of diagnostic measures are available with which to make this determination, for instance, formal tests such as those devised by Arlin (1984) and Peel (1966) and informal means of assessing the complexity of students' thinking.

If your orientation is Piagetian, you might obtain a very rough estimate of your students' concrete and formal thinking from the Arlin and Peel or tests by posing hypothetical questions such as: "What if it started snowing and never, ever stopped? What do you suppose would be the consequences?"

As students list numerous possible answers, they reveal what Torrance calls their ideational fluency (the number of responses), flexibility (the different perspectives reflected in each response), and originality. Students' answers also reveal their reflection of abstract thought. Young students tend to limit their responses to things they might have experienced close to home: "No school," "No shopping," "We would all die," "Lots of snowmen," "Daddy wouldn't go to work," and so on.

Older students are more able to foresee complex future possibilities and think in abstract collectivities: "People would become less selfish and more survival oriented, and that would be a good thing." "Building underground cities would help us cope." Their ability to foresee remote consequences allows older students to be more positive and less tied to immediate and limiting possibilities.

Teachers who are more inclined toward the conceptual levels of complexity model (Hunt, 1967) can use a simple essay question to observe students' abilities along a continuum from a simple, one-point-of-view orientation to more complex, multiple points of view. A question such as "Should our government prevent its citizens from smoking?" can be examined to see if students recognize more than one point of view, analyze each, and relate ideas within each point of view. Students who can accomplish this more complex thinking, according to Hunt, are more independent and require less structure than those whose thinking is more authoritarian and oriented toward absolutes of right and wrong.

Following assessment is the more difficult task of learning how to present intellectual challenges that are neither overly simplistic nor complex. For example, expecting 3rd graders to learn mathematical operations without benefit of concrete objects would overlook their concrete reasoning abilities. Similarly, expecting 6th graders to build and understand a model of an atomic reactor may be too complex a challenge; it may involve understanding relationships that are too abstract for them. The other side of the problem is to avoid all but the literal meanings of a play such as *Macbeth* with high school students who, because of their emerging formal thought, should be challenged to search for and create meanings of the symbols and metaphors that abound within the play.

There is no easy way to gauge the level of intellectual challenge. A rule of thumb is to present a problem of sufficient complexity for students of varying abilities to become involved, perhaps at different levels of difficulty. We want our students to be confronted with a discrepant experience that is difficult enough to stimulate inquiry. The more our instructional experiences are problem oriented, the better our chances of providing a challenge of slightly greater complexity than any one student can immediately master. Furth's *Thinking Goes to School* (1974) and Mosher's *Adolescent Development and Education* (1979) provide examples of the kinds of challenges that are appropriate at each level of schooling.

One of the best ways to stretch students' thinking is to present content in the form of problems that stimulate complex thinking: such content is likely to have some or all of the following characteristics:

● Conceptual complexity.
● Novelty.
● Dissonance (or presenting the discrepancy between expectations and reality that fosters inquiry).
● Significance.
● Multiplicity of levels or facets of meaning (capable of being approached or analyzed from a number of different perspectives).

Students' cognitive abilities need not impede thinking. We should and must assess the quality of students' thinking and design learning experiences to match and slightly exceed the level of complexity at which they currently function.

Teachers' Difficulties with Challenging Students to Think

Those of us who wish to challenge our students to think may encounter limitations of our own. We may lack knowledge of the nature of thinking, professional skills and behaviors required to challenge students to think, and problem-solving skills that can help us adapt our new knowledge to the classroom setting.

Knowledge of the Nature of Thinking

Without a solid foundation in the nature of reflective, critical, and creative thinking, teachers are unable to present meaningful and complex problems that stimulate thinking. They are also unable to recognize the products of such thinking when students ask intelligent questions or make thoughtful comments.

There are many ways to define critical thinking. We might define it, as Dewey did, as essentially problem solving; as "the process of reasonably deciding what to believe" (Ennis, 1982); or as a search for meaning, not the acquisition of knowledge (Arendt, 1977). These are only three possible definitions. With a clearer idea of what critical thinking is, teachers might be better able to interpret the following two classroom incidents:

● A kindergarten teacher asks her students, "Who was at the first Thanksgiving dinner?" After hearing the desired response—Pilgrims and Indians—one child says, "And cowboys came later." The teacher says "right" and moves on to the next phase of the lesson without acknowledging that this student is seeking—perhaps in a novel fashion—the meaning of facts and concepts.

● A 12th grade history teacher is checking his students' knowledge of the facts surrounding Germany's preparation for World War I when a student raises her hand and asks, "Was Kaiser Wilhelm the Hitler of World War I?" Her teacher says, "No, I wouldn't make that comparison" and continues with the facts and figures.

In both instances students exhibited the kind of thinking that, at a minimum, warranted a clarifying question, "What made you think of that?" In the latter example the student displayed complex, comparative, analytic thinking similar to that poets engage in when constructing metaphors and scientists exhibit when designing models for complex and invisible phenomena.

Without knowing something about the nature of thinking, teachers are in danger of denigrating or overlooking the marvels of students' contributions as well as making thinking in the classroom the presentation of very discrete lessons on equally specific skills such as classification, concept development, inferencing, and so on.

Professional Skills and Behaviors

The most important skills to be mastered quickly are those related to the teacher's ability to stimulate and nurture inquiry: the abilities to identify and present a discrepant experience and to initiate and manage discussions. The discrepant experience is one that puzzles us because we observe phenomena that conflict with our expectations or views of how the world works.

A role reorientation is involved here—one that Freire aptly described as *Pedagogy of the Oppressed*. He articulated the notion of "problem posing" education (in contrast to the "banking concept"), where teachers are no longer merely those who teach, but are themselves taught in dialogue with students, "who in turn while being taught also teach" (1974, p. 67). I observed an English teacher exemplify these skills by presenting students with the challenge of hypothesizing alternative courses of action for the colonists in Howard Fast's *April Morning*. Once students had presented two hypotheses, the teacher assumed the role of manager as they critiqued each other's thinking. This is a very different role from that of sole possessor of truth and wisdom! Skills related to this role reorientation include:

- Posing questions at various cognitive levels.
- Posing clarifying questions: "What makes you think that?" "How did you arrive at that conclusion?"
- Listening and building on student answers.
- Fostering student questions.
- Stimulating interaction and critique of other people's thinking (for example, asking Jane to critique Robert's conclusion and then challenging Robert to critique his own thinking).

When teachers enter the classroom to foster thinking, they will, of necessity, supplement their information-dispensing role with those of honest inquirer and problem-solving participant. Self-reflection about their own teaching is one strategy for improving these skills. Audio or videotape recordings can aid teachers in analyzing their abilities to stimulate and manage inquiry.

Problem Solving Needed to Adapt New Knowledge and Skills

No program can be transplanted into your classroom exactly as it was designed. As the Rand Change Agent Study (Berman and McLaughlin, 1978) noted, successful change in schools is an "adaptive" and "heuristic" process. This means that programs designed for one setting need to be modified to fit the constraints of a different workplace. It also means that teachers and administrators must work at making a program meet their own needs by finding varied ways to meet program objectives.

One way to do this is to establish peer support groups for coaching and problem posing and resolving. These groups could be in the form of seminars, additional workshops, and informal meetings before, during, and after school. Such a peer strategy is essential to the success of any change program and especially for those that involve such complex role reorientation as programs to foster thinking.

Kurt Lewin is one of the major theorists of a change strategy known as re-education, which is based on the notion that behavior change requires more than infusing new knowledge. Such changes as role reorientations require alterations in how one sees oneself, the situation, and others involved in situations. Teachers' work environments also need to be altered. Lewin noted that "effective re-education of a person requires changes in his environing society and cultures as well"; we need to "establish groups of concerned persons with norms that contrast in significant ways with those of the group to which a person previously belonged" (Benne, 1976). The support group's new norms and values should include openness to communications, inquiry for problem posing and resolving, risktaking, and willingness to experiment with varied alternative solutions.

Support groups foster intellectual growth for teachers by providing a secure environment where problems may be presented and rational problem-solving processes used to best advantage. They also help teachers encounter the realities of challenging students to transcend the hidden curriculum and their own cognitive developmental stages. Sarason (1982) and others have noted the absence of teachers in selecting solutions to school-related problems, identifying the underlying causes, setting objectives, and searching for that "universe of alternatives."

Problem-posing and -resolving support groups need to be built into the staff development process from the very beginning. These groups may be led by teachers, staff developers, consultants, or supervisors. Persons conducting seminars should possess the qualities that Lewin identified: openness, trust, willingness to confront difficulties, searching for causes and the universe of alternative solutions. They must exemplify trust, good communications processes, and, above all, be removed from the evaluative process. Teachers must be able to confront their own strengths and weaknesses in an atmosphere free from the fear or threat of subsequent evaluation.

Ideally, seminars should be conducted on school time. As Griffin (1983) pointed out, spending time with one's colleagues in a problem-posing and -resolving situation should be considered part of one's daily professional activities. These kinds of activities cannot satisfactorily be conducted during lunch.

The number of times teachers need to meet depends, of course, on the duration of inservice activities and the complexity of the knowledge and skills being considered. Opportunities are needed to debrief and evaluate after every major, new strategy has been introduced.

In summary, problem-posing and -resolving groups as envisioned by Freire (1974) and Lewin and practiced in the change strategies of Griffin (1983), for instance, provide us with the means for resolving real and immediate difficulties challenging students to think: difficulties related to instructional practice and management as well as more personal problems related to our own psychological comfort with venturing into the unknown.

Supervisors' Routines and Organizational Constraints

Sustaining any change in instructional practice requires supervision and collaborative problem solving. It is the latter process that is too often neglected in favor of the usual performance evaluation that may use observation criteria mismatched with the new and more desirable classroom behaviors.

The following suggestions include possibilities for day-to-day assistance, observation to improve instruction, and observation for evaluation. Some focus more directly on how teachers can help supervisors understand what they are attempting to do.

Day-by-Day Assistance

Supervisors or department chairs can communicate their support to teachers without observing them by:

1. Creating opportunities for two teachers to exchange visits and time to critique each other's performances. Peer observation and collaboration help to break down the barriers of teacher isolation created by our "egg crate" existence. Sparks (1984) indicates that peer observation can be more effective in promoting teacher professional development than working with an outside consultant.

2. Providing opportunities for teachers to plan together and to implement and evaluate these plans. Arrange schedules so that teachers participating within a specific program can be free at the same time to engage in problem posing and resolving.

3. Providing teachers with research reports and articles related to effective teaching behaviors. Often, just placing such items in mailboxes will foster inquiry and communicate interest and support.

4. Taking over a teacher's class occasionally to permit

that teacher to observe someone who practices the desired teaching behaviors.

5. Providing professional days for teachers to visit other districts where teachers practice the desired teaching behaviors within a specific program.

6. Providing in-class technical assistance—or coaching—to teachers interested in their own professional development. Coaches might be in-house teachers and supervisors or persons from other districts.

7. Using departmental or staff meetings to address instructional problems and issues rather than administrative affairs. Showing videotapes of classroom interactions can provide a stimulus for focusing on instructional issues and a setting within which to introduce related research on teaching.

8. Demonstrating knowledge of effective teaching behaviors in post-observation conferences, departmental meetings, and informal communications with teachers.

9. Linking teachers to technical assistance outside the school setting by identifying persons from other schools and colleges who can conduct inservice or provide coaching services.

10. Actively promoting teachers' self-reflection on performance and using that reflection as the basis for decisions about instructional improvement.

These practices have been derived from large-scale reports on change in educational settings and have been found to be related to positive teacher change. If practiced separately or in conjunction with each other, they can have a significant impact on teachers' behavior (Griffin, 1983).

Observation for Evaluation

The most important observation to make about evaluation of nontenured and tenured teachers is that the criteria for such judgments must be brought into alignment with district philosophy and goals regarding the fostering of critical and creative thinking. We cannot logically and fairly evaluate teachers using criteria that focus on classroom appearances, noise levels, and the presence of a behavioral objective on the chalkboard, or students' politeness, decorum, and ability to generate correct responses.

District evaluative criteria can and should be based as much as possible on what research says about teaching behaviors that are foundational—pertinent to all who teach the basics—and those that are found to be conducive to fostering higher levels of thinking (Barell, 1985). We can create instruments that include the foundation as well as the superstructure: those items that help students read with comprehension (posing questions at various cognitive levels and the use of metacognitive strategies) and those that help foster more complex reasoning (critiquing each other's reasoning processes).

Developing observational criteria that support what teachers are attempting in the classroom presents an excellent opportunity for the organization to engage in collaborative problem solving. Without such organizational sanction and support, teachers may justifiably think that the administration does not really value what the evidence and research say about thinking in the classroom: that there are very specific practices and strategies teachers can exhibit to challenge students to do more than read, recite, and recall factual knowledge.

Strategies to Help Teachers Communicate with Supervisors

I know an English teacher who went through a complex program of staff development, returned to her classroom, and started challenging students' thinking with various kinds of writing experiences—including composing a class newpspaper. Her supervisor immediately began to berate her: "You're using too much paper! There goes my budget!"

This incident illustrates the problem with all re-educative experiences: if they do not include people in supervisory and subordinate roles, confusion results. When one group—in this case, teachers—learns and adapts new expectations and role definitions and other groups—including supervisors—do not, we can expect conflict and confusion to be communicated to students and to be experienced by everyone involved. Intelligent planning can reduce tensions. Here are some suggestions for teachers:

1. Communicate with your supervisor the concerns you have about students' thinking. Present specific, concrete evidence of their difficulties from your own observations and tests as well as evidence from national reports. Stress what is observable and, therefore, less debatable.

2. Enlist the supervisor's support by presenting the situation as a large-scale problem requiring everybody's best thinking. Work toward a collegial problem-posing and -resolving approach: "How can we collaborate and work toward the best kinds of solutions? I have some ideas, but I need your assistance and the benefit of your experience."

To some this may sound like pie-in-the-sky. But never underestimate another person's desire *to be asked, to be included* in problem solving. At the very least they may be flattered—hopefully, they will recognize that you have identified a real need warranting further consideration.

3. Share your information with colleagues. Communicate need identification and possible solutions. Work toward building a constituency of people who share your concerns; this is a necessary step in the change process, and you may have to do a fair amount of it.

4. Invite the supervisor to observe a lesson during which you are practicing specific strategies. Ask him or her:

- What did you see?
- May I tell you what I saw happening?
- Would you like to know my evaluation—what I liked and didn't like?
- Can we discuss why these things happened and what we might do to alter the situation?
- This is what I think I'll do differently next time. I'll work on it. Will you return soon so we can continue this dialogue?

By using this process, teachers may control more of the discussion than they usually do. The point is that supervision for improved thinking in the classroom must engage all parties in rational problem solving—identifying a problem, understanding causes, and searching for and mutually selecting alternative solutions.

5. Team up with a colleague to exchange observations. Discuss your findings using an observation form or posing questions such as: "What occurred? Why? What seemed to impede or facilitate thinking? What can we do about it?" Share your discussion with your supervisor. Such peer observations will make challenging departmental meeting topics, especially if you include small portions of the research on teaching.

6. Share workshop curricular materials with your supervisor so that he or she can share such information with others. This can also be useful for departmental meetings.

7. Offer to share your classroom experiences in a departmental meeting. Videotape your implementation of a specific strategy and offer to have others view and critique it—again emphasizing the identification of specific, observable behaviors and searching for viable alternatives. Unless you have previously developed interest in other members of your department, your performance might be viewed as the concerns of one person, too much work with little reward, or a passing fancy. Having at least a modest constituency of likeminded persons will give you comfort and support and may convince others to re-examine what goes on in their classrooms.

8. Remember than changing how another person—child or adult—thinks is difficult and time consuming. Too often we embark on change in educational settings without regard for the complexities of affecting how others think about us, themselves, or the situation.

Community Expectations and Pressures

Too often we undertake an innovative program and neglect to inform the parents and community of our new expectations for students. This could be especially unfortunate in a program designed to foster thinking in the classroom. Parents can, if sufficiently informed, become allies in the struggle to overcome the passivity inculcated by the implicit curriculum. They can reinforce the thinking strategies teachers are working with during the day, thereby confronting students with not one but two settings in which they are challenged to do more than take in information and repeat it almost verbatim.

Some viable informational strategies involving parents include:

1. Communicating the intention to include their children in a new program early in its development and, if necessary, asking their permission.

2. Conducting informal briefings with interested and concerned parents early in the life of the project to inform them of the new expectations and behaviors. Providing parents with opportunities to practice the new behaviors so they can become resources for teachers helping to foster the desired outcomes within another setting—the home.

3. Involving parents in planning ways of overcoming the implicit curriculum. Engaging their thinking about how to challenge students to think in ways supported by the program.

4. Advising parents of difficulties as they arise and results of program implementation.

5. Enlisting the help of parents in collecting evidence of students' growth in rational behaviors.

These and other strategies will do more than communicate expectations to parents. They will actively involve them in the problem-solving process and thereby give parents a stake in the life and development of the new program.

Conclusion

The suggestions set forth here have been derived from personal experience and research on teacher and student growth and development. There is no prescription for dealing with the difficulties identified here. Nevertheless, there are significant principles that seem to apply to the kinds of changes we have been discussing:

1. Recognize that growth in thinking occurs over a long period of time, because we are concerned with changes in habits, dispositions, attitudes, and role perceptions. Teachers and students must unlearn old ways of thinking and learn new approaches to confronting the world.

2. Teachers engaged in teaching thinking require support from other teachers, supervisors, administrators, and parents. This support should facilitate the challenging task of posing and resolving instructional problems.

3. If teachers are to challenge students to think, they must, in turn, be challenged to think critically and crea-

tively by colleagues, supervisors, and administrators. They should be encouraged to be self-reflective, analytic, and evaluative with respect to their own teaching performances. This also means that, when appropriate, teachers should be involved in decision making and not merely be recipients of mandated changes (see Sarason, 1982).

4. Challenging students to think requires a systemic, holistic perspective. All elements of the school system should be involved—philosophy and goals, curriculum, instructional practices, supervisory services, and interpersonal relations and communications with the community.

Underlying these four principles is one overriding consideration when contemplating change: those most directly involved in the change should play an active, reflective role in formulating goals, practices, and programs. Teachers, therefore, will become more involved in decision making when planning and implementing programs that challenge students to think critically and creatively.

REFERENCES

Arendt, Hannah. "Thinking II." *The New Yorker,* November 28, 1977, pp. 114-163.

Arlin, Pat. *The Arlin Test of Formal Reasoning.* East Aurora, N.Y.: Slosson Educational Publications, Inc., 1984.

Barell, John. "You Ask the Wrong Questions!" *Educational Leadership* 42 (May 1985).

Benne, Kenneth. "The Process of Re-Education: An Assessment of Kurt Lewin's Views." In *The Planning of Change.* Edited by Warren Bennis, Kenneth Benne, Robert Chin, and Kenneth Corey. New York: Holt, Rinehart and Winston, 1976.

Berman, Paul, and McLaughlin, Milbrey. *Federal Programs Supporting Educational Change* (8 Volumes). Santa Monica, Calif.: Rand Corporation, 1978.

Ennis, Robert. *Manual for Two Tests: Cornell Critical Thinking Test Level X and Cornell Critical Thinking Test Level Z.* Champaign, Ill.: University of Illinois, 1983.

Freire, Paulo. *Pedagogy of the Oppressed.* New York: The Seabury Press, 1974.

Furth, Hans, and Wachs, Harry. *Thinking Goes to School.* New York: Oxford University Press, 1974.

Griffin, Gary. *Changing Teacher Practice—Final Report of an Experimental Study.* Austin, Tex.: Research and Development Center for Teacher Education, 1983.

Hunt, David. See *Human Information Processing.* Edited by Harold Schroder, Michael Driver, and Siegfried Streufert. New York: Holt, Rinehart and Winston, 1967.

Johnson, Roger, and Johnson, David. "Conflict in the Classroom: Controversy and Learning." *Review of Educational Research* 49 (Winter 1979): 51-70.

Johnson, David, and Johnson, Frank. *Joining Together—Group Theory and Group Skills.* Englewood Cliffs, N.J.: Prentice-Hall, Inc., 1982.

Mosher, Ralph. *Adolescents' Development and Education—A Janus Knot.* Berkeley, Calif.: McCutchan, 1979.

Peel, E.A. "A Study of Differences in The Judgments of Adolescent Pupils." *British Journal of Educational Psychology* 36 (1966): 77-86.

Roby, T. W. "Bull Sessions, Quiz Shows, and Discussion." Paper presented at the annual meeting of the American Educational Research Association, Los Angeles, 1981.

Sarason, Seymour. *The Culture of the School and the Problem of Change,* 2nd ed., Boston: Allyn and Bacon, Inc., 1982.

Sparks, Georgea Mohlman. "Inservice Education: The Process of Teacher Change." Paper presented at the annual meeting of the American Educational Research Association, Montreal, 1984.

Yinger, Robert, ed. "Can We Really Teach Them to Think?" In *Fostering Critical Thinking.* San Francisco: Jossey-Bass, Inc., 1980.

PART III

What Is Thinking? Deciding On Definitions

CRITICAL THINKING

One of the major tasks of improving or installing a thinking skills program is deciding what thinking is.

Schools should have a somewhat common vision of what it is they are striving for in order to teach it.

CREATIVE THINKING

LATERAL THINKING

If you don't know what it is you're teaching for, how can you measure it? How do you know if kids are getting better at it?

Isn't BLOOM'S TAXONOMY enough?

HIGHER-LEVEL THINKING

The field of cognitive education today is fraught with different interpretations. The purpose of this part of this resource book is

NOT to provide you with the definition. Rather, it is intended to stimulate discussion. From these several definitions, you must adapt, modify, and decide which definition is most appropriate to your situation:

METACOGNITION

There is not unanimity.

REMEDIAL THINKING

There is confusion.

INTELLIGENCE

But the decision on definition is part of the inquiry process. That makes the process consistent with the product.

Just what do human beings do when they behave intelligently?

REASONING

8

Thinking Skills: Meanings and Models

Barbara Z. Presseisen

It is not best that we should all think alike; it is differ-ence of opinion which makes horse races.

—Mark Twain

Of the many tasks that confront educators in plan-ning for thinking skills in the curriculum, few are more critical than determining what is meant by thinking or developing a model of the thinking process.

Currently, there is a great deal of interest in improving student thinking abilities, but there is also a great deal of confusion about what thinking is, the kinds of experiences or programs that advance it, and the implications of such efforts for school personnel and policies. This chapter pro-vides a glossary of working definitions of thinking skills and some practical models to help form a taxonomy to ex-plain the working relationships among different levels and different kinds of thought processes.

Definitions of Essential Thinking Skills

Thinking is generally assumed to be a *cognitive* pro-cess, a mental act by which knowledge is acquired. Al-though cognition may account for several ways that some-thing may come to be known—as in perception, reasoning, and intuition—the current emphasis on thinking skills em-phasizes *reasoning* as a major cognitive focus. Consider, for example, the following definitions of thinking:

This chapter is based on work funded by the National Institute of Education, Department of Education. The opinions do not neces-sarily reflect the position of the National Institute of Education, and no official endorsement by NIE should be inferred.

- "The mental derivation of mental elements (thoughts) from perceptions *and* the mental manipulation/ combination of these thoughts."[1]
- "The mental manipulation of sensory input to for-mulate thoughts, reason about, or judge."[2]
- "The extension of evidence in accord with that evi-dence so as to fill up gaps in the evidence: and this is done by moving through a succession of interconnected steps which may be stated at the time, or left till later to be stated."[3]

Several interesting aspects underlie these definitions of thinking. Thinking processes are related to other kinds of behavior and require active involvement on the part of the thinker. Notable products of thinking—thoughts, knowledge, reasons—and higher processes, like judging, can also be generated. Complex relationships are devel-oped through thinking, as in the use of evidence over time. These relationships may be interconnected to an organized structure and may be expressed by the thinker in a variety of ways. If anything, these definitions indicate that thinking is a complex and reflective endeavor as well as a creative experience. Such meanings are highly reminiscent of Dew-ey's original 1910 writing.[4]

Current literature on thinking presents multiple lists of cognitive processes that can be considered thinking skills. It is dangerous to confuse one level of thinking with another in terms of its power or significance. Beyer stresses the importance of defining skills accurately and suggests reviewing the work of researchers like Bloom, Guilford, and Feuerstein to find useful definitions.[5] Clear definitions, Beyer maintains, do not confuse distinctly dif-ferent processes like inquiry and simple recall. Further-more, consistent with other researchers of cognitive pro-cesses, Beyer distinguishes between lower, essential skills and complex, multiple-process strategies. For example, there is a great difference between picking identical examples of a particular insect and finding the antidote to the sting of the same insect. One task involves the basic processes of identification and comparison; the other requires multiple, sophisticated, replicable, and sequential steps of problem solving.

What are the basic or essential skills of thinking? Nickerson suggests that no one taxonomy exists.[6] Educators would be wise, he advises, to select abilities that represent what they want students to be able to do and incorporate these particular skills into their curriculums and school programs. Researchers' lists can be the basis of such selections. Consider, for example, the categories of skills suggested by Bloom and others[7] and Guilford[8] over 25 years ago:

Bloom's Taxonomy	Guilford's Structure of Intellect
Knowledge	Units
Comprehension	Classes
Application	Relations
Analysis	Systems
Synthesis	Transformations
Evaluation	Implications

Each of Bloom's cognitive categories includes a list of a variety of thinking skills and indicates the kind of behavior students are to perform as the objectives or goals of specific learning tasks. For example:
- *Knowledge:* Define, recognize, recall, identify, label, understand, examine, show, collect.
- *Comprehension:* Translate, interpret, explain, describe, summarize, extrapolate.
- *Application:* Apply, solve, experiment, show, predict.
- *Analysis:* Connect, relate, differentiate, classify, arrange, check, group, distinguish, organize, categorize, detect, compare, infer.
- *Synthesis:* Produce, propose, design, plan, combine, formulate, compose, hypothesize, construct.
- *Evaluation:* Appraise, judge, criticize, decide.

Some of these tasks are also evident in Guilford's six categories. For example:
- Recognizing a particular object is a *units* skill.
- Showing a group of similarly colored or shaped objects is a *classes*-based task.
- Forming a geometric structure out of six match sticks is a *systems* task.

In both researchers' work, there are some unstated dimensions to the thinking skills sequence. Tasks generally move from simpler to complex operations, from more observable and concrete to abstract dimensions, and from an emphasis on working with known materials toward creating or inventing new, previously unknown approaches or materials. Guilford is interested in both convergent and divergent operations, and his ultimate goal is a thorough exposition of the nature of intelligence.

Since the initial work of Bloom and Guilford, a greater concern for the developmental appropriateness of tasks or thinking skills has emerged. Hudgin's study of thinking and learning emphasizes Piaget's research on the development of thinking processes as the child grows intellectually.[9] This research assumes that there is a regular sequence to children's cognitive development, but not precisely in direct age correlates. Piaget suggests that youngsters first entering school are mostly "preoperational" or dominated by their perceptions.[10] Gradually they develop systematic explanations or concrete rules for resolving conflicting situations or explaining diverse phenomena; they form conceptualizations. By their early teens, most students develop the ability to perform higher forms of cognitive operations; they learn to vary interpretations or descriptions in abstract form and to construct formal explanations of cause and effect. Somehow, says Hudgins, the scope of thinking skills expressed in a K-12 curriculum needs to relate to this developmental and cumulative sequence, as well as to the empirical research it represents. The relationships of particular subject matter to the specific skills to be learned may also be of developmental consequence.

Another issue regarding essential thinking skills is the concern for various models of thinking that are available to the learner, such as types of symbol systems. Much school learning involves linguistic or verbal abilities as well as quantitative, numerical reasoning. Spatial or visual depictions of mental processing are becoming more significant to instruction, especially with the advent of video technologies in the classroom. How do these different modalities or modes of thinking influence cognitive development? That is an open research question. But the testing of cognitive abilities already reflects the appreciation of multiple modes of thinking to the instructional process and the learning of essential thinking skills. The *Developing Cognitive Abilities Test* is designed around a content format that uses Bloom's Taxonomy and a three-mode organization of content—verbal, quantitative, and spatial—for grade 3-12 subjects.[11]

Ideally, then, there are a host of candidates for a basic thinking skills taxonomy. In planning a curricular sequence, it's wise to consider the developmental level of the learners, the mode of presenting information to them, and the subject matters ultimately to be related to. At least five categories of thinking skills merit consideration. Figure 1, which draws from the work of Bloom and Guilford, is a basic framework for a first-order, operational taxonomy.

FIGURE 1

A Model of Thinking Skills: Basic Processes

CAUSATION—*establishing cause and effect, assessment:*

Predictions
Inferences
Judgments
Evaluations

TRANSFORMATIONS—*relating known to unknown characteristics, creating meanings:*

Analogies
Metaphors
Logical inductions

RELATIONSHIPS—*detecting regular operations:*

Parts and wholes, patterns
Analysis and synthesis
Sequences and order
Logical deductions

CLASSIFICATION—*determining common qualities:*

Similarities and differences
Grouping and sorting, comparisons
Either/or distinctions

QUALIFICATIONS—*finding unique characteristics:*

Units of basic identity
Definitions, facts
Problem/task recognition

Complex Thinking Processes

The five categories suggested in Figure 1 are essential thinking skills. The complex processes involved in thinking skills programs—the "macro-process strategies"—are based on the essential skills but use them for a particular purpose. Cohen distinguishes processes that rely on external stimuli and seek to be productive, such as making judgments or problem resolution, from processes that depend about equally on external and internal stimuli and seek to be creative.[12] He suggests at least four different complex thinking processes:

● *Problem Solving*—using basic thinking processes to resolve a known or defined difficulty; assemble facts about the difficulty and determine additional information needed; infer or suggest alternate solutions and test them for appropriateness; potentially reduce to simpler levels of explanation and eliminate discrepancies; provide solution checks for generalizable value.

● *Decision Making*—using basic thinking processes to choose a best response among several options; assemble information needed in a topic area; compare advantages and disadvantages of alternative approaches; determine what additional information is required; judge the most effective response and be able to justify it.

● *Critical Thinking*—using basic thinking processes to analyze arguments and generate insight into particular meanings and interpretations; develop cohesive, logical reasoning patterns and understand assumptions and biases underlying particular positions; attain a credible, concise, and convincing style of presentation.

● *Creative Thinking*—using basic thinking processes to develop or invent novel, aesthetic, constructive ideas or products, related to percepts as well as concepts, and stressing the intuitive aspects of thinking as much as the rational. Emphasis is on using known information or material to generate the possible, as well as to elaborate on the thinker's original perspective.

These complex processes obviously draw on and elaborate on the underlying essential skills. Certain of the essential skills may be more significant to one complex process than others, but current research has not clarified a discrete understanding of such relationships. What seems most important is that young learners develop competence in the essential skills during the early years of schooling, and then—in middle or junior high school—are introduced to the more complex processes in specific content matter that is fairly closely related to the use of such skills.

Late middle school or early junior high school is an appropriate time for introducing instruction about higher-order skills or complex thinking processes. The adolescent learner's growing cognitive capacities offer ripe opportunities for the challenge of more complex thinking.[13] Elementary students can benefit from early exposure to varied thinking processes and to different media of presentation, but probably can only approach more complex sequences as they gain experience and apply similar skills in multiple content areas. Beyer suggests that an effective thinking skills curriculum will introduce only a limited number of skills at a particular grade level, will teach these across all appropriate content areas, and will vary the media and contents of presentation.[14] Subsequent grades should enlarge the thinking skills base and provide additional and more elaborate applications of skills already introduced.

Some complex thinking processes may be more relevant to certain subject areas than to others. For example, problem-solving thinking skills seem ideal for mathematics or science instruction. Decision making may be useful for social studies and vocational studies; critical thinking may be more relevant for the debate team, language arts class, and problems of democracy or American government courses. Creative thinking might enhance all subjects, as well as be particularly meaningful to art, music, or literature programs. Most important, the goals of the specific complex process and objectives for learning in the particular subject area should be parallel and reinforcing.

Figure 2 presents a suggested model of complex thinking processes. The relationship of any one process to the underlying essential skills is tentatively drawn and is relative to the skills presented in Figure 1. Other potential complex processes might be examined as to how they compare to the four strategies presented in terms of underlying characteristics and ultimate outcomes.

Metacognition and Thinking

A useful taxonomy of thinking must somehow account for metacognitive aspects of the current thinking skills movement. " 'Metacognition' refers to one's knowledge concerning one's own cognitive processes and products."[15] Learners must actively *monitor* their use of thinking processes and *regulate* them according to their cognitive objectives. Henle considers such regulation the essence of autonomous self-education.[16] Costa suggests that this ability to "know what we know and what we don't know" is a uniquely human trait, but not necessarily one that all adults acquire. He proposes metacognitive skills as a key attribute of formal thinking or higher-process skills instruction and stresses that the teacher's classroom methodology must constructively deal with metacognition.[17] Other researchers maintain that metacognitive skills are also significant factors in developing subject-skilled performers.

One of the most salient characteristics of metacognition is that it involves growing consciousness. One becomes more aware of the thinking processes themselves

and their specific procedures, as well as more conscious of oneself as a thinker and performer. As learners acquire an understanding of what the various thinking processes are, they can better understand and apply them. Some researchers suggest that is why, initially, thinking skills should be taught directly and in relatively content-free situations.[18]

Metacognitive thinking has two main dimensions. The first is task-oriented and relates to monitoring the actual performance of a skill. The second dimension is strategic; it involves using a skill in a particular circumstance and being aware of getting the most informative feedback from carrying out a particular strategy. Figure 3 elaborates on these dimensions.

Monitoring task performance requires learners to watch their own activities. Students cannot tell if they are at the right place if they are not aware of the assigned task and the directions for completing it. They might be advised to discriminate subgoals of a task and relate to ultimate objectives. In mathematics problems involving reading, for instance, students might identify addition or subtraction as an appropriate operation prior to actually determining a final answer. Detecting errors while working may involve checking or proofreading, rereading passages, or recalculating or retranslating material. Allocating time across work or checking coverage in qualitative dimensions ("Is my outline extensive enough?") are aspects of pacing the completion of an assignment. The metacognitive thesis is that any and all of these behaviors can enhance the success of particular task performance. Often these same behaviors are also characteristic of sound study skills programs.

In terms of selecting appropriate strategies to work by,

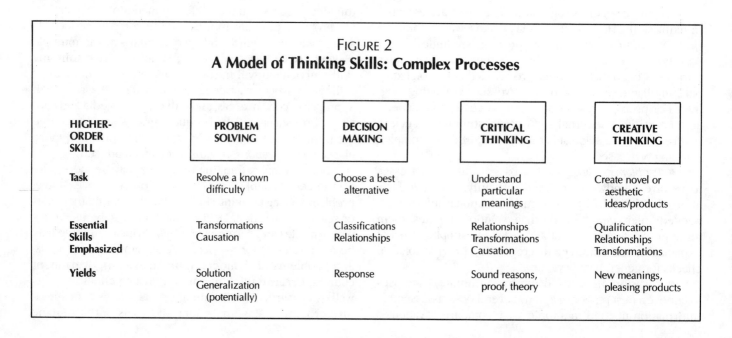

FIGURE 2
A Model of Thinking Skills: Complex Processes

HIGHER-ORDER SKILL	PROBLEM SOLVING	DECISION MAKING	CRITICAL THINKING	CREATIVE THINKING
Task	Resolve a known difficulty	Choose a best alternative	Understand particular meanings	Create novel or aesthetic ideas/products
Essential Skills Emphasized	Transformations Causation	Classifications Relationships	Relationships Transformations Causation	Qualification Relationships Transformations
Yields	Solution Generalization (potentially)	Response	Sound reasons, proof, theory	New meanings, pleasing products

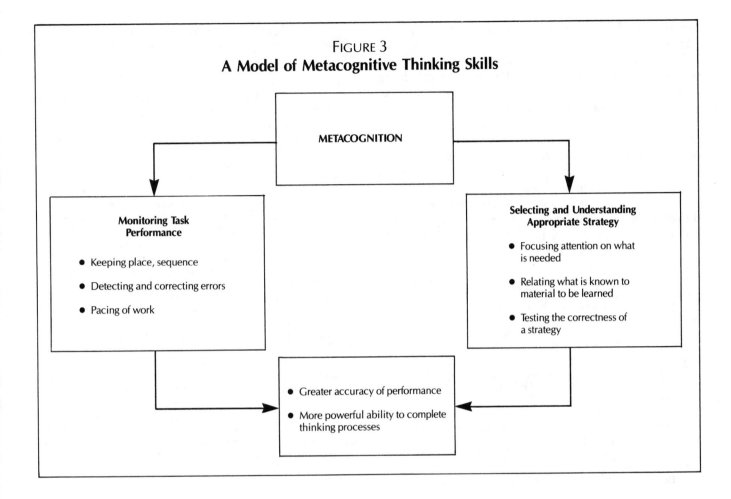

FIGURE 3
A Model of Metacognitive Thinking Skills

metacognitive theory suggests that the first order of learning is to recognize the particular problem and determine what information is needed to resolve it and where to obtain it. Through such consideration, the student comes to recognize the limitations of the learning and the ultimate boundaries of the solution being sought. Sternberg considers these the "executive processes" of sound reasoning.[19] Flavell refers to the various aspects of information retrieval in learning to think—remembering, monitoring, and updating information—and draws parallels between classroom learning and experiences involving thinking in the world outside school.[20] Henle suggests that recognizing what is understood and to what degree ultimately helps learners come to terms with the power of their own thoughts.[21] Consider, for example, the importance of knowing the difference between a wild guess, an informed guess, a hypothesis, an intuition, and a fact. Finally, testing the accuracy of a strategy provides an opportunity to apply varying sets of evaluative criteria and to determine if, in fact, the right approach is being employed. The learner has an opportunity to assess the initial selection of strategy, as well as to develop insight into a potentially better choice. A more holistic understanding of strategy and the development of fluency or competence in a particular strategy are involved in this type of learning. From the metacognitive viewpoint, the thinker becomes more autonomous as these skills are developed and refined.

Toward a Common Understanding

When we focus on what we mean by thinking, we need to consider the various levels of thought that humans are capable of. The complexity of the cognitive process becomes evident. A three-level model has been generated by this examination:

- *Cognition*—the skills associated with essential and complex processes.
- *Metacognition*—the skills associated with the learner's awareness of his or her own thinking.
- *Epistemic Cognition*—the skills associated with understanding the limits of knowing, as in particular subject

matter, and the nature of problems that thinkers can address.

Once this taxonomy is considered, educators can examine the kinds of material available to them for enhancing thinking instruction in the classroom. They may also become aware of the need to devote attention to relating thinking to current school programs and to teachers' understanding of what thinking is and what it means to student development and classroom instruction. How to assess student achievement in the various abilities related to thinking is also a prominent issue.

Without a common understanding of what we mean by thinking, we cannot even begin to address the extensive problems associated with the development of students' higher cognitive performance.

FOOTNOTES

[1]Jozef Cohen, *Thinking* (Chicago: Rand McNally & Co., 1971), p. 5.

[2]Barry K. Beyer, consultant at an ASCD National Curriculum Study Institute, "Practical Approaches to Teaching Thinking Skills in Every Classroom," February 1984.

[3]Frederick C. Bartlett, *Thinking: An Experimental and Social Study* (London: Allen and Unwin, 1958), p. 75.

[4]John Dewey, *How We Think* (Boston: D. C. Heath & Co., 1933).

[5]Barry K. Beyer, "Improving Thinking Skills—Defining the Problem," *Phi Delta Kappan* 65 (March 1984): 487.

[6]Raymond S. Nickerson, "Thoughts on Teaching Thinking," *Educational Leadership* 39 (October 1981): 21.

[7]Benjamin S. Bloom, ed; Max D. Englehart; Edward J. Furst; Walker H. Hill; and David R. Krathwohl, *Taxonomy of Educational Objectives, Handbook I: Cognitive Domain* (New York: David McKay, 1956).

[8]J. P. Guilford, *The Nature of Human Intelligence* (New York: McGraw-Hill, 1967).

[9]Bryce B. Hudgins, *Learning and Thinking: A Primer for Teachers* (Itasca, Ill.: F. E. Peacock, 1977), pp. 10-20.

[10]Jean Piaget, "Piaget's Theory," in *Carmichael's Manual of Child Psychology, Volume 1,* ed. Paul H. Mussen (New York: John Wiley & Sons, Inc., 1970), pp. 703-732.

[11]*Developing Cognitive Abilities Test,* Teacher's Manual (Glenview, Ill.: Scott, Foresman and Co., 1980).

[12]Jozef Cohen, p. 26.

[13]Barbara Z. Presseisen, *Understanding Adolescence: Issues and Implications for Effective Schools* (Philadelphia, Pa.: Research for Better Schools, Inc., 1982).

[14]Barry K. Beyer, "Improving Thinking Skills—Practical Approaches," *Phi Delta Kappan* 65 (April 1984): 559.

[15]John H. Flavell, "Metacognitive Aspects of Problem Solving," in *The Nature of Intelligence,* ed. Lauren B. Resnick (Hillsdale, N.J.: Lawrence Erlbaum, 1976), p. 232.

[16]Mary Henle, "Cognitive Skills," in *Learning About Learning: A Conference Report,* ed. Jerome S. Bruner (Washington, D.C.: U.S. Department of Health, Education and Welfare, 1966), pp. 53-63.

[17]Arthur L. Costa, *Mediating the Metacognitive,* Sacramento, Calif.: California State University, n.d., 7 pp., photocopy, published in *Human Development* 26 (July-August 1983).

[18]Barry K. Beyer, "Common Sense About Teaching Thinking Skills," *Educational Leadership* 41 (November 1983): 44-49.

[19]Robert J. Sternberg, "What Should Intelligence Tests Test? Implications of a Triarchic Theory of Intelligence for Intelligence Testing," *Educational Researcher* 13 (January 1984): 5-15.

[20]John H. Flavell, p. 234.

[21]Mary Henle, p. 57.

9

The Good Thinker

Allan A. Glatthorn and Jonathan Baron

Thought alone is eternal.
—Owen Meredith

Schools that are planning to teach critical thinking are surrounded by what seems to be a bewildering variety of programs. It would be helpful to have a theory of critical thinking that would allow educators to assess the theoretical soundness and effectiveness of such programs. In this chapter we describe one such theory and discuss its implications for educational practice.

Baron's Model of the Good Thinker

The model proposed by Baron (in press) is based on a philosophical argument in the tradition of Dewey (1933), but is consistent with empirical evidence as well. Before we describe it in detail, we would like to point out two important features.

First, it is a model of *conscious* thinking. In conscious thinking, we are aware of thinking; we can follow instructions about its processes and evaluate our use of those processes. In unconscious thinking, much of the thinking work is taken over by subconscious processes. Baron's model focuses on conscious thinking because only conscious thinking can be influenced directly by pedagogical interventions.

Second, it is a *general* model that provides insight into several types of thinking; it is not domain- or discipline-specific. It presents a picture of, for instance, how a mechanic diagnoses a problem with a car engine and how a principal chooses a method to improve school attendance.

In essence, the model involves several closely related processes or phases.

- *Thinking begins with a state of doubt about what to do or believe.* As Dewey (1933) noted, all conscious thought has its genesis in uncertainty; the individual is confronted with a problematic situation.
- We *usually have a goal in mind when the doubt arises, but we may search for new goals, subgoals, or a reformulation of the original goal.* The goal is the state we wish to achieve, such as a new insight or an effective solution. Implicit in each goal is a question that we want to answer: "What is wrong with the car?" "What methods will increase attendance?"
- We *search for possibilities.* Possibilities are possible answers to the question implicit in the goal. They are the alternative routes or options to solution. Each possibility has a strength—a measure of the value we accord that possibility. The strength is a subjective assessment of the closeness of the solution to the goal, and is always determined from our personal perspective, not from an outsider's viewpoint. While we may be influenced by the views of others, it is our own assessment of strength that makes the difference.
- We *search for evidence relative to the possibilities.* Evidence is needed to evaluate possibilities. We search for arguments, scenarios, analogies, and facts that bear on the possibilities.
- We *use the evidence to revise the strengths of the possibilities.* Each piece of evidence has a subjective weight for each possibility. We may either overreact or minimize this weight.
- We *decide that the goal is reached and conclude the search.* At a certain point we terminate the search for goals,

possibilities, and evidence, deciding that further searching would be counterproductive.

The most important components of the model are the three search processes—the search for goals, the search for possibilities, and the search for evidence. At times these searches are active—we exclude all other conscious activities. At other times they are inactive—we postpone judgment while pursuing other activities. Note also that while the processes are presented here in a linear form, they do not all occur consciously in every thought sequence and are ordinarily not used in a linear order.

Some Common Types of Thinking

When we examine the types of thinking that are essential to certain activities, we need to ask whether there is too much or too little thinking (relative to a range that would be optimal for the thinker's rational goals), but we usually cannot ask whether thinking occurs at all. There are nine types of thinking:

Diagnosis is troubleshooting, for which we use our hypotheses about the source of the problem. The evidence may consist of the results of tests we have performed. The goal is usually fixed. "My car stalls at corners—what's going wrong?"

Hypothesis testing is the process of forming and testing theories, just as scientists test theories. During hypothesis testing, the goal is often changed. Scientists frequently discover the real question while trying to answer some other question.

Reflection is the search for general principles or rules based on evidence gathered largely from memory: "What general principle might explain why teachers often ignore curriculum guides?" "What are the rules for simplifying algebraic expressions?" We search for possible answers, new questions, and evidence that supports the possible answers. Here the search for evidence is under considerable control; we might direct our memories to provide evidence either for or against a given possibility. Philosophers and other scholars spend most of their time reflecting. It is a major component of Lipman's "Philosophy for Children" program (Lipman, Sharp, and Oscanyon, 1980).

Insight is the "eureka" phenomenon. Solutions come suddenly and with certainty. In insight problems it is only the search for possibilities (possible answers or approaches) that seems under control; the search for and use of evidence are usually immediate. In this sense, insight problems are atypical of most thinking.

Artistic creation is also an important type of conscious thinking. The possibilities are the components of the work itself, such as the images in a poem, the colors in a painting, or the movements in a dance. The weight of the evidence for a given possibility is the artist's critical reaction to the evidence itself. In creative tasks the search for goals is under full control and is usually crucial for success.

Prediction is similar to reflection, but the search for goals may not be as controllable. The evidence usually consists of memories of past situations and analogous cases.

Decision making is a type of thinking in which the possibilities are courses of action or plans. The evidence usually consists of imagined consequences. Decision making may be one of the most important types of thinking, since it includes the selection of strategies for other mental tasks.

Behavioral learning involves learning about the effects of one's conduct. When we learn behaviorally, we try to accomplish two goals—to learn about the situation (for example, to learn how to cook) and to obtain success with the task at hand (to produce an edible meal). Often these goals compete. Repeating some action that has worked in the past might result in success, but it might also preclude the experimentation that is needed for learning. The same issues come up when we learn specific heuristics for problem solving or writing.

Learning from observation includes all cases in which we learn about the environment through observation alone, without voluntary experimentation. In this sense most language learning is a type of learning from observation, as are most types of culturally transmitted knowledge. In this type of thinking, the search for evidence is not controllable at all.

Good Thinking vs. Bias

Without corrective intervention, there are two general biases that may occur. First, we might search too little, give up too soon, or be too satisfied with the first possibilities, evidence, and goals that enter our minds. We tend to do this because the cost of thinking—time, effort, and lost opportunity—is immediate, but the benefits of thinking—increased knowledge and better decisions—are usually in the future. Thus, learning to think well is a problem of self-control, just like saving money.

The second bias is that we may not be sufficiently self-critical. We might seek evidence that supports, rather than conflicts with, our initial ideas, and we might ignore contrary evidence or fail to try to think of alternatives. This bias allows us to stop thinking early. Thus the first bias reinforces the second.

Both biases are difficult to correct without help, for those of us who are not self-critical or who give up early will never have a chance to experience the beneficial effects of better thinking. Of course, there are people who think too much or are too self-critical. But according to the theory, those people are victims of too much education.

Good Thinking vs. Poor Thinking

This model helps us make some valid and useful distinctions between good and poor thinking. Here we wish to distance ourselves from those who equate good thinking with a long list of discrete mental operations and those who describe poor thinking in terms of several logical errors. We argue for the analysis summarized in Figure 1. This analysis enables researchers and educators to focus attention on a smaller number of critical attributes. For clarity, Figure 1 contrasts good thinkers with poor thinkers; however, we do not mean to suggest that individuals should be so categorized. A person can be, for example, a good thinker in financial matters and a poor thinker in personal matters.

Given this caveat, we begin by noting that there are some general traits that characterize good thinkers. Good thinkers are willing to think, and may even find thinking enjoyable. They can carry out searches when necessary and supend judgment. They value rationality, believing that thinking is useful for solving problems, reaching decisions, and making judgments. Poor thinkers, in contrast, need certainty, avoid thinking, must reach closure quickly, are impulsive, and rely too heavily on intuition.

These traits are predictably manifested throughout the three searches. When searching for goals, good thinkers are deliberative and take the time necessary to reflect on several possible goals; poor thinkers are impulsive and choose one of the first goals that comes to mind. Like scientists, good thinkers can identify new goals while working on others; they can put aside the original question when a more basic one appears. Poor thinkers are reluctant to change goals, believing that changing one's course is a mark of weakness.

When searching for possibilities, good thinkers again manifest deliberateness; they can wait to find additional possibilities, and they are open to multiple options since most problems permit several solutions. Poor thinkers prefer to consider only a few possibilities—"There are only two sides to every question"—or, even worse, only one.

When searching for and using evidence, the differences are marked. Good thinkers deliberately search for evidence that opposes the favored possibilities, as well as

---

FIGURE 1
Good Thinking vs. Poor Thinking

ASPECT:	THE GOOD THINKER:	THE POOR THINKER:
General Traits	• Welcomes problematic situations and is tolerant of ambiguity.	• Searches for certainty and is intolerant of ambiguity.
	• Is sufficiently self-critical; looks for alternate possibilities and goals; seeks evidence on both sides.	• Is not self-critical and is satisfied with first attempts.
	• Is reflective and deliberative; searches extensively when appropriate.	• Is impulsive, gives up prematurely, and is overconfident of the correctness of initial ideas.
	• Believes in the value of rationality and that thinking can be effective.	• Overvalues intuition, denigrates rationality; believes that thinking won't help.
Goals	• Is deliberative in discovering goals.	• Is impulsive in discovering goals.
	• Revises goals when necessary.	• Does not revise goals.
Possibilities	• Is open to multiple possibilities and considers alternatives.	• Prefers to deal with limited possibilities; does not seek alternatives to an initial possibility.
	• Is deliberative in analyzing possibilities.	• Is impulsive in choosing possibilities.
Evidence	• Uses evidence that challenges favored possibilities.	• Ignores evidence that challenges favored possibilities.
	• Consciously searches for evidence against possibilities that are initially strong, or in favor of those that are weak.	• Consciously searches only for evidence that favors strong possibilities.

evidence that supports them. Poor thinkers, on the other hand, search only for confirming evidence. Good thinkers use evidence, whether or not it supports the favored possibilities; poor thinkers ignore negative evidence. Psychologists who have studied the persistence of irrational beliefs attribute such persistence to this bias in searching for and using evidence. (See, for example, Nisbett and Ross, 1980; Baron, in press.)

Fostering Good Thinking: The Classroom Climate

Our goal as educators is to foster the development of the "good thinker" attributes while helping students understand the limitations of contrary dispositions and behaviors. One fundamental approach is to provide a classroom climate conducive to and supportive of the attributes of good thinking. The model suggests three crucial elements.

A spirit of inquiry. The classroom where thinking is fostered is one where inquiry is valued. The teacher admits uncertainty: "We're not really sure how evolution works." "I'm not sure about my interpretation of the poem—I continue to see other things in it." The teacher welcomes intellectual challenges: "You're right in raising that issue—I need to re-think that matter." The teacher also emphasizes education in all subjects as an exploration into the unknown, as well as teaching what is known. And the teacher repeatedly conveys his or her own belief in the value of thinking. Intuition is valuable, but intelligent people look beyond their hunches.

An emphasis on problem finding. Most classrooms are places where answers are sought and solutions are valued. In a thinking-centered classroom, students are taught and encouraged to find problems, to wonder, and to speculate. The unthinking person observes graffiti and either smiles or frowns. The thinking person wonders: "Why is graffiti in Europe so often political—and in the United States, more commonly scatological?" The teacher nurtures the problem-finding attitude by encouraging students to ask questions, not just answer them: "Here are some data about income distribution in the United States—what questions could we ask?" "We'll be studying family life in Israel—what questions would you like to have answered?"

A more deliberative pace. Many classrooms seem to encourage impulsiveness—the teacher asks a question, expects an immediate answer, and calls on the first student who waves a hand. Such rapid-fire recitations are useful in several ways. They facilitate assessment of student knowledge, permit rehearsal of facts, and keep students attentive; yet they can be counterproductive when thinking is the focus. Students need time to deliberate—to reflect about alternate possibilities, to weigh the evidence, and to come to a tentative conclusion. One useful way to reinforce such deliberation has been suggested by David N. Perkins (personal communication, 1984): wait until all students have raised their hands before calling on anyone; then call on three and discuss the differences in their answers.

Whenever possible, examinations should allow time for reflection and discourage guessing. Some students will refuse to learn to think, despite strong encouragement, unless they are convinced that thinking will improve their grades. It is inconsistent to encourage thinking in the classroom and discourage it on tests.

Teaching Good Thinking: Methods That Might Work

We will not pretend that we have worked out all the pedagogical implications of the model; much more research and development need to be done. However, our review of previous research on teaching thinking and our educational analysis of Baron's model lead us to believe that certain approaches might be effective.

1. *Teach thinking in all subjects, wherever appropriate.* Evidence suggests that such multidisciplinary approaches are more effective than single courses in critical thinking. The model is sufficiently general in scope that it can be used in a variety of school subjects: the student designing a bookcase in industrial arts and the student interpreting a poem in English class are both engaged in thinking—or can be if the task is presented in a manner that encourages thinking. Of course, there are important differences that should be emphasized: evidence sought to support a given bookcase design is quite different from that offered for a particular interpretation of a poem. Students need to understand both the general model and its particular applications. In some cases, prepared materials designed with thinking in mind may be helpful, but materials alone will not be effective.

2. *Present students with case studies of good thinkers.* Students can learn a great deal by studying detailed examples of good thinkers at work. They can see the model at work and understand why the processes are used differently in each course. They can understand that good thinking is not limited to a given sex, to a particular social class or ethnic group, or to scientific endeavors. They can see that the best thinkers are often wrong, and the path to truth is often tortuous and uncertain. Watson searching for the DNA helix, Frost struggling with a poem, and Boorstin trying to find patterns in the discoverers are all examples of imperfect humans engaged in exciting quests.

3. *Present students with subject-related problems that require them to use the processes.* Not all learning should

be discovery learning; there is a time for presenting formulas, explaining concepts, and conveying information. But in each subject the teacher should develop a unit of study in which the students occasionally use the model—first with teacher coaching and then on their own. Some subjects, such as language arts, can be presented primarily from a thinking vantage point.

4. *Focus selectively on the relationships of the important search processes to particular subjects.* We do not argue here for the teaching of discrete skills; however, there is educational merit in giving selective attention to setting goals, searching for possibilities, and weighing evidence as occasions present themselves in the classroom—"The present goal of our foreign policy seems to be one of expanding our sphere of influence. What other goals might we have?" "Recent research suggests that cancers are virus-related. What other possibilities might be investigated?" "The manufacturer reports that this medicine is more effective than aspirin. How reliable is that evidence? What type of evidence might be more helpful?"

5. *Provide appropriate opportunities for applying the model to personal decision making.* Most educators agree that children and adolescents need help with personal de-cision making. The model has direct application to a variety of personal issues, such as moral choices, consumer decisions, and career options. In appropriate subjects students could be taught how to apply the model to these and other types of personal decisions.

We do not claim that this model is the best, nor do we guarantee that its methods will be effective. We know, however, that the model is sound in theory and consistent with available evidence. And we believe that the classroom climate and teaching methods we have suggested have a good chance of helping students become better thinkers.

REFERENCES

Baron, J. *Rationality and Intelligence.* New York: Cambridge University Press, 1985.

Dewey, J. *How We Think: A Restatement of the Relation of Reflective Thinking to the Educative Process.* Boston: D. C. Heath, 1933.

Lipman, M.; Sharp, A. M.; and Oscanyon, F. S. *Thinking in the Classroom.* 2nd ed. Philadelphia: Temple University Press, 1980.

Nisbett, R., and Ross, L. *Human Inference: Strategies and Short-comings of Social Judgments.* Englewood Cliffs, N.J.: Prentice-Hall, 1980.

10

Goals for a Critical Thinking Curriculum

Robert H. Ennis

There are two ways to slide easily through life; to believe everything or to doubt everything. Both ways save us from thinking.

—Alfred Korzybski

This chapter presents an overall content outline for a critical thinking curriculum. It does not incorporate suggestions for grade level, sequence, repetition in greater depth, emphasis, or infusion in subject matter areas (which might be exclusive or overlapping).

WORKING DEFINITION: *Critical thinking* is reasonable, reflective thinking that is focused on deciding what to believe or do.[1]

Critical thinking so defined involves both dispositions and abilities:

A. Dispositions
1. Seek a clear statement of the thesis or question
2. Seek reasons
3. Try to be well informed
4. Use credible sources and mention them
5. Take into account the total situation
6. Try to remain relevant to the main point
7. Keep in mind the original or basic concern
8. Look for alternatives
9. Be open-minded
   a. Consider seriously other points of view than one's own ("dialogical thinking")
   b. Reason from premises with which one disagrees—without letting the disagreement interfere with one's own reasoning ("suppositional thinking")
   c. Withhold judgment when the evidence and reasons are insufficient
10. Take a position (and change a position) when the evidence and reasons are sufficient to do so
11. Seek as much precision as the subject permits
12. Deal in an orderly manner with the parts of a complex whole
13. Be sensitive to the feelings, levels of knowledge, and degree of sophistication of others.[2]

B. Abilities
Elementary clarification:
1. Focusing on a question
   a. Identifying or formulating a question
   b. Identifying or formulating criteria for judging possible answers
   c. Keeping the situation in mind
2. Analyzing arguments
   a. Identifying conclusions
   b. Identifying stated reasons
   c. Identifying unstated reasons
   d. Seeing similarities and differences
   e. Identifying and handling irrelevance
   f. Seeing the structure of an argument
   g. Summarizing
3. Asking and answering questions of clarification and challenge, for example:
   a. Why?
   b. What is your main point?
   c. What do you mean by . . . ?
   d. What would be an example?

FIGURE 1
An Application of Critical Thinking in Real Life

The Charges of Murder and Voluntary Manslaughter, as Presented to Jurors at a Trial in the State of Illinois

The Charge of Murder

To sustain the charge of Murder, the State must prove the following propositions:

First: That the Defendant performed the acts that caused the death of the victim, or

Second: That when the Defendant did so, she intended to kill or do great bodily harm to the Victim, or she knew that her acts would cause death or great bodily harm to the Victim, or she knew that her acts created a strong probability of death or great bodily harm to the Victim, and

Third: That the Defendant was not justified in using the force that she used.

If you find from your consideration of all the evidence that each of these propositions has been proved beyond a reasonable doubt, then you should find the Defendant guilty.

If, on the other hand, you find from your consideration of all the evidence that any of these propositions has not been proved beyond a reasonable doubt, then you should find the Defendant not guilty.

The Charge of Voluntary Manslaughter

To sustain the charge of Voluntary Manslaughter, the State must prove the following propositions:

First: That the Defendant intentionally or knowingly performed the acts that caused the death of the Victim, and

Second: That when the Defendant did so, she believed that circumstances existed that would have justified killing the Victim, and

Third: That the Defendant's belief that such circumstances existed was unreasonable, and

Fourth: That the Defendant was not justified in using the force that she used.

If you find from your consideration of all the evidence that each of these propositions has been proved beyond a reasonable doubt, then you should find the Defendant guilty.

If, on the other hand, you find from your consideration of all the evidence that any of these propositions has not been proved beyond a reasonable doubt, then you should find the Defendant not guilty.

e. What would not be an example (though close to being one)?

f. How does that apply to this case (describe case, which might well appear to be a counterexample)?

g. What difference does it make?

h. What are the facts?

i. Is this what you are saying: _____?

j. Would you say some more about that?

Basic support:

4. Judging the credibility of a source; criteria (that are often not necessary conditions):
   a. Expertise
   b. Lack of conflict of interest
   c. Agreement among sources
   d. Reputation
   e. Use of established procedures
   f. Known risk to reputation
   g. Ability to give reasons
   h. Careful habits

5. Observing and judging observation reports; criteria (that are often not necessary conditions):
   a. Minimal inferring involved
   b. Short time interval between observation and report
   c. Report by observer, rather than someone else (that is, the report is not hearsay)
   d. Records are generally desirable. If report is based on a record, it is generally best that:
      (1) The record was close in time to the observation
      (2) The record was made by the observer
      (3) The record was made by the reporter
      (4) The statement was believed by the reporter, either because of a prior belief in its correctness or because of a belief that the observer was habitually correct
   e. Corroboration
   f. Possibility of corroboration
   g. Conditions of good access
   h. Competent employment of technology, if technology is useful
   i. Satisfaction by observer (and reporter, if a different person) of credibility criteria

Inference:

6. Deducing and judging deductions
   a. Class logic—Euler circles
   b. Conditional logic
   c. Interpretations of statements
      (1) Negation and double negation
      (2) Necessary and sufficient conditions
      (3) Other logical words: "only," "if and only if," "or," "some," "unless," "not both," and so on

7. Inducing and judging inductions
   a. Generalizing
      (1) Typicality of data: limitation of coverage
      (2) Sampling
      (3) Tables and graphs
   b. Inferring explanatory conclusions and hypotheses
      (1) Types of explanatory conclusions and hypotheses
         (a) Causal claims
         (b) Claims about the beliefs and attitudes of people
         (c) Interpretations of authors' intended meanings

(d) Historical claims that certain things happened

(e) Reported definitions

(f) Claims that something is an unstated reason or unstated conclusion

(2) Investigating

(a) Designing experiments, including planning to control variables

(b) Seeking evidence and counterevidence

(c) Seeking other possible explanations

(3) Criteria—given reasonable assumptions:

(a) The proposed conclusion would explain the evidence (essential)

(b) The proposed conclusion is consistent with known facts (essential)

(c) Competitive alternative conclusions are inconsistent with known facts (essential)

(d) The proposed conclusion seems plausible (desirable)

8. Making and judging value judgments

a. Background facts

b. Consequences

c. Prima facie application of acceptable principles

d. Considering alternatives

e. Balancing, weighing, and deciding

Advanced clarification:

9. Defining terms and judging definitions; three dimensions:

a. Form

(1) Synonym

(2) Classification

(3) Range

(4) Equivalent expression

(5) Operational

(6) Example and nonexample

b. Definitional strategy

(1) Acts

(a) Report a meaning

(b) Stipulate a meaning

(c) Express a position on an issue (including "programmatic" and "persuasive" definition)

(2) Identifying and handling equivocation

(a) Attention to the context

(b) Possible types of response:

(i) "The definition is just wrong" (the simplest response)

(ii) Reduction to absurdity: "According to that definition, there is an outlandish result"

(iii) Considering alternative interpretations: "On this interpretation, there is this problem; on that interpretation, there is that problem"

(iv) Establishing that there are two meanings of a key term, and a shift in meaning from one to the other

c. Content

10. Identifying assumptions

a. Unstated reasons

b. Needed assumptions: argument reconstruction

Strategy and tactics:

11. Deciding on an action

a. Define the problem

b. Select criteria to judge possible solutions

c. Formulate alternative solutions

d. Tentatively decide what to do

e. Review, taking into account the total situation, and decide

f. Monitor the implementation

12. Interacting with others

a. Employing and reacting to "fallacy" labels (including)

(1) Circularity

(2) Appeal to authority

(3) Bandwagon

(4) Glittering term

(5) Namecalling

(6) Slippery slope

(7) Post hoc

(8) Non sequitur

(9) Ad hominem

(10) Affirming the consequent

(11) Denying the antecedent

(12) Conversion

(13) Begging the question

(14) Either-or

(15) Vagueness

(16) Equivocation

(17) Straw person

(18) Appeal to tradition

(19) Argument from analogy

(20) Hypothetical question

(21) Oversimplification

(22) Irrelevance

b. Logical Strategies

c. Rhetorical strategies

d. Presenting a position, oral or written (argumentation)

(1) Aiming at a particular audience and keeping it in mind

(2) Organizing (common type: main point, clarification, reasons, alternatives, attempt to re-

but prospective challenges, summary—including repeat of main point)

Footnotes

¹For an elaboration of the ideas in this set of proposed goals, see: Robert H. Ennis, "Rational Thinking and Educational Practice," in *Philosophy and Education* (Eightieth Yearbook of the National Society for the Study of Education, Part I), ed. Jonas F. Soltis (Chicago: NSSE, 1981); and Robert H. Ennis, "A Conception of Rational Thinking," in *Philosophy of Education 1979,* ed. Jerrold Coombs (Bloomington, Ill.: Philosophy of Education Society, 1980). A note on terminology: "rational thinking," as used here is what I mean by "critical thinking/reasoning." In deference to popular usage and theoretical considerations as well, I have abandoned the more narrow, appraisal-only sense of "critical thinking" that I earlier advocated.

²Item "13" under "Dispositions" is not, strictly speaking, a critical thinking disposition. Rather, it is a social disposition that is desirable for a critical thinker to have.

11

What Creative Thinking Is

D. N. Perkins

Creativity is the encounter of the intensively conscious human being with his world.

—Rollo May

Creativity is a messy and myth-ridden subject. Many of our casual beliefs have prevented an adequate understanding of creative thinking and have thwarted efforts to nourish its development in schools, businesses, and homes. Before addressing what creativity is, it's useful to examine two things creativity is not: a single distinctive ability, and a matter of talent.

Intelligence as measured by IQ is one possible explanation for creativity in terms of ability. However, within a profession, creative achievement correlates poorly with IQ (Barron, 1969; Wallach, 1976a, b). Another ability theory of creativity implicates "ideational fluency"—the ability to produce a large number of appropriate and unusual ideas efficiently. Although plausible, this theory has not withstood empirical testing. Correlations between ideational fluency measures and various biological measures of real-world creative accomplishment are unimpressive (Crockenberg, 1972; Mansfield and Busse, 1981; Wallach, 1976a, b). Various other ability theories of creativity also fall short empirically or logically (Perkins, 1981, Chapter 9).

The second myth, that creativity depends on great talent in a particular field, conflicts with everyday experience. It's not unusual to find individuals with great *technical* talent in a field who are not notably creative. Moreover, iden-

tifying creativity with great talent suggests that we recognize as creative only the major innovators like Beethoven or Einstein. But, clearly, creativity is a matter of degree: it can be modest as well as grand. Moreover, if we only think of creativity on the grand scale, we may miss opportunities to foster modest creative achievements that can provide both practical payoffs and personal rewards.

What Creative Thinking Is

Creative thinking is thinking patterned in a way that tends to lead to creative results. This definition reminds us that the ultimate criterion of creativity is output. We call a person creative when that person consistently gets creative results, meaning, roughly speaking, original and otherwise appropriate results by the criteria of the domain in question.

There is no obvious reason that creative results should depend on a single trait like ideational fluency. The pattern of creative thinking is not simple and neat—not just a matter, for instance, of generating ideas and selecting among them. Rather, the pattern involves a number of components that contribute to the creative outcome. These components can be categorized according to six general principles of creative thinking.

1. *Creative thinking involves aesthetic as much as practical standards.* Creative people *strive* for originality, and for something fundamental, far-reaching, and powerful. For instance, Einstein's contributions were shaped substantially by his intense commitment to parsimonious theories lacking any element of arbitrariness; the same aesthetic led him to view quantum mechanics with distaste, despite his own early contributions to the development of the theory (Holton, 1971-72).

This chapter is an excerpt from D. N. Perkins, "Creativity by Design," *Educational Leadership* 42, 1 (September 1984): 18-24.

Creative results do not just bubble up from some fecund swamp in the mind. Creative individuals tend to value stated qualities and try quite straightforwardly to achieve them. Getzels and Csikszentmihalyi (1976) have documented this trend in creative student artists. Various studies have identified similar explicit commitments in creative scientists (Helson, 1971; Mansfield and Busse, 1981; Pelz and Andrews, 1966; Roe, 1952a, 1952b, 1963; Perkins, 1981).

2. *Creative thinking depends on attention to purpose as much as to results.* Creative people explore alternative goals and approaches early in an endeavor, evaluate them critically, understand the nature of the problem and the standards for a solution, remain ready to change their approach later, and even redefine the problem when necessary.

For an apt example of the latter, NASA scientists during the early days of the space program tried to solve the problem of heat of re-entry by devising a substance that could withstand the heat. They failed in their quest and had to abandon this definition of the problem. Their ultimate solution—the ablative heat shield that burns away as the space vehicle penetrates the atmosphere, taking the heat with it—turned upside down the original goal of finding a heat-resisting substance. The attention creative artists give to choosing what work to undertake has been documented by Getzels and Csikszentmihalyi (1976) for student artists. Skilled practitioners' understanding of problems has been extensively demonstrated for problem solving in science and mathematics. In brief, experts perceive problems in terms of possible solution paradigms, whereas novices perceive the same problems in terms of superficial surface features. (Chi, Feltovitch, and Glaser, 1981; Larkin, 1983; Larkin, McDermott, Simon, and Simon, 1980; Schoenfeld and Herrmann, 1982).

3. *Creative thinking depends on mobility more than fluency.* As noted earlier, efforts to relate measures of ideational fluency to real world creative achievement have been disappointing. Instead, when difficulties arise, creative people may make the problems more abstract or more concrete, more general or more specific. They may use analogies—as Charles Darwin did when he arrived at the notion of natural selection by reading Malthus on population growth and contemplating the intense struggle that would result from human overpopulation—or they may project themselves into different roles—the viewer of a painting rather than the painter, the user of an invention rather than the inventor.

Clement (1982, 1984) has documented the role of analogy in skilled solving of math and physics problems. Working backwards from answer to solution is a widespread tactic in skilled problem solving. (Newell and Simon, 1972). Reformulating a problem in various ways is one tactic used in Schoenfeld's successful demonstrations of teaching mathematical problem solving (Schoenfeld, 1982; Schoenfeld and Herrmann, 1982). These sorts of mobility are, of course, features of high competence as much as of creativity.

4. *Creative thinking depends on working at the edge more than at the center of one's competence.* Creative people maintain high standards, accept confusion, uncertainty, and the higher risks of failure as part of the processes, and learn to view failure as normal, even interesting, and challenging. An anecdote about Mozart illustrates performance under pressure. Mozart supposedly wrote the overture to *Don Giovanni* in a blitz effort the night before the opera opened. Although the orchestra performed it opening night without rehearsal, the overture was well received. Of course, many artists have taken risks of another sort, venturing well beyond the accepted canons of taste. Many works now considered notable received a dim reception from a public accustomed to more conventional styles, as happened, for instance, with Stravinsky's *Rite of Spring* and Monet's *Déjeuner sur l'herbe* and *Olympia*.

The career of Marie Curie presents a striking case of persistent research conducted under sometimes appalling conditions (Perkins, 1981, Chapter 8; Reid, 1974). Of course, dedication to success and the stamina to withstand setbacks are characteristics of many sorts of achievement, not just creative achievement.

5. *Creative thinking depends as much on being objective as on being subjective.* Creative people consider different viewpoints, set final or intermediate products aside and come back to them later, so that they can evaluate them with more distance, seek intelligent criticism, and subject their ideas to practical and theoretical tests.

Evidence on the relevance of criticism and the willingness to seek it out comes from my own studies of the practices of professional and amateur poets (see Perkins, 1981, Chapter 4). Contrary to the popular image of poets as utterly private individuals, many routinely sought feedback from colleagues. Moreover, these poets produced poetry judged by a panel of critics to be better than those who did not seek criticism.

6. *Creative thinking depends on intrinsic, more than extrinsic, motivation.* Creative people feel that *they,* rather than other people or chance, choose what to do and how to do it. They perceive the task as within their competence (although perhaps close to its edge); view what they are undertaking as worthwhile in itself, not just a means to an end; and enjoy the activity, its setting, and context.

Numerous studies discussed by Amabile (1983) argue the importance of intrinsic motivation. In one study she biased the attitudes of a group of poets by asking them to list their reasons for writing before they composed haikus.

The instructions for one group of poets led them to mention pragmatic reasons, such as holding a job as a professor, whereas the instructions for the second group produced a list of intrinsic reasons, such as writing for the sake of the art or for self-exploration. Remarkably, this simple preliminary activity produced a (presumably temporary) set that influenced the quality of the haikus the poets wrote immediately thereafter. As rated by judges who did not know which poets had received which treatments, the haikus produced by the intrinsic group ranked considerably higher.

In summary, it seems reasonable to say the more these six principles guide one's thinking, the more creative it will be. However, not all the principles specifically reflect creativity as much as intellectual competence or motivation in general. For example, the ability to grasp the nature of a problem quickly is characteristic of skilled problem solvers, whether notably creative or not. The willingness and even desire to work at the edge of one's competence is striking in champion athletes, who may or may not be particularly creative. Other characteristics, on the other hand, are specifically associated with creative performance, such as attention to purpose or an emphasis on originality.

The creative pattern of thinking is an interesting mix of strategies, skills, and attitudinal factors. For instance, attention and effort are allocated in certain ways—to purposes, to transformations of the problem, to gathering and processing feedback, to the originality and other aesthetic qualities of the product. At least to some extent, such allocational patterns can be viewed as strategies that teachers might directly encourage the students. On the other hand, there are aspects of skill involved, such as the ability to quickly grasp the nature of a problem. By and large, only considerable experience in the domain in question will impart such expertise. Finally, an individual would not maintain creative behavior without some commitment to aesthetic principles, without an involvement in the problem for its own sake, without pleasure in pushing a problem into different patterns, and so on.

How Education Falls Short

There are many books and courses designed to teach creativity, but the case for their effectiveness is thin. A review by Mansfield, Busse, and Krepelka (1978) examined the literature on several courses for definitive evidence of gains and transfer. In general, the results were disappointing. Some undramatic gains occurred on tasks close to the training task; transfer was little in evidence.

The six characteristics of creative thinking discussed earlier help to explain why brief special-purpose instruction may have little impact on creativity. Most such instruc-

tion focuses on strategies for creative thinking. These strategies probably help, but creativity benefits from skill as well.

The skills described in the six principles of creative thinking require extensive practice in a particular field. Although extreme competence may not be necessary, indeed may even be counterproductive, moderate skill seems essential. Thus, some efforts to impart creative problem solving may falter not so much because they fail to give enough emphasis to the creative side of the matter but because they do not provide sufficient guidance and experience on the competence side.

Moreover, attitudes as well are critical to creative thinking. They cannot be taught directly, any more than one can teach students to like Shakespeare. Teaching creativity must involve exposing students to the flavor and texture of creative inquiry and hoping they get hooked.

Another problem with special-purpose programs is the very limited time usually invested. We seem to assume that normal education equips students with the knowledge base for a creative pattern of thinking and that they need only a few quick tips about how to marshal existing knowledge and know-how to creative ends. Experience does not bear this out.

The deeper difficulty may be that schooling in general works against the creative pattern of thinking. Accordingly, instruction designed to foster creativity has to make up for the shortcomings of normal instruction. While the usual reasons—that schooling is too "right answer" oriented and has little tolerance for the maverick—are relevant, they are part of a much more pervasive syndrome. The six general principles of creative thinking yield a good map of the problem.

1. *Attention to aesthetics.* Outside of literature and the arts, conventional schooling pays little attention to the aesthetics of the many products of human inquiry that are addressed—for instance, scientific theories, mathematical systems, historical syntheses. How often, for example, do teachers point out the beauty of Newton's laws or the periodic table? How often do they highlight the originality of thinking of history as shaped by geography rather than skillful and willful leaders, or the originality of proving a theorem by *reductio ad absurdum* rather than by a constructive proof? Likewise, how often do teachers comment on the aesthetics of students' work in math and science?

2. *Attention to purpose.* Most assignments are so narrow that students have little opportunity to generate, or even select among, different purposes. The treatment of scientific theories, for instance, often concentrates on the result to the exclusion of the broader purposes of explanation and understanding that motivated their initial development. For example, what range of phenomena spurred

Newton to develop his laws, and where, historically, did that concern come from? How do Newton's laws affect our everyday lives? Some instruction in physics gives full play to such questions, but much does not.

3. *Mobility.* Most school problems are so narrow and convergent that, except for "working backwards," mobility doesn't count for much. Mobility applies most when a task presents major choices—for instance, selecting a problem, revising a problem, choosing between empirical and theoretical methods, or in a more humanistic context, choosing to treat a writing assignment either discursively or as a dialogue or drama, or trying to distill from one's knowledge a particular thesis to defend. For the most part, school problems lack the elbow room for exercising mobility.

4. *Working at the edge of one's competence.* Especially gifted students may become discouraged if they do not find school challenging enough. But perhaps the broader difficulty is this: school does not challenge students to be creative. If they have the motivation, students can work at the edge of their competence in other directions—by precision, remembering all the facts, solving textbook problems—but not so much in the direction of creative accomplishment.

5. *Objectivity.* Schools typically do highlight objectivity, although not always very successfully in the arts.

6. *Intrinsic motivation.* It's no news that conventional schooling does not do a very good job of fostering intrinsic motivation. Teachers, understandably discouraged by inattentive students and an often unsupportive society, often project an offhand or mechanical attitude toward knowledge and teaching. Students pick this up and project it back, continuing the vicious circle. Also, textbooks usually give little play to the most interesting features of subject areas. Finally, students have few opportunities to select the problems they address or the direction their instruction takes.

In summary, conventional schooling gets a mixed report card for its influence on creative thinking. Most of the problems trace back to two pervasive practices. Schooling generally presents knowledge as a given, rather than as the product of a creative effort to accomplish something. And schooling generally poses to students tasks that do not exercise or even allow creative effort.

REFERENCES

Amabile, T. M. *The Social Psychology of Creativity.* New York: Springer-Verlag, 1983.

Barron, F. *Creative Person and Creative Process.* New York: Holt, Rinehart, & Winston, 1969.

Chi, M.; Feltovich, P.; and Glaser, R. "Categorization and Representation of Physics Problems by Experts and Novices." *Cognitive Science* 5 (1981): 121-152.

Clement, J. "Analogical Reasoning Patterns in Expert Problem Solving." In *Proceedings of the Fourth Annual Conference of the Cognitive Science Society.* Ann Arbor, Mich.: University of Michigan, 1982.

Clement, J. "Non-formal Reasoning in Experts' Solutions to Mathematics Problems." Paper presented at the annual meeting of the AERA, New Orleans, April 1984.

Crockenberg, S. B. "Creativity Tests: A Boon or Boondoggle for Education?" *Review of Educational Research,* 1972, 42(1), 27-45.

Getzels, J., and Csikszentmihalyi, M. *The Creative Vision: A Longitudinal Study of Problem Finding in Art.* New York: John Wiley and Sons, 1976.

Helson, Ravenna. "Women Mathematicians and the Creative Personality." *Journal of Consulting and Clinical Psychology* 36 (1971): 210-220.

Holton, G. "On Trying to Understand Scientific Genius." *The American Scholar* 41 (Winter 1971-72):95-110.

Larkin, J. "The Role of Problem Representation in Physics." In *Mental Models.* Edited by D. Gentner and A. S. Stevens. Hillsdale, N.J.: Erlbaum, 1983.

Larkin, J.; McDermott, J.; Simon, D.; and Simon, H. "Modes of Competence in Solving Physics Problems." *Cognitive Science* 4 (1980): 317-345.

Mansfield, R. S., and Busse, T. V. *The Psychology of Creativity and Discovery.* Chicago: Nelson-Hall, 1981.

Mansfield, R. S.; Busse, T. V.; and Krepelka, E. J. "The Effectiveness of Creativity Training." *Review of Educational Research* 48,4 (1978): 517-536.

Newell, A., and Simon, H. *Human Problem Solving.* Englewood Cliffs, N.J.: Prentice-Hall, 1972.

Parnes, S. J.; Noller, R. B.; Biondi, A. M. *Guide to Creative Action.* New York: Charles Scribner's Sons, 1977.

Pelz, D. C., and Andrews, F. M. *Scientists in Organizations: Productive Climates for Research and Development.* New York: John Wiley and Sons, 1966.

Perkins, D. N. *The Mind's Best Work.* Cambridge, Mass.: Harvard University Press, 1981.

Reid, R. *Marie Curie.* New York: Saturday Review Press, 1974.

Roe, A. "A Psychologist Examines 64 Eminent Scientists." *Scientific American* 187, 5 (1952a): 21-25.

Roe, A. *The Making of a Scientist.* New York: Dodd, Mead & Co., 1952b.

Roe, A. "Psychological Approaches to Creativity in Science." In *Essays on Creativity in the Sciences.* Edited by M. A. Coler and H. K. Hughes. New York: New York University, 1963.

Schoenfeld, A. H. "Measures of Problem-Solving Performance and of Problem-Solving Instruction." *Journal for Research in Mathematical Education* 13, 1 (1982): 31-49.

Schoenfeld, A. H., and Herrmann, D. J. "Problem Perception and Knowledge Structure in Expert and Novice Mathematical Problem Solvers." *Journal of Experimental Psychology: Learning, Memory and Cognition* 8, 5 (1982): 484-494.

Wallach, M. A. "Psychology of Talent and Graduate Education." In *Individuality in Learning.* Edited by Samuel Messick & Associates. San Francisco: Jossey-Bass, 1976a.

Wallach, M. A. "Tests Tell Us Little About Talent." *American Scientist* 64 (1976b):57-63.

12

Toward a Model of Human Intellectual Functioning

Arthur L. Costa

Learning and memory are influenced by the sets, intentions, and plans generated in the neocortex of the brain, as well as by the information received from the immediate environment and from internal states, drives, and muscular responses. The reality we perceive, feel, see, and hear is influenced by the constructive processes of the brain, as well as by the cues that impinge upon it.
—Merlin C. Wittrock, 1978

The information processing model described in this chapter serves as a basis for the definitions of thinking, instructional strategies, and teaching behaviors discussed in later chapters. Such a model serves as a guide to curriculum and instructional development, *not* as a neurobiological definition of thinking. Such a definition is still open to interpretation. In fact, brain researchers are attempting to discover whether thinking is a natural bodily function similar to the heart pumping blood or whether it is the result of intense effort, strict discipline, and careful programming of instructional outcomes.

While there are numerous models of human intellectual functioning, it is best to adopt a familiar one as a guide. For example, if you're familiar with Bloom's Taxonomy (Bloom, 1956) or Guilford's Structure of the Intellect (Guilford, 1967), you can use them as a guide in materials selection, staff development, and defining thinking. Adopting a description of human intellectual functioning can help you recognize and develop teaching methodologies, curriculum sequences, learning activities, and assessment procedures that go beyond superficial learning.

An examination of several models of thinking yields more similarities than differences. Many authors distinguish three to four basic thought clusters (Smith and Tyler, 1945): (1) *input* of data through the senses and from memory; (2) *processing* those data into meaningful relationships; (3) *output* or application of those relationships in new or novel situations; and (4) metacognition. Figure 1 presents a comparison of several authors' constructs.

Thinking is the receiving of external stimuli through the senses followed by internal processing. If the new information should be stored, the brain attempts to match, compare, categorize, and pattern it with similar information already in storage. This process is done extremely quickly in an apparently random order, and either at the conscious or unconscious level.

Thus, every event a person experiences causes the brain to call up meaningful, related information from storage—whether the event is commonplace or a carefully developed classroom learning experience. The more meaningful, relevant, and complex the experience is, the more actively the brain attempts to integrate and assimilate it into its existing storehouse of programs and structures. According to this model of intellectual functioning, the most complex thinking occurs when external stimuli challenge the brain to (1) draw upon the greatest amount of data or structures already in storage; (2) expand an already existing structure; and (3) develop new structures.

A problem may be defined as any stimulus or challenge, the response to which is not readily apparent. If there is a ready match between what is perceived by the senses and what is an existing structure or program already in storage, no problem exists. Piaget calls this *assimilation*. If, however, the new information cannot be explained or resolved with knowledge in short- or long-term memory, the information must be processed, action taken to gather more information to resolve the discrepancy, and

Figure 1
Comparison of Thinking Models

DATA INPUT PHASE	PROCESSING PHASE	OUTPUT PHASE	SOURCE
Internal and external input	Central Processing	Output	Atkinson & Shiffrin, 1968, pp. 90-122
Participation and awareness	Internalization	Dissemination	Bell & Steinaker, 1979
Knowledge	Comprehension Analysis Synthesis	Application Evaluation	Bloom & others, 1956
Descriptive	Interpretive	Evaluative	Eisner, 1979, pp. 203-213; Great Books Foundation
Input	Elaboration	Output	Feuerstein, 1980, pp. 71-103
Fluency	Manipulation	Persistence	Foshay, 1979, pp. 93-113
Cognition and memory	Evaluation	Convergent and divergent production	Guilford, 1967
Fact	Concept	Value	Harmin, 1973
Receiving	Responding Valuing Organizing	Characterizing	Krathwohl & others, 1964
Alertness	Information processing	Action	Restak, 1979, p. 44
Learning	Integrating	Applying	Sexton & Poling, 1973, p. 7
Intuitive	Awareness	Function	Strasser & others, 1972, pp. 46-47
Intake storage	Mediation	Action	Suchman, 1966, pp. 177-187
Concept formation	Interpretation Inference	Application	Taba, 1964, pp. 30-38
Detailed information, recall of previous knowledge	Comparison	Rule generation Auto-criticism	Whimbey, 1976, pp. 116-138
Pre-exposure	Exposure	Re-creation	Barazakov, 1984

From *Toward a Model of Human Intellectual Functioning*

the ultimate resolution evaluated for its "fit" with reality. Piaget refers to this as *accommodation*. Our brains seem to dislike disequilibrium and constantly strive to satisfy and resolve discrepancies perceived in the environment.

Inputting information alone seems to be brain-dysfunctional. Information that the brain has not processed remains in memory for very short periods of time. Merely experiencing or memorizing without acting on that information commits it to short-term memory. Finding a pattern through comparisons, classifications, and causal, sequential, or hierarchical relationships apparently forms

or expands a structure in the brain so that the information is available for application in situations other than that in which it was learned. For example, try to remember which direction Lincoln, Kennedy, Roosevelt, and Jefferson are facing on their respective coins. Only when comparisons are made, relationships drawn, and connections built will this information stay in long-term memory.

Figure 2 provides a simplistic visual presentation of this complex model of intellectual functioning. It deletes such important factors as affect, motivation, and perceptual abilities.

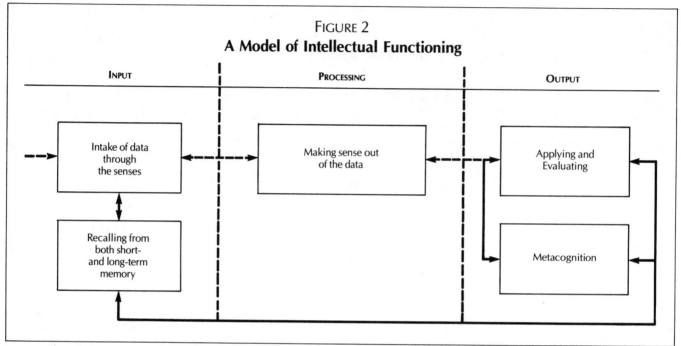

FIGURE 2
A Model of Intellectual Functioning

From *Toward a Model of Human Intellectual Functioning.*

Our brains never stop. We process information during sleep and even under anesthesia. The brain actively engages in these processes regardless of the external input that is presented. The brain does *not* remain inactive when it is not fully engaged in learning specific information. When learning tasks are presented that are insufficiently organized, unmotivating, or are not meaningful enough to engage these thought processes, the brain seeks stimulation in other ways: random thoughts, feelings, physical sensations, daydreaming, fantasy, problem solving, creative inspiration, and spontaneous memories. Instead of focusing on a lecture on igneous, sedimentary, and metamorphic rocks, for example, the brain may focus on the teacher's blue dress and start daydreaming about what to wear to the dance next Saturday. Thus, the brain continues to find patterns and relationships but not necessarily in the direction that the teacher intends.

Teachers and parents are crucial mediators of these intellectual behaviors. They can present or call attention to discrepancies and pose problems intended to invite more than a memory (assimilation) type response. Teachers can arrange the classroom and learning experiences to cause the exercise of these intellectual functions.

REFERENCES

Atkinson, R. C., and Siffrin, R. M. "Human Memory: A Proposed System and Its Control Process." In *The Psychology of Learning and Motivation,* Vol. 2. Edited by K. W. Spence and J. T. Spence. New York: Academic Press, 1968.

Bell, M., and Steinaker, N. *The Experiential Taxonomy: A New Approach to Teaching and Learning.* New York: Academic Press, 1979.

Bloom, B. S.; Engelhart, M. D.; Furst, E. J.; Hill, W. H.; and Krathwohl, D. R. *Taxonomy of Educational Objectives: Handbook I: Cognitive Domain.* New York: David McKay, 1956.

Eisner, E. *The Educational Imagination.* New York: Macmillan, 1979.

Feuerstein, R. *Instrumental Enrichment.* Baltimore: University Park Press, 1980.

Foshay, A. W. "Toward a Humane Curriculum." In *Education in Flux: Implications for Curriculum Development.* Edited by J. J. Jelenek. Tempe: University of Arizona Press, 1979.

Guilford, J. P. *The Nature of Human Intelligence.* New York: McGraw-Hill, 1967.

Harmin, M.; Kirschenbaum, H.; and Simon, S. *Clarifying Values Through Subject Matter.* Minneapolis: Winston Press, Inc., 1973.

Krathwohl, D.; Bloom, B. S.; and Masia, B. B. *Taxonomy of Educational Objectives: Handbook II: Affective Domain.* New York: David McKay, 1964.

Restak, R. *The Brain: The Last Frontier.* New York: Warner Books, 1979.

Sexton, T. G., and Poling, D. R. *Can Intelligence Be Taught?* Bloomington, Ind.: Phi Delta Kappa Educational Foundation Fastbook Series #29, 1973.

Smith, E. R., and Tyler, R. W. *Appraising and Recording Student Progress.* New York: Harper, 1942.

Strasser, B. B.; Babcock, R. W.; Cowan, R.; Dalis, G. T.; Gothold, S. E.; and Rudolph, J. R. *Teaching Toward Inquiry.* Washington, D.C.: National Education Association, 1972.

Suchman, J. R. "A Model for the Analysis of Inquiry." In *Analyses of Concept Learning*. New York: Academic Press, Inc., 1966.

Taba, H.; Levine, S.; and Elzey, F. *Thinking in Elementary School Children*. San Francisco: San Francisco State College, Cooperative Research Project No. 1574, 1964.

Whimbey, A., and Whimbey, L. S. *Intelligence Can Be Taught*. New York: Bantam Books, 1976.

Wittrock, Merlin C. In *Cognitive Processes of the Brain, 1978 Yearbook of the National Society for the Study of Education, Part II*. NSSE, 1978.

13

The Behaviors of Intelligence

Arthur L. Costa

As a result of observing, describing, analyzing, and classifying the behaviors of efficient scientists, successful entrepreneurs, accomplished artists, capable workers, effective managers, and so forth, we have been able to synthesize a list of pervasive behaviors that seem to be characteristic of intelligent action. What follows is an interpretation of those indicators, which draws heavily from Feuerstein's definitions in the Instrumental Enrichment Curriculum. (Figure 1 shows how a 5th grade teacher charted this information for her students.)

1. *The basis of all thinking involves taking in information through the senses. Listening, smelling, observing, tasting, and feeling are the processes through which all information is passed to the brain.* Intelligent human beings:
- Use these senses to gather complete information (perceiving clearly).
- Are alert to problems, discrepancies, and conflicts in the information perceived.
- Are tolerant of ambiguous situations.
- Have a system or plan to collect all information, and do not need to repeat observations (exploring systematically).
- Name the objects, conditions, and events being observed and experienced with precision so that they can be remembered and discussed (labeling).
- Describe objects, conditions, and events in terms of where and when they occur (perceiving temporal and spatial relationships).
- Identify which characteristics of an object, event, or condition remain the same when changes take place (observing constancy).
- Consider more than one variable when organizing and reorganizing the information gathered (using more than one frame of reference).
- Strive to be precise and accurate.

2. *Some meaning must be derived from all the received information. Intelligent human beings act on that information in ways to make sense of it.* Intelligent human beings:
- Define the problem, determine what is needed to resolve the problem, and design strategies to solve it (analyzing discrepancies).
- Select from the information gathered that which is relevant and applicable and that which is not (perceiving relevance).
- Have a goal—a picture, vision, or image of what to look for and how to find it, and change or alter that image when necessary (interiorizing).
- Identify data needed to accomplish goals and generate strategies to produce those data (strategic reasoning).
- Develop a plan or strategy that includes the steps needed to reach the goal (systematic planning).
- Remember the various pieces of information needed (broadening the mental field).
- Search for relationships (hierarchical, temporal, sequential, comparative, syllogistic, causal, and so on) among disparate objects, conditions, events, and past experiences (projecting relationships).
- Search for similarities and differences among objects, conditions, and events (comparing and contrasting).

FIGURE 1
**Behaviors Characteristic of Intelligent Action—
5th Grade Class**

1. **GETTING WHAT WE NEED**
   - Use our senses (listen, see, smell, taste, and touch) to get information.
   - Use a plan (system) so we do not miss or skip anything important.
   - Give what we do a name.
   - Tell where and when.
   - Tell what stays the same even when things seem to change.
   - Be able to use more than one idea at a time.
   - Be careful when it matters.

2. **USING INFORMATION**
   - Know what we are asked to do.
   - Use only the information we need.
   - See a picture in our mind of what we must do.
   - Plan our steps.
   - Keep all the facts in mind.
   - Find out how things go together.
   - Tell what is the same and what is different.
   - Find where things belong.
   - Think things out in our heads—then choose.
   - Prove our ideas.

3. **SHOWING WHAT WE KNOW**
   - Think before we answer—don't rush.
   - Tell it clearly.
   - If we "know" the answer but can't tell it right away, wait—then try again.
   - Don't panic.

4. **WE DO OUR BEST**
   - Check to make sure our job is finished.
   - Think about your own thinking.
   - Listen to others tell about their ideas.
   - Tell how we solved the problem.

- Think through a solution or answer, thus decreasing mistakes and repetition (overcoming trial and error).

- Use memory and past experiences to draw forth relevant data and strategies that are needed to solve the problem at hand (overcoming an episodic grasp of reality).

- Pause to formulate an idea before saying the first thing that comes to mind (restraining impulsivity).

- Invent novel, creative images, solutions, and relationships (fluency, flexibility, originality).

- Use alternate strategies to find answers when they are not immediately apparent, and do not give up in panic or despair (persistence, perseverance, overcoming blocking).

- Check to see if the results of the strategy (product) match the intended outcome (image) (checking for accuracy).

- Strive for quality, craftsmanship, and accuracy.

4. *Being conscious of their own behaviors (metacognition) and their effects on others is not only a characteristic of mentally healthy people, but also an attribute of effective problem solvers.* Intelligent human beings:

- Plan a strategy to solve a problem, monitor their progress along the way, and evaluate their strategy before, during, and after the conclusion is reached (metacognition).

- Know when they need additional information and devise systematic strategies to gather it.

- Use environmental cues to determine which behaviors are appropriate in certain situations (rational/intuitive, playful/purposeful, cooperative/competitive, and so on).

Toward a Hierarchy of Thinking: Skills, Strategies, Creativity, and Attitudes

Obviously, there is no one way to classify thinking skills. The following four-tier system summarizes what has been presented in Part III of this resource book. It has been found helpful as a way to organize for teaching, select programs, and adopt and develop instructional materials. A well-rounded instructional program that promotes thinking should attempt to develop all four levels.

Level I: The Discrete Skills of Thinking

This category includes individual, discrete mental skills that are prerequisite to more complex thought, such as:

1. Input of data:
   - Gathering data through the senses (listening, observing, smelling, tasting, and feeling)
   - Being alert to problems, discrepancies, and dilemmas

- Find the class or set to which a new object, condition, or event belongs (classifying, categorizing).

- Explore alternate solutions and project what might happen if one or another were chosen (hypothesizing).

- Defend an opinion with logical evidence, seek evidence to support more than one hypothesis, and are critical of their own and others' propositions that lack logical evidence.

- Have a repertoire of problem-solving strategies to select from when one does not produce desired results (flexibility and perseverance).

3. *The meaning derived from acting on environmental data is communicated to others, applied in novel situations, and constantly evaluated for accuracy.* Intelligent human beings:

- Communicate accurately and precisely (using precise language).

- Express another person's ideas, point of view, and feelings accurately (overcoming egocentrism).

- Being fascinated by the environment

2. Elaborating (processing) the data:
   - Comparing/contrasting
   - Analyzing/synthesizing
   - Classifying/categorizing
   - Inducing/deducing
   - Perceiving relationships (temporal, analogous, seriational, spatial, hierarchical, syllogistic, transitive, symbolic)

3. Output of the products of elaboration:
   - Inferring
   - Hypothesizing
   - Predicting/forecasting/extrapolating
   - Concluding/generalizing/summarizing
   - Evaluating

Level II: Strategies of Thinking

This category involves the linkage of the discrete skills to strategies. People employ these tactics when faced with situations to which the resolution or answers are not immediately known:

- Problem solving
- Critical thinking
- Decision making
- Strategic reasoning
- Logic

Level III: Creative Thinking

These are the behaviors of novelty and insight. We use them to create new thought patterns, unique products, and innovative solutions to problems. Because they are so idiosyncratic, they are difficult to define and reproduce. It is believed, however, that with properly designed instruction, they can be developed:

- Creativity
- Fluency
- Metaphorical thinking
- Complexity
- Intuition
- Model making
- Insight
- Imagery

Level IV: The Cognitive Spirit

With all the above skills identified and defined, there is still something missing. The thinking person must have the willingness, disposition, inclination, and commitment to think. Some of the attitudes and tendencies that demonstrate this internalization of the thinking spirit include:

- Being open-minded
- Withholding judgment
- Being honest
- Seeking to become more informed
- Searching for alternatives
- Dealing with ambiguity
- Striving for precision, definition, and clarity
- Remaining concerned with the central issue or main points
- Perceiving relationships between the basic concern and the discussion at hand
- Being willing to change with the addition of more information or for compelling reasons
- Taking a stand when the evidence and reasons are sufficient to do so
- Being sensitive to the feelings, level of knowledge, and concerns of others

PART IV

A Curriculum For Thinking

There is no doubt that it would be helpful to include in this book a "scope and sequence" chart identifying which cognitive functions should be taught at which grade levels and in what order. Indeed, many school districts have made such valiant attempts at curriculum development. These endeavors have proved to be highly instructive for the participants, extremely helpful in the placement of learning activities and materials, basic to lesson planning, and crucial to the assessment of student progress. Such local curriculum development is strongly encouraged.

Numerous researchers and teachers believe that thinking skills can and should be the focus of special exercises, texts, and programs. In *Cognitive Process Instruction*, Lochhead and Clement (1972) speak of the need "to isolate specific cognitive skills and to design instructional material appropriate for each skill." Edward de Bono claims that "generalizable thinking skills" can and should be taught in addition to "local skills" required in particular subject areas. Howard Citron believes that we must "systematically develop students' thinking and reasoning abilities in a 'purer' sense and directly build transfer of these abilities to academic learning and real behavior." The idea that certain generic cognitive functions underlie all school learning is basic to the thinking skills programs described in Part VIII of this resource book.

There is little agreement among psychologists, however, on what constitutes thinking. There are several compelling taxonomies of thinking skills to be used in building a curriculum. The ones developed by Feuerstein, Bloom, Guilford, Upton, Kohlberg, and Erickson are the most persuasive. The research on the effectiveness of these approaches is advanced cautiously, and the placement of grade or age level and the sequence in which each thinking skill should be learned is disputed vigorously.

In fear of suggesting a "national curriculum for thinking skills," no such scope and sequence chart is included here. In keeping with the philosophy of this resource book—that teaching for thinking should itself be an inquiry—guidelines for local decision making are presented instead. These guidelines include building a curriculum that is consistent with children's biological and psychological development, analyzing materials and matching learning activities to students' cognitive maturation, and constructing lessons with appropriate cognitive objectives.

REFERENCE

Lochhead, J., and Clement, J., eds. *Cognitive Process Instruction.* Philadelphia: Franklin Institute Press, 1979.

14

The Biological Basis for Thinking

Lawrence F. Lowery

We may be the universe's way of looking at itself. Aside from ourselves, we know of no other organism that can contemplate the outer edges of the universe or the inner workings of the atom. No other creature can imagine the future or reconstruct the past beyond the limits of its own life. How have humans become uniquely able to attain such a level of thinking? What knowledge about our thinking is important for educators to contemplate as they look to the future of schooling in light of the present and past?

Most people act as though thinking and the brain are synonymous. A fine thinker is often referred to as "brainy." "Brains over brawn" clearly equates the brain to clever thinking. A "brainless" person lacks intelligence. But thinking and the brain are not synonymous. They are quite distinct.

The brain is a physical organ, which at birth is about one third its eventual mass. Its estimated number of 100 billion cells will double within two years following birth, and many cells in the following 15 years will develop 600,000 connections between themselves and other cells (Maranto, 1984). In the past ten years we have learned much about the physiology of the brain—its electroconductivity, chemistry, and anatomy.

Thinking, however, is the ghost in the machinery. It is something beyond the physiological attributes. Imagine looking at a chess board at midgame. The physical placements of the pieces can be described, but where are the strategies of offense and defense? Similarly, imagine touring the chambers of a court and locating where the jury, judge, defendant, and prosecutor reside. Can you point to the "justice" that is carried out there? Strategies of chess and courtroom justice are processes within physical configurations. And so, too, is thinking with the brain. Neurobiologists may identify one or more factors actively engaged among cells during a thought process, but with the more than 100 billion interactions that are possible within our heads, it is the *process* of thinking that is of prime importance, not the particular mechanism.

By piecing together research information obtained from anthropologists, biologists, neurobiologists, psychologists, and psychobiologists, we know that thinking depends on our other physical attributes. We are not born with our thinking capabilities completely in place; they develop sequentially over time. There is a biological foundation for all human thinking.

Biological Structures and Thinking

With a head that swivels and tilts and eyes that perceive color and depth, the human structure is built to move about and explore unknown territory. The upright stance frees the forelimbs, and the hands, with their opposable thumbs, can manipulate the environment. These biological structures provide the means by which our thinking is imposed on the world to test or alter it. In so doing, we learn about our environment by noting what happens. There is no separating the intricate relationship of bipedalism, hand manipulation, sensory input, and brain development. Their interdependency is important to us all our lives. Just as young children observe objects in their environment by looking, touching, tasting, smelling, and throwing them, adults place a space probe on the surface of Mars and turn on the TV eye to see what it can see. A mechanical hand touches the surface and fondles the soil. Antennae listen.

Sensors "smell" the atmosphere. With each of these actions—the youngster's firsthand, sensory experiences and the adult's inventive extension of the senses—humans gather knowledge about the world.

Educators have long praised the hands-on approach to teaching. But in spite of the praise, a visit to most classrooms reveals a different environment in which learning is taking place. Books replace experience very early and are almost the exclusive way by which students are taught from grade 4 through 12. When not doing assignments in books, children spend time listening to teachers or responding to their questions. Classrooms are primarily environments in which symbols are manipulated and substituted for experience.

Books are important. We can learn from them. But books can only do this if our experiential foundation is well prepared. To learn geometry, we must have experience in handling geometric forms and comparing them for similarities and differences. To learn about electricity, we must explore relationships among batteries, wires, and bulbs.

At one time the particular biological adaptations that enabled humans to generate, hear, and recognize sounds were important for survival. It took a long time for humans to invent ways to convey information using marks as symbols. Humans were not biologically designed for the purpose of reading or writing. Reading and writing are fortunate extensions of biological attributes that were designed for other purposes. The only way we can learn anything is through our biological structures.

Biological Stages and Thinking

Compared to other living organisms that we know about, humans enter this world quite emptyheaded. Many species of birds, fish, and other animals are born with brains preprogrammed with information that enables them to survive, gather food, and reproduce their own kind. Some can travel to locations they never experienced directly. Others behave in ways that are independent of learning. But the human baby is quite helpless. It must construct a view of the world for itself.

From a biological perspective, the lack of having a view is superb. It has survival value. Humans can reproduce their kind in virtually any environment, and the offspring will learn that environment through observations and interactions with it. We have been endowed with a powerful genetic gift—a set of thinking capabilities that are programmed to appear at intervals and spaced well enough apart to let the current capability establish itself.

One might view these capabilities as maps, one overlayed on another to depict more complexity of surfaces, streets, cities, terrains, and continents. But they are maps

without content; the names, terms, and qualities are not yet in place. The individual's interactions with the environment gradually fill in the content—first one map, then another, and another.

The nature of thinking capabilities and the sequence in which they appear have been well established on two research fronts. The *biological* basis underlying their appearance is established by periodic increases in brain size (Epstein, 1974), brain weight (Epstein, 1974), cellular growth within the brain (Winick and Ross, 1969), electrical functioning within the brain (Monnier, 1960), and head circumference (Eichorn and Bayley, 1962). The *psychological* basis is established through (1) evidence of the individual's capacity to deal with independent ideas and to relate them in increasing combinations in two- or three-year spurts from about age three through 17 (Pascual-Leone, 1970; Case, 1974); and (2) the individual's tendency to exhibit the same kinds of behaviors as other individuals within two- to three-year ranges, and as they grow older to replace each view by a more sophisticated view, which, in turn, is replaced (Piaget, 1969). Although researchers have provided various descriptions of the unfolding of the thinking phenomenon (Bruner, 1966; Erikson, 1950; Gagne, 1970; Vygotsky, 1974), the sequence is described here in terms of classroom usefulness.

Stage 1: Building a Repertoire

A baby begins life with the first thinking capability ready to go. Although quite passive until motor development is in place, the baby receives information through all his senses. He organizes the information into mental structures of what is seen, heard, smelled, tasted, and felt. As muscle coordination becomes functional, his thinking leads him to reach out to touch objects and later to move into unexplored territories. When he can grasp an object, he pulls it to himself, fondling, tasting, and maybe throwing it. Each action and interaction provides more information about the world. His mind organizes the information, and he contemplates other actions to impose on the world. In his first few months, he acts only on objects that he sees. When an object is placed out of sight, he seems not to think about it. At one year of age, he actively seeks objects that he knows exist behind barriers, such as in drawers, behind cabinet doors, or in boxes.

The most important aspect of this first stage of thinking is the establishment of *object permanence*—that is, objects that have been experienced are known to exist even though they are out of sight. Such an important development for thinking and so fundamental to all that we do! We would not know where to go home at night if we did not have object permanence. We would not know where we

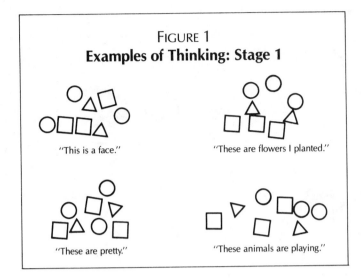

FIGURE 1
Examples of Thinking: Stage 1

"This is a face."

"These are flowers I planted."

"These are pretty."

"These animals are playing."

stopped reading a book if we could not trust that the print on the pages would remain the same when we are not looking at them. Knowing that the world can be trusted to keep things in place and as they are is important to all later learnings.

The way thoughts are structured during the opening stage is best revealed through a child's behaviors. When given objects to play with, the child will explore them one at a time, attracted by their perceptual feature. When the child has finished exploring it, the object will be discarded. The thinking capability at this stage is highly sensory, and actions are imposed on objects one at a time: perceiving aspects of color, size, and shape; touching it and sensing textures and firmness; pushing, pulling, or throwing it and noting how it behaves from such actions; tasting it and noting its flavor, firmness, and texture. These experiences provide the fundamental repertoire for future stages. Biologically, we have been given about three years in which to establish the repertoire.

Stage 2: Comparing the Known to the Unknown

The second thinking process begins to unfold at about age three. Now, when the child thinks about objects and acts upon them, she produces pairings as groups, piles, or chains on the basis of size, shape, color and so on, from her previous experiences (repertoire). In so doing, she establishes additional mental constructs about the world and how the objects and events in it are related. All her thinking is characterized by the ability to group two objects together on the basis of a common attribute or to link two events on the basis of a relationship. This will continue to be the dominant way in which she thinks and solves prob-

lems until about age six (Kofsky, 1966; Allen, 1967; Lowery, 1981a).

The power of thinking at this stage is amazing. The child will construct fundamental concepts about the physical world and its properties (similarity and difference comparisons based on sizes, shapes, colors, and so on); about ordinal and cardinal numbers (one-to-one correspondences of varying degrees); about all measures (comparisons of a known measure, such as a meter stick, to an unknown measure, such as the dimensions of a table); and about the use of symbols to stand for meaning (word recognitions). The child will learn more words during this stage than she will over the rest of her life. She can also learn to read music and, with proper motor coordination, play musical instruments, dance complex patterns, or carry out gymnastic or other athletic routines.

Educators have seldom provided instruction that allows the potential of this stage to develop. When we do challenge children to use this stage of thinking ability, the challenge usually takes the form of a rote-memory/recall routine. And we continue to teach toward this type of routine throughout all the school years. It is matching, sorting, pairing, and seriating real objects, illustrations, and symbols. To realize what is possible for the child, educators should consider the potential of the computer. The computer, which can only make simple comparisons on a one-to-one basis, does not use a stage of "thinking" beyond this one. But we appreciate the computer's capability and are in awe of what it can do. Why not also appreciate the child's capability at this stage (which will soon surpass the computer's current capability) and provide experiences that will develop it?

Stage 3: Putting Things Together

The next thinking process begins at about age six and is established for most children by age eight (Lovell and others, 1962; Smedslund, 1964; Bruner and Kenney, 1966). The process enables the child to group all objects in a set on the basis of one common attribute. For the first time, the resulting construct is comprehensive and has a rationale or logic to it. Without formal instruction, the child will put all the blue objects together from any array of objects, and then continue to sort the yellows, reds, and other colors into groups. If asked whether or not the objects can be arranged in another way, the child will rearrange them on the basis of some other attribute. If earlier experiences have provided a rich repertoire, the child will have many possibilities available to impose on any set of objects using this new thinking capability.

In formal schooling, the concepts of "all" and "some" can be easily taught at this stage. Upon these concepts, the

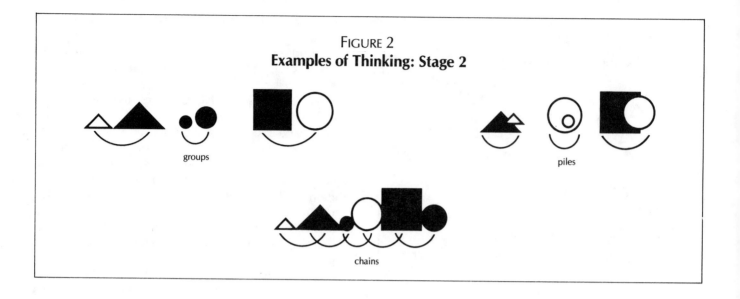

FIGURE 2
Examples of Thinking: Stage 2

groups

piles

chains

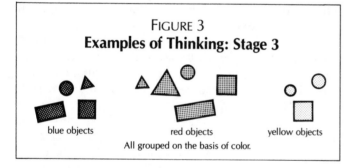

FIGURE 3
Examples of Thinking: Stage 3

blue objects   red objects   yellow objects
All grouped on the basis of color.

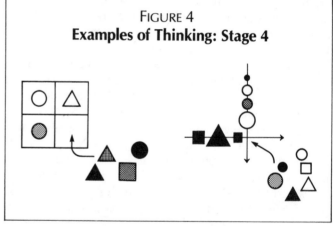

FIGURE 4
Examples of Thinking: Stage 4

child can build an understanding of all the fundamental operations of mathematics. Simple rules can be understood and generated by the child if given the opportunity. In our everyday existence, we seldom need to use thinking any higher than this stage.

Stage 4: Simultaneous Ideas

When children exhibit thinking that indicates they can mentally combine more than one idea at a time, they have entered Stage 4. For most children this takes place at about age eight and continues to develop until age ten (Inhelder and Piaget, 1964; Vernon, 1965).

Students begin to enjoy puns and can easily understand homonyms. Their creative writing moves from "It is an old house; it is a brown house; it is an empty house" (descriptions of a house, one property at a time) to "It is an old, brown, empty house" (multiple descriptors for the same noun). Their scientific reasoning moves from trial and error thinking or following an experimental "recipe" to contemplating the effects of comparing two situations si-

multaneously under different conditions. In mathematics, place and value can now be understood.

If the earlier levels have been properly established, the youngster can now exibit sophisticated products in all fields. Complex problems involving more than one idea at a time can be tackled. The essence of quality writing becomes apparent both through analysis of an author's writings and the youngster's own work.

Stage 5: Superordinate/Subordinate Relationships

Thinking about the relationships among groups of objects and a superordinate conception of them marks the stage of development that appears at about age ten. Such thinking realizes that if one collection of objects is included in another, then all the objects in the smaller grouping are but a part (some) of the larger. Conversely, some (a part) of the larger class is all of the smaller.

One use of this stage of thinking is evident as deductive reasoning that logically makes inferences between the more general and the less general: *All women are mortal. All queens are women. Thus all queens are mortal.*

The conclusion of a deductive argument is simply an explicit statement of something that is implicit in the premises. Its validity or consistency can be certified by logical considerations alone, usually through a transitivity of implications.

Some callytoots are herbitods. All herbitods have four legs. Therefore, which of the following must be true?

1. All callytoots have four legs.
2. All herbitods are callytoots.
3. Some callytoots have four legs.
4. It cannot be determined whether any of the above are true.

Teachers can substitute real concepts for make-believe ones (try "mammals" for "callytoots" and "dogs" for "herbitods") without interfering with the logic of the thinking represented by this stage.

Prior to this stage, children use superordinate words synonymously with subordinate words. For example, they use the word "bird" (which does not exist in any real way)

FIGURE 6
Examples of Thinking: Stage 6

$$24 + 32 = (3 \times 8) + (4 \times 8)$$
$$= (3 + 4) \times 8$$
$$= 7 \times 8$$
$$= 56$$

for a particular bird, such as a canary, a robin, or an eagle. At this stage, children can conceptualize the abstractness of "bird" and similar superordinate terms such as "justice," "freedom," "specific gravity," or "phyla," but only if the proper experiences have been made available for the conceptualization to take place.

The logic required to understand relationships is the major thrust of thinking at this stage. For it to develop and be useful to the student, curriculum materials must provide opportunities to do such thinking. For educators, this is the time to provide a curriculum that moves students from the real objects and experiences to the abstractions that can be derived from them or the abstractions that represent them (such as metaphors). This cannot be done by memorizing definitions. It can be done only by encouraging students to think about the relationships among objects or ideas.

Stage 6: Combinatorial Reasoning

As the next stage unfolds, at about age 13 (Lawson and Renner, 1975; Lowery, 1981b), the student becomes more flexible in her thinking. She can organize and then reorganize a collection of objects or ideas in different ways, while realizing that each way is possible at the same time and that the choice for an organization depends on one's purpose. For example, if a student is given a set of books with the identifying characteristics of size (number of pages), shape, color, and content, she realizes that the books can be organized on the basis of: size; shape; color; content; size and shape; size and color; size and content; shape and color; shape and content; color and content; size, shape, and color; size, shape, and content; shape, color, and content; size, shape, color, and content. Given the goal of locating information, she selects only the content as the organizing attribute because the other attributes are not useful to achieving the goal. Given a different goal, such as the determination of the ratio of books with fewer than 100 pages to those with more than 100 pages, she reclassifies the books for a different attribute to achieve that goal.

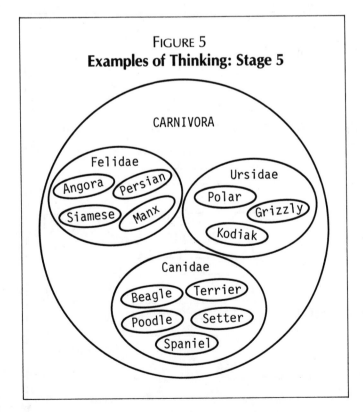

FIGURE 5
Examples of Thinking: Stage 5

CARNIVORA

Felidae
Angora Persian
Siamese Manx

Ursidae
Polar
Grizzly
Kodiak

Canidae
Beagle Terrier
Poodle Setter
Spaniel

Similarly, solving problems that involve the identification and systematic testing of each variable requires this stage of ability to separate variables by exclusion. For example, factors that influence the rate of swing of a pendulum are determined by isolating possible factors and testing them one at a time, while all others are held constant.

Schools must not continue to teach at the upper grade levels the way they teach at the earlier levels, making only the content more abstract. Students need experiences appropriate to the thinking they are learning. If such experiences are not provided at this stage, many students, as adults, will be unable to identify and isolate the possible combinations of relationships involved in complex problems they will face in their personal and professional lives.

Stage 7: Flexible Thinking

When flexible thinking appears, about age 16 (Karplus and Karplus, 1972; Lowery, 1981a; Lowery, 1981b), the student becomes able to develop a framework based on a logical rationale about the relationships among the objects or ideas in the taxonomy, while at the same time realizing that the arrangement is one of many possible ones that eventually may be changed based on fresh insights.

This stage of thinking can deal very flexibly with complex situations. Each field of endeavor produces new knowledge and further ideas. Resolutions to problems and knowledge generation often take many forms. The field of science is noteworthy for its examples. Darwin organized ideas concerning how all living organisms are related and formulated a comprehensive theory. Einstein did the same for the physical world. Mendeleev demonstrated this stage of thinking when he logically ordered the more than 50 different elements known in his day. His first *Periodic Chart of the Elements* clearly indicated the existence of elements not yet identified. Mendeleev predicted, in advance of seeing the elements, their weight and other important properties. This biological sequence of human thinking capabilities takes us wonderously from the early establishment of object permanence to the conceptualization of permanence and consistency among objects and events we have never, and may never, experience because of distance in time and space!

Educational Implications

The notion of stages is more than the sequential progression of thinking development. It includes the patterning of responses throughout the sequence and the time periods necessary for consolidating each capability.

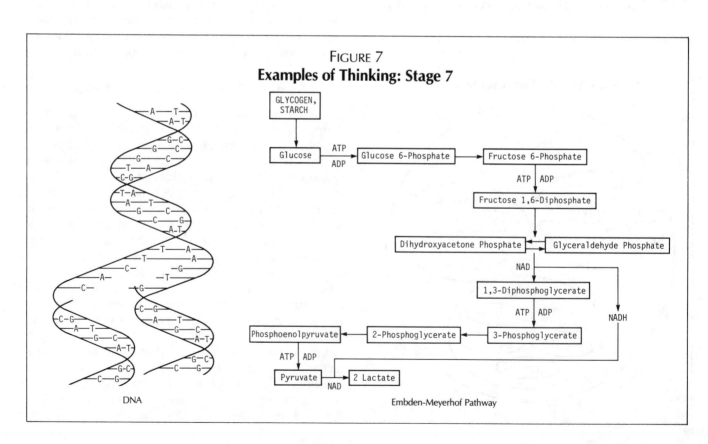

FIGURE 7
Examples of Thinking: Stage 7

DNA

Embden-Meyerhof Pathway

Development of the seven biologically based stages described here is invariant (Inhelder and Piaget, 1964; Kofsky, 1966; Allen, 1967; Hooper and Sipple, 1974; Kroes, 1974; Cowan, 1978) and involves a sequence common to all cultures (Bruner and others, 1956; Price-Williams, 1962; Lovell and others, 1962; Schmidt and Nzimande, 1970; Wei and others, 1971; Lowery and Allen, 1978; Cowan, 1978); a hierarchical integration of lower to higher levels; and a gradual consolidation in formation that unifies behaviors, concepts, and skills. The result is a broad structural network of interrelated capabilities appearing, not all at once, but within a fairly narrowly defined period followed by a plateau of several years. For thinking to develop properly, a very long childhood is necessary—one in which the youngster is free from having to carry out survival activities until all the stages are in place. This is why humans have a longer, biologically determined childhood than any other animal on earth. Pierce (1977) said it this way:

Although at any stage of development, nature is preparing us for the next stage, the beauty of the system is that we are conscious of none of this. Ideally, we must fully accept and exist within our developmental stage and respond fully to its content and possibilities. This means that every stage is complete and perfect within itself. The three-year-old is not an incomplete five-year-old; the child is not an incomplete adult. Never are we simply on our way; always we have arrived. Everything is preparatory to something else that is in formation.

The importance of this biological basis for the development of thinking is too often overlooked by educators. The periodic rapid increases in brain growth (perhaps the establishment of cellular networking) coupled by the appearance of new, content-free thinking capabilities (which overlay earlier capabilities containing content) are followed by plateaus (time periods that allow new capabilities to become integrated, used, and made functional). Unfortunately, the organization of curriculum and teaching in American schools and textbooks reflects an assumed, constant continuum of the thinking capacities of learners.

Most teachers are familiar with and trained in the vertical sequencing of content: skills and concepts constantly increase in complexity as students move through the grades; curriculum expectations for a student's performance are constructed upon the indices of school grade, chronological age, or achievement scores rather than upon individual cognitive and affective development indices.

In the competitive, social context of schools, educators try to accelerate the stages of development through school intervention (Furth, 1977). They act as if the distance from childhood to intellectual adulthood is measured only in terms of quantity—students acquire more experience, greater information, and broader knowledge as they grow older. This is an incomplete view of intellectual growth. The most significant differences between youngsters and adults rest in the nature and quality of their understanding. As youngsters develop, they pass through ways of thinking, each representing a different organization of experience, information, and knowledge, and each leading to a very different view of the world.

In our current educational system, many students progressively lose control over their own rate and sense of success (Collins, 1974; Covington and Berry, 1976). The reasons for this are highly complex, but two aspects related to the biology of thinking seem to be constructive:

1. The potential for success diminishes in relation to the degree of mismatch between content and thinking capability during a plateau period.

2. As personal evaluation becomes official evaluation in formal schooling, the mistakes and errors that are a natural part of learning become misinterpreted as failures. Students become motivated to work for extrinsic, symbolic rewards, such as gold stars and grades or to please adults, rather than for the sake of exploration and learning.

When cognitively mismatched content is accompanied by external expectations and rewards, the standards for successful performance are extended beyond the reach of many students. Over time, students are likely to lose confidence and develop a sense of failure. The result may contribute to developmental dysfunction—a slowing down or solidifying of stages plus asynchrony (very good performance in some things and very poor in others).

It is important for curriculum and instruction to reflect the biological basis for thinking. A *horizontal curriculum* is one in which students are challenged to use a particular stage of thinking with different materials at various levels of abstraction without the progressive requirement of having to be at a more and more advanced developmental stage. The model allows students at an identified stage of development to explore many experiences within and near that stage. Teachers do not compare a student's progress with that of other students, but rather select worthwhile experiences appropriate to his or her stage, organize them for meaningful interpretation, and orchestrate them to provoke the student's thinking. Numerous researchers have helped to validate this model in the sciences (Askham, 1972; Loggins, 1972; Lowery and Allen, 1978) and in mathematics (Ginsburg, 1977; Langbort, 1982; Rupley, 1981).

The essence of the approach is derived from the biological basis for the thinking—the thinking capability is independent of the objects involved in a given task. Students experience small, sequential steps of equilibration through an inexhaustible set of possible experiences. For example, a teacher might design sorting tasks to challenge a student who is at or beyond Thinking Stage 2 (comparing the known to the unknown) by asking the student to find from

FIGURE 8
Examples of Thinking

Concrete

Pictorial

Symbolic

an array of marbles two that are alike on the basis of first one color and then another. The activity can be done with other objects using colors or other physical properties. In each variation, the thinking capability required remains the same—pairing two objects on the basis of a single property. Studies show that when instructed in this way, students' thinking capabilities become more proficient and transfer more easily to new tasks.

The horizontal curriculum approach can also be used to extend students toward abstractions without requiring a higher stage of thinking. For example, if a student who is at or beyond Thinking Stage 3 (putting things together) can group all objects within a set so that they logically belong together, the action is considered to be firsthand or concrete. The action involves manipulations of real objects and not abstractions of reality. The student who can do the logical, concrete action has the potential to impose the same thinking on pictorial representations of reality without having to be at a more advanced stage. Pictorial representations are considered to be one step removed from reality. Again, without having to be at a more advanced stage, the same student has the potential to successfully carry out the same thinking on symbols and abstractions that are several steps away from reality.

Experiences designed to make use of thinking capabilities may provide significant cognitive and affective benefits by allowing students to perform progressively challenging tasks that are within a realm of potential success, while the accelerated and often mismatched vertical schemes may be inviting failure and eroding self-worth. The horizontal curriculum model allows teachers to be *teachers* having purpose for and power over materials rather than *managers* who keep track of places and pages in order not to interrupt the sequence dictated by the materials.

Our biological heritage provides us with a sequence of thinking capabilities and a set of physical tools that contribute to the establishment of each thinking capability. Originally designed to enhance our chances for survival, the interplay between thinking and actions has brought about understandings about the world that transcend the immediacy of survival. We have the leisure to fantasize and contemplate. We create through art, music, and construction; we imagine and communicate through books. We explore frontiers that are beyond the tangible and experiential. Educators must understand the heritage in order to appropriately select and sequence worthwhile experiences for students and to enhance their ability to think well. An understanding of the biological basis for thinking can lead to the conceptualization of a school curriculum far more responsive to the realities of how humans learn and to the intellectual differences among students at all grade levels, from early childhood through adolescence.

REFERENCES

Allen, L. R. "An Examination of the Classificatory Ability of Children Who Have Been Exposed to One of the 'New' Elementary Science Programs." Doctoral dissertation, University of California, Berkeley, 1967.

Askham, L. R. "Classification of Plants by Children in an Outdoor Environment." Doctoral dissertation, University of California, Berkeley, 1972.

Bruner, J. S.; Goodnow, J. J.; and Austin, G. A. *A Study of Thinking.* New York: John Wiley and Sons, 1956.

Bruner, J. S., and Kenny, M. J. *Studies in Cognitive Growth.* New York: John Wiley and Sons, 1966.

Case, R. "Structures and Strictures, Some Functional Limitations on the Course of Cognitive Growth." *Cognitive Psychology* 16 (1974): 544-573.

Collins, M. E. "Dependence and Independence in Young School-Age Children." Doctoral dissertation, University of California, Berkeley, 1974.

Covington, M., and Berry, R. *Self-Worth and School Learning.* New York: Holt, Rinehart and Winston, 1976.

Cowan, P. A. *Piaget With Feeling.* New York: Holt, Rinehart and Winston, 1978.

Eichorn, D., and Bayley, N. "Growth in Head Circumference from Birth Through Young Adulthood." *Child Development* 33 (1962): 257-271.

Epstein, H. T. "Phrenoblysis: Special Brain and Growth Periods I—Human Brain and Skull Development." *Developmental Psycho-Biology* 17 (1974): 207-216.

Erickson, E. H. *Childhood and Society.* New York: Norton, 1950.

Furth, H. "Piagetian Theory and Its Implications for the Helping Professions." Paper presented at the Annual Piagetian Conference, University of Southern California, 1977.

Gagne, R. M. *The Conditions of Learning.* New York: Holt, Rinehart and Winston, 1970.

Ginsburg, H. "The Psychology of Arithmetic Thinking." *The Journal of Children's Mathematic Behavior* 14 (1977): 1-89.

Hooper, F., and Sipple, T. "A Cross-Sectional Investigation of Children's Classificatory Abilities." Technical Report. Madison, Wisc.: Research and Development Center for Cognitive Learning, University of Wisconsin, 1974.

Inhelder, B., and Piaget, J. *The Early Growth of Logic in the Child.* Translated by A. Lunzer and D. Papert. New York: W. W. Norton and Co., 1964.

Karplus, R., and Karplus, E. "Intellectual Development Beyond Elementary School III: A Longitudinal Study." *School Science and Mathematics* 8 (1972): 735-742.

Kofsky, E. "A Scalogram Study of Classificatory Development." *Child Development* 37 (1966): 190-204.

Kroes, W. "Concept Shift and the Development of the Concept of Class in Children." *Journal of Genetic Psychology* 125 (1974): 119-126.

Langbort, C. R. "An Investigation of the Ability of Fourth Grade Children to Solve Problems Using Hand-Held Calculators." Doctoral dissertation, University of California, Berkeley, 1982.

Lawson, A. E., and Renner, J. W. "Piagetian Theory and Biology Teaching." *American Biology Teacher* 37 (1975): 336-343.

Loggins, P. "Visual Multiple Class Membership Sorting Abilities Among Second Grade Children—Tasks of Increasing Difficulty Across Categories of Sex and Socio-Economic Status." Doctoral dissertation, University of California, Berkeley, 1972.

Lovell, K.; Mitchell, B.; and Everett, I. R. "An Experimental Study of the Growth of Some Logical Structures." *British Journal of Psychology* 53 (1962): 175-188.

Lowery, L. F. *Learning About Learning: Classification Abilities.* Berkeley: University of California Department of Education, 1981a.

Lowery, L. F. *Learning About Learning: Propositional Abilities.* Berkeley: University of California Department of Education, 1981b.

Lowery, L. F. "Visual Resemblance Sorting Abilities Among First Grade Pupils." *Journal of Research in Science Teaching* 6 (1969): 248-256.

Lowery, L. F., and Allen, L. R. "Visual Resemblance Sorting Abilities of U.S. and Malaysian First Grade Children." *Journal of Research in Science Teaching* 15 (1978): 287-292.

Maranto, G. "The Mind Within the Brain." *Discover* 4 (1984): 34-43.

Monnier, M. "Definition of Stages of Development." In *Discussions on Child Development*, pp. 175-188. Edited by J. Tanner and B. Inhelder. New York: International Universities Press, 1960.

Pascual-Leone, J. "A Mathematical Model for the Transition Rule in Piaget's Developmental Stages." *Acta Psychologica* 63 (1970): 301-345.

Piaget, J. *Psychology of Intelligence.* Totowa, N.J.: Littlefield, Adams, and Company, 1969.

Pierce, J. C. *The Magical Child.* New York: E. P. Dutton, 1977.

Price-Williams, D. R. "Abstract and Concrete Modes of Classification in a Primitive Society." *British Journal of Educational Psychology* 32 (1962): 50-62.

Restak, R. M. *The Brain, The Last Frontier.* New York: Warner Books, 1979.

Rupley, W. "The Effects of Numerical Characteristics on the Difficulty of Proportional Reasoning Tasks." Doctoral dissertation, University of California, Berkeley, 1981.

Schmidt, W. H. O., and Nzimande, A. "Cultural Difference in Color/Form Preferences and in Classificatory Behavior." *Human Development* 13 (1970): 140-148.

Smedslund, J. "Concrete Reasoning: A Study of Intellectual Development." *Monographs of the Society for Research in Child Development* 29 (1964).

Vernon, P. E. "Environmental Handicaps and Intellectual Development." *British Journal of Educational Psychology* 35 (1965): 9-20.

Vygotsky, L. "The Problem of Age-Periodization of Child Development." *Human Development* 17 (1974): 24-40.

Wei, T.; Lavatelli, T.; and Jones, C. "Piaget's Concept of Classification: A Comparative Study of Socially Disadvantaged and Middle Class Young Children." *Child Development* 42 (1971): 919-977.

Winick, M., and Ross, P. "Head Circumference and Cellular Growth of the Brain in Normal and Marasmic Children." *Journal of Pediatrics* 74 (1969): 774-778.

15

Cognitive Levels Matching and Curriculum Analysis

Esther Fusco

There are one-story intellects, two-story intellects, and three-story intellects with skylights. All fact collectors who have no aim beyond their facts are one-story men. Two-story men compare, reason, generalize, using the labor of fact collectors as their own. Three-story men idealize, imagine, predict—their best illumination comes from above the skylight.

—Oliver Wendell Holmes

Five years ago the staff of the Shoreham-Wading River School District developed an inservice program designed to promote students' cognitive development. Initially, five staff members attended a course at Brandeis University designed by P. K. Arlin and H. T. Epstein. The course, Cognitive Levels Matching (CLM), refers in its broadest sense to teachers' ability to employ both formal and informal assessments to determine students' cognitive levels. Based on these assessments, the teachers adapt curricular tasks and guide students' acquisition of knowledge and problem-solving abilities in ways consistent with their cognitive abilities. To do so, teachers need to:

1. Understand cognitive developmental principles.
2. Understand the methods of assessing students' cognitive abilities.
3. Develop the ability to analyze and modify the cognitive demands of school-based experiences.

Thus, acquisition of a developmental perspective and creation of a "match" are central tenets of the inservice program. The term "match" recognizes and stresses the importance of fitting learners' abilities with certain tasks.

"The environmental circumstances force accommodative modifications in schemata only when there is an ap-

propriate match between the circumstances that a child encounters and the schemata that he already assimilated into his repertoir" (Hunt, 1961).

Hunt's approach stresses the matching process in teaching by encouraging the analysis of already assimilated schemata of an individual and the newly presented task or circumstance. Hunt considered this process difficult since such assessment can only be conducted through observing behavior, listening as individuals express themselves on particular matters, and awareness of individuals' past experiences. This is further complicated by the need to analyze individuals' potential intellectual ability.

The first CLM course presented at Brandeis was consistent with Hunt's viewpoint and also embodied Piaget's stages of intellectual development. The course has been expanded since then and now incorporates the work of other cognitive developmentalists (Arlin, 1977; Elkind, 1976; Sigel, 1978).

Such an approach requires that teachers become responsible educational leaders and model reflective thinking by designing environments consistent with the principles of cognitive development. To create this environment, they must assess the cognitive demands of the task and the cognitive abilities of the students, and then systematically (and often spontaneously) match the two. From this approach, another tenet emerges—one that seems somewhat revolutionary: the teacher is responsible for the development of thinking in the classroom. Thus, the teacher serves as the instructional leader and decision maker, mediates learning, and structures the classroom environment in a developmentally appropriate fashion. This goal is currently being accomplished in our system.

The dynamic matching process advocated here has been coined "thinking on your feet." Acquiring this thinking/teaching ability does not involve massive school reorganization, but instead, recognizing the classroom's multi-dimensional components. Teachers in such classrooms understand the cognitive demands of the task and then shift, refocus, extend, create, elaborate, and shape the learning to enable students to construct their own knowledge. There is an admission here that knowledge does not reside outside the children, nor can it be poured into them. Rather, learning is viewed as a constructed process that unfolds within each student.

Over the years, the CLM course has been restructured as we have learned more about the relationship of developmental perspective to the teaching/learning process. The initial six-credit graduate course presents theoretical background. Advanced courses are designed to implement the first course's goals. One major component teachers must focus on is cognitive assessment of the curriculum.

To assess the cognitive demands of curriculum, teachers must first decide what concept or task they want to present and recognize the steps involved in the presentations. Once this is accomplished, teachers consider the cognitive schemata (Inhelder and Piaget, 1958) that the curriculum demands of the students. Teachers who have completed the introductory course may initially refer to the Concrete and Formal Stage Concepts table for assistance in determining the schemata necessary for understanding the thinking a concept or task requires, but eventually they will be able to do this automatically (Figure 1).

Examples of Cognitive Assessment

Several illustrations may help clarify the cognitive assessment process. The first deals with understanding alphabetization, which requires students to be able to:

1. Recognize letters.
2. Comprehend the word "initial."
3. Recall the order of the alphabet.
4. Understand the words, "before," "after," "beginning," "middle," and "end."
5. Understand what to do with words that have the same initial letters.

The cognitive prerequisites for alphabetizing are:

1. Simple classification (these are all "g" words).
2. Simple and double seriation ("g" words in order: ga, ge, gi).
3. Class inclusion when alphabetizing to second and third letters (these "g" words are in the correct group and order: game, gate, gave; great, green, greet).

FIGURE 1
Concepts Associated with the Concrete and Formal Stages

CONCEPT DEFINITION	ASSESSMENT	EXAMPLE	OWN EXAMPLE
Simple classification: the ability to spontaneously group objects by one attribute and be able to shift to another attribute and regroup the same objects.	Attribute blocks—make groups that are the same, go together, or are alike in some way.	1. Finding the "short e" and "long e" words in a list. 2. Classifying animals as meat eating or non-meat eating. 3. Discussing how two pictures of patterns are alike and how they are different.	
Two-way classification: the ability to simultaneously coordinate two attributes of objects and group objects by that coordination.	Matrices: apple/flower; circle/square Venn diagrams; "I-shaped" classification task.	1. Comprehending similes. 2. Applying a grammatical rule that has two conditions.	
Three-way classification: the ability to simultaneously coordinate three attributes of objects and group objects that share three attributes.	Matrices: shape/color/direction.	1. Identifying countries that have the same three natural resources. 2. Grouping words.	
Class inclusion: the ability to understand and coordinate, in a hierarchical sense, part-whole relationships.	Flowers (plastic vs. colors); blocks (wooden vs. colors); cards (animals vs. types).	1. Fractions. 2. Recognizing the main idea of a paragraph. 3. States and capitals. 4. Missing addends.	

Developed by P. K. Arlin, University of British Columbia, and the staff of Shoreham-Wading River in the Cognitive Levels Matching project.

FIGURE 1
Concepts Associated with the Concrete and Formal Stages
(Continued)

CONCEPT DEFINITION	ASSESSMENT	EXAMPLE	OWN EXAMPLE
Simple Seriation: the ability to order a set of objects along some relevant dimension such as size.	Sticks of graduated sizes. Stacking cups. People pieces.	1. Getting in line according to size. 2. Putting events in a story in order.	
Double Seriation: the ability to order one set of objects according to some relevant dimension and to order a second set of objects along a relevant dimension in relation to that set of objects.	Cups ordered by size and in relation to sticks, which are also ordered by size or some other dimension.	1. One-to-one correspondence. 2. Copying words from the board to paper. 3. Alphabetical order.	
Number Conservation: recognizing that the property of number does not change in relation to a set of objects regardless of how those objects are arranged as long as no operation $(+,-)$ is performed on them. (The operation of reversibility supports this understanding.)	Two rows of 8-10 blocks, which are set up in a 1-1 correspondence and then one row is pushed together. . .	1. Basic addition and subtraction facts. 2. Different representations of the same number.	
Quantity Conservation: recognizing that the property of quantity does not change . . . (as above)	Two balls of clay; the size of a ball is changed after child establishes that both balls have the same amount of clay.	1. Pouring coke into different sized glasses. 2. Distributing materials.	
Length Conservation: recognizing that the property of objects called length does not change . . . (as above). (The operation of compensation also supports this concept.)	Two pipe cleaners of equal length. Displacement of one of the pipe cleaners or the curling up of one.	1. Concept of units of measure. 2. Distances of cities and countries from each other. 3. Number lines and time lines.	
Weight conservation: the ability to recognize that weight does not change when the shape and form of an object is altered unless the object is operated on by addition or subtraction. Requires the operation of compensation.	Two balls of clay, a pan balance. Establish equivalence and then alter the shape of one ball so that it "feels" lighter.	1. Scientific concepts of density, mass, and gravity. 2. The solar system. 3. Stress on bridges, and so on.	
Volume conservation: the recognition that volume does not change even if the form of an object is changed, unless it is operated on. Requires multiplicative compensations—namely, even though the form of the object is changed, what the volume gains or loses in one dimension is compensated for by what it gains or loses in the other two.	Two cylinders of equal size, one of brass, the other of aluminum; and two breakers of water with equal water levels. The islands problem with two sets of blocks. Clay balls with the two beakers of water.	1. Interior and exterior volume. 2. Displacement of volume. 3. Mathematical understanding of volume. 4. Analysis of closed systems. A change in one part of the system affects all other parts.	
Formal scheme—Multiplicative compensations: see definition above.	Same as above.	Same as above. 5. Centrifugal force.	
Formal scheme—Probability: the ability to develop a relationship between confirming and possible cases, with both beginning to be calculated as a function of the combinations, permutations, or arrangements compatible with the given elements.	Five red, five blue, and five yellow beads in an open box.	1. Figuring the odds in a game of chance. 2. The likelihood that a particular political event will occur given several preconditons.	

Continued

FIGURE 1

Concepts Associated with the Concrete and Formal Stages
(Continued)

CONCEPT DEFINITION	ASSESSMENT	EXAMPLE	OWN EXAMPLE
Formal scheme—Correlations: the ability to conclude that there is or is not a causal relationship, whether negative or positive, and to explain the minority cases by inference of chance variables. The task for the subject is to find out whether there is a relationship between the facts described by two or more variables when the empirical distribution is irregular.	Cards with people who have brown or black hair and blue or brown eyes. Different sets of cards with objects that vary in two or more dimensions.	1. Is there a relationship between economic condition and social protest? 2. Is there a relationship between hours of sunshine and plant growth? 3. Is there a relationship between movie genre and socio-historic and cultural events?	
Formal scheme—Combinations: the ability to systematically generate all possible combinations of the givens when a problem's solution demands that all possibilities be accounted for.	Electronic analog with five buttons and a light source. Chemical combinations tasks. Tokens tasks.	1. Qualitative analysis problems—chemistry. 2. Variation of ingredients for a specific recipe. 3. Meaningful combinations of beginnings, middles, and ends in writing tasks.	
Formal logic: the ability to reason using propositions based on a formal system.	Most tasks that assess formal schemes employ various logical propositions.	1. Syllogistic reasoning. 2. "If/then." 3. Making inferences. 4. Separating facts. 5. Literary criticism.	
Formal scheme—Proportional reasoning: the ability to discover the equality of two ratios that form a proportion.	Balance beam problem. Projection of shadows. "Mr. Big/Mr. Small."	1. Understanding analogies. 2. Ratio and proportions. 3. Making drawings to scale.	
Formal scheme—The coordination of two or more systems of reference: the ability to coordinate two systems, each involving a direct and an inverse operation, but with one of the systems in a relation of compensation or symmetry with respect to the other. This represents a type of relativity of thought.	Snail/path problem. Cyclists problem.	1. Understanding and comparing political or economic systems. 2. Developing a political ideology. 3. Generating multiple solutions to problems depending on multiple contexts. 4. Interpreting alternate historical accounts or interpretations.	
Formal scheme—Mechanical equilibrium: the ability to simultaneously make the distinction and the intimate coordination of two complementary forms of reversibility—inversion and reciprocity.	Piston problem.	1. Developing an understanding of work and energy.	
Forms of conservations beyond direct verification: the ability to deduce and verify certain conservations from their implied consequences. Developing a chain of inferences through which conservation can be verified by observing only effects.	Conservation of momentum problem with six suspended lead spheres.	1. Developing an understanding of momentum.	

4. Hierarchical classification (these are ordered properly: fee, fit, got, grace, help).

In constructing the learning experience, teachers consider the task analysis and cognitive prerequisites. Students' understanding of alphabetization can be assessed when such information is available, since the teacher can observe their performance and determine whether their demonstrated knowledge is appropriate to the task.

Examples of cognitive assessment are numerous in literature. Seventh graders read *Sounder* and engage in an active class discussion. The teacher asks what Armstrong (1972) meant when he wrote, "Cabin quiet was long and sad." In asking this question, the teacher recognizes that the students must comprehend the imaginary relationship and comparison the writer has created. The ability to understand this analogy or metaphor involves transposing the qualities of people, time, and cabins. Determining this comparison requires the students to first organize and classify the information and then reason proportionally. Thus, the cognitive demands require the use of the schemata classification and proportional reasoning.

Social studies provides still another curriculum example for determining cognitive levels. Suppose an 8th grade history teacher discusses the concept of tariffs. The teacher's goal is to enable students to comprehend what tariffs are and how they serve as another source of revenue for the government.

The cognitive schemata for comprehending tariffs and related concepts include:

1. Classification (qualities and attributes of terms such as import, export, free trade, tariff, foreign trade, and revenue).

2. Coordination of two or more reference systems (comprehending the symmetrical relationships that exist in free trade; international trade, reciprocal trade agreements, and government revenues).

3. Conservation beyond direct verification (understanding the balance of trade and payment).

4. Proportional reasoning (understanding the relationship of taxes to quantity, rates, and needs of country).

5. Correlational reasoning (developing an awareness of kinds of tariffs, their purpose, and how they are levied; their effects on industrial development, job protection, and prices).

As a final example, science courses also offer opportunities for cognitive assessment. Photosynthesis is an abstract concept that requires some understanding of the physics of light, chemical structure and reactions, diffusion, and the biochemical basis of organismic activities. The comprehension of this concept requires formal logical reasoning because it presupposes that students are able to use the following processes:

1. Classification, to comprehend the attributes of terms such as chloroplasts, molecules, energy related to work, wavelengths, photosynthesis, glucose, chlorophyll, and electromagnetic radiation.

2. Correlational reasoning, to comprehend the causal relationships between white light and the band of colored light, and CO_2 and blue/yellow bromthymol.

3. Combinatorial reasoning, to recognize what is required in plants for photosynthesis to take place, the types of light essential for plant growth, and activities that are necessary for plants to produce sugar or starch.

4. Proportional reasoning, to understand the number of chloroplasts in each cell and the quantities and substances necessary for photosynthesis.

5. Conservation beyond direct verification, to deduce and verify the consequences of chlorophyll's reaction to white light.

Applications of Cognitive Abilities

Once assessment is complete, the teacher constructs activities that reflect an understanding of students' various cognitive abilities. Suppose the teacher has had a group of students read *Twenty-One Balloons,* by William Rene du Bois (1947). The teacher has assessed the students' cognitive levels and thus might use the following activities to deal with the group's cognitive range as students read *Twenty-One Balloons.* The cognitive schemata listed next to the activity indicates the thinking skill the teacher anticipates emphasizing and each activity specifically related to the book's content.

1. How many different ways, both old and new, can you think of that people use to get from one place to another? (Classification)

2. Create a club you would like to join. Describe the rules and regulations for granting membership. Choose two people as honorary members, and tell us who they are and why you selected them. (Classification, correlational reasoning)

3. Imagine that an emergency has just happened and you only have ten minutes to get out of your house safely. What would you do first? Second? What would you take with you? Why? (Spatial-temporal relationships, seriation, correlational reasoning)

4. You are Thomas the Travel Agent. Andrea the Adventurer comes into your office with a request. She wants you to design the most unusual itinerary you can for her trip. Be as creative as you like; just remember that your plans should begin with the date of departure and include all the necessary information for it to be a successful trip for this famous customer. You may want to call a travel agent for helpful information. Have fun with this. (Correlational rea-

soning, frames of reference, classification, spatial-temporal relationships, and formal logic)

Conclusion

This chapter has focused on the cognitive analysis of curriculum, which is merely one dimension of the process. Other components of Cognitive Levels Matching are the informal and formal assessment of students' cognitive abilities and the systematic matching of students and curriculum. Each component is vital and integral in constructing classrooms that are dedicated to facilitating cognitive development.

REFERENCES

Arlin, P. K. "Piagetian Operations in Problem Finding." *Developmental Psychology* 13 (1977): 297-298.

Armstrong, William H. *Sounder.* New York: Harper and Row, 1969.

du Bois, William Rene. *Twenty-One Balloons.* New York: Viking Press, 1947.

Elkind, D. *Child Development and Education.* New York: Oxford University Press, 1976.

Hunt, J. M. *Intelligence and Experience.* New York: Ronald Press, 1964.

Inhelder, B., and Piaget, J. *The Growth of Logical Thinking from Childhood to Adolescence.* New York: Basic Books, 1958.

Sigel, I. "A Comparison of Two Teaching Strategies: Didactic and Inquiry." In *Proceedings of the Seventh Interdisciplinary Conference of Piagetian Theory and the Helping Professions.* Vol. 2, pp. 10-18. Edited by G. I. Lubin, M. K. Poulsen, J. F. Margary, and M. Soto-McAlister. Los Angeles: University of Southern California, 1978.

16

Developing Lesson Plans With Cognitive Objectives

S. Lee Winocur

Solutions to the significant problems facing modern society demand a widespread, qualitative improvement in thinking and understanding. We are slowly and painfully becoming aware that such diverse contemporary challenges as energy, population, the environment, employment, health, psychological well-being of individuals and meaningful education of our youth are not being met by the mere accumulation of more data or the expenditure of more time, energy or money. In view of the increasing pressures imposed on our society by these problems, many responsible thinkers have realized that we cannot sit back and hope for some technological invention to cure our social ills. We need a breakthrough in the quality of thinking *employed both by decision-makers at all levels of society and by each of us in our daily affairs.*

—Robert Ornstein

For the past six years, the Center for the Teaching of Thinking of the Orange County Department of Education has been designing and testing curriculum materials and instructional strategies to help students acquire higher-order thinking skills. This effort, called Project IMPACT (Improve Minimal Proficiencies by Activating Critical Thinking), has resulted in a professional training program for teaching thinking skills supported by 120 model lessons.

Enhancing Student Thinking

The goal of teaching thinking skills is based on a very different set of assumptions than those inherent in traditional practices. Teachers who successfully teach the IMPACT program assume that:

- All students are capable of higher-level thinking.
- Thinking skills can be taught.
- Thinking skills can be learned.
- Thinking skills are basic to the learning process.
- Thinking is best introduced in a social context.

To accomplish our goal of enhancing student thinking, we needed to bridge the gap between traditional instructional design, which is rooted in behavioral science, and the new designs of cognitive psychology. The IMPACT model serves as a framework for integrating behavioristic lesson elements—such as performance indicators, direct instruction, practice, and evaluation—with cognitive strategies for describing mental processes. Although primitive and imperfect, the lessons provide evidence that thinking skills can serve as both the purpose and the product of learning experiences.

The instructional design concentrates on three specific factors of cognitive theory that affect decisions by the teacher in planning the lesson: content, constructs, and conditions. Content involves separating the curriculum into its component parts so that it can be assimilated easily by the learner. Constructs are factors that ensure that learners bring the appropriate schemata or cognitive constructions to the learning situation. Conditions have to do with sequencing learning events and supplementing instructional approaches to include those that have been shown to promote cognitive growth.

Content

Our intention was to weave the teaching of knowledge of mathematics and language arts with instruction in the thought processes underlying those disciplines. In determining our strategy, two positions emerged. First, although specific cognitive skills had been isolated, the lessons were to emphasize the interrelatedness of reasoning processes with content. For knowledge to be translated to new situations, thinking must not be addressed as a separate subject. We would look for ways to promote higher-level reasoning as an integral part of any lesson. Second, the lessons were to focus on existing educational goals. The teaching-writing team was adamant that no new content be added to their already overburdened curriculum.

To systematically organize the teaching events related to thinking, we hypothesized that specific skills might be sequenced to create an overreaching structure, a framework possessing internal coherence. Ausubel (1957) had proposed that cognitive structure could be organized hierarchically with highly inclusive concepts subsuming less inclusive subconcepts. We found that it was possible to sequence thinking skills in this way.

The Universe of Critical Thinking Skills (Figure 1) organizes the skills so that we can teach the application of thinking in any content area. Derived from the work of Piaget (1958) and Ennis (1962), and Winocur (1981) and validated procedurally by IMPACT teachers in their classrooms, the placement of skills into categories is based on the idea that some less complex skills are prerequisite to the understanding and application of others. The rationale for the arrangement, therefore, depends on a factor of inclusiveness. The more inclusive of other skills, the higher it is placed on the model. The arrangement of skills also rests on the assumption that thinking is based on an ability to apply each skill independently and combine and sequence them to form a strategy. Although the position of skills within each category remains somewhat arbitrary, the three levels of the taxonomy reflect the theoretical development of cognitive ability.

The design or organization of skills can be easily related to each discipline. Reading, for example, makes use of skills listed in all three levels. Good readers make predictions as they read. We found that the ability to predict accurately presupposes and depends on the ability to observe, distinguish relevant data, identify patterns, and infer cause-effect relationships. Systematic attention to the process of predicting and to explicit instruction in that skill and its prerequisites is fundamental to better comprehension. The identification and ordering of the skills in the taxonomy allows a teacher to select, blend, and sequence the skills and thus manage the teaching-learning event.

To prepare lessons aimed at developing cognitive skills, teachers must understand each skill and how it relates to both the curriculum at hand and to other skills. Use of the framework simplifies the task of developing cognitive objectives for lessons because it allows us (1) to break down complex learning outcomes into component parts (for example, analyze standard objectives to determine whether or not sufficient instruction has been provided to complete a task), and (2) to identify the thinking skills prerequisite to the learning if re-teaching is necessary.

Not all disciplines emphasize all skills. Standard mathematics content, for example, may not require instruction in fact and opinion or identification of points of view. However, it does incorporate all of the enabling skills; some of the processes including identifying relevant vs. irrelevant information, cause-and-effect relationships, and the forming of generalizations, as well as deductive logic at the operations level. Although it may not be appropriate to teach all the skills in each course, it is possible to coordinate the effort so that students are exposed to instruction in each of the skills during one class or another.

The taxonomy serves instruction in two ways. First, if prerequisite component skills can be taught by a known method, the model can be used to prepare the task analysis of a complex skill as a way of reaching the entire objective. This approach of reducing complex objectives into sets of simply taught ones is popular among behavior-oriented educators; it works well with students who enter instruction with little or no knowledge of the skill being taught. In this case, the skill is explicitly described and modeled by the teacher and practiced by the student during the initial phase of the lesson followed by application to content material.

A second application, more appropriate for students familiar with skills, is to provide direct instruction only when student performance indicates that application is lacking or incorrect. In this case, the teacher begins the lesson by focusing on the content and uses of taxonomy to diagnose which skills are the sources of error. The teacher can then focus instruction on the processes in question.

From the viewpoint of an instructional designer, it is important that there be continuity and relevance between the objectives that are being developed for a particular lesson and overall curriculum objectives. This is equally true for process instruction as for content. The planner plays a critical role in coordinating, stimulating, and ensuring the use of cognitive skills.

Constructs

In our search for instructional techniques for transmitting rational thought processes, we found that cognitive psychology provided a powerful tool—graphic organizers. This instructional method involves the use of visual constructs or diagrams as a communication aid for systematically mapping the organization of ideas and guiding internal dialogue. IMPACT lessons incorporate a number of

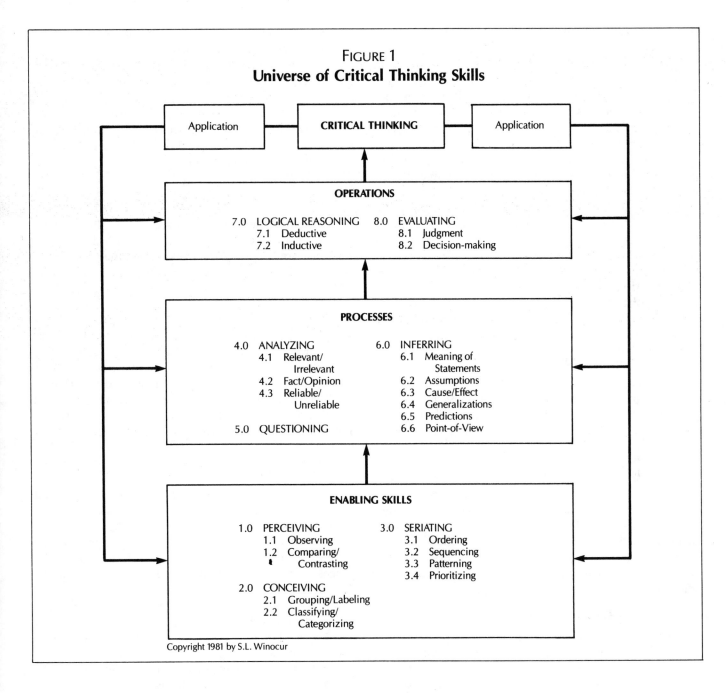

FIGURE 1
Universe of Critical Thinking Skills

Application   CRITICAL THINKING   Application

OPERATIONS

7.0 LOGICAL REASONING   8.0 EVALUATING
     7.1 Deductive   8.1 Judgment
     7.2 Inductive   8.2 Decision-making

PROCESSES

4.0 ANALYZING   6.0 INFERRING
     4.1 Relevant/   6.1 Meaning of
           Irrelevant   Statements
     4.2 Fact/Opinion   6.2 Assumptions
     4.3 Reliable/   6.3 Cause/Effect
           Unreliable   6.4 Generalizations
                                 6.5 Predictions
5.0 QUESTIONING   6.6 Point-of-View

ENABLING SKILLS

1.0 PERCEIVING   3.0 SERIATING
     1.1 Observing   3.1 Ordering
     1.2 Comparing/   3.2 Sequencing
           Contrasting   3.3 Patterning
                                 3.4 Prioritizing
2.0 CONCEIVING
     2.1 Grouping/Labeling
     2.2 Classifying/
           Categorizing

these constructs at various stages of the learning experience.

Research on memory has produced some valuable generalizations. First, the mind can concentrate on only a small number of elements at any one time. To be remembered, complex information must be grouped and stored intact so that attention can be focused on other topics. Second, the task of searching the memory for manageable amounts of related information is easier if that information was stored with reference to some kind of framework. A frame, or cognitive organizer, acts as a checklist, ensuring that the student searches through appropriate areas of memory in a systematic way.

To write an essay, solve a mathematics problem, or summarize a reading passage requires more than locating the correct answer. Students need a systematic plan for retrieving information, and for interpreting and recreating it in a coherent fashion (Calfee, 1981). Explicit training with reference to some kind of framework makes students consciously aware of the need to search for, compare, and evaluate various ideas in order to comprehend their relationships.

Collins and Loftus (1975) identified several methods for conveying and restructuring the relationships of concepts within any domain. In addition, the following instructional theories are useful: advanced organizers (Ausubel, 1968); digraph analysis (Harary, Norman, and Cartwright, 1965); graphic organizers (Jonassen and Hawk, 1984); cognitive maps, concept maps, spider maps, concept hierarchies, semantic feature analysis, and cross-classification tables (Jones and Friedman, 1984). Based on research on the scaling of similarity judgments, these schemes require the learner to consciously map the interrelationship of prior knowledge, locate anchors for new ideas, and identify gaps or deficiencies in their own cognitive structures.

Performance objectives for cognitive lessons require the learner to correctly apply these frames as conditions of learning. The following are three basic examples of constructs used in remedial language arts lessons with 7th and 8th graders.

Construct 1—Compare/Contrast

The teacher introduces a lesson in writing business letters by giving students copies of a business letter and a personal letter and asking them to identify similarities and differences, which they then plot on a Venn diagram (Figure 2).

Construct 2—Cause/Effect

A combination of a Venn diagram and mind-mapping helps students organize concepts surrounding the identification of cause-and-effect relationships in a reading assignment. In small groups, students first discuss the hypothetical causes for and long-range effects of school dropout. Next, students analyze a reading passage and apply the frame to elements of the story (Figure 3).

Construct 3—Concept Formation

A third scheme that has met with widespread acceptance is based on the principle of concept attainment. To use this diagram appropriately, the teacher constructs two lists. The "In" list contains words or phrases related to a specific concept or rule, in this case adverbial clauses. The "Out" list contains words or phrases unrelated to that concept. Students are instructed to hypothesize specific examples for the "In" column, and are cautioned not to disclose the rule. By applying such thinking skills as observing, comparing and contrasting, identifying relevant and irrelevant attributes, and generalizing hypotheses, students generate additional examples for the "In" column. As students offer suggestions, the teacher writes them in the appropriate column, either "In" or "Out" (Figure 4, p. 92).

The activity concludes when the majority of students can state the governing concept or rule.

In addition to its unique and game-like quality, use of a frame encourages students to consider each element of a situation separately, searching their memories for related ideas. This is particularly helpful for learners at the concrete stage of cognitive development, who have difficulty considering the multiple aspects of one element while holding several other elements constant.

Conditions

The IMPACT lesson format, based on the Hunter (1983) model, incorporates the use of frames to introduce, model, reinforce, transfer, and evaluate the thinking process during any of the following four stages of the learning experience.

Stage 1—Orientation

In those lessons in which a thinking skill is to be taught directly, teachers begin by presenting a situation designed to perk student curiosity. The teacher graphs key concepts and supporting details generated by large- or small-group discussions, using the same advanced organizer that the students subsequently will learn and practice. The construct in Figure 3 represents part of an orientation experience.

Stage 2—Instruction

During instruction, the teacher labels a thinking skill used by the students during the discussion and then uses a frame to model its application. Whether the topic is complex or simple, it is important that the teacher explicitly describe the mental strategies being performed while the process is under way. For example, for the "In/Out" frame, the teacher might describe the process as follows:

- Focus on several examples and nonexamples.
- Identify relevant attributes of each example.
- Compare and contrast attributes of the examples, noting commonalities.
- Generalize a commonality of all the examples.
- Compare the commonality to the nonexamples and note the differences.
- Verify the attributes that distinguish the examples from the nonexamples.

Due to the subjective nature of the complex mental performance, this description is imperfect. Yet we agree with Beyer (1984) that this verbal sharing of the reasoning process provides a model of performance needed by some students, and encourages each student to interiorize the strategy. When the description of thinking skills performance is accompanied by application of a frame to the con-

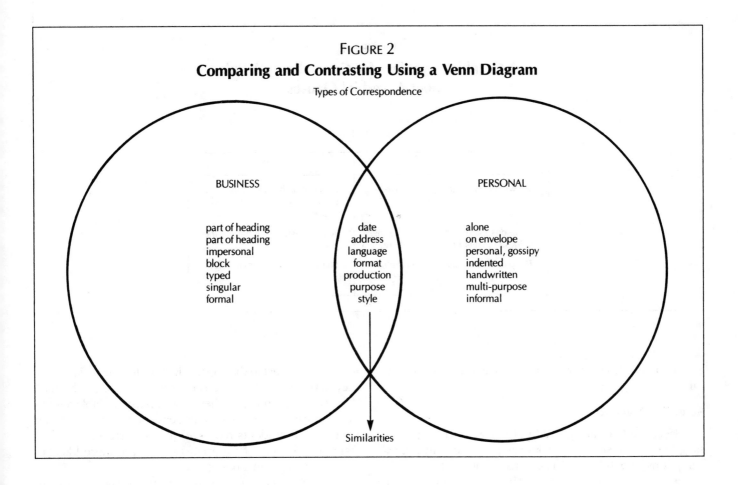

FIGURE 2

Comparing and Contrasting Using a Venn Diagram

Types of Correspondence

BUSINESS

part of heading
part of heading
impersonal
block
typed
singular
formal

date
address
language
format
production
purpose
style

PERSONAL

alone
on envelope
personal, gossipy
indented
handwritten
multi-purpose
informal

Similarities

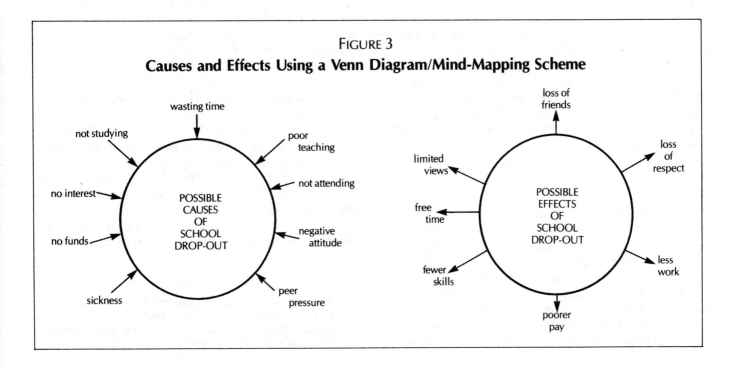

FIGURE 3

Causes and Effects Using a Venn Diagram/Mind-Mapping Scheme

wasting time
not studying
poor teaching
not attending
no interest
negative attitude
no funds
sickness
peer pressure

POSSIBLE
CAUSES
OF
SCHOOL
DROP-OUT

loss of friends
limited views
loss of respect
free time
fewer skills
less work
poorer pay

POSSIBLE
EFFECTS
OF
SCHOOL
DROP-OUT

FIGURE 4
A Graphic Organizer for Generalizing A Rule About Adverbial Clauses

What's The Rule?

IN	OUT
We will eat *when the guests arrive*.	Because of the grain shortage, cereal products have doubled in price.
If you don't know where you're going, it doesn't matter how you get there.	You understand the rules *of the game.*
The pass was completed *even though the quarterback had been tackled*.	I have a *friend who may help.*

tent area, the demonstration becomes all the more powerful.

Stage 3—Practice

Here students are guided in the construct to specific sample items or situations. For example, to identify the assumptions imbedded in an advertisement, students might use a mind-mapping organizer. The teacher monitors the performance, and students receive feedback from either the teacher or from a small group. For some students, further application of the skill might be necessary prior to applying the strategy to subject-matter content.

How do students acquire mental routines that are the basis for skilled performance? Irion (1966) recommends practice with feedback. If guidance was adequate, the number of times a student has performed a task is a good index to skill level. It is also important for students to perform the task in different situations so that they have experience in adapting the performance to a variety of contexts.

Stage 4—Transfer

The teacher introduces the application of the thinking skill and the frame to new material from the content area, carefully indicating those aspects of the learning closely akin to the prior application. Use of the graphic organizer during this stage greatly facilitates identification of the similarity of the two learning situations and promotes application of the thinking process to the new material.

Students describe, in their own words, the steps of the skill application, and demonstrate application of the

graphic construct to the appropriate content material. Since they have participated in discussions and have symbolized their thinking on paper, they should have available a strategy that can then be used independently in the follow-up exercises. If students have had the opportunity to use a frame in a variety of experiences, they are more likely to consider using it in a new setting.

Note that at every stage, use of a frame encourages students to employ a thinking skill in a conscious way. Although each skill undoubtedly is used in combination with other mental processes during any lesson, direct instruction and application of the organizer emphasize one particular skill during each occasion.

Development of the IMPACT curriculum has broadened our view of the capability of teachers and students to deal effectively and efficiently with information. Neither lesson design nor curriculum materials have required radical change. Rather, in applying the principles of information processing theory to instructional development, we have found that the educational impact has had more to do with instructional emphasis than with program reformation, more to do with an implicit view of students and learning than with the details of a particular learning experience.

REFERENCES

Ausubel, D. P. *Educational Psychology: A Cognitive View.* New York: Holt, Rinehart and Winston, 1957.
Beyer, Barry. "Improving Thinking Skills—Practical Approaches." *Phi Delta Kappan* 65, 8(1984): 556-560.

Calfee, Robert. "Cognitive Psychology and Educational Practice." In *Review of Educational Research.* Edited by D. A. Berliner. American Educational Research Association, 1981, p. 21.

Collins, A., and Loftus, E. "A Spreading Activation Theory of Semantic Processing." *Psychological Review* 82(1975): 407-428.

Ennis, R. "A Concept of Critical Thinking." *Harvard Educational Review* 32, 1 (Winter 1962): 81-111.

Harary, F.; Norman, R. A.; and Cartwright, D. *Structural Models: An Introduction to the Theory of Directed Graphs.* New York: John Wiley, 1965.

Hunter, M. *Mastery Teaching.* El Segundo, Calif.: Tip Publications, 1983.

Irion, A. L. "A Brief History of Research on the Acquisition of Skill." In *Acquisition of Skill.* Edited by E. A. Bilodeau. New York: Academic Press, 1966.

Jonassen, D. H., and Hawk, P. "Using Graphic Organizers in Instruction." *Information Design Journal* 61, 3 (1984): 58-68.

Jones, B. F., and Friedman, L. B. *Content-Driven Comprehension Instruction and Assessment.* (Technical Report). Alexandria, Va.: Army Research Institute, 1984.

Piaget, J. *The Growth of Logic From Childhood to Adolescence.* New York: Basic Books, 1958.

Winocur, S. L. *The Impact of a Program of Critical Thinking on Reading Comprehension Remediation and Critical Thinking of Middle and High School Students.* San Diego, Calif.: U.S. International University, 1981.

PART V
Thinking Pervades the Curriculum

You are a high school principal. Your school district has adopted a "thinking across the curriculum" approach, and all teachers will teach for thinking. Your P.E. department chairperson says, "No way." Your voc-ed teacher says, "That's the role of the science and math departments." Your foreign language department chairperson says, "It comes later, when they are fluent." Your counseling staff shuns the task because "it's outside their domain." You have to convince your entire staff that each of their disciplines is based on cognitive functions, the mastery of which permits the achievement of that discipline and its contents.

—Thomas Kimball

Accounting to Ed Gordon, Professor of Music at Temple University, to create, recreate, enjoy, or remember music is a form of thought. His term, "audiation," is to music what "metacognition" is to speech. Whenever we internally rehearse a tune, compose a melody, predict an ending, or feel a beat, we are *audiating*.

During the last Olympic games, it was reported that there were more psychologists attending the players than physicians. The athletes were already perfect physically; mental "pumping" is what gave them the edge. Mental rehearsal of athletic performance (the "Carpenters Effect"), freedom from stress, and not being overly confident are cognitive conditions that seem to enhance physical performance.

Increasing amounts of research show that mastery of any subject area or basic skill depends on students' possession of certain prerequisite cognitive abilities. For example, if students do not spontaneously analyze, compare, and infer, they will never master the skill of decoding. More drill and practice would prove to be of little help.

All teachers would agree that such intelligent behaviors as following instructions, striving for precision, checking for accuracy, perseverance, listening to others' points of view, and innovation are basic to their discipline. Regardless of their subject area, teachers want students to perform intelligently: measuring twice before cutting is an indication of reduced impulsivity practiced in the shop and home economics classrooms. Installing, remembering, executing, and evaluating a strategic plan of action is as basic to the football field as it is to the science laboratory. Being alert to, interpreting, and responding appropriately to environmental cues is as much a survival skill in driver training as it is in a successful marriage.

Pervasiveness implies that thinking skills are to be emphasized within existing subjects instead of being added as a separate subject. In this chapter, several commonly taught subjects and skills are examined to determine the thinking processes on which they are based. We will not examine *all* subject areas and skills; rather, we wish to emphasize that process and content are interdependent and inseparable. To teach one without the other is meaningless indeed. Learning is a process that engages and alters the mind.

17

Some Thoughts About Mathematics and Problem Solving

Robert Wirtz

The note from school said Marcia needed extra work with flash cards. " . . . she is still counting on her fingers, and that's not fast enough in 4th grade." Marcia's parents were surprised; they had learned that children who are dependent on their fingers can test out "at grade level"—until 4th grade.

Marcia's father found out quickly what the teacher had reported. When the card "3 + 7 = _____ " came up, Marcia used her fingers: "8, 9, 10 . . . it's 10." Her father complimented her for getting the right answer, but with a note of moral judgment, asked, "Why don't you remember that?"

There was considerable finger counting and more, "Why don't you remember that?" Frustration was mounting.

When the card with "5 + 5 = _____ " came up, Marcia beamed and said "10," without hesitation. "Ah," her father thought, "an entry point." So he found "5 + 6 = _____ " and put the cards side by side on the table. He then asked, "Now, how much is 5 + 6?" Marcia counted on her fingers from 6 to 11 and said, "It's 11."

"But Marcia, you know that 5 + 5 = 10; 6 is one more than 5. So if 5 + 5 = 10, how much is 5 + 6?"

Marcia was confused and troubled. With brows knit tightly, she counted on her fingers from 6 to 11 and asked, "Isn't it 11, Daddy?"

"Marcia, don't you see any connection between 5 + 5 and 5 + 6?"

"Yes, they both begin with a 5."

This chapter is excerpted from articles by the late Robert Wirtz. Permission to reprint has been granted by Curriculum Development Associates of Washington, D.C., and Monterey, California.

This first session ended with Marcia knowing she was an "I don't get it," and her father realizing he was an "I can't help her."

Everyone will agree rote memory and understanding are both essential ingredients of mathematical fluency. Any disagreements are limited to the relative importance of these two factors. It is enough for us to begin by recognizing the importance of both. Any math curriculum must suggest well-developed strategies for (1) helping all children remember more in less time, and (2) helping all children understand more mathematics. The standard curriculum is silent on both questions—or if not silent, certainly fuzzy and not at all specific.

If one were to look for implied strategies in the traditional curriculum, the following might be noted:

- Rote memory "is a matter of sufficient repetitions."
- Understanding "is telling about an idea often enough so all children will eventually understand it."

Such implications suggest an almost complete lack of understanding of both aspects of learning. They seem to rest on some kind of accumulated wisdom and are useless as strategies to overcome children's difficulties.

Rote Memory

Why is it Marcia can encounter "3 + 7 = _____ " countless times over four years and not remember the answer?

Clearly, "sufficient repetitions" is not a productive tactic for many children. A bit of analysis reveals that Marcia has been practicing counting on her fingers and that she needs no more practice at that method of problem solving. What she has always needed and almost never experienced was saying the complete sentence—"three plus seven equals ten"—and hearing that sentence from teachers, parents, and other children.

The unit of rote memory is a verbal pattern that, once begun, "rolls off the tongue" as a TV commercial or line of poetry. And this is true whenever rote memory is involved. Consider these questions:

- What is your phone number and area code?
- In the *Pledge of Allegiance to the Flag of the United States,* what words come just before and just after the word "Republic"?
- How many days are in the month of April?
- What is the fourth letter of your last name?
- How does this sentence end? "Hey, diddle, diddle, the . . . ."

No trouble: once begun, the rest rolls off your tongue with no conscious act of mind. It is in your rote memory—as a verbal pattern, a unit of memory.

This insight into the nature of rote memory leads to productive strategies and tactics. When Marcia encountered "3 + 7 = ____," she began immediately to read the card, "three plus seven equals ____." If the answer didn't roll off her tongue, she would find out on her fingers that 7 + 3 = 10. "It didn't roll off my tongue that time, Daddy, but I know what to do. I'm going to say the whole sentence three times—I'll say it as if I were angry" (or happy or fast or with a beat—any way she has decided to say it).

When rote memory is involved, classroom teachers and parents need to police their own language, never settling for answers, but requiring *complete sentences*—repeating over and over again the *full unit of memory*. And we might reinstate to good standing "chanting" or "choral response," which not only promotes memory but can also embrace the powerful and positive dynamic of group singing. The "I don't get its" and "I get its" respond together—and the latter group ought not be excluded because "they know the words of the song."

Understanding

Piaget (1965) provides powerful insight into the source of difficulty that "I don't get its" experience—and indicates strategies we must develop to overcome those difficulties and prevent them from arising:

The true cause of failure in formal education is that we begin with language rather than beginning with real and material action.

Language is a repository of experiences. It begins as children respond to the sensory data flooding into their minds as they encounter the three-dimensional world around them—a world of people and things. They see connections and relationships and talk about them—to themselves and to others. They use words and language patterns as organizers to draw together various aspects of their experiences. They build mental images and develop language patterns that persist in their minds after the experience passes.

Language grows out of "real and material action"—its meaning depends exclusively on the experience. Unfortunately, it is possible to begin with language that has no referent, no meaning. And this is doubly destructive: it develops a language as limited and capricious as the vocabulary of parrots; it also hides the fact that no meaningful language is being developed—the worthless counterfeit is being accepted at face value. This is the plight of "I don't get its."

Marcia could not comprehend her father's language, which focused on relationships, because it had no referent for her. Shortly thereafter her father introduced her to tenframes—an array of wire or plastic mesh. He asked Marcia to put five beans in each of two frames as shown in Figure 1a.

He asked her whether or not she counted the beans as she put them in.

"No, I just filled up one row in each; and I know you want me to say 5 + 5 = 10."

"That's right. Now will you please put another bean in the bottom frame?" She did (Figure 1b), and without hesitation, said, "Now you want me to say 5 + 6 = 11."

"How did you find that out so easily?"

"Don't you see, Daddy, the two 5s make 10 and one more is 11?"

A little later he asked her to put four beans in the top frame and five in the bottom frame (Figure 1c).

"Did you count those nine beans as you put them in?"

"No, I just left one hole, and you want me to say 4 + 9 = 13. That's easy: you take one of the four and fill up the hole in the bottom frame, and then you have 10 and 3, or 13."

She thought a minute and said, "Hey, Daddy, that'll work for all the nines . . . you can always fill up the hole and have 10 plus one less than you started with the other frame."

And she proceeded to make up examples without using the frames or beans: "7 + 9 will be 6 and 10, or 16" and so on.

Marcia smiled, "From now on, the nines are my 'cinchy' numbers."

She thought for a minute and continued, "And I can use the same trick with the eights—you move over two to fill up the ten frame: 8 plus 7 must be the same as 10 and 5 more, or 15."

"You know, I think I'll call the eights my almost cinchy numbers."

FIGURE 1
Ten-Frames

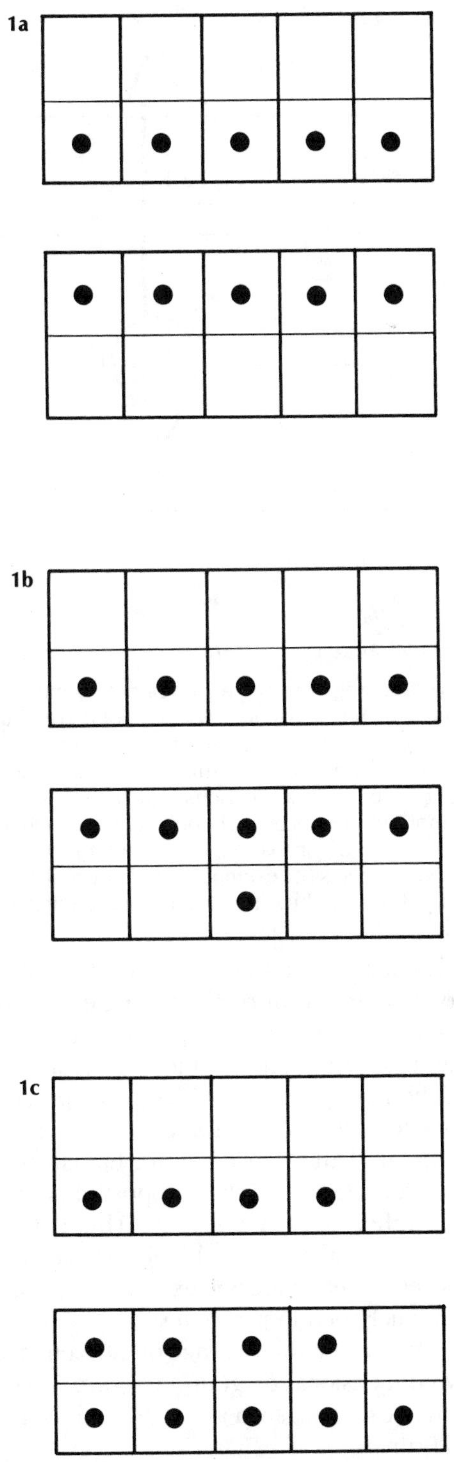

1a

1b

1c

Not long afterward, she asked, "Daddy, will the nines be cinchy in subtraction?"

She was building a language of connections as it grew out of "real and material action" and now was asking "global questions" searching for broad generalizations.

"I don't get its" are not naturally language deficient. Rather, they are failing because they were initiated to language that was not rooted in real and material action.

"I don't get its" are victims of a curriculum that fails to appreciate the central role of language experience and language development in mathematics or fails to help teachers and parents with their responsibility to help children develop the crucial language of connection and relationships.

"I don't get its" suffer a common difficulty. To them, each bit of arithmetic stands by itself. The subject is a maze of unrelated items. They never learned the language of connections or relationships. The "I get its" learned that language—they can talk their way from what they know into nearby, less familiar terrain.

Children As Learners

Children are experts at learning through trial and error. They come to school as seasoned inventors, full of the aspirations, dreams, and self-confidence that distinguish human beings from all other animals.

The extension of these natural learning abilities is awesome. At age two or three, children fathom the basic structure of their mother tongue. When they ask, "Will you read me the same story you *readed* me yesterday," they are not mimicking—they are inventing a new word according to the standard rule of forming the past tense of regular verbs in English. Early on, they learn to read body language and develop several reliable ways to control adults.

They have also had many experiences with the four basic operations of arithmetic: subtraction ("take away"), addition ("some more"), multiplication ("so many for everyone"), and division with remainders ("fair shares"). However, they are not yet able to verbalize all they know; consequently, the math curriculum must start by providing opportunities for language experiences. As the need begins to be fulfilled, another need arises naturally—to learn more about the "neat" and efficient ways arithmetic provides to record what they have learned to describe with language. But the ability to learn is unquestionable.

Many researchers, notably Piaget, report their observations of this natural learning process the ways children who are on their own learn without adult intervention. These researchers remain outside, uninvolved in the activity, thereby preserving its "naturalness." They are careful that they do not "contaminate" the process they are observing.

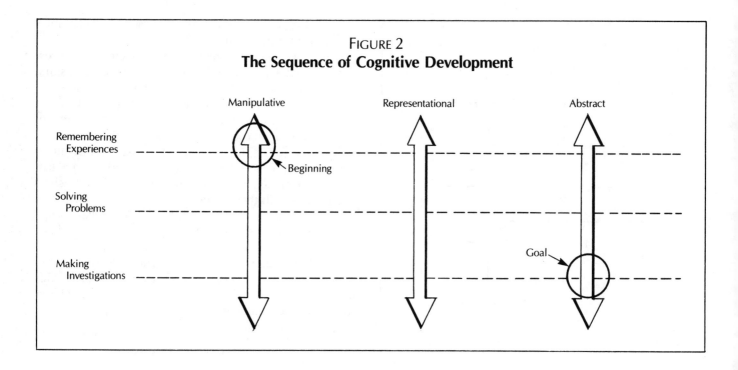

FIGURE 2
The Sequence of Cognitive Development

They report that children follow a common developmental pattern, maturing slowly through several stages according to some kind of innate timetable. They describe the basic development of ideas that children internalize and learn to use. All such notions are born out of "real and material action"—children responding to the sensory input that flows from the world about them. As familiarity grows, language begins. Gradually, children replace the three-dimensional context in which the idea originates with two-dimensional representations such as pictures, diagrams, sketches, and graphs. The language already developed is used to talk about things that can no longer be moved around. Eventually, these representations of the real world also fade out, and the idea is retained as a combination of visual images and language patterns. This slow transition from concrete to abstract is dependent on the continuing development of visualization, language, and thinking.

Other researchers, notably Jerome Bruner, are not content with observing and describing the natural learning process. They want to intervene in that process to help maximize children's development at higher cognitive levels—developing those potentials that are uniquely human. Only human beings can organize what we remember, enabling us to tackle problems and solve them. Moreover, human beings can progress to an even higher level—initiating and carrying on our own independent investigations.

In *The Relevance of Education,* Bruner (1971) wrote:

Discovery teaching generally involves not so much the process of leading students to discover what is "out there," but rather, their discovering what is in their own heads. It involves encouraging them to say, "let me stop and think about that"; "let me use my head"; "Let me have some vicarious trial and error." There is a vast amount more in most heads (children's heads included) than we are usually aware of, or that we are willing to try to use. You have to convince students (or exemplify for them, which is a much better way of putting it) of the fact that there are implicit models in their heads which are useful.

At a single sitting children can move from one cognitive level to another—from remembering experiences, to solving problems, to making independent investigations. Children can move from one level to another and back regardless of their progress along the developmental axis from concrete to abstract. Children can use their heads.

Any math curriculum that is fit for human consumption must provide a great variety of opportunities for activity at these higher cognitive levels. (This is true even though test makers have been able to monitor progress only at the levels of remembering experiences.) And mathematics is uniquely rich in problem-solving situations that can be tailored to meet a wide range of different needs.

The two-dimensional diagram in Figure 2 accommodates both the observers, such as Piaget, and the intervenors, such as Bruner.

Movement from left to right suggests a slow developmental process—ideas born in real and material action mature through a representational stage and finally grow into useful abstractions. This is essentially a one-way route. Movement back and forth from top to bottom suggests that higher levels of appropriate cognitive activities are available to all children at all times. Both movements have their origins in real and material action. The ultimate goal of education is shown as helping to provide all children with opportunities to enjoy making independent investigations at the abstract level.

Every strategy, every tactic, every activity in the math curriculum can be evaluated in terms of its contribution to continuous development of the process mapped by this diagram. This theory suggests there are always two optional ways to move ahead—toward increasing levels of abstraction and toward higher cognitive levels. It also suggests useful strategies to help learners who are confused or frustrated move back toward a less abstract level or to a lower cognitive level to build a more firm foundation before moving out again.

Conclusion

The math curriculum for the 80s must assume the responsibility to help children memorize what they need to memorize and to help all children understand the relationships that weave all of mathematics into a single tapestry. It must provide strategies that are responsive to the unique characteristics of rote memory—strategies designed to build understanding and to develop the language upon which understanding depends. Finally, it must offer suggestions for weaving the cognitive functions together in all learning activities.

REFERENCES

Bruner, Jerome. *The Relevance of Education.* New York: W. W. & Norton Company, Inc., 1971.
Piaget, Jean. *A Child's Concept of Number.* New York: W. W. & Norton Company, Inc., 1965.

18

The Thinking/Writing Connection

Carol Booth Olson

In his report on the current state of secondary education in America entitled *High School*, Carnegie Foundation President Ernest Boyer advocates that writing should be taught across the curriculum because "clear writing leads to clear thinking; clear thinking is the basis of clear writing." Perhaps more than "any other form of communication," he adds, "writing holds us responsible for our words and ultimately makes us more thoughtful human beings." In essence, Boyer's statement recognizes the thinking/writing connection—that depth and clarity of thinking enhance the quality of writing, while at the same time, writing is a learning tool for heightening and refining thinking.

This renewed emphasis on writing as a reflection of thinking comes at a time when the reasoning skills of American school children appear to be on the decline. For example, *Reading, Thinking and Writing*, a recent report of a national reading and literature assessment of over 100,000 nine-, thirteen-, and seventeen-year-olds cites as its "major and overriding" finding that although students at each age level had little difficulty making judgments about what they read, most lacked the problem solving and critical thinking skills to explain and defend their judgments in writing. According to the authors of this report (Applebee, Brown, Cooper and others), the results of this assessment do not point to any cognitive inability on the part of students to respond analytically. Rather, because of the current emphasis in testing and instruction on multiple choice, true/false and short answer responses, students are simply unused to undertaking critical thinking tasks. A separate study (Applebee, Auten, Lehr), corroborates these findings. In an intensive one year observation of two high schools,

researchers reported that 44 percent of the lesson time in six major subject areas involved writing activities of some kind; yet only 3 percent of that time was spent in writing tasks of a paragraph or longer.

What is important to note is that thinking and writing are interdependent processes—ways of making meaning out of experience. Both take *practice*. And that practice must be *sustained*. When one contrasts the current emphasis on teaching to the proficiency test with the expectations of higher education, one has to wonder when, where and how students will get the wide ranging practice in thinking and writing that will enable them to tap the full range of their cognitive potential.

Hilda Taba acknowledges the crucial role the teacher can play in providing students with the kind of practice that will facilitate cognitive growth when she concludes that "how people think may depend largely on the kinds of 'thinking experience' they have had. Writing is a complex and challenging thinking experience. In fact, researchers Flower and Hayes have observed, "Writing is among the most complex of all human mental activities." In order to produce a composition, writers must tap their memory to establish what they know, review the information they have generated and translate it into inner speech or print, organize main ideas, re-see the whole to find a focus, construct a structural framework for communicating an intended message, transform this network of thought into a written paper, and evaluate the product.

This description of the writing process mirrors the stages of the thinking process as portrayed in Bloom's Taxonomy of the Cognitive Domain—knowledge, comprehension, application, analysis, synthesis, evaluation. All of Bloom's levels of thinking recapitulate the writing process and vice versa (Figure 1).

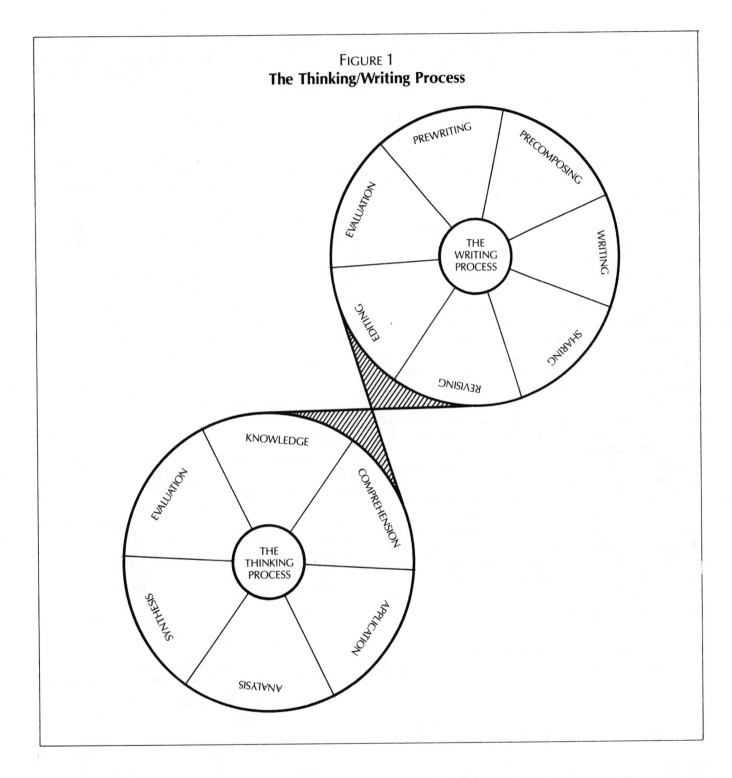

FIGURE 1
The Thinking/Writing Process

Thinking and writing are recursive processes in which one often has to go backward to go forward. It is admittedly somewhat appropriate, then, to describe the act of composing in a strictly linear fashion. However, whether evaluation should precede synthesis, whether one has to analyze in order to apply, or whether stages in the writing process can simultaneously tap two or more thinking levels does not alter the important point that composing involves all of the skills in the taxonomy.

Writing demands complex, intellective activity whatever the order of levels of thinking because while composing, writers must simultaneously entertain two main questions. The first is a content-oriented concern: What do I have to say? The second, a procedural concern that deals with transforming thought into print, focuses more on form and less on substance: How will I get my ideas into writing? Whether a student describes in rich sensory detail what it's like to eat an orange (a primarily comprehension-level task) or interprets and comments on the significance of the "Turtle Chapter" in *The Grapes of Wrath* (a predominantly analysis-level task), balancing the twin demands of the writing process taps all the levels of thinking.

Flower and Hayes have likened the writer in the act of composing to "a busy switchboard operator," juggling "constraints" and "working on cognitive overload."[1] Because students must grapple with such constraints as the limited knowledge they have to construct and express meaning, the imprecision of language they have to communicate what they know, the challenge of assessing their audiences and purposes for writing, and the demands of the contexts in which writing occurs,[2] it is not enough to simply *assign* writing tasks and anticipate spontaneous improvement in thinking. Practice in writing alone will not necessarily lead to enhanced thinking and writing skills. To facilitate the growth of problem-solving ability, teachers must carefully structure lessons that gradually increase the intellectual complexity and provide guided practice that makes the *what* in a paper more accessible to students and also allows them to focus more on the *how* of composing.

Virginia Baldwin, a teacher and consultant with the University of California, Irvine, Thinking/Writing Project, carefully crafted the lesson seen here (with annotations).[3] The lesson is organized according to the stage process model of composition—prewriting, precomposing, writing, sharing, revising, editing, and evaluating—and moves students through all of the levels of thinking—from knowledge through evaluation.

Writing Domain: Analytical/Expository

Thinking Level: Evaluation   Grade Level: Elementary (4-6)

PERSUASIVE LETTERS

Lesson:
Predicting possible reactions and meeting them with logical arguments, students will write a letter designed to persuade a specific audience to do something.

Objectives:
Thinking Skills—Students will function at the EVALUATION level by PREDICTING AND PERSUADING

Writing Skills—Students will be expected to write a persuasive letter that contains a well-supported argument directed toward a particular audience.

Although the lesson described here was designed for students in grades 4-6, it has been used successfully with a wide range of students, including adults, to guide the evaluation skills of predicting and persuading.

Prewriting

1. As a class, ask students to brainstorm *who* they have tried to persuade in the past, *what* they have tried to persuade them to do, *how* they tried to persuade them, and *what* the *results* were on the following chart:

What	Who	How	Results
Take me to the movies.	Big brother	Begged	Was mad but took me anyway,
Let me take skating lessons.	Mom	Panted and whined	Said, "No."
Stay all night.	Friend	Asked politely	Stayed
Buy me a bike.	Parents	Cried	Didn't buy it

2. Ask students to describe and explain orally their situations (*what, who*) to the class. Discuss the *how* and *results* columns.

3. Ask the class if anyone has ever tried writing a persuasive letter. If nobody has, suggest it and explain that letter writing can be a very effective tool for persuasion.

Prewriting activities generate ideas for writing. In any of its wide range of forms—class discussion, brainstorming, visualizing, free writing, and so on—prewriting aims to stimulate the free flow of thought. In this lesson, Baldwin asks students to share experiences in which they tried to persuade someone to do something, to allow something, or to give something. This activity stimulates student interest, elicits a wealth of examples, and sets the stage for introducing the prompt; that is, the writing assignment.

The Prompt

Choose one thing that you would like to persuade someone to do. Write a letter to persuade your chosen audience. Your letter should show that you have:

- Clearly stated what you want and why.
- Used a tone suited to your audience.
- Predicted two possible objections your audience might have.
- Shown logically that those objections have been considered and resolved.
- Followed the standard letter form of greeting, body, and closing.

Notice that the lesson now moves from past to present as students are asked to think of something they would like to persuade someone of *now*. Perry noted that one sign of cognitive growth is the ability to move from the stage of Basic Duality, where the world is perceived in absolutes, to a recognition that there is more than one approach to or perspective on a problem in the stage of Multiplicity.[4] In our sample lesson, the teacher encourages this transition in young children by asking them to anticipate the objections of their audience, presumably a parent, other trusted adult, teacher, or friend.

Precomposing

Focusing

4. Students may work in pairs, in groups, or individually. Ask students to choose one thing they would like to persuade someone to do (who, what) and enter the information in the first two columns of this chart:

Who	What	Possible Objections	Possible Arguments
Mom	Let me take three friends to Farrell's for my birthday.	1. 2. 3.	1. 2. 3.

Predicting objections of audience and experimenting with tone:

Oral Persuasion

5. Introduce the concept of tone by presenting students with this situation: Suppose you were certain that you had put your favorite record album in a special spot in your bedroom, and it's not there. After searching your room thoroughly and feeling frustrated, you must set out to question the following people about whether they've moved, misplaced, or taken your record:
- The housekeeper
- Your mom
- Your younger brother or sister
- A neighborhood friend who is always "borrowing" things without asking.
   a. What words and tone of voice would you use to inquire about the whereabouts of your record with each specific audience?
   b. How would your language and tone differ depending on your relationship with each person?
6. Explain to students that tone is used in writing as well as speaking. The tones one might verbally use can also be conveyed in writing, depending on nuances of chosen words.
7. Ask two students to role play the situation they chose during the Focusing Stage (see Step 4) in front of the class. Ask the students to identify which person is the *audience* and which person is the *persuader*. Before the role play begins, brainstorm characteristics of the *audience* that might influence their reactions. (For example, if a student wanted to persuade his mom to let him buy a boogie board, it would help the partner who is playing the role of his mom to anticipate her objections if she knew that Mom had earlier refused to let her son buy a skateboard because she was afraid he might fall and hurt himself.) *Persuaders* can experiment with different tones in attempting to persuade the chosen *audience*. Discuss which tones the *persuader* used that were most effective, and why.

8. Students should enter the possible reactions of audiences and possible arguments of the persuader on the chart:

Who	What	Possible Objections	Possible Arguments
Mom	Let me take three friends to Farrell's for my birthday.	1. It's too expensive. 2. 3.	1. I'll help pay with my allowance. 2. 3.

Transition from oral persuasion to written persuasion:

9. Help students make the transition from oral role play to written expression by conducting the following activity:

   a. On a lined sheet of paper, the persuader should request the audience to do something. Example: "Mom, will you let me take three friends to Farrell's for my birthday?"
   b. The audience should read the question silently, write a response according to his or her first possible reaction, and return it to the persuader. Example: "No, Farrell's is too expensive."
   c. The paper is passed back and forth in this manner until the audience is convinced or the persuader gives up.
   d. The persuader should then read over the dialogue and enter on another chart new possible reactions and possible arguments.
   e. Have the students switch roles and do the exercise again so that both students' charts are complete.

Who	What	Possible Objections	Possible Arguments
Mom	Let me take three friends to Farrell's for my birthday.	1. It's too expensive. 2. I don't know where Farrell's is.	1. I'll help pay with my allowance. 2. There's a Farrell's only two blocks from school.

10. Review the prompt and proper letter format with the class. Discuss possible opening statements they could use in their letters. (It is helpful to list them on the chalkboard.) Sample letter format:

	(date)
Greeting:	*Dear Mary,*
Body:	*It is really important to me that . . . .*
Closing paragraph:	*So, you see, this is why . . . .*
Closing:	*Sincerely,*
	(Signature)

11. Read a model to the class emphasizing the structure followed. Students may use their own structure but should include:
- What is wanted
- Reasons for wanting it
- Two possible objections
- Reasons to overcome the objections
- Closing summary

The following is a sample of the model.

(Continued)

(date)

Dear Mom,

    This year I would like to have my birthday party at Farrell's with three of my best friends. I've always wanted to go there because they sing "Happy Birthday" and play the big drum if you tell them it's your birthday.

    I know you probably will think that it will be too expensive, but it really won't be because I will pay for my friends' ice cream with my allowance. You won't need to give me any extra money because my ice cream will be free just because it's my birthday. That's why everyone likes to go to Farrell's on their birthday.

    You might not know where there is a Farrell's and be worried about driving with kids in the car. Guess what? There is a Farrell's just two blocks from school. We could walk and meet you there.

    I hope you will think about my idea and say "Yes." The only thing I really want for my birthday is to have a party at Farrell's. Please let me know what you decide.

                        Love,

                        Molly

Helping students generate ideas for writing is often not enough to enable them to organize and articulate their thoughts. **Precomposing** activities help students focus on the specific requirements of the prompt as well as formulate a writing plan. Since Baldwin's lesson calls for sophisticated critical thinking on the part of young students, it includes a very extensive precomposing stage to prepare them for writing. Students work in pairs and role play, first orally and then in writing, to generate a list of the possible objections they may encounter and to formulate reasons to overcome those anticipated objections.

Writing

12. Students write their letters referring to their lists of possible reactions of audience and possible arguments of persuader.

Writing is the stage in which thought is transformed into print. But more than that, it is an act of discovery. Often it is only as we write about what we think (and vice versa) that we grasp what it is that we truly want to communicate. Precomposing activities should facilitate and not inhibit the growth of thought that occurs in writing. The goal of the first draft should be fluency rather than refinement of ideas or expression.

In order for students to perceive writing as genuine communication and not just a chore to accommodate the teacher, opportunities must be provided for sharing writing—for giving and receiving feedback on work in progress. **Sharing** enables students to discover how their words affect other readers. **Responding** assists them in internalizing the criteria for good writing.

Sharing

13. Students share letters and help each other decide whether or not the letter will persuade the intended audience. Partners should underline the objections of the audience in red and arguments to overcome objections in green. Partners should also discuss whether or not the tone is appropriate for the audience. *Optional:* Partners may indicate a preliminary primary trait score (see Evaluation section).

Revising

14. Based on the feedback received, students should revise letters to make them more persuasive. They should consider the following questions:
- Is what I want clearly stated?
- Have I stated the reasons why I want it?
- Do the words I chose create the right tone for my audience?
- Did I include two possible objections?
- Are my arguments against those objections persuasive?
- Is my closing paragraph effective?

Editing

15. Students may edit their own letters or exchange them with a friend. The secondary trait scoring guide should be used as a reference (see Evaluation section).

Evaluation

16. *Primary Trait Scoring Guide:*

  3 This letter clearly states what is wanted and why, anticipates objections and meets them with logical arguments. It probably would persuade your audience because the arguments are presented in a tone suited to them.

  2 This letter presents persuasive arguments but does not anticipate the possible reactions of your audience. It might persuade them, but then again it might not.

  1 This letter would probably not persuade your audience since it is not presented in a tone suited to your audience and does not anticipate possible reactions or meet them with specific arguments.

17. *Secondary Trait Scoring Guide*

  2 This letter follows proper letter format, is neat and easy to read, and has no errors in spelling, mechanics, or usage. A letter like this is a pleasure to receive. Your audience will be impressed with your writing skills.

  1 This letter follows most of proper letter format but is not as neat and easy to read. It has a few errors in spelling, mechanics, or usage. If your primary trait score is high, your audience still *might* be persuaded.

  0 This letter is not neat or easy to read. It has many errors in spelling, mechanics, or usage. Even if your primary trait score is high, your audience probably would not do what you want them to since they might not be able to read it.

For many writers, editing occurs automatically as they compose. For those writers, editing is simply proofreading for minor errors in grammar, punctuation, spelling, and so forth. For students who have not acquired (or young writers who are still acquiring) the conventions of written English, it requires more conscious attention to correctness.

Although any revision is an act of self-evaluation, the evaluation stage of the composing process involves assessment of the final written product. Whether this rating comes in the form of a letter grade, holistic score, or analytic comment, the criteria on which the paper is to be judged should be clearly delineated and communicated early on in the writing process. Primary and secondary trait scoring guides allow the teacher to rank clarity and logic over details of format and correctness.

As mentioned previously, students need to see writing as a mode of genuine communication rather than as something artificially imposed. Positive perceptions of writing

as a useful, personal tool are fostered by a postwriting activity like publishing the writing in some form or, in this case, delivering the final product to the person for whom it is intended.

Finally, working from the premise that there is a developmental sequence in the growth of thought—that this sequence progresses from concrete to abstract levels, and that "the mental structures developed at a preceding stage are," as Taba says, "prerequisite to success in a subsequent one and are incorporated into it[5]—the teacher can use the Persuasive Letters lesson as a stepping stone to two other writing assignments that will provide additional practice in higher-level thinking and writing skills.

Regardless of whether one uses the stage process model of composition described in the Persuasive Letters lesson or another technique for facilitating written expression, the important point is that writing can and should be used as a learning tool across the curriculum for expanding and refining thinking. The most successful teachers of writing will think critically about critical thinking before designing curriculums. Writing develops thinking, after all, not so much from having students perfect any single written product or reaching the top of a critical thinking hierarchy, as much as from providing enough guided practice to cause students to internalize a workable problem-solving process.

Extension Activities

Application

Deliver the final letter to the audience it was intended for. Ask your audience to write back and tell you if your arguments were persuasive.

SUBSEQUENT EXTENSION ACTIVITIES

Analysis

Prompt: After reading Mark Twain's *Tom Sawyer*, explain how Tom persuaded his friends to whitewash the fence for him. How would you characterize the tone he used with his friends? Why do you think his approach to persuasion was effective?

Evaluation

Prompt: Choose a real audience at home or at school and try to convince them of something by writing a letter or composing a speech. You might try convincing:
- The teacher to give the class an extra recess.
- The principal to allow the class to raise money for a special field trip.
- The custodian to take you as a morning helper.
- Other classes to write letters and send art to homebound children or a children's hospital.
- Another school to exchange letters and art with your class.
- A community club to sponsor an activity at your school.
- Students at your school to write letters about endangered species legislation to members of Congress.
- Students at your school to write letters stating a position on the nuclear arms race to members of Congress.

FOOTNOTES

[1]Linda Flower and John R. Hayes, "The Dynamics of Composing," in *Cognitive Processes in Writing*, ed. Lee W. Gregg and Erwin R. Steinberg (Hillsdale, N.J.: Lawrence Erlbaum Associates, 1980), p. 33.

[2]Carl H. Frederiksen and Joseph F. Dominic, eds. "Introduction: Perspectives on the Activity of Writing," in *Writing: The Nature, Development, and Teaching of Written Communication* (Hillsdale, N.J.: Lawrence Erlbaum Associates, 1981), pp. 39-40.

[3]This letter appears in *Thinking/Writing: Fostering Critical Thinking Through Writing*, edited by Carol Booth Olson (Fund for the Improvement of Postsecondary Education, 1985). It was written by Virginia Baldwin, a teacher at Del Cerro Elementary School in Saddleback Valley United School District, and Teacher/Consultant from the University of California, Irvine, Thinking/Writing Project.

[4]William Perry, *Forms of Intellectual and Ethical Development in the College Years* (New York: Holt, Rinehart and Winston, 1970).

[5]Hilda Taba, *Thinking in Elementary School Children* (Washington, D.C.: U.S. Department of Health, Education and Welfare, Cooperative Research Project No. 1574, 1967), p. 12.

19

Reading and Thinking

Beau Fly Jones

Knowledge is the most powerful problem-solving tool there is. If I want to solve problems in mathematics I've got to have mathematical concepts. But there's a difference between teaching knowledge as a tool that facilitates problem solving and teaching it simply as a thing to be memorized.

—John Bransford

The definition of reading that arises from schema theory argues that meaning is not contained in the text (Rumelhart, 1980; Spiro, 1980). It is not enough for the reader merely to decode words in order to determine their meaning. Rather, reading involves an interaction of the reader, the information suggested in the text, and the characteristics of the context. The goal of reading, in this view, is to construct meaning from text.

This definition of reading raises two key questions: (1) What are the key characteristics of the reader, the text, and the context that affect comprehension? and (2) How do students process text-based instruction?

Characteristics of the Reader, the Text, and the Context

First, the reader's prior knowledge is critical and includes knowledge of content as well as learning strategies. Clearly, the greater the reader's knowledge of content and repertoire of reading and learning strategies, the greater the comprehension. Second, the reader's ability to control his or her own learning contributes significantly to the capability to comprehend. This capability, called metacognition (Armbruster and Brown, 1984), includes the capability

to plan, monitor comprehension, and evaluate what is learned. There is strong evidence that direct instruction in the use of metacognitive strategies can markedly improve comprehension (Paris, Cross, and Lipson, in press). There also appear to be individual differences in the ability to access prior knowledge and mediate one's own comprehension (Spiro, 1980).

Extensive research, conducted largely at The Center for the Study of Reading at the University of Illinois at Urbana, has shown that existing commercial materials often hinder comprehension because they lack appropriate connectives, pronoun references, and highlighting and signaling devices that help students understand the text (Anderson and Armbruster, 1984; Davison, 1984; Osborn, Jones, and Stein, 1985). Other comprehension problems arise from poor text design (Duchastel, 1982; Hartley, 1982).

Anderson and Armbruster have distinguished "considerate" from "inconsiderate" texts. The latter hinder or prevent comprehension because they are poorly written and are therefore inconsiderate to the reader. Considerate texts include various features that are intended to help readers learn. Four characteristics of considerate texts are *structure*—text structures that are well-organized and clearly signaled throughout the text; *cohesiveness*—the flow of

This chapter is a summary of a paper presented at the annual meeting of the American Educational Research Association, Chicago, April 1985. For further elaboration, see Jones, 1985, and Jones, Friedman, Tinzmann, and Cox, 1984.

The original research was conducted for the U.S. Army Research Institute, Contract No. MDA-903-82-069. The opinions and findings contained herein are those of the author and should not be construed as those of the Department of the Army or the North Central Regional Educational Laboratory.

ideas that is guided by text markers, connectives, and pronouns that help identify the text structure and the flow or arrangement of ideas; *unity*—the absence of irrelevant information and remarks; and *age appropriateness*.

Research on text design emphasizes additional features to help the reader learn:

● *Before reading*—reviews, previews, advance organizers, graphics, titles, subtitles, and paragraph headings emphasize the macro-structure or overall organizational pattern;

● *During reading*—underlining, boldfacing, italics, boxes, and marginal notes identify and emphasize important information from segments of the text;

● *After reading*—summaries and graphic organizers help students select important information and integrate information from diverse segments of text.

In schema-theory literature, context is traditionally defined in terms of the nature of the task and purpose for reading. Undoubtedly, these are powerful variables that influence reading rate, reading and study strategies, planning, and so on. Another context variable discussed at length in the research literature is the amount of knowledge about the text and the task that readers have access to as they read the text. Specifically, the information given about the task and setting of the story or message, the author's purpose, ancillary text features, and the reader's cultural background all influence his or her interpretation of the text.

More powerful than these variables, however, is the role of the teacher. According to the Commission on Reading (1985), the effects of the teacher are far more significant than the effects of instructional materials, curriculum alignment, and other variables. Specifically, the teacher is important as manager of instruction, with the ability to make effective decisions about content, pacing, grouping, and use of time (Berliner, 1984). Equally important, the teacher is a mediator of learning, providing instruction that is explicit, sustained, and interactive, guiding the students to construct meaning from text.

The Process: Comprehending and Responding to Text

The reader engages in different activities before, during, and after reading (Collins, Brown, and Larkin, 1980; Tierney, 1983). And in responding to essay questions about the text, the student progresses through various phases of planning, drafting, editing, and revising (Graves, 1978).

Before reading, a reader may use any of a variety of strategies to link new information to prior knowledge and to predict the gist of what the text will contain. These strategies include mentally reviewing previously acquired information; skimming the title, headings, subheadings, questions, and graphics; making hypotheses or predictions about the text's content or structure; self-questioning; prelearning new vocabulary; and so on. All of these strategies activate existing schemata or knowledge structures. Further, the reader determines the purpose of reading (for pleasure or for information) to plan the appropriate rate of reading and strategy (notetaking, for example).

During reading, the reader begins to refine earlier predictions and hypotheses, noting what is important and unimportant, what is clear and unclear, and possibly what analogies are relevant to the content. Depending on the purpose, the reader may use any of several strategies to encode and recall what is read: generative underlining (Rickards and August, 1975), inferring the main idea (Pearson and Leyes, in press; Wittrock, 1984), elaborating the text (Weinstein and Mayer, in press), forming analogies (Alexander and White, 1984; Sternberg, 1977), answering questions associated with the text (Brown and Palincsar, 1982), and so on. The reader may also engage in a number of innovative notetaking activities, such as matrix outlining (Jones, Amiran, and Katims, 1985) and fix-up strategies when the text is unclear (Anderson, 1980).

In this stage, readers also evaluate word meanings. Is a given word important? Can it be defined in the immediate context? In the distant context? Is it important enough to disrupt reading and look up in a dictionary? For words whose meaning is given, the reader may use various strategies to link the new word to prior knowledge, such as identifying a synonym or visualizing.

After-reading activities, like those during reading, depend on the purpose for reading. If the information is not to be processed in depth, memorized, or assessed for comprehension and retention, there may be few after-reading activities. If it is to be learned, however, the reader may engage in a number of activities to study what was read or monitor his or her own comprehension. Here the reader might outline or summarize the text, look back to check for mislearning, or reread what was unclear (Winograd, 1984).

Responses to essay questions are often part of the reading/thinking process. The teacher assigns essay questions to assess what the student has learned and to facilitate comprehension and writing skills. Throughout the country, the emphasis in writing instruction is largely process oriented (Applebee, 1981). While I fully support this emphasis in the context of language arts courses, other considerations obtain in the context of content courses. It is important to distinguish learning to write from writing to learn, which is obviously analogous to the distinction between learning to read and reading to learn (Herber, 1978). In learning to write, the focus of instruction should be process oriented.

However, it is important to be product oriented when

FIGURE 1
The Interaction of the Teacher, the Reader, and the Text
Stage I. Before Reading—Readiness Processing

Teacher Behaviors

1. Explains objectives (such as reading to learn) and identifies text to be read
2. May preteach or mention critical vocabulary
3. Asks students to skim title, subtitles, graphics, and questions, and to respond by making predictions/hypotheses
4. May generate questions to focus the students' attention
5. May provide or elicit extended review of previously acquired information
6. May provide advance organizers (such as outlines, graphics, previews, summaries)
7. Stimulates readers to generate the questions they want the selection to answer
8. May suggest or explain specific reading/learning strategy

Reader Behaviors

1. Mentally reviews prior knowledge of author, topic, and skills; considers reading rate
2. Becomes aware of new vocabulary and word meanings
3. Makes predictions/hypotheses about
   a. content and text structure
   b. type of responses indicated by the questions (such as compare/contrast, details)
4. Relates frame questions to titles, subtitles, graphics, and so on
5. May take notes
6. Begins to construct ideas about the text content and its relation to prior knowledge
7. Asks own questions
8. Recalls prior knowledge of reading/learning strategy

Learner Outcomes

1. Establishes purpose(s) of reading
2. Estimates rate of reading
3. Activates existing knowledge structures
4. Forms some rudimentary ideas about meaning

Stage II. During Reading—On-Line Processing

Text Characteristics

Context Text
1. Considerate/inconsiderate text
   a. structure
   b. cohesiveness
   c. unity
   d. age appropriateness
2. Vocabulary
3. Text condition
   a. explicit/literal
   b. implicit/inferential
   c. inadequate
4. Graphics
5. Questions

Instructional Text
1. Horizontal and vertical sequencing
2. Examples/models/explanations
3. Different modes of presentation
4. Guided and independent practice
5. Reviews/tests
6. Correctives/enrichment

Reader Behaviors

1. Decodes words; may visualize meaning
2. Pays special attention to new vocabulary words
3. Seeks to define unfamiliar words in context or with a dictionary
4. Begins to confirm or reject predictions and hypotheses
5. Searches for links to prior knowledge
   a. synonyms for new vocabulary
   b. analogies
6. Elaborates text by self-questioning and explanation, visualizing, taking a particular perspective, and so on
7. Searches for information to answer questions
8. May underline or take notes in prose or graphic form
9. Monitors comprehension; notes gaps and contradictions
10. Seeks to distinguish important from unimportant information

Learner Outcomes

1. Engages in reading and thinking
2. Generates surface-level understanding
3. Becomes aware of gaps in knowledge, possible errors
4. Refines hypotheses regarding content and responses to questions

Stage III. After Reading—In-Depth Processing

Teacher Behaviors

1. Discusses word meanings
2. Evaluates predictions/hypotheses made before reading
3. Monitors comprehension
   a. fills in gaps; corrects notes
   b. clarifies confusions
4. Guides students to construct
   a. graphic outlines
   b. graphic organizers
   c. explanations
5. Discusses author's purpose/different perspectives
6. Explains applications of comprehension strategy
7. Focuses on higher-order questioning strategies

Reader Behaviors

1. Links new word meanings to prior knowledge
2. Confirms/rejects earlier predictions/hypotheses
3. Evaluates comprehension; identifies important information; may engage in review or other fix-up strategies
4. Organizes notes, diagrams, and so on
   a. categorizes
   b. labels
   c. restructures
5. Analyzes author's purpose/perspective
6. Thinks about appropriate strategy
7. Engages in inferring, application, analysis, reasoning; tries to defend answers

Learner Outcomes

1. Constructs in-depth, organized meaning
2. Increases knowledge of concepts and facts
3. Gains knowledge of author's purpose, text structure, and content (idea) structure
4. Increases awareness of comprehension strategy taught and the process of comprehension monitoring

Stage IV. After Reading—Response Processing

Teacher Behaviors

1. Guides students to summarize passage and answer questions using notes, graphics, and so on
2. Discusses essay purpose and text structure (such as compare/contrast)
3. Guides students to organize notes for response to essay question(s)
4. Establishes criteria for prewriting, drafting, revisions, and editing; provides model response
5. Monitors writing process for class
6. Holds conferences with students
7. Reads/publishes selected essays

Reader Behaviors

1. Summarizes content orally or in writing; generates overviews
2. Plans text structure for essay; reviews appropriate text markers
3. Converts notes into outline for longer questions requiring a paragraph or essay; generates analogies, examples, and so on
4. Discusses notes, criteria; engages in self-questioning regarding audience, focus, point of view
5. Engages in prewriting, drafting, revising, and editing
6. Discusses ideas with teacher and other students
7. Reads other students' essays

Learner Outcomes

1. Increased in-depth processing
2. Increased comprehension of content
3. Increased retention
4. Increased knowledge of text structures and frames
5. Increased awareness of writing process and applications
6. Increased control over writing process

writing to learn if the student is expected to complete essay questions containing specific information and text structures in literature and other content courses. Observations of instruction in some of the most outstanding public and private schools in the country clearly show that good teachers provide what I term *response instruction* (Jones, 1985). Such teachers have very specific content and text structure objectives in mind when they give essay assignments (for example, compare/contrast two characters or situations in a novel). Moreover, teachers communicate these ideas to students in various ways: through course objectives, handouts, verbal explanations, modeling, comments on exam questions, and so on. I have even seen such teachers provide explicit essay writing instructions before testing. These efforts are to be commended, because writing objectives are often a hidden agenda in content courses as well as in language arts courses.

Model of Instruction

If comprehension is a process that involves different activities at different stages of reading—before, during, and after reading, and in responding to questions—then instruction should assist the reader at each of these stages (Anderson, 1980). Specifically, instruction, provided in materials or by the teacher, should help the reader construct meaning from text and should teach the reader to become an independent learner at each stage of the learning process. In many instances, instruction should teach readers a repertoire of reading and encoding strategies to use before and during reading, as well as in-depth study or learning strategies and writing skills they can use after reading. Additionally, instruction should provide students opportunities to learn which strategy is most appropriate for a given task or text condition, and it should give the criteria by which they will be judged and can judge themselves.

Figure 1 is a model of the interaction of the reader, the text, and the teacher at each stage of student cognitive processing. It provides an in-depth look at this interaction and identifies specific behaviors related to the role of the teacher as mediator.

Conclusions

The model of student cognitive processing I have presented incorporates research in reading, thinking, teaching, and instructional materials. It has led to three conclusions:

First, the teacher is critical in helping students process information from texts—whether the texts are for literature, content subjects, math, or problem solving; whether they are in print or electronic media; and whether they are

verbal or graphic. Given the importance of text-based instruction in all course areas and at all grade levels, it would be useful to researchers and practitioners alike to use the interaction model to document precisely what teachers do and say that helps students construct meaning from the various texts they read (Duffy, 1985).

Second, reading to learn—the act of constructing meaning from text—*is* fundamentally higher-order thinking at every stage of comprehending and responding to text. Therefore, it is as critical to define thinking skills with reference to research on reading and instructional materials as it is to define reading comprehension with reference to research on depth of processing and higher-order thinking. I hope the proposed model will facilitate this integration of ideas and data among researchers and practitioners.

Third, it is simply impossible to understand fully the teaching process or the model of instruction in any course without first understanding the characteristics of the textual materials and the interaction of the teacher, the reader, and the text. Given the preponderance of text-based instruction, this conclusion has implications for instructional design and research on teaching in all subject areas including those in higher-order thinking.

REFERENCES

Alexander, P. A., and White, C. S. "Effects of a Componential Approach to Analogy Training on Fourth Graders' Performance of Analogy and Comprehension Tasks: An Exploratory Investigation." Texas A&M University, College Station, Tex., 1984.

Anderson, T. H. "Study Strategies and Adjunct Aids." In *Theoretical Issues in Reading Comprehension*, pp. 483-502. Edited by R. J. Spiro, B. C. Bruce, and W. F. Brewer. Hillsdale, N.J.: Erlbaum, 1980.

Anderson, T. H., and Armbruster, B. B. "Content Area Textbooks." In *Learning to Read in American Schools: Basal Readers and Content Texts*, pp. 193-226. Edited by R. C. Anderson, J. Osborn, and R. J. Tierney. Hillsdale, N.J.: Erlbaum, 1984.

Applebee, A. N. *Writing in the Secondary Schools: English and the Content Areas*. NCTE Research Report No. 21. Urbana, Ill.: National Council of Teachers of English, 1981.

Armbruster, B. B., and Brown, A. L. "Learning from Reading: The Role of Metacognition." In *Learning to Read in American Schools: Basal Readers and Content Texts*, pp. 273-283. Edited by R. C. Anderson, J. Osborn, and R. J. Tierney. Hillsdale, N.J.: Erlbaum, 1984.

Berliner, D. C. "The Half-Full Glass: A Review of Research in Teaching." In *Using What We Know About Teaching*, pp. 51-77. Edited by P. L. Hosford. Alexandria, Va.: Association for Supervision and Curriculum Development, 1984.

Brown, A. L., and Palincsar, A. S. *Inducing Strategic Learning from Texts by Means of Informed Self-Control Training*. Technical Report No. 262. Urbana, Ill.: University of Illinois, Center for the Study of Reading, 1982.

Collins, A.; Brown, J. S.; and Larkin, K. M. "Inference in Text Understanding." In *Theoretical Issues in Reading Comprehension.* Edited by R. J. Spiro, B. C. Bruce, and W. F. Brewer, Hillsdale, N.J.: Erlbaum, 1980.

Commission on Reading. *Becoming a Nation of Readers.* Springfield, Ill.: Phillips Bros., 1985.

Davison, A. "Readability—Appraising Text Difficulty." In *Learning to Read in American Schools: Basal Readers and Content Texts.* Edited by R. C. Anderson, J. Osborn, and R. J. Tierney. Hillsdale, N.J.: Erlbaum, 1984.

Duchastel, P. C. "Textual Display Techniques." In *Principles for Structuring, Designing, and Displaying Text.* Englewood Cliffs, N.J.: Educational Technology Publications, 1982.

Hartley, J. "Designing Instructional Text." In *The Technology of Tests.* Englewood Cliffs, N.J.: Educational Technology Publications, 1982.

Herber, H. L. *Reading in the Content Areas.* (Text for Teachers.) Englewood Cliffs, N.J.: Prentice-Hall, 1978.

Jones, B. F. "Student Cognitive Processing of Text-Based Instruction: An Interaction of the Reader, the Text, and the Context." Paper presented at the annual meeting of the American Educational Research Association, Chicago, Ill., April 1985.

Jones, B. F.; Amiran, M. R.; and Katims, M. "Teaching Cognitive Strategies and Text Structures." In *Thinking and Learning Skills: Relating Instruction to Research.* Volume 1, pp. 259-296. Edited by J. Segal, S. F. Chipman, and R. Glaser. Hillsdale, N.J.: Erlbaum, 1985.

Jones, B. F.; Friedman, L. B.; Tinzman, M.; and Cox, B. E. *Content-Driven Comprehension Instruction: A Model for Army Training Literature.* (Technical Report.) Alexandria, Va.: Army Research Institute, 1984.

Osborn, J.; Jones, B. F.; and Stein, M. "The Case for Improving Textbooks." *Educational Leadership* 42 (1985): 9-17.

Paris, S. G.; Cross, D. R.; and Lipson, M. Y. "Informed Strategies for Learning: A Program to Improve Children's Reading Awareness and Comprehension." *Journal of Educational Psychology* (in press).

Pearson, P. D., and Leyes, M. "Application of an Explicit Skills Model in Developing Comprehension Instruction." In *Reading, Thinking, and Conceptual Development: Strategies for the Classroom.* Edited by E. J. Cooper and T. L. Harris. New York: The College Board, in press.

Rickards, J. P., and August, G. J. "Generative Underlining Strategies in Prose Recall." *Journal of Educational Psychology* 67 (1975): 860-865.

Rumelhart, D. E. "Schemata: The Building Blocks of Cognition." In *Theoretical Issues in Reading Comprehension.* Edited by R. J. Spiro, B. C. Bruce, and W. F. Brewer. Hillsdale, N.J.: Erlbaum, 1980.

Spiro, R. J. "Constructive Processes in Prose Comprehension and Recall." In *Theoretical Issues in Reading Comprehension.* Edited by R. J. Spiro, B. C. Bruce, and W. F. Brewer. Hillsdale, N.J.: Erlbaum, 1980.

Sternberg, R. J. *Intelligence, Information Processing, and Analogical Reasoning: The Componential Analysis of Human Abilities.* Hillsdale, N.J.: Erlbaum, 1977.

Tierney, R. J. *Learning from Text.* Reading Education Report No. 57. Urbana, Ill.: University of Illinois, Center for the Study of Reading, 1983.

Weinstein, C. E., and Mayer, R. E. "The Teaching of Learning Strategies." In *Handbook of Research on Teaching.* 3rd ed. Edited by M. C. Wittrock. New York: Macmillan, in press.

Winograd, P. N. "Strategic Difficulties in Summarizing Texts." *Reading Research Quarterly* 19 (1984): 404-425.

Wittrock, M. C. *Generative Reading Comprehension* (Ginn Occasional Reports). Boston: Ginn and Company, 1984.

20

How Scientists Think When They Are Doing Science

Arthur L. Costa

The mere formulation of a problem is often far more essential than its solution, which may be merely a matter of mathematical or experimental skill. To raise new questions, new possibilities, to regard old problems from a new angle requires creative imagination and marks real advances in science.

—Albert Einstein

What follows is a scientist's description of what he did and how he felt as he was working to solve a problem that perplexed him. In his description, he uses some names of objects and pieces of equipment with which you may be unfamiliar; however, the emphasis here is not on the equipment, but on the *thought processes* he used.

The scientist's description is accompanied by annotations that identify the cognitive processes of inquiry he used in solving his problem. The annotations are intended to illuminate the mental processes that are prerequisite and pervasive throughout the scientific process of inquiry.

Reading through the scientist's description first will give an overall picture of the scenario. A second reading, with attention to the annotations should help illuminate the process.

The Scientist's Description	**Annotations**
While supervising a student optical laboratory one afternoon, I was asked by a student using a Michelson interferometer what would happen if the light that had passed through the interferometer were dispersed by a grating. I replied that I thought the grating would merely diffract the light into its usual spectrum, and I suggested that he try it.	*The student is curious. He questions. The scientist draws on past knowledge and predicts what may happen.*
Using an inexpensive transmission grating, the student looked at the light coming from the Michelson interferometer and agreed that it produced the usual spectrum.	*The student observes the data.*
On closer observation, however, he noticed some dark bands in one region of the spectrum. The bands appeared only on the left side and covered a very limited region of the spectrum.	*When observations are made with greater precision, a discrepancy is noted.*

We found that when one light path in the interferometer was changed by adjusting the position of one mirror, the dark bands shifted to another region of the spectrum.

They experiment by changing one of the variables to determine its effect on the problem.

This immediately suggested an application for the dark-band phenomenon. It could be used to locate the white light fringes and bring them readily into the field of view of the interferometer—an adjustment that is usually tedious to make.

The scientist applies his initial explanation to solve an analogous problem.

For the next couple of days I was too busy to make further observations of the dark bands, but in spare moments I kept wondering what might be causing them.

Although he was able to arrive at an immediate explanation, he continues to ponder.

Suddenly, a couple of the observations that already had been made suggested to me that the dark bands might be white light fringes produced in the spectrum, even when the interferometer was not properly adjusted for white light fringes. It is well known that white light fringes are observed in an interferometer only when the paths traveled by the two interfering light beams are exactly equal.

Based on his observations, he draws a cause-effect relationship between the dark bands and the adjustment of the interferometer. He compares previously learned generalizations with this relationship to determine if they support each other.

I decided that the grating must somehow compensate for the unequal path lengths in the interferometer and equalize the total lengths for the light seen in the dark bands.

He theorizes, then concludes with an explanation of the cause of the event he originally observed.

With this idea in mind, I began to think about the problem even when I should have been doing other things. I scribbled drawings on pieces of scratch paper; repeated the observation in the laboratory; showed the phenomenon to colleagues, asking them if they had any explanations; and looked through a number of optics books to see if the effect had been observed and explained by others. No one seemed to have an explanation.

He makes drawings or models to represent his ideas. He seeks verification from others he thinks might have information. He does research hoping to gain further information.

As I struggled to find further relations between observations, I became more and more convinced that my idea about the compensating path lengths was correct. Finally, a sketch I drew during an airplane flight gave me a hint as to how the grating could equalize the path lengths and suggested an effect that I had not observed: moving the light source should cause the bands to shift.

He becomes increasingly intrigued with the problem; it consumes his attention. His theory is supported by information he gathers. He feels his explanation is gaining power.

That night I hurried to the laboratory to test my latest data. Quickly I set up a light source beside the interferometer and watched the dark band while moving the source.

He generates data to test his idea and observes the results.

Nothing happened. The position of the dark bands remained unchanged even when the light source was moved through large distances. My theory was no good, and I went to bed disgusted with the whole affair.

He compares the data generated with his theory. It does not fit; so he rejects his theory.

The next day, however, I redrew the sketch I made on the airplane and was struck with another idea. If moving the light source had no effect, then it must be the position of the grating that determines the location of the bands.

The scientist persists. He again draws models of his ideas. He makes another hypothesis—an "if-then" statement.

A more careful drawing of how the light traverses the interferometer and is diffracted by the grating convinced me that the location of the dark bands would change as the distance between the grating and the interferometer was changed, and as the angle of the interferometer mirror was changed.

He draws a more precise model, on which he bases another hypothesis of what should happen when variables are changed.

Again, I hurried into the laboratory to test this hypothesis.

He experiments to generate more information as a test of his hypothesis. He observes.

This time it worked!

The data he collected supports his explanation.

Now I knew I was on the right track and that I should be able to predict—quantitatively as well as qualitatively—where the dark bands would appear and how they would shift. With an even more careful drawn figure based on my new observations, it was not difficult to derive a mathematical formula that related the location of the dark bands to the path difference in the interferometer, the location of the grating, the angle of the interferometer mirror, the wavelength of the light, and the ruling spacing of the grating.

Now, knowing which variables are significant and how they interact, he is able to make a prediction. He formulates a mathematical model of the relationship.

The next day I was again scheduled to supervise the optics laboratory, so I decided to let the student who first asked about the phenomenon make the crucial test. I told him briefly about my theory and wrote down the formula I had derived. With excitement equal to mine, he set up the apparatus and made the necessary measurements.

He tests his theory by setting up the experiment and making observations.

We then entered the numbers in the computer and calculated where the bands should appear. His first calculation came out right on the nose.

They observe and record their information, and find that the data they gather "fit" the mathematical formula.

Since then the student has made many measurements to check the theory, and has found that it agrees with all observations.

The student continues to repeat the experiment to gather more data, thereby strengthening his explanation.

He is now engaged in a more thorough search of the literature to see if the theory has been published in any scientific journal. Even if he finds that it has, both of us will always remember the thrill we experienced that afternoon when the mathematical theory correctly predicted the phenomenon that we observed.

The student investigates other sources for agreement with his explanation. The scientist and his student are satisfied with their process.

In this description, we have traveled with a scientist as he discovered a problem, formulated possible theories, tested his explanations, rejected certain explanations, developed an explanation that corresponded to the data he generated, and converted the explanation into a mathematical formula.

Thus we have seen the intellectual processes of inquiry used to solve a rather simple scientific problem. Not everyone would have worked through that problem in the same way, nor would this scientist use the same processes in exactly the same way on his next problem. The important point is how this scientist applied effective thinking skills and attitudes that are basic and prerequisite to the scientific endeavor.

Author's note: My thanks to Graydon Bell, Physicist, Harvey Mudd College, Claremont, California, for permission to use this description.

21

Aesthetics: Where Thinking Originates

Arthur L. Costa

All information gets to the brain through our sensory channels—our tactile, gustatory, olfactory, visual, kinesthetic, and auditory senses. Those whose sensory pathways are open, alert, and acute absorb more information from the environment than those whose pathways are withered, immune, and oblivious to sensory stimuli. It is proposed, therefore, that *aesthetics* is an essential element of thinking skills programs. Cognitive education should include the development of sensory acumen.

Permeating the spirit of inquiry, inherent in creativity and prerequisite to discovery, the aesthetic dimensions of thought have received little concern or attention as a part of cognitive instruction. The addition of aesthetics implies that learners become not only cognitively involved, but also enraptured with the phenomena, principles, and discrepancies they encounter in their environment. In order for the brain to comprehend, the heart must first listen.

Aesthetics, as used here, means sensitivity to the artistic features of the environment and the qualities of experience that evoke feelings in individuals. Such feelings include enjoyment, exhilaration, awe, and satisfaction. Thus, aesthetics is the sensitive beginning of rational thought, which leads to enlightenment about the complexities of our environment. It may be that from within the aesthetic realm the skills of observing, investigating, and questioning germinate. These are bases for further scientific inquiry. Aesthetics may be the key to sustaining motivation, interest, and enthusiasm in young children; since they must become aware of their environment before they can explain it, use it wisely, and adjust to it. With the addition of

aesthetics, cognition shifts from a mere passive comprehension to a tenacious quest.

Children need many opportunities to commune with the world around them. Time needs to be allotted for children to reflect on the changing formations of a cloud, to be charmed by the opening of a bud, and to sense the logical simplicity of mathematical order. They must find beauty in a sunset, intrigue in the geometrics of a spider web, and exhilaration in the iridescence of a hummingbird's wings. They must see the congruity and intricacies in the derivation of a mathematical formula, recognize the orderliness and adroitness of a chemical change, and commune with the serenity of a distant constellation.

We need to observe and nurture these aesthetic qualities in children. Students who respond to the aesthetic aspects of their world will demonstrate behaviors manifesting such intangible values. They will derive more pleasure from thinking as they advance to higher grade levels. Their curiosity will become stronger as the problems they encounter become more complex. Their environment will attract their inquiry as their senses capture the rhythm, patterns, shapes, colors, and harmonies of the universe. They will display cognizant and compassionate behavior toward other life forms as they are able to understand the need for protecting their environment; respecting the roles and values of other human beings; and perceiving the delicate worth, uniqueness, and relationships of everything and everyone they encounter. After the period of inspiration comes the phase of execution; as children explore, investigate, and observe, their natural curiosity leads them to ask "What?" "How?" "Why?" and "What if?"

Children need help in developing this feeling for, awareness of, and intuitiveness about the forces affecting the universe—the vastness of space, the magnitude of time, and the dynamics of change. But can this attitude be taught in specific lesson plans and instructional models? Are steps for its development written in method books? Can we construct instructional theory for cognitive education that includes aesthetics as a basis for learning? Or do children derive this attitude from their associations and interactions with significant other adults who exhibit it?

Perhaps we need to identify teachers who approach thinking with an aesthetic sense. It may be teachers who generate awareness of the outside world in children. They are often the underlying inspiration for children to become ardent observers and insatiable questioners. Teachers may be the ones who develop in others a compassionate attitude toward the environment and a curiosity with which they go wondering through life—a prerequisite for higher-level thought.

22

Thinking Across the Disciplines: Publications and Programs

Arthur L. Costa

Publications

The following is a selected list of publications emphasizing the interrelationships between thinking and the various disciplines commonly taught in schools.

GENERAL

Eisner, E., ed. **Learning and Teaching the Ways of Knowing.** 84th Yearbook of the National Society for the Study of Education, Part II. Chicago: University of Chicago Press, 1985.

THE ARTS

Getzels, Jacob, and Csikszentmihalyi, M. **The Creative Vision: A Longitudinal Study of Problem Finding in Art.** New York: Wiley, 1976.

Howard, V. A. **Artistry, The Work of Artists.** Indianapolis: Hackett, 1982.

Perkins, David, and Leondar, Barbara, eds. **The Arts and Cognition.** Baltimore: Johns Hopkins University Press, 1977.

Sinatra, R. **Visual Literacy Connections to Thinking, Reading, and Writing.** Springfield, Ill.: Charles C Thomas, 1986.

LANGUAGE ARTS

Eco, Umberto. **A Theory of Semiotics.** Bloomington: Indiana University Press, 1976.

Hays, Janice, and others. **The Writer's Mind.** Urbana, Ill.: National Council of Teachers of English, 1983.

Jones, B. F. **Chicago Mastery Learning: Reading** (2nd ed.) Watertown, Mass.: Mastery Education Corp., 1982.

Sinatra, R., and Stahl, Gemake. **Using the Right Brain in the Language Arts.** Springfield, Ill.: Charles C Thomas, 1983.

Thaiss, Christopher, and Suhor, Charles, eds. **Speaking and Writing, K-12: Classroom Strtegies and the New Research.** Urbana, Ill.: National Council of Teachers of English, 1984.

SOCIAL SCIENCES

Branson, M. **Inquiry Experiences in American History.** Lexington, Mass.: Ginn and Co., 1975.

Carpenter, H. M., ed. **Skill Development in Social Studies.** Washington, D.C.: National Council for the Social Studies, 1963.

Ehman, L; Mehlinger, H.; and Patrick, J. **Toward Effective Instruction in Secondary Social Studies.** Boston: Houghton Mifflin, 1974.

Fair, Jean, and Shaftel, Fannie. **Effective Thinking in the Social Studies.** 37th Yearbook of the National Council for the Social Studies. Washington, D.C.: N. C.S.S., 1967.

Kurfman, D., and Soloman, R. **Measurement of Growth in Skills in Selected Social Studies Skills.** Boulder, Colo.: Social Science Education Consortium, 1963.

Phillips, R. C. **Teaching for Thinking in High School Social Studies.** Reading, Mass.: Addison Wesley, 1974.

MATHEMATICS

Whimbey, Arthur. **Analytical Reading and Reasoning.** Stamford, Conn.: Innovative Science Inc., 1983.

Whimbey, A., and Lochhead, J. **Developing Math Skills:**

Computation and Problem Solving. New York: McGraw Hill, 1982.

SCIENCE

Rowe, Mary. **Teaching Science as Continuous Inquiry.** New York: McGraw Hill, 1978.

Harms, Norris, and Yager, R. E. **What Research Says to the Science Teacher,** Vol 3. Washington, D.C.: National Science Teachers Association, 1981.

Hufstedler, S., and Langenberg, D. **Science and Engineering Education for the 1980's and Beyond.** Washington, D.C.: Superintendent of Documents, U.S. Government Printing Office, 1980.

PHYSICAL EDUCATION

Gallwey, T. **Inner Game of Golf.** New York: Random House, 1981.

Gallwey, T. **Inner Game of Tennis.** New York: Bantam Books, 1981.

Gallwey, T. **Inner Skiing:** New York: Bantam Books, 1982.

Garfield, C., and Bennett, H. **Peak Performance: Mental Training of the World's Greatest Athletes.** New York: Random House, 1974.

Programs

The following is a list of some of the major curriculum programs that teach thinking skills and methods of inquiry through subject matter. Brief annotations as well as sources for more detailed information are provided.

GENERAL

Thinking and Learning, developed by Selma Wassermann, Simon Fraser University, Burnaby, British Columbia, Canada. Published by Coronado Publishers, Inc., San Diego, California.

Includes a teacher's manual, teacher cards that describe how to use the program, posters, and over 100 student color-keyed cards. Each cognitive operation—observing, comparing, classifying, imagining, identifying assumptions, making hypotheses, solving problems, and making decisions—is identified by a different color. Using a variety of curriculum areas (including social studies, language arts, mathematics, music, and science), students follow the directions on their cards and perform the thinking skills involved in each activity.

SCIENCE AND HEALTH

Individualized Science Instructional System (ISIS), developed by the Florida State University, College of Education, 414 Monroe St., Tallahassee, FL 32301. Project Director, Ernest Burkman. Published by Ginn and Co., Lexington, Massachusetts.

ISIS is an individualized science program designed to provide direct experience in planning and conducting investigations, observing, interpreting data, keeping records, checking conclusions, and making hypotheses.

Health Activities Project (HAP), developed by Lawrence Hall of Science, University of California, Berkeley, CA 94720. Project Director, Robert Knott. Published by Hubbard Publishers, Northbrook, Illinois.

Involves 4th through 8th graders in an investigative/discovery approach to health, safety, and bodily functions.

Outdoor Biology Instructional Strategies (OBIS), developed by Lawrence Hall of Science, University of California, Berkeley, CA 94720. Project Director, Robert Knott. Published by Delta Education Inc., Tyngsboro, Massachusetts.

Through games, simulations, crafts, experiments, and data analysis, OBIS emphasizes the interaction of organisms with each other and the environment. It is intended for 10- to 15-year-olds but can be adapted for younger and older participants, including families.

Unified Sciences and Mathematics for Elementary Schools (USMES), developed by Educational Development Center, 55 Chapel St., Newton, MA 02158. Project Director, Earl L. Lomon. Published by Moore Publishing Co., Durham, North Carolina.

An interdisciplinary program that challenges students to solve real problems that occur naturally in their school and community environments.

Human Sciences Program (HSP), developed by Biological Sciences Curriculum Study, P.O. Box 930, Boulder, CO 80306. Project Director, Norris Ross. Published by C & F Associates, Batavia, Illinois.

Intended for 10- to 14-year-olds and designed to expand the experiential base required for transition to Piaget's stage of formal operational thinking.

Science Curriculum Improvement Study (SCIS), developed by Robert Karplus and Herbert Thier, Lawrence Hall of Science, University of California, Berkeley, CA 94720. Published by Delta Education Inc., Nashua, New Hampshire.

Materials and teacher guides help elementary school children explore a variety of scientific concepts, including interactions and systems, material objects, relative positions, subsystems, and variables. Develops students' abilities to observe, hypothesize, predict, and solve problems.

Elementary Science study (ESS), developed by Educational Development Center, 55 Chapel St., Newton, MA 02158. Published by McGraw-Hill, Novato, California.

Consists of over 40 instructional units with materials and teacher guides. Teacher guides suggest open-ended questions that lead students to observe, investigate, gather information, test hypotheses, and solve problems.

Voyage of the Mimi, developed by Bank Street College, New York.

A multicomponent system of software, videotapes, and printed material that requires students to solve problems encountered on a sailing voyage (including navigation and searching for whales).

MATH

CDA Math, developed by Robert Wirtz, Curriculum Development Associates, 1211 Connecticut Ave., N.W., Washington, DC 20036. Published by Curriculum Development Associates, Washington, D.C.

Based on the theories of Bruner and Piaget, develops language and problem-solving ability of students in a logical/developmental manner.

Comprehensive School Mathematics Program. Project Director, Claire Heidema, 470 N. Kirkwood Rd., St. Louis, MO 63122.

An experimental (but not strictly Piagetian) approach to teaching mathematics that uses a spiral curriculum.

British Primary Schools Materials, developed by Nuffield Mathematics. Published by John Wiley & Sons, Inc., 605 Third Ave., New York, NY 10158.

Includes directions for teachers in conducting and organizing science and mathematics instruction in the British primary schools. It is intended for 5- to 13-year-olds.

SOCIAL STUDIES

Law in a Free Society (LFS), developed by Center for Civic Education, 5115 Douglas Fir Rd., Suite I, Calabasas, CA 91302. Project Director, Charles N. Quigley. Published by the Center for Civic Education, Calabasas, California.

Students from grades K-12 engage in reading, writing, and discussion involving Socratic inquiry techniques; simulations of appellate court, administrative, and legislative hearings; and the use of "intellectual tools" to understand and apply the fundamental concepts of authority, justice, responsibility, and privacy.

Man: A Course of Study (MACOS), developed by Jerome Bruner, Education Development Center, 55 Chapel St., Newton, MA 02158. Published by Curriculum Development Associates, Washington, D.C.

Organized around the conceptual question, "What makes man human?" MACOS aims to develop students' questioning processes, research methodologies, discussion skills, reflective thought, and hypotheses development and substantiation skills using a variety of data sources. It shifts the role of the teacher to one of a resource/facilitator rather than authority.

U.S. History Data Base for P.F.S. File, published by Scholastic Inc., P.O. Box 7502, Jefferson City, MO 65102.

Consists of a series of six disks, each with a corresponding activity unit. Three teach students how to use the data files, and the other three teach students to build their own files. Students become actively involved in manipulating data, building and testing hypotheses, and perceiving relationships and trends over time among events, people, and places in U.S. history.

One World: Countries Data Base, developed by Active Learning System, P.O. Box 197, Indooroopilly, Queensland, Australia 4068.

Begins with the input of simple data and advances to the analysis of information, perception of new relationships, and comparisons among data. Uses formal logic and syllogistic thinking to interpret data. (Other data base curriculums under development include USA Profile; Rocks and Classification; The Whales; Ecology and Environmental Studies; Town Planning; Man's Major Achievements in the Sciences and Arts; Voyages of Discovery; Space Exploration; and Time Lines in Modern, Asian, Australian, European, and American History.)

Critical Analysis and Thinking Skills (CATS), developed by Terry Applegate, 4988 Kalani Dr., Salt Lake City, UT 84117.
Instruction may be integrated into existing social studies and language arts courses in grades five and above. Teaches research skills, critical reading, discriminating between fact/opinions/inferences/implications; predicting consequences, assessing credibility; and promotes effective oral and written communication.

THE ARTS

Developing Creative Thinking Skills, developed by Institute for Creative Education, Educational Improvement Center, Box 209, Rt. 4, Sewell, NJ 08080.
Student exercises using imagery, sensory awareness, brainstorming, relaxation, meditation, analogy, and so on may be used at any grade level and with any ability level. Useful in creative writing and visual arts programs.

PART VI

Teacher Behaviors That Enable Student Thinking

Arthur L. Costa

Teachers are the ones who touch students and interact with them. They are the ones who implement educational policy and curriculum content, scope and sequence. And—most important—they are the ones who establish the educational climate and who structure learning experiences. In short, they have almost complete power over the process that takes place in the classroom. And it is my contention that process is more important than content in education.

—J. J. Foley

What the teacher says and does in the classroom greatly affects student learning. Over the past 15 years much research has demonstrated that certain teacher behaviors influence students' achievement, self-concept, social relationships, and thinking abilities.

This chapter attempts to explain and justify the use of certain teacher behaviors that invite, maintain, and enhance students' thinking in the classroom. These behaviors fall into four major categories:

1. *Questioning* to help students collect and recollect information, process that information into meaningful relationships, and apply those relationships in different or novel situations.

2. *Structuring* the classroom by arranging for individual, small-group, and total-group interaction; managing the resources of time, energy, space, and materials to facilitate thinking, and legitimizing thinking as a valid objective for students.

3. *Responding* to help students maintain, extend, and become aware of their thinking.

4. *Modeling* desirable intellectual behaviors in the day-to-day problems and strategies of the classroom and school.

Dillon (1984) distinguishes two types of classroom interaction: recitation and discussion. Recitation is characterized by recurring sequences of teacher questions plus student answers, where students "recite" what they already know or are learning through the teacher's questioning. The interaction is teacher-centered. The teacher controls by asking the questions and reinforcing responses.

Discussion, on the other hand, involves group interaction in which students discuss what they don't know; students put forth and consider more than one point of view on a subject. The teacher, the discussion leader, facilitates by creating an atmosphere of freedom, clarity, and equality. John Goodlad in his Study of Schooling (1984) found that only 4 to 8 percent of classroom time was spent in discussion. Less than 1 percent of teacher talk was intended to elicit a student response.

This latter definition of classroom interaction—discussion—must be kept in focus as we consider which teacher behaviors are facilitative. Analyses of major programs and instructional strategies intended to enhance thinking, creativity, cooperation, and positive self-worth stress the need for this dialectic discussion strategy (Costa, 1984; Paul, 1984).

Teachers' Questions and Statements That Cause Thinking

Early in their school experience, children learn to listen and respond to the language of the teacher. From questions and other statements that the teacher poses, students derive their cues for expected behavior. Questions are the intellectual tools by which teachers most often elicit the de-

A Teacher's Testimonial

After the inservice on teacher behaviors and their consequences on students' thinking, I decided to test some of the theories in the sophomore biology class I teach. I was particularly interested in examining my questioning behaviors and students' responses to them. I was also curious about the effects of silence and nonjudgmental acceptance. When I began the grand experiment, I immediately discovered how difficult it is to structure questions and watch for reactions at the same time.

Given this limitation, I consciously practiced my questioning and response behaviors during a two-week period and began to notice a number of things evolving in the class.

First, the time I spent on lecturing to students declined. There was a shift to a more Socratic format as students became accustomed to processing and applying information. They appeared to become actively involved in what was going on, rather than passively taking notes and listening.

Second, some students who did not participate in class began to join in the discussions. These students seemed to come to an understanding of the material after they had the opportunity to talk about it. The number of "relevant" student questions increased, and students generally began to accept the position that it is not necessary for an answer to be right to be acceptable. More than one answer may solve the same problem.

Third, as I began "accepting" solutions to problems as plausible, more students risked answers. The level of anxiety decreased as students realized their answers wouldn't be classified as either right or wrong. I think that in the process, students were getting much needed practice in using their higher-order cognitive skills.

Finally, I've noticed an increase in test scores on inquiry/application questions. I'm not sure that this increase is due to students becoming more familiar with the test format or to gaining experience in solving these types of questions in class. I hope that it is the latter. Maybe it's a combination of both.

Although this "experiment" in no way reflects the scientific model, it has increased my sensitivity to the need for me to monitor my own behaviors in the classroom. What I do and the manner in which I do it has direct bearing on student behavior and learning.

Ron Edwards, Teacher
Jesuit High School
Sacramento, California.

sired behavior of their students. Thus, they can use questions to elicit certain cognitive objectives or thinking skills. Embedded in questions and other statements are the cues for the cognitive task or behavior the student is to perform (Davis and Tinsley, 1967).

There is a relationship between the level of thinking inherent in teachers' verbal behavior and the level of thinking of their students (Measel and Mood, 1972). Correlations have been found between the syntax of the teacher's questions and the syntax of the student's response (Cole and Williams, 1973). Furthermore, teachers whose questions more frequently require divergent thinking produce more divergent thinking on the part of their students, in contrast

to teachers who use more cognitive memory questions (Gallagher and Ashner, 1963). Students score higher on tests of critical thinking and on standardized achievement tests when teachers use higher-level cognitive questions (Newton, 1978; Redfield and Rousseau, 1981).

Realizing that teachers can cause students to think by carefully designing the syntax of questions and other statements, let us now return to the Model of Intellectual Functioning, described in Part III, Chapter 12. This model will serve as a basis for the composition of questions. Teachers can cause students to perform the intellectual functions represented in this model (Figure 1) by composing questions and other statements with certain syntactical arrangements.

Thus, with a model of intellectual functioning in mind, the teacher can manipulate the syntactical structure of questions and other statements to invite students to accept information, to process or compare that information with what they already know, to draw meaningful relationships, and to apply or transfer those relationships to hypothetical or novel situations.

The following sections provide examples of questions or statements that the teacher might pose to cause students to take in information—through the senses or from memory; to process that information; and to apply, transfer, or evaluate relationships in new or hypothetical situations.

Gathering and Recalling Information (Input)

To cause the student to *input* data, the teacher can design questions and statements to draw from the student the concepts, information, feelings, or experiences acquired in the past and stored in long- or short-term memory. Questions can also be designed to activate the senses to gather data that students can then process at the next higher level. There are several cognitive processes included at the *input* level of thinking. Some verbs that may serve as predicates of behavioral objective statements are: completing, counting, matching, naming, defining, observing, reciting, selecting, describing, listing, identifying, and recalling.

Examples of questions or statements designed to elicit these cognitive objectives are:

Question/Statement	*Desired Cognitive Behavior*
Name the states that bound California.	Naming
How does this picture make you feel?	Describing
What word does this picture go with?	Matching
What were the names of the children in the story?	Naming

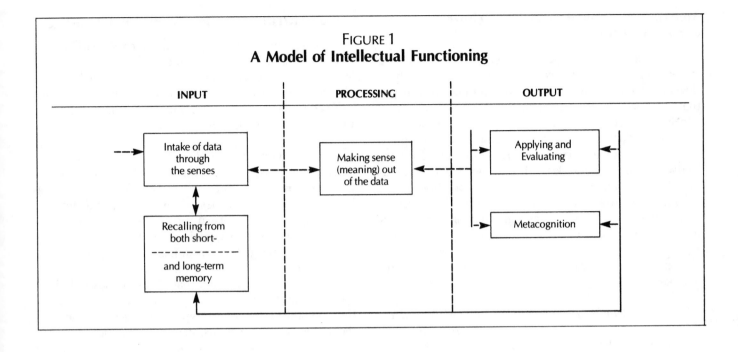

FIGURE 1
A Model of Intellectual Functioning

| INPUT | PROCESSING | OUTPUT |

How many coins are in the stack?	Counting
Which words on this list are rhyming words?	Selecting
Mexican houses were made of mud bricks called _____.	Completing
List the first four numbers in a set of positive integers.	Listing
How did you feel about the grade you received in algebra?	Recalling

Making Sense of Gathered Information (Processing)

To help students process the data gathered through the senses and retrieved from long- and short-term memory, teachers' questions and statements should prompt students to draw relationships of cause and effect, to synthesize, analyze, summarize, compare, contrast, or classify the data they have acquired or observed. Following are some verbs that may serve as the predicates of behavioral objective statements if the desired cognitive behavior is at the processing level: synthesizing, analyzing, categorizing, explaining, classifying, comparing, contrasting, stating causality, inferring, experimenting, organizing, distinguishing, sequencing, summarizing, grouping, and making analogies.

Examples of questions or statements designed to elicit these cognitive objectives are:

Question/Statement	*Desired Cognitive Behavior*
Why did Columbus believe he could get to the east by sailing west?	Explaining
What do you think caused the liquid to turn blue?	Stating causality
What other machines can you think of that work on the same principle as this one?	Making analogies
How can you arrange the blocks to give a crowded feeling?	Organizing
How are pine needles different from redwood needles?	Contrasting
How does the formula for finding the volume of a cone compare with the formula for finding the volume of a pyramid?	Comparing
Arrange the following elements of a set in ascending order: 13/4, 3/2, 5/6, 32/5.	Sequencing
From our experiments with food coloring in different water temperatures, what can you infer about the movement of molecules?	Inferring

Applying and Evaluating Actions in Novel Situations (Output)

Questions and statements that lead to *output* require students to go beyond the concepts or principles they have developed and to use this relationship in novel or hypothetical situations. Application invites students to think creatively and hypothetically, to use imagination, to expose or apply value systems, or to make judgments. Following are some verbs that may serve as predicates for behavioral objective statements if the desired cognitive behavior of students is at the application level: applying a principle, imagining, planning, evaluating, judging, predicting, extrapolating, creating, forecasting, inventing, hypothesizing, speculating, generalizing, model building, and designing.

Examples of questions designed to elicit these cognitive objectives are:

Question	*Desired Cognitive Behavior*
If our population continues to grow as it has been, what will life be like in the 21st century?	Speculating
What can you say about all countries' economies that are dependent on only one crop?	Generalizing
What would be the fairest solution to this problem?	Evaluating
From what we have learned, which painting is the best example of modern art?	Judging
What do you think might happen if we placed the saltwater fish in the freshwater aquarium?	Hypothesizing

Teachers have awesome power. Through the careful and selective use of questions and other statements, they can elicit, invite, and cause students to perform these cognitive behaviors. As a result of such questions, over time students should be able to:

1. Develop the relationship between the verbal syntax and the mental processes.

2. Experience and thus exercise these mental functions.

3. Become aware of these cognitive processes.

4. Apply these cognitive processes beyond the classroom.

5. Understand and appreciate teachers' invitations to think.

6. Increase their own inclination and desire to ask a range of questions.

Structuring the Classroom for Thinking

Structuring may be described as the way teachers control such classroom environmental resources as time, space, human energy, and materials. Every teacher in every classroom structures those resources, either consciously or unconsciously, directly or indirectly. Even the "unstructured" classroom imposes a structure to which and within which students interact.

Research on school and teaching effectiveness has repeatedly demonstrated that higher student achievement is produced in a well-structured classroom where students know the objective of the lesson, time is used efficiently, the teacher is clear about the directions, the classroom environment conveys a congenial sense of order, and student energies are engaged in a meaningful learning task.

Structuring the classroom for thinking should be conscious, deliberate, clear, and based on the desired objectives for the students. Knowing what learning tasks are to be accomplished and what type of interaction is desired, the teacher gives directions, states ground rules, describes objectives, places limits and constraints, and creates a classroom organizational pattern intended to best accomplish the desired cognitive performance of students.

There are three central aspects of teacher structuring:

1. The clarity of verbal and written instructions.

2. The structuring of time and energy.

3. Different ways of organizing and arranging interaction patterns.

Instructional Clarity

Teacher: "Why do you think Robert Frost repeated the last line of this verse?"

Student: (No response)

Teacher: (After a long pause) "Well, what feelings did *you* have as you read the poem?"

Student: "Why don't you just tell us the answer?" (Wasserman, 1978)

Students expend great amounts of energy trying to figure out teachers' intentions. Because some students come from homes, previous teachers, or other schools where thinking skills were not valued, they often are dismayed and resistant to the teacher's invitations to think. Such resistance and reluctance to respond should be taken as an indication that a program to develop intellectual skills is sorely needed.

Teachers must convey to students that the goal of instruction is thinking, that the responsibility for thinking is theirs, that it is desirable to have more than one solution, that it is commendable when they take time to plan, that an answer can be changed with additional information.

Research in classroom management seems to indicate that the clarity and purposefulness of the teacher's directions concerning a new learning task affect student behavior. If the messages and directions presented by the teacher are confused, garbled, and unclear, then students will have a more difficult learning task. Similarly, providing too many details at one time and repeating information that the students already know increases class restlessness and the possibility for nonattentiveness (Kounin, 1970).

Rosenshine and Furst (1971) placed teacher clarity at the top of their list of effective instructional behaviors. Teacher clarity is consistent and positively associated with student achievement. Some of the observations of instructional clarity focus on teachers' vagueness, redundancy, and use of mazes. Conversely, students increase their understanding of directions when the teacher frequently repeats concepts from one sentence to the next or says the same thing in more than one way; reviews prior work; prepares students for upcoming tasks by describing the work to be done and how to do it; allows time for students to think about, respond to, and synthesize what they are learning; uses visual and verbal examples; reviews difficult concepts on the chalkboard; and models the type of performance required in the task.

It seems imperative, therefore, that teachers convey to students their objectives, instructional strategies, and assessment procedures so that students will realize thinking is a legitimate goal of education.

Structuring Time and Energy

While much research has demonstrated that achievement (in basic skills at certain grade levels as measured by standardized tests) correlates highly with the amount of *time* students are successfully engaged in learning (Borg, 1980; Stallings and Kaskowitz, 1974; McDonald, 1976), this same proposition holds true for teaching thinking.

But how much time is enough? This can only be answered in terms of the needs of a particular population of students. A survey of the most popular curriculums and programs for teaching thinking suggests that at least two to three hours per week with carefully designed materials and well-planned and executed lessons are needed to permanently affect students' cognitive abilities. Furthermore, it seems this intensity needs to be maintained for at least two years for mastery of these mental functions.

With an educational organization that typically tracks students in one-year or -semester segments and 55-minute periods, it may prove difficult to provide such intense instructional continuity. Furthermore, emphasis on thinking cannot be viewed by the student as an isolated event occurring only when an itinerant teacher arrives, or from 2:00 to 2:53 each Thursday. Rather, students must repeatedly receive instruction in cognitive skills and encounter situations requiring the need to think throughout the school day, across academic content areas, and over extended periods of time. As a result, there is greater possibility for transference, generalization, and application of that cognitive skill (Sternberg and Wagner, 1982, pp. 50, 53). For some schools, this may require a reconsideration of curriculum goals, school organization, allocation of time, and assessment procedures.

Structuring time alone, however, is inadequate. Consideration must also be given to the quality of the task during that time: the degree that students' *energies* are engaged. According to Piaget's constructivist theory, all knowledge arises—or is constructed—from interactions between learners and their environment. That is, to the extent that teachers mediate the interaction of pupils with instructional materials and with the content of the lesson, those skills are likely to be learned. Much research has also shown that *active* learning has a positive effect on students' development of decision-making and problem-solving skills (Thomas, 1980), and their attitude toward school, teachers, the content to be learned, and learning itself (Kahn and Weiss, 1973).

This research strongly suggests that teachers organize their classrooms in a variety of ways so that students become actively involved in thinking—not passive. This might include teacher-led, Socratic-type discussions, individual manipulations, and cooperative small-group or total-group investigations.

Structuring Classroom Organizational Patterns for Thinking

Of all the various patterns of classroom organization that a teacher might use, some seem to get better results than others for certain students at certain grade levels and for certain goals of instruction. Gage (1976) and McDonald (1976) report that students learn more in a question-and-answer discussion strategy. Greater gains were found for 5th grade reading when teachers spent time discussing, explaining, asking higher-level questions, and stimulating cognitive processes. Group work with individual monitoring by the teacher seemed best for reading while less group work proved best for math.

Individual work seemed very ineffective if not carefully monitored by the teacher. Students were "off-task" more and a greater number of errors went uncorrected if the teacher did not constantly monitor individual students' learning.

The lecture method has long been found wanting in terms of student learning. Early studies have shown that there are vast individual differences in the amount of learning assimilated by students through lecture (Jones, 1923).

But . . . Do I Have The Time To Do It Right?

Dave Schumaker

Teachers should ask themselves, "Have my students really been learning what I have been teaching them, and can they put that knowledge to work in creative and critical thinking situations?" When I asked myself that question, the answer was, "No, my students have short-term memories; what they seem to learn one week is gone the next. I have to teach complex concepts such as photosynthesis and genetics over and over again, and the students still don't seem to understand them." It does not matter how much material you cover; if the students don't understand it and can't use it when you are finished teaching, it is useless to them.

If you want to change your students' attitudes toward learning, you should have them listen to each other and give them time to think before speaking. You should design your lessons around the basic questioning format that requires students to gather facts and process them using higher cognitive skills. I am convinced that good questioning skills improve student learning, and I have been trying to pass this notion on to other teachers.

The question that comes up at almost every workshop I conduct is, "But . . . it sounds like it takes too much time. I have to get through the book or my curriculum, and how will I be able to do that if I spend so much time questioning?" Since I have changed my method of questioning students, I have found that my students have changed their attitudes toward learning. This change, very subtle at first, is now quite startling. They pay attention; they listen to each other and give answers that show they are thinking about what they are going to say. I find that the quality of their questions has also improved; they seem to have a better understanding of the concepts and are showing improvement on tests and written work. Since I have become used to this new style, the amount of material I cover seems to be about the same now as it was in the past, although I must admit that when I was learning to use good questioning techniques the process did take longer.

The other question that I commonly hear is, "Do I have to change my teaching strategies?" Of course not! All teaching strategies require teachers to ask questions and students to answer them. The only thing you will change is your style of questioning, and that alone will allow your students to take a quantum jump in their ability to learn the material presented and truly understand how to apply it to problem-solving situations.

Let's face it—education has been under fire for some time, and we need to do all we can to improve our product. Our product is educated students, and through the implementation of sound questioning practices we can improve the quality of student education without the addition of a single dollar to our budgets or an extra minute to our teaching day.

Furthermore, students forget much content that is presented through lecture. Ebbinhous (1913) found that the curve of retention dropped from about 60 percent of immediate recall after the lecture to about 20 percent after eight weeks.

Different students need different classroom organizational patterns. Some students learn best individually; some learn best in groups. There are students who can only learn when an adult is present to constantly encourage and reinforce them; others can't learn when another person is nearby. Some students need noise; others need quiet. Some need bright light; some need subdued light. Some need formal settings; others need informal situations. Some need to move; others need to be stationary (Dunn and Dunn, 1978).

Similarly, some students need a great deal of structure while others need minimal structure. Less able students seem to do better in highly structured situations where direct help is generous than do more able students for whom less structured situations seem preferable (Sternberg and Wagner, 1982, p. 51).

What kind of classroom structure, then, produces the greatest achievement of cognitive skills and strategies? Thomas (1980) states:

Where the locus of control over learning-related behaviors is entirely vested in the teacher, where maximum structure is provided for carrying out learning activities, and where the motivation to perform is provided for through external rewards, praise, and/or fear of reprisal, there is little latitude or opportunity for students to develop a sense of agency and subsequently, to become proficient in using learning strategies . . . . What may be required is an instructional procedure replete with tasks for which strategies have some payoff and perhaps a deliberate attempt to teach and/or allow for the discovery of varieties of cognitive strategies appropriate to these tasks (Thomas, 1980, p. 236).

The Johnsons found that having students work cooperatively in groups promotes the use of higher reasoning strategies and greater critical thinking competencies more than do competitive and individualistic learning strategies (Johnson and Johnson, 1983).

What most authorities in curriculum and instruction promote, and what the authors above support with research, is that when higher-level thinking, creativity, and problem solving are the objectives, students must be in a classroom climate where they are in the decision-making role—where they decide on strategies to solve problems; where they determine the correctness or error of an answer based on data they produced and validated; where they are involved in setting their own goals and means of assessing the accomplishment of those goals.

Furthermore, the reward system in such a classroom should be intrinsic rather than extrinsic—derived from an internal motivation to learn—an intellectual curiosity about phenomena, an internal striving for craftsmanship and accuracy, a sense of responsibility to be a productive and interdependent member of a community of scholars, and a desire to emulate significant, respected others (Lepper, 1978; Bruner, 1956).

Teachers who value internal rather than external rewards, who engage students in structuring their own learning, who realize human variability in learning, and who can teach toward multiple goals use a repertoire of classroom organizational patterns. Classrooms organized for thinking are characterized by:

• *Individual students* working alone, engaged in a task requiring one or more cognitive skills: comparing, classifying, sorting, and evaluating. During individual work, teachers monitor student progress and mediate their experiences.

• *Groups* working cooperatively, in pairs or small groups, on such collaborative problem solving as: planning strategies for group projects, contributing data and ideas to the progress of the project, identifying information that needs to be gathered, devising strategies to generate that information, and evaluating individual and group social skills. During group work, teachers monitor students' progress, assess growth in social and cognitive abilities, and mediate both the intellectual skills required of the task and the cooperative group skills.

• At other times, *total group* engagement in listening to presentations by and interacting with the teacher, resource people, media, and other students. Such total-group interactive strategies as the Socratic, the dialectic, and class meetings are also employed when the teacher or a student raises a dilemma, problem, or discrepancy for all to participate in debating and resolving.

To learn to think, students must engage in, discuss, and come to value thinking. If schools are to value thinking, they must engage students in interacting individually, in small groups, and in total groups with problem-solving and creative activities that students design and evaluate themselves.

Response Behaviors that Create a Climate for Thinking

Teachers can create a classroom climate for thinking. It is the quality of certain teacher interactions that determines the degree of trust, risk-taking level of cognition, warmth, rapport, openness, and psychological safety in the classroom (Kahn and Weiss, 1973). Basically, it is the way the teacher responds to students that creates this classroom climate. Teachers' *responsive behaviors* are those actions taken after the student answers the teacher's questions or follows directions. In other words, the teacher

initiates a behavior through questioning or structuring, the student performs the behavior, then the teacher responds to the student's performance.

Lowery (1979) found that the way the teacher responds is more influential in determining students' behavior than what the teacher asks or tells students to do. Because students are constantly anticipating how their teacher will respond to their actions, teacher responses seem to exert greater influence than structuring or questioning. Flanders (1965) found that teacher responses have a great deal of influence on the development of students' self-concept, their attitude toward learning, their achievement, and their classroom rapport.

Response behaviors may be categorized according to their effect on students: those that tend to terminate or close down thinking, and those that maintain, open up, and extend thinking. There are six behaviors that can be classified under those two categories.

Terminal or closed responses:
    1. Criticism (and other put downs)
    2. Praise

Open or extending responses:
    3. Using silence (wait time)
    4. Accepting—passively, actively, or emphatically
    5. Clarifying—of both concept and process
    6. Facilitating data acquisition

Much research accumulated over several years supports the beneficial effects on students when teachers use these behaviors selectively.

Criticism (and other putdowns)

Criticism may be defined as negative value judgments. When a teacher responds to a student's performance with the use of such negative value words as "poor," "incorrect," or "wrong," it tends to terminate student thinking. Negative value judgments can sometimes be inferential or subtle signals of inadequacy, for instance, "You're *almost* right," "Who has a *better* answer?" or "You're getting *close*." Other criticism may be value judgments in the form of ridicule: "What a dumb idea" or "You're not good enough."

Other put downs include responses that imply sarcasm or rejection. These are sometimes subtle cues to students by the teacher's voice intonation or inflection that their performance was inadequate: "Who would want to help you when you act *that* way?" "Where on earth did you get *that* idea?" "Now that Mary is finished, who will show us the way it *should* be done?"

An abundance of research demonstrates that criticism is not helpful in promoting cognitive or affective learning.

Soar (1972) synthesized much research on the effects of criticism and found no evidence to support negative criticism as positively affecting learning. In fact, Flanders (1970) found that greater teacher criticism was related to less positive pupil attitudes and lower pupil achievement.

Criticizing students and making them feel failure obviously does not enhance thinking. There are numerous responses that teachers can use that are more helpful in promoting student thinking.

Praise

Praise may be defined as the opposite of criticism in that it employs the use of positive value judgments such as "good," "excellent," "great," and so forth.

Surprisingly, while many teachers advocate the use of praise in attempts to reinforce behaviors and to build self-worth, the research on praising seems to indicate that in reality, the opposite is more often the case. Praise builds conformity at a time when our goal is diversity. It tends to make students depend on *others* for their worth rather than on *themselves* for their worth.

Some teachers use praise so often and so indiscriminately that it tends to become a meaningless response providing little benefit. Praise does seem to be appropriate under certain conditions. It would be desirable for teachers to learn to recognize and use praise sparingly and judiciously and only in those circumstances, with only those students, and for only those objectives for which it is suitable. Teachers can replace praising with an enlarged repertoire of response behaviors that research indicates are more conducive to developing students' thinking skills.

Praising seems best used with only certain students and for certain tasks. Following are some circumstances in which praise seems warranted:

1. *Reluctant, unmotivated, dependent learners.* Some students are difficult to motivate. They depend on the teacher for reinforcement and need constant reminders to stay on task. These are often students who, when given an assignment, soon lose interest, have a limited attention span, and quickly seek redirection. While praise often benefits this type of learner, a goal for them should be to replace external reinforcement with internal motivation. Therefore, the amount and frequency of praise must gradually be reduced and replaced with the satisfaction derived from solving intriguing problems, accuracy and craftsmanship of tasks completed, and with the responsibility for contributing to group accomplishment. Thus, with this type of learner, the teacher must consciously withdraw praise over time (fading). Often when new or difficult learning is begun, praise will need to be used again briefly until the student has a feeling of confidence and mastery.

2. *Lower grade level students.* Kohlberg has described a sequence through which students grow in their understanding of social justice and moral reasoning. During early stages, children understand right and wrong because of the rewards and punishments given by adults and others in authority. These rewards and punishments are the consequences of their behavior. In later life, students can understand the consequences of their behavior because of their effect on others or because they understand "morally ethical" behavior.

While students are still in the early stages of moral development, praise and rewards may be appropriate. These states are not necessarily determined by chronological maturity, but rather by observation of students' behavior in situations requiring social decision making and by analyzing discussions with children about appropriate behavior in varying problem situations. Higher levels, more autonomous, and more appropriate, kind, and just behaviors will develop in students if they are involved in decisions and problem situations that require making choices. It is helpful if their behaviors are discussed and analyzed with them, and if significant adults in their environment model those more appropriate social behaviors.

While praise may seem to be more appropriate with young, morally immature students, we want to help them progress beyond that stage. Teachers, therefore, must soon abolish praising and replace it with the type of internal motivation system that is consistent with the higher stages of moral development.

3. *Low level cognitive tasks.* As indicated earlier, input questions help a student confirm or produce an answer from memory or from sensory observations. It is probable that the answer the student gives is predictable and therefore "correct."

If praise is used, there are some guidelines that can help students decrease their dependence on it:

● *Giving the criteria or rationale for the value judgment.* It is important that the criteria for praise be described. What makes an act "good" or "excellent" must be communicated along with the praise. The student then understands why the act is acceptable and can repeat the performance.

● *Helping students analyze their own answers.* For example,

Teacher: "Jane says San Francisco is the largest city in California. Bill says Los Angeles is the largest. Would each of you please tell us what is the population of the two cities? One way to find out is to compare our data."

In the long run, the teacher's goal should be to *decrease* the use of these terminal behaviors and use other response behaviors that have a more instructive effect on students' cognitive development.

Which instructional objectives warrant praise? Flanders (1970) stated:

> The pupil growth index which involves memory, a relatively low level cognitive task, can tolerate lower levels of teacher indirectness ... yet higher levels of cognitive reasoning are associated with more indirect ... teacher influence patterns: Creativity appears to flourish most with the most indirect patterns.

McGraw (1978) and Condry and Chambers (1978) found that student performance on routine, familiar procedures was not adversely affected by rewards and praise. In fact, when students did not particularly like assignments that were repetitious and of a practice nature, rewards enhanced their performance. In contrast, McGraw and Thomas (1980) found that rewards had a detrimental effect on student performance of tasks requiring higher-level problem solving. Condry and Chambers (1978) emphasize that the learning process is different from the learning product and indicate that the process is detrimentally affected by rewards. They suggest that effects of rewards differ depending on the extent to which the student had already learned the subject matter. Thus, rewards for tasks already learned are not detrimental because learning has already occurred and the focus is now on learner production of what he or she already knows.

In contrast, the process of learning *is* detrimentally affected by rewards. The performance of new tasks, skills, and processes requires cognitive risks and exploration, which are inhibited by praise and promised reward. Thus, these findings seem to indicate that rewards are best administered for well-learned tasks where specific rules need to be followed, as opposed to tasks that are in the process of being learned or are problem solving or exploratory in nature. Seatwork, which is of a practice nature, is likely to be facilitated by rewards, while rewards for learning a new skill are likely to have a detrimental effect.

Silence

Rowe (1974) found observable differences in classroom behaviors of students whose teachers waited after asking a question or after a student gave an answer.

If the teacher waits only a short time—one or two seconds—students will give short, one-word responses. On the other hand, if the teacher waits for longer periods, the students tend to respond with whole sentences and complete thoughts. There is a perceptible increase in the creativity of the response as shown by greater use of descriptive and modifying words. There is also increased speculativeness in the students' thinking. Research has also shown that student-to-student interaction is greater, the number of questions students ask increases, and shy students begin to contribute.

Good and Brophy (1973) report that teachers communicate their expectancies of students through the use of silence. Teachers who ask a question and then wait for a student's answer demonstrate that they not only expect an answer but also that they have faith in the student's ability to answer given enough time. Teachers who ask a question, wait only a short time, and then give the answer, call on another student, or give a hint, demonstrate their belief that the student really can't answer the question and is considered too poor a student to offer an answer or reason independently.

Accepting Responses

Teachers who are accepting are those who are nonevaluative and nonjudgmental. They give no clues through posture, gesture, or words as to whether the student's idea, behavior, or feeling is good, bad, better or worse, right or wrong. The intent of *accepting* is to provide a psychologically safe climate in which students can take risks, are entrusted with the responsibility of deciding for themselves, and can explore the consequences of their own actions. An accepting atmosphere in a classroom encourages students to examine and compare their own data, values, ideas, criteria, and feelings with those of others as well as those of the teacher. Even though students' values and feelings may differ from those of the teacher, teachers can still accept these differences because they know that only the student is able to modify them and make them consistent with their reality.

Thus, an alternative way of responding to a student's answer is by paraphrasing it, applying it, acknowledging it, comparing it to another idea, or summarizing what was said. Among the numerous ways of demonstrating acceptance are passive acceptance, active acceptance, and empathic acceptance.

Passive acceptance is demonstrated when the teacher merely receives and acknowledges what the student says, without making a value judgment. It demonstrates that the student's ideas have been heard. Passive acceptance might be:

Verbal, by saying: "Um-hmm," "That's one possibility," "Could be," or "I understand."

Nonverbal, by nodding the head or writing the student's statement on the chalkboard.

Active acceptance demonstrates an understanding of what the student says or does. The teacher actively accepts by reflecting (not merely repeating), rephrasing, paraphrasing, recasting, translating, or summarizing what the student said or did. It occurs when the teacher extends, builds on, compares, or gives an example based on the student's response. While the teacher may use different words, the teacher strives to maintain the intent and accurate meaning of the student's idea. Active acceptance is more than passive acceptance because the teacher demonstrates not only that the student's message has been received, but also that the message is understood. Examples of active acceptance are:

"Your explanation is that if the heat were increased, the molecules would move faster and therefore disperse the food coloring faster."

"I understand. Your idea is that we should all write our legislators rather than send them one letter from the group."

Empathic acceptance is the acceptance of feelings in addition to cognition. Often teachers can show empathy when they express similar feelings from their own experiences. It means that the teacher not only hears the student's ideas; the teacher also hears the *emotions* underlying the ideas. Some examples of empathic acceptance are:

"I can see why you're confused. Those directions are unclear to me, too."

"You're frustrated because you didn't get a chance to share your idea. We've all got to take turns, and that requires patience. It's hard to wait when you're anxious to share."

The student enters the room and slams a math workbook on the desk. The teacher responds empathically to this behavior by saying, "Something must be upsetting you today. Did you have difficulty with the assignment?"

Empathic acceptance does not mean that the teacher condones acts of aggression or destructive behavior. It does, however, demonstrate an understanding and acceptance of the emotions that produce those behaviors.

Clarifying

Clarifying is similar to accepting in that both behaviors reflect the teacher's concern for fully understanding the student's idea. While active acceptance demonstrates that the teacher truly *does* understand, clarifying means that the teacher *does not* understand what the student is saying and, therefore, needs more information.

Rosenshine and Furst (1971) report that when a teacher responds to students' comments by encouraging them to elaborate, there is a significant and positive correlation with student achievement.

Kleven (1968) found that when teachers use clarification, students tend to increase their consistency of thinking as measured on a scale-of-beliefs test. Students become more purposeful in their thinking and behaving.

Flanders' research (1960) supports the use of clarifying behavior. It shows that achievement is higher in classrooms where teachers use, build on, extend, or clarify students' ideas.

One of the most compelling reasons why teachers should clarify is that it contributes to the development of students' metacognitive abilities. Brown (1978) found a correlation between the degree of metacognitive awareness and the level of performance on complex problem-solving tasks. Students seem to become better problem solvers if they are able to become aware of and talk about the strategies and steps they use to solve problems.

Often students follow instructions or perform tasks without questioning why they are doing what they are doing. They seldom question themselves about their own learning strategies or evaluate the efficiency of their own performance. They may have virtually no idea what they are doing when they perform a task and are often unable to explain their strategies in solving problems (Sternberg and Wagner, 1982).

When the teacher clarifies by asking students to explain their answers and how they arrived at them, or to share the rationale behind them, the teacher causes the students to metacogitate. Much evidence suggests that causing students to talk about their thinking processes and problem-solving strategies before, during, and after enhances their ability to think. Evidently, thinking and talking about thinking begets more thinking (Whimbey, 1980; Bloom and Broder, 1950).

Facilitating the Acquisition of Data

If one of the objectives of cognitive education is for students to process data by comparing, classifying, inferring, or drawing causal relationships, then data must be available for the student to process. To facilitate the acquisition of data, the teacher must perceive students' information needs and provide data or make it possible for students to do so themselves. Thus, it is classified as a response behavior.

The teacher, therefore, creates a climate that is responsive to the student's quest for information. Teachers do this in a variety of ways.

● By providing data (feedback) about a student's performance: "No, three times six is not 24. Three times eight is 24." "Yes, you have spelled 'rhythm' correctly."

● By providing personal information or data (self-divulgence). (These are often in the form of "I" messages.): "I want you to know that chewing gum in this classroom really disturbs me." "John, your pencil tapping is disturbing me." "The way you painted the tree makes me feel like I'm on the inside looking out."

● By making it possible for students to experiment with equipment and materials to find data or information for themselves: "Here's a larger test tube if you'd like to see how your experiment would turn out differently." "We can see the film again if you want to check your observations."

● By making primary and secondary sources of information accessible: "Mary, this almanac gives information you will need for your report on the world's highest mountain ranges." "Here's the dictionary. The best way to verify the spelling is to look it up."

● By responding to a student's request for information:

Student: "What's this thing called?"
Teacher: "This piece of equipment is called a bell jar."

● By surveying the group for its feelings or for input of their information. "On this chart we have made a list of what you observed in the film. We can keep this chart in front of us so that we can refer to it as we classify our observations." "Let's go around the circle and share some of the feelings we had when we found out the school board decided to close our school."

● By labeling students' performance of a cognitive operation: "When you shared your crayons, that was an example of *cooperation*." "Your statement, 'If there is water found on Mars, then there could be life' is a *hypothesis*." "That was an *assumption* you made."

Knowledge of results is the single most important variable governing the acquisition of skillful habits (Irion, 1966).

There is a difference between rewards and feedback. Rewards can either control behavior or give information about competence. If students perceive the teacher's rewards as controlling, their intrinsic motivation will likely decrease. If students perceive rewards as providing feedback about their knowledge or competence, however, their intrinsic motivation is likely to increase (Deci, 1976, 1978).

Feedback or a response to a student's behavior should be given within seconds if learning is to progress rapidly (Kimble, 1961). Feedback need not always come from the external situation but may arise from other concepts, data, and principles recalled or gathered by the learners themselves—for example, by providing a model with which the student checks for accuracy or correctness, by comparison with other students' answers, or with rules stated in the instructions (Feuerstein, 1980). In other words, the teacher needs to provide an opportunity for students to check their ideas against the data being gathered so that they can decide for themselves if their ideas or answers are correct. This self-checking can furnish some immediate feedback and satisfaction that in turn reinforces learning (Gagne, 1967).

Suchman (1964), in his studies of Inquiry Training, found that students need a "responsive environment." Data of all kinds need to be available in great abundance. It should be possible for inquiring students to obtain whatever data they want as easily and quickly as possible from many sources: manipulation of materials, tools, and references; the teacher; and other resource people (Andre, 1979).

In Summary

In a poll conducted by the University of Northern Colorado, 87 percent of the parents surveyed said that teachers needed the ability to communicate, understand, and relate. The Colorado Department of Education concluded that the top concern of high school students was teachers' lack of acceptance and involvement. Students felt no one cared and no one listened to their needs (*Education USA*, 1978).

Probably the main reason why all the open response behaviors described in this chapter create a warm climate for learning is that they require teachers to listen. The teacher's use of silence communicates to students the value of reflective, thoughtful, crafted answers over impulsive answers. The use of accepting behaviors demands that teachers be sensitive to and understand students' ideas. Clarifying and probing demonstrates a desire to go deeper and to further explore the students' ideas. Facilitating data requires teachers to listen to and sense the students' need for information so that the proper data may be supplied. Performance of all these behaviors presents a model of the type of rational behaviors that teachers desire in students as well.

Modeling: Behaving Consistently With Cognitive Goals and Objectives

What you do speaks so loudly, they can't hear what you say.
—Emerson

Students are quick to pick up the inconsistency between what a teacher verbalizes as ideal behavior and the demonstration of that behavior. Powerful teachers of thinking constantly strive to bring their words, actions, beliefs, values, and goals for students into harmony.

Research in modeling substantiates the fact that children acquire much of their behavior, feelings, attitudes, and values without direct instruction but through imitation of both adult and peer models (Bandura and Walter, 1963; Good and Brophy, 1973). A considerable number of studies conclude that students adopt new behavior patterns or modify their own behavior on the basis of observation alone. Thus, since there is such extended contact between teacher and student, the teacher is one of the most significant and influential models in the student's life.

Modeling tends to reinforce students' perceptions of the values and goals stated by the teacher or by the school. Adults, by exhibiting the kinds of behavior desired in students, strongly influence students in those behavior patterns in regard to the desired actions and reactions. For example:

● If listening to one another is a valued behavior of cognitive education, teachers who listen to students will greatly enhance the probability of achieving this objective.

● If solving problems in a rational, scientific manner is valued, students must observe teachers and administrators solving problems in rational, scientific ways when problems arise in the school or classroom (Belcher, 1975).

● If restraining impulsivity is a characteristic of intelligent problem solving, students must witness teachers and administrators reacting calmly and patiently during stressful situations.

● If teachers desire students to understand others' points of view, values, and differences (overcoming egocentrism), they will accept students' differences.

● If teachers want students to become enthusiastic about thinking, they will demonstrate enthusiasm about challenges, puzzles, and complex tasks requiring thought (Rosenshine, 1970).

● Emulation of significant others is a basic motive for learning. Yet if we are "do as I say, not as I do" educators, then students will easily and quickly sense this incongruence between our behaviors and our stated values. The credibility gap that results can lead to hostility, frustration, and confusion. In the last analysis, there is probably only one person's behavior we have the power to control, train, and modify: our own!

Readings on Teachers' Questions and Student Cognition

Andre, T. "Does Answering Higher Level Questions While Reading Facilitate Productive Learning?" *Review of Educational Research* 49, 2 (Spring, 1979): 280-318.

Bloom, B., and others. *Taxonomy of Educational Objectives, Handbook I: Cognitive Domain.* New York: David McKay Co., 1956.

Carin, A., and Sund, R. *Developing Questioning Technique: A Self-Concept Approach.* Columbus, Ohio: Charles E. Merrill Co., 1971.

Crump, C. "Teachers, Questions, and Cognition." *Educational Leadership* 27, 7 (April 1970): 657-660.

Costa, A. *The Enabling Behaviors.* Morristown, N.J.: General Learning Press, 1976.

Egan, K. "How to Ask Questions to Promote Higher Level Thinking." *Peabody Journal of Education* (April 1975).

Gall, M. "The Use of Questions in Teaching." *Review of Educational Research* 40, 5 (December 1970): 207-220.

Hunkins, F. *Questioning Strategies and Techniques.* Rockleigh, N.J.: Allyn and Bacon, 1972.

Saunders, Norris. *Classroom Questions: What Kinds?* New York: Harper and Row, 1966.

Servey, R. E. *Teacher Talk: The Knack of Asking Questions.* Belmont, Calif.: Fearon Publishers, 1974.

Wease, H. "Questioning: The Genius of Teaching and Learning." *High School Journal* (March 1976).

Winne, P. H. "Experiments Relating Teachers' Use of Higher Cognitive Questions to Student Achievement." *Review of Educational Research* 49, 1 (Winter 1979): 13-50.

REFERENCES

Andre, T. "Does Answering Higher Level Questions While Reading Facilitate Productive Learning?" *Review of Educational Research* 49 (Spring 1979): 280-318.

Bandura, A., and Walter, R. H. *Social Learning and Personality Development.* New York: Holt, Rinehart and Winston, 1963.

Belcher, T. "Modeling Original Divergent Responses: An Initial Investigation." *Journal of Educational Research* 67 (1975): 351-358.

Bloom, B. S., and Broder, L. J. *Problem-Solving Processes of College Students.* Chicago: University of Chicago Press, 1950.

Borg, W. R. "Time and School Learning." In *Time to Learn.* Edited by C. Denham and A. Lieberman. Washington, D.C.: National Institute of Education, 1980.

Brophy, J. E. "Teacher Praise: A Functional Analysis." East Lansing: Michigan State University Institute for Research on Teaching, 1981. (Occasional Paper No. 28.)

Brophy, J. E. "Supplemental Group Management Techniques." In *Helping Teachers Manage Classrooms.* Edited by D. Duke. Alexandria, Va.: Association for Supervision and Curriculum Development, 1982.

Brown, A. L. "Knowing When, Where, and How to Remember: A Problem of Meta-Cognition." In *Advances in Instructional Psychology.* Hillsdale, N.J.: Erlbaum, 1978.

Bruner, J.; Goodnow, J. J.; and Austin, G. A. *A Study of Thinking.* New York: Wiley, 1956.

Cole, R. A., and Williams, D. "Pupil Responses to Teacher Questions: Cognitive Level, Length, and Syntax." *Educational Leadership* 31 (1973): 142-145.

Condry, J., and Chambers, J. "Intrinsic Motivation and the Process of Learning." In *The Hidden Cost of Rewards: New Perspectives on the Psychology of Human Motivation.* Edited by M. Lepper and D. Greene. New York: Erlbaum, 1978.

Costa, A. "Mediating the Metacognitive." *Educational Leadership* 42, 3 (November 1984): 57-62.

Daily, F. "A Study of Female Teachers' Verbal Behavior and Peer-Group Structure Among Classes of Fifth-Grade Children." Doctoral dissertation, Kent State University, 1970.

Davis, O. L., and Tinsley, D. "Cognitive Objectives Revealed by Classroom Questions Asked by Social Studies Teachers." *Peabody Journal of Education* 45, pp. 21-26.

Deci, E. L. *Intrinsic Motivation.* New York: Plenum Press, 1976.

Deci, E. L. "Application of Research on the Effect of Rewards." In *The Hidden Cost of Rewards: New Perspectives on the Psychology of Human Motivation.* Edited by M. Lepper and D. Greene. New York: Erlbaum, 1978.

Dewey, J. *Democracy in Education.* New York: Macmillan, 1944.

Dunn, R., and Dunn, K. *Teaching Students Through Their Individual Learning Styles*. Reston, Va.: Reston Publishing Company, 1978.

Ebbinhous, H. *Memory*. New York: Teachers College, Columbia University, 1913.

Education U.S.A. Arlington, Va.: National School Public Relations Association, 1978.

Feuerstein, R. *Instrumental Enrichment*. Baltimore: University Park Press, 1980.

Flanders, N. *Analyzing Teacher Behavior*. Reading, Mass.: Addison Wesley, 1970.

Flanders, N. *Teacher Influence, Pupil Attitudes and Achievement*. (Cooperative Research Monograph 112, OE 25040). Washington, D.C.: Department of Health, Education and Welfare, 1965.

Flanders, N. "Teacher Effectiveness." In *Encyclopedia of Educational Research* (4th ed.). Edited by R. Ebell. New York: Macmillan, 1960.

Foley, J. J. "Teaching and Learning in the Affective Domain." In *Removing Barriers to Humaneness in the High School*. Edited by J. G. Saylor and J. L. Smith. Washington, D.C.: Association for Supervision and Curriculum Development, 1971.

Gage, N. L. "A Factorially Designed Experiment on Teacher Structuring, Soliciting, and Reacting." *Journal of Teacher Education* 27, 1 (Spring 1976): 35-38.

Gagne, R. *Conditions for Learning*. New York: Holt, Rinehart and Winston, 1967.

Gallagher, J., and Ashner, M. J. "A Preliminary Report: Analysis of Classroom Interaction." *Merill Palmer Quarterly* 9 (1963): 183-194.

Good, T. L., and Brophy, J. E. *Looking in Classrooms*. New York: Harper and Row, 1973.

Good, T. L., and Grouws, D. "Teacher Effects: A Process-Product Study in Fourth-Grade Mathematics Classrooms." *Journal of Teacher Education* 27, 3 (May/June 1977): 49-54.

Goodlad, J. *A Place Called School: Prospects for the Future*. New York: McGraw Hill, 1983.

Irion, A. L. "A Brief History of Research on the Acquisition of Skill." In *Acquisition of Skill*. Edited by E. A. Belodeau. New York: Academic Press, 1966.

James, M., and Jongeward, D. *Born to Win*. Addison Wesley, 1971.

Johnson, R., and others. *Circles of Learning: Cooperation in the Classroom*. Alexandria, Va.: Association for Supervision and Curriculum Development, 1984.

Jones, H. E. "Experimental Studies of College Teaching." *Archives of Psychology* 68 (November 1923): entire issue.

Kahn, S. B., and Weiss, J. "The Teaching of Affective Responses." In *Second Handbook of Research on Teaching*. Edited by R. Travers. Chicago: Rand McNally, 1973.

Kimble, G. A., and Hilgard, E. R. *Conditioning and Learning*. New York: Appleton-Century Crofts, 1961.

Klevan, A. "An Investigation of a Methodology for Value Clarification: Its Relationship to Consistency of Thinking, Purposefulness, and Human Relations." Doctoral dissertation, New York University, 1968.

Kounin, J. S. *Discipline and Group Management in Classrooms*. New York: Holt, Rinehart and Winston, 1970.

Lepper, M., and Greene, D., eds. *The Hidden Costs of Rewards: New Perspectives on the Psychology of Human Motivation*. Hillsdale, N.J.: Erlbaum, 1978.

Lowery, L., and Marshall, H. *Learning About Instruction: Teacher Initiated Statements and Questions*. Berkeley: University of California, 1980.

McDonald, F. J. "Report on Phase II of the Beginning Teacher Evaluation Study." *Journal of Teacher Education* 27, 1 (Spring 1976): 39-42.

McGraw, K. "The Detrimental Effects of Rewards on Performance: A Literature Review and Prediction Model." In *The Hidden Costs of Rewards: New Perspectives on the Psychology of Human Motivation*. Edited by M. Lepper and D. Greene. New York: Erlbaum, 1978.

Measel, W., and Mood, D. "Teacher Verbal Behavior and Teacher and Pupil Thinking in Elementary School." *Journal of Educational Research* 66 (1972): 99-102.

Newton, B. "Theoretical Basis for Higher Cognitive Questioning—An Avenue to Critical Thinking." *Education* 98 (March/April 1978): 286-291.

Redfield, D., and Rousseau, E. "A Meta-Analysis on Teacher Questioning Behavior." *Review of Educational Research* 51 (Summer 1981): 234-245.

Rosenshine, B. "Enthusiastic Teaching, A Research Review." *School Review* 78 (1970): 279-301.

Rosenshine, B., and Furst, N. "Current and Future Research on Teacher Performance Criteria." In *Research on Teacher Education, A Symposium*. Edited by B. O. Smith. Englewood Cliffs, N.J.: Prentice Hall, 1971.

Rowe, M. B. "Wait Time and Rewards as Instructional Variables: Their Influence on Language, Logic and Fate Control." *Journal of Research in Science Teaching* 11 (1974): 81-94.

Soar, R. "Pupil Teacher Interaction." In *A New Look at Progressive Education*. Edited by J. Squire. Washington, D.C.: Association for Supervision and Curriculum Development, 1972.

Sprinthall, N., and Theis-Sprinthall, L. "The Teacher as an Adult Learner: A Cognitive Developmental View." In *Staff Development*. Edited by G. Griffin. 82nd Yearbook of the National Society for the Study of Education. Chicago: University of Chicago Press, 1983.

Stallings, J., and Kaskowitz, D. *Follow Through Classroom Observation Evaluation, 1972-1973*. Menlo Park, Calif.: Stanford Research Institute, 1974.

Sternberg, R., and Wagner, R. "Understanding Intelligence: What's In It For Education?" Paper submitted to the National Commission on Excellence in Education, 1982.

Suchman, J. R. *The Elementary School Training Program in Scientific Inquiry*. Urbana, Ill.: University of Illinois, 1964.

Taba, H.; Levine, S.; and Elzey, F. *Thinking in Elementary School Children*. Cooperative Research Project No. 1574. San Francisco: San Francisco State College, 1964.

Thomas, J. "Agency and Achievement: Self-Management and Self-Regard." *Review of Educational Research* 50, 2 (Summer 1980): 213-240.

Wallen, N. W., and Woodke, J. H. *Relationships Between Teacher Characteristics and Student Behavior, Part I*. Salt Lake City, Utah: University of Utah, Department of Educational Psychology, 1963.

Wasserman, S. *Put Some Thinking in Your Classroom*. New York: Benific Press, 1978.

Whimbey, A. "Students Can Learn to be Better Problem Solvers." *Educational Leadership* 37, 7 (April 1980): 56-65.

PART VII

Teaching Strategies Intended to Develop Student Thinking

A teaching strategy is a sequential pattern of instructional activities that are employed over time and are intended to achieve a desired student learning outcome. Incorporated within a teaching strategy are specific teaching skills such as questioning, communicating directions, structuring, and responding to students' answers. Within a teaching strategy, the teacher also employs a repertoire of instructional techniques, such as unique classroom arrangements and grouping patterns, ways of causing interaction, and various approaches to the use of instructional materials.

You will find, therefore, that the use of those basic instructional skills described in Part VI—questioning, structuring, responding, and modeling—are present in each of the teaching strategies described. They are used, however, in differing amounts, sequences, combinations, and for different purposes. For example, teacher questioning is present in every strategy. In the *Discussion* strategy, the teacher presents only one question; in the *Concept Development* strategies, the teachers asks three major types of questions in a hierarchical sequence; in the *Inquiry* and *Deep Process* strategies, the syntactical structure of the questions are selected because of a particular cognitive process that the teacher desires the students to perform.

In this section, the characteristics of various strategies are described. they are intended to develop students' thinking skills, but each strategy does so in different ways. Generally, there are four distinct categories of teaching strategies:

● *Directive* strategies help students acquire and retain important facts, ideas, and skills.

● *Mediative* strategies help students develop reasoning, concepts, and problem-solving processes.

● *Generative* strategies help students develop new solutions, insights, and creativity.

● *Collaborative* strategies help students learn to relate to each other and work cooperatively in groups.

The distinguishing characteristics of these four categories are their different purposes for students, the varied roles of students and the teacher, and the human motivations to learn on which each strategy capitalizes.

In the ensuing sections we will discuss each of these strategic styles in depth, give several detailed examples of strategies from each of the four categories, describe the goals toward which they aim and the roles they assign to teachers and students, and specify the curriculum areas in which they may be used.

23

Building a Repertoire of Strategies

Arthur L. Costa, Robert Hanson, Harvey F. Silver, and Richard W. Strong

The vast majority of problems, decisions and situations which confront us daily are those which do not have just one answer. Several solutions are usually possible. Logic suggests that if one can mentally generate many possible solutions, the more likely it is that an optimum solution will be reached. This is a creative process—the formation of new and useful relationships.

—Richard E. Manelis

Teaching strategies are nothing new. They are simply the various forms that teaching may take: Socratic/didactic, inductive/deductive, direct/indirect. By definition, a teaching strategy is a sequential arrangement of instructional activities that is employed over time and is intended to achieve a desired student learning outcome.

What *is* new is that over the last 30 years teachers and researchers have worked together to identify or create a wide repertoire of teaching strategies. Each of these strategies is intended to model, focus on, and develop a unique form of thinking.

Different Thoughts—Different Strategies

In Part III several definitions of thinking were presented: discrete skills, linkages of those skills into strategies, creative thinking, and attitudes of thought. One reason we need a repertoire is that there are many forms of thinking, and they are learned under differing conditions. For example, six different forms of thinking might be:

1. *Remembering:* Recalling specific facts, ideas, definitions, concepts, and generalizations; for example, giving the definition of a denominator.

2. *Repeating:* Using models (either present in the environment or stored in memory) to imitate in mastering a skill; for example, following the directions of how to add two fractions with unlike denominators.

3. *Reasoning* (critical thinking): Relating specific instances to general principles or concepts according to norms of provability and acceptable argument; for example, explaining why unlike denominators need to be changed.

4. *Reorganizing* (creative thinking): extending knowledge to new and different contexts in order to solve problems and create original products; for example, a student inventing a new way to add fractions with unlike denominators.

5. *Relating:* Establishing a connection between the knowledge being acquired and our own personal experience; for example, a student trying to justify spending one-third of his or her day watching television.

6. *Reflecting* (metacognition): Exploring thought itself and describing how a particular thought comes into being; for example, a student aware of and looking over the results of any of the previous styles of thought and trying to understand the processes that brought him or her to a particular conclusion.

Each of these styles of thinking makes use of knowledge in its own way, but all are normal human functions. In the same way that almost all humans can walk, run, skip, and hop, they can remember, repeat, relate, reason, reorganize, and reflect.

Different Styles—Different Strategies

Students have different styles and preferences for learning. Some students learn best alone, others learn best in pairs. Some learn best in small groups, some in large groups. Some learn with adults present, and others learn without adults. Some need constant structuring, but for others such structuring would be a distraction (Dunn and Dunn, 1978). Students with "field independent" learning styles learn best through an inductive approach while "field dependent" students learn best deductively. Some are auditory learners—they learn by hearing; some are visual learners—they learn by seeing; others are kinesthetic/tactile learners—they learn best by doing. Still others need all of the above.

Furthermore, different teachers have different styles. Just like students, some teachers are more comfortable teaching holistically while others are more comfortable with a step-by-step, analytical approach. Some teachers like to use diagrams, charts, the chalkboard, videotapes, films, and vivid examples—they focus on bright and clear images. Other teachers use discussions, tape recordings, listening games, and lectures—they stress classroom interaction. Still other teachers employ manipulatives, role playing, dramatizations, and hands-on experiences—they want students to be actively engaged.

Different Goals—Different Strategies

A balance of educational goals might include academic skills, physical agility, a positive self-concept, a sound value system, social abilities, reasoning, problem solving, and creativity. Basic skills are not learned in the same way as cognitive processes; values are not learned in the same way as creativity; physical agility is learned in a different manner than are social skills.

Thomas (1980) found striking differences in outcomes under different forms of instructional strategies. Those strategies that give the teacher control—to decide what should be learned and how and when it should be learned, to determine the criteria for success, and to control the reward system for correct performance—produce greater gains on low-level cognitive achievement test scores. They do not, however, go far in producing higher-level cognition, creativity, or autonomous behavior in students.

If, on the other hand, students are involved in determining what should be learned and how it should be learned, deciding on the criteria for success, and assessing themselves on those criteria; and if the reward system is intrinsic; greater problem solving, creativity, and internal locus of control in students is produced.

Different Motives—Different Strategies

In his book, *Toward A Theory Of Instruction,* Bruner (1966) states that almost all humans possess "intrinsic" motives for learning. An intrinsic motive is one that does not depend on outside reward; reward is inherent in the successful termination of that activity or even in the activity itself. He identified four such motives:

Curiosity is almost a prototype of the intrinsic motive. Our attention is attracted to something unclear, unfinished, or uncertain. We sustain our attention until the matter becomes clear, finished, or certain. The achievement of clarity, or merely the search for it, is what satisfies.

Competence is getting interested in what we become good at—an instinct for workmanship. It is usually difficult

FIGURE 1
Comparison of Instructional Strategies

Strategy	Decisions			
	Goals set by:	Methods, means, and materials determined by:	Evaluation/completion effectiveness determined by:	Source of motivation for learning:
Directive	Teacher	Teacher	Teacher	Teacher
Mediative	Teacher	Student	Student	Curiosity about the task
Generative	Teacher ↓ Student	Student	Student	Competency and craftsmanship
Collaborative	Teacher ↓ Group	Group	Group	Interdependence, reciprocity, and a sense of community

to sustain interest in an activity unless one achieves some degree of competence. To achieve a sense of accomplishment requires a task that has some beginning and some end point. Unless there is some meaningful unity in what we are doing, and a way of measuring our performance, we are not very likely to strive to excel. From the beginning of human history, we have not been able to leave a cave wall or a gold nugget alone—we have a strong drive to embellish, enhance, perfect, craft, and detail.

Reciprocity involves a deep human need to respond to others and to operate jointly with them toward an objective. It is probably the basis of society. Where joint action is needed and reciprocity is required for a group to attain an objective, there seem to be processes that carry individuals along into learning and sweep them into a competence that is required in the group setting. We sometimes endure hours of exhaustive labor while performing a group task that we would quickly give up on alone. The need to reciprocate can provide a driving force to learn.

Emulation refers to the strong human tendency to model oneself and one's aspirations on some other person. When we feel we have succeeded in being like significant identification figures—our heroes—we derive pleasure for the achievement. Conversely, we suffer when we have let them down. The teacher must be an effective competence model—the day-to-day, working model whose actions and values the student can emulate.

Different Problems—Different Strategies

Students will encounter a variety of problems in their lives. Some of the major types of problems, and methods to solve them, include:

1. Finding answers, through the use of:
   - Data sources (timetables, dictionaries, almanacs, and so on)
   - Memory or analogous experiences
   - Simple operations
   - Short-term memory
   - Mnemonics

2. Developing strategies to solve puzzling situations, using:
   - Inductive and deductive reasoning
   - Hypotheses and experimental designs
   - Data production
   - Strategic reasoning
   - Logic
   - Syllogistic reasoning

3. Coping with value-based problems, by:
   - Selecting from multiple, alternative solutions
   - Making decisions with little or no data or precedent
   - Interpreting data under different value systems (point of view)
   - Dealing with a lack of data and feedback (ambiguity)
   - Selecting the best alternative
   - Prioritizing from a value base
   - Understanding and appreciating others' values

4. Innovating, through:
   - Generation of novel solutions
   - Creative problem solving
   - Creativity, novelty, fluency, insight
   - Artistic expression
   - Invention

Our instructional task is to create opportunities that focus on and develop these innate and cultural cognitive functions. A variety of teaching strategies are the tools that will best equip us to accomplish this task. Figure 1 graphically displays the comparisons of the characteristics of the four categories of strategies.

REFERENCES

Bruner, Jerome. *Toward A Theory Of Instruction*. Cambridge: Harvard University Press, 1966, pp. 114-128.

Dunn, R., and Dunn, K. *Teaching Students Through Their Individual Learning Styles*. Reston, Va.: Reston Publishing Co., 1978.

Thomas, John W. "Agency and Achievement: Self-Management and Self-Regard." *Review of Educational Research* 509, 2 (Summer 1980): 213-240.

24
Directive Strategies

Arthur L. Costa, Robert Hanson, Harvey F. Silver, and Richard W. Strong

Tell a child WHAT to think, and you make him a slave to your knowledge. Teach a child HOW to think, and you make all knowledge his slave.

—Henry A. Taitt

The directive strategies are intended to help students acquire and retain the information, knowledge, and skills most likely to be useful to them as literate, effective citizens. They are termed "directive" because they require students to accurately imitate those behaviors or skills that are modeled, presented, or instructed by the teacher. Whether the teacher is presenting the correct way to spell a word, perform a mathematical operation, or adjust a microscope, the goal is for students to perform this skill or demonstrate ability to reproduce the behavior in a manner that closely or exactly resembles the way the teacher presented it.

Roles and Motivation

Directive strategies place teachers in the role of presenter of information. In this role, teachers may use a wide variety of materials (such as films, tapes, tests, lectures, and the work of other students), but their primary responsibility involves:

● Structuring the information so that it illicits the students' need to know.

● Selecting the goals and objectives to be achieved, the methods of achieving them, and the conditions under which and the criteria by which mastery will be demonstrated and evaluated.

● Providing an organization that permits easy storage and retrieval.

● Checking for understanding and retention.

● Rewarding correct performance of the desired behaviors.

Student Outcomes

Goals are often phrased in terms of recall or students' ability to demonstrate understanding. Directive strategies attempt to provide all students with a common well of information and resources that they can use to establish relationships with other members of our culture. Behavioral objectives of the directive strategies are often stated in such terms as "to understand," "to demonstrate," "to acquire," "to recall." They are usually at the "knowledge" level of Bloom's Taxonomy. Much research has shown that when these attributes of the strategies are employed, students score higher on standardized tests of basic skills.

Instructional Strategy

The following description of *Direct Instruction* is from one of its chief proponents, Barry Beyer. Beyer presents this strategy by comparing two ways of teaching discrete thinking skills—inductively and deductively—and by identifying and comparing the critical attributes of both methods.

Practical Strategies for the Direct Teaching of Thinking Skills

Barry K. Beyer

Many teachers today believe that they teach thinking skills. In most instances, however, what they actually do involves putting students into situations where they are simply made to think and expected to do it as best they can. Most methods teachers customarily use to "teach" thinking are indirect, rather than direct.[1] These methods are based on the questionable assumption that by doing thinking, students automatically learn how to engage in such thinking.

Educational researchers have pointed out time and again that learning how to think is not an automatic by-product of studying certain subjects, assimilating the products of someone else's thinking, or simply being asked to think about a subject or topic.[2] Nor do youngsters learn how to engage in critical thinking effectively by themselves.[3] As Anderson has noted, there is little reason to believe that competency in critical thinking can be an incidental outcome of instruction directed, or that appears to be directed, at other ends.[4] By concentrating on the detail of the subject matter being studied, most common approaches to teaching critical thinking so obscure the skills of how to engage in thinking that students fail to master them.

If we want to improve student proficiency in thinking, we must use more direct methods of instruction than we now use.[5] First, we must establish as explicit goals of instruction the attitude, skill, and knowledge components of critical thinking—as Glaser recommended.[6] Second, we must employ direct, systematic instruction in these skills prior to, during, and following student introduction to and use of these skills in our classrooms.

A Framework for Teaching Critical Thinking Skills

Research on skill learning and teaching suggests that teachers should, for example, provide students with opportunities to identify examples of a skill—or products of its use—before asking them to use the skill to develop similar products of their own.[7] They should also introduce components of a skill as systematically as possible[8] and explicitly introduce and demonstrate its basic attributes and procedural operations. Additionally, students should frequently discuss these operations and how to employ them.[9] They need repeated practice in the skill over an extended period of time with corrective feedback provided by peers or teacher and by analyzing the results and how they were derived.[10] Skills need to be broadened beyond their original components and operations. At this point more subtle or content-specific components need to be added, and the skills should be used in combination with other skills.[11] To facilitate generalization and transfer, students need to apply and practice skills—with instructional guidance—in a variety of settings and with a variety of data and media.[12] Finally, teachers should present lessons in a skill using the course content.[13] What we should do, in a nutshell, is keep the teaching/learning focus continuously and explicitly on the skills we are trying to teach and not let them get smothered by the content with which we use them.

Teachers can apply these principles by organizing instruction in each skill in terms of a five-stage framework:

1. Where appropriate, teachers should provide students with several opportunities to select examples of a specific skill by focusing on the products of that skill rather than on its nature. This helps develop readiness for more specific instructional introduction of the skill.

2. In a single 30- to 40-minute lesson, teachers should introduce, present, and demonstrate the skill components in as much step-by-step detail as possible.

3. Three to six lessons that provide guided, instructive practice should then follow, each with explicit reference to the skill components as originally introduced and each us-

A slightly different version of this chapter was published as "Teaching Critical Thinking: A Direct Approach," *Social Education* 49, 4 (April 1985): 297-303. Copyright © 1985 by Barry K. Beyer.

ing data and media identical in form and type of content to those used when the skill was introduced.

4. Next, in a new 20- to 30-minute lesson, teachers should review and transfer the skill to media or data that differ from those used when the skill was introduced.

5. Finally, teachers should provide students with additional opportunities to apply the skill—with appropriate corrective feedback—until they can individually initiate and employ the skill and evaluate their use of it.

Over the duration of any course, then, a single newly introduced skill may well be the focus of eight to 12 lessons.

Strategies for Introducing a Thinking Skill

Each stage of teaching any thinking skill is important to effective instruction and learning. However, the introduction is the most important stage. A detailed introduction should focus specifically on the skill's attributes and make the skill a subject of the students' continuing and conscious attention. Two kinds of classroom teaching strategies can serve this purpose. The first—an inductive strategy—allows students to articulate for themselves the key attributes of the skill. The second—a more directive strategy—gives students the components of the skill right from the start. Teachers may vary the two approaches to avoid monotony in learning as well as to suit the content, the specific skill, or students' ability levels and learning styles.

An Inductive Introduction

In executing an inductive strategy, teachers and students proceed through five major steps.

The teacher:

1. Introduces the skill.

Next, the students:

2. Experiment with using it.

3. Reflect on and articulate what goes on in their heads as they execute the skill.

4. Apply their new knowledge of the skill to use it again.

5. Review what goes on in their heads as they execute the skill.

All of this can be done in a way that advances subject matter learning. Such a lesson need not be a special event or in a "content free" context. It can—and indeed should—be presented when using a new skill is necessary in order to understand the content being taught.[14]

Suppose a teacher is introducing the skill of *detecting bias* in written documents in a world history course. The students have already studied the causes of England's late 18th century industrial revolution and are about to investigate its results. This subject provides an excellent opportu-

nity for the teacher to introduce this skill and help students learn how to use it. Students are motivated to attend to this learning objective because they need to be able to find out the real impact of this economic and social revolution.

Step 1. To *introduce* the skill the teacher states its label, defines it or has the students define it, gives a synonym or two, and identifies several examples. Such an introduction provides a purpose for learning and a focus for the lesson.

Step 2. Without any further instruction, the students *experiment* with the skill—use it—as best they can to achieve a substantive learning goal; in this case, determining the impact of the industrial revolution. Given an excerpt from a historical document, students examine it to see if it is biased:

EXCERPT A

Some of these lords of the loom . . . employ thousands of miserable creatures . . . [who are] kept, fourteen hours in each day, locked up, summer and winter, in a heat of from *eighty to eighty-four degrees.* . . .

What then must be the situation of these poor creatures who are doomed to toil day after day . . .? Can any man, with a heart in his body . . ., refrain from cursing a system that produces such slavery and cruelty?

. . .[T]hese poor creatures have no cool room to retreat to . . . [and] are not allowed to send for water to drink; . . . even the rain water is locked up, by the master's order. . . . [A]ny spinner found with his window open . . . is to pay a fine. . . .

. . .[T]he notorious fact is, that well constitutioned men are rendered old and past labour at forty . . . and that children are rendered decrepit and deformed . . . before they arrive at the age of sixteen. . . .[15]

Step 3. Students then *reflect* on how they used this skill. At this point, most remark that this document certainly is biased. They usually cite the numerous, emotionally charged terms—"miserable creatures," "locked up," "poor creatures," "doomed," "slavery," "rendered decrepit"—all with exploitative connotations and all identified with workers. On the other hand, terms such as "lords of the loom" and "masters" are applied to the factory owners or their actions—thus putting them in a rather negative light. Overgeneralizations ("any spinner . . .") also lead to this judgment. Moreover, even the rhetorical question ("Can any man, with a heart . . .?") seems loaded. And the author's emphases (italicized words) show bias even more. "Is there," students ask, "nothing of merit on the side of the mill owners?" One-sided accounts might well indicate bias.

As students engage in this analysis, they also discover procedures for finding such clues and making sense of them. As this occurs, they begin to articulate inductively some of the major attributes of the skill of detecting bias.

Step 4. Using another documentary excerpt, the students next deliberately *apply* and "test out" the clues and procedures they have just inferred to see if a pattern emerges among their findings.

EXCERPT B

I have visited many factories . . . and I never saw . . . children in ill-humor. They seemed to be always cheerful and alert, taking pleasure in the light play of their muscles—enjoying the mobility natural to their age. The scene of industry . . . was exhilarating. It was delightful to observe the nimbleness with which they pieced the broken ends as the mule carriage began to recede from the fixed roller-beam and to see them at leisure after a few seconds exercise of their tiny fingers, to amuse themselves in any attitude they chose. . . . The work of these lively elves seemed to resemble a sport . . . [T]hey evidenced no trace of exhaustion on emerging from the mill in the evening; for they . . . skip about any neighborhood playground. . . .[16]

Step 5. Finally, the students *review* what they did as they used for the second time the clues and procedures of detecting bias—as they have identified them—to clarify the components of this particular skill.

By the end of this introductory lesson, students have articulated the key attributes of the skill of detecting bias as well as discussed effects of the industrial revolution. Both kinds of knowledge can be used in future assignments and serve as the basis for subsequent lessons, but what they have expressed about the skill of detecting bias is crucial, and it is on this note that the lesson should conclude. By engaging in these five steps—*introduction, experimentation, reflection, application,* and *review*—students and teacher have, in effect, invented some major attributes of the skill and begun to learn how to execute it. This strategy allows field-independent students to share their intuitive insights about a skill with their field-dependent peers, who rely more often on teacher direction to accomplish a task.[17]

A Directive Introduction

A more direct introduction may prove useful for teachers who know the essential attributes of a skill, or when a new skill is complex and students require additional guidance.

To use a directive strategy, the teacher:

1. Introduces the skill.
2. Explains the procedure and rules of which the skill consists.
3. Demonstrates how the skill is used.

Then the students:

4. Apply the skill.
5. Reflect on what occurs as they execute the skill.

Here's how a teacher might use a directive strategy to introduce world history students to the same thinking skill described above, that of detecting bias.

Step 1. The teacher can *introduce* the skill by writing its name on the chalkboard and defining it in terms of examples and synonyms. Dictionary definitions are also useful at this point. This introduction allows students sufficient time to prepare to deal with this skill by recalling anything they might know about bias and by making connections to previously learned or related knowledge or experience.

Step 2. The teacher should *explain* the key procedures and clues that constitute the skill, writing these on the chalkboard or sharing a ditto outline of them with the students. In addition to listing clues that distinguish this skill (use of loaded words, overgeneralizations, one-sidedness, and so on), the teacher also outlines a procedure by which students can execute this skill. For example:

1. State your goal: to see if something is biased.
2. Identify some clues to bias.
3. Search the material line-by-line or phrase-by-phrase to find these clues.
4. Identify any pattern of relationships among these clues.
5. State and give evidence to support the extent to which the source is biased.

Step 3. Using an example of biased data—in this instance, Excerpt A—the teacher can *demonstrate* the skill by walking the students step-by-step through the above procedure and then reviewing the process.

Step 4. The students, individually or in pairs, *apply* the skill as modeled by the teacher to examine a second example of biased information (Excerpt B), deliberately employing the procedures, rules, and clues presented and demonstrated by the teacher.

Step 5. Finally, students should *reflect* on what they did in executing the skill in order to articulate its essential attributes. Such reviews serve to set up further learning that requires using the newly introduced skill to achieve further content objectives.

The directive strategy starts with attributes of the skill to be introduced already known to the teacher and presented to the students—not as the *only* attributes of this skill, but as basic ones to be used, learned, and then modified as students practice the skill in future lessons. Like the inductive approach, this strategy should not be used all the time nor with all skills. The complexity of the skill, the teacher's knowledge of the skill, and the kinds of data needed or available, as well as student abilities and teacher instructional goals, determine where and when this strategy should be used.

Guidelines for Introducing Thinking Skills

These two introductory teaching strategies are useful not simply because they may appeal to different personal teaching styles, but because they also incorporate important findings of research on and thoughtful practice of skill teaching and learning. To minimize the negative effects of interference, both strategies place obvious and continuing emphasis on the skill being introduced. Student attention is repeatedly focused on the skill throughout each strategy. To enhance student motivation and to make learning the skill easier, teachers introduce students to the skill when they need competence in it to accomplish a content-related task. Students also either invent a model for the skill or participate in a "dry run," consciously attempting to articulate components of the skill. Each strategy includes repeated student discussion of the skill, which takes precedence over discussion of subject matter—although as students discuss the skill they simultaneously talk about the subject matter. Each strategy also gives students an opportunity to apply the skill and receive immediate feedback.[18]

These two strategies have subtle implications for teachers. For example, use of a directive introductory strategy presupposes that a teacher knows the skill. Such knowledge is not easy to come by, however. Descriptions of the key attributes of critical thinking skills are exceedingly sparse, yet there are several ways teachers can identify them. One, of course, is to search for descriptions in the literature or in instructional materials. Another is to perform the skill and reflect on the results in order to articulate the steps employed and the rules or principles followed.[19] Third, students or adults who demonstrate competence in a particular skill may engage in the skill and report aloud what they are thinking or mentally doing and why (metacognition). A subsequent analysis of their transcribed remarks—usually called protocols—can help identify key elements of the skill. All of these approaches take time, of course, and additional resources.[20]

Teachers may also "discover" key attributes of a skill by joining their students in studying and practicing the skill. Using the inductive strategy above as a jumping-off point, teachers can use student responses and their own insights to hypothesize a description of a skill's major procedures and rules. As teachers reintroduce the skill via this same strategy in successive classes, they gain additional insights and can continue to build and refine a more detailed concept of the skill. This inductive introductory strategy thus serves two major functions: to aid teachers and students in inventing a hypothetical skill model, and to serve as the initial strategy for providing instruction in a skill.

Although transfer is not inherent in these two strategies, it is a crucial aspect of skill teaching. Notice that in each example introductory lesson, the data used in the second task application are identical in form and genre to those used in the initial demonstration or inference-making task. The reason for this is important: transfer is best facilitated when students initially *overlearn* the skill;

this initial learning requires repeated guided practice in the *same context* (form and media) as that in which it was introduced.[21] However, once students have demonstrated mastery of a skill in a given context, the teacher can then vary the context to induce those cues needed to facilitate transfer to new contexts.

Strategies for Guided Practice in Thinking Skills

Teaching thinking, of course, requires more than a lesson utilizing one of the introductory strategies outlined here, and use of either strategy does not eliminate the need for repeated follow-up guided practice. Guided practice consists of students' reviewing the skill attributes *before* they use the skill, *while* they use it, and *after* they have used it. Through deliberate attention to the skill at these three points of a practice lesson, students can become more aware of what goes on in their heads as they engage in thinking.

Teachers can use at least two different strategies to guide students in such reflective skill practice. In the first, teachers:

1. Introduce the skill.
2. Have students review the skill procedure, rules, and associated knowledge.
3. Have students employ the skill to achieve the assigned subject matter objective.
4. Help students reflect on and review what they did in their heads as they executed the skill—and why.

A second strategy engages students in even more deliberate reflective analysis of their thinking. In this strategy teachers have students:

1. State what they expect to achieve by using a specific critical thinking skill.
2. Describe the procedure and rules they plan to use as they employ the skill.
3. Predict the results of their use of the skill.
4. Check the procedure they use as they employ the skill.
5. Evaluate the outcome of using the skill and the way they employed it.

This latter strategy helps students become more aware of their own thinking and thus gain the kind of conscious control over it that skill teaching experts claim is crucial to learning thinking skills.[22]

Additional Strategies for Teaching Thinking

Student mastery of various thinking skills requires continued instruction beyond a single course. In lower grades, the skill teaching framework should extend across a sequence of courses and over a period of years—starting, as Dwyer suggested, with a simplified version of the skill at a readiness and then introductory level. More attributes, applications to new data, and student-initiated use of the skill can follow in later years.[23] Thinking skills grow and develop gradually as students have repeated experiences with them in a variety of contexts.

Thus, it may be most productive to introduce some skills before others. The skill of distinguishing statements of facts from value judgments, for example, ought to be introduced before that of detecting bias in data.[24] At first these skills can be practiced directly and explicitly as discrete skills. Then, in subsequent grades, guided practice and extension of these skills can be integrated with other thinking processes as the skills are themselves broadened by instruction in their subtleties and more complex attributes and used with a variety of content and media.

No one engages in thinking by employing a single cognitive thinking skill. One does not separate relevant from irrelevant data, for instance, and then stop. This skill may be used with other thinking skills, such as identifying unstated assumptions, separating statements of verifiable facts from value judgments, and so on. Instruction needs to focus on how to know when it is appropriate to use a particular skill and how to apply skills in combination in order to make meaning. The directive or inductive strategies described here can be used to introduce such skill instruction. Guided practice in identifying where and when to employ specific thinking skills should follow. Students need instruction and guided practice in critical thinking as a whole as well as in the discrete skills that constitute thinking.

Teaching thinking skills also involves teaching students the analytical concepts that inform these skills.[25] This means providing instruction in the knowledge base in which they are to be employed. McPeck[26] and others[27] assert that thinking is intimately connected with the specific fields of knowledge in which it is used; it cannot be taught—or learned—in complete isolation from any body of content. The better informed we are about a subject, the better able we are to think about it. How a specific skill may be used and when it is appropriate to use it are decisions closely tied to a specific body of information as well as to the goals of the individual learner.[28]

Although we may not now know all there is to know about teaching thinking skills, we can improve the teaching and learning of these skills if we use techniques of direct instruction. One way to do so is to employ the skill teaching framework, skill teaching strategies, and guidelines for teaching presented here. If these approaches can be incorporated into our teaching, I suspect that students can and will make major strides toward improving their competen-

cies in thinking and in better understanding the world in which we live—both major goals of education today.

FOOTNOTES

[1]Catherine Cornbleth and Willard Korth, "In Search of Academic Instruction," *Educational Researcher* 9, 5 (May 1980): 9; and "If Remembering, Understanding, and Reasoning are Important . . ." *Social Education* 45, 4 (April 1981): 276, 278-279.

[2]Hilda Taba, "Teaching of Thinking," *Elementary English* 42, 5 (May 1965): 534; Edward de Bono, "The Direct Teaching of Thinking as a Skill," *Phi Delta Kappan* 64, 10 (June 1983): 104; John E. McPeck, *Critical Thinking and Education* (New York: St. Martin's Press, 1981), p. 104; Edward M. Glaser, *An Experiment in the Development of Critical Thinking* (New York: Bureau of Publications, Teachers College, Columbia University, 1941), p. 69; Donald W. Oliver and James P. Shaver, *Teaching Public Issues in the High School* (Boston: Houghton Mifflin Company, 1966), p. 246; James P. Shaver, "Educational Research and Instruction for Critical Thinking," *Social Education* 26, 1 (January 1962): 14, 16.

[3]David Russell, *Children's Thinking* (Boston: Ginn and Company, 1956), p. 287.

[4]Howard Anderson, ed., *Teaching Critical Thinking in Social Studies: 13th Yearbook of the National Council for the Social Studies* (Washington, D.C.: National Council for the Social Studies, 1942), p. vii.

[5]Bryce Hudgins, *Learning and Thinking* (Itasca, Ill.: F. E. Peacock Publishers, Inc., 1977), p. 180; Barak V. Rosenshine, "Content, Time and Direct Instruction," in *Research on Teaching*, ed. Penelope L. Peterson and Herbert J. Walberg (Berkeley: McCutchan Publishing Corporation, 1979), pp. 28-56; Glaser, op. cit., pp. 69-71.

[6]Glaser, op. cit., pp. 69-70.

[7]Ralph Tyler, "Measuring the Ability to Infer," *Educational Research Bulletin* 9, 17 (November 19, 1930): 475-480; Hudgins, op. cit., p. 182.

[8]Hudgins, op. cit., p. 180.

[9]Taba, op. cit., pp. 533, 538; Russell, op. cit., p. 368. Michael Posner and Steven W. Keele, "Skill Learning," in *Second Handbook of Research on Teaching*, ed. Robert M. W. Travers (Chicago: Rand McNally College Publishing Company, 1973), p. 824; Ann Brown and others, "Learning to Learn: On Training Students to Learn from Texts," *Educational Researcher* 10 (February 1981): 14-21; Robert J. Sternberg, "Teaching Intellectual Skills: Looking for Smarts in All The Wrong Places," unpublished paper, Yale University, 1984, p. 16.

[10]Posner and Keele, op. cit., pp. 816, 820.

[11]Frances M. Dwyer, Jr., "Adapting Visual Illustrations for Effective Learning," *Harvard Educational Review* 37, 2 (Spring 1967): 250-263; Hudgins, op. cit., pp. 167-168.

[12]Hudgins, op. cit., pp. 147, 151, 205; Herbert A. Simon, "Problem Solving and Education," in *Problem Solving and Education: Issues in Teaching and Research*, ed. D. T. Tuma and F. Relf (Hillsdale, N.J.: Lawrence Erlbaum Associates, Publishers, 1980), p. 82.

[13]Horace T. Morse and George H. McCune, with Lester E. Brown and Ellen Cook, *Selected Items for the Testing of Study Skills and Critical Thinking: Bulletin 15* (Washington, D.C.: National Council for the Social Studies, 1940, 5th ed., 1971), pp. 4, 17.

[14]Ibid., p. 4.

[15]Excerpted from William Cobbett, *Political Register* L11, November 20, 1824 (italics in the original).

[16]Excerpted from Andrew Ure, *The Philosophy of Manufacturers: or An Exposition of the Scientific, Moral and Commercial Economy of the Factory System of Great Britain,* 3rd ed. (London: H. G. Bohn, 1861), p. 301.

[17]Peter Martorella, "Cognition Research: Some Implications for the Design of Social Studies Instructional Materials," *Theory and Research in Social Education* X, 3 (Fall 1982): 1-16.

[18]Posner and Keele, op. cit., pp. 808, 811-812, 816, 824.

[19]Harold Berlak, "The Teaching of Thinking," *The School Review* 73, 1 (Spring 1965): 1-13.

[20]Barry K. Beyer, "What's In A Skill? Defining the Skills We Teach," *Social Science Record* 21, 2 (Fall 1984): 19-23.

[21]Hudgins, op. cit., pp. 143, 147, 151.

[22]Carl Bereiter, "How To Keep Thinking Skills from Going the Way of All Frills," *Educational Leadership* 42, 1 (September 1984): 76; Robert J. Sternberg, "How Can We Teach Intelligence?" *Educational Leadership* 42, 1 (September 1984): 47; Judith W. Segal and Susan F. Chipman, "Thinking and Learning Skills: The Contributions of NIE," *Educational Leadership* 42, 1 (September 1984): 86; Elizabeth Bondy, "Thinking About Thinking," *Childhood Education* (March/April 1984): 234-238; Ann Brown and others, op. cit.

[23]Dwyer, op. cit.; McPeck, op. cit., p. 18; Hudgins, op. cit., pp. 167-168.

[24]Hudgins, op. cit., pp. 182, 205; Morse and McCune, op. cit., pp. 5-6.

[25]Hudgins, op. cit., pp. 174, 179.

[26]McPeck, op. cit., pp. 7-8, 17-18.

[27]Morse and McCune, op. cit., p. 8; Hudgins, op. cit., p. 189; William H. Burton, Roland B. Kimball, and Richard L. Wing, *Education for Effective Thinking* (New York: Appleton-Century-Crofts, Inc., 1960), p. 438; Harold Berlak, "New Curricula and the Measurement of Thinking," *Education Forum* 30, 3 (March 1966): 306.

[28]Berlak, op. cit., p. 304.

25

Mediative Strategies

Arthur L. Costa, Robert Hanson, Harvey F. Silver, and Richard W. Strong

Mediative teaching strategies help students act on and inductively transform information, skills, and concepts into new meanings and practice and understand the rational processes of problem solving, decision making, and critical thinking. They are intended to enable students to learn to evaluate different points of view in controversial issues, respect the opinions and beliefs of others, and use alternative problem-solving processes—sometimes called "heuristics," from the Greek *eureka*, meaning "I have found it."

Roles and Motivation

Mediative strategies may employ the dialogical approach discussed in Richard Paul's chapter. They are sometimes referred to as "Socratic" because, like Socrates, the teacher mediates by raising questions and dilemmas that tease students' curiosity and stimulate their inquiry, and by causing them to arrive at and test their own conclusions, apply the concepts they have induced, consider alternative theories or explanations, and experiment with alternative problem-solving approaches. The teacher refrains from making value judgments about students' ideas and invites them to evaluate ideas for themselves. After gathering the necessary information, students process it to form their own concepts and generalizations.

Students are motivated by the curiosity inherent in the cognitive task: explaining phenomena, finding patterns, designing systems for generating needed information, explaining causality, inducing concepts (such as metamorphosis, conductors, or prime numbers), establishing proof, considering alternative points of view, confronting real problems to solve, and hypothesizing.

Student Outcomes

Students, in turn, are expected to examine the problems posed and the discrepancies illuminated by the teacher and to use inductive and deductive reasoning to produce an explanation and to support that explanation with both logical and evidentiary proof. Students are also expected to articulate the understandings and cognitive processes they are developing and using.

By employing these strategies over time with skill, patience, and close adherence to their attributes, students become more autonomous, increase their problem-solving skill, and show greater respect for the varying opinions and points of view of others.

Instructional Strategies in this Category

Mediative strategies include *Open-Ended Discussion, Concept Development* (which includes *Concept Attainment* and *Concept Formation*), *Values Awareness/Clarification, Inquiry, Moral Reasoning,* and *Deep Process Instruction.* We have selected Bruner's and Taba's *Concept Attainment* and *Open-Ended Discussion*, and Suchman's *Inquiry* as strategies to present in greater detail.

Dialectical Reasoning

Richard W. Paul

Education is training in HOW to think rather than in WHAT to think; it is a confrontation, a dialogue between ways of assessing evidence and supporting conclusions. It implies that the teacher's primary job is that of making clear the bases upon which he weighs the facts, the methods by which he separates facts from fancies, and the ways in which he discovers and selects his ultimate norms ... This concept of teaching ... requires that the purported facts be accompanied by the reasons why they are considered the facts. Thereby the teacher exposed his methods of reasoning to test and change. If the facts are in dispute ... then the reasons why others do not consider them to be facts must also be presented, thus bringing alternative ways of thinking and believing into dialogue with each other.

—Emerson Shideler

The "critical thinking" movement whose early stirrings can be traced back to and beyond Edward Glaser's *An Experiment in the Development of Critical Thinking* (1941) and his development with Watson of the *Watson-Glaser Critical Thinking Test* (1940), is now, after a long and halting start, building up a head of steam. Predictably, a variety of quick-fix, miracle cures have sprung up. Turning to them is a distinct temptation, especially given the increasing variety of imperatives and mandates under which schools are operating. I advocate both a short- and a long-term strategy, based on a global analysis of where we now stand and of what ultimately we should strive to achieve. Our strategy should reflect a realistic appraisal of (1) the basic cognitive and affective "tendencies" of the human mind in its "normal" uncritical state; (2) the categorically different modes of problem types and reasoning appropriate to them; (3) the social and personal conditions under which cognitive and affective processes develop; (4) the present critical thinking skills of teachers and students; and (5) the fundamental intellectual, affective, and social obstacles to the further development of such skills.

I emphasize the importance of recognizing and high-lighting a fundamental difference between two distinct conceptions of critical thinking skills; that is, a conception of these skills in a weak sense and in a strong sense. Conceived of in a *weak sense*, critical thinking skills are understood as a set of discrete micro-logical skills ultimately extrinsic to the character of the person; skills that can be tacked onto other learning. In the *strong sense*, critical thinking skills are understood as a set of integrated macro-logical skills ultimately intrinsic to the character of the person and to insight into one's own cognitive and affective processes. If we opt for the latter, we will concern ourselves not only with the development of *technical reason*—skills that do not transform one's grasp of one's basic cognitive and affective processes—but also with the development of *emancipatory reason*—skills that generate not only fundamental insight into but also some command of one's own cognitive and affective processes. Also in the strong sense, we emphasize comprehensive critical thinking skills essential to the free, rational, and autonomous mind. In the weak sense, we are content to develop what typically comes down to "vocational" thinking skills, which by themselves have little influence on a person's intellectual, emotional, or moral autonomy.

By aspiring to strong-sense critical thinking skills for long-term goals, and by taking stock of where we now stand, careful consideration of the evidence will eventually convince us that:

1. There are deep-seated tendencies in the human mind to reason in order to maximize getting, and to justify getting, what we often unconsciously want. This typically involves using cognitive and affective processes to maintain self-serving or pleasant illusions, to rule out or unfairly undermine opposing ideas, to link our identity with ideas that are "ours" (such that disagreement is experienced as ego-threatening), and otherwise to distort or "misinterpret" our experience to serve our own advantage.

This chapter is excerpted from Richard W. Paul, "Critical Thinking: Fundamental to Education for a Free Society," *Educational Leadership* 42, 1 (September 1984): 4-14.

2. There is a fundamental difference between the kinds of problems one faces in technical domains and those in the logically messy "real world." Solutions to technical problems are typically determined by *one* self-consistent close-textured system of ideas and procedures. In contrast, the problems of everyday life are rarely settled in a rational manner as a result of opposing points of view, contradictory lines of reasoning, and the realities of power and self-delusion.

3. To this point the schools, to the extent they have addressed problem solving, have focused their efforts on technical problems and technical reason and procedure, and have either illicitly reduced real-world problems to them or have tacitly inculcated into students the prefabricated "apodictic answers" of the dominant social majority or some favored minority.

4. Our capacity to command our cognitive and affective processes is heavily influenced by the character of our early lives, both at home and school. Very special preparation is necessary if we want children to develop into adults who are comfortable with and skilled in weighing, reconciling, and assessing contradictory arguments and points of view through dialogue, discussion, and debate.

5. Teaching strategies need to be revamped across the board—especially in social studies and basic academic competencies—to stress the development of dialectical knowledge and skills, and thus self-formed, self-reasoned conviction.

The Short-Term Strategy

The best short-term strategy is to facilitate the understanding and the teaching of micro-logical, analytic critical thinking skills within established subject areas. At the base of this is the importance of skill in the elementary critical/analytic vocabulary of the English language: a working knowledge of such mundane terms as *premise, reason, conclusion, inference, assumption, relevant/irrelevant, consistent/contradictory, credible/doubtful, evidence, fact, interpretation, question-at-issue, problem,* and so on. Teachers should be encouraged to take at least one university level course in critical thinking that provides practice in the basic micro-logical skills associated with these terms. Such a course can teach them how to isolate and distinguish issues, premises, assumptions, conclusions, and inferences, and to master the rudiments of argument assessment.

The nationally normed tests, such as the Watson-Glaser and the Cornell Critical Thinking Tests, should be available to teachers, who should learn how to formulate test questions modeled on them. A full range of critical thinking books and materials, both university level and "curricular," should also be available to teachers, along with brainstorming sessions on their use. Teachers need to begin to do some critical thinking about critical thinking programs, to gain a grasp of what makes sense to them and of what they can begin immediately to do.

An important caveat should be entered here, however. Unlike the case of computer skills or other technical skills, there is a natural disinclination for people to recognize the degree to which they themselves have not developed critical thinking skills. Educators tend to retreat to simplistic curriculum packages that do not lay an appropriate foundation for higher level (strong-sense) critical thinking skills, or to dismiss the need for any new curriculum materials or learnings at all ("All good teachers naturally teach critical thinking"). Most people, including the most uncritical, take offense at the suggestion that they lack skill in this area. This ego-identification with critical thinking (it is the *others* who need it) is a continual problem in the nurturing of such skills. To the extent that people lack critical thinking skills, they conceptualize those who have them as prejudiced, close-minded, overly academic, negative or nit-picky.

It is well, therefore, to emphasize from the outset that the ability to think critically is a matter of *degree.* No one is without *any* critical skills, and no one has them so fully that there are no areas of his or her life and thought in which uncritical thinking is dominant. Open-mindedness may be the proper, but it is not the "natural," disposition of the human mind.

Additional short-term goals should include the following:

1. Training master teachers in a few of the best programs available; for example, *Philosophy for Children* and *Law in a Free Society.*[1] Both programs were carefully designed by scholars, begin in the early elementary years, and aim at foundational critical thinking skills. Both also provide the kind of staff development that lessens the possibility of superficiality, and focus on much needed dialogue and discussion rather than lecture.

2. Encouraging teachers and curriculum specialists to attend the growing number of critical thinking conferences.

3. Working to develop a schoolwide attitude in which reasoning within unorthodox and conflicting points of view and respectful reasoned disagreement is considered essential and healthy (a very difficult goal to achieve).

4. Encouraging special attention to what Bloom (1981) has called "latent" curricula and "unspoken" values that may undermine the critical spirit (again, very difficult).

5. Establishing a working relationship with at least one university critical thinking instructor (not because he or she will grasp all of the difficulties you face but because it is useful to get the kind of feedback that will help to avoid

straying into what seems to be, but is not, critical thinking instruction).

The ideal is to take those first steps that initiate the teaching of relatively "self-contained" critical thinking skills: testing for inferences that explicitly do or do not follow, for recognition of assumptions and clear-cut contradictions, for initial formulations or reasons to support conclusions, for consideration of evidence rather than reliance on authority, and so forth, and that enhance the development of an environment conducive to strong-sense critical thinking skills. Wherever possible, students should be given every opportunity to advance ideas of their own and to give reasons to support them, as well as opportunities to hear the objections of other students. If this is done carefully in an atmosphere of cooperation and while learning critical analytic terms, students will begin to use critical distinctions when defending their ideas. This vocabulary integration sets in motion a very healthy process that, properly nurtured, can lead to at least primitive emancipatory thinking skills.

Long-Term Strategy

An effective long-range strategy should have two components: an explication of obstacles to the development of strong-sense critical thinking skills, and an increasing recognition of the distinctive nature and importance of dialectical issues and importance of dialectical issues and of the manner in which they can be brought into the traditional school curriculum.

It is not enough to recognize that all human thought is embedded in human activity and all human activity embedded in human thought. We need to recognize in addition that much of our thinking is subconscious, automated, and irrational. The capacity to explicate the roots of the thinking that is "hidden" from us and to purge it when irrational are crucial. Long-range strategy must have, in other words, an explicative/purgative, as well as a constructive/developmental, dimension.

Obstacle One: The Denial of the Need

Without ignoring the many ways in which they intersect, it is illuminating to recognize the degree to which we live in two very different noetic worlds: a world of technical and technological order and clarity, and a world of personal and social disorder and confusion. We are increasingly adept at solving problems in the first domain and increasingly endangered by our inability to solve problems in the other.

Various explanations have been given for this unhappy state of affairs. One of the most popular identifies a two-fold root cause of the problem: first, a lack of willingness on the part of those who are right, and know they are, to "stand tall" and refuse to be pushed around by those who are wrong (and are being irrational, stubborn, or malevolent); and second, the difficulty of getting the others (our opposition) to see the rationality and fair-mindedness of our views and the irrationality, close-mindedness, or malevolence of theirs.

President Reagan, to take a recent striking example, put it succinctly when he claimed that one country, the USSR, is the "focus of all evil in the world," an "evil empire," which understands nothing but force and power and steel-eyed determination. That a one-dimensional explanation of this sort can still not only catch the public's fancy but seem intelligible to many national leaders, not to mention some "intellectuals," testifies to the primitive state of much of our thinking when it comes to nontechnical, nontechnological human problems.

President Reagan's nationalistic expostulations are reminiscent of a tendency to ethnocentrism deep in our own and perhaps in all cultures:

Fellow Americans, we are God's chosen people. Yonder at Bunker Hill and Yorktown His providence was above us. At New Orleans and on ensanguined seas His hand sustained us. Abraham Lincoln was His minister, and His was the altar of Freedom the boys in blue set on a hundred battlefields. His power directed Dewey in the East and delivered the Spanish fleet into our hands on the eve of Liberty's natal day, as he delivered the elder armada into the hands of our English sires two centuries ago. His great purposes are revealed in the progress of the flag, which surpasses the intentions of congresses and cabinets, and leads us like a holier pillar of cloud by day and pillar of fire by night into situations unforeseen by finite wisdom, and duties unexpected by the unprophetic heart of selfishness. The American people cannot use a dishonest medium of exchange; it is ours to set the world its example of right and honor. We cannot fly from our world duties; it is ours to execute the purpose of a fate that has driven us to be greater than our small intention. We cannot retreat from any soil where Providence has unfurled our banner; it is ours to save that soil for liberty and civilization. For liberty and civilization and God's promise fulfilled, the flag must henceforth be the symbol and the sign to all mankind—the flag! (Beveridge, 1898).

These sentiments remind us of the views articulated by children interviewed by Piaget in his study for UNESCO of the causes of war (Campbell, 1976).

Piaget: Have you heard of such people as foreigners?

Michel M. (9 years, 6 months old): Yes, the French, the Americans, the Russians, the English . . .

Piaget: Quite right. Are there differences between all these people?

Michel: Oh yes, they don't speak the same language.

Piaget: And what else?

Michel: I don't know.

Piaget: What do you think of the French, for instance? Do you like them or not? Try and tell me as much as possible.

Michel: The French are very serious, they don't worry about anything, an' it's dirty there.

Piaget: And what do you think of the Americans?

Michel: They're ever so rich and clever. They've discovered the bomb.

Piaget: And what do you think of the Russians?

Michel: They're bad, they're always wanting to make war.

Piaget: And what's your opinion of the English?

Michel: I don't know . . . they're nice . . .

Piaget: Now look, how did you come to know all you've told me?

Michel: I don't know . . . I've heard it . . . that's what people say.

Piaget: If you didn't have nationality and you were given a free choice of nationality, which would you choose?

Maurice (8 years, 3 months old): Swiss nationality.

Piaget: Why?

Maurice: Because I was born in Switzerland.

Piaget: Now look, do you think the French and the Swiss are equally nice, or the one nicer or less nice than the other?

Maurice: The Swiss are nicer.

Piaget: Why?

Maurice: The French are always nasty.

Piaget: Who is more intelligent, the Swiss or the French, or do you think they're just the same?

Maurice: The Swiss are more intelligent.

Piaget: Why?

Maurice: Because they learn French quickly.

Piaget: If I asked a French boy to choose any nationality he liked, what country do you think he'd choose?

Maurice: He'd choose France.

Piaget: Why?

Maurice: Because he was born in France.

Piaget: And what would he say about who's the nicer? Would he think the Swiss and the French equally nice or one better than the other?

Maurice: He'd say the French are nicer.

Piaget: Why?

Maurice: Because he was born in France.

Piaget: And who would he think more intelligent?

Maurice: The French.

Piaget: Why?

Maurice: He'd say that the French want to learn quicker than the Swiss.

Piaget: Now you and French boy don't really give the same answer. Who do you think answered best?

Maurice: I did.

Piaget: Why?

Maurice: Because Switzerland is always better.

Piaget: If you were born without any nationality and you were given a free choice, what nationality would you choose?

Marina (7 years, 9 months old): Italian.

Piaget: Why?

Marina: Because it's my country. I like it better than Argentina where my father works, because Argentina isn't my country.

Piaget: Are the Italians just the same, or more, or less intelligent than the Argentinians? What do you think?

Marina: I can see the people I live with, they're Italians.

Piaget: If I were to give a child from Argentina a free choice of nationality, what do you think he would choose?

Marina: He'd want to stay an Argentinian.

Piaget: Why?

Marina: Because that's his country.

Piaget: And if I were to ask him who is more intelligent, the Argentinians or the Italians, what do you think he would answer?

Marina: He'd say Argentinians.

Piaget: Why?

Marina: Because there wasn't any war.

Piaget: Good. Now who was really right in the choice he made and what he said, the Argentinian child, you or both?

Marina: I was right.

Piaget: Why?

Marina: Because I chose Italy.

For both the President of the United States and these children, the world is a nationalistically simple one in which the forces of good (embodied in ourselves) stand opposed by the forces of evil (those who oppose us). The need for emancipatory reason is a need of "the other," the stranger, the foreigner, the opposition.

From this vantage point the task of the schools is that of passing on our way of thinking to children, exposing them to all the reasons why we are right and superior and unquestionable and, at the same time, developing technical abilities and technological power to defend (enforce) our views. The school's task, in short, is to inculcate cultural patriotism and facilitate vocational training.

The distinguished American anthropologist, William Graham Sumner (1959), conservative though he was, sharply challenged this way of thinking, though he had no illusion about the difficulty of transforming the schools into vehicles for human and social emancipation:

School education, unless it is regulated by the best knowledge and good sense, will produce men and women who are all of one pattern, as if turned in a lathe . . . The examination papers show the pet ideas of the examiners . . . An orthodoxy is produced in regard to all the great doctrines of life . . . (There is a desire) that children shall be taught just that one thing which is "right" in the view and interest of those in control, and nothing else.

Sumner even had a conception of what a society would be like if critical thinking—in what I am calling the strong sense—were a fundamental social value:

The critical habit of thought, if usual in a society, will pervade all its mores, because it is a way of taking up the problems of life. People educated in it cannot be stampeded by stump orators and are never deceived by dithyrambic oratory. They are slow to believe. They can hold things as possible or probable in all degrees, without certainty and without pain. They can wait for evidence and weigh evidence, uninfluenced by the emphasis and confidence with which assertions are made on one side or the other. They can resist appeals to their dearest prejudices and all kinds of cajolery. Education in the critical faculty is the only education of which it can be truly said that it makes good citizens.

Sumner's concept of a "developed critical faculty" is one that clearly goes much beyond that envisioned by those who link it to a shopping list of atomic academic skills. It is a pervasive organizing core of mental habits, and a shaping force in the character of a person. It is fair-mindedness brought into the heart of everyday life, into all of its manifold dimensions. As a social commitment, it transforms the very nature of how life is lived and human transactions mediated.

Obstacle Two: The Failure of Cognitive Psychology and Problem Solving Theorists to Call Attention to the Logic of Dialectical Issues

One of the major weaknesses in cognitive psychology and in problem solving theory today is the failure to highlight the striking difference between the logic of technical problems and those of a dialectical nature. Until one recognizes this difference, there is a tendency to reduce all problems to technical ones and so to render all knowledge and all problems procedural, if not algorithmic. Susceptibility to operationalism is both the virtue and the limitation of technical crafts and disciplines. Progress is made in technical domains by severely narrowing what qualifies as appropriate subject matter and appropriate treatment of it. All concepts developed are specifically designed to serve restricted disciplinary purposes. Additionally, scope is typically further limited to what is quantifiable. For these reasons many of the concepts and attendant skills of application are relatively subject-specific.

Consider the wide variety of technical disciplines that can be brought to bear on the study of humans: physics, chemistry, neurology, physiology, biology, medicine, psychology, economics, sociology, anthropology, history, and philosophy. Put another way, humans are physical, chemical, neurological, biological, psychological, economic, sociological, historical, and philosophical beings, but they are all of these at once. Each person is *one* being, not many. To the extent that a problem about humans is rendered *technical* it is reduced to a relatively narrow system of exclusionary ideas; technical precision and manageability are achieved by excluding a variety of other technical and nontechnical features. Specialized disciplines develop by generating ever more specialized subdisciplines, abstracting further and further form the "wholeness" of things.

This is made more evident when we reflect upon those disciplines whose study of humankind does not appear to admit, beyond a range of foundational premises, to discipline-wide unanimity: history, psychology, sociology, anthropology, economics, and philosophy. In each of these social "sciences" and humanities, there are a variety of alternative systems or competing viewpoints. Generate a question within them, and you typically generate a field of possible conflicting lines of reasoning and answers. Raise questions about their application to everyday life problems, and the debate often intensifies. The issues are properly understood as dialectical, as calling for dialogical reasoning, for thinking critically and reciprocally within opposing points of view. This ability to move up and back between contradictory lines of reasoning, using each to critically cross-examine the other, is not characteristic of the technical mind. Technical knowledge is typically developed by restriction to one frame of reference, to one standpoint. Knowledge arrived at dialectically, in contrast, is like the verdict, with supporting reasoning, of a jury. There are at least two points of view to entertain. It is not, as problem-solving theorists tend to characterize all problems, a movement from an initial state through a series of transformations (or operations) to a final (answering) state.

Despite the need for nontechnical, dialectical, integrative thinking, most of the work in cognitive psychology and problem-solving theory seems to be premised on the notion that all problem solving can be understood on the model of processes appropriate to technical disciplines. Since each technical domain generates a dominant logical system, which in turn creates criteria and procedures for cognitive moves within them, there is a tendency to try to reduce problem solving to a technical or scientific model. This was true from the earliest beginnings of problem solving theory.

For example, Dewey (1933, 1938) thought that one could approach all problems through the following ordered scientific steps: (1) identify the problem, (2) establish facts, (3) formulate hypotheses, (4) test hypotheses, and (5) evaluate results. Polya (1957) formulated a similar general procedure.

Barry Beyer (1984) identifies insufficient proceduralization as a major problem in instruction in thinking skills. He advises teachers to provide "... step-by-step instructions on how to use specific thinking skills," indeed to spell out "... exactly how to execute a skill." He demands that "the crucial part of teaching a skill is discussing its operational procedures." There is no apparent recognition on his part that the largest and most important form of human thinking—dialectical thinking—cannot, by its very nature, be reduced to an operational procedure. When we think dialectically we are guided by *principles*, not *procedures*, and the application of the principles is often subject to discussion or debate.

The most vexing and significant real life problems are logically messy. They span multiple categories and disciplines. They are typically not *in* any one of them. The general attitude of mind, for example, that enables one with apparent peace and tranquility to confuse egocentric dogmatism with genuine conviction, to accept vague avowals as true beliefs, to take sentimental credulity for moral insight, to harmonize technical truths with pleasant delusions and superstitions, to wander in and out of a vast panoply of self-serving reifications, to use confusion to one's advantage, to perform social roles that one does not know one is performing—is not a problem whose solution lies in a discipline, or in a procedure, or in finding the connection between the data and the unknown, or in considering an auxiliary problem or in using special operators, or in performing a cost-benefit analysis, or in learning mnemonic techniques or memory codes or study systems or protocol analysis.

Once into the ebb and flow of mundane life, into its messy criss-crossing of categories, values, and points of view, its inevitable blending of the intellectual, the affective, and the moral, its embodying of irrationality in social practices and beliefs, there is little room for the neat and abstract procedures of technical reason. What is called for is dialogic, point-counterpoint, argument for and argument against, scrutiny of individual event against the background of this or that global "totalizing" of it into one's life. What is called for is liberating emancipatory reason, the ability to reason across, between, and beyond the neatly marshalled data of any given technical domain. Because it cannot presuppose or restrict itself to any one system or technical language or procedure, it must be dialectical. That is, it must move back and forth between opposing points of view. It must consider how this or that situation might be handled if we looked at it this way, or how if we looked at it that way, of what follows from this construal and what from that, of what objection can be raised to this and what objection to that. It is the logic that is mocked in the typically closed-minded exchanges of mundane human arguments about the personal and social affairs of life. It is the logic that is concept-generating as well as concept-using (since our point of view is shaped as we use it in a way parallel to case law).

Now, precisely because it is not procedural, not susceptible to a decision-procedure or a set of technical maneuvers, there is the temptation to retreat either to apodictic self-righteousness (let us pass on to our children our heritage, our wisdom, so they like us can recognize the folly of those who oppose us) or to vacuous or self-contradictory relativism (we cannot teach dialectical thinking skills for they are in the realm of opinion or faith). Both choices fail to give due recognition, or any recognition at all, to the proper role of dialectical reason, which, when used as a means of penetrating and assessing the logic of our mundane lives, alone creates the possibility of becoming intellectually, emotionally, and morally autonomous persons.

Obstacle Three: Childhood Ego-Identification With Adult Beliefs: A Foundation For Closed-Mindedness

If we do not control the fundamental logical structures—the assumptions, values, and beliefs—that shape our own thought, feeling responses, and moral judgments, then in a significant sense we are not free. Close scrutiny of the process by which most children come to imbibe those structures and of the evidence that can be adduced to demonstrate that most adults are both oblivious to them and typically unable to resist them mandates the recognition that we have not yet learned how to make fundamental intellectual, emotional, and moral emancipation a probable outcome of parenting or schooling. The ultimate court of appeal of a free and open mind is, and must be, the principles of comprehensive reason and evidence, not external authority, ego-identification, or technical expertise, the willingness to listen to and empathize with all contending perspectives on an issue without presupposing any connection between the truth and any preselected line of reasoning. The foundation for this capacity, if it is to flourish, must be laid in the early years of life. It is determined by what behavior is rewarded and penalized, by the process that is used to shape children's identities. It depends on whether and to what extent children are persuaded that their goodness as human beings depends on believing what those in authority believe. When love and affection are contingent on specific belief states, those belief states become an integral part of children's identities. They become egocentric extensions of children, who are thus denied opportunities to separate their own beings from the belief structures that adults are, in effect, imposing. Children become literally dependent, intellectually and emotionally, on them and are unable later, without trauma, to subject them to serious critical scrutiny. In this way, children are condemned to closed-mindedness.

Our present process of raising and teaching children is having precisely this unhappy effect. Children come to

adulthood today as intellectual, emotional, and moral crip-
ples. They are not whole or free persons in the sense delineated in this article, and they have no conception that they
are not. Like all persons whose belief states are ego-identi-
fications, they conceive of those who disagree with them—
independently of how rationally the case is put against the
favored point of view—as *biased*. They may have learned
how to affect an adult veneer, how to put on socially accepted masks; at root, however, infantile egocentric identi-
fications and commitments rule their minds. They do not
know how to conduct a serious discussion of their own
most fundamental beliefs. Indeed, they do not know in
most cases what those beliefs are. They are unable to empathize with the reasoning of those who seriously disagree
with them. If adept at conceptual moves at all, their adept-
ness is in dodges such as transforming the reasoning of
those who seriously disagree with them into caricatures.
They know, like politicians, how to retreat into vagueness
to protect their challenged beliefs.

This need not be the case. Children can be raised to
value the authority of their own reasoning capacities. They
can be taught comprehensive principles of rational thought.
They can learn to consider it natural that people differ in
their beliefs and points of view. And they can learn to grasp
this not as a quaint peculiarity of people but as a tool for
learning. They can learn how to learn from others, even
from their objections, contrary perceptions, and differing
ways of thinking.

But how is this to be done? How are these obstacles to
be overcome? How are we to teach dialectical reasoning
and pave the way for human emancipation?

Teaching Basic Academic Competencies As Incipient Higher Order Thinking Skills

Let's focus on a central feature; namely, that strategies
"be designed to achieve an understanding of the relationship of language to logic leading to the ability to analyze,
criticize, and advocate ideas." The important assumption
here is that unless one achieves an understanding of the relationship of language to logic, one will not develop the
ability to analyze, criticize, and advocate ideas. It is essential to recognize that there are differences between the
structure and purposes of technical languages, the nature
and use of concepts within them, and those of a natural
language like English, German, or French. The differences
are parallel to those between technical and dialectical issues, and the divergent modes of reasoning they require.
Teachers should realize when, on the one hand, they are in
essence teaching a technical language, and so presupposing *one* standpoint and a specialized technically defined hierarchy of problems and when, on the other, they are in a

domain where multiple standpoints are possible, and so
where some key concepts are being used in a nontechnical
way, and where opposing lines of thought need to be considered. Whenever we think, we conceptualize and make
inferences from our conceptualization, based upon assumptions. In technical domains like math, physics, and
chemistry, however, the concepts and assumptions are
given. They are not in the standard case to be challenged
by an alternative point of view. The logic, on the one hand,
and the technical language, on the other, are virtually opposite sides of the same coin. But the affairs of everyday
life, including the inner life of the mind, are fundamentally
conducted within the logic of a natural language, and the
key concepts are inevitably used nontechnically and (when
properly handled) dialectically.

How we read, write, speak, listen, and reason varies,
or should vary, in accordance with these fundamental distinctions. Do I read, write, speak, listen, and reason so as
to throw myself totally into one well-defined point of view
and make its rules, regulations, and operations the controlling variables in my thinking? Or do I read, write, speak,
listen, and reason so as to entertain comparisons and contrasts between ideas in competition from different competing perspectives? Do I reason monologically or dialogi-
cally?

Most of our students have virtually no experience in
this second and crucially important mode of reading, writing, speaking, listening, and reasoning, even though many
of their everyday experiences presuppose such abilities. In
their everyday lives they often talk and listen to people who
are looking at events and situations in a variety of ways.
Their parents and their peers often see situations differently from them. They are often frustrated by their inability
to come to terms with these conflicts and dilemmas.

If we understand speaking and writing as constructing
a point of view, developing ideas in some logical relation to
each other, and listening and reading, as entering into
someone else's point of view, into *his* or *her* organization of
ideas, then we are in a better position to grasp how the
teaching of basic academic competencies ought to be
understood as incipient higher order thinking skills.

Furthermore, we will recognize that when we are listening to or reading ideas that conflict with our ego-identi-
fied belief states, we have a different problem to combat
than when the difficulty is not a matter of resistance but of
technical complexity. Learning how to listen to and read
(without distortion) lines of reasoning whose possible
truth we egocentrically wish to rule out is an essential experience and should constitute a significant element at all
ages and at all levels of educational development. As in all
areas of intellectual and emotional competency, these reading and listening capacities must be built up progressively

and over a long time. They are acquired by degrees. They are always amenable to further development.

Dialectical Knowledge Is Not Opinion But Macro-Logical Synthesis

It may be thought that dialectical reasoning (the reasoning called for whenever we are confronted by issues that cross categories or disciplinary lines, by issues for which different possible points of view can plausibly be developed) limits one by definition to *opinions*. This would be a mistake. To say, as a jury must ultimately, that a given defendant is innocent or guilty is not to imply that we seek their opinion as such. We are seeking their *reasoned judgment*, and we expect them to use the best comprehensive canons of reasoning and evidence to get it. We expect them to enter emphatically into the arguments of both prosecution and defense, and we want the strongest possible case to be made on both sides. A juror who fulfills these standards and in the end concludes that the accused is guilty or innocent may properly be said to *know* what the verdict enunciates. He or she may know it as well as he or she knows this or that technical truth. The knowledge is conditional, of course, but so too is technical knowledge.

A scientific experiment, for example, produces scientific knowledge to the extent that (1) its conditions were carefully and appropriately controlled, (2) its results were accurately recorded, and (3) accurately interpreted. Put another way, most of the important knowledge we have is the result of integrative acts of the mind; and inevitably the more we integrate, the more we must scrutinize what is left out, what is highlighted, and how the whole is being interpreted. The process is always subject to error. There are mistakes possible in all processes that lead to knowledge. Whenever we claim to know anything, our confidence is justified to the degree we have carefully attended to possible mistakes.

Synthesis across or beyond technical categories can be well or poorly justified. When outside the purely technical, part of the dues we must pay to justify rational confidence is empathy into the strongest case that can be made against our conclusion. These, unfortunately, are dues rarely paid. When they are, a person is not expressing a mere opinion, but rendering a rational verdict.

Finally, it should be emphasized that dialectically achieved synthesis is based on comprehensive rational principles, not on specialized procedures and concepts. It is *principled*, not procedural, thought. Like the law, it is based on the capacity of the mind to marshal cases and examples that illustrate principles; unlike the law, it does not require any technical concepts or procedures to do this. It is based on our capacity to achieve command of a natural language and our own minds and to use both as resources to make rational assessments of experience and human life, to create a standpoint in life that is neither egocentric nor ethnocentric.

A Final Plea

When, as the result of a trial, the jury comes to a verdict of guilty or innocent; when, as a result of political debate, a citizen decides to vote for one of the candidates; when, as a result of reading the case for alternative political systems, one concludes that one is superior to the others; when, as a result of hearing various sides of a family argument, one becomes persuaded that one way of putting things is more justified and accurate; when, as a result of reading many reports on the need for educational reform, one is prepared to argue for one of them; when, as a result of entertaining various representations of national security and the building of more nuclear weapons, one reasons to a position on the issue; when, after reading and thinking about various approaches to the raising of children, one opts for one; when, after "knowing" a person for a number of years and exploring various interpretations of his or her character, one decides that he or she would make a good marriage partner—*one is reasoning dialectically*. Dialectical thought is the master-principle of all rational experience and human emancipation. It cultivates the mind and orients the person as technical training cannot. It meets the need of persons to bring harmony and order into their lives; to work out an amalgamation of ideas from various dimensions of experience; to achieve, in short, intellectual, emotional, and moral integrity. The proper doing of it is our ultimate defense against closed-mindedness.

Collectively reinforced egocentric and sociocentric thought, conjoined with massive technical knowledge and power, are not the foundations for a genuine democracy. The basic insight that was formulated over a hundred years ago by John Stuart Mill (1858) is as true today, and as ignored, as it was when he first wrote it:

In the case of any person whose judgment is really deserving of confidence, how has it become so? Because he has kept his mind open to criticism of his opinions and conduct. Because it has been his practice to listen to all that could be said against him; to profit by as much of it as was just, and expound to himself, and upon occasion to others, the fallacy of what was fallacious. Because he has felt, that the only way in which a human being can make some approach to knowing the whole of a subject, is by hearing what can be said about it by persons of every variety of opinion, and studying all models in which it can be looked at by every character of mind. No wise man ever acquired wisdom in any mode but his; nor is it in the nature of human intellect to become wise in any other manner.

If the schools do not rise to meet this social need, what social institution will? If this is not the fundamental task and ultimate justification for public education, what is?

FOOTNOTE

[1]See Chapter 35 for information about *Philosophy for Children*. *Law In A Free Society* was developed by the Center for Civic Education in cooperation with the State Bar of California and UCLA.

REFERENCES

Beveridge, Albert J., U.S. Senator. "The March of the Flag," 1898.

Beyer, Barry. "Improving Thinking Skills—Defining the Problem." *Phi Delta Kappan* (March 1984).

Bloom, Benjamin. *All Our Children Learning*. New York: McGraw-Hill, 1981, pp. 22-24.

Campbell, Sarah, ed. *Piaget Sampler: An Introduction to Jean Piaget Through His Own Words*. New York: John Wiley & Sons, 1976.

Dewey, John. cf. *How We Think*. Boston: D.C. Heath & Co., 1933.

Dewey, John. *Logic: The Theory of Inquiry*. New York: Holt, Rinehart, & Winston, 1938. Chapters VI and XXIV.

Giere, Ronald. *Understanding Scientific Reasoning*. New York: Holt, Rinehart & Winston, 1978.

Hayes, John R. *The Complete Problem Solver*. Philadelphia: The Franklin Institute Press, 1981.

Jammer, M. *Concepts of Space: The History of Theories of Space in Physics*. Cambridge: Harvard University Press, 1957, p. xi.

Milgram, Stanley. *Obedience to Authority*. New York: Harper & Row, 1969.

Mill, John Stuart. *On Liberty*. Edited by Alburey Castell. Illinois: AHM Publishing Co., 1947, p. 20.

Polya, Gyorgy. *How To Solve It*. New York: Doubleday Anchor, 1957.

Sumner, William G. *Folkways and Mores*. Edited by Edward Sagarin. New York: Schocken Books, 1959.

Concept Development

Sydelle Seiger-Ehrenberg

Despite much talk about concept-centered curriculum, too many students still just learn facts. Teachers report, and tests show, that even those students who seem to have learned concepts often fail to apply them to new but similar situations.

Let's explore some of the possible reasons.

Different Concepts of "Concept"

One reason may be that educators haven't been sufficiently clear and consistent about what they think a concept is. They haven't distinguished between concepts and other things they want students to learn, such as facts, principles, attitudes, and skills. Fuzziness or lack of common understanding among curriculum developers, teachers, and testers about what a concept is could well account for disparity among what is taught, learned, and tested.

Lack of Understanding of Concept Learning/Teaching Processes

Another reason may be the assumption that concepts are learned (and therefore should be taught) in the same way facts are learned. While much attention has been given to differences in individual student learning "styles" (preferences related to *gathering* information), very little has been focused on the differences in various learning "strategies" (procedures for *processing* information). The process for learning and teaching concepts differs significantly from those appropriate for fact, principle, attitude, and skill learning. Lack of understanding of those differences on part of the curriculum developer or the teacher could certainly contribute to student failure to learn concepts.

Inadequate or Inappropriate Curriculum Material

Curriculum guides, teachers' manuals, and student materials may not contain enough of the right kind of information. Neither commercial nor locally developed curriculums may be thorough enough in identifying, defining, and relating the concepts students are expected to learn; of outlining appropriate concept-learning processes; or of presenting the kind of information students need in order to form concepts. Too often, the concept is just "presented" (as though it were a fact). Teachers who have to work with an inadequate or inappropriate curriculum may well be misled as to how to help students learn concepts, or, if they know better, are burdened with the task of revising or even developing the curriculum from scratch.

These may not be the only reasons students are not learning concepts as well as we think they should, but since these factors are under control, they should be addressed and, to the extent possible, eliminated.

Following are some ideas about concept learning and teaching which over the past 12 years many educators have learned and successfully applied. Their success came not from merely reading about or listening to these ideas, but as a result of hard work during and after intensive training in a staff development program called BASICS. This program and its predecessor, *The Hilda Taba Teaching Strategies Program*, focus on the thinking strategies students need to learn to achieve each of the basic types of learning objectives of any curriculum: concepts, principles, attitudes, and skills.

What Is a Concept?

Following are three *examples* of concepts.

1. Any plane, closed figure having just three sides
2. Any body of land bordered on all sides by water
3. Any invertebrate having just three body parts and exactly six legs

First, observe what each statement says. Note the *differences* among them. Then decide what is *true of all three statements*. What is true of all three is what makes all of them examples of "concept."

This subchapter originally appeared in Sydelle D. Ehrenberg, "Concept Learning: How To Make It Happen In The Classroom," *Educational Leadership* 39, 1 (October 1981): 36-43.

Now focus on the following three items. *None* of the three is a concept.

    a. ABC is a plane, closed figure having three sides.

    b. island

    c. ant

Consider items "a," "b," and "c" one at a time. Compare and contrast each with the concept examples (#1, #2, and #3) and decide why "a," "b," and "c" are not examples of a concept. Item "a" states certain facts about figure ABC—its characteristics—but it does not state the characteristics common to any and all examples of that type of figure. Item "b" gives the English label for a type of thing but does not state the set of characteristics common to any and all examples. Item "c" gives the name of one example of concept #3, insect, but it does not state the characteristics common to any and all examples of insects, distinguishing all insects from any non-insect.

Based on the above, consider the following definitions and examples:

Concept—the set of attributes or characteristics common to any and all instances (people, objects, events, ideas) of a given class (type, kind, category) *or* the characteristics that make certain items examples of a type of thing and that distinguish any and all examples from nonexamples.

Concept Label—one or more *terms* used to refer to any and all examples of a given concept.

Examples—any and all *individual items* that have the characteristics of a given concept (class).

Nonexamples—any and all *individual items* that may have some but not all the characteristics that make items examples of a given concept (class).

The concept is the set of characteristics, not the label. A person can know the label for a concept without knowing the characteristics of any and all examples and vice versa. A concept is not the same as a fact. A fact is verifiable information about an individual item, while a concept is a generalization in a person's mind about what is true of any and all items (even those the person has never seen) that are examples of the same class.

A few additional points about concepts:

All concepts are abstract. This is so because a concept constitutes a generalized mental image of the characteristics that make items examples. However, the characteristics of individual items may be either concrete (*all* of the characteristics are perceivable, as in an apple) or represented in some way. A representation may be quite "concrete" (many of the characteristics are perceivable, as in a model, film, or photo) or quite "abstract" (few or none of the characteristics are perceivable, as in a diagram, symbol, spoken or written description). A common misconception is that young children cannot conceptualize because they cannot yet form abstract ideas. Actually, young children can and do conceptualize but only when the characteristics of examples of the concept are perceivable directly through the senses and they have the opportunity to perceive those characteristics firsthand in several individual items. They need these sense perceptions to form the generalized mental picture of the characteristics. (Is it any wonder that young children have so much trouble forming such concepts as "sharing" and "tidiness"?)

Concepts cannot be verified, like facts, as being "right" or "wrong." Although it is difficult for us to realize, our concepts are not what is but what we have learned to think is. As a cultural group, over time, we decide what things are and what to call them. We store our current sets of characteristics and the concept labels that go with them in the dictionary and this becomes our "authority" to arbitrate any dispute. However, we all know how dictionaries

---

Figure 1
Concept Examples

CONCEPT LABEL	CONCEPT CHARACTERISTICS	EXAMPLES	NONEXAMPLES
Compound Word	Any word whose meaning is a combination of the meaning of the root words of which it is composed.	Nightgown Oversee Doorknob	Carpet Begun Understood
Fruit	The part of any plant that contains the seed(s).	Apple Tomato Squash	Potato Celery Carrot
Improper Fraction	Any fraction whose numerator is equal or greater than its denominator.	$8/7$ $16/16$ $4/1$	$7/8$ $4/16$ $1/4$

differ and that dictionaries need to be updated periodically to keep up with our changing concepts that are newly-developed and commonly agreed on.

If you want to test this idea about concepts, see how many different explanations you get when you ask several people whether each of the following is a "family" and why they think it is or is not:

—A husband and wife with no children
—Several friends sharing the same home
—Roommates at college
—A separated husband and wife each having one of their children
—A mother and grown daughter living together.

Concepts are hierarchical; that is, some classes include other classes. Living things include plants and animals; animals include vertebrates and invertebrates; vertebrates include mammals, fish, birds, amphibians, and reptiles; and so on. My dog Spot is a specific example of every one of the classes in the hierarchy until he separates out into the canine class because some of his characteristics distinguish him from examples of feline, equine, and so forth. Not only that but, by virtue of the unique characteristics that distinguish him from other mongrels in the world, Spot is himself a concept (in a class by himself).

We've already made the distinction between "concept" and "fact." Let's now consider the relationship between concepts and the other types of learning: principles, attitudes, and skills.

1. *Fact:* Verifiable information obtained through observing, experiencing, reading, or listening. Evidence of acquisition, comprehension, retention, and retrieval of information is the learner's expression of the specific, accurate, complete, relevant information called for.

2. *Concept:* Mental image of the set of characteristics common to any and all examples of a class. Evidence of conceptualization is the learner's demonstrated ability to consistently distinguish examples from nonexamples by citing the presence or absence of the concept characteristics in individual items.

3. *Principle:* Mental image of the cause-effect process which, under certain conditions, occurs between examples of two or more concepts. Evidence of understanding of the principle is the learner's demonstrated ability to make well-supported and qualified inferences of either cause or effect in new or changed situations.

4. *Attitude:* Mental set toward taking some action based on the desirability of anticipated consequences. Evidence of attitude learning is newly-acquired willingness to take (or refrain from) an action based on the learner's concept of what the action is and his or her predictions as to the desirable or undesirable effects of taking (or not taking) the action.

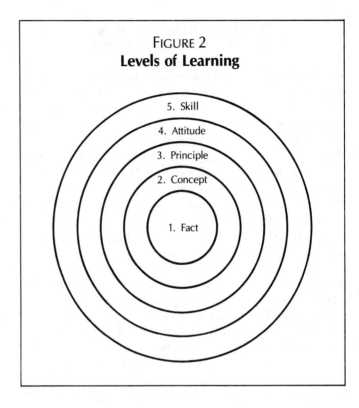

FIGURE 2
Levels of Learning

5. Skill
4. Attitude
3. Principle
2. Concept
1. Fact

5. *Skill:* Proficiency and speed in performing a mental or physical action or set of procedures. Evidence of skill learning is the learner's performance of the action/procedures at the desired level of proficiency or speed and, where applicable, a product that meets desired standards for quality and/or quantity. This performance is based on the learner's concept of the action, his or her predictions as to the effects of performing one way or another, and his or her internalization of the procedures through repeated practice.

It is important to note, in Figure 2, that concept learning is distinctly different from any of the other levels of learning; therefore, the evidence of achievement is different. You can't, for example, appropriately test understanding of a concept by having the learners state facts or perform a skill. Note also that each level is prerequisite to and an important component of the next level of learning. This being the case, fact-learning is necessary but not sufficient to concept learning, and concept learning is necessary but not sufficient to the learning of principles, attitudes, and skills. (Paradoxically, the learner needs to develop a certain degree of thinking, listening, and reading *skill* before achieving even the fact-learning level.)

What Learning/Teaching Strategies Develop Concepts?

Fundamental to helping students learn concepts is understanding that conceptualizing has to take place in the mind of the learner. That is, the learner needs to establish in his/her own mind a mental image of the set of characteristics that makes something an example of the concept and that distinguishes examples from nonexamples. If the learner has access only to the concept label and a definition (all words), his/her mental image of the characteristics of examples of the concept may be vague, inaccurate, or nonexistent. Being able to accurately state a definition one has read or heard amounts only to fact-level learning, not conceptualization; the learner is only recalling words.

One who has conceptualized, on the other hand, is able to consistently identify new examples, create new examples, distinguish examples from nonexamples, change nonexamples into examples, and, in every case, is able to explain what he/she has done by citing the presence or absence of the concept characteristics. The learner can do this because he/she is guided by a clear mental image of the characteristics that should be there.

There are a number of strategies through which the learner can be guided so that he/she gathers the appropriate information, processes the information appropriately, and ends up with his/her own clear mental image of the concept characteristics.

For example, using an inductive strategy from the BASICS Program, a teacher might have students record on worksheets information about the physical characteristics and life cycles of ants, grasshoppers, moths, and mantises. When the information has been reported, verified, and recorded on a large wall chart, the teacher would ask questions intended to direct students' attention to differences among the examples and then to characteristics common to all examples. Students would be asked to formulate a statement specifying "What is true of all invertebrates like these?"

After giving (or asking students for) the concept label "insect," the teacher might have students complete another worksheet calling for information about the characteristics of spiders, centipedes, scorpions, and earthworms. The learning sequence would be completed by having students respond to:

According to this information, what are some of the characteristics of these invertebrates that make them like insects?
What was true of the insects that is not true of any of these other insect-like invertebrates?
Based on what you've said here, finish the statement, "What makes insects different from other insect-like animals is _____ ."
Identify the animals shown here which you think are insects and the ones you think are not. For each be ready to tell what about the animal made you decide it was or was not an insect.

Using a deductive (classifying) strategy a teacher would first present information about characteristics of all examples of the concept (a definition) along with the concept label. For the concept "contraction," for instance, the teacher might ask students to state in their own words what they had read was true of all contractions. Next, students would be asked to identify and verify the characteristics in each of several examples of the concept. For instance the teacher might say, "In the sentence, 'The girl's here,' the word *girl's* is an example of a contraction. Referring to the definition we just discussed, what about *girl's* in this sentence makes it an example of a contraction?"

Next, students would be asked to note the absence of one or more of the concept characteristics in each of several nonexamples. For example, the teacher might say, "In the sentence, 'The girl's coat is here,' the word *girl's* is not a contraction. Referring to our definition, what about *girl's* in this sentence makes it not a contraction?"

Then students would develop generalized personal statements giving characteristics of all examples of the concept and characteristics that distinguish examples from nonexamples. Finally, the teacher might have students identify which underlined words in a group of sentences were contractions and which were not. Students would be expected to explain what made each an example or a nonexample of contractions.

From these examples you can see there are certain common elements to concept-learning strategies:

1. Students must focus on several examples of the concept.

2. Students must gather and verify information as to the *concept-relevant characteristics* of each individual example and nonexample.

3. Students must note how the examples vary and yet are still examples of the concept.

4. Students must note what is *alike* about all the examples of the concept.

5. Students must generalize that what is alike about all the examples they've examined is also true of all other examples of the concept.

6. Students must note how the nonexamples resemble examples, but, particularly, how they *differ* from them.

7. Students must generalize about the characteristics that *distinguish* all examples of the concept from any item that might resemble them in some way.

What Should Curriculum Materials Provide?

You might find it useful and enlightening to check a number of curriculum guides and text materials to see how concepts are introduced. How often is there nothing more than words: the concept label and a definition? If examples are presented, are the concept characteristics clearly identified in each example, or is it assumed that the reader can and will identify the right ones?

For curriculum materials to promote concept development:

1. Concepts should be clearly identified as concepts (not facts, principles, attitudes, and skills).

2. Concepts should be clearly stated in terms of the set of characteristics by which examples are identified and by which examples can be distinguished from nonexamples.

3. Several good examples and nonexamples should be suggested or provided for use with students.

4. One or more appropriate concept development learning sequences should be outlined for each concept. These should state clearly what the learner needs to do at each step of the sequence and what the teacher might provide, do, or say to guide students through the conceptualizing process.

5. Appropriate concept testing and reinforcing activities should be included (as in our example of having students distinguish contractions from possessives). Each should require students not only to identify new examples but also to cite the presence (or absence) of the concept characteristics.

None of the foregoing ideas is new. Nor is reading and understanding them all that is needed to make concept learning a consistent reality in the classroom. To concep-

tualize these ideas, the reader needs to encounter and deal with a number of examples and nonexamples of their use in the classroom. To develop skill in the use of concept learning/teaching strategies requires not only conceptualization, but firsthand experience with their results with students, willingness to take the required action to achieve the desired results, and enough practice and application to make the learning and teaching strategies an integral part of both curriculum and instruction.

REFERENCES

Durkin, Mary, and Hardy, Patricia. *Hilda Taba Teaching Strategies Program*. Miami, Fla.: Institute for Staff Development, 1972.

Ehrenberg, Sydelle D., and Ehrenberg, Lyle M. *BASICS: Building and Applying Strategies for Intellectual Competencies in Students, Participant Manual A.* Coral Gables, Fla.: Institute for Curriculum and Instruction, 1978.

Project BASICS. *Final Report*. Ann Arbor, Mich.: Washtenaw Intermediate School District, 1975.

Sigel, Irving. *The Attainment of Concepts*. Princeton, N.J.: Educational Testing Service Research Center, 1976.

Sigel, Irving. *Logical Thinking in Children: Research Based on Piaget's Theory*. New York: Holt, Rinehart, & Winston, 1968.

Taba, Hilda. *Teacher's Handbook*. Palo Alto, Calif.: Addison-Wesley Publishing Company, 1967.

Taba, Hilda. *Teaching Strategies and Cognitive Functioning in Elementary School Children*. San Francisco: San Francisco State College, 1966.

Wallen, Durkin, and others. *The Taba Curriculum Development Project in Social Studies, Final Report*. Project No. 5-1314, OE6-10-182. Washington, D.C.: HEW, Office of Education, Bureau of Resarch, 1969.

Other Mediative Strategies

Arthur L. Costa, Robert Hanson, Harvey F. Silver, and Richard W. Strong

The Open-Ended Discussion Strategy

Goal: To promote all students' effective expression of opinions, support their opinions with rational and logical evidence, and to actively listen to and appreciate the opinions of others.

Critical Teacher Behaviors:

• Pose one question or assign a task to the total group.

• Assign students to work independently (covertly) to visualize or think about an answer.

• Assign students to work independently and overtly by writing down their answers, demonstrating them, role playing, construction, and so on.

• Assign students to small groups to explain and critique their own and others' ideas.

• Conduct total-group discussions. Establish and maintain a nonjudgmental environment that encourages voluntary participation and open, personal communication.

• Refrain from influencing students' responses, avoid summarizing the discussion, and resist stating a personal opinion about the question.

Design a task.

Internalize the task (see it, think about it).

Share your response with another person.

Communicate in small groups.

Use principles of active, nonjudgmental participation.

Stimulate discussion.

Students summarize the discussion.

Evaluation: As a result of using the open-ended discussion strategy over time and with close adherence to its attributes, students will think and visualize covertly, express their ideas and opinions overtly, seek the ideas and opinions of others, provide logical evidence to support their ideas, become better listeners, and appreciate another person's point of view even though it may differ from their own.

The Inquiry Strategy

Goal: To develop students' awareness of and ability to apply a range of problem-solving and critical thinking behaviors when confronted with a problem to which the answer is not readily known.

Critical Teacher Behaviors:

• Pose or identify a problem that is not explainable with students' present store of knowledge. The problem is "discrepant" with students' expectations, beliefs, or predictions.

• Establish and maintain a nonjudgmental environment in which students are free to offer theories or explanations that might resolve problems.

• Hold students responsible for building and testing their own theories or explanations by determining what data are needed and how they may be obtained.

• Facilitate students' acquisition of needed information and data.

• Assist students' growth in their experiencing, becoming aware of, applying, and evaluating various inquiry problem-solving processes and strategies (metacognition).

• Refrain from influencing students' theories or explanations, avoid summarizing or judging their inquiry problem-solving processes and strategies, and resist stating personal explanations or solutions to the problem.

Evaluation: As a result of repeated experiences with the inquiry strategy, students will become better able to autonomously and voluntarily build and test theories and explanations to problems, and discuss the strengths and weaknesses of various problem-solving strategies in a wide range of topic areas. They should demonstrate greater awareness of their own problem-solving strategies and spend more time planning rather than reacting impulsively; they should demonstrate increased inventiveness in designing experimental approaches that will produce and verify the information needed to support a theory.

Background: In 1933, John Dewey described the process of teaching intended to develop the progressive states of what he called "reflective thinking." These states are: suggestion, formation of a problem, hypothesis, reasoning, and testing of the hypothesis. When students engage in reflective thinking, they must utilize and process data to test answers they have posed to problems. Inquiry is an approach to teaching and learning that encourages students to ask questions that will lead them to the answers they seek.

In the models of intellectual functioning constructed by Bloom, Piaget, Taba, and others, students must use significant skills in reflective thinking. They must pass the input-recall stage and enter the higher levels of thinking; they must possess and apply data. As students make meaning of data through process and application, there is an increased chance that the material will enter long-term memory and become lasting, durable, and applicable to new situations.

The inquiry methods of teaching purposely creates situations for students to use and extend the reflective thinking process. Fenton (1967) described six major steps of inquiry:

1. Recognizing a problem from data.
2. Formulating hypotheses.
3. Recognizing the logical implications of hypotheses.
4. Gathering data on the basis of logical implications.
5. Interpreting, analyzing, and evaluating data.
6. Evaluating hypotheses in light of the data.

The process begins with a problem situation. The problem must be discrepant to the students—they are unable to explain the problem using existing knowledge. The learner creates a hypothesis to explain the problem, and gathers, organizes, and verifies information to test the hypothesis for its power to explain and resolve the problem.

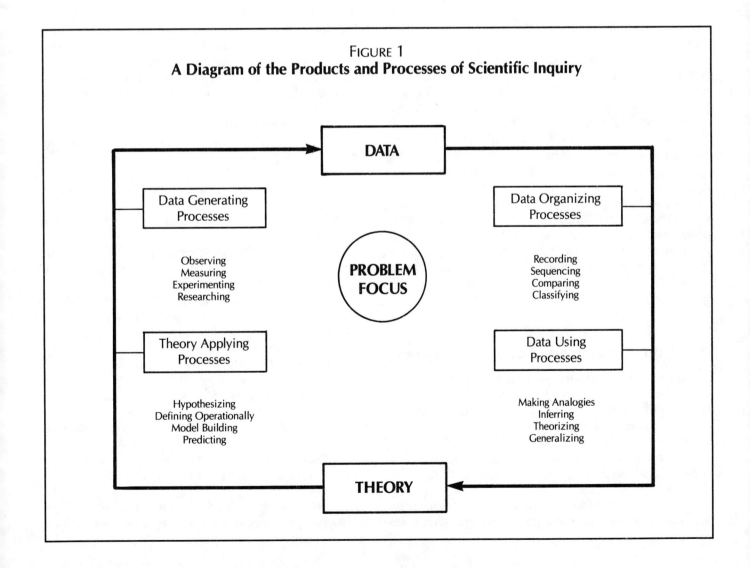

FIGURE 1
A Diagram of the Products and Processes of Scientific Inquiry

Suchman (1966) wrote, "It is clear from the research on teaching strategies that the more active and autonomous the learner becomes in a learning process and the more he/she takes responsibility for decisions regarding the collection and interpretation of information, the more meaningful the learning becomes and the more motivated the learner becomes." In the inquiry method, the responsibility for initiative and control rests squarely with the inquirers. Learners control the process so that cognitive gains match their own goals, thus building learner autonomy.

According to Bruner (1961), the potential benefits of the inquiry process include an increase in learner motivation as inquiry brings a shift from extrinsic to intrinsic rewards plus an increased comprehension of the heuristics of discovery. Other potential benefits noted by Bruner include an increase in intellectual potency and the development of a useful aid in memory by helping students organize material in terms of their own interests and cognitive structures.

Goldmark (1968) suggests that the main value of the inquiry method is that it teaches learners how to learn. The objective of the method should be to develop in learners a commitment to inquiry as a useful process. In order to gain maximum insight into their thinking, Goldmark would include in the process a step in which learners analyze what they do, how they do it, and how an inquiry would differ if they were to take a different viewpoint or pose the problem in a different context.

To teach for inquiry, the teacher must create and sustain the conditions that stimulate the process. Learners must be faced with an event that is discrepant with their idea of the universe. The teacher may manage presentation of the problem, but must not provide an explanation that narrows learners' thinking. Working in a climate that allows freedom to successfully gather data and test ideas, learners are allowed to come to grips with the problem in their own terms.

The Values Awareness/Clarification Strategy

Goal: To cause students to become aware of and to clarify their own values and those of others; and to appreciate the divergent values of others (overcoming ethnocentrism and ego-centrism).

Critical Teacher Behaviors:

● Arrange an activity or pose a value-laden question (of a somewhat controversial nature) as a stimulus for discussion.

● Invite students to make judgments and evaluations and to provide reasons or justifications for their judgments and actions.

● Identify the values underlying students' reasons, actions, or judgments.

● Maintain a nonjudgmental environment in order to encourage open, responsible, and personal communication.

● Refrain from influencing students' responses; avoid summarizing the discussion; and resist stating personal opinions, values, or courses of action.

Evaluation: As a result of repeated values awareness/clarification sessions, students will be able to report their own values and beliefs; relate their values to their actions, decisions, or judgments; and appreciate the diverse values, actions, and judgments of others.

The Concept Development Strategies: Concept Formation/Concept Attainment

Goal: To promote students' conceptual knowledge, including concept definition, the ability to describe the attributes of members of the concept, to distinguish between members subsumed within that concept and those that are not, to apply the concept in settings other than in which it was learned, and to become aware of the cognitive processes of conceptualizing.

Critical Teacher Behaviors:

● Make the concept definition available to the student or provide opportunities for them to "discover" the definitions.

● Provide practice for students to recall the concept definition.

● Monitor their practice and provide appropriate feedback.

● Provide practice for students in distinguishing the attributes of the concept, to build or design a product, to explain, to categorize, or to predict.

● Use an evaluation method designed to test students' ability to recall the concept definition and to use that concept in a setting or condition different from that in which it was learned or practiced.

Steps in the Concept Formation Strategy:

1. Provide or have students generate data relevant to a particular question or problem. Teacher collects data on retrieval chart.

2. Ask students to group data according to common attributes.

3. Have students label groups with a word or phrase that most precisely describes the attributes of the members of that group.

4. Ask students to subsume items under other labels or labels under more conclusive categories. Have students give reasons for their groupings.

5. Have students suggest different ways of grouping, labeling, and subsuming items based on other relationships.

Generate data.

Record data.

Organize data into groups.

Use labels to describe each group.

Place additional items into categories.

Subsume items and labels into larger groups.

Evaluation: As a result of use of this strategy over time and with close adherence to the attributes, students should be able to recall concepts, to use the concepts correctly, and to use that concept in the construction of a model, categorization, prediction, or explanation.

Take a concept and identify its essential attributes.

Review attributes and develop positive and negative examples.

Arrange examples into a sequence.

Identify the concept according to its attributes.

Try to generate additional examples of the concept.

FIGURE 2

Steps in the Concept Attainment Strategy

Phase I. Introduction of the Concept:

● The teacher presents unlabeled examples, such as:

● Students inquire which examples, including their own, are positive ones.

> Gazelle?
> Mosquito?

● The teacher places examples in the appropriate list.

Phase II. Testing Attainment of the Concept:

● The students generate and test hypotheses:

> Bugs you swat?

● Students identify additional unlabeled examples.

● Students generate examples.

● The teacher confirms hypotheses, names concepts, and restates definition according to essential attributes.

Phase III. Analysis of Thinking Strategy:

● Students describe thoughts.

● Students discuss role of hypothesis and attributes.

● Students discuss type and number of hypotheses.

Hypotheses	
In	Out
Butterfly Fly Grasshopper	Mouse
Mosquito	Gazelle
Frog	Baboon
Clam	Shark
METAMORPHOSIS	

REFERENCES

Inquiry Strategy:

Bruner, J. S. "The Act of Discovery." *Harvard Educational Review* 31 (1961): 21-32.

Dewey, J. "Reflective Thinking." In *How We Think.* Boston: D. C. Heath, 1933.

Fenton, E. "Inquiry and Structure." In *Inquiry in the Social Studies.* Edited by R. Allen and J. Fleckenstein. Washington: D.C.: National Council for the Social Studies, 1967.

Goldmark B. *Social Studies: A Method of Inquiry.* Belmont, Calif.: Wadsworth Publishing Co., 1968.

Suchman, R. "A Model for the Analysis of Inquiry." In *Analysis of Concept Learning.* Edited by H. Klausmeier and C. Harris. New York Academic Press, 1966.

Values, Awareness/Clarification Strategy:

Raths, L.; Harmin, M.; and Simon, S. *Values and Teaching.* Columbus: Charles E. Merrill, Co., 1966.

Harmin, M.; Kirchenbaum, H.; and Simon, S. *Clarifying Values Through Subject Matter.* Minneapolis: Winston Press, Inc., 1973.

Simon, S.; Howe, L.; and Kirchenbaum, H. *Values Clarification: A Handbook of Practical Strategies For Teachers and Students.* New York: Hart Publishing Co., 1972.

Concept Development Strategies:

Bruner, J. "Some Elements of Discovery." In *Learning By Discovery.* Edited by L. Shulman and E. Keisler. Chicago: Rand McNally, 1966.

Bruner, J. *Toward A Theory of Instruction.* Cambridge: Harvard University Press, 1966.

Bruner, J.; Goodman, J.; and Austin, G. *A Study of Thinking.* New York: George A. Austin Science Editions, 1967.

Taba, H.; Levine, S.; and Elzey, F. *Thinking in Elementary School Children.* Cooperative Research Project No. 1574. San Francisco: San Francisco State College, 1964.

26
Generative Strategies

Arthur L. Costa, Robert Hanson, Harvey F. Silver, and Richard W. Strong

Generative strategies help students create new knowledge and develop novel and insightful ways of approaching and solving problems.

Roles and Motivation

Using generative strategies, teachers stimulate students' imaginations by inviting creative imagery, using metaphors, and posing hypothetical and seemingly bizarre situations. They withhold value judgments so as not to stifle students' "creative juices." They elicit and explore multitudes of answers, products, and solutions in an attempt to make them more generalized, specific, detailed, parsimonious, or elegant and crafted. Planning is essential and includes developing standards, making criteria explicit, and exploring alternative strategies.

Students are motivated to participate in the generative strategies by their natural, human drive toward competence and craftsmanship. We want to get better at what we do.

Student Outcomes

These strategies may well be used in expressive writing processes, developing solutions to nonroutine problems, and in artistic expression. By employing these strategies under low-risk conditions, research has shown that, over time, students become more creative in their use of new materials, more insightful and intuitive in offering solutions to problems, and more metaphorically descriptive in their vocabulary.

Instructional Strategies

Generative strategies include Osborne's *Brainstorming*, Buzan's *Mind Mapping*, Gordon's *Synectics*, Perkins' *Creativity by Design*, and de Bono's *Lateral Thinking*. We have selected *Synectics* and *Creativity by Design* as examples to describe in greater detail.

Creativity by Design

D. N. Perkins

Education for creativity is nothing short of education for living.

—Erich Fromm

Courses that focus on creative thinking, address strategies, skills, and attitudes and offer plenty of time-on-task can have a significant impact on creative thinking. Such courses, slipped into the curriculum where possible, would be worthwhile. But by far the better, although more difficult, path is to revise normal schooling to foster creative thinking in all subjects.

As noted earlier, part of the problem is that conventional instruction usually presents knowledge as given, when it should encourage a view of knowledge as the product of creative effort. An approach well suited to this aim can be summed up in three words: knowledge as design.

The notion is that pieces of knowledge are designs shaped by human invention, designs not so unlike a screwdriver or a can opener. Although this stance may seem peculiar at first, it offers a powerful metaphor for unifying the range of human productive activities under a common framework. To put it succinctly, virtually any product of human effort, including knowlege, can be understood better with the help of four design questions: What is the purpose? What is the structure? What are some model cases (concrete examples that bring the matter in question closer to perceptual experience)? What are the arguments for or against the design?

For instance, we can easily see a thumbtack as a structure adapted to a purpose. *The purpose:* temporarily attaching materials, usually paper, to surfaces like bulletin boards and walls. *The structure:* a short point and a wide head. *A model case:* an actual thumbtack. *The argument:* why is the head so wide? So the thumb can push it, and so it holds the paper well with its breadth. Why is the point so short? So the thumb can push the tack all the way in, and so that it isn't hard to remove. As this simple example shows, the design questions require that we understand the thumbtack as a design and from four perspectives at the same time: purpose, structure, model, and argument.

The design perspective is a flexible tool because abstract concepts can also be treated as designs. Consider the organization of a sentence as an invention. *The purpose:* to package linguistic information in an orderly way that promotes production and comprehension. The latter can be demonstrated by stripping syntax, sentence, and phrase divisions from text, which makes it much harder to read. *The structure:* nouns, verbs, adjectives, and so on put together in accordance with the rules of grammar. *Model cases:* the sentences in this paragraph, for instance. *The argument:* the structure of a simple sentence makes a neat package of information—what thing (the subject) exercises what action (the verb) on what other thing (the direct object) with what qualifications on the things (adjectives) and on the action (the adverbs)? The grammatical ordering and the case endings help the hearer to discern what does what to what, and which qualifiers limit which things and actions.

This example is far too sketchy to serve students well, of course. It is but an outline of what would be necessary for a thorough view of sentences from a design perspective. But perhaps it conveys a sense of how the design perspective could be used to discuss grammar.

Now consider a very different example—the Pythagorean theorem. *The structure:* the square of the hypotenuse of a right triangle equals the sum of the squares of the other two sides. *Model case:* perhaps the most familiar model case is a right triangle with squares constructed on all three sides. *The argument:* one of the many proofs of the Pythagorean theorem is based on just such a construction.

As the *purpose*, this theorem has come to have a number of important purposes in mathematical contexts. It provides the basis for measuring distance in an n-dimensional Cartesian coordinate system. As such, it underlies vector calculus concepts such as the dot and cross products. The Pythagorean theorem plays a role in applying the calculus

This subchapter is an excerpt from D. N. Perkins, "Creativity by Design," *Educational Leadership* 42, 1 (September 1984): 18-24.

to compute the lengths of curves in space. The trouble is that it is difficult to convey this wide-ranging import to students encountering the theorem for the first time.

This difficulty is a pervasive problem in mathematics instruction, where quite commonly the purpose of newly introduced concepts and theorems do not become fully apparent until much later in the instructional sequence. But having some grasp of the purpose of anything is crucial to understanding it as a design and indeed, to feeling it to be important. Mathematics teachers must forecast and make vivid for students the import of mathematical findings and concepts when they are introduced, even by use of analogy and even if the message is not fully understood.

Virtually every other topic dealt with in schools can be viewed as a design and discussed as such; for example, historical claims, mathematical notations, Newton's laws, short stories and poems, legal codes, biological organisms, mathematical algorithms, newspaper layout, and moral principles. If all knowledge were presented and discussed from the perspective of design, education would yield a much more creative view of knowledge.

Learning to Design

If design provides a useful way of thinking about knowledge, it offers an even greater hold on the nature of creative thinking. One can view creative thinking as the process of designing something and provide advice on how to do so. This might be done in many ways; I will describe one.

Over the past few years, I have helped to develop a course on thinking skills for the 7th grade level in Venezuela (Final Report, Project Intelligence, 1983). The course consists of six lesson series. The series on inventive thinking (Perkins and Laserna, 1983) begins with nine lessons that teach students strategies for analyzing everyday designs (like chairs and tacks), evaluating them, planning improvements, and inventing useful gadgets that do not already exist. It continues with a second set of six lessons that takes the same approach to daily procedures, such as shopping, which can also be viewed as designs. The lesson series emphasizes most of the six characteristics of creative thinking identified earlier.

The extensive summative evaluation of the course, which yielded generally favorable results, included a design task administered both to students who had received the first nine inventive thinking lessons and the other lesson series and to control students. The students' designs were rated on a number of dimensions by two judges. The treatment group outperformed the control group considerably on a number of measures. For instance, treatment students included in their designs an average of two features to help

solve the given problem, while control group students incorporated an average of only 1.2. Treatment students described their designs in much more detail, an average of 83 words as compared to the control students' average of 46. Treatment students also included much more detail in their sketches in a number of categories of detail (Final Report, Project Intelligence, 1983).

Obviously, these results do not imply that students learned to be creative in the course of nine lessons. The treatment was not long enough nor comprehensive enough to warrant such a conclusion. But the students do appear to have learned some patterns of creative thinking as they apply to simple design tasks. The results suggest that with continued treatment to increase such skills and extend them to other contexts, creative thinking might be enhanced.

Wide-Ranging Products of Inquiry

One of the most interesting features of the above experiment is that it emphasized working on *whole* creative products—the deisgns of simple objects. After all in real life, the outcome of a creative endeavor is almost always a complex product rather than a brief answer to a question. School knowledge also deals largely in complex products. Theorems, theories, definitions, classification systems, arguments, analyses, field notes, interpretations, and evaluations are among many products of inquiry found in the study of the various disciplines. However, although students learn about scholars' products of inquiry, they do very little creating on their own. Students function primarily as consumers of products of inquiry, not producers.

A look at the kinds of products students normally attempt quickly reveals the limits. Broadly speaking, students are asked to produce three kinds of things: *short answers*, as in grammar or arithmetic exercises or fill-in-the-blank quizzes; *problem solutions,* as in physics or mathematics; and *essays.* The first of these hardly deserves to be called a product at all. Solving given problems does involve substantive thinking, but it is only a small part of the activity of the mathematician or scientist, who also routinely formulates problems, devises classification systems, constructs definitions, analyzes phenomena, and so on.

The essay is in principle an enormously flexible medium of expression. However, students do not know how to exploit its flexibility, and teachers do little to help them. Most students compose essays by writing what they know about a given topic. This "knowledge telling" approach, as researchers have called it (Bereiter and Scardamalia, in press), is a very narrow, not very creative use of the essay vehicle.

The narrow range of products of inquiry produced by

students reflects tradition and convenience more than necessity. Here are some examples of assignments that call for rather different written products: an analysis, a prediction with argument, a classification system, a plan.

1. *Analysis of a tool according to physical principles.* After learning about basic physical principles such as the lever and the inclined plane, pick a tool—for instance, a screwdriver or a hammer—and write an analysis of how the tool works by identifying the physical principles underlying it. Many tools involve several such principles.

2. *Prediction of a political event.* Wait for an international incident, and then predict what actions the nations involved will take over the ensuing weeks. Base your predictions on as much information as you can find in newspaper accounts, plus historical analogies. Give not only your prediction but the argument for it. Then see what happens. If your prediction does not pan out, explain at what point events diverged and suggest why.

3. *A classification system for sources of slang.* Slang words enter the language in many ways. Special dictionaries often give their derivations. After learning some important characteristics of classification systems, use these special dictionaries as resources to design a classification system for the ways slang words arise.

4. *Strategic planning in history.* Select a famous battle, and learn as much as you can about it. Then using hindsight, make the best plan you can for the strategy of the losing side. In light of this plan, might the losing side have won, or was the loss an inevitable consequence of resources and position? Present not only your plan but also your argument on this point.

As these examples show, it's relatively easy to formulate both short assignments, like analyzing a tool, and term projects, like the strategy planning project above, that engage students in designing products of inquiry. Note also that the rubric of design leads to a much broader concept of creative activity. When we think of creativity in school contexts, we usually think of creative writing and art, which are far too narrow. As soon as one thinks in terms of de-

sign, one realizes that all sorts of things in the various subject matters are designed and hence can become objects of creative thinking for students. Accordingly, a drastic expansion in the range of products of inquiry asked of students should be a key element in promoting creative thinking in schools.

Of course, an emphasis on products of inquiry is not enough. Just because students work on such products does not mean that they will do so creatively. But we can help them by providing instruction in various strategies, skills, and attitudes appropriate to creative thinking and design.

In summary, creative thinking turns out to have a discernible pattern that we can put to work throughout education. The passive view of knowledge fostered by conventional instruction can be replaced by the more active perspective of knowledge as design. Students can learn about the art and attitudes of design, and they can work on a far greater range of products of inquiry than they normally do.

Although questions certainly remain about creative thinking, it is no longer so mysterious as to excuse neglect on the grounds of ignorance. The only excuse is inertia—education's favorite but not a good one. With a vigorous push, perhaps we can set schools in motion toward worlds of invention, which now seem not so far away.

REFERENCES

Bereiter, C., and Scardamalia, M. "Cognitive Coping Strategies and the Problems of Inert Knowledge." In *Thinking and Learning Skills, Volume 2: Current Research and Open Questions.* Edited by S. Chipman, J. W. Siegel, and R. Glaser. Hillsdale, N.J.: Erlbaum, in press.

Final Report, Project Intelligence: The Development of Procedures to Enhance Thinking Skills. Cambridge, Mass.: Harvard University and Bolt Beranek and Newman, Inc., 1983.

Perkins, D. N., and Laserna, C. *Inventive Thinking. Lesson Series VI, Project Intelligence Course.* Cambridge, Mass.: Harvard University and Bolt Beranek and Newman, Inc., 1983.

Synectics: Making the Familiar Strange

Arthur L. Costa, Robert Hanson, Harvey F. Silver, and Richard W. Strong

To him whose elastic and vigorous thought keeps pace with the sun,
The day is a perpetual morning.
—Henry David Thoreau

To make the familiar strange is to distort, invert, or transpose the traditional ways of experiencing our surroundings. The result is a new look at the world. In the familiar world, objects are always right side up, children who bend over and peer at the world from an upside-down position are experimenting with the familiar made strange.

Art and literature have long recognized the role of metaphor for seeing the world in a new way. Metaphor can also be used as the basis for a new approach to teach creative thinking and writing. In synectics exercises, analogies and metaphors are the mechanisms for finding ideas and putting them into words. As connectors, they permit comparisons to be brought out in order to develop new ways to see ourselves and our surroundings.

Background

Since 1944, the Cambridge Synectics Group has directed its efforts toward the possibility of increasing the creative output of individuals and groups by uncovering the psychological mechanisms basic to creative activity. This investigation resulted in the synectics system for the conscious use of metaphor in problem solving and hypothesis formation. Synectics theory holds that:

1. Creative efficiency in people can be markedly increased if they understand the psychological process by which they operate (metacognition).

2. In creative processes, the emotional component is more important than the intellectual, the irrational more important than the rational.

3. It is these emotional, irrational elements that can and must be understood in order to increase the probability of success in a problem-solving situation.

Originally, synectics research emphasized creative process in the sciences. This was a research decision based on the fact that the innovative degree of a technical invention can be judged more objectively than any other area of innovation. In spite of substantial assistance from such diverse, creative groups as the Department of Defense, the Institute of Contemporary Art, the Rockefeller Foundation, Harvard University, and the Massachusetts Institute of Technology, the industrial world was synectics' laboratory until 1960.

Industry presented a variety of pragmatic scientific problems. Through research, it became apparent that the most important element in creative problem solving is making the familiar strange. Innovative breakthroughs depend on strange, new contexts through which to view familiar problems. Synectics research identified three operational mechanisms, each metaphorical in character, for deliberately making the familiar strange. They are:

1. Direct analogy—simple comparison:
    How is a teacher like a tuna fish sandwich?

2. Personal analogy—being the thing:
    A candle is not alive
    But it looks alive when it burns.
    How would you feel
    If you were a candle,
    Burning in a camping tent?

3. Symbolic analogy—compressed conflict (oxymoron):
    What is an example of a careful collision?

Since 1961, synectics theory has become increasingly operational. An investigation was launched based on more operational tools to examine ways to teach young people how to use metaphors to understand the world around them and write creatively about their world. In the fall of 1964, synectics' metaphorical approach was used experimentally as a teaching device in science, social studies, and creative writing. These successful experiments led to more concrete conclusions than any other research to date. The

---

FIGURE 1
A New Design for
Creative Thinking and Writing

Choose a subject and a metaphor. Present the students with an image that in some ways resembles and in other ways differs from your subject: *Summer is like a bridge because. . . .*

Record students' descriptions of both the subject and the image.

Establish the relationship between the familiar subject and the unfamiliar image.

Ask students to personalize: *Be a summer. How do summers feel?*

Take two words from the student discussion and make them oppose each other (oxymoron): *Vacation loneliness.*

Establish a new metaphor.

Summarize new learnings.

---

results of this research were developed into a new design for creative thinking and writing (Figure 1).

REFERENCES

Gordon, William. *Synectics.* New York: Harper Brothers, 1961.

27

Collaborative Strategies

Arthur L. Costa, Dee Dishon, and Pat Wilson O'Leary

Collaborative strategies provide a way to structure student groups for learning. They help students think and solve problems together, successfully accomplish tasks, both academic and nonacademic, and employ and process the social skills necessary to student success.

Roles and Motivation

The elements of successful cooperative learning are discussed below.

• *Positive interdependence* is created if the success of the individual is related to others in the group by distributed leadership, a group product, group materials and resources, and a group reward.

• *Verbal interaction and communication skills* are required to build and maintain positive interdependence.

• *Individual accountability* results when students take responsibility for their own accomplishment of the task and for assisting and encouraging all members of the group to understand and accomplish.

• *Social skills* are necessary for accomplishing the task and maintaining the group in working order, and must be practiced by all group members.

While the teacher structures learning, assigns tasks, composes the group, monitors the processes, and invites evaluation of group skills, the main emphasis is for students to become aware of, practice, and evaluate their own employment of cooperative group skills.

The motivation in the collaborative strategies is the reciprocity of group effort, about which Bruner speaks. Students soon realize that the product of group thinking is often superior to that of individual thinking. Thus, they take responsibility, for their own roles in and contributions to the group's functioning and productivity.

Student Outcomes

It takes time and practice for teachers and students to learn the skills required of the collaborative strategies. However, the results make the efforts worthwhile. Research has shown that students not only learn the academic content, but also develop and employ higher-level thinking skills. They develop greater appreciation of group members, and learn to apply social skills in groups beyond the classroom.

Instructional Strategies

The collaborative strategies include Johnson and Johnson's *Cooperative Learning*, Slavin's *Jigsaw, Jigsaw II, Student Teams and Academic Divisions (STAD), Rutabaga, Teams-Games-Tournaments (TGT)*, Glaser's *Class Meetings (Circles of Knowledge)*, and Whimbey's *Paired Problem Solving*. Dee Dishon and Pat Wilson-O'Leary, two proponents of Johnson and Johnson's *Cooperative Learning*, describe this strategy in greater detail.

REFERENCES

Dishon, D., and O'Leary, P. *A Guidebook for Cooperative Learning: A Technique for Creating More Effective Schools.* Holmes Beach, Fla.: Learning Publications, 1984, pp. 10-11.

Johnson, D.; Johnson, R.; Holubec, E.; and Roy, P. *Circles of Learning: Cooperation in the Classroom.* Alexandria, Va.: Association for Supervision and Curriculum Development, 1984.

Johnson, D., and Johnson, R. *Learning Together and Alone: Cooperation, Competition, and Individualization.* Englewood Cliffs, N.J.: Prentice-Hall, 1979.

Sharan, S. "Cooperative Learning in Small Groups: Recent Methods and Effects on Achievement, Attitudes, and Ethnic Relations. *Review of Educational Research* 50, 2 (Summer 1980): 241.

Slavin, R. E. *Using Student Team Learning, The Johns Hopkins Team Learning Project.* Baltimore, Md.: Center for Social Organization of Schools, 1978.

Cooperative Learning

Pat Wilson O'Leary and Dee Dishon

It is good to rub and polish our brain against that of others.

—Montaigne

Cooperative strategies provide a way to structure student groups for learning. The purposes of cooperative strategies are to help students successfully accomplish tasks (both academic and nonacademic) and to use social skills necessary for success. Successful cooperative experiences are based on five principles:

1. *The Principle of Distributed Leadership.* All students are capable of understanding, learning, and performing leadership tasks.

2. *The Principle of Heterogeneous Grouping.* Effective student groups are those that are heterogeneous, including students of different genders, social backgrounds, skill levels, and physical capabilities.

3. *The Principle of Positive Interdependence.* Students need to learn to recognize and value their dependence on one another. Positive interdependence is promoted through common subject matter tasks, group and individual accountability, shared materials and rewards, or the creation of one group product.

4. *The Principle of Skill Acquisition.* The ability of students to work effectively in a group is determined by the acquisition of specific social skills that promote collaboration and group maintenance.

5. *The Principle of Group Autonomy.* Student groups are more likely to resolve their own problems if they are not "rescued" by their teacher. Students solving their own problems are more autonomous and self-sufficient (Dishon and O'Leary, 1984).

Teacher Behaviors

The teacher's role is critical in transferring these principles to classroom practices. For instance, before a cooperative learning lesson begins, the teacher:

1. States instructional goals, both academic and social.

2. Provides verbal and written subject matter objectives.

3. Supplies materials to be used and shared by all groups.

4. States that individual and group accountability will be checked and explains criteria to be used.

5. Describes any rewards available and how to obtain them.

6. Announces and teaches the assigned social skills, providing "looks like/sounds like" examples collected from the class.

7. Describes the teacher's role as one of an observer; states what is to be collected, why, and how it will be shared.

8. Organizes each group in the optimal size and composition for the assigned task and available time and materials.

9. Assigns the groups to a specific area, arranging the room to promote group sharing and noise control.

During the lesson, the teacher:

10. Observes students' social skills and tallies those being used.

11. Monitors student behavior and takes notes to be used later in giving feedback to students.

12. Provides assistance by responding to group questions.

After the lesson, the teacher:

13. Checks students, in follow up to step 4.

14. Provides questions about subject matter and social skills, which individual groups discuss and report to the whole class.

15. Hands out the observation form, which each group compares with their own findings before reporting to the whole class.

16. Offers comments about positive and negative behaviors, avoiding mentioning specific groups or individuals.

17. Privately critiques the lesson in writing, including the best and worst features and what to change next time.

Evaluation

It takes time and practice for teachers and students to learn the skills necessary for cooperative learning. However, the results are worth the effort. Over time students who use cooperative learning strategies attain higher achievement; employ superior learning strategies; experience greater learning retention; exhibit more positive atti- tudes toward peers, the school, teachers, and the principal; demonstrate a greater liking for subject areas that use groups; and transfer social skills beyond the classroom. Cooperation means higher motivation, interest in others, increased self-esteem, constructive conflict management, and acceptance and appreciation of the differences in others.

28

Summing Up

Arthur L. Costa, Robert Hanson, Harvey F. Silver, and Richard W. Strong

Looking over the ground we've covered, we are struck by the diversity of strategies available to teachers. This raises the question of why strategies have not become an integral part of most teachers' practices. Are the strategies too theoretical? Is there adequate time in the real life of classrooms to use them? Do some teachers' personalities and teaching styles better accommodate certain strategies? Or is it that we have, until now, simply lacked the structure that could show us how to put them to use?

A strategy is appropriate when it stimulates, elicits, and models a form of thinking that the teacher seeks to encourage. In particular, when we work toward mastery of discrete cognitive skills, the directive strategies seem most powerful. When working toward problem solving, decision making, and inductive reasoning, the mediative strategies seem productive. When creativity is the goal, the generative strategies prevail. And when students need to learn to share, listen to one another, and work cooperatively, the collaborative strategies are best employed.

The brilliant men and women who developed these strategies invested in them heavily and were committed to their dissemination. *Direct Instruction, Concept Formation, Values Clarification, Inquiry,* and *Lateral Thinking* all became more than teaching techniques, they are ways of life. Each of these strategies reflects a philosophical preference, a mode of behaving, and a perception of learning.

Acknowledgements

We would like to thank the following educational leaders for their ideas, research, and development of teaching strategies, from which we have generously drawn:

Barry Beyer, George Mason University, Fairfax, Virginia; Sema Brainin, Teachers College, Columbia University, New York City; Jerome Bruner, Harvard University, Cambridge, Massachusetts; Edward de Bono, The Cognitive Research Trust, England; Reuven Feuerstein, Bar Elan University, Ramat Gan, Israel; Madeline Hunter, University of California at Los Angeles; Roger Johnson and David Johnson, University of Minnesota; Bruce Joyce, University of Oregon; David Perkins, Harvard University; Sid Simon, Howard Kirchenbaum, Ben Strasser, and Gus Dalis, The Teaching Strategy Center, Los Angeles County Superintendent of Schools Office; J. Richard Suchman, Santa Cruz, California; and Hilda Taba (deceased).

Further References on Teaching Strategies

Bruner, Jerome. *Towards A Theory of Instruction.* Cambridge: Harvard University Press, 1966.

Costa, A. *Teaching for Intelligent Behavior.* Orangevale, Calif.: Search Models Unlimited, 1985.

Eggen, P.; Kauchak, R.; and Harder, J. *Strategies for Teachers.* Englewood Cliffs, N.J.: Prentice-Hall, 1978.

Gage, N. *The Psychology of Teaching Methods.* Yearbook of the National Society for the Study of Education, Part I. Chicago: University of Chicago Press, 1976.

Hudgins, B. *The Instructional Process.* New York: Rand McNally, 1971.

Hyman, R. *Ways of Teaching.* Philadelphia: Lippincott Co., 1974.

Joyce, B. *Flexibility in Teaching.* New York: Longman, 1981.

Joyce, B. *Selecting Learning Experiences.* Alexandria, Va.: Association for Supervision and Curriculum Development, 1978.

Joyce, B. *Three Teaching Strategies for the Social Studies.* Chicago: Science Research Associates, 1972.

Joyce, B., and Weil, M. *Information Processing Models of Teaching.* New York: Prentice-Hall, 1978.

Joyce, B., and Weil, M. *Models of Teaching.* New York: Prentice-Hall, 1972.

Joyce, B., and Weil, M. *Personal Models of Teaching.* New York: Prentice-Hall, 1978.

Lamm, Z. *Conflicting Theories of Instruction.* Berkeley: McCutchan Publishers, 1976.

McClosky, J., and others. *Teaching Strategies and Classroom Realities.* New York: Prentice-Hall, 1971.

Mosston, M. *Teaching: From Command to Discovery.* Belmont, Calif.: 1972.

Reigeluth, C., ed. *Instructional Design Theories and Models.* New York: Lawrence Erlbaum Inc., 1983.

Silver, H., and Hanson, R. *Teaching Styles and Strategies.* Moorestown, N.J.: Hanson Silver Strong and Associates Inc., 1983.

Weil, M., and Joyce, B. *Social Models of Teaching.* Englewood Cliffs, N.J.: Prentice-Hall, 1978.

PART VIII

Programs for Teaching Thinking

Educators considering the selection and installation of one or more of the available cognitive curriculum programs are often confused by having to make a selection from a vast array of alternatives. Each program serves a different purpose and audience, is lodged in a different theoretical home, and produces different outcomes.

Because of this overload of complexity, educators are often tempted to make simplistic decisions based on cur- sory examinations or for reasons of political urgency, financial economy, or ease of installation. Sometimes schools have shunned the decision and chosen to develop their own programs.

This section will help you make intelligent decisions by (1) providing criteria for examining any curriculum intended to enhance intelligent functioning, (2) describing many of the major programs designed to develop the intellect, (3) identifying the audience for whom each program is intended, and (4) distinguishing among the several theoretical and philosophical assumptions on which each is based.

29

Choosing the Right Program

Robert J. Sternberg

Do we really need intervention programs for teaching students intellectual skills? The answer is clearly "yes." During the last decade or so we have witnessed an unprecedented decline in the intellectual skills of our school children (Wigdor and Garner, 1982). This is evident, of course, from the decline in scores on tests such as the Scholastic Aptitude Test (SAT); but college professors don't need SAT scores to be apprised of the decline: they can see it in poorer class performance and particularly in the poorer reading and writing of their students. Moreover, thinking skills are needed by more than the college-bound population. Perhaps intellectual skills could be better trained through existing curricula than they are now. But something in the system is not working, and I view programs such as those described here as exciting new developments for reversing the declines in intellectual performance we have witnessed in recent years.

How does one go about choosing the right program for one's particular school and student needs? I believe that wide-ranging research is needed before selecting any one of several programs for school or districtwide implementation. Which program to select will depend on the grade level, socioeconomic level, and intellectual level of the students; the particular kinds of skills one wishes to teach; the amount of time one can devote to training students; one's philosophy of intellectual skills training (that is, whether training should be infused into or separated from regular curricula); and one's financial resources, among other things. Clearly, the decision of which program to use should be made only after extensive deliberation and out-side consultation, preferably with people who have expertise, but not a vested interest, in the implementation of one particular program or another.

The following general guidelines can be applied in selecting a program (see also Sternberg, 1983):

• The program should be based on a psychological theory of the intellectual processes it seeks to train and on an educational theory of the way in which the processes will be taught. A good pair of theories should state what processes are to be trained, how the processes work together in problem solving, and how the processes can be taught so as to achieve durability and transfer of training. Innumerable programs seek to train intelligence, but most of them are worth little or nothing. One can immediately rule out large numbers of the low-value programs by investigating whether they have any theoretical basis.

• The program should be socioculturally appropriate. It should be clear from the examples described here that programs differ widely in terms of the student populations to whom they are targeted. The best intentions in such a program may be thwarted if the students cannot relate the program both to their cognitive structures and to the world in which they live.

• The program should provide explicit training both in the mental processes used in task performance (performance components and knowledge-acquisition components) and in self-management strategies for using these components (metacomponents). Many early attempts at process training did not work because investigators as-

This chapter is an excerpt from Robert J. Sternberg, "How Can We Teach Intelligence?" *Educational Leadership* 42, 1 (September 1984): 38-48.

sumed that just teaching the processes necessary for task performance would result in improved performance on intellectual tasks. The problem was that students often did not learn when to use the processes or how to implement them in tasks differing even slightly from the ones on which they had been trained. In order to achieve durable and transferable learning, it is essential that students be taught not only how to perform tasks but also when to use the strategies they are taught and how to implement them in new situations.

● The program should be responsive to the motivational as well as the intellectual needs of the students. A program that does not adequately motivate students is bound not to succeed, no matter how excellent the cognitive components may be.

● The program should be sensitive to individual differences. Individuals differ greatly in the knowledge and skills they bring to any educational program. A program that does not take these individual differences into account will almost inevitably fail to engage large numbers of students.

● The program should provide explicit links between the training it provides and functioning in the real world. Psychologists have found that transfer of training does not come easily. One cannot expect to gain transfer unless explicit provisions are made in the program so as to increase its likelihood of occurrence.

● Adoption of the program should take into account demonstrated empirical success in implementations similar to one's own planned implementation. Surprisingly, many programs have no solid data behind them. Others may have data that are relevant only to school or student situations quite different from one's own. A key to success is choosing a program with a demonstrated track record in similar situations.

● The program should have associated with it a well-tested curriculum for teacher training. The best program can fail to realize its potential if teachers are insufficiently or improperly trained.

● Expectations should be appropriate for what the program can accomplish. Teachers and administrators often set themselves up for failure by setting expectations that are inappropriate or too high.

Programs are now available that do an excellent, if incomplete, job of improving children's intellectual skills. The time has come for supplementing the standard curriculum with such programs. We can continue to use intelligence tests, but we will provide more service to children by developing their intelligence than by testing it.

REFERENCES

Sternberg, R. J. "Criteria for Intellectual Skills Training." *Educational Researcher* 12 (1983): 6-12, 26.
Wigdor, A. K., and Garner, W. R., eds. *Ability Testing: Uses, Consequences, and Controversies* (2 volumes). Washington, D.C.: National Academy Press, 1982.

30

SOI

Mary N. Meeker

Guilford's theory of intelligence, the Structure of Intellect (SOI), was first applied as a measure of human intellectual abilities in 1962. Today many administrators regard SOI as a program primarily for the gifted because its first use was with identifying intellectual abilities that differentiated gifted students in California.

But all students have intelligence. The SOI answers "what kind" instead of "how much." That is, the SOI-LA assessments determine 26 intellectual abilities in all kinds of students. Educators and psychologists can obtain a complex documentation of at least 96 of the 120 kinds of thinking abilities (Meeker, 1962, 1963, 1969, 1975), including the preparation abilities that lead to the higher-level critical thinking abilities. Since 1962 SOI has been used to:

- Teach thinking skills and abilities.
- Teach creativity (divergent production).
- Teach reasoning and higher-level critical thinking skills and abilities.
- Identify SOI learning abilities and teach them to students who have not yet developed these abilities.

In 1962, I applied the SOI theory to analyses of the Binet and WISC tests and derived a profile of intelligence by basing these IQ tests on a theory of intelligence (rather than on their probability-based foundation). This profile enabled psychologists to determine in which areas students were gifted and which of their abilities seemed undeveloped (Meeker and Bonsall, 1962).

By 1974, we had validated 26 (of the known 96) factored abilities necessary for successful learning. This research led to the development of various SOI Learning Abilities Tests. (See the 1985 Buros Tests in Print and the 1986 Buros Mental Measurements Yearbook.)

Relationship of SOI Abilities to Higher-Level Thinking Abilities

In designing new curriculums to develop higher-level thinking abilities, it is necessary to differentiate between *basic* and *higher-level* critical thinking abilities. Just as basic reading differs from advanced reading, basic thinking abilities differ from critical thinking abilities. The developmental aspects of scope and sequence are shown in Figures 2 and 3 (R. Meeker, 1984). Each shows how reasoning abilities are differentiated between the two fundamental curriculums for language arts and arithmetic-math-science, and how basic learning abilities are differentiated (and fundamental) for advanced critical thinking and reasoning abilities. The top portion of each figure lists the learning abilities required to achieve mastery of basic reading (Figure 1, p. 188) and basic arithmetic (Figure 2, p. 189).

Start at the top of the chart in Figure 2, which shows the sequence of foundational abilities involved in learning each discipline, which, if developed, leads to curriculum mastery for knowledge. These SOI abilities lay the basic foundation for sequencing the learning abilities; once mastered, they allow the teaching of higher-level reasoning or critical thinking abilities. The scope of the critical thinking will be determined by the knowledge of subject matter.

Figure 2 lists six reading and language arts foundation abilities. If any one is undeveloped, specific reading problems occur. (The Teacher's Guide explains how to use SOI test results.) Once these abilities are developed, students can develop the intermediate abilities, which lead to accomplishment of the critical thinking activities requiring

FIGURE 1
Abilities Identified as Being Necessary
For Success in Reading and Arithmetic*

READING (Foundational abilities):

_____ **CFU**—Visual closure

_____ **CFC**—Visual conceptualization

_____ **EFU**—Visual discrimination

_____ **EFC**—Judging similarities and matching of concepts

_____ **MSU (visual)**—Visual attending

_____ **MSS (visual)**—Visual concentration for sequencing

READING (Enabling skills):

_____ **CMU**—Vocabulary of math and verbal concepts

_____ **CMR**—Comprehension of verbal relations

_____ **CMS**—Ability to comprehend extended verbal information

_____ **MFU**—Visual memory for details

_____ **NST**—Speed of word recognition

WRITING:

_____ **NFU**—Psycho-motor readiness

ARITHMETIC:

_____ **CFS**—Constancy of objects in space (Piaget)**

_____ **CFT**—Spatial conservation (Piaget)**

_____ **CSR**—Comprehension of abstract relations**

_____ **CSS**—Comprehension of numerical progressions

_____ **MSU (auditory)**—Auditory attending

_____ **MSS (auditory)**—Auditory sequencing

_____ **MSI**—Inferential memory**

_____ **ESC**—Judgment of arithmetic similarities

_____ **ESS**—Judgment of correctness of numerical facts

_____ **NSS**—Application of math facts

_____ **NSI**—Form reasoning (logic)**

**pre-math abilities

CREATIVITY:

_____ **DFU**—Creativity with things (figural-spatial)

_____ **DSR**—Creativity with math facts (symbolic)

_____ **DMU**—Creativity with words and ideas (semantic-verbal)

*See ERIC 11-0-2822 for confirmatory studies.

Structure of the Intellect (SOI)

Developer:	Mary Meeker (based on Guilford)
Goal:	Equip students with the necessary intellectual skills to learn subject matter and critical thinking.
Sample skill:	NMI: coNvergent production of seMantic Implications (choosing the best word)
Assumptions:	• Intelligence consists of 120 thinking abilities that are a combination of *operations* (such as comprehending, remembering, and analyzing); *contents* (such as words, forms, and symbols); and *products* (such as single units, groups, relationships).
	• Twenty-six of these factors are especially relevant to success in school.
	• Individual differences in these factors can be assessed with the SOI-LA tests and improved with specifically designed SOI materials.
Intended audience:	All students and adults.
Process:	Students use materials (some three dimensional) prescribed for them based on a diagnostic test. Computer software gives analyses and prescriptions.
Time:	Varies, but can be 30-minute lessons twice a week until abilities are developed on post-assessment.
Available from:	SOI Institute 343 Richmond Street El Segundo, CA 90245

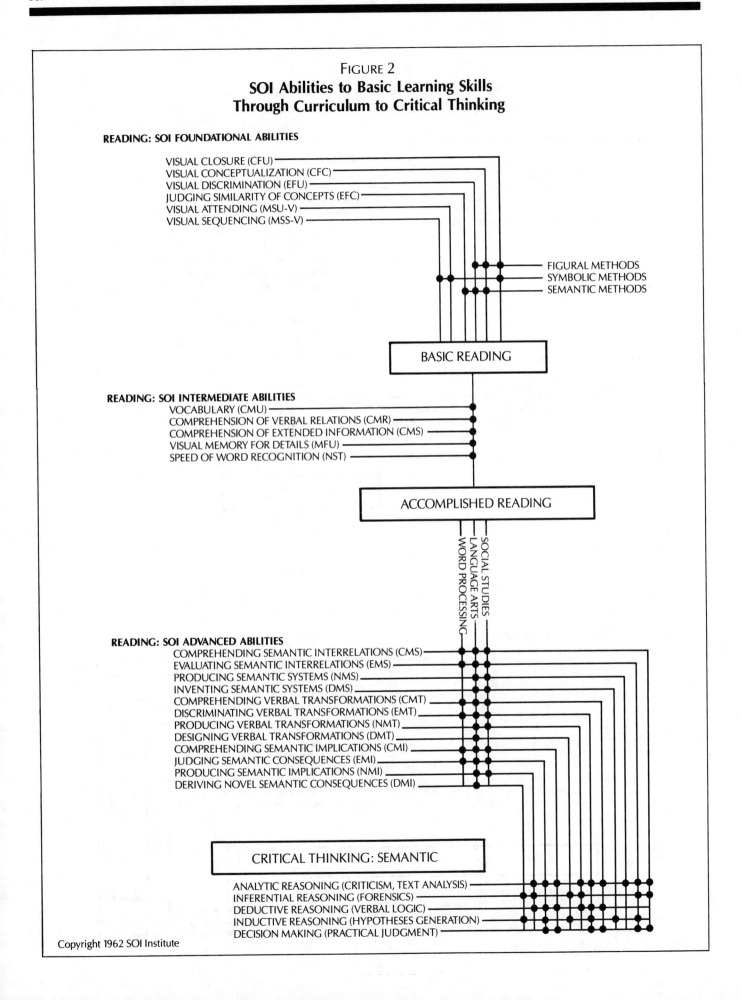

FIGURE 2
**SOI Abilities to Basic Learning Skills
Through Curriculum to Critical Thinking**

FIGURE 3
SOI Abilities to Basic Learning Skills
Through Curriculum to Critical Thinking

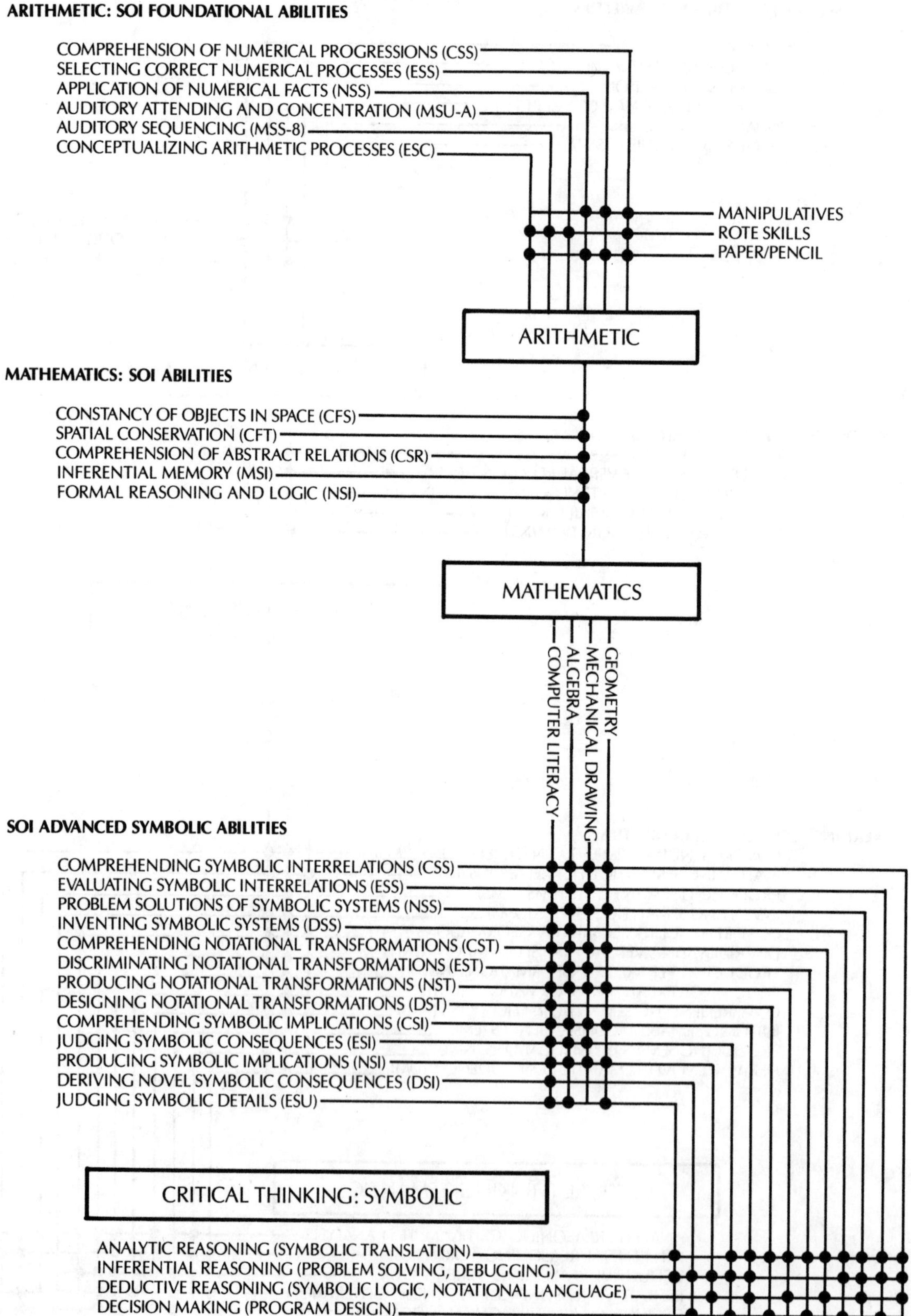

ARITHMETIC: SOI FOUNDATIONAL ABILITIES

COMPREHENSION OF NUMERICAL PROGRESSIONS (CSS)
SELECTING CORRECT NUMERICAL PROCESSES (ESS)
APPLICATION OF NUMERICAL FACTS (NSS)
AUDITORY ATTENDING AND CONCENTRATION (MSU-A)
AUDITORY SEQUENCING (MSS-8)
CONCEPTUALIZING ARITHMETIC PROCESSES (ESC)

MANIPULATIVES
ROTE SKILLS
PAPER/PENCIL

ARITHMETIC

MATHEMATICS: SOI ABILITIES

CONSTANCY OF OBJECTS IN SPACE (CFS)
SPATIAL CONSERVATION (CFT)
COMPREHENSION OF ABSTRACT RELATIONS (CSR)
INFERENTIAL MEMORY (MSI)
FORMAL REASONING AND LOGIC (NSI)

MATHEMATICS

COMPUTER LITERACY
ALGEBRA
MECHANICAL DRAWING
GEOMETRY

SOI ADVANCED SYMBOLIC ABILITIES

COMPREHENDING SYMBOLIC INTERRELATIONS (CSS)
EVALUATING SYMBOLIC INTERRELATIONS (ESS)
PROBLEM SOLUTIONS OF SYMBOLIC SYSTEMS (NSS)
INVENTING SYMBOLIC SYSTEMS (DSS)
COMPREHENDING NOTATIONAL TRANSFORMATIONS (CST)
DISCRIMINATING NOTATIONAL TRANSFORMATIONS (EST)
PRODUCING NOTATIONAL TRANSFORMATIONS (NST)
DESIGNING NOTATIONAL TRANSFORMATIONS (DST)
COMPREHENDING SYMBOLIC IMPLICATIONS (CSI)
JUDGING SYMBOLIC CONSEQUENCES (ESI)
PRODUCING SYMBOLIC IMPLICATIONS (NSI)
DERIVING NOVEL SYMBOLIC CONSEQUENCES (DSI)
JUDGING SYMBOLIC DETAILS (ESU)

CRITICAL THINKING: SYMBOLIC

ANALYTIC REASONING (SYMBOLIC TRANSLATION)
INFERENTIAL REASONING (PROBLEM SOLVING, DEBUGGING)
DEDUCTIVE REASONING (SYMBOLIC LOGIC, NOTATIONAL LANGUAGE)
DECISION MAKING (PROGRAM DESIGN)

Figure 4
Developmental Aspects of Presenting Critical Thinking Abilities

SUBJECT MATTER	REASONING ABILITY	SOI TEACHING MODULES	GRADE
Language Arts/Reading	Basic		
	Concept formation	CFC	Primary
	Differentiating concepts	EFC	Primary
	Comprehending verbal relations	CMR	Primary
	Comprehending verbal systems	CMS	Elementary
	Enrichment		
	Memory for implied meanings	MMI	Elem.-H.S.
	Judging verbal implications	EMI	Elem.-H.S.
	Problem solving	NST	All
	Interpreting verbal meanings	NMR	H.S.
	Using analogical ideas	NMI	Elem.-H.S.
	Creative writing	DMU	All
	Creative interpretation	DMT	High School
	Creative grammatics	DMS	Elem.-H.S.
Arithmetic, Mathematics, Science Preparation	Basic		
	Comprehending space	CFS	All
	Conserving abstracts in spatial perspectives	CFT	All
	Deduction/formal logic	NSI	Elem.-H.S.
	Inductive reasoning	ESS	Elem.-H.S.
	Decision making	ESC	All
	Enrichment		
	Discriminating notational transformations	EST	High School
	Producing notational transformations	DST	High School
	Comprehending inferences	CMI	High School
	Judging symbolic results	ESI	High School
	Producing symbolic implications	NSI	High School
	Creative consequences	DSI	High School

verbal (semantic) intelligence. Figure 2 defines specific kinds of thinking abilities.

Just as IQ tests are global and nonspecific, a general, unspecified critical thinking program does not provide information as to kinds of thinking or their requisites. For this reason we need a roadmap for teaching higher-level thinking abilities and an assessment method to chart diagnostically where students are and where we have taken them.

Figure 3 lists the sequence of abilities required for bringing students to critical thinking competency, which builds on arithmetic and mathematics knowledge. Once students have mastered the foundational abilities necessary for learning basic arithmetic, they can perform successfully in mathematics provided they have also developed the intermediate spatial abilities. Figure 3 lists the kinds of thinking abilities students need for competency in computer literacy, algebra, mechanical drawing, and geometry. By mastering the contents of these disciplines, students are prepared to develop the abilities necessary for critical thinking: analytic reasoning, inferential reasoning, deductive and inductive reasoning, and decision making. At this stage, content is symbolic and notational and sometimes figural-spatial.

A Plan for A Critical Thinking Curriculum

There are differences between critical thinking abilities and learning abilities and between the kinds of critical thinking abilities required for a verbal curriculum and a quantitative curriculum. There are also developmental differences in the sequence and levels of difficulty of those abilities. The *developmental* aspects of presenting critical thinking abilities are shown in Figure 4.

Educators are always faced with choosing the kind of program best suited to the needs of their students and their budgets. This brief description of the Structure of Intellect attempts to show the complexity of critical thinking abilities and the importance of separating verbal and quantitative preparation. SOI allows us to start even our youngest students on the ladder of developing higher-level reasoning and critical thinking abilities. More importantly, because SOI assessments are teacher-group administered, they allow administrators to evaluate the effectiveness of any change in the curriculum by providing assessment information both before and after the change has been made.

The negative aspect of using SOI assessments and materials concerns their comprehensiveness. To use SOI requires training and retraining: (1) teachers need training in diagnostic procedures, and (2) SOI materials require specific methodology. Educators hold many notions about the immutability of intelligence. Retraining requires, at the least, a two-day staff development seminar.

The advantage of using SOI is that it defines 90 thinking abilities ranging from the basic foundational level to advanced higher-order thinking abilities. The greatest pay-off is increased academic achievement as measured by standardized achievement tests. SOI is complex and at the same time precise. It is this very precise clarity that makes it such a powerful tool for education.

REFERENCES

Guilford, J. P. *Way Beyond the IQ.* Great Neck, N.Y.: Creative Synergetic Associates, 1977.

Meeker, Mary, and Bonsall, Marcella. "The NSWP." Los Angeles County Department of Education, Research, and Guidance, 1962. Paper given at APA, Philadelphia, 1963.

Meeker, Mary. *The SOI: Its Uses and Interpretations.* Columbus, Ohio: Charles Merrill, 1969.

Meeker, Mary, and Meeker, Robert. *Teachers' Guide to Using SOI Test Results.* El Segundo, Calif.: SOI Institute, 1975.

Meeker, M., Meeker, R., and Roid, Gayle. *The Basic SOI Test Manual.* Los Angeles: WPS, 1984.

Meeker, R. Prepared for Bill Honig, California State Superintendent of Schools, 1983, and presented to the Urban Task Force of Superintendents, Puerto Rico, Havana, 1983.

31

Instrumental Enrichment

Frances R. Link

There is no curriculum development without staff development.

—Frances Link

Improving the overall cognitive performance of the low-achieving adolescent demands a broad-scale strategy of intervention that focuses not on any specific skills or subject, but rather on the process of learning itself. Instrumental Enrichment is such a program: a direct and focused attack on those mental processes which, through absence, fragility, or inefficiency, are to blame for poor intellectual or academic performance.

The core of the Instrumental Enrichment program—which was developed by Reuven Feuerstein, an Israeli clinical psychologist—is a three-year series of problem-solving tasks and exercises that are grouped in 14 areas of specific cognitive development. They are called instruments rather than lessons because in themselves they are virtually free of specific subject matter. Each instrument's true goal is not the learner's acquisition of information but the development, refinement, and crystallization of those functions prerequisite to effective thinking (see Figure 1, p. 194). In terms of behavior, Instrumental Enrichment's ultimate aim is to transform retarded performers, to alter their characteristically passive and dependent cognitive style to that of active, self-motivated, independent thinkers.

The Instruments

The instruments provide sufficient material for one-period lessons given two to five days a week. Although a three-year sequence is recommended, the program may be implemented in two years, depending on the class curriculum and students' needs. Instrumental Enrichment is intended not to replace traditional content areas, but as a supplement to help students get the most out of all opportunities to learn and grow, and to make bridges to all subject areas.

In the first-year curriculum students use the following instruments:

Organization of Dots—helps students find the relationships—shapes, figures, and other attributes—among a field of dots, much the way one picks out constellations in the night sky. In this way they begin developing strategies for linking perceived events into a system yielding comprehensible information that can be a basis for understanding and logical response.

Orientation in Space I—promotes the creation of specific strategies for differentiating frames of reference in space, such as left, right, front, and back.

Comparison—fosters precise perception, the ability to discriminate by attribute (equal/unequal, similar/dissimilar), and the judgment necessary to identify and evaluate similarities and differences.

Analytic Perception—addresses the ability to analyze component parts in order to find how they relate to each other as well as how they contribute to the overall character of the whole they compose.

In the second-year curriculum, students use these instruments:

Categorization—helps students learn the underlying principles and strategies for creating conceptual sets and categories, a vital prerequisite for higher mental processing.

Figure 1
Instrumental Enrichment Cognitive Functions

I. GATHERING ALL THE INFORMATION WE NEED (INPUT)
1. Using our senses (listening, seeing, smelling, tasting, touching, feeling) to gather clear and complete information (clear perception).
2. Using a system or plan so that we do not skip or miss something important or repeat ourselves (systematic exploration).
3. Giving the thing we gather through our senses and our experience a name so that we can remember it more clearly and talk about it (labeling).
4. Describing things and events in terms of where and when they occur (temporal and spatial referents).
5. Deciding on the characteristics of a thing or event that always stays the same, even when changes take place (conservation, constancy, and object permanence).
6. Organizing the information we gather by considering more than one thing at a time (using two sources of information).
7. Being precise and accurate when it matters (need for precision).

II. USING THE INFORMATION WE HAVE GATHERED (ELABORATION)
1. Defining the problem, what we are being asked to do, and what we must figure out (analyzing disequilibrium).
2. Using only that part of the information we have gathered that is relevant, that is, that applies to the problem and ignoring the rest (relevance).
3. Having a good picture in our mind of what we are looking for or what we must do (interiorization).
4. Making a plan that will include the steps we need to take to reach our goal (planning behavior).
5. Remembering and keeping in mind the various pieces of information we need (broadening our mental field).
6. Looking for the relationship by which separate objects, events, and experiences can be tied together (projecting relationships).
7. Comparing objects and experiences to others to see what is similar and what is different (comparative behavior).
8. Finding the class or set to which the new object or experience belongs (categorization).
9. Thinking about different possibilities and figuring out what would happen if we were to choose one or another (hypothetical thinking).
10. Using logic to prove things and to defend our opinion (logical evidence).

III. EXPRESSING THE SOLUTION TO A PROBLEM (OUTPUT)
1. Being clear and precise in our language to be sure that there is no question as to what the answer is. Putting ourselves into the "shoes" of the listener to be sure that our answers will be understood (overcoming egocentric communication).
2. Thinking things through before we answer instead of immediately trying to answer and making a mistake, and then trying again (overcoming trial and error).
3. Counting to ten (at least) so that we do not say or do something we will be sorry for later (restraining impulsive behavior).
4. Not fretting or panicking if for some reason we cannot answer a question even though we "know" the answer. Leaving the question for a little while and then, when we return to it, using a strategy to help us find the answer (overcoming blocking).

Instructions—emphasizes the use of language as a system for both encoding and decoding operational processes on levels of varying complexity. Exercises focus on critiquing instruction, rewriting instructions to supply missing relevant data, and creating instructions and directions for others to follow.

Temporal Relations—addresses chronological time, biological time, and other temporal relations. Students learn to isolate the factors involved in evaluating or predicting outcomes—time, distance, velocity—and to find the interrelationships among those factors.

Numerical Progressions—promotes the ability to perceive and understand principles and formulas manifested in numerical patterns.

Family Relations—promotes understanding of how individual roles in hierarchical organizations define the network of relationships that are encountered in daily life and work.

Illustrations—encourages spontaneous awareness that a problem exists, analysis of why it exists, and projection of cause-and-effect relationships.

In the third-year curriculum, students are introduced to four instruments:

Transitive Relations and *Syllogisms*—foster higher-level abstract and inferential thought. *Transitive Relations* deals with drawing inferences from relationships that can be described in terms of "greater than," "equal to," or "less than." *Syllogisms* deals with formal propositional logic and aims at promoting inferential thinking based on local evidence. Students learn to critique analytic premises and propositions.

Representational Stencil Design—requires students to analyze a complex figure, identify its components, and then recreate the whole mentally in color, shape, size, and orientation.

Orientation in Space III—complements earlier instruments by extending students' understanding of relative positions from a personal orientation to the stable external system represented by the points of the compass.

Mediated learning experience may be viewed as the means by which nascent, elementary cognitive sets and habits are transformed into the bases for effective thinking. Consequently, the earlier and the more children are subjected to mediated learning experience, the greater will be their capacity to efficiently perceive, understand, and respond to information and stimulation in and out of school.

Teacher Training

Whatever the particular focus of an instrument, its larger purpose is always the further development of students' conscious thought processes and their discovery of practical applications of those processes in and out of school. In this effort, teachers play the crucial role as mediating agents.

Teacher training involves a minimum of 45 hours of inservice annually, plus on-the-job use of exercises in the classroom, if possible, while training is in process. Training programs are custom-designed to fit the inservice schedules of school systems.

Instrumental Enrichment

Developer:	Reuven Feuerstein
Goal:	To develop thinking and problem-solving abilities in order to become an autonomous learner.
Sample skills:	Classification/comparison, orientation in space, recognizing relationships, following directions, planning, organizing, logical reasoning, inductive and deductive reasoning, synthesizing.
Assumptions:	• Intelligence is dynamic (modifiable), not static. • Cognitive development requires direct intervention over time to build the mental processes for learning to learn. • Cognitive development requires *mediated* learning experiences.
Intended audience:	Upper elementary, middle, and secondary levels.
Process:	Students do paper-and-pencil "instruments," which are introduced by teachers and followed by discussions for insight to bring about transfer of learning. The teacher becomes the mediating agent. The cognitive tasks in the materials of instruction are not subject-specific but parallel the subject matter being taught by the teacher.
Time:	Two to three hours a week (plus bridging to subject matter and life skills) over a two- to three-year period.
Available from:	Curriculum Development Associates, Inc. Suite 414, 1211 Connecticut Avenue, N.W. Washington, DC 20036

32
Strategic Reasoning

John J. Glade and Howard Citron

Educators have long realized that major advances in education begin with sound educational theory that can be translated into practical, easy-to-implement instructional methods and materials. Any effort to improve students' thinking and reasoning abilities must necessarily meet the stringent test of hands-on classroom application, and can do so only by satisfying key criteria inherent in the school setting.

The University Urban Schools National Task Force—a committee of professors, researchers, school superintendents, and curriculum directors—has developed a list of criteria for thinking improvement programs (Anderson, 1983). These are:

1. The program can be taught to teachers in a relatively short time.

2. The program has available materials for use by students.

3. The program provides a balanced approach to the treatment of content and mental operations or processes.

4. The program can be integrated into the current organizational framework of schools (that is, courses organized around subject matters).

5. Research evidence exists concerning the effectiveness of the program in enabling students to reason well.

The Strategic Reasoning program satisfies each of these criteria. It is designed for use with students from the 4th grade through community college level, and can be used in English, reading, math, social studies, and science courses. For any given population of students, appropriate instructional levels are identified and assigned.

Program Goals

Strategic Reasoning is a cognitive skills program for teaching students the fundamental thinking skills, reasoning abilities, and problem-solving techniques for functioning effectively in and out of school. Students learn how to process, analyze, and create information that helps them make sense of the world; solve problems of all kinds; and meet their personal life goals. The program has four specific goals:

1. Build students' metacognitive awareness of their fundamental thinking skills and reasoning abilities, which can be applied and transferred to all areas of learning and problem solving.

2. Improve students' ability to use their fundamental thinking skills for critical thinking and higher-order problem solving.

3. Increase students' ability to verbalize their thinking by stating reasons, explanations, arguments, and questions.

4. Develop students' ability to consciously apply and transfer their natural thinking skills to nonacademic (IQ-type) material, interdisciplinary subject matters, and real-life problem solving.

Strategic Reasoning addresses the needs of teachers, as well. The program contains all student and teacher materials required to fulfill the above instructional goals; no teacher-developed materials are necessary. Further, the teacher materials are designed so that extensive teacher training is not needed. However, an experienced cadre of consultants is available to provide staff development when desired.

Program Philosophy

The program is based on the hypothesis that deliberate cognitive development can be taught to all students within the regular classroom. Its methodology for fulfilling this goal is grounded in the theoretical and practical research of Albert Upton, Professor Emeritus of Whittier College. Upton's work has shown that through formalized education, training, and exercise in the performance of six fundamental thinking skills—with emphasis on the verbalization of thinking processes—students can become better learners, reasoners, and problem solvers. In addition, students can learn to generalize the performance of their thinking skills: to transfer their thinking skills to any situation involving intellectual functioning, including academic subject areas and real-life behavior (Upton, 1961; Upton and Samson, 1963; Brunelle, 1967).

A major strength of the Upton methodology lies in its linking of several discrete, successful cognitive development strategies. Various elements of the approach are supported by the work of Gordon (1961), Inhelder and Piaget (1958), Levi (1965), and Osborn (1963). Whimbey (1975, 1980) has confirmed the importance of students' conscious verbalization of their thinking processes.

Upton's Research

For over 20 years, Upton researched the role of conscious thinking in learning tasks involving information processing, language comprehension and usage, problem solving, and creativity. He focused on how individuals consciously used their minds in performing these tasks. This research produced two main findings (Upton, 1961):

1. There are six primary, natural thinking skills that underlie performance of learning, reasoning, and problem solving.

2. Although everyone has the capacity to perform these six thinking skills, the ability to use them productively depends on experience and training.

In 1960 Upton designed a thinking improvement course that came to be called "Graded Exercises in Analysis." The course objectives were to make students aware that they use a basic set of six thinking skills when they think; improve their ability to use these skills; enhance their verbalization of their thinking processes; and increase their ability to use the skills as a model for processing information and solving problems.

Upton and his graduate student assistants taught this course to 280 college freshmen over an eight-month period using a standardized intelligence test as the pre- and post-measure of students' overall thinking ability. The results showed that the average IQ score increased by 10.5 points, with some students gaining 20 points and one gaining 32 points (Hechinger, 1960). As Upton explains:

> [The approach] teaches the relationship between "words and things." It applies the scientific method to language and communication and thereby to thinking and understanding. . . . We don't know whether "native intelligence" may be increased, because we don't know what it is, but we can train people to solve problems they could not solve before.

The Six Thinking Skills

The results obtained from the "Graded Exercises in Analysis" course revealed that instruction and practice in six fundamental thinking skills result in overall improvements in mental performance. The six thinking skills Upton isolated are:

1. *Thing-Making*—perceiving and mentally identifying things through word names, symbols, or mental images. For example: identifying that a structure in which you store money is called a *bank* but that there is also a thing identified as a river *bank*, or that a skull-and-crossbones symbolizes danger. This skill is the basis for vocabulary development, context inferencing, and all communication because it embodies word-reference, knowledge, perception, and association.

2. *Qualification*—analyzing the characteristics of things. For example: analyzing that a certain pen is six inches long, cylindrical, smooth, easily held, and produces blue ink; characterizing the United States as democratic, civilized, large, and powerful. The better we describe the characteristics of things, the better we comprehend them, fit them to purposes, compare and contrast them with other things, and creatively change or improve them.

3. *Classification*—organizing things into groups according to shared characteristics. For example: classifying a pen with a pencil, typewriter, and word processor as writing instruments; grouping the United States with England and France as Western nations; organizing specific statements under a general idea or heading. The better we classify, the better we organize any set of data, form general concepts, and perform such reasoning as syllogistic logic.

4. *Structure Analysis*—analyzing and creating part-whole relationships. For example: analyzing that a chair is a structure physically composed of and defined by a seat, back, two arms, and four legs; that a dry cell has chambers, a zinc electrode, and a copper electrode; that an essay can be created by arranging individual paragraphs. Competently analyzing and creating part-whole relationships underlie our comprehension of the composition and structure of things, reveal key ingredients, and build spatial reasoning skill.

5. *Operation Analysis*—sequencing things, events, or thoughts into a logical order. For example: ordering people

from tallest to shortest; arranging criteria from most important to least important; completing a timeline; planning the steps for an experiment or solving a problem. The more logically we order things, the better we comprehend serial relationships of all types, follow the steps of any process, identify cause-effect relationships, and make plans and predictions.

6. *Seeing Analogies*—recognizing similar relationships. For example: recognizing that a writer uses a pen as an artist uses a paintbrush; that Vietnam was to the United States what Angola was to Cuba; that the structure of an atom is similar to the structure of an egg. This skill is the application of the information produced by all of the other thinking skills. It provides the basis for problem-solving insight when we recognize similar problems, for comprehending metaphors when we recognize the analogy being expressed, and for understanding the mathematical concepts of ratio and proportion.

These six thinking skills are fundamental elements of *all* learning, reasoning, and problem solving, regardless of content. "Poor" thinkers perform these skills weakly; "good" thinkers perform them well. "Poor" thinkers do not know how to apply the skills to different subject areas; "good" thinkers do so consciously.

The Stages of Strategic Reasoning

Strategic Reasoning incorporates Upton's methodology into a formal, easy-to-implement classroom program. Specifically, Strategic Reasoning includes four stages of thinking improvement instruction (Figure 1). Each stage represents a central objective essential to improving students' cognitive functioning. Most important, each stage has a complete set of student and teacher materials required for fulfilling its objective; no additional materials are needed.

Stage 1

Objective: To build students' metacognitive abilities by developing their knowledge of the six fundamental thinking skills and how they use these skills to communicate, learn, reason, and solve problems.

The focus in this stage is on making students aware that their thinking involves systematically using the six basic thinking skills and that they can learn to become better thinkers. Instruction involves using the following materials and strategies.

Components and Strategies. Instructional materials consist of an eight-lesson multimedia kit entitled *Introducing Thinking Skills* and an accompanying *Thinking Skills Poster Set*. Each lesson is designed to take approximately one class period, with supplemental activities included for teachers wishing to expand their instruction. Throughout the eight lessons, the teacher guides students to an awareness of their possession and use of the six basic thinking skills. Students explore examples of how they use these skills in their everyday thinking, and the teacher outlines metacognitive strategies needed to use the skills most effectively.

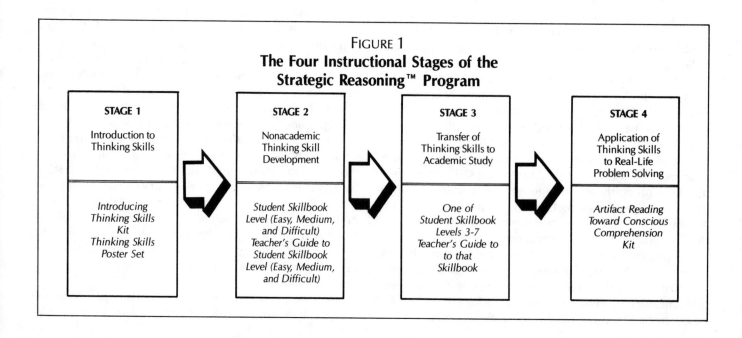

FIGURE 1
**The Four Instructional Stages of the
Strategic Reasoning™ Program**

STAGE 1	STAGE 2	STAGE 3	STAGE 4
Introduction to Thinking Skills	Nonacademic Thinking Skill Development	Transfer of Thinking Skills to Academic Study	Application of Thinking Skills to Real-Life Problem Solving
Introducing Thinking Skills Kit *Thinking Skills Poster Set*	*Student Skillbook Level (Easy, Medium, and Difficult)* *Teacher's Guide to Student Skillbook Level (Easy, Medium, and Difficult)*	*One of Student Skillbook Levels 3-7* *Teacher's Guide to to that Skillbook*	*Artifact Reading Toward Conscious Comprehension Kit*

FIGURE 2
A Sample of Nonacademic Exercises

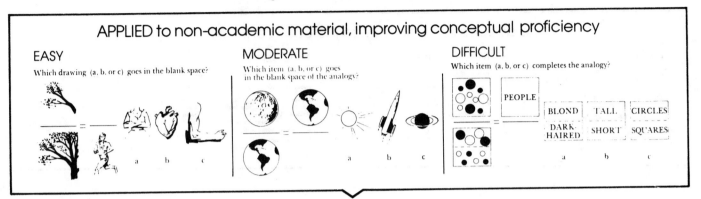

The Teacher's Manual for this kit includes all lesson plans needed to complete this stage. All activities are teacher directed, with whole-class participation; brief in duration, inductive/exploratory in nature; oriented around group discussion; and designed to accommodate students of all ability levels and to draw on the creative thinking talents of students and teachers alike.

Stage 2

Objective: To increase the level of students' cognitive proficiency through structured training in the performance of each of the six fundamental thinking skills as a tool for communication, learning, reasoning, and problem solving.

The focus is on improving students' ability to perform each of the six thinking skills while processing and solving a structured set of nonacademic, IQ-type exercises.

Components and Strategies. Students first study a skillbook entitled *EASY* and later progress to skillbooks *MEDIUM* and *DIFFICULT*. There is a detailed Teacher's Guide, including an expanded solution key, for each skillbook. Each student skillbook requires about six to ten hours of classroom time. In each skillbook, students solve approximately 100 carefully sequenced, nonacademic exercises, such as the samples in Figure 2. Through individual work and teacher-guided group discussion, students progressively improve their ability to use each of the six thinking skills when interpreting information and solving problems.

An oral group discussion of all exercises is a key element in this thinking improvement process for several reasons. First, the results of Upton's work indicate that students think better and more clearly when they put their thinking into spoken words. Second, many of the exercises are divergent in nature, allowing for more than one correct answer. Group discussion allows students to share their personal thinking and reasoning with one another. Third, students often learn more about problem-solving styles and strategies from their peers than from the teacher. Finally, when a student's answer is incorrect, asking that student to explain his or her reasoning will often result in "hearing" the mistake in thinking and lead to a self-correcting solution.

Strategic Reasoning embodies an innovative instructional feature within the expanded solution key of the Teacher's Guide. Unlike most answer keys, this guide provides the teacher not only with the correct or most appropriate answer to a given exercise, but also with the following teacher aids:

● The specific thinking skill(s) required to solve any exercise.

● The reasoning supporting the correct answer.

● Possible alternative answers, both correct and incorrect.

● The reasoning supporting or refuting those answers.

● The reason why one answer is more appropriate than others.

● Ideas for expanding the exercise.

The sample in Figure 3 (p. 200) is an excerpt from the expanded solution key.

Stage 3

Objective: To develop students' ability to consciously transfer and apply their thinking skills to learning, comprehending, analyzing, communicating about, and solving problems with academic material.

Because conscious application and transfer of thinking skills to academic study do not seem to be intuitive or au-

FIGURE 3
Sample From the Expanded Solution Key

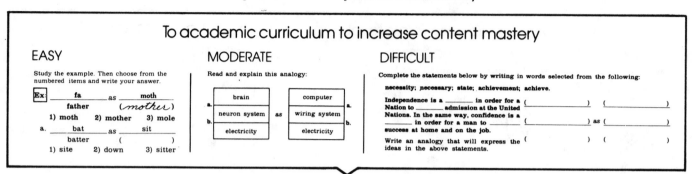

tomatic in many cases, and because it is typically unrealistic to rely on the teacher to develop necessary materials, Strategic Reasoning includes a series of exercises drawn from a variety of academic disciplines. These exercises integrate students' mastery of academic content with their thinking improvement. Transfer is concretely addressed and successively applied to increasingly complex material. The sample exercises in Figure 4 show three different academic disciplines to which the Seeing Analogies thinking skill is applied.

Components and Strategies. This stage entails about 15-20 classroom periods. Students study an appropriate ac-

ademic skillbook determined by their grade reading level. There are seven skillbooks, numbered from Level 3 through Level 9, with corresponding Teacher's Guides. Each skillbook contains five units of academic content-based thinking improvement instruction. Each unit consists of a short reading selection followed by a set of exercises called "Logic and Comprehension." The reading selections have been carefully chosen to represent diverse subject areas. The "Logic and Comprehension" exercises are thinking skills exercises and problems designed to build students' ability to master the information presented in the selections. Through completing these units, the goal of

FIGURE 4
Sample Applications of the Seeing Analogies Thinking Skill

11. Which drawing (a, b, or c) goes in the blank space?

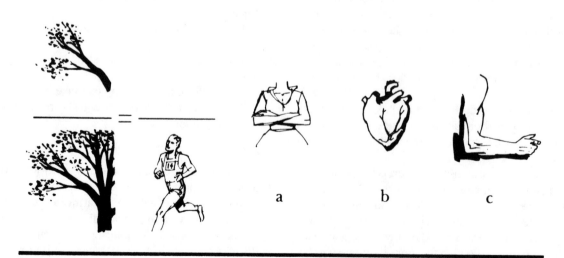

transferring thinking ability from nonacademic to academic material is achieved. Transfer becomes conscious and natural.

Stage 4

Objective: To improve students' ability to consciously apply and transfer their thinking skills to analyzing, comprehending, communicating about, and solving problems involving real-life situations.

The ultimate role of all education is to improve the quality of an individual's life; that is, to make that individual successful in the real world and not merely able to survive. Strategic Reasoning ensures that students are provided with formal instruction in the conscious application and transfer of thinking ability to everyday problems. Thus, Stage 4 is the culmination of the cognitive improvement accomplished during the preceding three instructional stages.

This stage involves the use of one of the two multimedia instructional kits outlined below. Each kit presents a major social or emotional problem and includes important concepts that challenge students' lives every day.

Components. Kit #1—"2087 A.D." (Theme: Identity). We all experience some loss of identity in a world that treats the individual as a computer entry; we are known by our social security numbers, student ID's, and so on. We talk to and are instructed by machines. We struggle for personality in a world increasingly impersonal in nature.

Kit #2—"Bug Off" (Theme: Rivalry). Rivalry affects all of our actions in school, on the job, and in our social lives. It is a concept that is built into our world system and that we must deal with effectively to successfully achieve our life goals.

Strategies. Each of these kits is a multimedia, whole-class learning experience. They give students the chance to use their thinking skills in personal, unstructured, real-life situations. In each case, a real-life situation is dramatized on audiotape and through a collection of "artifacts" (letters, photos, personal notes, and so on).

Students start by listening to the audiotape and examining the artifacts in order to discern and identify the problem represented and the features of that problem. Then, through a set of teacher prompts and questions included in the Teacher's Guide to the kit, students apply their thinking skills to analyzing the problem, interpreting the information presented, drawing on personal experiences, and suggesting potential solutions to the problem. Throughout, the students must verbalize the thinking skills they are using to ensure that thinking has now truly become a conscious, controllable talent.

Strategic Reasoning

Developer:	John Glade, based on Albert Upton's "Design for Thinking" model.
Goal:	Teach the conscious thinking skills students must have to function effectively in school and in real life.
Skills:	Thing-making (identification) Qualification (description) Classification (organization) Structure Analysis (part-whole relations) Operation Analysis (sequencing) Seeing Analogies
Assumptions:	• Six thinking skills form the fundamental core of *all* thinking and problem solving. • Instruction in the six thinking skills improves both school and real-life performance and success. • Thinking instruction must be integrated with, not separated from, regular classroom learning.
Intended audience:	All types of students from the 4th grade up.
Process:	Students do group activities and paper-and-pencil exercises. Teachers lead discussions of problem-solving processes and rationales. Program materials provide for transition from developmental IQ-type exercises to subject-matter exercises, then to life applications.
Time:	One period per week.
Available from:	Innovative Sciences, Inc. Park Square Station P.O. Box 15129 Stamford, CT 06901-0129

Field Effectiveness Data

The effectiveness of the Strategic Reasoning program has been demonstrated by a wealth of test data such as the following:

• Orin Glick (1975), Director of Program Evaluation for the Franklin Pierce Schools in Tacoma, Washington, reports that nine of ten instructional groups scored gains in IQ, measured by the verbal and nonverbal intelligence subtests of the Short Form Test of Academic Aptitude.

• Barbara Spear and others (1977) report that an Orange Coast College student population having IQ's lower than 94 increased their scores on the Peabody Individual Achievement Test.

• In a study by Raul Besteiro (1980), Superintendent of the Brownsville Independent School District in Texas, below-average junior high students achieved a mean gain five times that expected on the SRA Achievement Series in Reading.

• Laura D. Harckham (1979), independent evaluator for the New Rochelle School District in New York, has conducted a longitudinal study assessing the effectiveness of continued study by the same students over three successive school years. Below-average 7th grade students who successively studied the system in 7th, 8th, and 9th grade achieved mean gains two and one-half times those expected for that period on the Iowa sub-tests in both vocabulary and comprehension.

• In Tulsa, Oklahoma, Superintendent Larry Zenke and Larry Alexander (1984) report that 251 regular 6th graders increased on average from the 32nd to 40th percentile in Growth Scale Value and from 95 to 99 in Intelligence Quotient, as measured by the Educational Abilities Series of the SRA Test Battery. In a separate Chapter I program, 287 junior high students achieved in two and a half instructional months mean gains on the Gates MacGinitie Reading Test of five months in Vocabulary, seven months in Comprehension, and seven months in Total Score.

Mastering Thinking

Strategic Reasoning satisfies each of the five criteria for thinking improvement programs identified by the University Urban Schools National Task Force. It requires minimal staff development; supplies all of the student and teacher materials needed to provide the full scope of thinking improvement instruction; effectively links nonacademic thinking improvement with the direct transfer of thinking to academic and real-life content; is easily implemented within regular school courses, by regular subject area teachers; and has a proven history of thinking improvement gains.

Through the careful, guided instruction in thinking provided in the cognitive exercises of Strategic Reasoning, students will strain their mental muscles in much the same way that weightlifters and runners strain their muscles to improve their performance. What might this increased strength do for students? Evidence indicates that when students master the methods of thinking, they develop greater self-confidence and a better self-image. Also, they are motivated to apply themselves to learning and solving problems in all areas, and they become more successful at both. Finally, they discover that virtually any subject area, problem, or goal can be mastered with success.

REFERENCES

Anderson, L. W. "Introduction." In *Proceedings: The Fourth Conference of the University Urban Schools National Task Force; The Fourth R: Reasoning.* Edited by R. Bossone. New York: Center for Advanced Study in Education, The Graduate School and University Center of The City University of New York, 1983, pp. 1-7.

Besteiro, R. A. *An Evaluation of Think and Intuitive Math.* Brownsville, Tex.: Brownsville Independent School District, 1980.

Brunelle, E. A. "An Experiment in Exposition." *California English Journal* 3, 1 (1967): 58-65.

Glick, O. *Experimental Schools Project: Evaluation Report No. 27.* Tacoma, Wash.: Franklin Pierce Schools, 1975.

Gordon, W. J. J. *Synectics.* New York: Harper, 1961.

Harckham, L. D. *Evaluation of the Think Program.* New Rochelle, N.Y.: City School District of New Rochelle, 1979.

Hechinger, F. "Student IQ's Rise in California Test." *The New York Times,* June 27, 1960.

Inhelder, B., and Piaget, J. *The Growth of Logical Thinking from Childhood to Adolescence.* New York: Basic Books, 1958.

Levi, A. "Treatment of a Disorder of Perception and Concept Formation in a Case of School Failure." *Journal of Consulting Psychology* 29 (1965): 289-295.

Osborn, A. *Applied Imagination,* 3rd ed. New York: Scribners, 1963.

Spear, B. E.; Ortiz, K. K.; Cowperthwait, S. M.; and Bosse, D. A. *Second Annual Report—1976-1977—Educational Testing and Learning Clinic.* Costa Mesa, Calif.: Orange Coast College, 1977.

Upton, A. *Design For Thinking.* Palo Alto: Pacific Books, 1961.

Upton, A., and Samson, R. *Creative Analysis.* New York: E. P. Dutton, 1963.

Whimbey, A. *Intelligence Can Be Taught.* New York: E. P. Dutton, 1975.

Whimbey, A. "Students Can Learn to be Better Problem Solvers." *Educational Leadership* 37 (April 1980): 560-565.

33

The CoRT Thinking Program

Edward de Bono

Creativity involves breaking out of established patterns in order to look at things in a different way.
—Edward de Bono

A major trend may be developing in education toward the direct teaching of thinking as a skill. I intend in this article to answer two basic questions related to this trend. First, what is thinking? And second, how can we teach thinking directly? My answers spring from 16 years of experience in the field. During this time I developed an instructional program on thinking skills that is now used by several million schoolchildren in many different countries and cultures.

Of course, some educators believe that thinking is simply a matter of innate intelligence. Two corollaries follow from this belief: 1) we do not have to do anything specific to help highly intelligent individuals learn how to think, and 2) there is little we can do to help less intelligent individuals learn how to think. Thus those who hold this belief rest content. Yet many highly intelligent individuals often seem to be rather ineffective thinkers. Such people are often good at reactive thinking and puzzle solving—but less able to think about topics that require a broader view. They may show cleverness, but not wisdom.

I prefer to see the relationship between intelligence and thinking as similar to the relationship between a car and its driver. Engineering determines the innate potential of the car, but the skill with which the car is driven must be learned and practiced. Thus I would define thinking as "the operating skill with which intelligence acts upon experience."

What, then, is the relationship of information to think-ing? It seems obvious to me that God can neither think nor have a sense of humor. Perfect knowledge precludes the need to move from one arrangement of knowledge to a better one. Thus perfect knowledge makes thinking unnecessary. Nonetheless, educators often seem to believe that we can attain such perfect knowledge. However, even if it were possible to absorb perfect knowledge about the past, we can only have very partial knowledge about the future. Yet, as soon as a youngster leaves school, he or she will be operating in the future. Every initiative, decision, or plan will be carried out in the future and thus will require thinking, not just the sorting and re-sorting of knowledge. I have coined the term "operacy" to stand along literacy and numeracy as a primary goal of education. Operacy is the skill of doing things, of making things happen. The type of thinking that my program (which I will describe later) teaches is very much concerned with operacy.

In short, information is no substitute for thinking, and thinking is no substitute for information. The dilemma is that there is never enough time to teach all the information that could usefully be taught. Yet we may have to reduce the time we spend teaching information, in order to focus instead on the direct teaching of thinking skills.

The relationship between logic and thinking is likewise not a linear one. The computer world has a saying, "Garbage in—garbage out." In other words, even if the computer is working flawlessly, this will not validate a given outcome. Bad logic makes for bad thinking, but good logic (like the flawless computer) does not insure good think-

This chapter originally appeared in Edward de Bono, "The Direct Teaching of Thinking as a Skill," *Phi Delta Kappan* 64, 10 (June 1983): 703-708. Reprinted with permission.

ing. Every logician knows that a conclusion is only as good as the premises. Mathematics, logic (of various sorts), and—increasingly—data processing are excellent service tools. But the deeper we advance into the computer age, the greater the need to emphasize the perceptual side of thinking, which these tools serve.

Meanwhile, emotions, values, and feelings influence thinking in three stages. We may feel a strong emotion (e.g., fear, anger, hatred) even before we encounter a situation. More usually, there is a brief period of undirected perception, until we recognize the situation. This recognition triggers emotion, which thereafter channels perception. The trained thinker should be operating in the third mode: perception explores the situation as broadly as possible, and, in the end, emotions determine the decision. There is no contradiction at all between emotions and thinking. The purpose of thinking is to arrange the world so that our emotions can be applied in a valuable manner.

The relationship of perception to thinking is, to my mind, the crucial area. In the past, far too many of our approaches to thinking (e.g., mathematics, logic) have concerned themselves with the "processing" aspect. We are rather good at processing but poor in the perceptual area.

What do I mean by perception? Quite simply, the way our minds make sense of the world around us. Language is a reflection of our traditional perceptions (as distinct from the moment-to-moment ones). Understanding how percep-

tion works is not so easy. But this is a crucial point—one that has a direct effect on the way we teach thinking.

Imagine a man holding a small block of wood. He releases the wood, and it falls to the ground. When he releases it a second time, the wood moves upward. This is strange and mysterious behavior. The third time he releases the wood, it remains exactly where it is—suspended in space. This is also mysterious behavior. If I were now to reveal that, in the second instance, the man was standing at the bottom of a swimming pool, then it seems perfectly natural for the wood to float upward. In the third instance, the man is an astronaut in orbit; thus it is perfectly natural for the wood to remain suspended, since it is weightless. Behavior that seemed strange and unaccountable suddenly seems normal and logical—once we have defined the "universe" in which it is taking place.

The traditional universe of information handling is a "passive" one. We record information through marks on paper or marks on magnetic tape. We can handle and process that information. The marks on the surface of the paper or tape and the information itself do not alter, unless we alter them.

An "active" system is totally different; here, the information actually organizes itself into patterns. We human beings have self-organizing information systems. I first wrote about them in 1969 in my book, *The Mechanism of Mind*.[1] I showed then how such systems work, and I suggested how the structure of a nerve network would pro-

---

CoRT (Cognitive Research Trust)

Developer:	Edward de Bono
Goal:	Teach thinking skills useful to everyone in and out of school.
Sample skills:	PNI: Positive, Negative, Interesting CAF: Consider All Factors
Assumptions:	• Lateral thinking, unlike vertical thinking, is not necessarily sequential, is unpredictable, and is not constrained by convention. • It is not necessary to be right at every stage of the thought process nor to have everything rigidly defined. • Intelligent people are not necessarily skillful thinkers.
Intended audience:	Ages eight to 22, all ability levels.
Process:	Students practice "operations" following "lesson notes." Teachers present and monitor the exercises.
Time:	One lesson 35 minutes or longer per week for three years.
Comments:	Evaluation results suggest that the program leads students to take a broader view of formally posed problems.
Available from:	Pergamon Press, Inc. Fairview Park Elmsford, NY 10523

duce such pattern-making effects. My hypothesis has since been simulated by computer, and the nerve network functions substantially as I had suggested.[2] In the world of information handling, the concept of self-organizing information systems is now coming to the fore.[3] Such systems are quite different from our usual computers.

Once we enter the "universe" of active, self-organizing systems, then the behavior of such things as perception and creativity becomes quite clear. The processes are no longer mysterious. Just as happened with the block of wood, phenomena that seemed to be unaccountable are suddenly seen to be explicable—once we have identified the appropriate universe.

The function of a self-organizing system is to allow incoming experience to organize itself into patterns. We could loosely compare these patterns to the streets in a town. The self-organizing system is immensely efficient; it allows us to get up in the morning, cross a road, recognize friends, read and write. Without such a pattern-making and pattern-using system, we would spend about a month just in crossing a road.

However, the advantages of a patterning system are also its disadvantages. "Point-to-point thinking" is a good example. In this kind of thinking, we follow a pattern from one point to the next—and then follow the dominant pattern from that next point onward. In an experiment that I conducted jointly with the Inner London Education Authority,[4] I asked 24 groups of 11-year-olds to discuss the suggestion that "bread, fish, and milk should be free." Although many of the children came from deprived backgrounds, 23 of the 24 groups opposed the idea of free bread, fish, and milk. The point-to-point thinking that led to this stand went as follows: 1) the shops would be crowded; 2) the buses going to the shops would be crowded; 3) the bus drivers would demand more money; 4) the drivers would not get more money, and they would go on strike; 5) other people would go on strike as well; and 6) there would be chaos—so giving away bread, fish, and milk is a bad idea. Thus can point-to-point thinking lead us astray, as we miss the forest while fixating on the trees.

However, direct teaching of thinking can offset the disadvantages of a patterning system. At the end of a pilot project on the teaching of thinking in Venezuelan schools, for example, we held a press conference. A journalist attending that conference claimed that all attempts to teach thinking are really a form of brainwashing in western capitalist values. The journalist happened to be wearing spectacles. So I removed her spectacles and asked what she used them for. She told me that she used the spectacles in order to see things more clearly. I then explained that the perceptual tools we were teaching in the lessons on thinking served the same purpose. The tools enable youngsters to scan their experiences so that they can see things more clearly and more broadly. A better map of the world is the result. These thinkers can still retain their original values and choices, however. Giving spectacles to nearsighted individuals enables them to see three glasses on a table—containing wine, orange juice, and milk. The individuals still exercise choice as to which drink each prefers. In the same way, our instructional program cuts across cultures and ideologies. The program is used in industrialized nations, such as Canada and Great Britain, and in developing nations, such as Venezuela and Malaysia; it will soon be used in Cuba, China, and Bulgaria—as well as in Catholic Ireland.

My point is that, in terms of perception, we need to achieve two things: 1) the ability to see things more clearly and more broadly and 2) the ability to see things differently (i.e., creativity or "lateral thinking"[5]). As I have said, perception takes place in an "active" information system. Such systems allow experience to organize itself into immensely useful patterns, without which life would be impossible. But, as I said above, the very advantages of the patterning system are also its disadvantages. We must overcome these disadvantages and improve perception in two ways: in breadth and in creativity or lateral thinking (both of which fall under the heading of "change").

Let me turn now to the second question that I posed at the beginning of this article. How can we teach thinking as a skill? Such teaching is going on right now; it is not tomorrow's dream, but today's reality. Millions of children are involved. In Venezuela, for example, 106,000 teachers have been trained to use my program, and every school child takes a course in thinking. By law, Venezuelan schoolchildren in every grade must have two hours of direct instruction per week in thinking skills. The contracts of some labor union members in Venezuela specify that their employers must make provisions to teach them thinking skills. My program is also in use in many other countries—including Australia, the U.S., and Israel, as well as those nations I have mentioned previously.

The program of which I speak is called CoRT. (The acronym stands for Cognitive Research Trust, located in Cambridge, England.) I have already outlined the theoretical foundation for the design of this program. The lessons themselves focus on the perceptual aspect of thinking. The design of the tools takes into account the behavior of self-organizing patterning systems.

The design criteria for a practical instructional program should include the following elements.

● The program should be usable by teachers who represent a wide range of teaching talents, not just by the highly gifted or the highly qualified. (The 106,000 Venezuelan teachers were not all geniuses.)

• The program should not require complicated teacher training, since it is difficult to generalize such programs. (The CoRT program can be used by teachers with no special training or with only simple training.)

• The program should be robust enough to resist damage as it is passed along from trainer to trainer—and thence from new trainer to teachers and, finally, to pupils.

• The program should employ parallel design so that, if some parts of the program are badly taught and other parts are skipped or later forgotten, what remains is usable and valuable in its own right. (This contrasts with hierarchical design, in which a student must grasp a basic concept before moving on to the next concept layer; failure at any concept layer in a program of this type makes the whole system unworkable.)

• The program should be enjoyable for both teachers and youngsters.

• The program should focus on thinking skills that help a learner to function better in his or her life outside of school, not merely to become more proficient at solving puzzles or playing games.

Before considering ways of teaching thinking, we must confront a prior question: Should thinking be taught in its own right? Certain practical considerations affect the answer to this question. For example, there are no gaps in the school schedule as it now exists. Thus it seems to make more sense to insert thinking skills into an existing subject area. English makes a good home, because a natural synergy exists between thinking and the expression of thought in language. In addition, the teaching style is often more open-ended in English classes than in some other subject areas. However, the CoRT program has been used effectively by science teachers, by music teachers, and even by physical education teachers.

Despite these practical considerations, I believe that we should have a specific place in the curriculum that is set aside for the teaching of thinking skills. This formal recognition is essential so that pupils, teachers, and parents all recognize that thinking skills are being taught directly. In time, I would certainly hope that the skills taught in the "thinking lessons" would find their ways into such subject areas as geography, history, social studies, and science. However, the first step is to establish "thinking" as a subject in its own right.

This brings me to the central problem: transfer and content. Does a generalizable skill of thinking exist? Many theorists think not. They believe instead that there is thinking in mathematics, thinking in science, and thinking in history—but that in each case the rules are different, just as the rules for Monopoly differ from those for chess. I do not see this as a point of view with which I must either agree or

disagree totally. Clearly, subject idioms exist. Nevertheless, it is possible to establish both habits of mind and specific thinking techniques that can be applied in any subject area. For example, the willingness to look for alternatives is a generalizable thinking habit. And deliberate provocation is a technique that can be applied to generate ideas in any situation.

Because we cannot succeed in teaching generalizable thinking skills through the use of specific content materials, some theorists believe that such skills cannot exist. But there is another way of looking at the situation: the view that generalizable thinking skills exist but cannot be taught using specific content. My experience has led me to the latter view. As I have already noted with regard to the "discussion method" of teaching thinking skills, little transfer of such skills seems to take place from one situation to another. Given the mechanics of perception and attention, this is hardly surprising. If the subject of a discussion is interesting, then—by definition—attention follows this interest. But this attention is not focused on the metacognitive level; that is, participants are not thinking about the *thinking* that they are using to discuss the subject. Moreover, it is very difficult to transfer a complex action sequence from one situation to another. That is why the CoRT program deliberately focuses on "tools" that can be transferred.

I have noticed among U.S. educators a tendency to try to teach thinking through content materials. This approach seems—to its proponents—to have two merits. First, this approach makes it easier to introduce thinking into the curriculum, because the material must be covered anyway (and it is already familiar to the teacher). Second, this approach seems to be killing two birds with one stone: teaching thinking *and* teaching content. But this approach is not effective. I am afraid that the nettle must be grasped. Either one wishes to teach thinking effectively or merely to make a token gesture. Attending to content distracts from attending to the thinking tools being used. Theory predicts this outcome: you cannot build meta-patterns on one level and experience patterns on another level at the same time. Experience backs up this expectation. Wherever there has been an attempt to teach thinking skills and content together, the training in thinking seems to be weaker than when those skills are taught in isolation.

So what is the CoRT method? It is best to illustrate this method with an example.

I was teaching a class of 30 boys, all 11 years of age, in Sydney, Australia. I asked if they would each like to be given $5 a week for coming to school. All 30 thought this was a fine idea. "We could buy sweets or chewing gum . . . . We could buy comics . . . . We could get toys without having to ask Mum or Dad."

I then introduced and explained a simple tool called the PMI (which I will describe later). The explanation took about four minutes. In groups of five, the boys applied the PMI tool to the suggestion that they should be given $5 a week for coming to school. For three to four minutes they talked and thought on their own. At no time did I interfere. I never discussed the $5 suggestion, other than to state it. I did not suggest that the youngsters consider this, think of that, and so forth. At the end of their thinking time, the groups reported back to me: "The bigger boys would beat us up and take the money. . . . The school would raise its charges for meals . . . . Our parents would not buy us presents . . . . Who would decide how much money different ages received? . . . There would be less money to pay teachers . . . . There would be less money for a school minibus."

When they had finished their report, I again asked the boys to express their views on the suggestion of pay for attending school. This time, 29 of the 30 had completely reversed their opinion and thought it a bad idea. We subsequently learned that the one holdout received *no* pocket money at home. The important point is that my contribution was minimal. I did not interact with the boys. I simply explained the PMI tool, and the boys then used it on their own—as *their* tool. My "superior" intelligence and broader experiences were not influences. The boys did their own thinking.

The PMI is a simple scanning tool designed to avoid the point-to-point thinking that I mentioned earlier. The thinker looks first in the *Plus* direction (good points), and then in the *Minus* direction (bad points), and finally in the *Interesting* direction (interesting things that might arise or are worth noting, even if they are neither good nor bad). Each direction is scanned formally, one after another. This formal scan produces a better and broader map. Thinking is used to explore, not merely to back up a snap judgment. The thinker then applies judgment to the better map. The PMI is the first of the 60 CoRT lessons.

For the rest of this particular lesson on thinking, I might have asked the boys to apply the PMI in various ways (e.g., one group doing only "Plus" or "Minus" or "Interesting") to a number of thinking items, such as: Should all cars be colored yellow? Would it be a good idea for everyone to wear a badge showing his or her mood at the moment? Is homework a good idea? Note that the items are not related. Moreover, the group would be allowed to spend only two or three minutes on each. This is quite deliberate and essential to the method.

The items are switched rapidly so that attention stays on the PMI tool and *not on the content*. Once skill in the use of the tool is developed, students can apply the PMI to other situations in other settings. One girl told us how she used the PMI at home to decide whether or not to have her long hair cut. Some children report that they have used the PMI with their parents, in discussing such major decisions as moving to a new town or buying a car. This is the sort of transfer that the CoRT program aims to achieve.

The PMI is a scanning tool, not a judgment tool. If a thinker spots 10 "Plus" points and only two "Minus" points, this does not necessarily mean that the idea is a good one. Like all scanning, the PMI is subjective, depending on the thinker's perspective. One boy said, as a "Plus" point, that yellow cars would be kept cleaner. Another boy stated this as a "Minus" point—because he had to clean his dad's car and would therefore have to perform this chore more often. Both were right.

The PMI is designed to be artificial, memorable, and easy to pronounce. At first, some teachers rejected "PMI" as pointless jargon. They preferred to encourage or exhort the youngsters to look at the good points and the bad points in any situation. The youngsters probably did so—at that moment. However, without the artificial term "PMI" to crystallize the process and to create a meta-pattern, the exhortation does not stick. One teacher told me how he had used the term "PMI" and how his colleague, in a parallel lesson, had used exhortation. His colleague was soon convinced of the value of the term "PMI."

One girl said that she initially thought the PMI a rather silly device, since she knew how she felt about a subject. But she noted that, as she wrote things down under each letter (she was doing a written exercise instead of the usual oral approach), she became less certain. In the end, the points she had written down did cause her to change her mind. Yet *she* had written down the points. That is precisely the purpose of a scanning tool.

It is important to realize that the description of thinking and the design of tools are two totally different things. It is possible to describe the process of thinking and to break it into components. But then one is tempted to turn each component into a tool, on the premise that, if the components are taught, thinking skills must surely be enhanced. However, teaching someone how to describe a flower does not teach him or her how to grow a flower. The purpose of analysis and the purpose of an operating tool are separate and distinct.

The CoRT tools are designed specifically as operating tools. Such a design has two components: 1) the tool must be easy to use, and 2) it must have a useful effect. Abstract analyses and subdivisions of the thinking process may be intellectually neat, but this does not guarantee usability or effectiveness. My many years of experience, working with thousands of executives and organizations in different countries, have given me some insight into those aspects of thinking that have practical value. I have also worked with scientists, designers, lawyers, and many others who are involved in the "action world" of thinking, as distinct from the "contemplative world."

The CoRT program[6] has six sections, each consisting of 10 lessons: CoRT I (breadth), CoRT II (organization), CoRT III (interaction), CoRT IV (creativity), CoRT V (information and feeling), and CoRT VI (action). All teachers who use the program should teach CoRT I. (Some teachers use *only* the 10 lessons of CoRT I.) Therafter, the sections can be used in any order. For example, a teacher might use CoRT I, CoRT IV, and CoRT V. The last section (CoRT VI) is somewhat different from the other sections, in that it provides a framework for a staged approach to thinking.

I believe that thinking is best taught to 9-, 10-, and 11-year-olds. Youngsters in the middle grades really enjoy thinking, and motivation is very high. They have sufficient verbal fluency and experience to operate the thinking tools. The curriculum is more easily modified in the middle grades to include thinking as a basic subject. But the CoRT materials have also been used with children younger than 9 and with students ranging in age from 12 to adult.

So basic is thinking as a skill that the same CoRT lessons have been used by children in the jungles of South America and by top executives of the Ford Motor Company, United Kingdom. The lessons have been taught to students ranging in I.Q. from below 80 to above 140. The lessons have also been used with groups of mixed ability.

David Lane, at the Hungerford Guidance Centre in London, found that the teaching of thinking to delinquent and violent youngsters brought about an improvement in behavior, as measured by a sharp fall in the number of disciplinary encounters these youngsters had with supervisors.[7] William Copley and Edna Copley, in preliminary work at an institution for young offenders, found similar changes.[8] They recounted how one youth, on the verge of attacking an officer with a hammer, brought to mind a thinking lesson concerned with consequences—and quietly put the hammer down. I mention these changes in behavior for two reasons. First, I believe that the true test of teaching thinking is the effect of such teaching on behavior. Second, we do not really have any adequate way of measuring thinking performance. Standardized tests are largely irrelevant, because they do not allow us to observe the thinker's composite performance.

John Edwards taught the CoRT program in lieu of a portion of the science syllabus to a class in Australia. Using an analysis-of-discourse approach to measurement, he found that the trained students did significantly better at thinking than untrained peers; the trained students even seemed to do better in science, although they had had less instructional time devoted to that subject.[9] It is not difficult

to show that pupils who have had training in thinking produce a wider scan when they are asked to consider some subject. In Ireland, Liam Staunton found that, before CoRT training, individuals produced an average of four sentences on a topic, whereas after CoRT training, they produced an average of 47.[10] We are currently analyzing data from the experiment in Venezuela and data from the Schools Council project in England.

I prefer that CoRT users carry out their own tests and pilot projects. Tests carried out by the designers of a program are of limited value for two reasons: 1) the conditions of teaching are ideal (and often far removed from those prevailing in schools where the program will be used), and 2) such studies always contain an element of bias.

It is impossible, however, to measure the soft data: the confidence of those who have had training in thinking, the focus of their thinking, their willingness to think about things, the effectiveness of their thinking, their structured approach and breadth of consideration. Teachers often sum up these factors as "maturity," in commenting about those children who come to their classrooms after some training in thinking.

I would expect four levels of achievement in the acquisition of thinking skills through use of the CoRT program:

● *Level 1.* A general awareness of thinking as a skill. A willingness to "think" about something. A willingness to explore around a subject. A willingness to listen to others. No recollection of any specific thinking tool.

● *Level 2.* A more structured approach to thinking, including better balance, looking at the consequences of an action or choice (taking other people's views into account), and a search for alternatives. Perhaps a mention of a few of the CoRT tools.

● *Level 3.* Focused and deliberate use of some of the CoRT tools. The organization of thinking as a series of steps. A sense of purpose in thinking.

● *Level 4.* Fluent and appropriate use of many CoRT tools. Definite consciousness of the metacognitive level of thinking. Observation of and comment on the thinker's own thinking. The designing of thinking tasks and strategies, followed by the carrying out of these tasks.

In most situations, I would expect average attainment to fall somewhere between levels 1 and 2. With a more definite emphasis on "thinking," this would rise to a point between levels 2 and 3. Only in exceptional groups with thorough training would I expect to find average attainment at level 4.

Perhaps the most important aspect of the direct teaching of thinking as a skill is the self-image of a youngster as a "thinker," however. This is an operational image. Thinking becomes a skill at which the youngster can improve.

Such a self-image is different from the more usual "value" images: "I am intelligent" (I get on well at school) or "I am not intelligent" (I do not get on well at school, and school is a bore). Value images are self-reinforcing. So are operational images—but the reinforcement goes in opposite directions at the negative end. In other words, the less intelligent students find repeated evidence of their lack of intelligence, but they also notice those occasions when they do manage to come up with good ideas.

FOOTNOTES

[1]Edward de Bono, *The Mechanism of Mind* (New York: Simon & Schuster, 1969).

[2]M. H. Lee and A. R. Maradurajan, "A Computer Package of the Evaluation of Neuron Models Involving Large Uniform Networks," *International Journal of Man-Machine Studies* (1982): 189-210.

[3]John Hopfield, "Brain, Computer, and Memory," *Engineering and Science* (September 1982).

[4]Unpublished material, Cognitive Research Trust.

[5]Edward de Bono, *Lateral Thinking* (New York: Harper & Row, 1970).

[6]CoRT Thinking Program, Pergamon, Inc., Maxwell House, Fairview Park, Elmsford, NY 10523.

[7]Personal communication from David Lane.

[8]William Copley and Edna Copley, *Practical Teaching of Thinking,* forthcoming.

[9]Unpublished paper by John Edwards, James Cook University, Queensland, Australia.

[10]Personal communication from Liam Staunton.

34

Project IMPACT

S. Lee Winocur

Project IMPACT (Improving Minimal Proficiencies by Activating Critical Thinking) seeks to improve student performance in mathematics, reading, and language arts by infusing critical thinking instruction into the content areas. In addition to the major goal of improved student achievement on district tests of basic competency, project objectives include improved performance on tasks requiring critical thinking and independent judgment and on standardized measures of reading and mathematics, improved instruction through staff inservice education, and trained coordination of program installation.

Program Components

The IMPACT curriculum includes three essential features of effective instruction:

1. Skills are clearly identified and placed in a hierarchical sequence of cognitive development.

2. Ten teacher behaviors that promote critical thinking are identified and practiced.

3. Skills are presented in a lesson-plan format that infuses critical thinking into the content areas, identifies the cognitive skill level of the lesson, labels classroom structure to promote critical thinking skills, and includes learning activities.

Although designed as an alternative approach to remedial reading and math at the junior and senior school levels, IMPACT accommodates individual development states and cognitive learning styles and is compatible with various content areas and grade levels. The learning activi-

ties allow all students to experience success as they actively participate in tasks that move from the concrete to the abstract.

Students receive classroom instruction using the IMPACT program two to three hours per week. Emphasis is on small-group and individualized instruction, but large-group instruction and discussion are also used. To provide appropriate learning experiences for students with varying educational backgrounds, interests, and skill achievement levels, study sheets accompanying each lesson use diverse instructional methodologies and are written at various levels of vocabulary and task difficulty. Learning activities include oral and written reports, research projects, art work, and dramatic presentations.

Program Materials

The Curriculum Materials Kit provides a language arts and a mathematics handbook. Each contain 60 teacher-developed lessons focusing on aspects of critical thinking skills that directly affect reading comprehension and mathematical problem solving. The kit's four filmstrips provide motivational experiences and information related to each of the major categories of the Universe of Critical Thinking Skills, including Enabling Skills, Processes, and Operations.

Home Enrichment Learning Packets reinforce selected aspects of skills in critical thinking identified as being the most difficult for students to grasp. These self-paced packets are sent home with students as supplementary materials. Packet topics include Reliable/Unreliable Sources, Cause and Effect, Assumptions, and Point of View.

The IMPACT Training Manual for teachers explores the program's theoretical base, provides sample lessons and exercises in implementation, examines ten teaching behaviors, and explains the Universe of Critical Thinking Skills.

Program Training

Teachers attend an intensive three-day training session that focuses on the Universe of Critical Thinking Skills, the theoretical base for implementing critical thinking, the IMPACT lesson plan, ten teaching behaviors, and social interactions that reinforce critical thinking in the classroom. Availability of all IMPACT materials is contingent on successful completion of the training.

Level I training is followed by peer-coaching in which teachers practice identified teaching strategies, teach the IMPACT thinking skills, observe one another in the classroom and record the use of each teaching strategy, and review feedback on observation findings.

One representative from each district is eligible for training as a district/site coordinator certified to conduct training for other teachers. Regional trainers certified by the project are contracted by the Orange County Department of Education to train in each state.

Project IMPACT has proliferated throughout California. It has been funded and sponsored by the National Diffusion Network as a model program in several other states. Project IMPACT's strengths lie in its clear theoretical base, its validated effectiveness, its ease of implementation, and its synthesis of theory and practice.

Project IMPACT

Developer:	S. Lee Winocur
Goals:	To improve students' performance in mathematics and language arts by facilitating their acquisition of higher-level thinking skills.
Sample skills:	Classifying and categorizing, ordering, identifying relevant and irrelevant information, formulating valid inductive and deductive arguments, rendering judgments.
Assumptions:	• All students are capable of higher-level thinking. • Thinking skills can be taught. • Thinking skills can be learned • Thinking skills are basic to the learning process. • Thinking is best introduced in a social context. • Thinking skills must be related to the curriculum.
Intended audience:	Middle and secondary levels.
Process:	Students' basic skills in language arts and mathematics improve through learning activities that include a critical thinking component infused into content area lessons through (1) a sequential and cumulative universe of critical thinking skills designed to help students reason, (2) a model lesson format, and (3) ten teaching behaviors that label and reinforce students' use of thinking in an interactive environment.
Time:	Two to three hours per week.
Available from:	S. Lee Winocur National Director Project IMPACT Orange County Department of Education P.O. Box 9050 Costa Mesa, CA 92628-9050

35

Philosophy for Children

Matthew Lipman

The aim of Philosophy for Children is to promote excellent thinking: thinking that is creative as well as critical, imaginative as well as logical, inventive as well as analytical. But to make children think *well*, we must first make them think. This involves an intellectual awakening, a strengthening of their ability to discriminate the relationships among things—to draw appropriate distinctions and make connections.

Unfortunately, the models of children available on television and in most children's stories do not offer much evidence that children do in fact reflect, consider, deliberate, infer, seek out underlying assumptions, define, or hypothesize, to name a few of the mental activities characteristic of people who think. Editors of children's readers evidently prefer story characters who have feelings, engage in physical actions, and note facts; references to thinking are considered superfluous. If the stone is flat, it's flat. What difference does it make that Jane *imagines* it's flat, Tom *infers* that it's flat, Bruce *wonders* if it's flat, Edna *supposes* it to be flat, and so on? In forming a model of thinking children, it *does* make a difference, and this is one objective of Philosophy for Children.

Program Materials and Goals

The following passage is from *Kio and Gus*, a novel for children in grades K-4:

There usually aren't many cars on the road that runs by the corral. Something's coming now, although it's still a long way off. Now I hear the siren! It's an ambulance, and it's speeding very fast. There must have been an accident somewhere.

Just as the ambulance gets near the corral, I hear Brad trying to quiet Tchaikovsky down. The siren terrifies him. Suddenly Tchaikovsky rears up on his hind legs and Kio is thrown on the grass! Face down. Brad and I bend over him. But he just lies there.

The ambulance stops and backs up. Two people hurry out, scoop Kio up, put him in the ambulance and drive off. Tchaikovsky stands around nibbling at some grass. It all seems so strange, that an ambulance on its way to the hospital should cause an accident!

Gus, the narrator, is blind. Apparently she has never seen. How much of what she has told us could she have perceived directly through her other senses? What could she have inferred? What could she not have observed? What might she have learned from the testimony of others? What might she have inferred from such testimony? How much of her story is description, and how much is explanation? These questions, reworded for young children, are the subject of lively classroom discussion. While the readers cannot perceive what Gus perceived, they can reenact her inferences. This is an example of how children in early elementary school can learn what inferring ("figuring things out") is and practice it at the same time. Inferring, in turn, is fundamental to a child's ability to acquire meanings. And that ability, in turn, is essential to academic success.

Kio and Gus is one of six novels currently available as part of the Philosophy for Children curriculum; it emphasizes reasoning about nature, especially animals and the environment. Another K-4 program, *Pixie*, stresses language and reasoning, particularly analogical thinking. Children in grades 5-6 who read and discuss *Harry Stottlemeier's Discovery* learn the principles of reasoning. The remainder of the curriculum requires students to apply the tools of intellectual inquiry acquired in the first three programs to specific subject areas. The *Lisa* program—for grades 7-8—applies them to ethical reasoning. The other two programs are for secondary school students; *Suki* stresses the unification of thinking and writing, and *Mark* takes a reflective approach to the social sciences.

Thus, the early elementary portion of the Philosophy for Children curriculum provides children with a broad array of situations that challenge them to practice their reasoning and inquiry skills; the middle school portion introduces them to the principles underlying such practices; and the later portion enables them to apply their cognitive skills, now sharpened and better understood, to a variety of academic and life situations. Whatever the grade level, Philosophy for Children is generally taught about two and one-quarter hours weekly for an entire year. It is not unusual for each program to extend over two years since much class time must be devoted to discussions and exercises.

Characters in the Philosophy for Children novels are shown discussing ideas. When, for example, the practice of taking turns comes up, they look for the underlying principle, which they may identify as *sharing* or *reciprocity*. When the question of what someone's "real name" is arises, they insist on examining what is meant by "real" as carefully as what is meant by "name." In other words, these fictional children display intellectual curiosity about concepts, principles, and ideals. The practice that elementary school children receive in discussing the general concepts philosophy deals with (such as *truth, justice, person, right,* and *education*) prepares them to understand the more specific concepts they will encounter in the secondary school curriculum. To students who are aware that truth is important but unsure just what truth is, the opportunity to discuss the concept is welcomed. Likewise, students who want to be treated "as persons" and who want to know how to treat others that way appreciate an opportunity to discuss what a person is.

Indeed, discussion of the readings is of crucial importance. Philosophical discussions differ from more conventional conversations in that the dialogues seek to conform to the rules of logic and inquiry as the children have learned them. Dialogues disciplined by logical considerations promote better thinking, because logic consists of the criteria through which better and worse thinking are distinguished. Philosophy for Children aims at producing scrupulous readers and reasonable discussants. It also aims at producing children disposed to wonder, inquire, deliberate, and speculate. Whether or not the children who do these things know the names of the skills they employ is relatively unimportant; what matters is that thinking becomes something they enjoy doing and do well.

Program Training and Effectiveness

Not every teacher is cut out to teach Philosophy for Children, including some teachers who, by other standards, are highly effective. Philosophical issues are generally problematic and have to be approached with an open mind and a readiness to admit that one doesn't know the answers. A teacher of philosophy must be self-effacing with

---

Philosophy for Children

Developer:	Matthew Lipman
Goal:	Improve children's reasoning abilities by having them think about thinking as they discuss concepts of importance to them.
Sample skills:	Drawing inferences, making analogies, forming hypotheses, classification.
Assumptions:	• Children are by nature interested in philosophical issues such as truth, fairness, and personal identity. • Children should learn to think for themselves, to explore alternatives to their own points of view, to consider evidence, to make careful distinctions, and to become aware of the objectives of the educational process.
Intended audience:	Children kindergarten through high school.
Process:	Students read special novels with inquisitive children as characters, followed by teacher-led discussion, using structured discussion plans, exercises, and games.
Time:	Three 40-minute periods per week.
Available from:	Institute for the Advancement of Philosophy for Children Montclair State College Upper Montclair, NJ 07043

regard to personal views and exercise patience with students' efforts to think for themselves. The teaching of philosophy demands mutual rather than unilateral respect.

Training in the use of the curriculum materials is indispensable for most teachers. On-site teacher training programs may extend as long as two years. More intensive workshops are also available, including a three-day introductory seminar, which covers one-half of a program.

Evidence supporting the effectiveness of Philosophy for Children has been derived from a series of ETS-conducted experiments, as far back as 1976, and involving as many as 5,000 students over a one-year period. Results indicate that 5th, 6th, and 7th grade students in experimental classes gained 80 percent more in reasoning proficiency than did comparable students in control classes. There was also an academic spinoff: experimental students showed a 66 percent greater gain in reading and a 36 percent greater gain in mathematics than control students.

Since it is generally conceded that reasoning is the common ingredient in all academic pursuits, we may infer that improved reasoning ability is the most promising avenue to improved academic performance. Since there is little being done in the way of diagnosing children's reasoning deficiencies with consequent remediation, it's not surprising that student performance on reasoning tests seems to reach a plateau between 4th and 5th grades and remains there at least until college. Given simple but fundamental reasoning tasks, students tend to answer correctly fewer than 75 percent of the questions. Nevertheless, as the 1980-81 ETS experiment demonstrated, a one-year intervention with Philosophy for Children can cut the experimental students' deficiency by a third. It would be wrong to infer that children's creativity is not stimulated by the emphasis on reasoning; a 1984 ETS experiment with 3rd graders showed that the control group's level of appropriate responses diminished over a year's time, while experimental students registered gains of 63 percent and 46 percent on the two test instruments.

A visit to a classroom where Philosophy for Children is being taught competently will reveal the exuberance with which children respond to the opportunity to discuss ideas that matter greatly to them and to think cooperatively in a community of inquiry. By promoting children's questioning and inquiry skills, Philosophy for Children enables them to discover the connections among the apparently fragmentary curriculums that make up the school day. In addition to this much-needed unifying function, the program sharpens the reasoning and concept-formation skills that students sorely need in later school years. Indeed, there is no better way of ensuring that schools produce reasonable citizens than to introduce reasoning skills at the beginning of the child's education and to reinforce such skills throughout the remainder of the schooling process.

36

The California Writing Project

Carol Booth Olson

The UCI Thinking/Writing Project integrates basic principles of learning theory, current research on the composing process, and practical strategies of the National Writing Project in a developmental approach to fostering critical thinking skills through writing. It is based on the premise that since writing is a complex, critical thinking activity, a training program consisting of lessons that gradually increase in intellectual difficulty and lead students through the levels of thinking will make the "what" in a paper more accessible and allow students to focus on the "how" of composing. Overall, helping students to become better thinkers will enable them to become better writers, and vice versa.

Project Activities and Services

The Thinking/Writing Project involves three main activities:

1. *Curriculum Development.* Teacher/Consultants from the project have created a 300-page notebook, *Thinking/Writing: Fostering Critical Thinking Skills Through Writing,* which contains:

● A rationale for why writing can and should be used as a tool for promoting cognitive growth.

● A thinking/writing taxonomy.

● A description of the sensory/descriptive, imaginative/narrative, practical/informative, and analytical/expository domains of writing.

● Thirty demonstration lessons (one for each primary, elementary, intermediate, high school, and college teachers/students for each level of Bloom's Taxonomy—knowledge, comprehension, application, analysis, synthesis, and evaluation) that provide explicit strategies for teaching each stage of the composing process—prewriting, precomposing, writing, sharing, revising, editing, and evaluation.

● Consideration of how the affective domain relates to the thinking/writing process.

● An explanation of how to create thinking/writing lessons.

● A summary of interviews with university faculty regarding their expectations of the thinking/writing abilities entering freshmen should possess.

● A thinking/writing bibliography.

2. *Teacher Training.* The Thinking/Writing Project offers a variety of staff development programs, which run from three hours to six days and can be tailored to specific teacher and student populations. A typical workshop combines one-third theory with two-thirds practice. Participants are introduced to the thinking/writing model and then experience a demonstration lesson by participating in each stage of the writing process. The project also has sample syllabi available for the following courses: Writing and Critical Thinking, Young Writers' Workshop, the UCI Thinking/Writing Project for Entering Freshmen, the Training of Trainers Project in Thinking and Writing, and Thinking/Writing/Computing.

3. *Evaluation.* In order to evaluate the project's impact on students, several instruments have been developed. The evaluation data and the evaluation design itself are available from the project.

Project Directors

The UCI Thinking/Writing Project is directed by Carol Booth Olson, Co-Director of the UCI Writing Project and

Coordinator of Project Radius; it is co-directed by Owen Thomas, Professor of English, Linguistics, and Teacher Education; and John Hollowell, Campus Writing Director. Twenty-seven Teacher/Consultants from the UCI Writing Project, representing all grade levels, are involved in the curriculum development, teacher training, and evaluation components of the project.

For more information write: Carol Booth Olson, UCI Writing Project, Office of Teacher Education, University of California at Irvine, Irvine, CA 92717.

37

Future Problem Solving

Anne B. Crabbe

The Future Problem-Solving Program helps youngsters think more creatively as they consider ways to solve predicted problems of the future. The program, which is based on the work of Alex Osborn and Sidney Parnes, was developed in 1974 by E. Paul Torrance, an internationally known expert in creativity. The plan has since expanded from a curricular unit for high school students to an international program that reaches an estimated 100,000 students annually.

Program Objectives

When Torrance created the Future Problem-Solving Program, his primary motives were to encourage youngsters to think more creatively and to help them develop richer images of the future. In addition to using the logical and sequential parts of their intellects, Torrance wanted students to develop, exercise, and use their intuition and imagination.

Since its earliest days, the program's objectives, like its scope and audience, have grown. The Future Problem-Solving Program now embraces several other objectives, which include helping youngsters (1) increase their written and verbal communication skills, (2) become better members of a team, (3) develop and improve their research skills, (4) integrate a problem-solving process into their daily lives, and (5) improve their analytical and critical thinking skills. Evidence indicates that the program is fulfilling its objectives.

Program Participants

The regular program has three grade-level divisions: Juniors, grades 4-6; Intermediates, grades 7-9; and Seniors, grades 10-12. A noncompetitive Primary Division is open to students in any grade, although it is designed for students in grades K-3.

To date, the program has appealed primarily to gifted students, but the materials and processes are appropriate for children at all ability levels. In fact, Parnes has even reported success in using the process with a mentally retarded youngster.

Program Components

1. *Practice Problems* are the heart of the program. Early in the school year, teams of four students receive a set of practice problems. Each problem begins with a "fuzzy situation" and instructions that indicate the steps to be followed. The first practice problem directs students to complete the first four steps of the problem-solving process. The second and third problems add more steps, so that by the third problem students are negotiating the full process developed by Osborn and Parnes.[1] The steps in the process are as follows:

● Students *research* the general topic by reading books and magazines, reviewing audiovisual materials, interviewing experts, visiting agencies, or using other sources of information.

● After reading and discussing the "fuzzy situation," students *brainstorm possible problems* related to the situation.

● Working from their list of problems, students *iden-*

tify one underlying problem they feel is central to the situation.

- Using the underlying problem as a focus, students *brainstorm alternative solutions*.
- Next, they *develop five criteria* for evaluating their alternative solutions.
- Students *rank their ten most promising alternative solutions* according to all five criteria.
- After they total the scores to *identify the best solution*, students write a few paragraphs describing it.

The results of these efforts are entered into booklets, which are mailed to trained volunteers who review, score, and return them to the team with comments and suggestions. Teams that have submitted the best work on the third practice problem are invited to compete in state bowls.

Topics for the three practice problems, as well as the state and national problems, are voted on by the participating students. Topics selected are as varied as they are complex; past topics have included UFO's, ocean communities, robotics, nuclear war, prisons, lasers, nuclear waste, genetic engineering, the greenhouse effect, drunk driving, education, and the militarization and industrialization of space.

2. *State and National Bowls.* A typical state bowl brings together about 30 teams to compete for the right to represent their state at the National Future Problem-Solving Bowl held in late spring. In addition to the problem-solving competition at the Bowls, participants engage in a full schedule of social activities and educational presentations.

3. The *Scenario Writing Contest* challenges students to envision the repercussions of suggested solutions to one of the three practice problems. Asked to project themselves 25 years into the future, many students have exhibited exceptional writing talent in their scenarios.

4. The *Advanced Division* was launched in the fall of 1983 to allow the most competent problem-solving teams to put their skills to work on real problems presented by business and governmental agencies. Nominated by their state program directors, these teams forward their recommendations to the cooperating business or agency, where they are reviewed and ranked. Winners compete in the national bowl.

5. *The Primary Division*, begun in the fall of 1984, is the noncompetitive program component designed to instruct children in grades K-3 in the problem-solving process. Three practice problems on themes related to school and home are presented to the youngsters, whose work is sent to trained evaluators for critique and suggestions for improvement.

The Future Problem-Solving Program takes a somewhat novel approach to teaching problem solving. Its procedures are formal and require specific training for the teacher-coaches (either by attending training sessions or through self-study of written program materials) and, ultimately, for the student participants. The next step after training is to register teams of students with either state or national program offices. Funding, teacher schedules, par-

---

Future Problem Solving

Developer:	E. Paul Torrance (based on the work of Alex Osborn and Sidney Parnes)
Goals:	Develop creative problem-solving skills while learning about the future.
Sample skills:	Creative problem-solving process, communication skills (verbal and written), teamwork skills, research techniques, critical and analytical thinking.
Assumptions:	• Problem-solving skills are necessary to function effectively. • In order to prepare for the future, young people need to consider issues related to that future. • Students can and should be taught to think more creatively.
Intended audience:	Regular program: grades 4-12. Primary division: K-3.
Process:	Students in teams of four follow a multiple step problem-solving process: gathering information about a topic, brainstorming problems from a given situation, identifying the major underlying problem, brainstorming solutions, selecting criteria by which to evaluate solutions, and evaluating the solutions to determine the best one.
Time:	Varies with individual schedules; one hour per week is normal.
Available from:	Future Problem Solving Program Coe College Cedar Rapids, IA 52402

ent involvement, transportation, advanced training, and so on, are dealt with according to local district guidelines. The program encourages flexibility in such matters and is a refreshing departure form the usual classroom instruction.

FOOTNOTE

[1]Alex F. Osborn, *Applied Imagination*, 3rd ed. (New York: Charles Scribner's Sons, 1963); and Sidney Parnes, *Creative Guidebook* (New York: Charles Scribner's Sons, 1967).

38

Teaching Decision Making With Guided Design

Anne H. Nardi and Charles E. Wales

A problem well stated is a problem half solved.
—Charles Kettering

Schools that plan to teach thinking skills must carefully consider both what to teach and how to teach it. The choice of what to teach should be based on the kind of skills graduates will be expected to use when they go to work in business, industry, or government. Whatever career is pursued, one thinking skill crucially affects success after graduation: *decision-making*. Other skills that support people's decision-making performance, such as creative thinking, analytical thinking, and dialectical reasoning, also deserve to be taught, but the decision-making process should be the focal point of what students learn.

What to Teach

The form of the decision-making process taught at each grade level is determined by the prior experience and developmental level of the students. In the primary grades, a process of only four operations is probably sufficient:
- State the goal.
- Consider the options
- Prepare a plan.
- Take action.

A teacher can determine what to teach about each of these operations by carefully examining the thinking process a person uses when solving a simple problem such as, "What shall I wear today?" The following example shows what to consider.

Goal. Good decision makers know that stating the goal is a critical step. A goal not only sets the direction for all succeeding steps, but it is also used to judge both the worth of the plan prepared and the result of the actions that follow. The goal of today's clothes might be merely to avoid what was worn yesterday, but it could also be to blend in or stand out, to influence others, or to feel very comfortable.

Options. Skilled decision makers search for all available options. In the dressing problem, the options include all the clothes and shoes a person owns or can borrow.

Plan. Even a relatively simple problem such as this requires a plan. Good decision makers develop a detailed plan for the chosen option which includes a combination of questions, answers, and an evaluation. Some of the questions might be: Are the chosen clothes clean? Torn? Pressed? Do they fit? Do zippers work? Are buttons missing? Skilled decision makers answer these questions, develop a plan, and test that plan mentally to ensure that the goal will be achieved.

Action. The completed plan is translated into action: the decision maker gets dressed. As events unfold, revisions of the plan may, of course, be necessary. And when the day is over, the results are checked to be sure the goal was achieved: Was the outfit just right? This information is stored for use in future decisions.

More Complex Problems

As students mature and their skills evolve, they should encounter and practice more sophisticated versions of the decision-making process. The four operations that students must eventually learn serve three different processes: (1) *find the cause* of a problem (the past), (2) *solve* the problem (the present), or (3) *anticipate* potential problems (the future). The relationship of these processes, as defined in

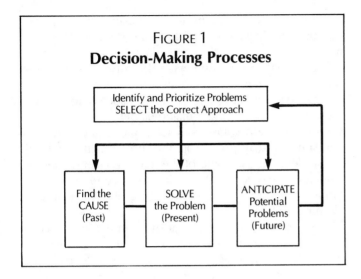

FIGURE 1
Decision-Making Processes

Identify and Prioritize Problems
SELECT the Correct Approach

Find the
CAUSE
(Past)

SOLVE
the Problem
(Present)

ANTICIPATE
Potential
Problems
(Future)

three steps are interrelated, as shown in the Goal triangle at the top of Figure 2, p. 222.

At the next level, students generate possible options and consider constraints: the time and clothes available, what others expect, the ability of the person to coordinate colors, and the effect a specific outfit might have on the person or others. Assumptions about the day's activities are made, the consequences of each choice considered, and the best outfit chosen. These three steps are shown in the Options triangle.

The Plan triangle includes the analysis questions that are asked, the synthesis of answers, the preparation of a detailed plan, and the evaluation of that plan. The Action triangle for a simple problem includes two steps: implement the plan and check the results. A recommendation report step is included when appropriate, and a detailed plan is prepared for the teacher.

the book *Successful Decision-Making* (Wales and Nardi, 1984), is shown in Figure 1.

The dressing problem can be used to show what might happen in a classroom where students use the complete decision-making process. At the outset, they identify the problem, give it top priority, and select the solve process. Next, they gather information to define the situation that exists, including the clothes, the amount of time available, and what others might wear. Then a goal is stated. These

How to Teach

Because of the way schools are organized, educators have been conditioned to think in terms of subjects, and some will want to treat decision making in that way. They may offer thinking skills as a new, required course, just as they did with values clarification when it was a popular topic. Decision making cannot be treated that way, it is not just another subject. It is a skill that transcends course and discipline boundaries. Because it is the process that relates

Guided Design

Developer:	Charles E. Wales
Goal:	To teach students the decision-making process and how to apply the subject matter they learn.
Sample skills:	Identify and solve open-ended problems; think critically; generate, classify, and explore alternatives; develop analogies; analyze issues; find the causes of problems; make careful distinctions; anticipate potential problems; and deal with issues of truth, fairness, and different viewpoints.
Assumptions:	Knowledge is a means, not an end; a necessary but insufficient tool for success after graduation. It is the ability to apply knowledge that is crucial.
Intended audience:	Upper elementary through college and adult learners.
Process:	The "complete" decision-making process is modeled step by step in slow motion using printed instruction-feedback materials. Students use current subject matter as they make decisions. The teacher is a mediator and manager.
Time:	Varies. There should be regular practice in at least one course at every level each term.
Available from:	The Center for Guided Design Engineering Sciences Building West Virginia University Morgantown, WV 26506-6101

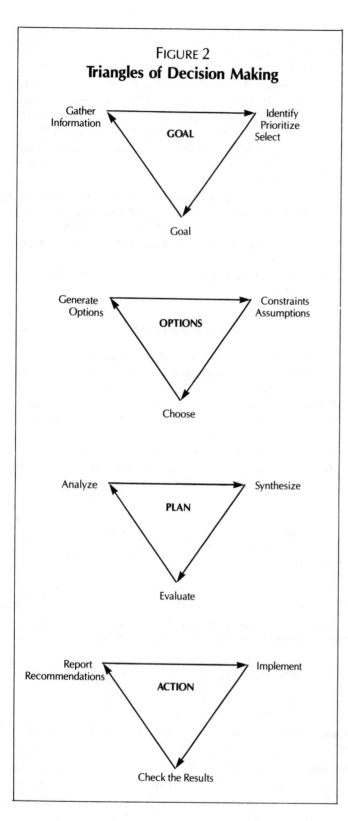

FIGURE 2
Triangles of Decision Making

subject matter fields and makes them useful, decision making must be directly and explicitly taught at all levels and integrated throughout the curriculum. Practice over time is an additional critical dimension because students need time to understand and internalize the process.

Decision making is a complex process so teachers must prepare appropriate materials before they enter the classroom. The first task is to select an open-ended problem situation that grows from the subject matter and calls for students to use some of the major concepts they are studying. The second task is to prepare an outline of the solution, similar to the one shown in Figure 3 for solving the clothing problem.

Since there are no right answers in decision making, the teacher's outline may not include all of the responses the students will make. That's no problem as long as all of the appropriate steps are included. Without an outline, teachers are likely to omit steps from the process. Experienced decision makers appear to omit steps because much of their thinking is subconscious. It occurs so rapidly inside their heads that they are unaware of everything they considered. Thus, while experienced people actually use all 12 steps, they are likely to be poor models for those who want to learn the process. A carefully prepared outline helps to solve that problem.

In the first few primary grades, students should learn to deal with both the solve and cause processes using the four basic operations of selecting Goals, sifting Options, laying Plans, and taking Action. The problems should be simple, the decision making verbal. The teachers should visibly record both the operations and the students' responses so that everyone can see the process. When their writing skills are sufficiently developed, the students should do the recording, either on the chalkboard, at their seats, or both. Eventually, students should work in small groups and produce their own outlines. If time permits, they may be asked to write a report on the class exercise or some parallel problem.

More complex problems that involve all of the process steps should be introduced in later grades and used throughout the secondary program. A proven teaching strategy that can provide the needed step-by-step guidance at any level is called Guided Design (Wales and Stager, 1977). This approach is based on printed instruction-feedback pages prepared in advance by the teacher. These pages go beyond an outline and actually model the decision making of a fictitious group.

The first instruction in a set of Guided Design materials presents the problem situation and may ask students, for example, to state the goal of their work. Students work in teams of five and six, so they have to deal with the alternatives that come from different values and divergent view-

FIGURE 3
Problem-Solving Steps

Identify the Problem	What to wear today.
Prioritize, Select	Use the solve process.
Gather Information	Clothing and time available. Place the person is going. What others will wear.
STATE THE GOAL	Avoid what was worn yesterday. To blend in or stand out. To influence others or feel most comfortable.
CONSIDER OPTIONS	All the clothes and shoes owned or borrowed.
Constraints, Assumptions	Time and clothes available. What others expect. A sense of color. The effect. The day's activities.
Choose	An outfit is selected.
PREPARE A PLAN	
Analysis	Are the chosen clothes clean? Torn? Pressed? Do they fit? Do zippers work? Are buttons missing?
Synthesis	The equations are answered and a plan is prepared.
Evaluation	The plan is evaluated. Is it likely to satisfy the goal? How could you tell?
TAKE ACTION	
Recommendations/Report	N/A
Implement	Get dressed.
Check the Results	Did the clothes achieve the goal?

points. When the team has agreed on a goal, the teacher checks the answer to be sure it goes in an appropriate direction. If the response is reasonable, the teacher gives the students a feedback page that describes what the fictitious group discussed and decided.

After the students consider any new viewpoints, they move on the next instruction, which might ask the students to begin the information gathering step by listing the questions they want answered about the situation. The next feedback provides a list of the questions that might have been asked and may also include some of the needed information, or the students may be asked to get the answers from their textbook, other people, or the library.

This pattern continues as the students think their way through the complete decision-making process. As they work, they learn how to think critically, draw inferences, devise analogies, explore alternatives, and make value judgments. Students also learn the crucial role that facts and

concepts play in decision making and why everyone must continue to learn throughout life.

These are important gains, but perhaps the most significant reasons to integrate subject matter and decision-making are (1) that students gain a new respect for facts and concepts, and (2) their motivation to learn and the amount they remember increases. Information is no longer just something to be remembered until the next test, but one of the tools that can be used to solve present and future problems.

REFERENCES

Wales, C. E., and Nardi, A. H. *Successful Decision Making*. Morgantown, W. Va.: West Virginia University Center for Guided Design, 1984.

Wales, C. E., and Stager, R. A. *Guided Design*. Morgantown, W. Va.: West Virginia University Center for Guided Design, 1977.

39

Odyssey: A Curriculum for Thinking

Elena Wright

Odyssey: *A Curriculum for Thinking* combines knowledge from current cognitive research with the methods of direct instruction. The overall goal of the program, which is intended for regular heterogeneously grouped classes in elementary and middle schools, is to enhance the ability of students to perform a wide variety of intellectually demanding tasks. These include careful observation and classification, deductive and inductive reasoning, the precise use of language, the inferential use of information in memory, hypothesis generation and testing, problem solving, inventiveness and creativity, and decision making.

While some lessons concentrate on increasing the students' ability to use the knowledge they already have, other lessons teach ways to acquire knowledge, including conventional classroom content. In either case, the lesson objectives are achieved through the application of such strategies as making classification hierarchies and generating alternative points of view. The application of these strategies across diverse problem domains is a critical part of internalizing the mental structures and assuring transfer of the formal, abstract procedures to the sorts of personal and classroom challenges students will face beyond the program.

The *Odyssey* approach to the teaching of thinking is deliberatively eclectic. Program materials reflect the more persuasive aspects of a number of theories of epistemology and cognitive development. Some lessons involve a Socratic inquiry approach, while others are based on a Piagetian-like analysis of cognitive activities. Still others emphasize exploration and discovery in a way reminiscent of Bruner. The overall design reflects the multi-faceted nature of intellectual performance and the focus on long-term effects that will transfer to content-area subjects as well as beyond school.

Lesson Design

Each of the approximately 100 lessons is organized in four sections:

1. Rationale—why the lesson is included in the course.

2. Objectives—what the lesson is intended to accomplish. Examples are:

● Increase skills in spatial orientation.

● Make students aware of the power of a strategic approach to problem solving.

● Introduce the relationships of contradiction and implication.

● Teach rules of antonymy.

● Show the importance of both negative and positive instances in testing hypothesis.

● Introduce a systematic procedure for choosing among options whose preferability differs along several dimensions.

● Teach a general strategy for analyzing any design.

3. Target abilities—a list of things the student should be able to do after completing the lesson, such as:

● Use a diagram to understand the meaning of a statement.

● Interpret a story from different characters' points of view.

● Identify pairs of assertions in which one assertion implies another.

• Test hypotheses about the essential characteristics of a class.

• Generate negative antonyms by adding or subtracting the appropriate prefix.

• Evaluate a procedure.

• Analyze a decision situation to determine what alternatives exist.

4. Classroom procedure—a detailed plan for conducting classes, usable by most teachers without extensive training. Plans for conducting the class include suggested teacher questions and possible student responses. These models are not intended to be memorized or read by the teacher, but simply illustrate how the dialogue *might* go. Most important, they are meant to convey the idea that every lesson should involve interaction between the teacher and students, and that active student participation is to be encouraged and reinforced throughout the course. The models show the different teaching strategies that can be used to teach the processes of divergent, synthetic, and inductive thinking as well as convergent, analytic, and deductive thinking.

Odyssey materials include six teacher manuals and six student books:

1. *Foundations of Reasoning*
2. *Understanding Language*
3. *Verbal Reasoning*
4. *Problem Solving*
5. *Decision Making*
6. *Inventive Thinking*

The six book titles are listed in the intended order of use. *Foundations of Reasoning* may be a full-year course in a 4th grade classroom, but it can be paced more rapidly in 5th through 6th grade classes. At grade levels above 4th grade, each book is intended for a semester course of approximately 20-minute lessons, four times a week.

Classes can begin *Foundations* as early as 4th grade, because the student book relies almost entirely on graphic representations. It is highly recommended that *all* students experience *Foundations* because, as its name implies, it is the basis for each of the other books. *Foundations of Reasoning* introduces the students to the processes of gathering, organizing, and interpreting information in systematic and critical ways. The processes introduced lead to analyzing and synthesizing information that students then use to formulate and verify hypotheses.

Building on the skills developed in the first book, *Understanding Language* extends analytical skills to the domain of vocabulary. Just as the students learned to analyze and describe objects in turns of configurations and characteristics, now they learn to analyze and describe dimensions of meaning and impact of written text in terms of choice, organization, and sequencing of words, sentences, and paragraphs.

Verbal Reasoning, the third *Odyssey* book, deals with assertions and arguments: how to recognize them, analyze them, produce them, and evaluate them. Several key concepts are developed: the distinction between form and meaning; the use of quantifiers; the relationships of contra-

---

ODYSSEY

Developers:	A team of researchers from Harvard University, Bolt Beranek and Newman Inc., and the Venezuelan Ministry of Education.
Goal:	To teach a broad range of general thinking skills.
Sample skills:	Careful observation, classification, precise use of language, analogical reasoning, hypothesis generation and testing, problem-solving strategies, and decision making.
Assumptions:	• Performance of intellectually demanding tasks is influenced by various types of factors: abilities, strategies, knowledge, and attitudes. • Some, perhaps all, of these factors are modifiable. • Teaching approach should ensure student participation and intellectual involvement.
Intended audience:	Middle level students.
Process:	Emphasis on discussion and student engagement in problem solving, reasoning, decision making, creative activities. Some paper-and-pencil exercises. Introspection on own thought processes.
Time:	Three to five 45-minute lessons per week.
Available from:	Mastery Education Corporation 85 Main Street Watertown, MA 02172

diction, implication and consistency; and the distinction between validity and truth.

In *Problem Solving,* the fourth book in the series, students learn to visualize problems with the help of drawings, graphs, diagrams, tables, simulation or enactment. They also learn systematic use of trial and error and how to think out the implications of a problem.

Decision Making begins with activities designed to create an awareness of the opportunities for and importance of decisions every day. Students learn to predict logical outcomes of alternatives, and to gather and sort information for relevance, consistency, and credibility. Ultimately, students learn to use a preference analysis strategy and to weight dimensions of complex problems.

Inventive Thinking introduces the concept of design and teaches three strategies for understanding a design: description, comparison, and experimentation. Students practice evaluating, improving, and inventing designs and conclude by learning similar steps with more abstract inventions called procedures and theories.

The *Odyssey* materials were originally developed for use in Venezuela as part of that country's Project Intelligence. A 1981-82 evaluation found that gains made by classes using the experimental materials ranged from 1.15 (Cattell Test) to about 2 (target abilities test) times those achieved by control classes.

For further details about Project Intelligence, see the Project's Final Report (Harvard, 1983); Adams, 1984; and Nickerson and others, in press a and b.

REFERENCES

Adams, M. J. "Project Intelligence." *Human Intelligence International Newsletter* (Winter 1984): 8.

Harvard University. Project Intelligence: the Development of Procedures to Enhance Thinking Skills. Final Report. Submitted to the Minister for the Development of Human Intelligence, Republic of Venezuela, October 1983.

Nickerson, R. S.; Herrnstein, R. J.; de Sanchez, M.; and Swets, J. A. *Teaching Thinking Skills,* in press a.

Nickerson, R. S.; Perkins, D.; and Smith, E. E. *Teaching Thinking.* Hillsdale, N.J.: Erlbaum Associates, in press b.

40

Learning to Learn

Marcia Heiman

Learning to Learn (LTL) is a system of critical thinking skills that students apply directly to their work in academic courses. It was originally designed for use with educationally disadvantaged college students. Externally validated studies have shown that LTL results in significant, long-term improvements in academic performance across the curriculum and retention in school for college students reading as low as the 6th grade level. As a result of these studies, LTL has been approved for national dissemination by the U.S. Department of Education's Joint Dissemination Review Panel.

LTL has recently been adapted for use in junior and senior high schools, and will be fully implemented in a number of public schools in fall 1985.

History and Theory

Learning to Learn has a 20-year history of research and practice. Its genesis was in the work of a group of researchers at the University of Michigan in the 1960s. This group attempted to identify critical thinking skills common to successful learners by asking good students to talk aloud their thinking while they were engaged in a variety of academic tasks. The group found that successful learners could "program" their learning, breaking up large tasks and complex ideas into components; engage in a covert dialogue with author or lecturer, reading or listening for confirmation; devise informal means of obtaining ongoing feedback on their learning progress; and focus on instructional objectives, directing their learning toward those objectives.

The group theorized that variations of these skills are fundamental to all learning, both academic and nonacademic. For example, the act of crossing a street involves aspects of these skills: one looks for feedback, engages in a covert dialogue about the possibilities of crossing against the light, breaks up the task into parts, and has a goal—getting across the street. These skills, however, are generally not explicitly developed, or the transfer demonstrated, when children come to school. Emphasis on memorizing facts and answering the teacher's rather than their own questions reinforces students' sense that "book learning" is somehow fundamentally different from other kinds of learning. Learning to Learn bridges the gap between students' out-of-school learning skills and those needed for school. The developers of the system believe that it is effective because it teaches students to harness skills they have long been using in informal learning situations.

LTL vs. Study Skills

Since LTL applies a set of strategies directly to academic work, it has a superficial relation to traditional "study skills," such as outlining or time management. However, when students stop actively using most study skills, they stop benefiting from them. In contrast, after students master LTL, they can stop overtly using the skills and still perform well academically; the process of learning how to learn becomes externalized. All of the LTL skills are taught in relation to each other, and to the four basic learning principles mentioned above. Students become more active learners because they continually generate questions about their work—increasingly more complex questions that reflect the field under study. Learning becomes a kind of game in which students "play" with the material, devising their own strategies for learning material from different academic disciplines.

Objectives

LTL is initially presented to students as separate but interrelated skills related to identifiable objectives. As students use the system, LTL becomes less a set of discrete "techniques" than variations on means of question-generating and talking aloud the thinking process.

LTL is taught in three stages: input, organization, and output; and includes both general and subject-specific skill areas. Students who fully implement the system achieve the following objectives:

Input Stage

1. *Generating questions from lecture notes.* Using notes taken in class or discussion groups, students create questions that are increasingly like the ones the instructor will include on examinations.

2. *Reading to answer questions I: Nontechnical textbooks.* Students learn to read to answer their own questions, break up chapters into learning units, and assess their mastery of chapter content.

3. *Reading to answer questions II: Reading without headings and subheadings.* Students learn to adjust the comprehensiveness of their questions relative to each course and its instructional objectives.

4. *Reading as problem solving.* Students learn to direct their reading toward finding solutions to mathematically based problems, discriminate textual information that facilitates problem solving, and assess their short- and long-term mastery of the material.

5. *Reading graphs, tables, and diagrams.* Students generate questions about illustrations, translate the illustrations into a series of statements, and use imaginary data to draw variations of the illustrations.

6. *Reading for examples.* Students learn to identify examples of general principles and ideas in their textbooks and use their own examples to construct definitions of these terms.

7. *Developing editing checklists.* Students learn to edit their own grammatical writing errors rather than completing textbook exercises. Students build and use their own error checklists. A similar exercise helps students find idiosyncratic math errors.

Organization Stage

1. *Flowcharting.* Given complex assignments, such as research papers or biology laboratory reports, students construct flowcharts to sequence their work activities.

2. *Information mapping.* Given two or more items

Learning to Learn

Developers:	Marcia Heiman and Joshua Slomianko
Goals:	To improve students' academic performance in content areas across the curriculum; and to improve students' skills in reasoning, reading, writing, and listening.
Sample skills:	Generating questions from notes, books, handouts; constructing information maps and flowcharts; reading for examples; reading to solve problems; using an editing checklist for math problem solving and written composition; systematic problem solving.
Assumptions:	All successful learning has the following elements. The learner is: • Generating questions, raising and testing hypotheses. • Breaking down complex tasks and ideas into manageable components. • Devising informal feedback mechanisms to assess progress toward goals. • Directed toward achieving specific goals.
Intended audience:	Junior and senior high school students.
Process:	In junior and senior high school, content area teachers incorporate LTL activities into classroom and homework assignments. In senior high, students take a year-long course in which they adapt the LTL skills to all their content area courses, learn the principles underlying LTL, and devise LTL exercises based on these principles.
Time:	No extra time when LTL is part of classroom instruction since the method helps students master the content material in an efficient way. A year-long course at senior high level.
Available from:	Learning Skills Consultants Box 493 Cambridge, MA 02138

that can be compared and contrasted, students construct information maps. They compare items with respect to questions generated from notes and readings, and insert key words (indicating answers to questions) in the maps.

3. *Scheduling.* Students perform weekly homework analyses. Using an LTL Task Checklist, they convert assignments into a series of small tasks.

Output Stage

1. *Writing to answer questions.* Students learn to write papers as a series of answers to student-generated questions, rather than following rigid outline formats.

2. *Systematic problem solving.* Given math-based problems, students use step-by-step procedures for working through the problems. They solve problems by answering a series of questions.

3. *Analyzing exams.* Students examine and categorize the types of questions asked on their midterms; they modify their questions accordingly for the remainder of the term.

4. *Writing mock exams.* Students generate and take mock exams prior to official, in-class exams. Given short-answer or essay questions, students write brief, key-word diagrams, outlining their answers.

As students work, they learn to recognize two basic skills: generating questions and breaking down complex ideas and tasks into manageable elements. Their learning becomes more goal-directed, and they are able to assess their own progress. They come to see the skills as tools that become automatic and are integral to learning. In addition, they begin to see the relationships between the kinds of learning that occur in school and out of school.

Instructional Settings

Learning to Learn is incorporated directly into content-area classrooms of junior and senior high schools. For example, a 9th grade social studies teacher might give a brief lecture on the main points of a chapter in the textbook, and ask students to take notes and then generate questions from those notes. The questions might then form the basis of discussions or more complex question building, or provide direction for students in reading the chapter itself. In chemistry class, students might work in pairs, using systematic problem-solving methods on assigned problems; in English, students might use individually derived checklists to edit their grammatical errors in writing.

On the senior high school level, Learning to Learn instruction is reinforced through a year-long course in which students apply the skills to all their content area courses. LTL is generally offered for credit in psychology and includes related readings on the psychology of learning. Students taking the course come to understand the skills in terms of learning principles they derive from, and become more independent learners, able to readily adjust the LTL skills to their future content courses.

Anticipated Results

Schools fully adopting the Learning to Learn system can anticipate several positive effects. These include:

● Improved student motivation, reflected by higher student attendance and retention in school through graduation.

● Improved student performance in academic courses.

● Higher scores on basic skills tests in the areas of reading, writing, and listening.

● Increased rates of student admission to post-secondary institutions.

41

Creative Problem Solving

Sidney J. Parnes

It appears that some people have experiences that de-velop their facility in intellectual processes associated with creativity and intelligence. Research seems to demonstrate that we can design educational programs for many of these experiences, rather than merely waiting and hoping for them to happen.

—Sidney J. Parnes

Perceptual, emotional, and cultural blocks to creative thinking are demonstrated and discussed in Creative Problem Solving (CPS). Perceptual blocks include matters such as difficulty in isolating problems, difficulty in narrowing problems, inability to define or isolate attributes, and failure to use all the senses in observing. Cultural and emotional blocks are evidenced by conformity; overemphasis on competition or cooperation; excessive faith in reason or logic; fear of mistakes, failure, or looking foolish; self-satisfaction; perfectionism; negative outlooks; and reliance on authority.

Early in the course, students are taught the deferred-judgment principle (artificially separating imaginative from judicial thinking in each of the steps) as applied to individual thinking and group brainstorming. Deferred judgment allows students more freedom to apply other techniques that are introduced. Students are taught to use their imagination first and judge afterwards.

Within the freewheeling atmosphere that the principle of deferred judgment provides, students learn to look at issues from a variety of viewpoints. When considering other uses for a piece of paper, for example, students are taught to look at each attribute of paper—its whiteness, its four corners, its straight edges, and so on. Each of these attributes then suggests a number of possible uses.

Checklist procedures are encouraged, such as Osborn's checklist of idea-spurring questions. In this procedure students are taught to analyze problems by asking questions, such as: How might we simplify? What combinations might be used? What adaptations might be made?

Forced relationship techniques are also applied in the course. For example, students produce a list of tentative solutions to a problem. Each of these ideas is then related to each of the other ideas on the list in order to force new combinations. Sometimes a somewhat ridiculous idea is used as a starting point. By associating the idea with the problem, a series of associations is produced that often leads to a solution for the problem.

The course emphasizes the importance of taking notes (recording ideas at all times, rather than just when trying to solve problems), setting deadlines and quotas for producing ideas, and allotting time for deliberate idea production.

Informal procedures are also used throughout the course. Students are placed in small groups to provide practice in collaboration, and are given opportunities to lead these groups.

Problem-Solving Practice

Students are provided many opportunities to practice solving problems, with emphasis given to problems from their personal lives and studies. They are taught to sense problems, challenges, and opportunities, and to effectively define them for creative attack.

During problem analysis, students are taught to list every fact that could conceivably relate to the problem.

They then apply their judgments to select the most important data. Next, students list the longest possible group of questions and sources of additional data that might help solve the problem; they then return to the process of selecting the most important questions and sources of data. This alternating procedure continues throughout the final stages of evaluating and presenting ideas.

Objectives

The major objectives of the Creative Problem Solving program are to assist students in developing:

1. Awareness of the importance of creative efforts—in learning, the professions, scientific and artistic pursuits, and personal living.

2. Motivation to use their creative potential.

3. Self-confidence in their creative abilities.

4. Heightened sensitivity to the problems that surround them—an attitude of "constructive discontent."

5. An open mind toward the ideas of others.

6. Greater curiosity—an awareness of the many challenges and opportunities in life.

7. Improved abilities associated with creativity, enabling them to:

- Sense problems, challenges, and opportunities.
- Observe, discover, and analyze relevant facts.
- See problems from different viewpoints and redefine them productively.
- Defer judgment and break away from habit-bound thinking.
- Discover new relationships.
- Use checklists to discover new ideas.
- Refine unusual ideas into useful ones.
- Evaluate the consequences of one's proposed actions—taking into account all relevant criteria.
- Develop and present ideas for maximum acceptability.
- Develop action plans and implement ideas and solutions.
- Check the effectiveness of actions and take corrective measures when advisable.

Creative Problem Solving (CPS)

Developer:	Sidney J. Parnes, based on Alex F. Osborn
Goals:	Develop abilities and attitudes necessary for creative learning, problem sensing, and problem solving.
Sample skills:	Setting goals and objectives; sensing problems, challenges, and opportunities; searching out data; defining and analyzing problems; generating ideas; discerning criteria for effective evaluating; developing and implementing solutions; developing feedback systems; planning and gaining acceptance; anticipating new challenges from actions taken.
Assumptions:	• Creativity involves the *application* of knowledge, imagination, and judgment to learning, problem sensing, and problem solving. • Everyone has the capacity, at their own mental level, for using creative approaches to learning, problem sensing, and problem solving. • Continuing practice in using these approaches leads to ever-increasing proficiency, whether the person is mentally retarded, average, or gifted. • CPS processes should be taught deliberately, both as general thinking skills and as applications to learning within all subject matter areas.
Intended audience:	Middle (especially for the gifted) and secondary levels (all). (Lower level materials based on CPS available from D.O.K. Publishers, Buffalo, N.Y.)
Process:	Students use activity book for practice exercises to strengthen CPS processes, under direction of the teacher using an instructor's guidebook. This guidebook offers additional exercises, readings, film listings, bibliographic sources, and test sources. Alternatively, students do independent self- or group-study and practice with specially designed test. Transfer of learning is emphasized in all materials.
Time:	A variety of flexible time patterns are suggested in the teacher's guide. Material is programmed for instructional blocks of approximately one hour. Plans are suggested for programs as short as eight hours or as long as two years. Programs are based on extensive research and field testing.
Available from:	Creative Education Foundation 437 Franklin Street Buffalo, NY 14202

The teacher of any subject may wish to emphasize a particular mental ability or attitude, using sessions specially designed for the specific objectives listed above. The program covers all of the objectives while teaching a methodical yet creative approach to problem solving. It has been scientifically evaluated in numerous research investigations.[1]

FOOTNOTE

[1]In one literature review, 20 of 22 research studies of the specific Osborn-Parnes CPS program showed consistent positive effects (Torrance, 1972). Rose and Lin (1984) used a new statistical technique, meta-analysis, on the creativity research literature. This procedure compiles data from a wide range of studies. The study concluded, "The substantial impact of Osborn and Parnes' CPS on verbal creativity, combined with the conclusions from both Torrance's and Parnes and Brunelle's reviews, provide strong evidence to support the effectiveness of this program."

REFERENCES

Osborne, A. F. *Applied Imagination.* New York: Scribner's, 1963.

Parnes, S. J. *The Magic of Your Mind.* Buffalo: Bearly Limited Publishers, 1981.

Torrance, E. P. "Can We Teach Children to Think Creatively?" *Journal of Creative Behavior,* 6, 2 (1972).

Rose, L. M., and Lin, M. T. "A Meta-Analysis of Long-Term Creativity Training Programs." *Journal of Creative Behavior* 18, 1 (1984).

42

Great Books

Howard Will

To read interpretively means to think independently and reflectively. If you are unwilling to think, it is almost impossible to read interpretively. That is why developmental reading remains the supreme challenge to teachers in language arts.

As far back as I can remember, my teachers and professors gave us what were then considered fairly sound interpretations of each of the books we read. Our task was to listen closely to their expositions and give them back on examinations. The more accurately we followed their interpretations, the more likely a high grade and the college and graduate school of our choice. There were few exceptions to this rule in my 20 years of formal education.

In contrast to this, the Junior Great Books program gives children a process of education that will enable them to learn to read interpretively on their own and to realize that other equally valid interpretations may be heard during their discussions. The goal, of course, is to give them a method for a lifetime of purposeful reading. The Great Books Foundation accomplishes this objective in three ways: by readings included in the program, by the method of discussion, and by a course on interpretive reading and discussion which is included in each volume of its Junior Series.

Reading Selections

The reading selections used in the program are outstanding works of literature of the past and present. These readings go back some 25 hundred years and are as recent as the present, giving youngsters the widest experience of literature possible. The Foundation's editorial staff constantly seeks good readings that will sustain thoughtful discussion. Thousands of well-written, delightful stories must be eliminated simply because they don't lead to thoughtful discussion. These readings are so explicit that analysis of the author's intention is never necessary or profitable. The editorial staff must find not only good readings that allow analysis, but also those which are enjoyable to discuss because they have meanings relevant to the grade levels for which they are recommended.

When the staff is engaged in debate about a book worthy of consideration, the big test comes in writing interpretive questions. The more good interpretive questions that can be written about the book, the more likely it comes up for possible inclusion in the Foundation's Series. Good interpretive questions, by the Foundation's definition, are those questions which have more than one possible answer that can be validated from the reading. Often good questions can be about the meaning of a word, a phrase or a sentence.

Since many children's classics have been rewritten over the years or even centuries, it often becomes a challenge for the editorial staff to find that version of the story which satisfies the above criteria. Often classics are rewritten to improve the morality of the story or to guard against political dissent. More often classics are rewritten to make them "easier" or more accessible to mass consumption. Al-

This chapter originally appeared in Howard Will, "You Must Think If You Wish To Read Interpretively," *Childhood Education* (March/April 1984): 246-248. Reprinted with permission.

though the Foundation has been criticized over the years for certain selections, it has adhered to the principle of not tampering with the author's product. Vocabulary has not been watered down or syntax simplified.

Method of Discussion

The method of discussion is based on the idea that discussion can be a mutual learning experience for leaders as well as participants. To ensure such a process, the Foundation gives intensive two-day training courses for teachers and parent volunteers. In these courses leaders are taught how to formulate interpretive questions for which they have real doubt about the answer. This practice is called "shared inquiry." Shared inquiry has a dual meaning in the program: the leaders are sharing a real problem of interpretation with the group, and the youngsters are sharing ideas and opinions with each other during the discussion in order to resolve the problem in the leader's question. To reinforce the idea of independent and reflective thinking, leaders are not permitted to give answers or make statements of any kind during the discussion.

Perhaps the most challenging part of the leader's role is asking spontaneous follow-up questions to most of the participants' responses. We do not regard discussion as oral recitation in which children tell us what they already know from their reading. Instead the discussion is a learning tool that furthers their understanding of the reading. The leader constantly asks participants questions based on the participants' responses, and their substantiation of interpretations from the readings rather than from personal experiences.

When they first start to lead Junior Great Books groups, leaders find it difficult to listen constantly to the participants' ideas and to recognize that the youngsters may come up with opinions about the books which had not occurred to the leaders. One of the supreme challenges facing any teacher who has worked with highly gifted students is to recognize that children may be saying something their peers do not understand and most adults may not even recognize. A good leader will sense this and try to get motivated students to clarify their leaps of mind so that others can understand what they are saying. Thus, by thoughtful follow-up questions, the leader has "caught up" to individual students, helped the students clarify thoughts and fostered other good answers to the leader's interpretive question. Each student has become a recognized participant in the group and not a mind lost in limbo because the leader failed to recognize the child's contribution.

Another skill encouraged in the Foundation's Basic Leader Training Course is the ability to rephrase a ques-

tion. In order to encourage every student to participate to the best of his/her ability, a leader learns to rephrase a question at any point in the discussion. Thus, if a youngster does not respond to a question of interpretation, that is no reason to exclude the child. Changing the question into a lower-level factual or evaluative question often allows the child to begin to make a contribution to the discussion. Also, this offers the leader the ability to involve all participants in the discussion.

Course on Interpretive Reading and Discussion

Included throughout the Foundation's Junior Series, which goes from the 2nd through the 12th grade, is a course on interpretive reading and discussion. This course has three main uses: 1) as a review for leaders on how they might carry out each session with the youngsters, 2) as an aid in preparing good questions for discussion, and 3) as a way of helping participants read the selections more carefully and get more involved in the discussions. In the best sense of the word, the students have "the teacher's edition."

In this course students have detailed descriptions of what they should do during their first reading and what they should do during their second reading which they could not have done during their first. During their first and second readings students are encouraged to mark up their paperbacks, underlining sections and writing down both their positive and negative reactions as they read. They are encouraged while reading to write down any questions they have and look up and write down definitions of words they do not understand. The Great Book Foundation believes that youngsters should not have to wait until college to learn and practice this very important skill. We want them to learn to read actively rather than passively.

Youngsters can then be taught the three kinds of questions we use in discussion: factual, interpretive and evaluative. They learn that factual questions depend more on memory than thinking; that interpretive questions depend more on thinking than memory; and that evaluation, if it is to be meaningful, can take place only after they have learned to interpret and understand the story. In several ways, by using the course, the students go through the same elements of shared inquiry as their leaders did in the Basic Leader Training Course. After much exposure to hundreds of examples of questions based on books they have read and discussed, the students can then begin to formulate their own questions about the authors. This is a decided reversal of traditional educational practice, where most students' primary efforts are directed toward answering questions.

The Junior Great Books program began on a nation-wide basis in the fall of 1963. Now, 20 years later, the Foundation conducts leader training in 49 of the 50 states and several other countries. Over 450,000 youngsters participate in the program; most of the groups meet during school time. The Foundation's fulltime staff conducts Basic Leader Training Courses in any district or school that has decided to adopt the program. The district or school must provide 24 adults for the training course who are committed to carrying out the Foundation's program with the youngsters. Often these classes are made up of combinations that include teachers, librarians, principals and parent volunteers.

43

Building Thinking Skills

John D. Baker

The Midwest Publications Analytic and Critical Thinking Program offers a sequential plan for direct instruction in analysis and critical thinking skills. The program fosters analysis skills at the elementary and secondary levels and critical thinking skills at the middle and high school levels. The analysis skills developed in the Building Thinking Skills series prepares learners for the formal and informal logic concepts in the Critical Thinking series (see Figure 1).

Building Thinking Skills

This series provides activities for cognitive skill development and analytical reasoning instruction in a carefully sequenced instructional plan. A variety of thinking skills required for better academic performance has been organized into four basic types—similarity and difference, sequence, classification, and analogy.

Each skill is developed in figural and verbal form. Figural similarities and differences take the form of visual discrimination, similarity, congruence, extrapolation (enlarging or reducing), and symmetry. Verbal similarities and differences include synonyms, antonyms, denotation, and connotation.

Figural sequences include arranging by size, color, marking, or shape. More elaborate versions include paths, rotations, folding, and reflection. Verbal sequences include degree of meaning, comprehending the meaning of transitive or negative statements, following sequential directions, putting statements in order of occurrence, recognizing cause and effect, and comprehending implicational statements.

Classification involves grouping by common characteristics. Figural classification allows the learner to practice observation and categorization skills regardless of vocabulary development. The learner uses graphics (Venn diagrams, branching diagrams, and matrices) to organize figural forms and later to organize words and ideas for clear comprehension. Verbal classification is primarily useful in learning and remembering new words and perceiving correct word relationships and inferences. A more complex form involves classifying concepts and abstract ideas, a form of classification commonly used in science and social studies curriculums.

Analogy involves relational thinking and drawing proper comparisons. Figural analogies give the learner concrete practice in relational and proportional reasoning. Verbal analogies involve the correct interpretation of word relationships. Analogies promote vocabulary development and test-taking skills. Analogous reasoning forms the basis for using and interpreting figurative language (simile, metaphor, and personification).

Book 1 utilizes a vocabulary level of the first thousand words of functional reading and is recommended for middle elementary or secondary students with limited vocabularies.

Book 2 employs vocabulary not exceeding the second thousand words and is recommended for upper elementary or secondary students in need of vocabulary development.

Book 3 Figural features complex figural and spatial perception exercises and is recommended for junior high school students or prevocational instruction in graphics, drafting, and design.

FIGURE 1

Instructional Plan for Developing Analytic and Critical Thinking Skills

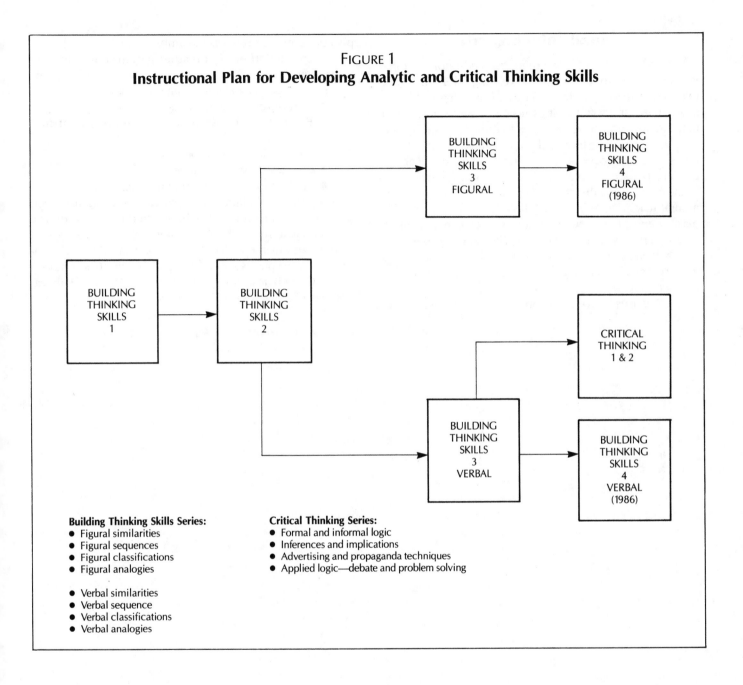

Building Thinking Skills Series:
- Figural similarities
- Figural sequences
- Figural classifications
- Figural analogies

- Verbal similarities
- Verbal sequence
- Verbal classifications
- Verbal analogies

Critical Thinking Series:
- Formal and informal logic
- Inferences and implications
- Advertising and propaganda techniques
- Applied logic—debate and problem solving

Book 3 Verbal utilizes vocabulary appropriate for junior high school use or as reading remediation for high school students or adults. It prepares students for formal logical thinking by introducing inferential statements using the logic connectives "and," "or," "not," and "if . . . then." Since complex thinking skills activities are presented at a relatively low vocabulary level, the items are more difficult than the vocabulary level suggests.

The books contain pencil-and-paper exercises on thinking skills basic to content objectives. These written exercises are followed by class discussions during which the thinking process is examined, clarified, and refined. Follow-up exercises provide practice and reinforcement.

Objective tests used to evaluate the Building Thinking Skills series include:
- Cognitive Abilities Test (Riverside Publishing Co.)
- Developing Cognitive Abilities Test (American Testronics)
- Ross Test of Higher Cognitive Processes (for use with Book 3 Verbal only, Academic Therapy Publications)

Critical Thinking Series

This series is a course in formal and informal logic, written at the 5th and 6th grade reading level. The objectives are discernment in reading and listening and clarity in speaking and writing. Students consider a variety of situations by performing exercises that draw on newspaper articles, letters to editors, advice columns, commentaries, newscasts, advertisements, political speeches, everyday conversations, and government regulations. The material is relevant and appealing to young adults because the fundamental teaching approach is class discussion. The books make a good mini-course or semester course and can be taught in one or more disciplines. The texts explain:

- Basic concepts in critical thinking—discussions, disagreements, and arguments; general statements and counterexamples.
- Misuses of words—connotation and denotation, implications and inferences, and ambiguity.
- Inconsistent, contradictory, and misleading statements.
- Propaganda and advertising schemes.
- Logical reasoning fallacies.
- Formal logic with and without quantified statements.
- Probability of truth and falsity.
- Characteristics of arguments.
- Applied logic—debate and problem solving.

For the past eight years Critical Thinking has been used widely in junior high school gifted programs or as a supplement to high school or junior college English, social studies, and mathematics. The Watson Glaser Test of Critical Thinking (published by the Psychological Corporation) or the Cornell Test of Critical Thinking (Midwest Publications) can be used to evaluate the series.

44

HOTS: A Computer-Based Approach

Stanley Pogrow

American educators have traditionally assumed that mastery of basic skills is prerequisite for engagement in sophisticated learning activities. As a result, students in compensatory programs are drilled heavily to achieve appropriate grade-level performance. The Higher-Order Thinking Skills (HOTS) program reverses this process, converting compensatory education to an enrichment program that employs no drill and practice. Instead, students systematically engage in higher-order thinking activities to strengthen their basic skills and social confidence.

The HOTS program was originally developed as an alternative to existing approaches to Chapter I education, which underestimate the abilities of compensatory students and do not teach appropriate or sufficient skills. A high percentage of compensatory students are bright yet still fail under conventional Chapter I programs. In addition, even when such programs are successful, they teach only basic, rote skills. This essentially relegates compensatory students to second-class citizenship in an information economy where rote work will be performed by robots, and individuals possessing higher-order thinking skills will be the only ones able to compete for better paying jobs.

There is no evidence that mastery of basic skills is prerequisite for engaging in higher-order thinking skills. Indeed, the evidence from animal research suggests quite the opposite—that higher-order thinking proceeds independently of basic thinking tasks. Thus, HOTS takes advantage of and taps the innate brightness of students by challenging them intellectually.

Basic Approach

HOTS is a pullout-type compensatory program with heavy reliance on computer activities combined with state-of-the-art teaching techniques. The computer is used for its motivational aspects and because it enables students to test the consequences of their ideas at the same speed at which they think. HOTS is implemented in grades 3-6 because of the belief that grades K-2 should focus on conventional programs and that instruction in thinking skills should be accomplished before grade 7, when thinking should be directed toward content areas.

Clearly, computers cannot produce cognitive gain without high-quality teaching or structured curricular strategies. HOTS is different from other computer curriculums in that it systematically uses a wide variety of commercially available software and equipment in accordance with a theory of learning. HOTS has identified the teaching and curriculum development techniques needed to take advantage of the computer's special modality. "Hi-teach" techniques often run counter to traditional teaching strategies and are designed to give students the space and responsibility to think. A philosophy of assertive thinking pervades the computer laboratory. The teacher's role switches from information provider and decision maker to one of guiding students to make decisions about the quality of their ideas and strategies by analyzing computer feedback.

The HOTS curriculum provides the teacher with a day-to-day script. It creates an instructional shell that takes advantage of nonliteral software usage to create linkages among concepts in various computer environments and between the computer environment and the classroom. The curriculum uses software to create an environment with maximum opportunity and incentive for developing generalizations, and where the teacher works with the students to help them realize and articulate those generalizations.

Thinking activities are organized in the same manner that the brain seems to organize information in long-term memory. Instead of teaching components of thinking or using frameworks such as Bloom's Taxonomy, the focus is on students' development of more sophisticated associations of ideas that seemingly have no relationship. This general ability to construct such associations and apply them to the development of a problem-solving strategy is viewed as the critical aspect of thinking. It is a symbol processing model rather than a specific content approach.

Specific content is taught by the classroom teacher, who is trained in effective teaching techniques rather than techniques of computer use. As such, HOTS does not replace effective schooling efforts and can be grafted onto such programs to provide the second dimension of improvement reform—the ability to think.

Evaluation and Future Direction

The HOTS program has grown from a single pilot school to more than 20 in the current school year. Former Secretary of Education Terrell Bell awarded the program a grant as an outstanding national technology demonstration project. It has been evaluated with respect to (1) basic skills as measured by the standardized CAT test, (2) higher-order thinking skills as measured by the Raven's Colored Matrices Test and criteria developed particularly for this program, and (3) social confidence as measured by sociograms. First-year evaluations of HOTS showed that reading scores had improved and that students in the HOTS school performed better on higher-order thinking tasks and had 50 percent more friends than did Chapter I students at the control schools. In fact, in the control school that had best implemented the effective school techniques that were geared only on improving scores on basic skills, students showed the poorest performance on all open-ended tasks and had the lowest levels of self-confidence and the fewest friends.

During the 1985-86 school year HOTS will be installed in about 10 districts throughout the country. In time, the program should be expanded to include average students. Preliminary evaluation data suggest that a higher-order thinking skills approach can improve basic skills and that responding to intellectual challenges is a powerful way to make students feel good about themselves. In virtually all cases, Chapter I students' capabilities exceeded our expectations.

Higher-Order Thinking Skills (HOTS)

Developer:	Stanley Pogrow, based on cognitive psychology theories of the organization of information in the brain.
Goal:	Use higher-order thinking activities to improve basic skills and social confidence, while also improving problem-solving ability.
Skills:	• Developing and testing strategies for the solution of problems. • Interpreting computer-generated feedback as to the quality of strategies. • Integrating and synthesizing information from a variety of subjects to the solution of problems. • Generalizing ideas across content areas and computer environments.
Assumptions:	• Most compensatory students are really quite bright and can and should be challenged intellectually. • The key to improving thinking ability is to increase the repertoire of strategies available to students and to increase the ability to develop sophisticated networks of associations between concepts.
Intended audience:	Chapter I students in grades 3-6; can be extended to average ability students in grades 3-6.
Process:	Students work in computer lab. Curriculum provided to lab teachers structures the problem-solving and linkage activities that students will engage in. Work on computer is preceded by a thinking discussion in which students articulate the consequences of their strategies and the teacher poses challenge questions for the students to work on.
Time:	Compensatory students have four lessons per week on a continuous basis, which replaces existing Chapter I services. Average ability students would attend lessons every other week.
Available from:	Stanley Pogrow College of Education University of Arizona Tucson, AZ 85721

45

BASICS

Sydelle Seiger-Ehrenberg

In the late 1960s, Hilda Taba culminated a 15-year research project on children's thinking with a social studies curriculum that incorporated particular thinking strategies into the learning process. Taba contended that through this type of curriculum, students would not only learn significant social studies ideas better, but that they would—at the same time—learn particular thinking strategies applicable to any learning or life situations.

After Taba's death in 1967, a commercial social studies textbook series reflecting Taba's ideas was published, and an accompanying staff development program that Taba had piloted was implemented in a large number of school districts. The BASICS Thinking/Learning Strategies Program, developed in 1971, grew out of that staff development effort, the Hilda Taba Teaching Strategies Program.

BASICS is a program of thinking strategies selected and organized to advance student achievement in each of the five major types of learning objectives of any curriculum—facts, concepts, principles, attitudes, and skills.

Since its inception, BASICS has been implemented in much the same manner as the Hilda Taba Teaching Strategies Program. In both, staff members who developed and implemented the program, under the auspices of the Institute for Curriculum Instruction, train local training leaders. They in turn conduct district-sponsored staff development programs in which teachers learn how to plan and conduct lessons that use BASICS Thinking and Learning Strategies as the means for achieving the content objectives of individual lessons. The focus of the training is not so much on

how to teach thinking as on how to guide students in doing to appropriate thinking for the task at hand.

Hundreds of school districts have used this BASICS staff development model during the past 14 years, including the Morristown (New Jersey) Public Schools, Southwestern City Schools (Grove City, Ohio), Long Beach (California) Public Schools, Austintown (Ohio) Local School District, King of Prussia Schools (Upper Merion, Pennsylvania), Public Schools of the Tarrytowns (New York), Lincoln (Nebraska) Public Schools, Marquette-Alger (Michigan) Intermediate School District, and Adams County School District #12 (Northglenn, Colorado).

Limitations of the Staff Development Model

Experience with the staff development model has revealed three limitations of using a staff development model to improve the quality of student thinking.

1. *Too little time and opportunity for trainers to train.* Successful implementation depends not only on the ability and commitment of those sent for training by the district, but also on trained people subsequently staying in the district in jobs that allow them time to train and coach teachers effectively.

2. *Optional teacher participation in training.* Since, ideally, teachers' participation should be optional, their involvement often depends on whether they need the credit offered or want the training. Thus, there is no way to ensure their continued involvement.

3. *No guarantee of cumulative instruction in the use of thinking strategies.* Incorporation of thinking strategies into the curriculum depends almost entirely on the teachers' willingness and ability to plan their lessons that way. If teachers, even after training, do not recognize opportuni-

ties to use certain types of thinking or don't have the time to develop appropriate plans, the students will not receive sufficient opportunities to use thinking strategies.

Despite these pitfalls, a remarkably large number of teachers have learned the BASICS teaching strategies and achieved considerable success in using them with their students.

In recent years ICI and certain participating school districts have experimented with Taba's original idea, which was to develop curriculum that incorporates the use of appropriate thinking strategies. QUEST, a reading comprehension program developed under the direction of Carolyn Hughes in Parma, Ohio, schools, exemplifies this curriculum model for BASICS implementation. The Global Education program of King of Prussia Schools in Upper Merion, Pennsylvania, and the 12th grade economics pro-

gram at the Sleepy Hollow High School in Tarrytown, New York, are other examples.

EXPLORE Curriculum in Colorado

I am currently working with Adams County District #12 in Northglenn-Thornton, Colorado, to develop and implement EXPLORE, a K-6 curriculum using BASICS strategies that integrates instruction in science, social studies, and thinking. EXPLORE promises to have a significant and lasting impact on students' thinking abilities because:

1. The curriculum provides the structure for important studies that are required for all K-6 students. Because it is not a narrow, optional unit or a curriculum designed for only certain students (the gifted, for example), all stu-

---

BASICS

Developers:	Sydelle Seiger-Ehrenberg and Lyle M. Ehrenberg (based on original work by Hilda Taba)
General goal:	Students use appropriate thinking strategies to achieve the five major types of learning objectives of any curriculum: facts, concepts, principles, attitudes, and skills. They apply these thinking strategies in dealing with outside-of-school learning and life situations.
Sample skills:	Observing, retrieving, comparing, contrasting, grouping, concept formation, classifying, inferring, generalizing, anticipating, making choices, attitude formation, skill development.
Assumptions:	• Practice of thinking skills out of context is not likely to result in consistent use of appropriate thinking in learning and life situations. • Achievement of curriculum learning objectives and transfer to life situations is most likely to occur if students have consistent practice in the use of appropriate thinking as they learn. • All curriculum objectives, regardless of specific content, can be classified by the type of learning (and thinking) required of students. • Thinking strategies can be incorporated into any curriculum so that students not only achieve the objectives better and faster but also learn strategies for learning, problem solving, planning, and so on. • Short of building or revising curriculum to incorporate appropriate thinking strategies, teachers can be trained to build such strategies into their teaching of the existing curriculum.
Intended audience:	Suitable for preschool through adult learners.
Process:	• In the *curriculum model* curriculum is developed or revised to include thinking strategies as the process for achieving the learning objectives. • In the *staff development model* teachers are trained to plan and conduct lessons that incorporate the use of appropriate thinking strategies.
Time:	• The *curriculum model* is developed and implemented in a three- to five-year process that includes periodic training and follow-up as curriculum is written and tested. • The *staff development model* requires a minimum of 15 to 20 full days of training over a two-year period with one-year periodic follow-up.
Available from:	ICI Services, Ltd. 301 South Third Street Coshocton, OH 43812 (614) 622-5344/5341

dents will learn thinking strategies on an ongoing, cumulative basis over a seven-year period.

2. The curriculum is not merely a syllabus or a list of objectives but is a real plan for learning, with the sequence of student thinking and accompanying learning experiences spelled out in detail. Yet it is not a binding prescription; teachers are free to select student materials or use whatever methods are effective in guiding their students through the processes. Suggestions are given for teacher questions, directions, resources, and so on, but the teachers are encouraged to be as creative and natural as possible, so long as students are doing the thinking as described in the curriculum.

3. Each grade level of the curriculum is developed and field-tested for one year with a few teachers, revised and piloted the second year with more teachers, and fully implemented and evaluated the third year. This gradual, deliberate implementation provides time for teacher training and input based on actual classroom experiences with the curriculum, so teachers are more likely to develop the skills they need to implement the curriculum effectively. Students, therefore, receive the planned, cumulative thinking and learning experiences they need to learn and apply the thinking strategies to all types of situations.

REFERENCES

Durkin, Mary, and Hardy, Patricia. *Hilda Taba Teaching Strategies Program.* Miami: Institute for Staff Development, 1972.

Ehrenberg, Sydelle D., and Ehrenberg, Lyle M. *BASICS: Building and Applying Strategies for Intellectual Competencies in Students.* Coshocton, Ohio: Institute for Curriculum and Instruction, 1982.

Taba, Hilda. *Teaching Strategies and Cognitive Functioning in Elementary School Children.* San Francisco: San Francisco State College, 1966.

Wallen, Durkin, and others. *The Taba Curriculum Development Project in Social Studies, Final Report.* Washington, D.C.: U.S. Government Printing Office, 1969.

46

Comparing Approaches to Teaching Thinking

Ronald S. Brandt

The programs described in this section demonstrate that teachers and administrators who want to improve their students' thinking have a multitude of approaches from which to choose. Some of these approaches are embodied in published materials, such as Strategic Reasoning (p. 196), while others depend on teachers' lesson planning. Some approaches, such as the strategies in Project IMPACT (p. 210), are ways to teach existing subjects, while others, such as Edward de Bono's CoRT (p. 203), are intended as additions or supplements to the existing curriculum. Some, such as SOI (p. 187), are ways to teach thinking skills directly as the primary aim of instruction, while others, such as Joyce and Weil's *Models of Teaching* (1980), stimulate students to *use* their thinking as they engage in discussions.

Figure 1 shows key features of selected approaches, including the authority who developed the approach (or on whose research it is based), a word or phrase that describes the approach (if in quotes, the term used by the author), and published materials that embody the approach. Figure 1 also shows another way in which the various approaches differ: in the kinds of thinking they seek to develop. Some, such as Matthew Lipman's Philosophy for Children (p. 212), are for teaching reasoning, while others, such as David Perkin's Creativity by Design (p. 172), emphasize imaginative thinking. Still others focus on fundamental cognitive skills prerequisite to higher-level thinking.

Most of these programs use special materials that are somewhat different from ordinary textbooks and work-books. For example, Instrumental Enrichment (p. 193) uses paper-and-pencil "instruments" to improve student intellectual functioning. With sufficient "mediation" (teacher-student interaction) in connection with use of the instruments, students are reported to become less impulsive, more persistent, more able to see relationships and make comparisons, better able to plan and relate past experiences to future ones. A number of other programs—SOI, Strategic Reasoning, and Odyssey (p. 224), for example—are also materials-based, but the way the materials are used varies. In some programs the exercises themselves are intended to improve students' cognitive abilities, while proponents of Instrumental Enrichment emphasize the teacher's mediation.

Barry Beyer (p. 145) contends that while special programs may be useful, such skills as detecting bias and distinguishing fact from opinion should be taught directly in existing classes. For example, the local curriculum might call for teaching classifying as part of the 4th grade science program. Beyer suggests that to formally introduce a thinking skill, teachers should use a five-step process derived from research on skills training.

In this approach a teacher (1) introduces the skill to be taught by describing an example of it in action or by having the students actually do it. Then referring to the introductory experience for examples, the teacher (2) explains specific steps and rules for executing the skill and (3) demonstrates how the skill works with the content being studied. Next, working in triads or pairs under the teacher's guidance, the students (4) apply the skill procedures and rules to data similar to—but not the same as—that used in the demonstration. Finally, the students (5) restate and explain the basic components of the skill as they have used them so far.

Beyer's approach seems reasonable to many educators because it is similar to the way school systems plan for the teaching of other skills, but Richard Paul (p. 152), who

FIGURE 1
Selected Approaches to Teaching Thinking

Authority	Approach	Materials	Type of Thinking
Whimbey	"precise processing"	(several)	problem solving
Feuerstein	"mediated learning experiences"	Instrumental Enrichment	mental operations
Meeker (Guilford)	assessment, practice	SOI	intelligence
Glade (Upton)	teaching	Strategic Reasoning	thinking skills
Beyer	"direct"	———	thinking skills
Paul (Ennis)	"dialectical"	———	critical thinking
Lipman	discussion	Philosophy for Children	reasoning
de Bono	heuristics	CoRT	perception
Perkins	"design"	Odyssey	creative thinking

teaches courses in critical thinking at the university level, contends that critical thinking is not simply a set of technical skills. Paul endorses the teaching of "micro-logical" analytical skills as a useful "short-term strategy," but he asserts that critical thinking is "intrinsic to the character of the person" and is "guided by *principles*, not *procedures*."[1] Teaching critical thinking, Paul says, requires a "dialectical" approach; "that is, it must move back and forth between opposing points of view."

As an example of a good way to teach critical thinking, Paul recommends Philosophy for Children. Rather than teaching skills directly, Philosophy for Children uses incidents from novels, such as *Harry Stottlemeier's Discovery*, to stimulate classroom discussions. The stories are written to raise perennial philosophical questions in children's terms. Students learn the principles of logic by talking about the activities and ideas of the characters in the novels.

Another approach to teaching thinking, Edward de Bono's CoRT program, uses quite different methods and is described as having different aims. de Bono portrays critical thinking as "reactive," calling it "the bane of society and education." Rather than having students judge other people's ideas, he says, schools should encourage students to develop original solutions to problems by learning to change their perceptions.

The 60 lessons in CoRT (for Cognitive Research Trust, de Bono's organization in Cambridge, England), provide practice in using such "tools" as the PMI (for Plus, Minus, Interesting), which is intended to help students develop the habit of considering new ideas without immediately judging them as good or bad, right or wrong. Students are taught to "do an OPV" (for "Other Point of View") or "do a CAF" (Consider All Factors) when making decisions.

It is interesting to note that Philosophy for Children, designed to teach logic, and CoRT, which teaches that productive thinking is often *not* logical, nevertheless both stress attention to alternatives. This suggests that, while some aspects of the various approaches are undeniably different, they also have some similarities, at least in their aims. Paul advocates teaching dialectically—deliberately exposing students to conflicting ideas—while de Bono would simply have them "do an OPV." Despite these differences in method, the aim of both authorities is for students to become more objective and empathetic. In other words, the proponents of quite different approaches may nevertheless have in mind a somewhat similar image of the thinking person they hope to produce.

Glatthorn and Baron (p. 49) describe "the good thinker" as being willing to think, persistent, objective, and rational. Development of these qualities is the explicitly stated or implied aim of many of the various approaches. For example, one of the goals of Instrumental Enrichment is "restraining impulsivity." Teaching students to be more precise and persistent is also the theme of Whimbey and Whimbey's *Intelligence Can Be Taught* (1957), which reports the authors' use of tutoring and paired problem solving to help college students with low academic aptitude scores improve their performance.

Selecting Approaches

There are numerous approaches to teaching thinking not shown in Figure 1. For example, Carol Booth Olson (p. 215) and her colleagues at the University of California-Irvine have prepared units for teaching higher-order thinking through writing. Developmental psychologists such as Irving Sigel (1984) and educators such as those in the Shoreham-Wading River, New York, schools (Brooks and others, 1984) favor a "constructivist" approach. Mortimer Adler and members of the Paideia Group (1982) advocate Socratic discussion of classic documents such as the Declaration of Independence to develop what Hirsch (1985) calls "cultural literacy." Robert Glaser (1984) also advises that thinking skills be developed in the context of the existing academic disciplines, stresssing the essential role of knowledge in intellectual functioning.

The choice of which these approaches to use depends on many factors, including the experience and competence of teachers and the availability of funds for special materials and inservice training. Other considerations are the age and background of one's students and the kinds of thinking sought. Two essential questions to ask when reviewing a published program are whether (1) it "is based on a theory of intellectual performance specifying mental processes that has received experiential verification outside the context of the training program" (Sternberg, p. 185) and (2) whether there is valid evidence of the program's effectiveness.

John Goodlad (1983) has noted that classroom activities should be related to their supposed purposes. Most schools, he points out, have adopted goals such as "develop the ability to use and evaluate knowledge" and "develop positive attitudes toward intellectual activity, including intellectual curiosity and desire for for further learning." Goodlad comments:

These goals convey to me an image of students writing essays and narratives, engaging in dialogue with one another and with their teachers, initiating inquiry into questions not resolved by teachers or in their own minds, and so on. But this is not the picture that emerges from our data. Indeed the picture is of students passively listening, reading textbooks, completing assignments, and rarely initiating anything—at least in the academic subjects (p. 10).

The point is, of course, that what students actually do day-by-day in classroom should be consistent with our goals for them. To become better thinkers, they need to engage in activities that develop thinking abilities. Authorities may not agree on what approaches to use, but they do agree that the teaching methods most commonly used—lectures, worksheets, and recitations—are not very effective.

Teachers and administrators considering the various approaches to teaching thinking may find it useful to first define their own conception of "the good thinker" and then match their definition with the expected outcomes of the various approaches. With a clear idea of their aims, they will be in a position to select learning activities that appear to have the most potential for achieving them.

FOOTNOTES

[1] Support for this contention is provided by Robert Ennis, who specializes in the study of critical thinking. Ennis (1985) defines critical thinking as "reasonable reflective thinking that is focused on deciding what to believe and do," and says it involves both "abilities and dispositions."

REFERENCES

Adler, Mortimer J. *The Paideia Proposal: An Educational Manifesto*. New York: Macmillan, 1982.

Brooks, Martin; Fusco, Esther; and Grennon, Jacqueline. "Cognitive Levels Matching." *Educational Leadership* 40 (May 1983): 4-8.

Ennis, Robert H. "Goals for a Critical Thinking/Reasoning Curriculum." Paper presented at the Annual Meeting of the American Educational Research Association, Chicago, April 1985.

Glaser, Robert. "Education and Thinking: The Role of Knowledge." *American Psychologist* 39 (February 1984): 93-104.

Goodlad, John I. "What Some Schools and Classrooms Teach." *Educational Leadership* 40 (April 1983): 8-19.

Hirsch, E. D., Jr. "Literacy and Formalism." In *Challenges to the Humanities*. Edited by C. E. Finn, D. Ravitch, and P. H. Roberts. New York: Holmes and Meier Publishers, Inc., 1985.

Joyce, Bruce, and Weil, Marsha. *Models of Teaching*. Englewood Cliffs, N.J.: Prentice-Hall, Inc., 1980.

Whimbey, Arthur, with Whimbey, Linda Shaw. *Intelligence Can Be Taught*. New York: Bantam Books, 1975.

PART IX

Computers and Thinking

I've finally come to the conclusion that computers are smarter than people. Not once have I ever seen one jogging.

—Bob Orben

Storing vast amounts of information in long-term memory, sorting and classifying data, detecting and correcting errors, extrapolating and simulating alternative outcomes—computers are constructed to perform many of the functions associated with human intellect; thus, they provide us with "artificial intelligence."

The outer limits of the instructional uses of computers and other technologies to develop students' intellectual abilities have yet to be fully explored. Technology and programs for intellectual development are still in their infancy. Because of the nature of our educational system, the state of the art of school computer usage may be perpetually behind the technology's instructional potential. Continued experimentation, creative development, and critical evaluation in this field are in store.

This section presents these potentials and provides assistance in selecting software that may challenge and exercise students' thinking.

47

The Potential of Computers for Teaching Thinking

Carolee Matsumoto

Computer technology and the systematic development of thinking skills have converged in the education world and exploded into high energy and chaos. Carefully fused, elements of these two new curricular additions promise great eventual benefits, but at present most of their potential synergy remains unrealized.

Can computers help us teach thinking? What can computers and thinking skills mutually contribute to help us achieve our educational goals? This chapter suggests some possible advantages of computer use for teaching thinking, defines issues and planning considerations, and points out resources that can help educators formulate appropriate initial directions.

Certainly many people believe that using computers to teach thinking has vast promise. Scientist Patrick Gunkel (1985) expressed the hope and confidence that many educators have vested in the computer when he said, "Computers will be the way of introducing the young mind directly into the world of thought."

How Can Computers Aid Thinking Instruction?

Though some people claim that software and hardware can partially think for the user by executing long, complicated thinking chores, such as calculation and graphic display, others believe that learning programming and software use can actually stimulate and teach thinking skills (Nickerson, 1983; Kurland and others, 1984). Whether the computer thinks for its operator, or stimulates the user to think—or both—it seems clear that computers will re-

duce or eliminate the drudgery of skills practice and create time for teacher and student to confront more complicated learning and thinking tasks (Dede, 1981).

Computers seem to present to many theorists a means of shifting from the pedestrian educational mode of amassing a body of information to a more sophisticated level of problem solving and decision making. The interactive nature of computers, some believe, stimulates thinking and self-reflection in ways that encourage students to progress from processing ideas in a serial fashion to simultaneous or parallel thinking. Dede (1981) proposes that access to data bases, communications networks, and information processing software restricts the need for knowledge transmission education and frees time for knowledge processing, application, evaluation, and communication. Gunkel (1985) believes that, with appropriate software, computers can help operators to generate ideas and extend thinking by providing swift and easy ways to manipulate, merge, and sort information that our physical energy and time constraints would ordinarily limit. Complex new software also offers the potential for users to "design, model, abstract, represent in different modes, and create metaphors for ideas" (Perkins, 1984).

Other observers see potential for these machines to teach people about their own minds. Creating structured (for example, simulations) or unstructured (such as LOGO) learning environments helps children experience thinking and learning in rich, complex, explorative manner.

Another exciting facet for computers is hardware and software programmed with artificial intelligence. Such systems can mimic human thinking, problem solving, reasoning, and language (Green, 1984). Artificial intelligence devotees believe the logic of such computer capabilities can help to coach human thinking and could be used to create "empowering" environments to "motivate, amplify, audit, and communicate creativity" (Brown, 1983).

New technologies, including computer hardware and software, offer a long continuum of possible applications for teaching thinking. Certainly some schools and teachers have already begun to stretch the powers of developing minds by capitalizing on students' enthusiasm for computers. Before we can even attempt to define a role for computers in honing incisive thought processes, however, some basic and highly charged educational and philosophical issues need to be settled.

An emerging difficulty lies in the absence of clear goals for computers and thinking in education. Until we establish what "thinking" should do and be, we cannot decide on a proper role for computers in advancing that effort. The overall quality of education will consequently be adversely affected. We must not yield, though, to the temptation to cut through to quick answers. If we are to truly master these areas and find the best possible solutions, we must act with deliberation and determination as well as with dispatch.

The Issues

Like surfers, many optimistic educators, researchers, and software publishers have paddled out to the "Thinking Wave" (Costa, 1982). It is a big wave, very attractive and very strong. Understanding its components and dynamics, though, will mean the difference between an inspiring ride and a costly fiasco. What, then, is there to understand about using computers in the teaching of thinking? To begin with, we must determine:

1. Educational goals for teachers and learners.

2. A vision of how technology, particularly computers, will be used in thinking skills education and what roles teachers and students will play.

3. The ways hardware and software will be supplied.

4. Processes used to develop and evaluate software.

5. Specialized computer and thinking skills training necessary for educators.

Educational Goals for Teachers and Learners

Most school systems aspire to some ambitious but vague notion of educating and developing the whole child in all the traditional domains. A definite plan for how students will apply their education and a clear idea of the future they are being educated for is usually (and unfortunately) missing. Given the overwhelming and confusing bombardment of national reports, studies, research revelations, future forecasts, economic imperatives and restrictions, fickle fights for priorities, and cyclical calls for curric-

ulum revision, it is not surprising that our goals and priorities are sometimes muddled.

We find, however, a surprising degree of accord among educators, educational reform proponents, demographers, futurists, economists, and employers who agree that higher-level thinking and competency with computers and related technologies are essential survival skills in the Information Society we have already entered. Some computer enthusiasts even reason that the omnipresence of computers forces the redefinition of basic skills to include higher-order thinking (Hunt, 1983; DeBevoise, 1984; Dede, 1981).

Skeptics with long memories will perhaps recall that many of these promises promoted educational television and teaching machines in the 1960s. Computer technologies, however, are clearly distinct from these precursors and offer far greater potential advantages. One difference is outside applicability. Computers have become widespread tools of our culture. Furthermore, computers' complexity, flexibility, interactive nature, and multiple modes (literal, audio, graphic, and kinesthetic) provide the user with a wide repertoire of tools we can use to work, learn, and communicate.

Education itself has come a long way since the '60s, too. Information about teaching, learning, and knowledge has advanced with intense societal interest in boosting achievement to prepare students for a complex future. Unlike the costly, static, and technologically primitive mechanical white elephants of the past, present-day computers are dynamic vehicles that can be continually upgraded to serve education in new, inexpensive, and expanded ways.

As important institutions of society, schools need to determine their proper role in exposing children to these tools and the most appropriate application of computers to aid the teaching and learning process.

Educators are now challenged to examine, redefine, and merge traditional goals with new information about neurological functions and learning processes; then we must recognize applications of the new knowledge, using present technological capabilities and anticipating future ones. If we are to attend to the more global aspects of teaching—developing specific cognitive powers, enhancing higher-level thinking, and applying useful technological advances—an ongoing synthesis of the previously known and the newly discovered will necessarily involve a reconceptualization of the nature of schools and education.

In view of the breadth of support for computer use to provoke sophisticated thought, it is very likely that computers will become as common in schools as they are in businesses. That being the case, some key questions need answers:

1. Have we developed goals and established definite

A Beginning List of Software Companies That Have Produced Thinking Skills Software

WARNING: These software packages have been recommended by many sources and have not been comprehensively evaluated.

Company	Skill Area	Title
Apple Computer 20225 Mariani Ave. Cupertino, CA 95014 (408) 996-1010	Problem Solving	Mix and Match
CBS Software One Fawcett Place Greenwich, CT 06836	Language Arts Logic and Problem Solving	Mystery Master: Murder by the Dozen
Chalk Board, Inc. 3772 Pleasantdale Rd. Atlanta, GA (404) 447-6711	Problem Solving	Logicmaster
Educational Materials P.O. Box 17 Pelham, NY 10803	Language Arts Social Studies Science Philosophy	Thinking and Learning (Tutorial on thinking, Socratic dialogue)
The Learning Company 4370 Alpine Rd. Portola Valley, CA 94025 (415) 851-3160	Problem Solving Critical Thinking	Gertrude's Secrets
	Critical Thinking Problem Solving Math and Reading Skills	Gertrude's Puzzles
	Reading and Language Arts Logic	Moptown Parade
	Math Science	Rocky's Boots
	Logic Problem Solving	
Minnesota Educational Computing Corporation 3490 Lexington Ave., N. St. Paul, MN 55112	Problem Solving Thinking Skills	Problem Solving Strategies Mind Puzzles
Midwest Publications Co. P.O. Box 448 Pacific Grove, CA 93950	Deductive Thinking Skills Logic Problem Solving	Mind Benders What's My Rule?
Spinnaker Software Corp. 1 Kendall Square Cambridge, MA 02139	Simulation Thinking Skills Deductive Reasoning	Snooper Troops I Snooper Troops II
	Math Science Language Arts	In Search of the Most Amazing Thing
	Miscellaneous Simulation Thinking Skills Deductive Reasoning	Snooper Troops Case #1 (The Granite Point Ghost)
Sunburst Communications 39 Washington Ave. Pleasantville, NY 10570 (914) 769-5030 (800) 431-1934	Prediction Analysis Science/Problem Solving/Predictions Math Problem Solving/Generalizations/Hypothesis testing Science/Problem Solving Problem Solving/Math/Visual Reasoning Social Studies/Problem Solving/Analysis Problem Solving/Pattern Recognition/Visual Perception Problem Solving/Pattern Recognition/Analysis/Synthesis Math/Problem Solving Math/Simulation/Judgments Science/Math/Problem Solving Puzzles/Problem Solving Math/Problem Solving/Thinking Skills	Gears The Pond The King's Rule The Incredible Laboratory The Factory Code Quest Fun House Maze Color Keys The King's Rule Survival Math Semcalc Tobbs Learns Algebra Amazing Think Tank

*The Concord Public Schools and the Concord-Carlisle Regional School District, 120 Meriam Road, Concord, MA 01742, have begun a collection and data base of thinking skills software. Contributions and suggestions are welcome.

priorities for computer use to promote intelligent behavior and higher-level thinking (Costa, 1982)?

2. Do we have a clear vision of what the merger of thinking instruction with computer capability can do for education and what the resultant teaching and learning will be like?

3. Do we have organizational structures to assemble and support computer use in thinking skills programs? To integrate such programs into curriculum and teaching practices?

4. How will administrators and staff be involved and trained in classroom uses of computers to teach thinking?

5. Is the community apprised of our goals and supportive of them?

6. Are we willing to secure and allocate adequate resources to support this expensive endeavor?

A Vision of Computers in Thinking Skills Education

If our goal is to meld thinking, computers, and learning, we must be able to envision the desired result in the classroom. One scenario of education in the 1990s describes learners as working at "electronic desks." Their computers would be connected to a variety of information sources, data bases, production peripherals, and networks. Students would assume responsibility for their own learning through the manipulation of a rich variety of technological tools and would gain the ability to communicate with an extensive network of people and information (Licklider, 1980).

Many believe these "electronic learners" will think on higher levels than their pencil-and-paper equivalents did previously. Dede (1981) predicts that "new kinds of person-tool learning partnerships will redefine new kinds of intelligence that demand higher-order skills of flexibility, creativity, decision making, complex pattern recognition, and evaluation of systems." Licklider's projection is consonant with the probable positive results Walker described in 1983: "more active learning, more varied sensory and conceptual modes, less mental drudgery, more independent learning, learning nearer the speed of thought, and learning better tailored to individuals and to abstraction." Seeley-Brown (1984) claims that the computer can also "act as a mirror for the user's thought processes, enabling him to reflect on his own thinking and improve his metacognitive skills."

The role implications of this picture clearly differ from those now present in schools. Teachers in this scenario would become orchestrators or coaches for learning. Instead of imparting information or teaching skills, teachers would inspire, reinforce, clarify, guide, and motivate learning. Students would take responsibility for arranging and pacing their own learning; they would use strategies that access and process information and draw on higher-level thinking powers, communication skills, and problem-solving and decision-making capacities.

Supplying Hardware and Software

Assuming decisions are reached to equip learners with electronic study systems, educators will face the challenge of supplying students with appropriate hardware and software, and it is clear that we are not talking just one computer per classroom. For some schools, the lack of sufficient funding will be slow progress. All schools must pick and choose among computer systems with care. While I can suggest no easy street leading to perfect future visions, I do urge clear goals and priorities, a commitment to equity, community education, and whatever political involvement is necessary for action.

Processes for Software Development and Evaluation

Software is available right now that teaches or can be adapted to teach, the many aspects of higher-level thinking—thinking strategies, logic, cognitive (learning) skills, problem solving, and so on. The recent interest in the systematic teaching of thinking has resulted in a frantic search for appropriate materials. Part of the attention has included a closer look at thinking skills software that exists now, is being developed, or could be developed.

A few companies have published software catalogs specifically including titles under "Thinking" (see sidebar), and some schools are trying to assemble soft- and hardware components to serve their thinking skills programs. Often, a hodge-podge of incompatible materials results.

Before schools can make valuable educational use of computers in thinking skills programs, some questions need firm answers:

1. Has thinking been defined?

2. Is there a place in the curriculum that accommodates and encourages the use of computers to teach thinking?

3. Has the use of instructional technology, which includes computers, been evaluated as to purpose, weighed against other priorities, and adequately supported?

4. Are teachers trained in computer use? Are they motivated to teach, encourage, and value a computer-assisted approach to thinking instruction?

5. Is there a system to evaluate, adopt, and implement appropriate software? Each school needs general criteria, perhaps like these:

   a. Selected software will be integrated into the curriculum at designated points.

b. A monitor system will coordinate the use of all computer-assisted instruction.

c. The goals and objectives of the software are clear.

d. The software is compatible with system curriculum objectives, pedagogy modes, and standards of quality. It is user interactive and fully child-tested.

e. The software capitalizes on computer capabilities to facilitate maximum learning.

These guidelines are neither comprehensive nor prescriptive. They cannot be. Each school system needs to draft its own guidelines, implement their use, and oversee the selection and use of software that satisfied local program requirements.

A model that may be helpful, however, is Project CompuTHINK, which compiled a glossary of different kinds of thinking and a matrix guide that cross-references appropriate teaching software. The project also devised teacher training exercises and produced rating sheets that describe and analyze the content and tasks in each piece of software. (See Chapter 49 for more information on CompuTHINK.)

The continued development of suitable software depends largely on school practitioners. Software will be of high quality only if educators decide on parameters for course materials, communicate their needs to software producers, and demand nothing less than the best. Producers try to be sensitive to such guidance; after all, what educators regard as valuable is what publishers know is marketable.

Training for Educators

Though many schools and teachers already use computers to develop thinking, the eventual involvement of all educators is at this point uncertain. As in all proposed educational improvements, the extent to which our endeavor will succeed will depend largely on staff attitudes, knowledge, and skills. In turn, the level of teacher support for this new approach will be determined in large measure by how visionary leadership can be, how creative school improvement efforts are, how effectively we settle issues, and how thoroughly we train staff in the new applications of teaching technology.

Learning how to use computers has been a major stumbling block for many administrators, teachers, and other school employees. Because computer literacy is a new and rapidly developing field, there is a general lack of clarity as to how computers could and should be used in schools. As a direct consequence, little consistency or qualitative knowledge exists about what administrators and teachers ought to learn about computers. The problem is compounded by the scarcity and variability of equipment and the lack of staff time for instructors to become so experienced with computers that they naturally integrate them into regular classroom use.

If we were to assess the level of administrative and teacher knowledge and skills with computers at this time, we would no doubt find many people with significant expertise and knowledge of how to apply computer technology in their work. Unfortunately, we would probably also find many who know that computers exist, but beyond that, are completely mystified about how computers might serve them.

Familiarity with computers is a significantly additional expectation we now place on teachers. It involves a new technological medium, altered classroom practices, and new learning and teaching modes for both students and teachers. Further, because interest in deliberately teaching thinking skills is relatively recent, many educators have neither a well-defined understanding of the field nor specific training in conveying its principles to students. Before computers can be harnessed to develop student thinking, teachers will have to learn these two related fields, internalize them, and sense how their new knowledge can be transferred into existing curriculums.

Merging thinking instruction with computer use thus becomes a formidable staff development hurdle. Before planning appropriate programs to satisfy this requirement, we face several decisions:

1. What kind of training will develop the ability to teach computer skills and thinking techniques? Then, what training can aid the instructor in using computers to teach thinking or using thinking to teach computers?

2. Should training in each area be separate, or should we take a "braid" approach, weaving the strands together?

3. How can educators learn to evaluate software and approaches for computer use in thinking skills programs?

4. When should we start training, and who needs it?

5. How can we assure and verify that training transfers to the classroom?

Without clear answers to these training issues and a sustained effort to make the transition in curriculum, we cannot expect to see teachers concertedly applying this promising innovative approach.

Looking Ahead

For over ten years, we have heard how computers would revolutionize education, yet the potential of computers in teaching is nowhere near realization. Some of the common excuses for the lack of prompt progress are valid—expense of hardware, lack of time for training, confusion over software selection.

If we are honest, though, some of the responsibility lies in our inability to articulate how and why we should use these new technologies. Computers are no panacea for all educational problems, but clearly they can help advance learning and teaching. If we can accept, believe, and act on the promises of many experts, the cultivation of acute thinking is one area where computers can have significant impact on multivarious ways. If we can produce students who can use technology to extend their thinking in preparation for life in a society that will demand intelligence, we will have served the future well.

REFERENCES

Brown, J. "Process versus Product: A Perspective on Tools for Communal and Informal Electronic Learning." In *Report from the Learning Lab: Education in the Electronic Age,* pp. 41-57. Edited by S. Newman and E. Poor. New York: WNET, 1983.

Costa, Arthur L. "Teaching for Intelligent Behavior." *Human Intelligence Newsletter* 3 (1982): 1-3.

Cradler, John. *Project CompuTHINK.* San Francisco: South San Francisco Unified School District, California, 1985.

DeBevoise, Wynn. "Education and Technology: Predicting the Needs of the Future." School Research Forum Report. Arlington, Va.: Educational Research Service, Inc., 1984, ppp. 69-70.

Dede, Christopher. "Educational, Social, and Ethical Implications of Technological Innovation." *Programmed Learning and Educational Technology* 18 (1981): 207.

Green, John O. "Artificial Intelligence and the Future Classroom." *Classroom Computer Learning* (January 1984): 26-31.

Gunkel, Patrick. Scientist, Cambridge, Massachusetts. Interview, January 11, 1985.

Hunt, James B., Jr. "Action for Excellence, Excerpts from the Task Force Report." *Educational Leadership* 18 (September 1983): 15-16.

Kurland, D. Midian; Clement, Catherine; Mawby, Ronald; and Pea, Roy D. "Mapping the Cognitive Demands of Learning to Program." Paper presented at the International Conference on Thinking at Harvard University, Cambridge, Mass., 1984.

Licklider, J.C.R. "Social and Economic Impacts of Information Technology on Education." *Information Technology in Education* 134 (Joint Hearings of the Committee on Science and Technology and the Committee on Education and Labor). Washington, D.C.: U.S. Government Printing Office, 1980.

Nickerson, Raymond. "Computer Programming as a Vehicle for Teaching Thinking Skills." *Thinking, The Journal of Philosophy for Children* 4 (1983): 42-47.

Papert, Seymour: *Mindstorms: Children, Computers, and Powerful Ideas.* New York: Basic Books, Inc., 1980.

Perkins, David. Co-Director, Project Zero, Harvard University, Cambridge, Mass. Interview, October 11, 1984.

Walker, Decker F. "Reflections on the Educational Potential and Limitations of Microcomputers." *Phi Delta Kappan* (October 1983) 103-107.

48

Uses of Computers for Teaching Thinking

Chuck Wiederhold

To gain both an appreciation for and an understanding of the various roles computers play in our learning environments, let's examine some of these roles functionally in terms of the computer's relationship to students, teachers, and the thinking and learning processes. This list is by no means exhaustive, and some functions overlap the categories.

1. *Computer as content*. Computer science classes deal with this theme. Topics include computer architecture, operating systems, and storage techniques.

2. *Computer as learner*. In this role, the computer has undefined possibilities. *Programming* gives the computer definition and dictates tasks to be performed. Computer languages (such as BASIC, LOGO, PASCAL) are vehicles for interacting with the computer as learner. When computer literacy was first introduced in the curriculums of the early 1980s, computer as content and computer as learner were the major components.

3. *Computer as teacher*. In this role, the computer sequentially presents lesson material to students either through drill and practice items or tutorials. The computer records results and provides instant feedback to the learner. In the more sophisticated applications of this role, the computer assesses learner performance and branches to material of appropriate difficulty.

4. *Computer as tool*. The computer is an extension of the user. For the writer, it is a word processor; for the manager, it is an electronic filing system or data base. For the accountant, it is an interactive electronic ledger or spreadsheet; and for the scientist, it can at once observe, record, and compare data. Using the computer as a tool in its various forms has become the major definition of computer literacy for students, teachers, and other users.

5. *Computer as data source*. The computer transcends the role of being a tool for individual users and becomes a common interactive electronic encyclopedia for multiple users. People who access electronic networks, centralized data bases, and news retrieval are using the computer as a data source. Teachers who develop lesson materials based on the retrieval of information contained within data bases enable students to use computers in this role.

6. *Computer as inquiry facilitator*. The computer is both data source and teacher. The user interacts with the program both to determine the content and the form of inquiry necessary to reveal it. Complex "adventure games" and "guess and rule" programs place the computer in this role. It is in this way that the computer has captured the imagination of problem solvers and offers the greatest potential for addressing higher-order thinking skills.

49

CompuTHINK and Criteria for Selecting Software

John Cradler

Project CompuTHINK is designed to assist educators in teaching and developing the thinking skills of their students with the aid of technology. Specifically, it provides educators with:

1. A conceptual framework that identifies and classifies 33 specific thinking skills ranging from simple recall to complex problem solving.

2. A tested strategy for identifying each of the cognitive skills emphasized in any educational software program.

3. A resource guide that matches the cognitive skills framework to existing computer programs.

4. Training and materials needed for using computers to facilitate the development of cognitive and critical thinking skills.

The CompuTHINK Cognitive Skills Framework is based on established models such as Bloom's Taxonomy and the Project IMPACT Universe of Critical Thinking Skills. Evaluating grade 1-8 software programs for cognitive skills content was an *immediate* project goal; however, the framework and analysis strategies provided can be used to identify the cognitive skills stressed in any educational program presented in any medium.

CompuTHINK Materials[1]

The CompuTHINK *Resource Guide* contains:
1. The Cognitive Skills Framework.
2. Definitions of each component.
3. Questions and examples to show how each skill might be illustrated or tested for students in K-3, 4-6, and 7-8.

4. Rating forms (with directions) for analyzing software programs using CompuTHINK criteria.

5. Extensive reviews of 30 programs evaluated by those criteria, rating each program's educational quality, ease of use, and cognitive skill content.

6. A matrix presenting the results of these evaluations in graphic form.

In addition, a CompuTHINK *Resource Diskette* (for Apple IIe and IIc) provides a quick reference to definitions of terms used in the skills framework and permits quick retrieval of programs reviewed by grade level and specific cognitive skills required.

CompuTHINK Training

One- and two-day workshops can be provided for schools, districts, and county offices. Workshop topics include (1) understanding specific cognitive skills included in the framework; (2) selecting computer software programs according to the thinking skills they emphasize; (3) analyzing software programs for their cognitive skills content, quality, and structure; and (4) incorporating cognitive skill instruction into existing curriculums with the aid of computers.

CompuTHINK Cognitive Skills Matrix

The matrix presented in Figure 1 is a graphic representation of quality rating, grade level range, and specific cognitive skills emphasize in 25 popular educational software programs. These ratings were made by triads of educators who had field-tested the programs with students and then evaluated them using CompuTHINK forms and procedures.

CompuTHINK has been certified as an EXEMPLARY project by the Educational Technology Unit of the California

FIGURE 1
CompuTHINK Cognitive Skills Matrix

Key:
Skill Emphasis: ■ = Major ● = Incidental
Rating: E = Excellent, VG = Very Good, G = Good

COGNITIVE SKILLS	1 BUMBLE GAMES	2 BUMBLE PLOT	3 CODE QUEST	4 COLOR KEYS	5 CREATURE CREATOR	6 THE FACTORY	7 FIRST THINGS FIRST/ DO THIS, DO THAT	8 GEOGRAPHY SEARCH	9 GERTRUDE'S PUZZLES/ GERTRUDE'S SECRETS	10 IGGY'S GNEES	11 MEMORY CASTLE	12 M_SS_NG L_NKS	13 MOPTOWN HOTEL	14 MOPTOWN PARADE	15 ODD ONE OUT	16 PICK THE PART	17 THE POND	18 REGROUPING	19 ROCKY'S BOOTS	20 SIMON SAYS	21 TEASERS BY TOBBS	22 TEDDY AND IGGY	23 TEDDY'S PLAYGROUND	24 WAS IT THERE? WAS IT MISSING?	25 WHAT'S IN A FRAME?
ENABLING SKILLS																									
PERCEIVING																									
Observing					■	●	■				●		●	■	■	■		■		■		■		■	■
Recalling					■		■				■					■		■		■	■	■		■	■
CONCEIVING																									
Comparing/Contrasting					■	■			■	■			■	■	■								■		
Grouping/Labeling									■					■	●			■					●		
Categorizing/Classifying								●		●			■	■				■					●		
SEQUENCING																									
Ordering	■	■			■	■	■	●						■					●	●		■			
Patterning				●	■			●						■			■		●	●	●		■		
Prioritizing								●											●						
PROCESSES																									
ANALYZING																									
Questioning	●	●	■					■					●		■				■		■				
Discriminating Fact from Opinion																									
Discriminating Relevant from Irrelevant			●					■																	
Discriminating Reliable from Unreliable																									
Recognizing Part to Whole Relationships			■	■	●	■		■				■		■		■		●	■				●	■	
INFERRING																									
Understanding Statements			■					■				●									■				
Identifying Cause/Effect			●			●		■											■		●				
Generalizing			■					■	●	●		●		■			●		●		●		■		
Making Predictions			■			●		■				●		●					■		●				
Identifying Assumptions			■					■													●				
Identifying Point of View			●					■																	
OPERATIONS																									
LOGICAL REASONING																									
Inductive	●	●	■			■		■	■	■		■	■	■	■		■		■		■		■		
Deductive			■	■		■		■	■					●					■		■		■		
CREATIVE THINKING																									
Demonstrating Fluency			■					■											●						
Demonstrating Flexibility			■					■											●						
Demonstrating Originality			■					■											●						
Elaborating			■					■											■						
Creating New Ideas Spontaneously			■					■											●						
PROBLEM SOLVING																									
Making Judgments/Decisions			■	●		■		■					●	●	●				■						
Defining a Problem			■					■											■		■				
Determining the Desired Outcome			■			■		■											■		■				
Searching for Possible Solutions			■					■						●					■		■				
Selecting and Applying a Trial Solution			■		●	■		■	●					●			●		■		■				
Evaluating Outcomes			■		●			■											■						
Revising and Repeating Steps as needed			■			■		■						●			●		■						
*Rating	VG	VG	E	E	VG	E	VG	VG	E	E	VG	G	E	E	VG	G	E	G	E	G	E	E	E	G	G
Grade Level Range	K-3	2-12	4-12	4-12	K-6	4-12	K-6	4-12	K-6	K-6	4-5	3-6	3-12	K-6	K-6	K-6	2-12	4-6	4-9	K-9	4-12	K-3	K-6	K-6	K-6

State Department of Education. The project is funded for dissemination to schools throughout California. For information regarding workshops and materials, contact John Cradler, Project Director, South San Francisco Unified School District, 398 "B" Street, South San Francisco, California 94080 (telephone: 415-877-8835 or 877-8768).

Criteria for Selecting Software

Evaluating computer software for classroom use generates many questions:

- Is the program worthy of serious consideration?
- Is it high in educational quality?
- Is it well-organized and presented?
- Is it convenient and efficient in use?
- What skills does it develop?

Among the goals of Project CompuTHINK is developing methods to evaluate computer software that show promise of developing specific cognitive skills. After a year of experiments, trial and error, strenuous debate, and continuous revision, the developers of CompuTHINK created a series of forms, definitions, and procedures to make such evaluations manageable.

FIGURE 2
Screening Form For Cognitive Skills Courseware

Program Title: _____ Publisher: _____

Package Title (if applicable): _____

Subject (Area(s): _____

Reviewer's Name/Title: _____ Date: _____

To recommend the program for further evaluation, the answers to questions 1-7 should all be "Yes."

Circle the appropriate answer.

1. Does the program emphasize cognitive skills? yes no
2. Is the computer a good medium for presenting this material? yes no
3. Does the program deserve a "good" to "excellent" rating in educational quality and program structure? yes no
4. Is the program likely to maintain high student motivation? yes no
5. Can the program be used by several students in a reasonable amount of time? yes no
6. Is the program accurate in content, grammar, and spelling? yes no
7. Is the program free from objectional material? yes no

This program *is* recommended for further evaluation. yes no
This program *is not* recommended for further evaluation. yes no

Comments:
_____
_____
_____
_____
_____

The process is challenging, lively, and thought-provoking. Participants report that skills gained and sharpened in these sessions are useful not only in selecting curricular materials but also in using them for maximum advantage in the classroom.

Evaluation Procedure

Every program is evaluated by a team of at least three educators. First, each team member rates the program independently. Team members then confer to reach consensus on how to rate each item. No phase of the evaluation is complete until the team members agree on the ratings, comments, and statements to be recorded. The evaluation sequence is as follows:

1. *Courseware screening*—to eliminate unsuitable programs from further consideration.

2. *Courseware field test evaluation*—to provide detailed, specific information for prospective buyers from educators who have used the program with students. This evaluation emphasizes the program's educational quality and convenience for classroom use.

3. *Cognitive skills task analysis*—to give clear answers to educators who want to know which programs to buy to exercise or develop specific thinking skills.

SCREENING COGNITIVE SKILLS COURSEWARE

Purposes:
- To identify programs that show promise of being useful for developing cognitive skills in classrooms.
- To eliminate unsuitable programs from further consideration.

Preparation:
- Examine the seven questions on the screening form. They represent minimum standards of program quality and suitability.

Evaluation:
- Run the program as many times as needed to become familiar with all sections and levels.
- Make deliberate mistakes to discover how the program responds.
- Keep standards in mind.

The Form (Figure 2):
- Working individually, consider each question and check *yes* or *no*. Confer to reach team consensus.
- The questions call for general impressions. A detailed examination of these points will follow if the program passes this initial screening.
- The program can be recommended for further evaluation only if the evaluation team answers *yes* to all questions.

- If the program is not recommended for further evaluation, provide the reasons and a brief explanation.

COURSEWARE FIELD TEST EVALUATION

Purpose:
- To provide detailed, specific information for prospective buyers from educators who have used the program with students.

Preparation:
- This form should *not* be used until at least one member of the evaluation team has used the program with ten or more students. The reliability and validity of the team's evaluation depend on field-testing the program with many children of different ages in a variety of settings.
- Study all manuals, documentation, and support materials that are available for the program.

Evaluation:
- Work through the program thoroughly, include all levels and branches.
- Purposely make mistakes to see what happens.
- Notice what prompts and cues are given if you make a mistake or get stuck.

The Form (Figure 3):
1. *Program title:* If the program is part of a set, note package title.
2. *Computer systems:* List brands and models for which the program is available. This information can be found in the documentation or vendor catalog.
3. *Subject areas:* Identify academic subjects for which the program is most appropriate (math, social studies, language arts).
4. *Retail price:* Note the approximate price on the date of review. If the program is only available as part of a package, enter the package price.
5. *Appropriate for:* Use your judgment and check student groups for whom the program is applicable.
6. *Can be taught by:* Use your judgment and check applicable groups.
7. *Publisher's targeted students:* Refer to documentation for this information.
    Evaluators' judgment: Use your judgment and check those applicable.
8. *Field test:* Enter approximate number of students who have used this program under team members' supervision.
9. *Input mode:* Check those applicable. If other modes are used, note which ones after "other."
10. *Program uses:* Check those applicable. Indicate additional uses after "other."

11. *System requirements and options:* Refer to documentation for accurate information.

12. *Program structure/educational quality:* Rate the following items *yes, no,* or *n/a* (not applicable). Check *n/a* if a possible feature is missing, but its absence does not diminish the educational value of the program.

    a. *Clear purpose:* Refer to documentation to make judgment.

    b. *Instructor adjustment:* Instructors can, for example, set the program for speed, number of problems, level of difficulty, and so on.

    c. *Menu adjustment:* Try each menu selection to determine level of difficulty.

    d. *Automatic adjustment:* Depending on student responses, program become harder or easier and faster or slower.

FIGURE 3
Evaluation Form For Courseware Field Test

1. Program Title: _____ Package Title: _____

2. Computer System(s): _____

3. Subject Area(s): _____ 4. Retail Price: $_____ $_____
                                                                           program   package

5. Appropriate for: a. Individual ____   6. Can be taught by: a. Teacher ____   c. Parent ____
                        b. Small group ____   b. Aide   ____   d. Self ____
                        c. Large group/class ____

7. Publisher's targeted students: In evaluator's judgment, appropriate for:

        Preschool _____   _____
        K-3   _____   _____
        4-6   _____   _____
        7-9   _____   _____
        10-12   _____   _____
        Regular _____   _____
        Remedial _____   _____
        Bilingual _____   _____
        Other   _____   _____

        Describe _____

8. Field Test.   Rater's Name/Title: _____ Date: _____

           Rater: a. Has used this program with _____(#) students.

                  b. Has received feedback from others who have used this program.   yes ____   no ____

                  c. Will continue to use this program.   yes ____   no ____

9. Input Mode: Keyboard _____   Graphics pad _____   Joystick _____   Other: _____

10. Program Uses (Check all applicable):	11. System Requirements and options	Required	Optional
Drill and practice _____	Memory required (48K, 64K, 128K, etc.)	_____	_____
Tutorial _____	Cassette	_____	_____
Simulation _____	Cartridge	_____	_____
Demonstration _____	Diskette	_____	_____
Instructional game _____	No. of disk drives	_____	_____
Cognitive skills _____	Monochromatic monitor	_____	_____
Informational _____	Color monitor	_____	_____
Other (describe):	Printer (graphics)	_____	_____
	Printer (text only)	_____	_____
_____	Other (describe):		
_____	_____		

Figure 3
Evaluation Form For Courseware Field Test (Continued)

12. Program Structure/Educational Quality

	Yes	No	n/a
a. Program's purposes and objectives are clearly defined.	——	——	——
b. Instructor can adjust the program for different levels of skills/abilities.	——	——	——
c. Menu allows choice of difficulty level.	——	——	——
d. Program automatically adjusts to student skill level.	——	——	——
e. Teacher can change program content.	——	——	——
f. An efficient management system is provided for monitoring student progress.	——	——	——
g. "Prompts" and "Help" options are provided.	——	——	——
h. Program is interactive.	——	——	——
i. Program integrates well with classroom curriculums.	——	——	——
j. Program is popular with students in choice-free situation.	——	——	——

Comments: _____

_____

13. Program Utility/Convenience

	Yes	No	n/a
a. Instructor's guide is clearly written.	——	——	——
b. Instructor's guide is comprehensive.	——	——	——
c. One disk can serve several computers simultaneously.	——	——	——
d. Requires little or no instructor training.	——	——	——
e. Program requires little preparation time.	——	——	——
f. Requires minimal instructor intervention.	——	——	——
g. Time per student is manageable and efficient for classroom use.	——	——	——
h. Ample support materials are provided.	——	——	——

Comments: _____

_____

14. Program Strengths: _____

_____

15. Program Weaknesses: _____

_____

16. Overall rating of program value: Good _____ Very good _____ Excellent _____

Comments: _____

e. *Change of content:* Instructors can enter their own word lists, questions, and so on.

f. *Management system:* Management systems may include student scores, level assignments, tests, progress records, and so on.

g. *Prompting:* Cues and "help options" are available if the user is confused or stuck.

h. *Interactive:* The program requires users to manipulate and control objects/features rather than to respond to multiple-choice type questions.

i. *Curriculum integration:* The program can be used to support and reinforce classroom instruction.

j. *Student interest:* When allowed to select from several programs, students often choose this one.

13. *Program utility/convenience:* Rate the following items *yes, no,* or *n/a.*

    a. *Clear guide:* The guide is easy to understand and follow.

    b. *Comprehensive guide:* All features are explained. Directions are provided for each operation.

    c. *Multiple use:* Disk can be removed after program is loaded.

    d. *Instructor training:* The instructor can learn to use the program in one hour or less.

    e. *Preparation time:* Minimal time is required to boot the system, enter content, prepare support materials, and so on.

    f. *Instructor intervention:* After initial instructions, students need little or no teacher assistance.

    g. *Time per student:* The program can be used effectively with several students in a reasonable period of time.

    h. *Support materials:* Ample support includes thorough documentation, useful teaching suggestions and ideas, and classroom activities to precede or follow computer use.

14. *Program strengths:* Describe the program's best features.

15. *Program weaknesses:* Describe any noteworthy shortcomings of the program.

16. *Overall rating:* Any program rated less than "good" should have been eliminated in the screening phase.

    ● *Good*—program is useful and free from serious flaws.

    ● *Very good*—program has some limitations but is better than most available.

    ● *Excellent*—program scores high in all or nearly all criteria—an exemplary purchase.

Comments: Note any points not adequately covered above.

COGNITIVE SKILLS TASK ANALYSIS

Purpose:

    ● To give clear answers to educators who want to know which programs to buy to exercise or develop specific thinking skills.

Informtion:

    ● The skills listed are categorized into three levels:
      1. Enabling Skills
      2. Processes
      3. Operations

    ● These skills are not necessarily hierarchical and need not be taught or learned in the order presented. However, some skills may be interdependent.

Preparation:

    ● Study the task analysis to familiarize yourself with the terms used.

    ● Become familiar with the *definitions of terms with examples.*

Evaluation:

    ● Work through the program thoroughly. Try all sections and levels.

    ● Continually ask yourself which thinking skills you are applying while using the program.

The Form (Figure 4):

    ● Evaluators should independently complete the checklist *before conferring to produce* the final team rating. Refer to *definitions of terms with examples* when disagreements arise.

    ● Rate the skill as *major* only if you would recommend purchase or use of the program to develop this skill.

    ● Rate the skill as *incidental* if the skill is exercised, but you would not recommend purchase or use of the program to develop this skill.

    ● Leave the line blank if the skill is absent or used to a slight degree. You may rate several skills as *major* and several as *incidental*, but do not rate any skill both *major* and *incidental*.

Program description:

    ● Briefly describe the type of program, its purpose, content, format, and features. The publisher's documentation, catalog descriptions, and available reviews may be helpful. *Support materials*—review accompanying documentation and rate as follows:

    ● *Instructions only*—directions are limited to program operation.

    ● *Brief manual*—a few teaching ideas or suggestions are included.

    ● *Extensive manual*—materials include many pre- and post-computer use activities for integrating the program into coursework.

Transfer:

    ● Transfer means learning a skill or concept in one context and applying it in another context.

    ● If the program or package has noteworthy features intended to facilitate transfer, describe them.

    ● Within a well-designed program, transfer is fostered by using the same (or similar) skills in man, different situations.

    ● Well-designed support materials facilitate transfer by providing follow-up lessons in which a skill is applied to classroom subjects or to everyday life. If such lessons are provided, note topics.

Figure 4
Evaluation Form For Cognitive Skills Task Analysis

Program Title: _____ Publisher: _____

Reviewer's Name/Title _____ Date: _____

	Emphasis	
	Major	**Incidental**

ENABLING SKILLS

1. *Perceiving*—the program requires students to:
   a. *Observe* carefully.. _____ _____
   b. *Recall*/remember things, ideas, events .... _____ _____

2. *Conceiving*—the program requires students to:
   a. *Compare/contrast*.. _____ _____
   b. *Group/label*—assign a descriptive label or phrase to a set of objects/ideas after grouping them according to a common attribute .... _____ _____
   c. *Categorize/classify*—group ideas or objects according to given criteria (labels are provided)... _____ _____

3. *Sequencing/seriating*—the program requires students to:
   a. *Order*—arrange things/ideas according to time, size, alphabetical order, and so on, or identify the scheme or standard by which they have been ordered .... _____ _____
   b. *Pattern*—arrange things/ideas according to an established, repeated scheme .... _____ _____
   c. *Prioritize*—arrange things/ideas by degree of personal importance .... _____ _____

PROCESSES

1. *Analyzing*—the program requires students to:
   a. *Question* (formulate relevant information).......................... _____ _____
   b. Discriminate *fact* from *opinion*................................... _____ _____
   c. Discriminate *relevant* from *irrelevant* information .... _____ _____
   d. Discriminate *reliable* from *unreliable* sources of information .... _____ _____
   e. Recognize *part to whole relationships*............................. _____ _____

2. *Inferring*—the program requires students to:
   a. *Understand* the meaning of *statements* .... _____ _____
   b. Identify probable *causes* and *effects*............................ _____ _____
   c. Use *generalizations* to solve problems or justify decisions........ _____ _____
   d. Make *predictions* .... _____ _____
   e. Identify one's own *assumptions* or those of others .... _____ _____
   f. Identify personal *point of view* or point of view of others .... _____ _____

OPERATIONS

1. *Logical reasoning*—the program requires students to:
   a. Use *inductive reasoning*—combine an assumption or hypothesis with provided information to draw a tentative generalization .... _____ _____
   b. Use *deductive reasoning*—draw a conclusion that can be proven or disproven by using only the information provided .... _____ _____

2. *Creative Thinking*—the program requires students to:
   a. Demonstrate *fluency*—product a variety of responses............. _____ _____
   b. Demonstrate *flexibility*—try several different approaches *or* apply a concept, idea, or rule to a variety of situations................................. _____ _____
   c. Demonstrate *originality*—produce novel, unexpected but related responses .... _____ _____
   d. *Elaborate*—extend or expand on a concept or idea .... _____ _____
   e. Spontaneously create new ideas or rules to fit available information (the *"aha!"* experience)... _____ _____

3. *Problem Solving*—the program requires students to:
   a. Make *decisions/judgments*—draw conclusions and/or determine what to do after discerning and comparing relevant facts .... _____ _____
   b. *Define*/describe the problem...................................... _____ _____
   c. *Determine desired outcome* .... _____ _____
   d. *Search for possible solutions*.................................... _____ _____
   e. Select and *apply a trial solution* .... _____ _____
   f. *Evaluate* outcome... _____ _____
   g. *Revise* and repeat above steps (except "a.") if desired outcome is not attained .... _____ _____

Continued

FIGURE 4
Evaluation Form For Cognitive Skills Task Analysis (Continued)

* * * * * * *

Program description: _____

_____

_____

_____

_____

_____

Support materials:

Instructions only _____   Brief manual _____   Extensive manual _____

Comments: _____

_____

Transfer (describe any attempts to encourage transfer of skills/concepts taught to other contexts): _____

_____

_____

_____

Summary:

a. List *major* thinking skills checked. Use the italicized words on the checklist as descriptors.

_____

_____

_____

b. List *incidental* thinking skills involved (no more than three).

_____

_____

c. List prerequisite skills. Note special skills students must have to work through the program.

_____

_____

Comments/Recommendations: _____

_____

_____

_____

_____

Summary:

● *Major skills*—list skills marked *major* on checklist. If all skills within a category are marked *major*, list the category heading. For example, if all skills under "Analyzing" are marked *major*, enter "Analyzing" as a major skill instead of listing all component skills.

● *Incidental skills*—enter the three most important incidental skills checked.

● *Prerequisite skills*—consider the age range of in-

tended users. Note any required skills that might cause problems if not previously learned.

● *Comments/recommendations*—note concerns and recommendations that would help prospective users.

FOOTNOTE

[1]The CompuTHINK *Resource Guide* is available for $25.00 and the *Resource Diskette* (Apple IIe and IIc) may be purchased for $20.00.

PART X

Assessing Growth in Thinking Abilities

Educators may have to undergo a "paradigm shift" when searching for indicators of improved thinking abilities in students. While behaviors are overt, thinking is covert. We make inferences about students' inner mental processes based on their performance of observable behaviors and language usage.

The development of thinking skills takes time. Many research studies show that demonstrable change in thinking skills occurs only after a two-year period of consistent and sustained instruction that employs a carefully designed curriculum and well-trained teachers. This is contrary to "quick-fix" concepts of educational evaluation.

Another problem stems from an obsession with quantifiable measures. Reducing thinking to a forced selection of multiple choice items, having to express mental functioning in a paper-and-pencil format, and trying to standardize creative insight may be antithetical to our goals.

This section presents the view that numerous assessment procedures must be employed at a variety of levels in many forms. Depending on your definition, different conceptions of thinking demand different assessment practices. We may not be able to assess *creative* thinking in the way that we assess *critical* thinking. Indeed, those intelligent behaviors of the good thinker may be displayed best in real-life problem situations. Thinking is not demonstrated by how many answers students know; rather, it is demonstrated by how they behave when they *don't* know.

50

Test Results From Teaching Thinking

Arthur Whimbey

What scholastic benefits can a school expect from focusing on thinking skills in classes? Data on this question have accumulated gradually, and include measures of improvement on standardized instruments such as the Scholastic Aptitude Test (SAT) and the Nelson-Denny, follow-up studies of course grades, and personal reports of new approaches in handling academic and even social problems.

One example is project SOAR (Stress on Analytical Reasoning), a five-week prefreshman program at Xavier University, a traditionally black university in New Orleans (Hunter and others, 1982). SOAR uses a procedure called Thinking Aloud Pair Problem Solving (TAPS), in which students work in pairs, taking turns reading problems aloud and explaining the thinking processes they use to reach conclusions. The acronym TAPS reminds students that the procedure is designed to *tap* thinking, bringing it out into the open where it can be seen and improved. The program begins with reasoning problems that are not content specific, such as these (Whimbey and Lochhead, 1982):

Verbal analogy: Elephant is to small as _____ is to _____.
a. large, little
b. turtle, slow
c. hippopotamus, mouse
d. lion, timid

Series analysis: 13R 16P 25L 31J _____ _____

Word problem: In a different language, *peg bo* means "green book," *sa bo mai* means "green old house," and *ja mai* means "old man." What is the word for house in this language?

After several hours of practice with such problems, students continue using TAPS but shift over to math problems (word problems, plane geometry, and elementary algebra, for example) and reading comprehension training with special exercises progressing from simple to complex, such as the following examples taken from a 50-exercise series (Whimbey, 1983):

● Of the famous 19th-century painters, Gauguin was born before van Gogh but after Whistler. Matisse was born after van Gogh. Write the names of the four artists in the order they were born.

● Two noteworthy documents for political freedom are the U.S. Constitution, written in 1787, and the French Constitution of 1791. The U.S. Bill of Rights was written after the U.S. Constitution. In contrast, the French Declaration of the Rights of Man was written before the French Constitution, perhaps because the U.S. Bill of Rights was already in existence as a model. The U.S. Declaration of Independence preceded the U.S. Constitution, and England's Petition of Right preceded the Declaration of Independence by about 150 years. Still earlier—by 400 years–England's Magna Carta planted the seeds for freedom from the tyranny of kings. Seven documents of political freedom are mentioned. List them in order.

Through SOAR training, scores of the Nelson-Denny Reading Test have increased an average of two grade levels. For students whose initial SAT total score fell below 700, there has been an average gain of 110 points (Hunter and others, 1982). These gains are now well established; SOAR has served about 175 students per summer for the last five years. But what impresses Xavier's staff more than test score gains are follow-up statistics showing that SOAR students are twice as likely as other Xavier students to pass their freshman science and math courses (Carmichael,

1982). Moreover, the cognitive approach has been incorporated into a number of pre-med courses, which the teachers feel contributes strongly to the fact that for the past two years more Xavier students have been admitted to medical and dental colleges than black students from all the other universities in Louisiana combined (AAMC, 1984).

Readers familiar with experimental design may notice that the SOAR project does not have a control group. However, an experimentally controlled study on the utility of thinking skills training for improving SAT scores was reported by Worsham and Austin in 1983. They found that a group of high school seniors that participated in a thinking skills program called Strategic Reasoning made significantly larger gains on the SAT than a comparable group that did not participate in the program. The Strategic Reasoning program teaches students to analyze cause-effect, serial order, classification, and other relationships through problem solving and extensive small-group discussion of solutions.

Another experimentally controlled study evaluating cognitive-oriented instruction was performed at Bloomfield College (Sadler, 1980). Two remedial math classes (for students scoring at or below the 7th grade level on a College Board standardized test) used TAPS during a portion of each class, with pairs of students taking turns solving problems and explaining their thinking. Two comparable classes used the conventional format of instruction and homework. The TAPS classes gained an average of three grade levels on the College Board test, whereas the other two classes averaged only a one-grade-level improvement. The TAPS procedure has been used since that experiment, and the director of the freshman program, William Sadler (in press), reports that follow-up studies show "most of these students go on to complete college level math and science courses successfully." This is a noteworthy achievement for students whose initial 7th grade math skills indicated that they had learned virtually no math during their four high school years.

What accounts for the improved test scores and grades following cognitive training? Woods (1984), who teaches a course strengthening the problem-solving skills of chemical engineering students, has found that students develop a different approach to processing information. One student wrote:

The course activities showed me the importance of being able to communicate to others what I am doing in a problem. To be able to explain to others, first you must be able to explain to yourself. Doing the TAPS activities made me slow down my thought process and explain everything to myself. This, in turn, makes it easier to realize if you made a mistake, you don't rush right past it.

Since the course, I have become more aware of the problem-solving process. Last week, when a friend came to me for help

with an assignment, I was able to listen to his problems and then explain to him what he had done wrong. Before the course, I would have just given him my assignment to copy what he needed.

Lochhead (1985) has reported similar comments made by students in cognitive-oriented courses ranging from remedial math to advanced physics and engineering.

The transfer of cognitive skills learned in the classroom to social situations has not been widely researched; yet one of the earliest studies in the area did find evidence of students developing a more reflective presence of mind in interpersonal relationships. In that study (Bloom and Broder, 1950), analytically weak students who were failing comprehensive exams in college participated in a "think aloud" program to work through information and answer questions similar to those on the exams. Students became more reflective in their reading and thinking; the change was noted by professors in other classes, and comprehensive exam scores improved significantly, with the degree of improvement correlated to the number of sessions students attended.

In addition, students reported benefits extending beyond the classroom. For instance, one student experiencing emotional difficulties with her family reported receiving a letter from her brother that would have ordinarily upset her. She said that on this occasion she found herself analyzing his arguments and breaking them down, until her brother's written rebuke no longer had a demoralizing effect on her. Another student said of her improved thinking: "I use this in my daily life as well as my problem solving. Now I take one thing at a time instead of having a finger in every pie. Even my mother has noticed this."

The studies reviewed so far concern high school and college students, but elementary school teachers have also found that focusing on mental processes can improve academic success. This is illustrated in the report of a 1st grade teacher working with a pupil who scored in the mastery range on word recognition and comprehension tests, but had difficulty with suffixes and scored below mastery level on this skill. The teacher felt that thinking aloud would be helpful (Short, 1977):

After a brief conversational period, I explained to Scott that I hoped to help him with a system to aid him in reading. We talked about word endings and how the meanings of words were changed by adding special word parts. Scott easily explained the ideas: -s, -es means more than one if added to a noun or right now if added to a verb, -ing means right now, and -ed means past time.

We then proceeded to work through a set of exercises. I asked Scott to (1) read each item aloud, and (2) explain to me how or why he chose each word needed to complete the blanks.

Scott made more accurate choices when he tried each alternative orally than when he read the items silently. He had to be reminded to read the items aloud frequently. Some errors were due to careless reading. Reading the exercises aloud and substituting each choice before picking an answer was helpful. Scott was forced, by oral reading, to listen to the sentence and the choices, and then select the one that made sense. Scott agreed that reading the examples aloud and listening to the choices had helped him. He felt that if he would whisper instead of read aloud, it would serve the same purpose. After the training, Scott was given a worksheet with 20 fresh exercises and was able to answer 18 correctly by employing his new method.

Though implementing this process with very young children may be difficult, I feel it well worth the effort. I plan to incorporate more verbalizing of problem solving, both teacher modeled and student modeled, in reading and math with my 1st graders during the coming year.

Taken together, the studies present a strong argument that focusing on thinking improves academic performance and problem-solving skills. In a world that is becoming increasingly technological, teaching analytical thinking may become a major component of education.

REFERENCES

Admission Action Summary Report. Washington, D.C.: Association of American Medical Colleges, 1984.

Bloom, Benjamin, and Broder, Lois. *Problem-solving Processes of College Students.* Chicago: University of Chicago Press, 1950.

Carmichael, J. W. "Including Problem Solving Skills: Minority Students in the Health Professions." *New Directions In College Learning Assistance* 10 (December 1982): 37-45.

Hunter, Jacqueline; Jones, Lester; Vincent, Harold; and Carmichael, J. W. "Project SOAR: Teaching Cognitive Skills in a Pre-College Program." *Journal of Learning Skills* 1 (Winter 1982): 24-26.

Lochhead, Jack. *Evaluation of Math Program.* Amherst, Mass.: Center for Cognitive Approaches to Mathematics Instructions, University of Massachusetts, 1985.

Sadler, William. "A Holistic Approach to Improving Thinking Skills." *Phi Delta Kappan* (in press, Spring 1985).

Sadler, William. "Teaching Cognitive Skills: An Objective for Higher Education." *National Forum* 40 (Fall 1980): 43-46.

Short, Nancy. *Case Study of Teaching Suffixes.* Bowling Green, Ky.: School Psychology Program, Bowling Green State University, 1977.

Whimbey, Arthur. *Analytical Reading and Reasoning.* Stamford, Conn.: Innovative Sciences, 1983.

Whimbey, Arthur, and Lochhead, Jack. *Problem Solving and Comprehension: A Short Course in Analytical Reasoning.* Philadelphia: Franklin Institute Press, 1982.

Woods, Donald. "Problem Solving Corner: One Major Resource Program." *Journal of College Science Teaching* (May 1984): 469-472.

Worsham, Antoinette, and Austin, Gilbert. "Effects of Teaching Thinking Skills on SAT Scores." *Educational Leadership* 41 (November 1983): 50-51.

51

Evaluating Efforts to Teach Thinking

Stuart C. Rankin

School districts embarking on new programs to improve student thinking need to evaluate them in order to make informed decisions and to communicate about them to the public.

The following guidelines for evaluation include a step-by-step procedure that can guide any evaluation through design to data collection and decision making.

Evaluation for Decision Making

Many educators see evaluation as beginning with objectives. A more useful rationale starts with consideration of what decisions are to be served by the evaluation findings and what kinds of information the decision makers will use.

About 20 years ago, Daniel Stufflebeam proposed a theoretical framework for the kinds and uses of evaluation. That framework, represented in Figure 1, is still appropriate and widely used. The model is often called the CIPP model—Context, Input, Process, and Product. This is the usual order in which these four kinds of evaluation occur when new programs are introduced.

Once a district has made the decision to give priority to the teaching of higher-order thinking, the next decision is what program to choose, adapt, or develop. At this point, formal or informal evaluation is required to judge possible program options. Consultants are sometimes used, materials examined, teacher skills and needs considered, costs reviewed, and the results of process and product evaluations of programs in other districts examined. This input evaluation informs the programming decisions that are made to select or develop particular programs for implementation with certain grades, subjects, and students.

Most educators are familiar with the concept of evaluation as depicted on the right side of Figure 1. Some use the terms "process evaluation" and "product evaluation;" others use "formative evaluation" and "summative evaluation." Either pair is acceptable, and they are used interchangeably here.

Process (formative) evaluation provides two kinds of information. First, it indicates whether the actual program implementation is consistent with the program's design. Second, it identifies adjustments that may be needed to make the program work in the classroom. Program developers cannot predict everything, and many decisions for refinement can come from ongoing process evaluation.

At some point the new program must be judged on its impact on students' ability to think. Are we reasonably certain that the objectives are being met? How well? For what students? At what cost? Should we continue the program, expand it, abort, or make major revisions? These are impact decisions that require summative (product) evaluation information.

Getting the Evaluation Started

Since many school districts today are well into input evaluation to determine which programs to implement, the recommendations of this chapter are devoted to process and product evaluations, which should come well before summative evaluations.

Conducting a summative evaluation too soon can be compared to pulling out a young plant to examine the growth of its root structure. Nothing useful is learned, and

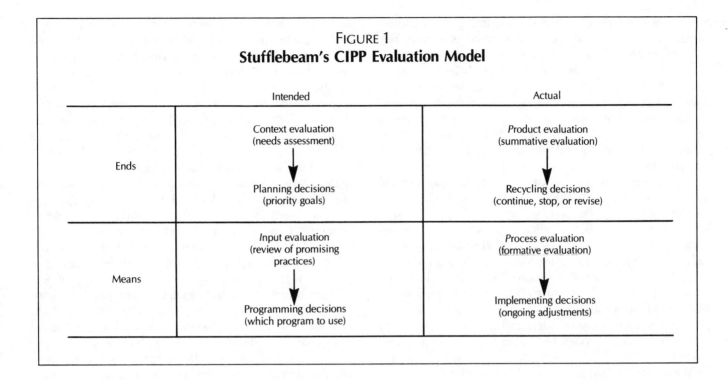

FIGURE 1
Stufflebeam's CIPP Evaluation Model

	Intended	Actual
Ends	Context evaluation (needs assessment) ↓ Planning decisions (priority goals)	Product evaluation (summative evaluation) ↓ Recycling decisions (continue, stop, or revise)
Means	Input evaluation (review of promising practices) ↓ Programming decisions (which program to use)	Process evaluation (formative evaluation) ↓ Implementing decisions (ongoing adjustments)

the uprooting process damages the growth. When funding restrictions or political pressures require premature product evaluation, there may be no choice but to comply. Otherwise, formal product evaluation should be delayed until after programs have been tried out and revised more than once.

After the programs have been tested and revised in the crucible of real classrooms, a scientific, summative evaluation will be appropriate. At that time the objectives must be clearly stated and measured as precisely as possible. Controls are needed for reliability, validity, objectivity, and comparison; and side effects and costs must be examined.

The time to conduct process or formative evaluation is when we begin to try out new methods of teaching higher-order thought. We need to look at student products, test results, and student behaviors, as well as observe the teaching/learning situation, talk to the teachers and students, keep track of progress and problems, and look for ways to improve the program. This process evaluation procedure ought not be left to chance. To be useful it, too, needs a careful design—although less rigid than a product evaluation design.

The same general steps are appropriate to both formative and summative evaluation. The examples that follow illustrate both formative and summative evaluation. The steps are organized into three stages: designing the evaluation, collecting the data, and using the findings.

Designing the Evaluation

1. *Appoint the evaluator.* Someone needs to be responsible for the evaluation. In large districts, this task is usually assigned to a member of the research and evaluation department. In small districts, evaluation will probably be an additional responsibility of a principal, teacher, or curriculum director; or an outside agency may be employed.

2. *Determine the decisions.* The evaluator's first job is to discuss the program with the superintendent or other decision makers to determine what decisions about the program will be made, the evidence on which they will be based, the timing of the report, the objectives of the program, who will receive the evaluation information, and any political constraints. The reason most evaluation reports gather dust is that no one agrees in advance on why they are being done.

3. *Indicators and objectives.* In product evaluation the indicators are usually limited to evidence of learning and program costs. Process evaluation is concerned with those factors but also with staff and student opinions, the fit between the intended program and the actual program, the practices that facilitate program implementation, and those that impede it. Time will be well spent at the evaluation design stage if teachers and other staff members can agree on the criteria for evaluating the program's effectiveness.

School people can develop some indicators of higher-order thinking from an examination of items on tests they use regularly. Such tests may be national, state, district, or teacher-made. Some questions to ask are: Which questions measure higher-order thought? How do they differ from questions that measure recall, low-level comprehension, or basic skills? What differences are seen when these results are disaggregated into two groups with one score for lower-level questions and another score for higher-order questions?

Another source of indicators are tests especially designed to measure thinking, such as the Cornell Critical Thinking Test, the Watson-Glaser, or the New Jersey Test of Reasoning Skills. A list of such tests is included in the "Resources for Teaching Thinking" section of this book. California, New Jersey, and Connecticut are among the states developing assessment procedures for higher-order thinking. Many states will soon have objectives and sample measurement items to share.

Students can show evidence of learning to reason in ways other than through tests, long reading samples, and word problems, although such approaches ought not be excluded. Rather than relying solely on word problems, the Detroit Public Schools have developed mathematics test items for grades 1-8 that emphasize problem solving and use diagrams, charts, pictures, and puzzles to present the problems.

Evaluation, especially at the early stages, need not depend on tests at all. Teachers can observe student use of inference, assumptions, criteria, evidence, and judgment. Teachers who ask open-ended questions, probe for higher levels of abstraction, seek counterexamples, and ask "why" provide opportunities not just for students thought, but for observation of such thought.

Student products can also indicate higher-order thinking. The sorting or re-sorting of objects or ideas according to some criteria is a product of thought. Drawings and paintings can symbolize ideas and be used to solve technical art problems. Writing samples are ideal products that can indicate higher-level understanding as well as complex writing skills and creative interpretation—and they need not be long.

Students' descriptions of their own thought processes are frequently used as indicators of higher-order thinking. This practice has merit for understanding one's one thinking patterns and for providing information from which teachers can evaluate the level of development. However, it may be disadvantageous at times because premature verbalization can impede solutions and understanding and prevent students from making discoveries for themselves. If students are to understand the concepts of mathematics—and not just calculate—we must evaluate their understanding of the concepts in their products, in our observations, on our teacher-made tests, and on our district tests.

When the goal is to develop critical thinking skills, the evaluation must require demonstration of whatever skills we choose. Students may be asked to distinguish among premises, inferences, assumptions, interpretations, conclusions, problems, and decisions. They may be asked to draw reasonable conclusions and defend them. They may be asked to clarify a problem or organize relevant information.

If the goal desired is creative thinking, the evaluation strategy must provide an opportunity for students to demonstrate growth in the relevant skills. The measure of such an ability is not shown by solving ten subtraction problems, for example, but might be found in the answer to: "The number four is the answer to what questions?"

Creative writing samples are sometimes returned to students with more comments on grammar than on new ideas or inventive use of language. We should not ignore bad form, but if we teach for substance, we should evaluate for it too. The listing of all possible uses of an object is another common indicator of inventive thought.

When the higher-order thinking skill is decision making, the evaluation task must require a decision. One approach is to provide a decision situation and ask the students what to do *next*. Evaluation of decision making can also be put into a test format by giving several choices from which students must select what to do next, with the wrong answer foils characterized by wrong order, ineffective action, or irrelevant action.

Careful attention to indicators of higher-order thought will help the evaluator state the objectives to be evaluated in a form that makes their measurement clear.

4. *Data collection.* The evaluation design should show how the information will be obtained. This may involve tests, observations, interviews, documentation, and other strategies. All instruments must be identified.

5. *Use of results.* The design should indicate how the findings will be compared, analyzed, and used to make decisions about the program.

6. *Implementation plan.* The evaluation design should specify the tasks to be completed, who will do them, the calendar, and the budget for the evaluation.

7. *Approval of design.* Before the design for evaluation is implemented, it should be reviewed by the participants and the decision makers to be sure that it is feasible and will be supported. This often-omitted step is a key to ensuring that evaluation findings are used.

Collecting Data

Once the design is approved, the evaluation can proceed. Controls are established and data are collected.

1. *Controls.* There are so many variables in education that it is hard to pinpoint the cause of changes in output. Sometimes variables such as highly able students or outstanding teachers who volunteered for the program can give false assurances that it is the *program* that makes the difference when it is really the *students* or the *staff members.* Objectivity in the evaluator helps. Matched or balanced control groups can help. Random assignment of students and teachers can help. Being very clear about the objectives and the measures can help. And repeating the treatment over time or with a different group or teacher can also help.

At the formative stages of developing a program for teaching thinking, it is all right to let enthusiasm outweigh skepticism. But in the long run we want to know what really works and what doesn't. If we are to develop programs that provide higher-order thinking capability for all students and that work for most teachers, then at some point we need to become skeptical, scientific, and rigorous about our program evaluation. This requires careful measurement controls.

2. *Data collection methods.* Since higher-order teaching methods can result in better thinking skills and also improve basic skills, both should be measured. Tests provide quick information, but observation can also yield a wealth of formative information. While outside observers are usually more objective than insiders, participating teachers can also provide insights on how to improve the program by observing each other, student behaviors, and student products.

A very effective technique for collecting process information is to convene participating staff members and answer three important questions: What features of the program are working well and should be kept? What features are inhibiting it and should be stopped? What features are missing and should be started? This "keep, stop, start" process produces useful formative information.

Documentation is a strategy that has recently found a legitimate place in the domain of evaluation. Assigning a documenter to observe and record decisions, events, problems, and progress can serve process evaluation needs very well and has the added benefit of helping with public relations. Documentation blends well with naturalistic observation, goal-free evaluation, and cost benefit evaluation. A part-time documenter is a worthwhile investment.

Using the Findings

1. *Analyzing data.* Test results, observation records, staff discussion summaries, and documentation comprise much of the evaluation data that the evaluator must organize before analysis. This may require tabulating responses; charting test scores; summarizing observation reports; or reviewing written, audio, or video recordings. Test scores may require statistical analyses. Student products, records of observations, and summaries are best analyzed by a team of curriculum experts or program participants for ideas to improve the program.

The analysis must determine the extent to which objectives have been met and, if possible, the reasons for the performance on objectives. Cost data must also be analyzed so that some price can be put on the benefits. Results are sometimes statistically significant but so small or costly that alternative programs should be considered. Any other evidence requested by the decision makers must also be analyzed.

2. *Implications and decisions.* The purpose of evaluation is to serve decisions. Now that the benefits, costs, progress, and problems are known, the information should be presented orally and in writing for decision making. Summative information is always results-oriented. Decisions will be made about whether to keep or abort the programs, based on their benefits and costs. Hard data are more effective than opinions.

On the other hand, formative decisions use all kinds of information, including observations, opinions, and even hunches. But they also require evidence of attainment and cost information. Decision makers need formative evaluation findings to strengthen their programs. The business of improving our ability to teach higher-order thought processes will benefit from careful and sensible evaluation. But the evaluation should serve the program, not the other way around.

52

California Assesses Critical Thinking

Peter Kneedler

I n 1985, 280,000 California 8th grade students will take a history-social studies test in which 40 percent of the questions will address critical thinking skills (CTS). The primary purpose of the test is to provide school personnel with detailed information about the performance of different groups of students.

Three different approaches will be used to assess students' critical thinking skills: objective questions, a student essay, and CTS vocabulary. Although the major part of the assessment consists of objective questions, the optional essay portion, which will be scored locally, is also integral. The third part of the test, the CTS vocabulary, requires students to demonstrate their understanding of terms associated with critical thinking, such as generalization, hypothesis, inference, and premise.

Critical Thinking Skills for Grade Eight

The critical thinking skills assessment was developed by the statewide History-Social Science Assessment Advisory Committee, which is composed of California's curriculum leadership and selected critical thinking advisors from across the country. These individuals agreed that critical thinking at the 8th grade level should focus on defining problems, judging information related to problems, drawing conclusions, and solving problems. The committee generally defines critical thinking as those behaviors associated with deciding what to believe and do.

The committee felt that 8th graders, in *defining prob-*

lems, should be able to identify central issues, compare similarities and differences, determine relevance of information, formulate appropriate questions, and express problems clearly and concisely. In *judging information*, students should be able to distinguish among fact, opinion, and reasoned judgment; check consistency and identify unstated assumptions; recognize and minimally reason within value orientations and ideologies; recognize bias, emotionalism, propaganda, and semantic slanting; and recognize stereotypes and cliches. In *solving problems and drawing conclusions,* students should be able to recognize the adequacy of data, identify reasonable alternatives or solutions, predict possible consequences, and test conclusions or hypotheses.

The CTS Process Model

The committee—using advice from its members, the state curriculum framework, teacher survey results, and CTS advisors—identified 12 essential skills for critical thinking, which are defined in Figure 1. These skills are taught as part of a larger process involved in solving problems and reaching conclusions. Although they are presented serially for clarity and understanding, students use them and others in a variety of combinations to solve problems.

The process model in Figure 2, (p. 278) begins with unassessed information that students and adults must deal with all their lives. Basic skills in social studies help students prepare and organize information. The skills that are assessed in the objective portion of the statewide test are italicized in the center of the process model. The remaining skills will be assessed in the essay portion of the test.

FIGURE 1
Twelve Essential Critical Thinking Skills

DEFINING AND CLARIFYING THE PROBLEM

1. **Identify central issues or problems**
   The ability to identify the main idea or point of a passage, an argument, or a political cartoon, for example. At the higher levels, students are expected to identify central issues in complex political arguments. Implies the ability to identify major components of an argument, such as reasons and conclusions.

2. **Compare similarities and differences**
   The ability to compare similarities and differences among two or more objects, living things, ideas, events, or situations at the same or different points in time. Implies the ability to identify distinctive attributes and to organize information into categories for different purposes.

3. **Determine which information is relevant**
   The ability to make distinctions between verifiable and unverifiable, relevant and nonrelevant, and essential and incidental information.

4. **Formulate appropriate questions**
   The ability to formulate questions that will lead to a deeper and clearer understanding of an issue or situation, and of different viewpoints from which an issue or situation can be approached.

JUDGING INFORMATION RELATED TO THE PROBLEM

5. **Distinguish among fact, opinion, and reasoned judgment**
   The ability to apply criteria for judging the quality of observation and inference.

6. **Check consistency**
   The ability to determine whether given statements or symbols are consistent with each other and their context. For example, the ability to determine whether the different points or issues in a political argument are logically connected and agree with the central issue.

7. **Identify unstated assumptions**
   The ability to identify what is taken for granted, though not explicitly stated, in an argument.

8. **Recognize stereotypes and cliches**
   The ability to identify fixed or conventional notions about a person, group, or idea.

9. **Recognize bias, emotional factors, propaganda, and semantic slanting**
   The ability to identify partialities and prejudices in written and graphic materials. Includes the ability to determine the credibility of sources (gauge reliability, expertise, and objectivity).

10. **Recognize different value orientations and ideologies**
    The ability to recognize the similarities and differences among different value orientations and ideologies.

SOLVING PROBLEMS/DRAWING CONCLUSIONS

11. **Recognize the adequacy of data**
    The ability to decide whether the information provided is sufficient in quality and quantity to justify a conclusion, decision, generalization, or plausible hypothesis.

12. **Predict probable consequences**
    The ability to predict probable consequences of an event or series of events.

Illustrative Objective Test Questions

Let's look at three of the critical thinking skills and the kinds of questions that are used to evaluate them.

Skill: Formulate appropriate questions (under the category of Defining and Clarifying the Problem). Questions related to this skill test students' ability to formulate questions that will lead to a deeper and clearer understanding of an issue or situation. Such questions can help turn a ponderous, general issue to a more specific, manageable one. For instance:

- Which of the following questions would be *most* important to ask in determining whether someone had a fair trial?
   - A. What was the ethnic background of the judge?
   - B. Was the accused guilty?
   - C. Was the judge a man or a woman?
   - *D. Was the accused represented by a lawyer?

To answer the following question, students are asked to look at two maps, one of central Europe in 1935, the other of central Europe in 1949. The test question then reads:

- Which of the following questions might lead to better understanding of the relationship between these two maps?
   - A. Who is the present political leader of Poland?
   - B. What are the main differences between the governments of Hungary and Rumania?
   - C. Is Czechoslovakia a major world power?
   - *D. What happened in central Europe between 1935 and 1949?

Skill: Recognize bias, emotional factors, propaganda, and semantic slanting (under the category of Judging Information Related to the Problem). Questions related to this skill test students' ability to identify partialities and prejudices in written and graphic materials, including the ability to determine the credibility of sources such as gauging reliability, expertise, and objectivity. In order to identify bias in written material, students should be able to examine political cartoons, pamphlets, and other symbolic materials and determine author intent. For instance:

- *"One of the most vicious movements that has yet been instituted by the crackpots, the Communists, and the parlor pinks of this country is trying to browbeat the American Red Cross into taking the labels off the blood bank they are building up for our wounded boys in the service so that it will not show whether it is Negro blood or white blood."* (John E. Rankin, during World War II.)

   Which of the following sets of words makes the above passage unfairly biased?

FIGURE 2
The Critical Thinking Skills Process Model

UNASSESSED INFORMATION

From school, home, community, books, magazines, television, newspapers, maps, and so forth.

BASIC SKILLS

Skills that help organize and prepare information, such as ability to understand and use written and symbolic materials, locate and organize information in textbooks and reference materials, and social studies vocabulary.

CRITICAL THINKING SKILLS*

Defining and Clarifying the Problem
a. Identify central issues or problems*
b. Compare similarities and differences*
c. Determine which information is relevant*
d. Formulate appropriate questions*
e. Express problems clearly and concisely

Judging Information Related to the Problem
a. Distinguish among fact, opinion, and reasoned judgment*
b. Check consistency*
c. Identify unstated assumptions*
d. Recognize stereotypes and cliches*
e. Recognize bias, emotional factors, propaganda, and semantic slanting*
f. Recognize value orientations and ideologies*

Solving Problems/Drawing Conclusions
a. Recognize the adequacy of data*
b. Identify reasonable alternatives
c. Test conclusions or hypotheses
d. Predict probable consequences*

*Assessed on the objective portion of the statewide test.

PROCESS OUTCOMES

Having learned critical thinking skills, students are able to:

● Assess information around them, define problems, weigh evidence, and draw conclusions.
● Participate effectively as citizens in a representative democracy
● Defend and justify intellectual and personal values, present and critique arguments, and appreciate the viewpoints of others.

A. "Movements," "instituted," "country," "service."

*B. "Vicious," "crackpots," "parlor pinks," "Communists."

C. "American Red Cross," "labels," "building," "blood."

D. "Blood bank," "show," "Negro," "white."

- Accompanying the following question is a cartoon drawing of a politician giving a speech in which he is saying, ". . . and so I say to you, if we continue to give in to the outrageous demands made by these young hoodlums, we will allow them to destroy every trace of law and order we now have." The question then reads, "Which two words make this politician's statement biased?"

A. "Demands," "order."

B. "Continue," "law."

C. "Young," "allow."

*D. "Outrageous," "hoodlums."

Skill: Predict probable consequences (under the category of Solving Problems/Drawing Conclusions). Questions related to this skill test students' ability to predict probable consequences of an event or series of events that might occur as the result of a particular action. This is a process of thinking through a decision and anticipating its effects. Many of the assessment items related to this skill deal with economic issues. In most cases, the test-taker is presented with a situation, given an additional factor, and then asked to select a response that might logically represent what would happen next. For instance:

- If the United States had only one political party, which one of the following problems might arise and pose a threat to our country?

*A. Elected officials would not be obliged to carry out the people's wishes.

B. Party conventions would no longer be necessary.

C. We would no longer have a military.

D. Having only one party is ideal.

- Suppose that United States farmers experienced several years of drought. Many cattle died because of lack of water and inadequate food. What do you think would happen to beef prices?

A. People would import less beef.

*B. The price of beef would rise.

C. The price of beef would drop.

D. Beef would completely disappear from grocery stores.

Critical Thinking Skills Vocabulary Questions

The assessment committee identified 103 vocabulary terms associated with critical thinking. In most of the test questions, CTS terms are placed in a social studies context. For example:

- Randy was to write a report on the Civil War, focusing on its battles and outcome. He included a detailed description of how General Lee was dressed when he surrendered to Grant. Randy's teacher told him that this information was *incidental* to the report. This means that it was:

A. Confusing.

*B. Not important information.

C. Not very interesting information.

D. In need of a graph or diagram.

- During a world history class, Mr. Johnson told his students that *propaganda* was an important tool of the Nazi regime. This means that the Nazi party:

*A. Used selected information to support one side of a story.

B. Used a secret process to manufacture weapons and machine tools.

C. Developed a network of spies in foreign countries.

D. Implemented a genetic selection process to ensure a "master race."

The Student Essay

In the future, districts will have the option of participating in the student essay component of the history-social science assessment. The state will provide an essay report based on a statewide sample, and will give districts procedures for local training and scoring, which are now in the developmental stage.

Limitations

Any test has its limitations. While tests may provide an overall view of content priorities, they cannot replace teachers' daily observations of their students' problem-solving and decision-making abilities. Statewide assessment should not replace teacher-made tests, which can be much longer and employ open-ended questions. Nor should statewide assessment supplant the many other ways students can demonstrate an understanding of history-social science, such as through oral or graphic presentation or the effective use of argument and group discussion.

One of the dangers of any testing program that assesses knowledge is the tendency to trivialize the content area and narrow the curriculum. Recall questions are easy to write and can be made more difficult by focusing on esoteric aspects of subject material. If what is tested is what is taught, teachers may then address trivial aspects of the content area in the classroom. The consequence is fact-based instruction that produces students who are more concerned with memorizing facts than with processing information and solving problems.

Testing programs that attempt to appeal to very large multistate audiences offer an additional danger. Tests, like textbooks, that cater to large and varied audiences often regress to a narrow mean. What suffers is critical thinking. CTS items are much more difficult to develop and require considerable staff development and new materials. Because of these dangers, the statewide assessment advisory committee decided to strongly emphasize the *process* of critical thinking rather than recall of information.

Rationale

While the knowledge explosion we have heard so much about can facilitate decisions by providing more relevant information, the sheer volume of information can render the task of making rational decisions more difficult. This is coupled with an increasing population that is better educated and occupies a world that is linked by satellites, computers, and television. Never before has the demand for ways to process information been greater, and never before has the need for schools to prepare students for effective participation been more critical.

Critical thinking can help students make the important journey to the other person's perspective. The ability to step outside of oneself and examine objectively the ideas and feelings of others who may be different than ourselves (in terms of sex, race, religion, or culture) is a skill that requires practice, but one essential to a successful democracy.

This ability to think critically is what distinguishes humankind from lower animals. We owe it to ourselves and future generations to occupy this world rationally, and to not accept what we hear and see on faith alone. Critical thinkers use critical thinking skills and possess an *attitude* that enables them to maintain an objective, constructive, and questioning stance toward all the information they receive. Finally, critical thinkers *participate*—they vote, examine issues, communicate without jargon, offer opinions, and value the viewpoints of others.

BIBLIOGRAPHY

Aubyn, G. *The Art of Argument.* New York: Emerson Books, 1980.
Branson, M. *Inquiry Experiences in American History.* Lexington, Mass.: Ginn and Company, 1975.
Ennis, R. H. *A Concept of Critical Thinking.* Cornell Social Science Research Center, Volume 32, Number 1, 1962.
History-Social Science Framework. Sacramento: California State Department of Education, 1981.
Hitchcock, D. *Critical Thinking—A Guide to Evaluating Information.* Toronto: Methuen, 1982.
Nosich, G. *Reasons and Arguments.* Belmont, Calif.: Wadsworth Publishing Co., 1982.
Phillips, R. C. *Teaching for Thinking in High School Social Studies.* Reading, Mass.: Addison-Wesley, 1974.

53

What Are We Looking For and How Can We Find It?

Joan Boykoff Baron and Bena Kallick

Tests of thinking skills are limited only by the thought that goes into their design. Statewide tests can provide a rich data source for classroom teachers if they are designed to measure higher-order thinking. They may include a variety of question formats—such as multiple-choice items; short constructed responses; and longer, more sustained tasks such as writing samples and design of experiments. However, there is a good deal more to our understanding of children's thinking than what can be measured by paper-and-pencil tests. This chapter provides some recommendations and insights to assessing higher-order thinking garnered from statewide and classroom experience, including both qualitative and quantitative measures.

Assessing Thinking on Statewide Tests

Although there is some truth in Arthur Costa's assertion that "standardized tests assess what is measurable but insignificant," it does not have to be true. It does not necessarily follow that all tests are, by their very nature, trivial. One need only look at the new California Social Studies test (see Chapter 52) to see some fine examples of critical thinking skills that are appropriately measured by multiple-choice items. Similarly, in Connecticut, we have been measuring higher-order thinking skills in a concerted way for the past four years. In 1982-83, we began by assigning a Bloom's Taxonomy level (Bloom, 1974) to every item on our Connecticut Assessment of Educational Progress (CAEP) social studies tests in order to be certain to adequately represent the higher levels of the taxonomy. In 1983-84, on our

CAEP English language arts tests, we measured text level writing skills (focus, organization, and support) through a variety of approaches designed to get an accurate picture of how well students can recognize and produce writing that exhibits these features. In 1984-85, on our CAEP science tests, we included multiple-choice items, open-ended written questions, and a series of practical exercises to ascertain how well students can recognize, understand, and apply the scientific method. In 1985-86, our new Fourth Grade Connecticut Mastery Test will include higher-order thinking items in reading, writing, and mathematics, and under development is a separate test designed to measure critical thinking, reasoning, and problem-solving skills.

The Connecticut assessment results are consistent with the findings of the National Assessment of Educational Progress as well as the findings of many blue ribbon panels. (See Education Commission of the States.) Like their national counterparts, Connecticut students have many facts at their command and can solve single-step problems. However, when they are asked to solve multi-step problems or do more sustained thinking, performance drops off. Specifically, students have difficulty when they are asked to infer, integrate, evaluate, condense, or synthesize several pieces of information or apply knowledge to new situations. In addition, when students are asked to develop and maintain a point of view and support it with reliable and sufficient evidence, performance is poor. (See CAEP English Language Arts Highlights brochure.)

In social studies, we learned that higher-level questions are not necessarily more difficult than lower-level questions. It is often more difficult to recall obscure facts than to make judgments about the best reason to believe a certain opinion. Often, the higher-order thinking questions contain within them all the information necessary to answer them. Therefore, it is often misleading to aggregate and report the scores for each of the cognitive levels separately (knowledge, comprehension, application, analysis, synthesis, and evaluation). In order to make a valid direct comparison, it is necessary to use a process called "nesting," which measures the same concept across different cognitive levels. For example, on our grade 8 test, 59 percent of the students recognized that the term "supply and demand" applies to the relationship between price and the

availability of a product as well as people's wants and needs. However, on a related question that asked students to apply that concept, only 38 percent knew that the highest price occurs when supply is low and demand is great.

Our social studies test demonstrated that students generally have little difficulty with simple, direct reading of data presented on graphs, tables, and charts. However, if they are asked to do anything more with the data, performance drops off. As illustrated in the top question in Figure

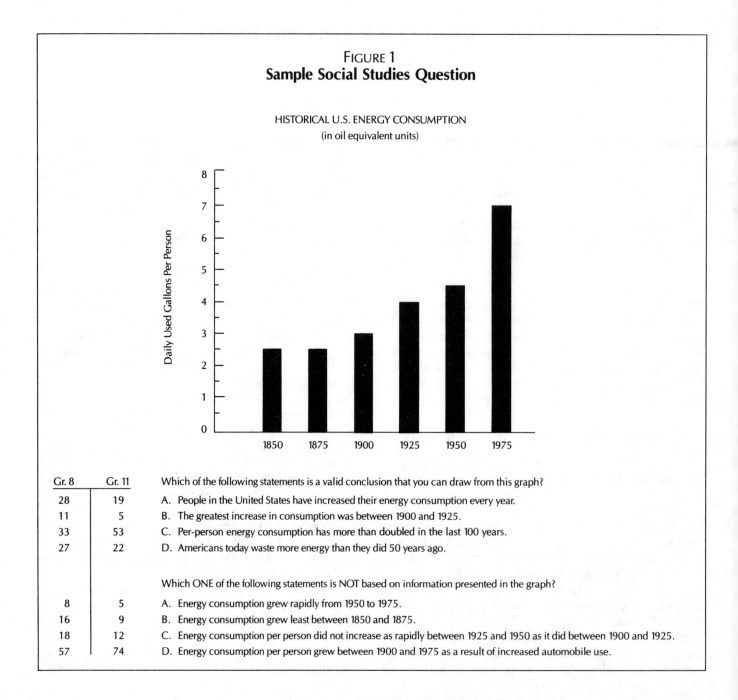

FIGURE 1
Sample Social Studies Question

HISTORICAL U.S. ENERGY CONSUMPTION
(in oil equivalent units)

Gr. 8	Gr. 11	Which of the following statements is a valid conclusion that you can draw from this graph?
28	19	A. People in the United States have increased their energy consumption every year.
11	5	B. The greatest increase in consumption was between 1900 and 1925.
33	53	C. Per-person energy consumption has more than doubled in the last 100 years.
27	22	D. Americans today waste more energy than they did 50 years ago.
		Which ONE of the following statements is NOT based on information presented in the graph?
8	5	A. Energy consumption grew rapidly from 1950 to 1975.
16	9	B. Energy consumption grew least between 1850 and 1875.
18	12	C. Energy consumption per person did not increase as rapidly between 1925 and 1950 as it did between 1900 and 1925.
57	74	D. Energy consumption per person grew between 1900 and 1975 as a result of increased automobile use.

1, almost half of the 11th grade students and two-thirds of the 8th grade students had difficulty in identifying a valid conclusion presented in a graph.

Another finding on our social studies test is that students have difficulty in dealing with pairs of ideas. If students are asked which two rights or values are in conflict in a particular situation, many are unable to answer correctly. The same is true when students are asked to draw logical conclusions from two statements.

Finally, students have difficulty with the concept of inverse variation. They seem to be unaware of the fact that one thing can go up while another thing goes down. Just over a third of the grade 11 students felt that an increase in either the rate of inflation or the sales tax was associated with increased buying power of consumers.

In our English language arts tests, one of the most important writing features assessed was the recognition and production of adequate support for a position statement. As illustrated in Figure 2, when students were confronted with an example of an essay with insufficient support, only 40 percent of the 8th graders recognized the deficiency. (The other 60 percent were equally divided among the other three distractors.)

On a different section of our language arts test, students were asked to write a persuasive letter to a television critic, either encouraging him to write more editorials like the one he had written or asking him to take back what he had written. Only 5 percent of the 8th graders and 2 percent of the 11th graders wrote essays that were considered strong enough to convince the critic. Fewer than 5 percent of the grade 8 students provided support that was judged adequately deep, sufficiently credible, or amply numerous.

The grade 11 students performed slightly better, with 17 percent providing sufficient support to validate the position and 31 percent explaining the stated reasons with ample explanation.

On any statewide writing assignment, the question always arises about whether to include the scoring criteria with the topic. Because we developed a 20-item scoring guide that included holistic, primary trait, and 18 separate analytic elements, our advisory committee felt that including it might intimidate students and cause some to be so fearful about being judged that they might not write at all. So, we did not provide the criteria. The problem inherent in our solution was that if performance was found to be poor on some of those elements (which it was) then we really would not know whether students did not use sufficient support or effective organization because they didn't know how or because we didn't specifically ask them for it. In order to address this problem, we isolated the separate elements of good writing (focus, organization, support, tone, mechanics, and so forth) and developed a separate set of exercises. These exercises were administered to a comparable group of students in our state sample. For example, in the exercise presented in Figure 3 (p. 284) students were asked to provide the support for a PTA drive for school computers. On this exercise, the 8th graders outperformed the 11th graders, with just over a quarter of the 8th graders providing two or more credible facts, examples, and/or reasons as support. The corresponding number of 11th graders was 12 percent.

These three different item types provide a consistent profile of students' inability to recognize inadequate support in someone else's writing and produce it themselves

---

FIGURE 2
Sample English Language Arts Question

Student #2 was asked to write an essay in response to the following question: "Should we always keep promises, or are there times when it is better to break them?" This is what the student wrote:

> We should always keep promises we make. We should not make promises we can't keep. If you make a promise, you should always keep it because you can get hurt. There are some people who will hurt you if you make a promise you can't keep.

2. Which of the following is probably this essay's greatest weakness?

   A. It refers to the audience as "you".
   B. It does not tell a story.
   C. It does not provide enough supporting examples.
   D. It does not answer the question that was asked.

FIGURE 3
Sample Writing Question

EDITOR'S NOTE: As it stands now, this editorial will not convince our readers to contribute money. The article needs to provide more specific reasons why people should donate money.

ASSIGNMENT: Add facts or examples to back up the opinions given in the editorial.

EXAMPLE: Original

> Send the recreation department one dollar to help build the new gym. Everyone will really enjoy using it. I know I will.

Revision

> Send the recreation department one dollar to help build the new gym. *It will be a place where young children and teens can play on rainy days. There will be Friday night dances and Sunday bingo for senior citizens.*
>
> Everyone will enjoy using it.

NOW ADD MORE SPECIFIC SUPPORT TO THE FOLLOWING EDITORIAL.

> Our next PTA drive will help our school buy computers. I think computers would be fun and useful, as well. _____
>
> _____
>
> _____
>
> _____
>
> _____
>
> _____
>
> _____
>
> Because computers are the wave of the future, give generously.

in either a persuasive letter or in a short, constructed response in which it is specifically requested.

In science, we again used several formats to obtain information about students' proficiency in the scientific method. These included multiple-choice items, open-ended short essays, as well as a test that asked students to conduct a practical experiment.

Our upcoming 4th grade Connecticut Mastery Test represents both a continuation and an extension in our thinking about thinking skills. Up until now, our assessment of thinking skills has been incorporated into content domains. We measured scientific thinking in the context of science and the application of economic concepts in the context of social studies. Similarly, on our forthcoming grade 4 tests in reading, writing, and mathematics, thinking skills have been incorporated. The reading test devotes a third of its items to evaluative comprehension in which many of the same critical thinking skills assessed in the California Social Studies test have been incorporated into reading passages. Thus, students are asked to judge the authority and validity of evidence; judge the consistency, relevance, and logical order of statements in a passage; judge the sufficiency of support based on evidence or reasoned judgment; and recognize consistent tone.

On the 4th grade Connecticut Mastery Test in mathematics, students are asked to identify problems that present insufficient information for their solution and problems that have extraneous information from which students must select the relevant information. They are also asked to complete number series.

An extension in our thinking comes about through our present attempt to isolate, separate from subject matter, significant and instructable thinking skills that are developmentally appropriate for most 4th grade students to master. The word "most" is critical because, unfortunately, many still confuse thinking skills with the concept of "giftedness." Virtually all students can and should learn to think. As Matthew Lipman stated, "Thinking is more basic than reading." To help us identify the criteria students should use in evaluating thinking, we have turned to a group of philosophers. Robert Ennis has begun the development of a multiple-choice Connecticut Critical Thinking Test for our grade 4 students. In addition, Matthew Lipman, Richard Paul, and Robert Swartz are helping to shape our thinking. For insights into thinking strategies, we have turned to several cognitive psychologists. Robert Sternberg is working on an application of his triarchic theory of intelligence to our 4th grade population. We are also looking for ways to include the characteristics of the IDEAL Problem Solver as defined by John Bransford. Further, David Perkins' knowledge as design model and Ray Nickerson's fine syntheses of thinking and reasoning skills are informing our efforts.

It should be clear from the above examples that statewide tests can provide a rich data source for classroom teachers if, during the design of these tests, care is taken to measure thinking skills. Statewide tests can include a variety of question formats, including multiple-choice items, short constructed responses, and longer, more sustained tasks such as writing samples and designing experiments. However, statewide tests are limited to pencil-and-paper and we all know that there is a good deal more to our understanding of children's thinking than what can be measured by paper-and-pencil.

Measuring Classroom Thinking

There are ways, other than tests, to measure what is taking place in classrooms conducive to critical thinking. What might we see in a classroom where thinking is encouraged? First, the room is arranged so that students can see and hear each other during a discussion. Second, students are engaged with one another and not just directing their comments to the teacher. Third, the teacher is a facilitator for students' ideas. The teacher clarifies, encourages, seeks explanations, requests illustrations, and suggests alternative ideas. In other words, the teacher models the behavior desired in students as they enter a critical thinking discussion. The following are four frequently used techniques for measuring thinking in the classroom.

1. *Observations.* Many teachers keep a journal or log to record classroom activities and ask students to keep one as well. Journals are a rich source of data about what takes place during a particular lesson, and time should be set aside to allow students to reflect on their thinking. Systematic observations over time are necessary to provide a sufficient lens for understanding and evaluating thinking.

Journals can be analyzed for themes or patterns. For instance, teachers can analyze their own journals by asking such questions as:

● Is there a difference over time in the quality of students' responses to materials?

● Are students showing evidence of their ability to deal with new situations by using thinking skills and strategies?

● Do class discussions take longer than they did a few weeks ago? Is this because there is more wandering or because the discussion reflects more thoughtful questioning?

● What is significant about my questions?

● What is significant about my students' questions?

When examining students' journals, teachers can ask:

● Are my students more aware of their own thinking processes? Do they know how they approach a new problem or situation?

• Is there evidence that students are able to build a more persuasive argument for their points of view?

• Do they pay attention to others' points of view?

• Are their points of view clear? Logical? Founded on evidence more than emotion?

• Do my students question how they and others know what they know?

2. *Tape recordings.* Video and audio recorders enable teachers to study students' verbal as well as nonverbal responses. Collected systematically over time, these data should be analyzed to find out:

• How many questions were teacher initiated. If our assumption is that student-initiated questioning is a sign of critical thinking, then this analysis will be informative.

• The quality of teacher-asked questions. Do the questions require higher-order thinking on the students' part? For example, do the questions begin with words like "distinguish," "contrast," "compare," and "analyze," and extend with "Can you give me an example? Do you know anything else that has the same attributes? What does this situation remind you of? Which do you prefer, and why?"

• The quality of students' questions. Do they appear to be asking questions to one another that force depth and understanding of the material? Are their questions relevant?

• Whether the teacher encourages and accepts different points of view. For example, one way to indicate acceptance of any view is to say, "Some people say that you need a special environment to be creative; others say that is not necessary. What do you think and why?" On the other hand, is the teacher too accepting, to the point that students are not being stretched to think more sharply?

• Which portions of the discussion were productive, and why.

• Which portions of the discussion reached a dead end, and why.

3. *Interviews.* Students who interview one another about their thinking strategies can record the results and analyze or compare how the other students' strategies fit into their own scheme and understandings.

Teachers can bring community members into the classroom to be interviewed. Preparation for the interview process (level of questions) as well as the interview itself (students' ability to develop probes) will be an excellent indication of critical thinking abilities.

Teachers can interview students about their thinking strategies. It is critical that teachers not make this an instructive conference in the typical "teaching" sense. They should draw the student out and try to evaluate both the student's thinking process and the content. These data may lead to insights about the student's instruction.

4. *Student work.* A portfolio for each student might include writings, drawings, and other work that can be examined from different perspectives—such as papers that reflect work assigned by the teacher as well as student-initiated work. The more variety in the samples, the deeper our understanding of the student's capacity for thinking. If selections show both a lateral and a vertical expansion of knowledge, we can see student growth in a new light. Student portfolios are especially useful for parent conferences.

Establishing Criteria

One of the most difficult aspects of evaluating thinking is selecting and establishing criteria. Most often, there is not a clear standard against which to measure thinking. First, teachers need to establish criteria that appear to be appropriate for their students. Students can help establish such criteria, for example, by discussing their own characteristics of a good essay. They might then write their essays and self-evaluate, peer evaluate, and have the teacher evaluate. Or they might read essays by well-known essayists and establish why those essays are excellent. Once again, they need to establish criteria that can be matched against what writers consider to be criteria for a good essay.

Implications for Staff Development

Reflecting on and evaluating children's thinking requires continuous inquiry into teaching and learning, and teachers need support in doing so. Experience indicates that study groups designed to examine what takes place in the classroom raise the level of professionalism among teachers. The Children's Thinking Seminar, founded in Cambridge, Massachusetts, brings teachers together to discuss concrete examples of children's work and conversations. Such study groups are based on a few common characteristics:

• The facilitator ensures that the presenter uses specific examples, not generalizations.

• Teachers describe—not interpret—situations.

• Teachers try to take some distance from their customary investments ("This is my best student; I'm surprised he couldn't do that") and look at the student anew.

• Teachers share insights, resources, and strategies for working with students.

• Teachers analyze students' learning in light of theory and practice.

Conclusion

The nature and quality of children's thinking can be observed and assessed in a variety of ways. Whereas paper-

and-pencil tests in the past have given thinking skills short thrift, this need not necessarily continue. It is certainly possible for nationally normed standardized tests, state- and district-developed criterion-referenced tests, and teacher-made classroom tests to include questions that assess students' thinking skills. For the fullest and most accurate picture of children's thinking, a variety of item formats should be used. The information obtained from tests can be used for improving instructional programs as well as providing information about individual students' strengths and weaknesses. Further, such tests can be used to monitor longitudinal changes in students' thinking.

For an accurate and more complete understanding of student thinking, however, tests are not enough. Teachers must carefully observe and listen to children. They must also let the children's work speak. Reflecting on and evaluating children's thinking is a continuous inquiry into teaching and learning. It is the soul of the classroom and needs to be cared for.

REFERENCES

Bloom, Benjamin S., and others. *The Taxonomy of Educational Objectives: Affective and Cognitive Domains.* New York: David McKay Company, Inc., 1974.

Connecticut Assessment of Educational Progress 1983-84 English Language Arts Highlights Brochure. Hartford: Connecticut State Department of Education.

Education Commission on the States. *The Information Society: Are High School Graduates Ready?* Denver: Education Commission of the States, 1982.

54

How Can We Recognize Improved Student Thinking?

Arthur L. Costa

After several years of intensive work on these matters, the improvements in students' higher mental process learning and achievement became very pronounced. These and other approaches made it clear that most students could learn the higher mental processes if they became more central in the teaching-learning process.

—Benjamin Bloom

When we consider how evidence of student achievement is collected, we most often think of testing—using some form of paper-and-pencil instrument to determine how many questions a student answers correctly. While there may be some types of thinking that can be measured in this fashion, we need more accurate means of determining intellectual growth. When we teach students to think, the emphasis is not on how many answers they know, but on how they behave when they *don't* know. We are interested in observing how students produce—not reproduce—knowledge. A critical characteristic of intellectual ability is not only having information, but knowing how to act on it.

By definition, a problem is any stimulus, question, or phenomenon for which an explanation is not immediately known. Thus, student performance is assessed under challenging conditions that demand strategies, insight, perseverance, and craftsmanship to resolve problems.

Many teachers are unimpressed with standardized tests (Harootunian and Yarger, 1981; Lazer-Morrison and others, 1980) and for good reasons (Anderson, 1981; Coffman, 1980):

- Results are often available for several weeks or months after the test is administered.

- Thinking skills are affected by the degree to which students are acquainted with the subject matter.
- Performance is influenced by the mental and emotional states of the students at the time of the test.
- Performance is subject to external stimuli.
- Scores do not yield diagnostic clues as to how students derived the answers (metacognition), how students processed the data, and emotions necessary to arrive at the best answer (cognitive mapping).

Teachers know that many students are deemed gifted because they test well, while others are often overlooked because they perform poorly on tests. While *competency* may be demonstrated in a single test, *effectiveness* is demonstrated by sustained performance in a variety of situations that demand selective and spontaneous use of different problem-solving strategies rather than singular, isolated behaviors.

Indicators of Intellectual Growth

As students face real-life, day-to-day classroom problems, what might teachers search for as indicators that their instructional efforts are paying off? Following are ten characteristics of intellectual growth that teachers can observe and record (Feuerstein, 1980). Keeping anecdotal records of a student's acquisition of these types of behaviors provides more usable information about growth in intellectual behaviors than typical norm-referenced, multiple-choice, standardized achievement tests.

1. *Perseverance*. Students often give up in despair when the answer to a problem is not evident. They are unable to analyze problems or develop systems, structures, or strategies to solve them.

Thinking students grow in their ability to use alternate

problem-solving strategies. If one strategy doesn't work, they know how to back up and try another. They realize that the first theory or idea must be rejected and another employed. They use systematic methods to analyze problems and know how to begin, what steps to perform, and what data to generate or collect.

2. *Decreased impulsiveness.* Students often give the first answer that comes to mind. Sometimes they shout out answers, start to work without fully understanding the directions, or do not use plans or strategies to approach problems.

As students become less impulsive, we observe a decrease in the number of erasures on their papers. They gather information and make sure they understand directions before beginning tasks, take time to reflect on answers before giving them, listen to alternate points of view, and plan problem-solving strategies.

3. *Flexible thinking.* Some students have difficulty considering alternate points of view or dealing with more than one classification system simultaneously. *Their* way to solve problems seems to be the *only* way. They are more interested in knowing whether their answers are correct than being challenged by the process of finding the answer, and are unable to sustain this process. They avoid ambiguous situations and have a need for certainty rather than an inclination for doubt.

As students become more flexible they can consider, express, or paraphrase the viewpoints or rationales of others. They can state several ways of solving the same problem and evaluate the merits and consequences of alternate courses of action.

4. *Metacognition.* Some people are unaware of their own thinking processes. They are unable to describe the steps or strategies they use during problem solving, cannot transform into words the visual images held in their minds, and seldom evaluate the quality of their own thinking skills.

We can determine that students are becoming more aware of their own thinking as they are able to describe what goes on in their heads when they think. When asked, they can list the steps and tell where they are in the sequence of a problem-solving strategy. They can trace the pathways and blind alleys they took on the road to the solution, and describe what data are needed and their plans for producing those data (Sternberg and Wagner, 1980).

5. *Careful review.* Students are often careless when turning in their completed work. They seem less inclined to reflect on the accuracy of their work, contemplate their precision, or take pride in their accomplishments. Getting the assignment over with quickly is more important to them than craftsmanship.

We can recognize growth in students' desires for ac-

curacy as they take time to check over their tests and papers and become more conscientious about precision, clarity, and perfection. They review the rules and models they were to follow and the criteria they were to employ to confirm the correctness of their finished products.

6. *Problem posing.* One of the distinguishing characteristics between humans and other life forms is our ability to *find* problems. Yet students often depend on others to ask questions and solve problems for them (Brown, 1983).

We want to see a shift from teachers asking questions and posing problems to students asking questions and finding problems themselves. The types of questions students ask should change and become more specific and profound. For example:

● We seek an increase in requests for data to support conclusions and assumptions, such as: "What evidence do you have?" or "How do you know that's true?"

● We want to hear more hypothetical problems. These are characterized by "iffy" questions: "What do you think would happen *if* . . .?" or "*If* that is true, then . . .?"

● We want students to recognize discrepancies and phenomena in their environment and to inquire about their causes: "Why do cats purr?" "What would happen if we put the saltwater fish in the freshwater aquarium?" "What are some alternate solutions to international conflicts other than wars?"

7. *Use of past knowledge and experiences.* Too often students begin tasks as if they were being approached for the very first time. Teachers are often dismayed when they ask students to recall how they solved a similar problem previously and students don't remember. It is as if each experience has no relationship to what has come before or what comes afterward.

Thinking students are able to abstract meaning from past experiences and apply it to new experiences. Students show growth in this ability as they say things like "This reminds me of . . ." or "This is just like the time when we . . ." They explain what they are doing now in terms of analogies with or references to previous experiences. They call on their store of knowledge and experiences as sources of data to support, theories to explain, and processes to solve each new challenge.

8. *Transference beyond the learning situation.* The ultimate goal of teaching thinking skills is for students to apply school-learned knowledge to real-life situations and content areas beyond those in which it was taught. Yet we find that some students who pass mastery tests in mathematics have difficulty deciding whether to buy six items for $2.38 or seven for $2.86 at the supermarket.

When parents and other teachers report how they have observed students thinking at home and in other classes, we know students are transferring. Parents may report increased interest in school; greater curiosity and questioning; more planning in their children's use of time and finances, or increased organization of their rooms, books, and desks at home. We might hear the social studies teacher describe how a student used a problem-solving strategy that was originally learned in the science class, or the wood shop teacher tell how a student volunteered a plan to measure wood accurately before cutting it: "measure twice and cut once"—an axiom learned in the geometry class.

9. *Precise language.* Some students' language is confused, vague, or imprecise. They describe attributes of objects or events with nonspecific words such as "weird," "nice," or "okay." Objects are referred to as "stuff," "junk," or "things." And sentences are often punctuated with "ya know," "er," and "um."

As students' language becomes more precise, they use more descriptive words to distinguish attributes. They use correct names and, when universal labels are unavailable, they use analogies such as "crescent-shaped" or "like a bowtie." They speak in complete sentences, voluntarily provide supportive evidence for their ideas, elaborate, clarify, and operationally define their terminology. Their speech becomes more concise, descriptive, and coherent.

10. *Enjoyment of problem solving.* Some children and adults avoid problems. We often hear them saying things like "Thinking games turn me off," "I was never good at brain teasers," or "Go ask your father, he's the brain in this family." Many people never enroll in demanding academic subjects after they meet their high school or college requirements. They perceive thinking as hard work and recoil from situations that they view as demanding too much of it.

We want to see students move toward not only an *"I can"* attitude, but also an *"I enjoy"* feeling. We will notice students seeking out problems they can solve themselves and pose to others. They will display increased independence and not need as much help and intervention from teachers. Statements such as "Don't tell me the answer, I can figure it out by myself," indicate growing autonomy.

Conclusion

Assessing thinking through the exclusive use of standardized, paper-pencil techniques is inadequate. Each teacher should look for indicators of growing intelligence. Most teachers neither need nor use standardized tests to determine the effectiveness of their teaching for thinking. Significant problem-solving behaviors are displayed and can be observed daily if we know how to recognize them.

As educators, we have the great responsibility of instilling intelligent behaviors in our students. We must teach them to value intelligent and rational action. To do so, we must provide conditions conducive to the practice and demonstration of intelligent behavior. We must believe that *all* students can continue to grow in their ability to behave more intelligently, and we must have faith in the ability of all humans to become increasingly more gifted. Finally, we must set an example by modeling these intelligent behaviors ourselves (Costa, 1983).

REFERENCES

Anderson, S. "Testing and Coaching." Paper presented at the annual meeting of the American Association of School Administrators, Atlanta, Ga., 1981.

Brown, I. *The Art of Problem Posing.* Philadelphia: The Franklin Institute Press, 1983.

Coffman, W. E. "Those Achievement Tests—How Useful?" *Executive Review* 1, 1 (1980): 2-5.

Costa, A. "Teaching Toward Intelligent Behavior." In *Thinking: The Expanding Frontier*, pp. 211-221. Edited by W. Maxwell. Philadelphia: Franklin Institute Press, 1983. This chapter further describes the teacher behaviors and classroom conditions that promote thinking.

Feuerstein, R. *Instrumental Enrichment.* Baltimore: University Park Press, 1980. Several of these behavioral indicators are derived from the curriculum *Instruction Enrichment.* Teachers who have taught this program report changes in student behaviors similar to those described herein.

Harootunian, B., and Yarger, D. *Teachers' Conceptions of Their Own Success.* Washington, D.C.: ERIC Clearinghouse on Teacher Education, 1981, No. SP 017 372.

Lazar-Morrison, C., and others. *A Review of the Literature on Test Use.* Los Angeles: Center for the Study of Education, 1980.

Sternberg, R., and Wagner, R. "Understanding Intelligence: What's in It for Educators?" Paper presented to the National Commission on Excellence in Education, July 1980.

Epilogue
It's Our Move

Rebecca van der Bogert

Give me a fish and I will eat today. Teach me to fish and I will eat for a lifetime.

—Chinese proverb.

Practitioners are smarter now—or at least older and wiser. At any rate, we aren't jumping as quickly as we have in the past. Despite all the pressure from the media, publishing companies, and parents, the people who run schools are looking cautiously at the latest trend of teaching thinking skills. They demand to know, "How do I know this isn't just another fad?"

My answer to them is that it *is* another fad. True, the term ordinarily carries a pejorative connotation, but are fads necessarily all bad? We need to take time to analyze a fad's origin, study how systems adapt the fad to particular situations, and anticipate what might remain after the fad is no longer in fashion. I would even take one more step and say what we really need to do is to determine what should remain and how we can influence what eventually does remain. The question we should be asking is, "How can we turn this fad to our own advantage?"

A quick answer to the latter question would be most gratifying. Schools feel pressured, and along with this pressure comes the need to act quickly. Unfortunately, moving quickly in education means looking to the outside for answers rather than taking the time to find and cultivate the unordered knowledge we already have. Furthermore, as Dewey's comments on reflective thinking pointed out in 1909, rushes to judgment do not produce sound and careful conclusions:

One can think reflectively only when one is willing to endure suspense and to undergo the trouble of searching. To many per-

sons both suspense of judgment and intellectual search are disagreeable; they want to get them ended as soon as possible. They cultivate an overpositive and dogmatic habit of mind, or feel perhaps that a condition of doubt will be regarded as evidence of mental inferiority. To be genuinely thoughtful, we must be willing to sustain and protract that state of doubt which is the stimulus to thorough inquiry, so as not to accept an idea or make positive assertion of belief until justifying reasons have been found.

If we practitioners are to be truly thoughtful about thinking, we must resist the pressure to follow a fad before enduring the suspense and undergoing the trouble of searching. We can't just grab the first package curriculum because it would get the search over with and satisfy the Board of Education. We have to accept that easy and fast answers do not last, and we, as individuals and as systems, have to ask ourselves some tough questions.

First, we need to clarify what we mean by thinking. We need to rely not only on what Torrance or Ennis or Dewey defined as thinking, but we must specify what we mean when claiming, "We teach thinking skills." Do we mean creative thinking? Productive thinking? Critical thinking? Are we using the term in a generic sense or talking about specific skills? Are we referring to a specific program, such as Instrumental Enrichment, or a change in teaching styles, or both? None of these choices is unequivocally superior to others; a district could be justified in using any of these approaches. It should be clear, however, which tack has been taken because the different choices entail very different curricular and staff development decisions.

Do we have the right conditions for thinking in our schools? Assuming that we know what teaching for thinking is and that we are able to do it, consider whether schools provide the right environment for thinking. Thinking takes time. How many schools are willing to grant students time to think without scheduling it from 9 to 10 on Wednesdays? Also, in the light of what we know about the powerful effects of modeling, we need to know if our schools encourage teachers and principals to be thinkers. Are they permitted to take risks, form new ideas, and try out new things in which mistakes might occur? We can't say such conditions exist if we mandate thinking skills programs with rigid scope and sequence charts and specified time blocks.

How might a new program work with what we already have in the system? Probably most of us have scars to vividly verify the futility of a program stamped "Top-Down" and mandated without regard to the context in which it is introduced. Besides building the necessary support for new programs, a crucial consideration is whether they are similar to what many teachers are already doing or demand a total switch in teaching styles. The latter case would require a great deal of staff development time, which in some cases may already be consumed by other concerns like learning about computers or new math programs.

Have we just created another way of indoctrinating our students? Are we really facilitating our students' *own* thinking or are we telling them what to think, how to think, and when to do it? We have to be aware of this danger, so that our enthusiasm for teaching thinking doesn't lead us down the missionary path of imposing our agenda and thereby actually suppressing student thinking.

Are we fragmenting the teaching of thinking skills (as we've fragmented teaching into subject areas), removing skills from the contexts in which they are useful? We adults have had a wonderful time in the past few years analyzing what thinking is, an effort essential to research and understanding, but one that could lead to the isolation of thinking skills. Do any of us spend time thinking creatively or thinking critically, apart from the context of real-life situations? I doubt it. To preclude the separation of thinking from its contexts, we should be looking at how various thinking skills become integrated in actual life experiences and how we can simulate such situations in classrooms.

Why are we interested in teaching thinking? Each of us must ask ourselves whether our interest in thinking skills stems from its status as the current trend or whether we have a genuine interest in teaching students to develop thoughtful behaviors. If you are tempted to undertake a thinking skills program because you are feeling pressure from your school committee or superintendent, I suggest you engage your repertoire of stalling techniques. Not only will all of this hubbub pass quickly, but most of what is being purchased quickly now will probably end up shelved next to the modern math textbooks and the attribute blocks from the open classrooms.

In all likelihood, two years from now thinking won't be gone, and neither will we. The likelihood that our students will leave school excited by new ideas, amenable to taking reasonable risks, able to detect propaganda, stoic in enduring suspense, and willing to take the trouble to search depends on practitioners and the way our systems respond to these challenging questions. Packaged thinking skills programs, scope and sequence charts, materials, and testing programs are all important steps. We may eventually end up using pieces of all of them. But the essence of what will remain after the fad fades is whatever school people do in the next few years that becomes imbedded in the culture of our schools.

Resources for Teaching Thinking

As soon as this list of resources is published it will be obsolescent. Addresses change, new books are published, more research is generated, and additional resources are developed and discovered. No such list is ever complete. While we have drawn from numerous sources to compile it, you should continue to supplement it with additional books, articles, other media, and human resources as they become known and available as you search to understand the nature of teaching for thinking.

This section categorizes numerous resources—in addition to those sprinkled throughout the text. The compilation of the bibliography was coordinated by Nelson "Pete" Quinby. Annotations, where they are given, were written by Robert Sternberg and Arthur Costa. Still others came from fly leaf data and publishers' catalogues. The bibliography is presented in 12 categories to assist in coping with such a vast array of material. As with any classification system, items may be grouped in various ways depending on needs. This classification system was developed by Inabeth Miller.

The resource list is divided into three sections: (A) an incomplete bibliography of books, (B) tests of critical thinking, and (C) a listing of media, newsletters, and networks.

Resource A

An Incomplete Bibliography

Arthur L. Costa, Inabeth Miller, and Nelson "Pete" Quinby

The study of thinking covers topics such as problem solving, creativity, decision making, intelligence, neurobiology, research, and more. Although the categories employed here are somewhat vague and overlapping, they provide serviceable, if rough, partitions of a complex field.

General

Among the many worthwhile readings in the area are a few that cut across several categories and provide a broad picture.

Anderson, John. *Cognitive Skills and Their Acquisition.* Hillsdale, N.J.: Lawrence Erlbaum Associates, 1981.

Bossone, Richard. *The Fourth R: Reasoning.* New York: City University of New York, 1983.

Cohen, Josef. *Thinking.* Chicago: Rand McNally and Co., 1971.

Chipman, S.; Siegel, J.; and Glaser R., eds. *Thinking and Learning Skills: Current Research and Open Questions* (2 vols). Hillsdale, N.J.: Lawerence Erlbaum Associates, 1984.

de Bono, Edward. *New Think.* New York: Basic Books, 1967.

Dewey, John. *How We Think.* Boston: D. C. Heath & Co., 1933.

Halpern, Diane E. *Thought and Knowledge: An Introduction to Critical Reasoning.* Hillsdale, N.J.: Lawrence Erlbaum Associate, 1984.
    Relates critical thinking to the current work by cognitive psychologists in problem solving, decision making, and intelligence.

Machado, Luis. *The Right to Be Intelligent.* New York: Pergamon Press, 1980.

Maxwell, William, ed. *Thinking: The Expanding Frontier.* Philadelphia: Franklin Institute Press, 1983.
    A collection of papers presented at the 1982 Conference on Thinking in Suva, Fiji.

Upton, Albert. *Design for Thinking: A First Book in Semantics.* Palto Alto, Calif.: Pacific Press, 1961.

Teaching for Thinking

Installing intelligent behavior in young people is the major challenge of educators and parents. There is not unanimity in the field of education to prescribe the best methods of instruction and what school and home conditions need to exist to produce thoughtful children and youth. This section includes several points of view on this subject.

Adams, M. J., and others. *Teachers Manual. Prepared for Project Intelligence: The Development of Procedures to Enhance Thinking Skills.* Cambridge: Harvard University Press, 1982.

Aylesworth, Thomas, and Reagan, Gerald. *Teaching for Thinking.* New York: Doubleday, 1965.

Bills, Robert. *Education: For Intelligence? Or Failure?* Washington, D.C.: Acropolis Books Ltd., 1982.
    Basing his analysis on a survey of 124,000 students in public, private, and parochial schools, Bills offers answers to the question, "Why are schools failing to educate our children?" and proposes a five-part plan for change.

Bloom, Benjamin. *All Our Children Learning.* New York: McGraw-Hill, 1981.

Bloom, Benjamin, and others. *Taxonomy of Educational*

Objectives. Handbook I: Cognitive Domain. New York: David McKay, 1956.

Bruner, Jerome. *The Process of Education.* New York: Vintage Books, 1960.

Chall, Jeanne, and Mirsky, Allan, eds. *Education and the Brain.* Seventy-seventh Yearbook of the National Society for the Study of Education. Chicago: University of Chicago Press, 1978.

Chipman, S.; Siegel, J.; and Glaser, R., eds. *Thinking and Learning Skills: Current Research and Open Questions* (2 vols.) Hillsdale, N.J.: Lawrence Erlbaum Associates, 1984.
A large collection of papers describing current programs for training intelligence and evaluating their strengths and weaknesses.

Copple, C.; Siegel, I.; and Saunders, R. *Educating the Young Thinker: Classroom Strategies for Cognitive Growth.* Hillsdale, N.J.: Lawrence Erlbaum Associates, 1984.

Costa, Arthur. *Teaching for Intelligent Behavior: A Course Syllabus.* Orangevale, Calif.: Search Models Unlimited, 1985.
Describes the teacher behaviors and strategies that support thinking. Presents and suggest ways of practicing the behaviors.

Covington, Martin; Crutchfield, R.; Davies, L., and Olton, R. M. *The Productive Thinking Program: A Course in Learning to Think.* Columbus: Charles Merrill Co., 1974.

Cronbach, L. J.; and Snow, R. E. *Aptitudes and Instructional Methods.* New York: Irvington, 1977.
The best and most comprehensive single account of the relations between patterns of aptitude and optimal instructional methods.

de Bono, Edward. *Teaching Thinking.* New York: Penguin Books, 1980.

Feuerstein, Reuven; Rand, Y.; Hoffman, M.; and Miller, R. *Instrumental Enrichment: An Intervention Program for Cognitive Modifiability.* Baltimore: University Park Press, 1980.
A thorough description of Feuerstein's Instrumental Enrichment program for training intellectual skills.

Frankenstein, C. *They Think Again.* New York: Van Nostrand, 1979.

Furth, Hans, and Wachs, Harry. *Thinking Goes to School.* New York: Oxford University Press, 1974.

Glaser, Robert. *Advances in Instrumental Psychology,* Vol. 1. Hillsdale, N.J.: Lawrence Erlbaum Associates, 1978.

Hart, Leslie. *Human Brain and Human Learning.* New York: Longman, 1983.
Suggests that schools and normal brain functioning are incompatible. Presents Hart's Proster Theory of intellectual processing.

Hunkins, Francis. *Questioning Strategies and Techniques.* Rockleigh, N.J.: Allyn Bacon, 1972.

Lipman, M.; Sharp, A.; and Oscanyan, F. *Philosophy in the Classroom.* 2nd ed. Philadelphia: Temple University Press, 1980.
An introduction to the principles behind Lipman's Philosophy for Children program for training thinking skills.

Lochhead, Jack, and Clement, John, eds. *Cognitive Process Instruction.* Philadelphia: Franklin Institute Press, 1979.
A collection of papers presented at the first conference on Thinking held at the University of Massachusetts in 1978.

Lochhead, Jack, and Whimbey, A. *Instructor's Guide for Problem Solving and Comprehension: A Short Course in Analytical Reasoning.* Philadelphia: Franklin Institute Press, 1982.

McPeck, John. *Critical Thinking and Education.* New York: St. Martin's Press, 1981.

Meichenbaum, D. *Cognitive Behavior Modification.* New York: Plenum Press, 1977.

Nickerson, Raymond; Perkins, David; and Smith, Edward. *Teaching Thinking.* New York: Academic Press, 1985.
A review of available programs for training thinking skills. Addresses the question of how one might go about trying to enhance thinking skills. Discusses concepts, courses, and experiences that are likely to enhance intellectual development and teaching strategies that can ease the transition from concrete to formal thinking.

Olds, H. F., and others. *Motivating Today's Students.* Palo Alto, Calif.: Learning Handbooks, 1974.

Raths, Louis; Wassermann, Selma; Jonas, Arthur; and Rothstein, Arnold. *Teaching for Thinking: Theory and Application.* Columbus: Charles E. Merrill Co., 1967.
An early seminal work on developing thinking skills. Suggests numerous ways teachers can cause and enhance students' thinking abilities.

Sanders, Norris. *Classroom Questions: What Kinds.* New York: Harper and Row, 1966.
Describes teacher questioning related to Bloom's taxonomical levels.

Schwebel, M., and Raph, Jane, eds. *Piaget in the Classroom.* New York: Basic Books, 1973.

Segal, J.; Chipman, S.; and Glaser, R. *Relating Instruction to Basic Research.* Hillsdale, N.J.: Lawrence Erlbaum Associates, 1983.

Silver, Harvey. *Teaching Strategies.* Moorestown, N.J.: Hanson Silver Strong Associates, 1983.

Wassermann, Selma. *Put Some Thinking in Your Classroom.* Chicago: Benific Press, 1978.

Problem Solving

Nearly any task people face, from the most mundane to the most creative, can be called a problem. However, in the fields of psychology and education, problem solving tends toward a narrower meaning. It ranges from solving academic problems in mathematics, physics, and other disciplines, to solving puzzle-like problems and riddles, and to solving everyday "how to" problems, such as how to foster better employer-employee relations.

Ackoff, R. L. *The Art of Problem Solving.* New York: John Wiley and Sons, 1978.

Anderson, Valerie, and Bereiter, C. *Thinking Games 2.* Belmont, Calif.: Pitman Learning, 1980.

Hayes, John R. *The Complete Problem Solver.* Philadelphia: The Franklin Institute Press, 1981.
   A useful course covering a wide range of problem-solving skills.

Hudgins, Bryce B. *Learning and Thinking: A Primer for Teachers.* Itaska, Ill.: F. E. Peacock, 1977.

Jacobs, Paul. *Up the I.Q.* New York: Wyden Press, 1977.

Jacobs, Paul, and Meirovitz, M. *Brain Muscle Builders: Games to Increase Your Natural Intelligence.* Englewood Cliffs, N.J.: Prentice-Hall, 1983.
   A set of games to improve thinking skills.

Mayer, Richard. *Thinking, Problem Solving, Cognition.* San Francisco: Freeman and Co., 1983.

Newell, A., and Simon, H. *Human Problem Solving.* Englewood Cliffs, N.J.: Prentice Hall, 1972.

Polya, Gyorgy. *How to Solve It.* Princeton, N.J.: Doubleday, 1957.

Rubenstein, M. F. *Patterns of Problem Solving.* Englewood Cliffs, N.J.: Prentice-Hall, 1975.

Schmuck, Richard; Chesler, M.; and Lippit, Robert. *Problem Solving to Improve Classroom Learning.* Chicago: SRA, 1966.

Snow, R.; Federico, P.; and Montague, W., eds. *Aptitudes, Learning and Instruction,* Vol. 1. Hillsdale, N.J.: Lawrence Erlbaum Associates, 1980.

Walberg, Franette. *Puzzle Thinking.* Philadelphia: Franklin Institute Press, 1980.

Whimbey, Arthur, and Lochhead, Jack. *Problem Solving and Comprehension: A Short Course in Analytical Reasoning.* 3rd ed. Philadelphia: Franklin Institute Press, 1982.
   Pair problem solving is explained in depth. Problems and step-by-step solutions follow each chapter. Also available are problem cards, which are taken from the text (40 different problems).

Whimbey, Arthur, and Lochhead, Jack. *Beyond Problem Solving and Comprehension.* Philadelphia: Franklin Institute Press, 1984.

A sequel to and advanced version of the previous entry. Suitable for secondary schools and adults.

Wickelgren, Wayne. *How to Solve Problems.* San Franicsco: W. H. Freeman, 1974.
   A course in how to solve complex problems.

Creativity

Creativity refers to the individual train of producing appropriate and original ideas or other products in any field. Appropriateness without originality is mundane, and originality without appropriateness is simply bizarre. The word creativity does not imply a single ability; it may be as much a matter of personality as ability and may involve a mix of diverse abilities, perhaps a different mix in different cases. The literature on creativity includes a variety of theoretical positions and numerous books oriented toward self-help and instruction. Some of each are represented on our list.

Adams, James. *Conceptual Blockbusting: A Guide to Better Ideas.* 2nd ed. New York: W. W. Norton, 1980.

Amabile, Theresa. *The Social Psychology of Creativity.* New York: Springer-Verlag, 1983.

Barron, Frank. *Creative Person and Creative Process.* New York: Holt, Rinehart and Winston, 1969.

de Bono, Edward. *Lateral Thinking: Creativity Step by Step.* New York: Harper and Row, 1970.

Getzels, Jacob, and Csikszentmihalyi, M. *The Creative Vision: A Longitudinal Study of Problem Finding in Art.* New York: Wiley, 1976.

Howard, V. A. *Artistry, The Work of Artists.* Indianapolis: Hackett, 1982.

Koberg, Don. *The All New Universal Traveler: A Soft-Systems Guide to Creativity, Problem Solving, and the Process of Reaching Goals.* Los Altos, Calif.: W. Kaufmann, 1976.

Koestler, Arthur. *The Act of Creation.* New York: Macmillan, 1964.

LeBoeuf, Michael. *Imagineering: How to Profit from Your Creative Powers.* New York: McGraw Hill, 1982.

MacKinnon, Donald W. *In Search of Human Effectiveness: Identifying and Developing Creativity.* Buffalo, N.Y.: The Creative Educational Foundation, Inc., in association with Creative Synergetic Associates, Ltd., 1978.
   This volume includes various papers on creativity and human effectiveness. The author's main goal was to find ways to help people become as fully functioning as possible.

Mansfield, R. S., and Busse, T. V. *The Psychology of Creativity and Discovery.* Chicago: Nelson-Hall, 1981.

Osborn, A. *Applied Imagination: Principles and Proce-*

dures of Creative Problem Solving. New York: Charles Scribner's Sons, 1963.

Parnes, Sidney, J.; Noller, R. B.; and Biondi, A. M. *Guide to Creative Action.* New York: Charles Scribner's Sons, 1977.

Perkins, David. *The Mind's Best Work: A New Psychology of Creative Thinking.* Cambridge: Harvard University Press, 1983.
A fascinating description of research on creativity, insightfulness, and giftedness.

Rothenberg, A., and Hausman, C. R., eds. *The Creativity Question.* Durham, N.C.: Duke University Press, 1976.

Rothenberg, A. *The Emerging Goddess: The Creative Process in Art, Science, and Other Fields.* Chicago: University of Chicago Press, 1982.

Simonton, Dean K. *Genius, Creativity and Leadership: Historiometric Inquiries.* Cambridge: Harvard University Press, 1984.

Von Oech, Roger. *A Wack on the Side of the Head: How to Unlock Your Mind for Innovation.* New York: Warner Books, 1983.

Philosophy of Mind and Thinking

Besides founding the critical thinking movement, philosophers have addressed the nature of mind, of knowledge, and of thinking directly, sometimes with an eye toward how students can be introduced to a philosophical perspective and style of inquiry.

Block, Ned. *Readings in Philosophy of Psychology.* Vol. L. Cambridge: Harvard University Press, 1980.

Cederbolm, J., and Paulsen, D. *Critical Thinking.* Belmont, Calif.: Wadsworth Publishing Co., 1982.
Emphasizes understanding and criticizing arguments and theories. Deals with the problems of the amateur in a world of specialization.

Hitchcock, David. *Critical Thinking: A Guide to Evaluating Information.* Ontario, Canada: Methuan Publications, 1983.
Uses informal logic and focuses on real-life rather than artificial examples.

Kahane, Howard. *Logic and Contemporary Rhetoric.* Belmont, Calif.: Wadsworth Publishing Co., 1980.
The best-selling college text; excellent chapters on how the "news" and "basic belief systems" are "managed."

Matthews, Gareth. *Philosophy and the Young Child.* Cambridge: Harvard University Press, 1980.

Radner, Daisie, and Radner, Michael. *Science and Unreason.* Belmont, Calif.: Wadsworth Publishing Co., 1982.
Focuses on recognizing the difference between science and pseudo-science.

Ruggerio, Vincent. *The Art of Thinking.* New York: Harper & Row, 1984.
Excellent general overview without technical detail.

Scheffler, Israel. *Conditions of Knowledge.* Glenview, Ill.: Scott, Foresman and Co., 1965.

Scriven, Michael. *Reasoning.* New York: McGraw-Hill, 1977.
An excellent college-level introduction to the problem of thinking critically. Closely reasoned and precise.

Weddle, Perry. *Argument: A Guide to Critical Thinking.* New York: McGraw-Hill, 1978.
Emphasizes argument mechanics and evaluation.

Learning to Learn

Learning to learn may sound odd at first, but it is a commonplace part of human development. For instance, most high school students have acquired strategies for memorizing that are unfamiliar to the second grader, such as the value of repetition, visualization, or organized time. Although some learning to learn happens spontaneously, much more might occur if education broadened its focus to address the learning process as well as content.

Baddely, A. *Your Memory: A User's Guide.* New York: Macmillan, 1982.

Brown, S., and Walter, M. *The Art of Problem Posing.* Philadelphia: Franklin Institute Press, 1983.
Offers practical methods that affect our view of learning and teaching. Includes many problems and specific strategies, such as the "what-if-not" approach to problem posing. Although set within the context of mathematical problems, the discussion is readily accessible to other problems as well.

Higbee, Kenneth L. *Your Memory: How It Works and How to Improve It.* Englewood Cliffs, N.J.: Prentice-Hall, 1977.

Novak, J. D., and Gowin, R. D. *Learning How to Learn.* New York: Cambridge University Press, 1984.

O'Neil, H. F., and Splielberger, C. D., eds. *Cognitive and Affective Learning Strategies.* New York: Academic Press, 1979.

O'Neil, H. F., ed. *Learning Strategies.* New York: Academic Press, 1978.

Sheinker, J., and Sheinker, A. *Study Strategies: A Metacognitive Approach.* Rock Springs, Wyo.: White Mountain Publishing Co.
Strategies book and trainers' manual.

Visual, Oral, and Symbolic Communication

Thinking is not just a matter of how we think but what tools we think with. The written or spoken word, pictures, and other symbol systems are instruments that often help us to formulate, edit, and preserve lines of thought. The way that various symbol systems aid and foster thinking has been explored by several contemporary thinkers.

Arnheim, Rudolf. *Visual Thinking.* Berkeley: University of California Press, 1976.

Bowen, Eleanor. *Return to Laughter.* Garden City, N.Y.: Natural History Press, 1964.

Chukovsky, Kornei. *From Two to Five.* Berkeley: University of California Press, 1963.

Gardner, Howard, and Kelly, Hope, eds. *Viewing Children Through Television.* San Francisco: Jossey-Bass, 1981.

Greenfield, Patricia. *Mind and Media: The Effects of Television, Video Games and Computers.* Cambridge: Harvard University Press, 1984.

Johnson-Laird, P. N. *Mental Models: Toward a Cognitive Science of Language, Inference and Consciousness.* Cambridge: Harvard University Press, 1983.

Luria, A. R. *Cognitive Development: Its Cultural and Social Foundations.* Cambridge: Harvard University Press, 1976.

Moffett, James. *Teaching the University of Discourse.* Boston: Houghton Mifflin, 1983.

Morris, P., and Hampson, P. *Imagery and Consciousness.* Orlando, Fla.: Academic Press, 1983.

Olson, David R., ed. *Media and Symbols: The Forms of Expression, Communication and Education.* Chicago: University of Chicago Press, 1976.

Paley, William. *Wally's Stories.* Cambridge: Harvard University Press, 1981.

Perkins, David, and Leondar, Barbara, eds. *The Arts and Cognition.* Baltimore: Johns Hopkins University Press, 1977.

Rose, Mike. *Writer's Block: The Cognitive Dimension.* Carbondale: Southern Illinois University Press, 1984.

Salomon, Gavriel. *Communication and Education: Social and Psychological Interactions.* Beverly Hills, Calif.: Sage Publications, 1981.

Salomon, Gavriel. *The Language of Media and the Cultivation of Mental Skills: A Report on Three Years of Research Submitted to the Spencer Foundation.* Jerusalem: Hebrew University, 1977.

Vygotsky, L. S. *Thought and Language.* Cambridge: Massachusetts Institute of Technology Press, 1962.

Artifical Intelligence and Computers

Artificial intelligence means the use of computers to perform tasks that—in a human being—would be considered intelligent. Among the tasks that have received special attention are playing chess, identifying objects in a scene from a visual input, and conducting a conversation in ordinary language via keyboard and monitor. Much of the work in artificial intelligence informs our understanding of how people think. More generally, artificial intelligence and related disciplines have led to research on how computers can help people learn to think better.

Boden, Margaret. *Artificial Intelligence and Natural Man.* New York: Basic Books, 1977.

Boden, Margaret. *Minds and Mechanisms: Philosophical Psychology and Computational Models.* Brighton, Sussex, England: Harvester Press, 1981.

Dreyfus, H. L. *What Computers Can't Do.* New York: Harper and Row, 1979.

Goldenberg, E. P. *Social Technology for Special Children.* Baltimore: University Park Press, 1979.

McCorduck, P. *Machines Who Think.* Van Nuys, Calif.: Freeman Press, 1979.

Papert, S. *Mindstorms: Children, Computers and Powerful Ideas.* New York: Basic Books, 1982.

Turkle, S. *The Second Self: Computers and the Human Spirit.* New York: Simon and Schuster, 1984.

Weizenbaum, J. *Computer Power and Human Reason. From Judgment to Calculation.* Van Nuys, Calif.: Freeman Press, 1976.

Winston, P. *Artificial Intelligence.* 2nd ed. Reading, Mass.: Addison-Wesley, 1984.

Brain Functioning and Neurobiology

As conscious beings, we cannot help but find it odd that our thinking and learning occur through the actions of a biochemical machine. This information provokes many questions: What parts of the brain do which jobs, or is the work distributed throughout? Is there any substance to the popular left-right brain theme? Can mental capacities and incapacities be treated to anatomical or chemical differences in the brain? Does the development of the brain tell us anything about what can or should be taught when?

Annett, Marian. *Left, Right, Hand and Brain: The Right Shift Theory.* Hillsdale, N.J.: Lawrence Erlbaum Associates, 1985.

Bloom, F. E.; Hofstadter, L.; and Arlyne, L. *Brain, Mind, and Behavior, A Major New Text.* New York: W. H. Freeman, 1984.

Gardner, Howard. *The Shattered Mind: The Person After Brain Damage.* New York: Vintage Books, 1976.

Heilman, K., and Valenstein, E., eds. *Clinical Neuropsychology.* New York: Oxford University Press, 1979.

Hampden-Turner, Charles. *Maps of the Mind: Charts and Concepts of the Mind and Its Labyrinths.* New York: Collier (Macmillan), 1981.

Hart, Leslie. *How the Brain Works.* New York: Basic Books, 1975.

Ornstein, R., and Thompson, R. *The Amazing Brain.* New York: Houghton Mifflin.
> Visual and intellectual exploration of the construction, evolution, and chemical and electrical operations of the brain. Illustrated by David Macaulay.

Penfield, Wilder. *The Mystery of the Mind.* Princeton, N.J.: Princeton University Press, 1975.

Restak, R. *The Brain.* New York: Bantam Books, 1984.
> Accompanies the television series broadcast on Public Television in 1984.

Restak, R. *The Brain: The Last Frontier.* New York: Warner Books, 1979.

Wittrock, M. C., ed. *The Brain and Psychology.* New York: Academic Press, 1980.

Reasoning and Critical Thinking

While the core discipline for most of the other categories in this bibliography is psychology, the core discipline for this category is philosophy. That is, the majority of the ideas and writings come from philosophy and philosopher-educators. Reasoning and critical thinking focus on the assessment of beliefs and products of thought. Is it clear? Is it sound? Has it been proved? The "critical" of critical thinking does not imply a negative posture but an objective, analytical, and evaluative one, a posture that most would agree education should foster.

Giere, Ronald. *Understanding Scientific Reasoning.* New York: Holt, Rinehart and Winston, 1979.
> Helps students learn to evaluate and utilize scientific information. Excellent introduction to the basic concepts of scientific reasoning.

Halpern, Diane. *Thought and Knowledge: An Introduction to Critical Thinking.* Hillsdale, N.J.: Lawrence Erlbaum Associates, 1984.

Kahneman, D., Slovic, P.; Tversky, A., eds. *Judgment Under Uncertainty: Heuristics and Biases.* New York: Cambridge University Press, 1982.

Nisbett, R., and Ross, L. *Human Inferences: Strategies and Shortcomings of Social Judgment.* Englewood Cliffs, N.J.: Prentice-Hall, 1980.

Samson, Richard. *Thinking Skills: A Guide to Logic and Comprehension.* Stamford, Conn.: Innovative Sciences, Inc., 1965.

Toutmin, S. E., and others. *An Introduction to Reasoning.* New York: Macmillan, 1979.

Cognitive Development

Cognitive development concerns long-term human intellectual growth and learning. A number of themes characterize the field, among them the question of whether development is stage-like or continuous, whether certain concepts can't be learned until learners have attained some general level of intellectual readiness, whether intellectual development depends on a few core operations or a multitude, whether direct instruction or a nourishing environment best foster development across a broad front.

Boden, Margaret A. *Jean Piaget.* New York: Viking Press, 1980.

Flavell, J. *Cognitive Development.* Englewood Cliffs, N.J.: Prentice-Hall, 1977.

Gardner, Howard. *Developmental Psychology: An Introduction.* Boston: Little Brown, 1982.

Kohlberg, Lawrence. *The Meaning and Measurement of Moral Development.* Worcester, Mass.: Clark University Press, 1981.

Kohlberg, Lawrence, and others. *Assessing Moral Stages: A Manual.* Cambridge: Harvard University, 1978.

Kohlberg, Lawrence, and others. *Moral Stages: A Current Formulation and a Response to Critics.* New York: Karger, 1983.

Levin, Joel R., and Allen, Vernon. *Cognitive Learning in Children.* New York: Academic Press, 1976.

Loevinger, J. *Ego Development: Conceptions and Theories.* San Francisco: Jossey-Bass, 1976.

Meadows, S., ed. *Developing Thinking: Approaches to Children's Cognitive Development.* London: Methuen, 1983.

Perry, W. G. *Formal Intellectual and Ethical Development in the College Years.* New York: Holt, Rinehart and Winston, 1976.

Sternberg, R., ed. *Mechanisms of Cognitive Development.* San Francisco: Freeman, 1984.

Sugarman, S. *Children's Early Thought: Developments in Classification.* Cambridge, England: Cambridge University Press, 1983.

Yussen, S. R., ed. *The Growth of Insight in Children.* New York: Academic Press, 1985.

Intelligence

In everyday terms, intelligence refers to a person's ability to solve problems, plan well, learn well, and deal flexibly and appropriately with situations. In other words, intelligence means general mental competence. Psychologists have long sought a simple model of what is most essential to intelligence and how it is measured. Is it really one trait or a product of several, influenced primarily by inheritance or learning, subject to change by instruction or not? Interpretations are so diverse that while some would say you can improve thinking without improving intelligence, others would say that to improve thinking is to improve intelligence.

Baron, J. *Rationality and Intelligence*. New York: Cambridge University Press, 1985.

A new view of intelligence as based on rational thinking.

Binet, A., and Simon, T. *Classics in Psychology: The Development of Intelligence in Children*. New York: Arno Press.

The best introduction to Alfred Binet's theory of intelligence, which served as the basis for the Stanford-Binet Intelligence Scale.

Block, N.J., and Dworkin, G., eds. *The I.Q. Controversy*. New York: Pantheon, 1974.

Cattell, R. B. *Abilities: Their Structure, Growth, and Action*. Boston: Houghton-Mifflin, 1971.

The most comprehensive single presentation of Cattell's psychometric theory of intelligence, according to which there are two major subfactors of general intelligence: fluid and crystallized abilities.

Eysenck, H. J., ed. *A Model for Intelligence*. Heidelberg: Springer-Verlag, 1982.

A collection of papers on the nature of intelligence, most of which emphasize the importance of mental speed in intelligence.

Feuerstein, Reuven. *The Dynamic Assessment of Retarded Performers*. Baltimore: University Park Press, 1979.

Gardner, Howard. *Frames of Mind: The Theory of Multiple Intelligences*. New York: Basic Books, 1983.

Gardner acknowledges that some capacities, like memory, common sense, and even wisdom, can cut across the lines between intelligences. He argues that human intelligence is actually a host of different intelligences that reside in various parts of the brain, develop more or less independently, and can bloom separately, skill by skill. Gardner sharply challenges the notion that any single measure of intelligence is sufficient to label someone smart or stupid.

Gould, Stephan Jay. *The Mismeasure of Man*. New York: McGraw-Hill, 1967.

Guilford, J. P., and Hoeptner, R. *The Analysis of Intelligence*. New York: McGraw-Hill, 1971.

A presentation of Guilford's Structure of the Intellect model, a widely cited psychometric theory of intelligence.

Herrnstein, R. J. *I. Q. in the Meritocracy*. London: Allen Lane, 1973.

Herrnstein, R., and others. *Matching and Maximizing Accounts*. Cambridge: Ballinger, 1982.

Jacobs, P. I., and Knapp, J. *Setting Standards for Assessing Experiential Learning*. Columbia, Md.: Council for the Advancement of Experiential Learning, 1981.

Jensen, Arthur. *Bias in Mental Testing*. Riverside, N.J.: Free Press, 1983

Jensen's well-known treatment of test bias; he claims that, in general, intelligence tests are not biased against subgroups and presents his information-processing theory of intelligence.

Jensen, Arthur. *Genetics in Education*. New York: Harper and Row, 1975.

Jensen, Arthur. *Straight Talk About Mental Tests*. Riverside, N.J.: Free Press, 1982.

Matarazzo, J. D. *Wechsler's Measurement and Appraisal of Adult Intelligence*. 5th ed. Baltimore: Williams and Wilkins, 1972.

An exposition of David Wechsler's theory of intelligence, and also of the basic nature of the Wechsler Adult Intelligence Scale.

Meeker, Mary N. *The Structure of Intellect: Its Interpretation and Uses*. Columbus: Charles E. Merrill, 1969.

Piaget, Jean. *The Psychology of Intelligence*. Totowa, N.J.: Littlefield Adams, 1972.

A presentation of Piaget's theory of intelligence.

Resnick, L. B., ed. *The Nature of Intelligence*. Hillsdale, N.J.: Lawrence Erlbaum Associates, 1976.

The first major collection of papers on the information-processing approach to intelligence.

Spearman, C. *The Abilities of Man*. New York: Macmillan, 1927.

A classic book on Spearman's "two-factor" psychometric theory of intelligence.

Stenhouse, D. *The Evolution of Intelligence: A General Theory and Some of Its Implications*. New York: Harper and Row, 1972.

Sternberg, R. J. *Advances in the Psychology of Human Intelligence*. Vols. 1 and 2. Hillsdale, N.J.: Lawrence Erlbaum Associates, 1982, 1984.

Two collections of papers on contemporary views of and programs of research studying human intelligence.

Sternberg, R. J. *Beyond I. Q.: A Triarchic Theory of Human Intelligence*. New York: Cambridge University Press, 1984.

A comprehensive presentation of the triarchic theory of intelligence.

Sternberg, R. J. *Intelligence, Information Processing, and Analogical Reasoning: The Componential Analysis of Human Abilities*. Hillsdale, N.J.: Lawrence Erlbaum Associates, 1977.

Sternberg describes his componential theory of intelligence.

Sternberg, R. J., ed. *Handbook of Human Intelligence*. New York: Cambridge University Press, 1982.

A comprehensive collection of papers on various aspects of human intelligence.

Sternberg, R. J., ed. *Human Abilities: An Information Pro-*

cessing Approach. New York: Freeman, in press.
An introduction to the information processing approach to human abilities.

Sternberg, R. J., and Detterman, D. K., eds. *Human Intelligence: Perspectives on its Theory and Measurement.* Norwood, N.J.: Ablex, 1979.
A collection of papers on various information processing approaches to intelligence and intelligence testing.

Vernon, P. E. *The Structure of Human Abilities.* London: Methuen, 1971.
Vernon presents his hierarchical theory of intelligence.

Whimbey, A., and Whimbey, L. *Intelligence Can Be Taught.* New York: E. P. Dutton and Co., 1975.
An early, well-known book, which argues that intelligence can be improved throught training.

Resource B

Tests That Could Be Called Critical Thinking Tests

Robert H. Ennis

This listing is divided into general critical thinking tests, which make an attempt to cover critical thinking as a whole, and aspect-specific critical thinking tests, which focus on one aspect of critical thinking. A second distinction—between multiple-choice tests and essay tests—is used here only for general critical thinking tests because of the dearth of such tests. A third distinction—between topic-specific and general-knowledge-based critical thinking tests—is not used here because I do not know of any topic-specific critical thinking tests.[1] I hope that in the near future there will be more critical thinking essay tests and a wide variety of topic-specific critical thinking tests.

The criterion for selection of the general critical thinking tests was that half of their items be critical thinking items, with "critical thinking" defined as "reasonable reflective thinking that is focused on deciding what to believe or do." Anyone considering any of these tests should examine the items with great care.

Wide grade ranges are listed for many of these tests, in part to accommodate both students who have had appropriate instruction and students who have not.

General Critical Thinking Tests

MULTIPLE CHOICE TESTS

Basic Skills for Critical Thinking (1979, 5 forms) by Gary E. McCuen. Aimed at high school students. Sections on sources of information, primary and secondary sources, fact and opinion, prejudice and reason, stereotypes, ethnocentrism, library card catalogue, and *Reader's Guide to Periodical Literature*. (Greenhaven Press, Inc., 577 Shoreview Park Rd., St. Paul, MN 55112.)

Cornell Critical Thinking Test, Level X (1985) by Robert H. Ennis and Jason Millman. Aimed at grades 4-14. Sections on induction, credibility, observation, deduction, and assumption identification. (Midwest Publications, P.O. Box 448, Pacific Grove, CA 93950.)

Cornell Critical Thinking Test, Level Z (1985) by Robert H. Ennis and Jason Millman. Aimed at advanced or gifted high school students, college students, and other adults. Sections on induction, credibility, prediction and experimental planning, fallacies (especially equivocation), deduction, definition, and assumption identification. (Midwest Publications, P.O. Box 448, Pacific Grove, CA 93950.)

New Jersey Test of Reasoning Skills (1983), developed by Virginia Shipman. Aimed at grade 4 through college. Syllogism (including A.E.I.O. statements) heavily represented. Several items apiece on assumption identification, induction, good reasons, and kind and degrees. (IAPC Test Division, Montclair State College, Upper Montclair, NJ 08043.)

Ross Test of Higher Cognitive Processes (1976) by John D. Ross and Catherine M. Ross. Aimed at grade 4 through college. Sections on verbal analogies, deduction, assumption identification, word relationships, sentence sequencing, interpreting answers to questions, information sufficiency and relevance in mathematics problems, and analysis of attributes of complex stick figures. (Academic Therapy Publications, 20 Commercial Blvd., Novato, CA 94947.)

Watson-Glaser Critical Thinking Appraisal (1980, 2 forms) by Goodwin Watson and Edward Maynard Glaser. Aimed at grade 9 through adulthood. Sections on induction, assumption identification, deduction, conclusion-logically-following-beyond-a-reasonable-doubt, and argument evaluation. (The Psychological Corporation, a subsidiary of Harcourt Brace Jovanovich, 7500 Old Oak Blvd., Cleveland, OH 44130.)

ESSAY TESTS

The Ennis-Weir Critical Thinking Essay Test (1985) by Robert H. Ennis and Eric Weir. Aimed at grade 7 through college; also intended to be used as a teaching material. Incorporates getting the point, seeing the reasons and assumptions, stating one's point, offering good reason s, seeing other possibilities (including other possible explanations), and responding appropriately to/avoiding equivocation, irrelevance, circularity, reversal of an if-then (or other conditional) relationship, overgeneralization, credibility questions, and the use of emotive language to persuade. (Midwest Publications, P.O. Box 448, Pacific Grove, CA 93950.)

Aspect-Specific Critical Thinking Tests

ASPECT: DEDUCTION

Cornell Class-Reasoning Test, Form X (1964) by Robert H. Ennis, William L. Gardiner, Richard Morrow, Dieter Paulus, and Lucille Ringel. Aimed at grades 4-14. Seventy-two items that each contain a premise asserting a class relationship, such as "No A's are B's." Each of 12 logical forms is represented by six items of varying types of con-

tent. (Illinois Critical Thinking Project, University of Illinois, 1310 S. Sixth St., Champaign, IL 61820.)

Cornell Conditional-Reasoning Test, Form X (1964) by Robert H. Ennis, William L. Gardiner, John Guzzetta, Richard Morrow, Dieter Paulus, and Lucille Ringel. Seventy-two items that each contain as a premise a conditional statement, such as "If A, then B." Each of 12 logical forms is represented by six items of varying types of content. (Illinois Critical Thinking Project, University of Illinois, 1310 S. Sixth St., Champaign, IL 61820.)

Logical Reasoning (1955) by Alfred F. Hertzka and J. P. Guilford. Aimed at high school and college students and other adults. Tests for facility with syllogisms, the premises of which include a statement asserting a class relationship, such as "No A's are B's." (Sheridan Psychological Services, Inc., P.O. Box 6101, Orange, CA 92667.)

ASPECT: OBSERVATION

Test on Appraising Observations (1983) by Stephen P. Norris and Ruth King. Aimed at grades 7-14. Pairs of statements are compared for their believability. The manual provides principles for judging observation statements, which the items serve to test. Two story lines are used. (Institute for Educational Research and Development, Memorial University of Newfoundland, St. John's, Newfoundland A1B 3X8, Canada.)

FOOTNOTE

[1] I would appreciate hearing from any readers who know of currently available critical thinking tests that do not appear on this list. Please contact Robert H. Ennis, Director of the Illinois Critical Thinking Project, University of Illinois, Urbana-Champaign, 1310 S. Sixth Street, Champaign, Illinois 61820.

Media, Newsletters, and Networks

Arthur L. Costa

MEDIA

Approaches to Teaching Thinking. Audiocassette. Ron Brandt compares several widely used approaches. (612-20475) Alexandria, Va.: ASCD, 1985.

Beyond the Three R's—Reasoning and Responsibility. Audiocassette. Jane Stallings accounts for how we teach children to ask key questions and what concepts—not merely facts and figures—we want them to learn. (612-20414) Alexandria, Va.: ASCD, 1984.

Classroom Conditions That Encourage Student Thinking. Audiocassette. Arthur Costa suggests ways teachers can stimulate thinking, including asking questions and responding appropriately to students. (612-20476) Alexandria, Va.: ASCD, 1985.

Direct Instruction and Teaching for Thinking. Theme issue of *Educational Leadership*. Articles by Bruce Joyce, John Barell, Richard Paul, and Stephen Norris explaining the relationship between effective teaching and critical thinking. Alexandria, Va.: ASCD, May 1985.

Direct Instruction and Teaching for Thinking. *Educational Leadership on Tape.* Recorded articles by Ron Brandt, Bruce Joyce, John Barell, and Janet Kierstad. (612-20435) Alexandria, Va.: ASCD, 1985.

Educating Better Thinkers (working title). Videotape. Designed for teachers and administrators at all levels, features interviews with Arthur Costa, Robert Sternberg, Reuven Feuerstein, David Perkins, Ernest Boyer, and others. Alexandria, VA.: ASCD, available late fall 1985.

Improving the Quality of Student Thinking. Videotape. Ron Brandt encourages teachers to analyze their own teaching to improve student thinking skills. Features actual classroom episodes, statements by researchers, psychologists, and other authorities. Alexandria, Va.: ASCD, 1984.

Knowledge As Design. Audiocassette. David Perkins explains how treating curriculum topics as designs could develop student creativity. (612-20478) Alexandria, Va.: ASCD, 1985.

Practice is Not Enough. Audiocassette. Barry Beyer suggests ways to incorporate thinking skills into regular academic course work and teach them directly. (612-20473). Alexandria, Va.: ASCD, 1985.

Problem Solving. Theme issue of *Educational Leadership*. Arthur Whimbey on paired problem solving; two articles on Instrumental Enrichment. Alexandria, Va.: ASCD, April 1980.

Put Some Thinking in Your Classroom. Sound filmstrip series by Selma Wasserman. Westchester, Ill.: Benefic Press, 1978.

Survey of the Thinking Skills Movement. Audiocassette. Sandra Black provides guidelines for developing a local district thinking skills program. (612-20474) Alexandria, Va.: ASCD, 1985.

Teaching for Intelligent Behavior. Audiocassette. Arthur Costa outlines 14 conditions that curriculum developers should consider when including thinking skills in curriculum and instruction. (612-20390) Alexandria, Va.: ASCD, 1984.

Teaching Thinking Skills. Theme issue of *Educational Leadership*. Includes symposium on brain research, articles by Robert Sternberg, Ray Nickerson, Arthur Costa, Sydelle Seiger-Ehrenberg, and others. Alexandria, VA.: ASCD, October 1981.

Thinkabout. Television series for school use. Designed to help students experience and become aware of their thinking and problem-solving processes. Bloomington, Ind.: Agency for Instructional Television.

Thinking As a Skill. Audiocassette. Edward de Bono argues that thinking is a skill that should be given direct attention in schools. (612-20477) Alexandria, Va.: ASCD, 1985.

Thinking Skills in the Curriculum. Theme issue of *Educational leadership*. Articles by Richard Paul on critical thinking, Matthew Lipman on reasoning, Robert Sternberg on intelligence, Edward de Bono on thinking as a skill, and David Perkins on creativity. Alexandria, Va.: ASCD, September 1984.

Training Intellectual Skills—A Triarchic Model. Audiocassette. Robert Sternberg explains a new three-part model for training intellectual skills. (612-20372) Alexandria, Va.: ASCD, 1984.

When Teachers Tackle Thinking Skills. Theme issue of *Educational Leadership*. Arthur Costa, Irving Sigel, Carol Booth Olson, Meredith Gall, and others discuss ways to help teachers prepare to teach thinking. Alexandria, Va.: ASCD, November 1984.

Why in the World? Television series by Elinor Richardson and Carlos E. Cortes. Uses national and international current events to stimulate critical analyses in high school students. Los Angeles: KCET Agency for Public Broadcasting.

NEWSLETTERS

All prices quoted are 1985 yearly subscription rates. Prices may change.

Applied Research in the Cognitive and Behavioral Sciences. A quarterly publication of Hanson Silver Strong and Associates Inc., P.O. Box 402, Moorestown, NJ 08057 ($8.00).

Cerebretics Society International. C/O Leslie A. Hart, 120 Pelham Road, 6-C, New Rochelle, NY 10805 ($16.00).

Cogitare. Newsletter of the Thinking Skills Network sponsored by ASCD. C/O John Barell, Montclair State College, Upper Montclair, NJ 07043 ($10.00).

Cognition and Instruction. Lawrence Erlbaum Associates, Publishers, 365 Broadway, Suite 102, Hillsdale, NJ 07642 (published quarterly; $50.00 institutional, $20.00 individual).

Human Intelligence International Newsletter. Oakland University, 544 O'Dowd Hall, Rochester, MI 48063 ($15.00).

Informal Logic. University of Windsor, Department of Philosophy, Windsor, Ontario, Canada N9B 3P4 (Vol. I, $10.00; Vols. I and II, $20.00).

Learning Styles Network. St. John's University, Jamaica, NY 11439 ($14.00).

Mind-Brain Bulletin. Interface Press, P.O. Box 4221, 4717 N. Figueroa Street, Los Angeles, CA 90042 ($25.00).

Noetic Sciences Newsletter. Institute of Noetic Sciences, 2820 Union Street, San Francisco, CA 94123 ($25.00).

On The Beam. New Horizons for Learning, P.O. Box 51140, Seattle, WA 98115 ($15.00).

The Philosophy for Children Newsletter. The First Mountain Foundation, Box 196, Montclair, NJ 07042 ($8.00).

Problem Solving. Franklin Institute Press, 20th and Race Streets, Box 2266, Philadelphia, PA 19103 ($24.00 institutional; $10.00 individual).

Professional Journal of Record: Informal Logic. Edited by Johnson and Blair. University of Windsor, Ontario, Canada N9B 3P4 ($10.00).

SOI Newsletter. SOI Institute, 343 Richmond Street, El Segundo, CA 90245 (published August, December, and April; $5.00).

The Tarrytown Letter. Published by the Tarrytown Group, Tarrytown House, Executive Conference Center, East Sunnyside Lane, Tarrytown, NY 10591 ($30.00).

Thinking Skills Newsletter. Pennsylvania Department of Education, c/o Stephanie Bowen or John Meehan, Harrisburg, Pennsylvania.

NETWORKS AND PROFESSIONAL ASSOCIATIONS

Association for Supervision and Curriculum Development Thinking Skills Network. C/O John Barell, Montclair State College, Upper Montclair, NJ 07042 ($10.00).

Research for Better Schools. C/O Barbara Presseisen, 444 N. Third Street, Philadelphia, PA 19123.

The Association for Informal Logic and Critical Thinking. Professor David Hitchcock, President, McMaster University, Canada.

National Council for Excellence in Critical Thinking Instruction. C/O Richard Paul, Center for Critical Thinking, Sonoma State University, Rohnert Park, CA 94928.

International Center for the Development of Thinking Skills. 5 Canal Road, Pelham Manor, NY 10803. Contact: Phyllis Calderaro, Director, at (914) 738-2189.

New Horizons for Learning. P.O. Box 51140, Seattle, WA 98115 ($15.00 per year).

Appendices

Almost every classification system has a "miscellaneous" category and what follows is ours. Included in this final section is a collection of checklists; a glossary of terms; and a set of overhead masters that you might use in presentations to staff members, school board members, or the community. We hope they will help you in your implementation of a "teaching for thinking" curriculum.

Appendix A

A Glossary of Thinking Skills

Arthur L. Costa and Barbara Presseisen

Although there is no one glossary of thinking terms that serves the many nuances of meaning associated with cognitive operations, a working definition is a useful base to further understanding. While some may take issue with these definitions, the following terms may be helpful to practitioners who are seeking to integrate thinking skills into their curricular and instructional tasks.

"Aha" experience: An instantaneous generation of ideas or rules.

Algorithm: A problem-solving procedure that, if followed exactly, will always yield the solution to a particular problem. Compare with heuristic.

Ambiguity: The result of more than one meaning or underlying representation in a communication or utterance.

Analogy: A problem-solving strategy in which linguistic or figural similarities are noted between two or more situations while simultaneously discerning that there are also differences in the relationship.

Analyze: To separate or break up a whole into its parts according to some plan or reason. Opposite of *synthesis. Structural analysis* is performed in random order. *Operational analysis* is performed in sequential steps.

Anticipate probabilities: To assess all of the factors in a situation in order to determine the likely effects or outcomes of that situation.

Assumption: A fact or condition taken for granted; a supposition that something is true without proof of evidence.

Brainstorming: A group or individual method for generating solution paths for problems. The goal is to produce multiple possible solutions.

Build hypotheses: To construct tentative assumptions that appear to account for an observed effect, which may be used more fully to examine a specified situation or to provide possible conclusions or proofs.

Categorical reasoning: Also known as syllogistic reasoning. Use of such quantifiers as "some," "all," "no," and "none" to indicate category membership.

Categorize: To arrange items in such a way that each possesses the particular properties, based on predetermined criteria, required to belong to a specific group.

Causation: The act or process that occasions or effects a result.

Cause/effect: A condition or event (cause) that makes something happen; the result (effect) or outcome created by the previous condition or event.

Change forms of concepts: To translate information into a different form or present information through a different medium.

Classify: To sort into clusters, objects, events, or people according to their common elements, factors, or characteristics. Includes giving that cluster a label that communicates those essential characteristics.

Cognition: Related to the various thinking processes characteristic of human intelligence.

Compare and contrast: To examine objects in order to note attributes that make them similar and different. To contrast is to set objects in opposition to each other or to compare them by emphasizing their differences.

Compare word meanings: To analyze the various uses of a word and the relationship of that word to other words.

Comprehension: The arrival at the speaker's or writer's intended meaning by a listener or reader.

Conceive: To organize information in order to form an idea or generalized rule; to conceptualize; to understand.

Conclusion: An inferential belief that is derived from premises.

Conditional logic: Also known as proportional logic. Logistical statements that are expressed in "if, then" format.

Conduct projects: To describe the important elements of a task and explain the ways in which the task can be completed successfully.

Consequent: In "if, then" statements, the information given in the "then" clause.

Contingency relationships: Relationships that are expressed with "if, then" statements. The consequent is contingent or dependent upon the antecedent.

Contradiction: A problem-solving strategy in which the problem solver shows that a goal cannot be obtained from the givens because of inconsistencies.

Contrasting: To set objects or ideas in opposition or to compare them by emphasizing their differences.

Convergent thinking: Thinking that requires a single correct answer to a question or problem. (Compare with divergent thinking.)

Creative thinking: The act of being able to produce along new and original lines. See also *flexibility, originality, elaboration, aha.*

Critical thinking: Using basic thinking processes to analyze arguments and generate insight into particular meanings and interpretations; also known as directed thinking.

Decision making: The process leading to the selection of one of several options after consideration of facts or ideas, possible alternatives, probable consequences, and personal values.

Deduce (deductive reasoning): To infer from what precedes; to lead or draw to a conclusion; to derive the unknown from the known. The opposite of *induce* (inductive reasoning).

Detect ambiguity: To recognize the existence of two possible interpretations of a sentence or phrase because (1) of the manner in which the words are arranged, or (2) a word may be interpreted in two or more ways within the same context.

Detect assumptions: To recognize that a supposition is being made or that a supposition underlies a statement.

Determine alternative actions: To explore and develop different approaches to the solution of problems.

Develop criteria: To create standards, rules, or tests for

judging ways in which one event, item, or person may be differentiated from another one.

Discriminate between definition and example: To identify a word, phrase, or term by stating its precise meaning or significance (definition) as contrasted with identifying it by giving instances of its occurrence (examples).

Discriminate between fact and opinion: To differentiate between statements generally accepted as true and those based on personal or unsubstantiated assumptions.

Discriminate between real and fanciful: To distinguish between that which is true or actual and that which is illusory, fictitious, or imaginative.

Divergent thinking: The kind of thinking required to generate many different responses to the same question or problem. (Compare with convergent thinking.)

Elaborate: To expand on concepts or ideas; to give an idea or object greater detail.

Epistemic thinking: Related to the collective knowledge produced by various forms of thinking: scientific, aesthetic, political, etc., and the ways these bodies of knowledge are developed and extended.

Error: The result of a mistake.

Estimate: To form a judgment about the worth, quantity, or significance of something—the implication being that the judgment formed is based on rough calculations.

Evaluate value conflicts: To assess the coherence of specific actions and ideals and determine the compatibility of personal desires and social sanctions.

Evaluation: To make an examination or judgment based upon a set of internal or external criteria.

Fact: A statement that can be proven or verified; information presented as having objective reality.

Fallacy: An error or mistake in the thinking process.

Flexibility: The ability to take alternate points of view; present a different perspective with each response; try several different approaches; apply concepts, ideas, or rules to a variety of situations.

Fluency: (See ideational fluency)

Generalization: A rule, principle, or formula that governs or explains any number of related situations.

Group: To assemble objects according to a unifying relationship or critical attribute.

Heuristic: A general strategy or "rule of thumb" that is used to solve problems and make decisions. While it doesn't always produce a correct answer, it is usually a helpful aid. ("Look before you leap" as an example.) (Compare with algorithm.)

Hypothesis: A tentative proposition or relationship assumed in order to draw out its logical or empirical consequences. An "if, then" statement that serves as a basis for testing through experimentation or gathering facts.

Hypothesize: To construct a hypothesis.

Ideational fluency: The ability to list many possible ideas—the more ideas, the more fluent. The ability to produce a variety of responses.

Identical: Sharing all attributes.

Identity: A sameness of essential or generic characteristics.

Identify relationships among events: To determine the particular ways that occurrences can be analogous.

Identify relevant principles: To assess the usefulness of specific theories in clarifying or solving a problem.

Identify steps in a process: To recognize and point out discrete yet ordered elements within a larger activity.

Identify structure: To describe patterns and relationships among the elements or parts of a work.

Illogical: Reaching conclusions that are not in accord with the rules of logic.

Induce (inductive reasoning): To combine one or more assumptions or hypotheses with available information to reach a tentative conclusion. Reaching a rule, conclusion, or principle by inference from particular facts. Opposite of *deduce* (deductive reasoning).

Infer: To arrive at a conclusion that evidence, facts, or admissions point toward but do not absolutely establish; to draw tentative conclusions from incomplete data. Inferring is the result of making an evaluation or judgment in the absence of one or more relevant facts. Inference requires supposition and leads to prediction.

Inquiry: Seeking information about a problem or condition.

Insight: Sudden knowledge of a solution to a problem. Finding a new relationship between seemingly unrelated events, conditions, or objects.

Interpret changes in word meanings: To detect and analyze alterations or extensions of word meanings.

Interpret the mood of a story: To assess or appraise the temper—the range of sensitive impressions—of a literary work.

Interpretation: Explanations of the meaning of a situation or condition.

Intuition: The power or faculty of attaining direct knowledge or cognition without rational thought and inference.

Irrelevant information: Data that are not useful in solving a problem or answering a question. May be a distraction.

Judge abstract or concrete: To determine whether words describe general or specific items or ideas. The distance from reality: real, pictorial representation of the real, symbolic representation of the real, verbal or auditory sound that stands for the real.

Judge completeness: To assess data to determine whether or not they are sufficient for thorough coverage of the subject or issue under consideration.

Judge elements of a selection: To analyze a work to determine the function and effectiveness of each major component.

Judge logic of actions: To assess the feasibility, utility, and applicability of a procedure or method.

Judge relevance of information: To decide whether or not data are connected logically with and are useful in the solution of a problem.

Judge story logic. To assess materials, actions, and events to determine whether or not episodes within them are related in a consistent manner and follow a logical pattern of development.

Judgment: The process of forming an opinion or evaluation based upon a value.

Knowledge: The condition of having information or of being learned.

Label: To assign a category name or phrase to a set of objects or ideas in which the name selected identifies the major attributes shared by the members of the set.

Lateral thinking: Thinking "around" a problem. Used to generate new ideas. (Compare with vertical thinking.)

Logical: Reaching conclusions that are in accord with the rules of logic; derived from valid (correct) conclusions.

Logical reasoning: To think in a systematic fashion in order to determine the truth or validity of an argument.

Memory: The power or process of reproducing or recalling what has been learned and retained. That portion of the brain or mind where information and knowledge is stored and from which it is retrieved.

Metacognition: Consciousness of one's own thinking processes.

Metaphor: Linguistic comparisons formed when similarities between things that are basically dissimilar are noted. Often used in creative thinking.

Mnemonics: Memory aids or techniques that are utilized to improve memory.

Observe: To use the senses to gather information; to notice qualities, quantities, texture, color, form, number, position, direction, and so on.

Opinion: A personal belief, judgment, or appraisal regarding a particular matter.

Order: To arrange objects, conditions, events, or ideas according to an established scheme or criterion or to identify the scheme by which they have been arranged.

Originality: The ability to generate novel, nontraditional, or unexpected responses.

Part to whole relationships: The elements of an object, condition, event, or idea and how they combine to form a complete unit.

Pattern: An artistic or mechanical design revealing constant traits or replicable characteristics.

Patterning: Arranging objects, conditions, events, or ideas according to an established, repeated scheme or recognized, repeated schemata.

Perceive: To become aware through the senses; to discern.

Point of view: A perception of the world based on a variety of physical, environmental, intellectual, cultural, and emotional factors.

Predict: To formulate possible consequences of a particular event or series of experiences.

Premise: A statement that allows the inference of logical conclusions.

Prioritize: To rank objects, ideas, persons, conditions, or events by importance or personal preference.

Problem solve: To define or describe a problem, determine the desired outcome, select possible solutions, choose strategies, test trial solutions, evaluate the outcome, and revise these steps where necessary.

Qualification: Finding unique characteristics of particular identity or description.

Question: To formulate relevant inquiries so as to evaluate a situation, guide hypotheses, verify information, seek logical evidence, clarify, and so on.

Reasoning: In two forms, deductive and inductive. *Deductive:* use knowledge of two or more premises to infer if a conclusion is valid. *Inductive:* collect observations and formulate hypotheses based upon them.

Recall: To bring from memory storage ideas, facts, terminology, formulas, or propositions.

Recognize "either-or" fallacies: To detect situations in which only two choices are offered as alternatives, although other possible courses of action may actually be available.

Recognize false analogies: To determine when two situations or sets of evidence have been falsely compared.

Recognize guilt by association: To detect situations in which individuals or groups are falsely assumed to possess all or most of the characteristics of people with whom they associate; to determine cases in which individuals or groups have been falsely assumed to have taken part in an action because of proximity.

Recognize slanted arguments: To determine when language has been purposely misused in order to create false impressions or to convert others to a certain point of view that may be biased.

Relate cause and effect: To find a relationship between two events—one, the source, producing the other; to distinguish between simultaneity, coincidence, and causality of events.

Relate hierarchically: To arrange objects, items, or events by rank, grade, or class according to some value.

Relationships: Detecting regularity between two or more operations: temporal, causal, syllogistic, transitive, spatial, mathematical, and so on.

Relevant information: Data useful in solving a problem or answering a question.

Rules: The principles or formulae that underlie or govern some problems or relationships.

Sequence/seriate: To arrange events, items, or objects in some order according to an ascending or descending relationship of size or value; to order according to a temporal relationship in which the events occurred.

Strategy: The art of devising or employing plans toward achievement of a goal.

Summarize: To present the substance of a complex idea in a more condensed or concise form.

Syllogistic reasoning: Drawing a logical conclusion from two statements or premises; using deductive logic to reason from the general to the particular.

Synthesize: To unite parts into a whole; to conclude; to move from principle to application; to reason deductively from simple elements into a complex whole.

Test generalizations: To determine whether or not declarations, conclusions, or systematically organized bodies of knowledge (prepared by others) are justified and acceptable on the basis of accuracy and relationship to relevant data.

Thinking: The mental manipulation of sensory input to formulate thoughts, reason about, or judge.

Transformations: Relating known to unknown characteristics, creating meanings.

Understand figural relationships: To compare representations of objects or ideas with concrete forms or objects in order to discern ways in which they are related.

Vertical thinking: Thinking that is logical and straightforward. Used in the refinement and development of ideas and solutions. (Compare with lateral thinking.)

---

*These definitions are taken from a variety of sources. Readers who are interested in more detailed explanations of these terms should refer to: Donald Barnes and others, *SEASCAPE Manual* (1978); Barry K. Beyer, "What's In A Skill? Defining the Thinking Skills We Teach," *Social Studies Review* 24 (1): 19-23; Commission on Science Education, *Science—A Process Approach* (Washington, D.C.: American

Association for the Advancement of Science, 1963); Diane F. Halpern, *Thought and Knowledge: An Introduction to Critical Thinking* (Hillsdale, N.J.: Lawrence Erlbaum Associates, 1984, pp. 357-372); Dana G. Kurfman, ed., *Developing Decision-Making Skills* (Arlington, Va.: National Council for the Social Studies, 1977); and George A. Miller and others, *Plans and the Structure of Behavior* (New York: Holt, Rinehart & Winston, 1960).

Appendix B
Classroom Observation Form

John Barell

This form has been developed using the most recent research on teacher effectiveness as it relates to improving students' complex thinking processes in the classroom.

Generic Teaching Methods

1. Sets high standards:
   - Expects students to think with complexity and creativity.
   - Models desired thinking skills in day-to-day conduct.
2. Structures the classroom for thinking:
   - Organizes the classroom with clearly delineated rules for managerial and academic tasks.
   - Informs students that thinking is the objective.
   - Organizes the class for individual, paired, small-group, or total-group interaction.
   - Communicates desired attitudes and behaviors to students, including specific objectives for thinking processes.
   - Models thinking processes for students verbally.

3. Presents complex problems for students to think about:
   - Provides rationale for new skill/concept being introduced.
   - Provides meaningful examples, models, and comparisons.
   - Relates new information to previously learned material and students' own experiences.
   - Poses questions at various cognitive levels.
4. Establishes a warm, supportive environment for risk-taking:
   - Encourages autonomy of thought and action.
   - Encourages peer listening and responsive interaction.
   - Accepts students' contributions nonjudgmentally.
   - Uses silence (wait time) effectively.
   - Probes for clarification, extension, or expansion of meaning.
   - Probes for clarification of process (metacognition)—"How did you arrive at your conclusion?"
   - Builds on and extends students' responses.
   - Encourages trust and cooperative behavior.
   - Provides an environment rich in data sources.
   - Responds with information when the student needs or requests it.
   - Identifies students' cognitive functions.

Appendix C

Self-Reflection on Your Teaching: A Checklist

John Barell

Using a scale of 1 to 5, rate your classroom and school according to the following items.

5 = Very Often   4 = Often   3 = Sometimes   2 = Seldom   1 = Hardly Ever

CLASSROOM

	5	4	3	2	1
1. When students pose unusual or divergent questions, I ask, "What made you think of that?"	5	4	3	2	1
2. Whatever the text says is accepted as the right answer.	5	4	3	2	1
3. When a decision has to be made between involving the class in a discussion of an intriguing student idea (topic related) or moving on to "cover" content, I choose the latter.	5	4	3	2	1
4. I encourage students to seek alternative answers.	5	4	3	2	1
5. Students give reasons for making statements.	5	4	3	2	1
6. I use subject matter as a means for students to generate their own questions (or problems), which we then seriously consider.	5	4	3	2	1
7. When teaching, I sit or stand behind my desk.	5	4	3	2	1
8. Most questions posed during class can be answered with short or one-word answers.	5	4	3	2	1
9. Students spontaneously engage in critiquing each other's thinking.	5	4	3	2	1
10. Students relate subject matter to experiences in other subjects or in their personal lives.	5	4	3	2	1

11. I stress *what* to think, not *how*.	5	4	3	2	1
12. Students often set objectives for their own learning.	5	4	3	2	1
13. Students spend time working collaboratively to solve subject matter questions.	5	4	3	2	1
14. One focus in my classroom is trying to understand how and why people (mentioned in texts) created ideas, solutions, experiments, rules, principles, and so on.	5	4	3	2	1
15. My classroom mirrors the patterns of involvement practices in most faculty meetings.	5	4	3	2	1
16. Students actively listen to each other.	5	4	3	2	1

SCHOOL

17. We talk about the nature of thinking.	5	4	3	2	1
18. My school stresses collaborative instructional problem solving.	5	4	3	2	1
19. I learn from my colleagues by observing their teaching.	5	4	3	2	1
20. My supervisor and I discuss how to challenge students to think in more complex fashions.	5	4	3	2	1

Appendix D
How Thoughtful Are Your Classrooms?

Arthur L. Costa

Using the following 14 questions as your criteria, rate your school's effectiveness in developing thinking skills.

	Degree of Effectiveness				
	(5 = high			1 = low)	
1. Do your community and staff value thinking as a primary goal of education?	5	4	3	2	1
2. Does the staff believe that with appropriate intervention human intelligence can continue to grow throughout life?	5	4	3	2	1
3. Have you reached consensus on or adopted a model of intellectual functioning?	5	4	3	2	1
4. Are students aware that intelligent behavior is an instructional objective?	5	4	3	2	1
5. Does the teachers' language (questioning and structuring) invite students to think?	5	4	3	2	1
6. Do the teachers' response behaviors extend and maintain higher levels of thinking?	5	4	3	2	1
7. Are learning activities arranged in order of increasing complexity and abstraction?	5	4	3	2	1
8. Do instructional materials support higher cognitive functioning?	5	4	3	2	1
9. Is adequate instructional time devoted to thinking?	5	4	3	2	1
10. Does instruction provide for differences in modality strengths?	5	4	3	2	1

	Degree of Effectiveness (5 = high 1 = low)				
11. Are concepts and problem-solving strategies encountered repeatedly throughout, across, and outside the curriculum?	5	4	3	2	1
12. Do students and teachers discuss their thinking (metacognition)?	5	4	3	2	1
13. Do evaluation measures assess intelligent behavior?	5	4	3	2	1
14. Do significant adults model intelligent behaviors?	5	4	3	2	1

Appendix E
A Thinking Skills Checklist

Barry K. Beyer

	Yes	In Progress	No
1. Does your school system have:			
a. A list of major thinking skills to be taught throughout the system?	_____	_____	_____
b. Agreement among all subject areas that these skills should be taught throughout the system?	_____	_____	_____
c. A K-12 curriculum document that clearly delimits which thinking skills are to be taught at each grade level in each subject area?	_____	_____	_____
d. A K-12 curriculum document that presents thinking skills to be taught in a developmental sequence based on the cognitive development of learners, nature of the target skills, and subject-matter needs?	_____	_____	_____
e. A thinking skills curriculum that provides for continuing instruction in these thinking skills across many grade levels and subjects?	_____	_____	_____
f. Detailed descriptions of the operating procedures, rules, and distinguishing criteria of each major thinking skill or process to be taught?	_____	_____	_____
g. Appropriate thinking skill descriptions in the immediate possession of every teacher and administrator?	_____	_____	_____
h. Provisions for instruction in each skill with a variety of media, in a variety of settings, and for a variety of goals?	_____	_____	_____

	Yes	In Progress	No
2. *Do your teachers:*			
a. Use a common terminology and instructional language to describe the thinking skills they are required to teach?	_____	_____	_____
b. Provide instruction in thinking skills when these skills are needed to accomplish subject-matter learning goals?	_____	_____	_____
c. Understand the major components of the thinking skills they are teaching?	_____	_____	_____
d. Provide continuing instruction in each thinking skill through the stages of readiness, introduction, guided practice, extension, practice, and application?	_____	_____	_____
e. Introduce thinking skills as explicitly as possible by explaining and modeling each skill and having students apply the skill with their guidance?	_____	_____	_____
f. Provide frequent, guided practice in each skill with appropriate instructive feedback?	_____	_____	_____
g. Require students to reflect on and discuss how they make each skill operational?	_____	_____	_____
h. Use instructional materials appropriate to learning thinking skills?	_____	_____	_____
i. Test on their own unit tests the thinking skills they are responsible for teaching?	_____	_____	_____
3. *Do your provisions for evaluating the learning of thinking skills include the:*			
a. Selection or development of instruments that measure student performance on skills taught in the school system?	_____	_____	_____
b. Use of instruments that are valid measures of thinking skill competency?	_____	_____	_____
c. Use of instruments that provide the maximum data for diagnostic or monitoring purposes?			
4. *Do your supervisors and instructional leaders:*			
a. Understand the nature of the thinking skills and how to teach and measure them?	_____	_____	_____
b. Provide inservice instruction in the nature of the thinking skills to be taught and in different ways to teach these skills?	_____	_____	_____
c. Help teachers in different subject areas and grade levels share methods for teaching thinking skills?	_____	_____	_____

	Yes	In Progress	No
d. Ensure that teachers follow the thinking skills curriculum?	————	————	————
e. Ensure the revision of the thinking skills curriculum, instructional strategies, and instructional materials as appropriate?	————	————	————

Appendix F

Classroom Observation Checklist

S. Lee Winocur

Teacher _____ School _____ District _____

Observer _____ Subject _____ Date _____

Directions:

Mark an "x" in the appropriate column for each classroom behavior. If the statement is generally true of this classroom, mark *yes*. If the statement is generally not true of this classroom, mark *no*. If you are unsure, mark the third column.

	Yes	*No*	*Unsure*

Affective Disorders

1. FOSTERS A CLIMATE OF OPENNESS
   - Eye contact is frequent between teacher and students, and students and students.   _____ _____ _____
   - Teacher moves around the room.   _____ _____ _____
   - Students listen attentively to others.   _____ _____ _____
   - Teacher calls on students by name.   _____ _____ _____

2. ENCOURAGES STUDENT INTERACTION/COOPERATION
   - Students work in pairs or small groups.   _____ _____ _____
   - Students respond to other students.   _____ _____ _____
   - Students help others analyze and solve problems.   _____ _____ _____

3. DEMONSTRATES ATTITUDE OF ACCEPTANCE
   - Teacher accepts all valid student responses.   _____ _____ _____

	Yes	No	Unsure
● Incorrect student responses elicit encouraging, supportive comments.	____	____	____
● Teacher acknowledges student comments with a nod or other signal.	____	____	____

Cognitive Indicators

4. ENCOURAGES STUDENTS TO GATHER INFORMATION

● Reference materials are readily available.	____	____	____
● Students use reference materials.	____	____	____
● Student mobility is allowed to obtain information.	____	____	____
● Teacher acts as facilitator.	____	____	____
● Students record data in notebooks or journals.	____	____	____

5. ENCOURAGES STUDENTS TO ORGANIZE INFORMATION

● Teacher works from organized lesson plans.	____	____	____
● Students classify and categorize data.	____	____	____
● Students take notes systematically.	____	____	____
● Teacher's presentation is logical, organized.	____	____	____
● Ideas are graphically symbolized during instruction.	____	____	____

6. ENCOURAGES STUDENTS TO JUSTIFY IDEAS

● Teacher probes for correct responses.	____	____	____
● Teacher seeks evidence for stated claims.	____	____	____
● Students analyze sources of information for reliability, relevance.	____	____	____
● Teacher frequently asks, "Why do you think so?"	____	____	____
● Students relate learning to past experience or similar situations.	____	____	____

7. ENCOURAGES STUDENTS TO EXPLORE ALTERNATIVES AND OTHERS' POINTS OF VIEW

● Teacher establishes expectations for divergent solutions.	____	____	____
● Teacher allows time to consider alternatives/points of view.	____	____	____
● More than one student is queried for point of view/solution.	____	____	____
● Teacher asks students to justify and explain their thoughts.	____	____	____

8. ASKS OPEN-ENDED QUESTIONS

● Teacher asks open-ended questions with multiple answers *as frequently as* single-answer questions.	____	____	____

9. PROVIDES VISUAL CUES FOR DEVELOPING COGNITIVE STRATEGIES

● Teacher appropriately uses a variety of visual media (charts, chalkboard, maps, pictures, gestures).	____	____	____

	Yes	No	Unsure
• Teacher uses symbolic language to illustrate a point (simile, metaphor).	_____	_____	_____
• Teacher uses outlining.	_____	_____	_____

10. MODELS REASONING STRATEGIES
   - Teacher uses "if/then" language.
   - Teacher poses "what if" or "suppose that" questions.
   - Teacher uses clear examples to facilitate logical thought.

11. ENCOURAGES TRANSFER OF COGNITIVE SKILLS TO EVERYDAY LIFE
   - Teacher encourages transfer at end of lesson with comments like, "This will help you in your everyday life in this way...."

12. ELICITS VERBALIZATION OF STUDENT REASONING
   - Teacher poses questions at different levels of Bloom's Taxonomy.
   - Teacher allows at least ten seconds wait time for student answer before restating or redirecting the question.
   - Teacher asks students to clarify and justify their responses.
   - Teacher probes "I don't know" responses.
   - Teacher reinforces students for responding to open-ended questions.

13. PROBES STUDENT REASONING FOR CLARIFICATION
   - Teacher asks questions to elicit reasoning by students.
   - Teacher requires students to expand on answers.
   - Teacher cues students for most logical answers.

14. ENCOURAGES STUDENTS TO ASK QUESTIONS
   - Teacher poses problematic situations.
   - Teacher withholds "correct" responses; encourages students to explore possibilities.
   - Teacher encourages students to answer other students' questions.

15. PROMOTES SILENT REFLECTION OF IDEAS
   - Teacher allows time for reflection.

Appendix G

Questionnaire: Are You Ready to Teach Thinking?

Arthur L. Costa

DIRECTIONS

1. Answer the first eight questions individually.
2. Share your answers with other staff members.
3. As a total staff, grade-level team, or department, compile one copy that reflects the consensus of the total group.
4. Sign the group's composite copy. Your signature indicates that:
   a. You understand it—not necessarily that you agree with it.
   b. You will support it—even though you may not agree with it.
   c. You feel comfortable enough to explain it and respond to questions about it from parents or visitors to your school.
5. Now answer question nine and repeat the above process.
6. Describe and evaluate the process and the time it took to complete this procedure.

THE QUESTIONNAIRE

1. **Why do you want to teach thinking?**

2. **What is it about your students that makes you think they need to learn to think?**

3. **What conditions are present in your school that make this a good time to begin teaching for thinking? What indicators of readiness, desire, and motivation exist?**

4. **What is the degree of your commitment? How much time, energy, and resources are you willing to give?**

5. What do you think human beings do when they are acting/behaving intelligently? Describe the vision of human intelligent behavior for which you are striving.

6. How do you think human beings learn to become more like this vision? What are the conditions in which intelligent behavior is learned?

7. What conditions must be created in your school to promote these intelligent behaviors?

8. What can classroom teachers do to promote these intelligent behaviors?

9. What changes do you think it would take to install a thinking skills curriculum?
    a. Time allocations: How much time in the school day, week, or year should be given to thinking skills?

    b. Instructional materials?

    c. Curriculum materials, organization, and development procedures?

    d. Staffing?

    e. School organization?

    f. Assessment tools, techniques, and procedures?

    g. Teaching skills?

    h. Staff development?

    i. Other?

Appendix H
Suggestions for Getting Started

Sandra Black

1. Review the objectives and methods of existing cognitive skills and logical reasoning programs.

2. Establish a hierarchy of thinking skills for identifying and sequencing instructional objectives.

3. Select a few skills identified by district objectives and identify how they are being taught in content areas.

4. Determine the form of regular student practice in thinking skills and methods to monitor such practice.

5. Identify or develop materials for classroom instruction and assume that their application is to be intradisciplinary rather than extradisciplinary.

6. Develop an inservice plan for administrators and teachers.

7. Organize a parent education plan and a community awareness program.

8. Identify techniques and materials that should be included in staff development programs.

9. Determine which teaching skills to observe when coaching and supervising.

10. Develop teacher and administrator assessment plans.

11. Develop and adopt methods to assess students' growth in cognitive abilities.

Appendix I

Questions System Planners Need to Ask

Carolee S. Matsumoto

The following are questions that system planners need to consider when incorporating higher-level thinking into teaching and learning.

INPUT

Development of a rationale:

1. Why should we be concerned with higher-level thinking?
2. Do we have a commitment to intelligent behavior?
3. Do school administrators and committees (boards) support, model, and promote higher-level thinking and intelligent behavior?

Input of outside data and information from research and practice:

1. What do the experts say about this (Costa, Paul, Perkins, Sternberg, and others)?
2. What are the various approaches that have been taken?
   a. Formal programs (Project Intelligence, Instrumental Enrichment, Philosophy for Children, and others)
   b. What outstanding school systems, state programs, and other plans exist?

ACTION

Definition, setting goals, and internal reflection:

1. What do we mean by higher-level thinking, cognitive development, and intelligence?
2. What elements/areas of thinking are we going to include as goals for the K-12 learning experience?
3. What are we already doing to promote thinking?
   a. What institutional structures and practices promote thinking?
   b. Does/will/how can the school culture support change to incorporate a priority to promote higher-level thinking?
   c. What teacher behaviors encourage thinking?
   d. What curriculums/programs expect, stimulate, or provide opportunities or contexts for higher-level thinking?
4. What do we do that inhibits or restricts thinking?
   a. What institutional structures and practices inhibit thinking?
   b. What teacher behaviors inhibit thinking?
   c. What curriculums/programs inhibit or restrict thinking?
5. How can and will we use computers/technologies to help us develop thinking?
6. What are our immediate goals and priorities?

PROCEDURES

Action:

1. How can we create expectations that demand higher-level thinking and cognitive development?

2. What are the training/development implications for:
   a. Administrators?
   b. Teachers?
   c. Schools and systems?
   d. Teacher training in universities?

3. How can we develop K-12 curriculums that expect, stimulate, or provide opportunities or contexts for higher-level thinking and cognitive development?

4. How can we infuse higher-level thinking and cognitive development across all disciplines and programs?

5. Who will support these expectations, training, and curriculum development efforts, and how will they do so?

6. Can our supervisors (principals, department chairs, or other administrators) cognitively coach, supervise, and evaluate?

7. How will the answers to all of these questions be conceptualized and realized in our schools and systems?
   a. What steps will we take?
   b. What additional support (human and financial) is necessary?
   c. How will we maintain a long-term commitment?

8. How can we continually inform, educate, and train parents and community members to understand and support their children's and our efforts?

PRACTICE

Evaluation:

1. How will we know if students have developed their thinking skills, strategies, and self-confidence?

2. What evidence/indicators will reflect staff (administrators and teachers) skills in thinking?

3. How will we access supervisors' (principals, department heads, and others) ability to coach cognitively?

4. What processes will continually develop and revise curriculums for the infusion of thinking and cognitive development?

INSTITUTE

School culture:

1. How will we know that thinking and cognitive development are a part of the school culture?

2. How can we be sure that everyone in the school system is committed, participating, and prioritizing this endeavor?

Appendix J

Overhead Transparency Masters

Ronald S. Brandt

These masters may be used with a copier to make overhead transparencies for a large-group presentation. Pages 331-335 highlight data from several sources documenting reasons for an emphasis on thinking (see Part I, "The Need to Teach Students to Think"). For background information on page 336, which explains differences among "Teaching For, Of, and About Thinking," see page 21.

"Ways to Improve Student Thinking," page 337, lists suggestions appropriate for teachers of any subject at any level. It is based on the videotape, "Improving the Quality of Student Thinking," which is available from ASCD.

The "Basics" of Tomorrow:

- Evaluation and analysis skills

- Critical thinking

- Problem-solving strategies (including mathematical problem-solving)

- Organization and reference skills

- Synthesis

- Application

- Creativity

- Decision-making given incomplete information

- Communication skills through a variety of modes

—Education Commission of the States, 1982

National Assessment Results

17 Year Olds

Reading
- Read for inferences   1971—64%   1980—62%
- Analyze a passage for mood   1971—51%   1980—41%

Writing
- Write persuasively   1974—21%   1979—15%
     competent   competent

Mathematics
- Understand mathematics   1973—62%   1978—58%
- Apply mathematics   1973—33%   1978—29%

Science
- Classify (physics)   1977—44%

"The pattern is clear: the percentage of students achieving higher order skills is declining."

Percent not competent ranges from 38% to 85%.

—Education Commission of the States, 1982

Reading, Thinking, and Writing

A four-step model of the comprehension process:

1. Initial comprehension, leading to
2. Preliminary interpretations, followed by
3. A reexamination of the text in light of these interpretations, leading to
4. Extended and documented interpretation

Only 5 to 10% move beyond Step 2.

"Students seem satisfied with their initial interpretations of what they have read and seem genuinely puzzled at requests to explain or defend their points of view. Few students could provide more than superficial responses to such tasks, and even the "better" responses showed little evidence of well-developed problem-solving strategies or critical-thinking skills."

—National Assessment of Reading and Literature, 1979-80

A Place Called School

—John Goodlad

Reports "A Study of Schooling"

- 38 schools, 13 communities, 7 regions

- 20 data collectors, 30 days per community

- over 1,000 classrooms

Classroom Talk

Instruction = 75% of class time

Talk = 70% of instruction

Teacher Talk

Invited open response (reasoning, opinion) = 1%

—John Goodlad, p. 229.

Teaching:

for thinking— Teaching academic content so as to strengthen students' cognitive abilities

of thinking— Teaching particular mental skills as the primary purpose of instruction

about thinking— Helping students be more conscious of their own thinking processes

Ways to Improve Student Thinking

1. Ensure that students <u>process</u> information.

2. Ask broad, open questions.

3. Wait before calling on students.

4. Follow up student responses by asking for: clarification, elaboration, evidence, thinking process.

5. Have a clear purpose, plan a sequence of activities to accomplish it.

6. Make students conscious of their own thinking processes.

7. Model problem solving and other thinking processes.

8. Have students ask questions of their own.

Contributing Authors

JOHN D. BAKER, President, Midwest Publications, PO Box 448, Pacific Grove, California 93950.

JOHN BARELL, Associate Professor of Education, Montclair State College, Upper Montclair, New Jersey 07043, and Coordinator, ASCD Network on Thinking.

JOAN BOYKOFF BARON, Project Director, Connecticut Assessment of Educational Progress, Connecticut State Department of Education, PO Box 2219, Hartford, Connecticut 06145.

JONATHAN BARON, Associate Professor of Psychology, Graduate School of Education, University of Pennsylvania, 3700 Walnut Street, Philadelphia, Pennsylvania 19104.

JAMES A. BELLANCA, Executive Director, Illinois Renewal Institute, Inc., 500 S. Dwyer, Arlington Heights, Illinois 60005.

BARRY K. BEYER, Consultant to school systems and state education agencies and Professor of Education, George Mason University, 4400 University Drive, Fairfax, Virginia 22030.

SANDRA BLACK, Adjunct Instructor, Department of Special Education, University of North Florida at Jacksonville, PO Box 468, St. Augustine, Florida 32085.

RONALD S. BRANDT, Executive Editor, Association for Supervision and Curriculum Development, 225 N. Washington Street, Alexandria, Virginia 22314.

HOWARD CITRON, Vice-President, Innovative Sciences, Inc., 300 Broad Street, Park Square Station, PO Box 15129, Stamford, Connecticut 06901-0129.

ARTHUR L. COSTA, Professor of Education, California State University, 6000 J Street, Sacramento, California 95819.

ANNE B. CRABBE, Director, Future Problem Solving Program, Coe College, Cedar Rapids, Iowa 52402.

JOHN CRADLER, Coordinator of Special Projects and Research, South San Francisco Unified School District, 398 "B" Street, South San Francisco, California 94080.

EDWARD DE BONO, Director, Cognitive Research Trust, Piccadilly, London, United Kingdom; and Director, International Center for the Development of Thinking Skills, 5 Canal Road, Pelham Manor, New York 10803.

DEE DISHON, Co-Director, Institute for Personal Power, PO Box 68, Portage, Michigan 49081.

RONALD EDWARDS, Teacher, Jesuit High School, Sacramento, California.

ROBERT H. ENNIS, Director, Illinois Critical Thinking Project, and Professor of Philosophy, Department of Educational Policy Studies, University of Illinois at Urbana-Champaign, 1310 S. Sixth Street, Champaign, Illinois 61820.

ESTHER FUSCO, Principal, Babylon Elementary School, 171 Ralph Avenue, Babylon, New York 11702.

ROBERT GARMSTON, Associate Professor of Education, Department of Educational Administration, California State University, 6000 J Street, Sacramento, California 95828.

JOHN J. GLADE, Director of Curriculum Development, Innovative Science, Inc., 300 Broad Street, Park Square Station, PO Box 15129, Stamford, Connecticut 06901-0129.

ALLAN A. GLATTHORN, Professor of Education, Graduate School of Education, University of Pennsylvania, 3700 Walnut Street, Philadelphia, Pennsylvania 19104.

ROBERT HANSON, Chief Executive Officer, Hanson Silver Strong & Associates, Inc., Box 402, Moorestown, New Jersey 08057.

MARCIA HEIMAN, Co-Director, Learning Skills Consultants, Box 493, Cambridge, Massachusetts 02138.

BEAU FLY JONES, Director, Instructional Improvement, North Central Regional Educational Laboratory, 295 Emroy Avenue, Elmhurst, Illinois 60126.

BENA KALLICK, Director, Weston Woods Institute, Weston, Connecticut 06883.

PETER KNEEDLER, Consultant, California State Department of Education, 721 Capitol Mall, Sacramento, California 95814-4785.

FRANCES R. LINK, Vice-President, Curriculum Development Associates, Inc., 1211 Connecticut Avenue, NW, Suite 414, Washington, D.C. 20036.

MATTHEW LIPMAN, Director, Institute for the Advancement of Philosophy for Children, Montclair State College, Upper Montclair, New Jersey 07043.

LAWRENCE F. LOWERY, Professor, University of California, School of Education, Tolman Hall, Room 4533, Berkeley, California 94720.

CAROLEE MATSUMOTO, Assistant Superintendent, Concord Public Schools, Concord-Carlisle Regional School District, 120 Meriam Road, Concord, Massachusetts 07142.

JAY McTIGHE, Specialist, Gifted and Talented Education and Thinking Improvement Program, Maryland State Department of Education, 200 W. Baltimore Street, Baltimore, Maryland 21201.

MARY N. MEEKER, President, SOI Institute, 343 Richmond Street, El Segundo, California 90245.

INABETH MILLER, Librarian to the Faculty of Education, Monroe C. Gutman Library, Harvard Graduate School of Education, Cambridge, Massachusetts 02138.

ANNE H. NARDI, Professor, Department of Educational Philosophy, and Co-Director, Center for Guided Design, West Virginia University, 137 Engineering Science Building, Morgantown, West Virginia 26506.

PAT WILSON O'LEARY, Instructional Consultant, Kalamazoo Valley Intermediate School District, 1819 E. Milham Road, Kalamazoo, Michigan 49002.

CAROL BOOTH OLSON, Project Director, UCI Writing Project, University of California, Irvine, California 92717.

SIDNEY J. PARNES, Professor of Creative Studies, State University of New York at Buffalo, and President, Creative Education Foundation, 437 Franklin Street, Buffalo, New York 14202.

RICHARD PAUL, Director, Center for Critical Thinking and Moral Critique, Sonoma State University, Rohnert Park, California 94928.

D. N. PERKINS, Co-Director, Harvard Project Zero, Harvard University, Cambridge, Massachusetts 02138.

STANLEY POGROW, Associate Professor of Educational Foundations and Administration, College of Education, University of Arizona, Tucson, Arizona 85721.

BARBARA Z. PRESSEISEN, Associate Director of Urban Development, Research for Better Schools, Inc., 444 N. Third Street, Philadelphia, Pennsylvania 19123.

NELSON "PETE" QUINBY, Director of Secondary Education, Joel Barlow High School, 100 Black Rock Turnpike, West Redding, Connecticut 06896.

STUART C. RANKIN, Deputy Superintendent, Division of Education Services, Detroit Public Schools, 5057 Woodward, Detroit, Michigan 48202.

JAN SCHOLLENBERGER, Consultant/Educator, 5782 Hobnail Circle, West Bloomfield, Michigan 48033.

DAVE SCHUMAKER, Consultant, University of California at Santa Cruz, and Mentor Teacher, San Lorenzo Valley High, Felton, California 95018.

SYDELLE SEIGER-EHRENBERG, Director, Institute for Curriculum and Instruction, PO Box 747, Coshocton, Ohio 43812.

HARVEY F. SILVER, Director of Programs and Operations, Hanson Silver Strong & Associates, Inc., Box 402, Moorestown, New Jersey 08057.

ROBERT J. STERNBERG, Associate Professor, Department of Psychology, Yale University, Box 11A, Yale Station, New Haven, Connecticut 06520.

RICHARD W. STRONG, Director of Curriculum, Hanson Silver Strong & Associates, Inc., Box 402, Moorestown, New Jersey 08057.

REBECCA VAN DER BOGERT, Director of Curriculum, Office of Superintendent, Groton Public Schools, Groton, Massachusetts 01450.

CHARLES E. WALES, Professor of Engineering and Education and Director, Center for Guided Design, West Virginia University, Engineering Sciences Building, PO Box 6101, Morgantown, West Virginia 26506-6101.

ARTHUR WHIMBEY, Educational Consultant, 3051 S. Atlantic Avenue, No. 503, Daytona Beach Shores, Florida 32018.

CHUCK WIEDERHOLD, Consultant, Placer County Office of Education, 360 Nevada Street, Auburn, California 95603.

HOWARD WILL, West Coast Director, Great Books Foundation, 40 East Huron Street, Chicago, Illinois 60611.

S. LEE WINOCUR, Director, Project IMPACT, Orange County Department of Education, PO Box 9050, 200 Kalmus Drive, Costa Mesa, California 92628.

ROBERT WIRTZ (deceased), Adjunct Professor, Department of Mathematics, University of Illinois, and Co-Founder, Curriculum Development Associates, Washington, D.C., and Monterey, California.

ELENA WRIGHT, Managing Editor, Mastery Education Corporation, 85 Main Street, Watertown, Massachusetts 02172.

Index

accepting responses, 133
aesthetics, 58, 60, 118
affective domain, 215
algorithms, 173
anecdotal records, 288
artificial intelligence, 249
artistic creation, 50
assessment, evaluation, 34, 37, 44, 163, 173, 180, 192, 202, 208, 214, 215, 227, 240, 272, 273, 279, 320, 329
attitudes, 163, 172, 280
audiation, 95

Baron, Jonathan, 245
BASICS, 161, 164
Beethoven, Ludwig von, 58
behavioral learning, 50
Bell, Terrell, 240
Beyer, Barry K., 20, 244
bias, 50, 146, 147, 149
Binet, 187
Bloom, Benjamin, 43, 44, 62, 69, 102, 167, 215, 240, 256, 281, 324
Bloom's Taxonomy, 44, 62, 102, 215, 240, 256, 281, 324
Boorstin, 52
Boyer, Ernest, 102
brain functioning, 21
Bransford, John, 285
Bruner, Jerome, 100, 151, 177, 287

CAT test, 240
Center for the Study of Reading, 4
change agent, 26, 36
change strategy, 36
Chapter I, 239, 240
clarifying, 34, 35
clarifying questions, 35, 36
clarity, 128
classroom climate, 131
classroom structure, organization, 129, 314
clear objectives, 34
climate, classroom, 131
clinical supervision, 19, 27
coaching, 17, 19, 27, 36, 329
    cognitive, 329
    peer, 17, 36

cognition, 47
Cognitive Abilities Test, 237
cognitive coaching, 27, 329
cognitive development, 33, 34, 44, 81, 86, 90, 300, 319
cognitive developmental levels, stages, 33, 34, 36, 44, 100
cognitive dissonance, 25
cognitive spirit, 68
collaborative strategies, 139, 177, 181
    Circles of Knowledge, 177
    Class Meetings, 177
    Cooperative Learning, 177
    Jigsaw, Jigsaw II, 177
    Paired Problem Solving, 177
    Rutabaga, 177
    Student Teams and Academic Divisions, 177
    Teams—Games—Tournaments, 177
College Board test, 270
communicating with parents/community, 38
community expectations, 38
computer hardware, 252
computer literacy, 253
computer software, 253, 258
computer technology, 249
concept attainment, 90, 168
concept development, formation, 161, 168, 214
concept development strategies, 168
concept labels, 161, 162, 164
concept learning, 163
concept learning/teaching strategies, 165
concepts, 161, 162, 163, 164, 172
conceptual complexity, 35
conceptual levels, 34
conceptualization, 163, 164, 165
conscious thinking, 49
convergent operations, 44
cooperative learning, 130, 177
cooperative strategies, 179
Cornell Test of Critical Thinking, 153, 238, 274
CoRT, 244, 245
Costa, Arthur L., 328
creative thinking, 45, 58, 68, 172, 173, 174, 212, 217, 220, 230, 274, 314

creativity, 58, 118, 205, 208, 214, 252, 297, 314
Creativity by Design, 244
criteria for selecting computer software, 252
critical thinking, 35, 45
criticism, 131
Curie, Marie, 59
curriculum guides, 161
curriculum, hidden, 33
    implicit, 33
    thinking skills in, 45
curriculum materials, 161, 164

Darwin, Charles, 59
de Bono, Edward, 20, 244, 245
decision making, 45, 50
deductive strategy, 164
definitions of thinking skills, 43
Developing Cognitive Abilities Test, 44, 237
developmental levels, stages, 44, 100, 162, 191
Dewey, John, 3, 33, 35, 43, 49, 156, 167, 291
diagnosis, 50
dialectical reasoning, 220
direct instruction, 20, 87, 88, 108, 145, 149, 203, 205, 300
directive strategies, 139, 144, 146, 147, 148, 149, 181
    direct instruction, 144, 181
discrepancy, 35
discrepant experience, 35
discrete mental operations, 51
discrete skills, 53, 67, 145, 148, 149, 152
disposition, 54, 68, 280
dissonance, 35
distinguishing fact from opinion, 149
distributed leadership, 179
divergent operations, 44

Education Commission of the States, 3, 281
Educational Testing Service, 214
egocentrism, 159, 168
Einstein, Albert, 58
Emerson, Ralph Waldo, 31
empathy, 31

enabling behaviors, 17, 19
encouragement, 17
Ennis, Robert H., 285, 291
epistemic cognition, 21, 22, 23, 47
equal cue, 17
equal distribution of student responses,
    17
Erickson, Eric, 69
ethical action, 7, 8, 9
ethics, 10
ethnocentrism, 154, 159, 168
evaluation, assessment, 34, 37, 44, 163,
    173, 180, 192, 202, 208, 214, 215, 227,
    229, 240, 272, 273, 279, 320, 329
evaluation, formative, 272, 273
    process, 272, 273
    product, 272, 273
    summative, 272, 273
executive process, 47
extrinsic motivation, 59
extrinsic rewards, 168

fact, 163
feedback, 59, 145, 148
Feuerstein, Reuven, 20, 24, 43, 66, 69, 193
field-dependent students, 147
field-independent students, 147
flowcharting, 228
fluency, 20, 34, 58
    ideational, 34, 58
formal thought, 35
formative evaluation, 272, 273
Freire, Paulo, 36

generative strategies, 139, 171, 181
    Brainstorming, 171
    Creativity by Design, 171
    Lateral Thinking, 171, 181
    Mind Mapping, 171
    Synectics, 171
gifted students, 61
Glaser, Edward, 152
Glatthorn, Allan A., 245
Gleichy, David, 25
goals, 3, 7
Goodlad, John, 26
Gordon, Ed, 95
group autonomy, 179
guided practice, 148, 149
guides, curriculum, 161
Guilford, J. P., 43, 44, 62, 69, 187

hardware, computer, 252
heterogeneous grouping, 179
heuristics, 168
hidden curriculum, 33
hierarchical, 163
higher-level questions, 33, 281
higher-order thought, 274
Hilda Taba Teaching Strategies Program,
    161
hypothesis testing, 50

ICI Curriculum Model, 10
ideational fluency, 34, 58
immorality, 10
IMPACT, Project, 87, 244, 256
implicit curriculum, 33
impulsivity, 10, 31
indirect instruction, 145
inductive strategy, 146, 147, 148, 149
information age, 3
information mapping, 228
information processing, 62, 92
information retrieval, 47
inquiry, 52, 118, 173, 174, 213, 246
insight, 50
Institute for Curriculum and Instruction
    (ICI), 7
instruction, direct, 145, 149
    indirect, 145
Instrumental Enrichment, 66, 244, 245,
    291, 328
integrity, lack of, 10
intellectual functioning, 27
intellectual growth of teachers, 26, 36
intelligence, 8, 9, 10
intelligent thought, 14
interpretive questions, 234
intrinsic motivation, 59, 61, 142
intrinsic rewards, 168
intuition, 45, 52
irrationality, 9
irresponsibility, 9

journals, 285

Kohlberg, Lawrence, 69, 132

language and thinking, 27, 98, 99, 101
lateral thinking, 205
Law in a Free Society, 153
learning from observation, 50
learning styles, 146, 147, 161
Lewin, Kurt, 36
linguistic abilities, 44
linguistic tools, 27
Lipman, Matthew, 20, 23, 50, 244, 285
Lipman's Philosophy for Children, 23, 50,
    153, 212, 244, 245, 328

macro-process strategies, 45
mediated learning, 24, 194
mediation, 244
mediative strategies, 139, 151, 166, 181
    Concept Attainment, 151
    Concept Development, 139, 151
    Concept Formation, 151, 181
    Deep Process Instruction, 139, 151
    Inquiry, 139, 151, 181
    Moral Reasoning, 151
    Open-Ended Discussion, 139, 151, 166
    Values Awareness/Clarification, 151, 168,
        181
memory, rote, 97, 98, 101

mental image, 164
metacognition, 15, 16, 19, 21, 22, 31, 46, 47,
    62, 67, 95, 108, 134, 141, 148, 166, 175,
    196, 198, 206, 208, 252, 274, 288, 289,
    314, 317
metacognitive discussion, 16
metacognitive strategies, 16, 17, 19, 37
metaphor, 35, 172, 323
metaphorical thinking, 20
micro-logical skills, 152
microskills, 19
mnemonics, 157
modeling, 17, 31, 34, 125, 135, 290, 314
Monet, Claude, 59
motivation, extrinsic, 59
    intrinsic, 59, 61, 142

NASA, 59
National Assessment of Educational
    Progress, 4, 281
National Commission on Excellence in
    Education, 4
National Council for the Social Studies, 5
National Council of Teachers of English, 5
National Council of Teachers of
    Mathematics, 5
National Education Association's
    Educational Policies Commission, 3
National Institute of Education, 4
National Science Board Commission on
    Pre-College Education in
    Mathematics, Science, and
    Technology, 3
National Writing Project, 215
Nelson-Denny, 269
New Jersey Test of Reasoning Skills, 14,
    274
Newton, Sir Isaac, 60, 61
Newton's laws, 60, 61, 173
Nickerson, Ray, 285
novelty, 35
numerical reasoning, 44

observation, learning from, 50
    peer, 37, 38
Odyssey, 244
Olson, Carol Booth, 246
Ornstein, Robert 4
Osborn, Alex, 217

Paideia Group, 246
parent education, 31, 327
parenting, 31
Parnes, Sidney, 217
Paul, Richard, 244, 245, 285, 328
Pedagogy of the Oppressed, 36
peer coaching, 17, 36
peer observation, 37, 38
perception, 204
Perkins, David, 20, 244, 285, 328
Philosophy for Children, 23, 50, 153, 212,
    244, 245, 328

Piaget, Jean, 34, 44, 62, 63, 81, 98, 99, 100, 167, 224
Piaget's stages of intellectual development, 81
positive interdependence, 179
practice, guided, 148, 149
praise, 132
prediction, 50
principle, 163
problem finding, 52
problem solving, 45
process evaluation, 272, 273
production evaluation, 272, 273
Project IMPACT, 87, 244, 256
Project Intelligence, 173, 328
Project SOAR, 269
Pythagorean theorem, 172

quantitative reasoning, 44
questioning, 125, 130, 234, 274, 279, 285, 314, 323
    techniques, strategies, 27, 130, 234
questions, clarifying, 35
    higher-level, 33, 281
    interpretive, 234
    recall, 279
    student, 34
Quiz Show Model, 33

Raven's Colored Matrices Test, 240
reasoning, dialectical, 223
    numerical, 44
    quantitative, 44
recall questions, 279
reciprocity, 213
recklessness, 9
reflection, 50
responding, 125
rewards, extrinsic, 168
    intrinsic, 168
Ross Test of Higher Cognitive Process, 237
rote memory, 97, 98, 101

Scholastic Aptitude Test (SAT), 4, 185, 269
scientific method, 285
selective reinforcement, 17
Sigel, Irving, 33, 246

silence, 17, 34, 133, 314
skill acquisition, 179
skills, 145, 146, 147, 148, 163, 172
    discrete, 53, 67, 145, 148, 149
    study, 227
SOAR, 159, 168
sociocentrism, 159, 168
Socratic, 151
Socratic inquiry, 224
software, computer, 252, 253, 258
SOI, 44, 62, 187, 244
SOI Learning Abilities Tests, 187
spatial depictions, 45
specific thinking skills, 145, 156
spirit of inquiry, 52
staff development, xii, 11, 27, 36, 186, 194, 202, 241, 329
Sternberg, Robert, 285, 328
strategic planning, 174
Strategic Reasoning, 244, 270
strategies, 172
    change, 36
    collaborative, 139, 177, 181
    concept learning, teaching, 168
    cooperative, 179
    deductive, 164
    directive, 139, 144, 146, 147, 148, 149, 181
    generative, 139, 171, 181
    inductive, 146, 147, 148, 149
    macro-process, 45
    mediative, 139, 151, 166, 181
    metacognitive, 16, 17, 37
    questioning, 27, 234
    teaching, 130
    thinking, 68
    transfer, 17, 19
Stravinsky, Igor, 59
Stress on Analytical Reasoning (SOAR), 269
Structure of the Intellect (SOI), 44, 62, 187, 244
structuring, 125
student questions, 34
study skills, 227
Stufflebeam, Daniel, 272
subconscious thinking, 49
Suchman, 151
summative evaluation, 272, 273

supervision, 11, 29, 37, 38
Swartz, Robert, 285

Taba, Hilda, 102, 107, 151, 161, 167, 241
TAPS, 269
task analysis, 88
taxonomy, thinking skills, 46, 48
teacher assessment, evaluation, 37
Teacher Expectations and Student Achievement (TESA), 17
teaching strategies, 130, 139, 141
teaching styles, 147
technologies, 44, 249
thinking aloud, 34
Thinking Aloud Pair Problem Solving (TAPS), 269
thinking, conscious, 49
    subconscious, 49
    unconscious, 49
    definition of, 203
    evaluation, assessment of 34, 44
thinking skills curriculum, 45
thinking skills, definitions of, 43
thinking skills taxonomy, 46, 48
thinking strategies, 68
Torrance, E. Paul, 34, 217, 291
transfer, 15, 16, 17, 19, 129, 148, 161, 185, 186, 196, 199, 201, 206
transfer strategies, 17
trust, 27, 36

unconscious thinking, 49
Upton, Albert, 69, 197, 198
U.S. Department of Education's Joint Dissemination Review Panel, 227

value judgments, 149
values, 10
verbal abilities, 44
visual depictions, 44
visualization, 100

wait time, 17, 34, 314
Watson-Glaser Test of Critical Thinking, 152, 153, 238, 274
Whimbey, Arthur, 20
WISC, 187
withholding impulsivity, 31
writing samples, 274